AF559663

# WETLANDS MANAGEMENT IN NORTH BIHAR

## About the Author

**R.B. Mandal** born on 7.5.1948 in Kharsam Village of Samastipur district, Bihar. He passed M.A. (1968) and Ph.D. (1973) from Patna University. He taught in the Universities of Patna, Bhagalpur and Dar es Salaam (Tanzania) and presented paper in Bristal University (U.K.) in 1994. Since 1973 uptil now Dr. Mandal has written and edited more than 20 books, 66 research papers and supervised more than 20 Ph.D. research scholars. His current interest is on aerial photograph and remote sensing. At present he is also editing a bi-annual magazine entitled 'East West Geographer' since 1990. At present Dr. Mandal is a University Prof. of Geography, Tilka Manjhi University, Bhagalpur.

# WETLANDS MANAGEMENT IN NORTH BIHAR

**RAM BAHADUR MANDAL**
*University Professor of Geography*
*T.M. Bhagalpur University*
*Bhagalpur-812007*

**CONCEPT PUBLISHING COMPANY PVT. LTD.**
**NEW DELHI-110059**

ISBN - 13-978-81-8069-707-4

First Published 2010

*Published and Printed by*

**Concept Publishing Company Pvt. Ltd.**
**Regd. Office:**
A/15-16, Commercial Block, Mohan Garden
New Delhi-110059 (India)
*Phones* : 25351460, 25351794, *Fax* : 091-11-25357109
*E-mail* : publishing@conceptpub.com
*Website:* www.conceptpub.com
**Editorial Office:**
H-13, Bali Nagar, New Delhi-110 015, India.

Cataloging in Publication Data--*Courtesy:* D.K. Agencies (P) Ltd. <docinfo@dkagencies.com>

Mandal, R. B. (Ram Bahadur), 1948-
Wetlands management in north Bihar / Ram Bahadur Mandal.
p. cm.
Includes bibliographical references (p. ) and index.
ISBN 9788180697074

1. Wetland management--India--Bihar. 2. Wetland ecology--India--Bihar. I. Title.

DDC 577.680954123 22

# PREFACE

Wetlands are areas of shallow water upto 3 metres depth whether they are rivers, tanks, ditches, lakes, swampy land and coastal areas of the ocean. North Bihar is endowed with wetlands as this area has been formed by Himalayan rivers which flow sluggishly and deposited sand and silt unevenly thereby forming varieties of wetlands. It is a case of stagnation of shallow water in the form of temporary permanent water bodies. In North Bihar some of the important wetlands are Gogabeel in Katihar, Barailatal in Vaishali, Kabartal in Begusarai, Hazarpanch lake in Katihar and Hardia Chaur in Saran district. Similarly in Darbhanga district Rajokhar, Pokharbhinda, Simardah, Narsar Chaur, Narail Chaur and Kusheswar Asthan are important.

In this project most of the works have been done on the basis of fieldwork. This is because the published data regarding wetland is not available. Most of the fieldwork have been done in the year 1994 and 1996. The fieldworks are related with the collection of data, consultation of people, taking photograph of representative items including library work.

The entire project has been divided into twenty-one chapters. The introductory chapter is related with meaning and scope along with hypothesis testing. The second chapter geographical background is devoted to physical, economic and demographic structure of North Bihar. The physical and cultural factors controlling wetlands are the subject matter of third chapter. Theoretical background is the delineation of different stages of wetlands formation, So far as the distribution of wetland is concerned it has been found that they are more prolific in areas of meandering courses of rivers and low-lying areas having annual visit of flood. So far as the types and patterns of wetland is concerned they are swampy land, flood plains, natural lakes, ditches, oxbow lakes and marginal area of rivers. So far as the patterns of wetland are concerned they may be elongated, circular, square and variety of shapes and sizes. The economic gains from wetlands are many e.g. work as pollution filter, produce *makhana*, mothi, purain leaves, fishes, varieties of medicinal plants and game birds as well. Besides these, it has social value, ecological value and economic value as well. The wetlands is disappearing fast due to its reclamation for agricultural and industrial expansion as well. The soil of wetland carries more humus material and the water is either polluted, more turbid and carries excess of Bio-chemical oxygen demand.

The wetland is highly helpful in agricultural development e.g., it is helpful in the production of rice, *makhana, singarhara* and bhent besides medicinal plants. In the Begusarai district of North Bihar Kabartal is a big natural lake where several species of plants, migratory birds from foreign lands visit each and every year but the agricultural activities of farmers, netting of birds and fishes by the local people have really disturbed the ecological balance of Kabartal. Regarding the productivity the wetland is unparallel as it can produce four times more in comparison with the dryland farming. The Himalayan wetlands have definite impact on the wetlands of North Bihar. In sample study the wetlands of Kabar, Paraila, Hardia, Chamra Chaur, Telia Chaur, Kusheshwar Asthan, Motijheel, Hazarpanch lake, Sowa jheel and several others have been delineated. The conservation of wetland is its continuance and betterment for the use of future generation. The problems are its reclamation, eutrophication, agricultural expansion and dump of garbage and refuge water in the wetland. The planning of wetland involves control of flood, beautification and digging of wetland besides remodelling for the better future. At the end the nature of analysis, the details of data to be collected, questionnaires and conclusions are given that for the maintenance, of ecological balance the wetland should be conserved, protected and planned in a better way for the survival of humanity and prosperity of future generations.

I am highly grateful to my honourable teachers Prof. P. Dayal, Retired Vice Chanceller, Magadh University, Bodh-Gaya.; Prof. L.N. Ram, Pro-Vice Chanceller, Patna University, Patna; Prof. G. N. Singh, Head of the Department of Geography,

R.D. & D.J. College, Munger for their kind help, suggestions and criticisms.

I am also thankful to Dr. Narain Prasad Singh, Ex. Principal, R.D. & D.J. College, Munger; Dr. S.P. Yadav, Principal, R.D. & D.J. College, Munger; Dr. B. P. Poddar, Principal, R.D. & D.J. College, Munger without whose help and cooperation this project may not have seen light of the day.

15th August, 2009

**R. B. Mandal**
*University Professor*
*T.M. Bhagalpur University*
*Bhagalpur, Bihar*

R.D. & D.J. College, Munger for their kind help, suggestions and criticisms.

I am also thankful to Dr. Narain Prasad Singh, Ex. Principal, R.D. & D.J. College, Munger, Dr. S.P. Yadav, Principal R.D. & D.J. College, Munger, Dr. B. P. Poddar, Principal, R.D. & D.J. College, Munger without whose help and cooperation this project may not have seen light of the day.

15th August, 2009 **R. B. Mandal**

*University Professor*
*T.M. Bhagalpur University*
*Bhagalpur, Bihar*

# CONTENTS


*Preface* v

*List of Figures* xi

*List of Tables* xv

1. Introduction 1
2. Geographical Background 20
3. Factors Controlling Wetlands 95
4. Theoretical Background 105
5. Distribution of Wetlands 130
6. Types and Patterns of Wetlands 144
7. Economic Gains from Wetlands 167
8. The Value of Wetlands 189
9. Endangered Wetland Ecology 224
10. Soil and Water of Wetlands 251
11. Eutrophication of Wetlands 278
12. Wetlands and Agriculture 300
13. Ecological Diversities of Kabar Tal 310
14. Productivity of Wetlands 323
15. Sample Studies 338
16. Conservation of Wetlands 435
17. Problems and Planning of Wetlands 451
18. The Nature of Wetland Data Analysis 476
19. The Details of Data to be Collected 480

20. All India Questionnaire for the Survey of Wetlands 484
21. Conclusions 495
*Bibliography* 500
*Index* 518

# LIST OF FIGURES


| | | |
|---|---|---|
| 1.1 | Model of Wetland Linkage | 3 |
| 1.2 | Relationship between Tanks and Orchards in Darbhanga Division | 14 |
| 2.1 | North Bihar : Regional Framework | 21 |
| 2.2 | Effect of 1988 Earthquake on Darbhanga Division | 24 |
| 2.3 | North Bihar : Epicentre of 1988 Earthquakes | 25 |
| 2.4 | Strata Chart (Log of Drilling) Location : Gorain Village of Kalyanpur Block | 26 |
| 2.5 | North Bihar : Relief Feature | 27 |
| 2.6 | Siwalik Hills of Champaran | 29 |
| 2.7 | North Bihar : Alluvial Geomorphology, Samastipur District | 30 |
| 2.8 | Gandak Alluvial Cone | 32 |
| 2.9 | Oxbow Lake in Vaishali District | 34 |
| 2.10 | Topographic Features of North Bihar | 36 |
| 2.11 | North Bihar : Geomorphic Regions | 37 |
| 2.12 | North Bihar : Sources of Irrigation | 39 |
| 2.13 | Kosi Basin : Drainage Lines | 42 |
| 2.14 | North Bihar Plain : Climographs (After G. Taylor) | 44 |
| 2.15 | North Bihar : Climographs (After E.M. Forster) | 46 |
| 2.16 | North Bihar : Distribution of Rainfall (1996) | 49 |
| 2.17 | Strata Chart of Singhara Village, Mahua Anchal | 51 |
| 2.18 | North Bihar : Land Utilization, 1995 | 53 |
| 2.19 | North Bihar : Crop Combination Regions, 1995 | 58 |
| 2.20 | Field and Cropping Pattern of Singhara Village (Mahua Anchal) | 60 |
| 2.21 | Strata Chart of Tubewell in Majarahia Village (Samastipur District) | 62 |
| 2.22 | Kosi Irrigation Project | 64 |
| 2.23 | Command Area of Gandak Project (1996) | 65 |

| | | |
|---|---|---|
| 2.24 | North Bihar : Major Roadways | 73 |
| 2.25 | North Bihar : Types of Rural Settlements | 77 |
| 2.26 | North Bihar : Spacing of Rural Settlements, 1991 | 80 |
| 2.27 | North Bihar : Density of Rural Settlements, 1991 | 81 |
| 2.28 | North Bihar : Distribution of Towns, 1991 | 82 |
| 2.29 | Muzaffarpur : Functional Zones | 85 |
| 2.30 | North Bihar : Parganas and Tappas, 1992 | 91 |
| 2.31 | North Bihar : Administrative Map | 92 |
| 3.1 | Factors Affecting Wetlands in North Bihar | 96 |
| 3.2 | Patterns of Landforms in North Bihar | 98 |
| 3.3 | Meandering Courses of Rivers and Diara lands in Samastipur District | 102 |
| 4.1 | Stages of Wetlands Formation Along Kamla River | 106 |
| 4.2 | North Bihar : Flood Affected Areas, 1994-97 | 115 |
| 4.3 | Alluviation and Diluviation as Forces of Wetland Formation | 116 |
| 4.4 | Socio-economic Diversities and Wetland | 117 |
| 5.1 | Kosi Alluvial Cone | 134 |
| 5.2 | North Bihar : Distribution of Tanks as Wetlands (1991) | 138 |
| 5.3 | North Bihar : Relative Magnitude of Ponds and Orchards, 1991 | 140 |
| 5.4 | North Bihar : Lorenz Curve showing Distributional Patterns of Wetlands (1991) | 141 |
| 6.1 | North Bihar : Distribution of Wetlands | 150 |
| 6.2 | Role of Rivers in Economic Development of an Area | 160 |
| 6.3 | Distribution of Tanks in the Division of Darbhanga (1971) | 161 |
| 7.1 | Economic Gains from Wetlands | 169 |
| 7.2 | North Bihar : Production of Fish in Wetlands, 1990-91 | 171 |
| 8.1 | Dimensions of Wetlands | 191 |
| 8.2 | North Bihar : Origin and Evolution of Wetland in the Division of Darbhanga | 192 |
| 8.3 | Types of Wetlands | 193 |
| 8.4 | The Concept of Wetland | 203 |
| 8.5 | Meandering Courses of the Kareha River | 207 |
| 8.6 | North Bihar : Distribution of Tanks as Wetlands, 1991 | 211 |

8.7 Pokharbhinda : Distribution of Tanks 212
8.8 Socio-economic Model for Wetlands Development 215
8.9 The Environs of Kabar Tal 216
8.10 Regional Location of Goga-Beel 217
10.1 Number of Wetland in Saharsa District 275
13.1 Kabartal Wetland Eco-system Transformed 312
13.1 (a) Bihar — Darbhanga and Monghyar Districts 313
13.2 Check List of Kabar Tal 314
13.3 Plan of Jaimanglagarh 317
15.1 Factors Affecting Wetlands 339
15.2 Kathra Wetland in Manigachhi 341
15.3 Kusheshwar Asthan Chaur (Darbhanga) 343
15.4 Sisulia Chaur in Manigachhi 347
15.5 Location of Pachkurba — Sahara Chaur 349
15.6 Belhi Wetland in Manigachhi 352
15.7 Masbasi Wetland, Darbhanga 353
15.8 Simardah Wetland, Darbhanga 355
15.9 Rajokhar Wetland of Narayanpur, Manigachhi Anchal 355
15.10 Udaipur Forest 357
15.11 Tilabai Moin (Supaul) 359
15.12 Lake Narha Wetland (Supaul) 361
15.13 Malkayan Wetland, Katihar Anchal 363
15.14 Hajarpanch Wetland 365
15.15 Wetlands of Simri-Bakhtiarpur Block 368
15.16 Wetlands of Bangaon Mahisi 371
15.17 Motijheel and Kararia Lakes of East Champaran 375
15.18 Basman Lake 379
15.19 Khagma Wetland (Saharsa) 381
15.20 Chamra Chaur (Vaishali District) 383
15.21 Phulbhasa Lake (Kishanganj) 385
15.22 Kanti Wetland (Muzaffarpur) 387
15.23 Hardia Chaur Wetland (Saran) 390
15.24 Suhagman and Basman Lake (Champaran) 391
15.25 Bharthua Chaur (Muzaffarpur) 393
15.26 Gothara Kanakpur Wetland (Kishanganj) 395
15.27 Manikaman Wetland (Muzaffarpur) 396

| | | |
|---|---|---|
| 15.28 | Telia Chaur (Muzaffarpur) | 397 |
| 15.29 | Mahbal Man Wetland (Muzaffarpur) | 399 |
| 15.30 | Kuleshra Chaur (Muzaffarpur) | 401 |
| 15.31 | Kharudah Wetland (Kishanganj) | 403 |
| 15.32 | Ruighasa Wetland (Kishanganj) | 414 |
| 15.33 | Bengadhasan Wetland (Supaul) | 418 |
| 15.34 | Berain Wetland (Vaishali District) | 428 |
| 15.35 | Wetlands near Vaishali Excavation Site | 429 |
| 15.36 | Lake Baraila of Vaishali | 430 |
| 15.37 | Dhima Makhnaha, Purnea | 431 |
| 16.1 | Satellite and Sensors | 442 |
| 16.2 | Stereoscopic Imaging | 442 |
| 16.3 | Nadir Viewing | 444 |
| 16.4 | Latitude and Local Solar Time | 444 |
| 16.5 | Off-nadir-viewing | 444 |
| 16.6 | Revisit capabilities | 445 |
| 16.7 | Viewing on successive days | 446 |
| 16.8 | Stereoscopic Viewing | 447 |
| 16.9 | Remote Sensing in Wetland Management | 448 |
| 16.10 | Himalayan foothills at the top, Alluvial Plains of Narayani River | 448 |
| 16.11 | The LANDSAT # MSS (Band 6) imagery of the Ghaghara-Gandak region. | 449 |
| 17.1 | Problems of Wetlands in North Bihar | 452 |
| 17.2 | Socio-economic condition and Damage to Wetland Environment | 454 |
| 17.3 | Darbhanga Division Relationship of Ponds and Orchards (1991) | 469 |
| 17.4 | Wetland Management | 470 |
| 17.5 | North Bihar : Planning of Wetlands | 473 |

# LIST OF TABLES

| | | |
|---|---|---|
| 1.1 | Relationship between Tanks and Orchards in Darbhanga Division | 15 |
| 2.1 | Certain Relevant Data on District Level of North Bihar (1991) | 22 |
| 2.2 | Meandering of River Kareh | 35 |
| 2.3 | Approximate Rate of Shifting of The River Kosi (1736 to 1950 A.D.) | 40 |
| 2.4 | North Bihar : Conditions of Soil in percentage | 50 |
| 2.5 | Pattern of Land Utilization in North Bihar (1995) | 54 |
| 2.6 | Area under Different Crops in '000 hectares of North Bihar (1995-1996) | 55 |
| 2.7 | Total Irrigated Area in '000 hectares (1995-96) | 61 |
| 2.8 | Sugar Mills of North Bihar, 1998 | 66 |
| 2.9 | Length of Roads and Railways in North Bihar in kms. | 74 |
| 2.10 | North Bihar : Number of Inhabited and Uninhabited Rural Settlements (1991) | 76 |
| 2.11 | North Bihar : Size Class of Rural Settlements, 1991 | 78 |
| 2.12 | Population Density of Urban Places in North Bihar (1991) | 83 |
| 2.13 | Growth of Urban Places in North Bihar (1901-1991) | 84 |
| 3.1 | Some of the Important Wetlands of Darbhanga Division | 97 |
| 4.1 | Taxonomy of Wetland as Riverine Origin | 112 |
| 5.1 | Wetlands under Environmental Study | 131 |
| 5.2 | Characteristics of the Distribution of Wetlands in North Bihar | 141 |
| 5.3 | Distribution of Tanks and Forests/Orchards in North Bihar (1991) | 142 |
| 5.4 | North Bihar : Lorenz Curve showing Distributional Patterns of Wetlands (1991) | 143 |

| | | |
|---|---|---|
| 6.1 | General Conditions of Wetlands in North Bihar | 145 |
| 6.2 | Number of Chaurs in Darbhanga District, 1998 | 154 |
| 6.3 | Some of the Important Chaur as Wetlands of Darbhanga District | 155 |
| 6.4 | Distribution of Tanks and Forests/Orchards in North Bihar (1991) | 159 |
| 6.5 | Chemical Analysis of the water of sampled wetlands | 162 |
| 6.6 | North Bihar : Lorenz Curve showing Distributional Patterns of Wetlands (1991) | 164 |
| 7.1 | Fish Production in the Wetlands of North Bihar, 1987 | 170 |
| 7.2 | Distribution of Tanks and Forests/Orchards in North Bihar (1991) | 184 |
| 7.3 | Production of various resources from Wetlands in North Bihar Production in M.T. (1991) | 185 |
| 8.1 | List of Wetlands in Bihar | 197 |
| 8.2 | General Conditions of Wetlands in North Bihar | 199 |
| 8.3 | Excessively Waterlogged Areas of Champaran Districts | 201 |
| 8.4 | Location and Threats to Wetland Resources in North Bihar | 202 |
| 8.5 | Production of various resources from Wetlands in North Bihar | 206 |
| 8.6 | Distribution of Tanks and Mango Orchards in North Bihar, 1991 | 213 |
| 9.1 | Some of the important Wetlands of Rajasthan (1993) | 239 |
| 10.1 | Surveyed Wetlands of North Bihar | 252 |
| 10.2 | Pooled Mean Soil Analysis of some of Wetlands in North Bihar | 256 |
| 10.3 | Chemical Analysis of some of the Water Sample of North Bihar | 264 |
| 10.4 | Physico-chemical Parametres of Wetlands Soil in North Bihar | 266 |
| 10.5 | Results available from Sampled Water Test in the Wetlands of North Bihar (1995-96) | 272 |
| 10.6 | Water Area of Wetland in Saharsa District (1994-95) | 276 |
| 11.1 | Basic Information of Wetlands in India | 294 |

| | | |
|---|---|---|
| 13.1 | Area and Population of Rural Settlements in the Watershed of Kabar Tal | 316 |
| 13.2 | Subsidiary Occupational Structure of Workers | 320 |
| 14.1 | Net Primary Product by Main Vegetation Units | 333 |
| 14.2 | Productivity of some North American Wetlands | 334 |
| 14.3 | Some of the important wetlands of Saharsa District (1994-95) | 335 |
| 15.1 | Birds and their weight | 348 |
| 15.2 | Birds and their weight in Sahara | 350 |
| 15.3 | General characteristics of Karma Man Wetland | 356 |
| 15.4 | The Characteristics of Villages in the Environs of Karma Man | 358 |
| 15.5 | Fishes and their weight | 362 |
| 15.6 | Birds and Weight in Sirdiha Chaur | 367 |
| 15.7 | Birds visiting the Area | 370 |
| 15.8 | Chemical Factors of Motijheel Lake, 1995 | 376 |
| 15.9 | Physical Factors of Motijheel Lake, 1995 | 382 |
| 15.10 | Incoming of birds in Chamra Chaur | 383 |
| 15.11 | Characteristics of Wetland in Muzaffarpur | 386 |
| 15.12 | The Weight and Price of Birds in Hardia Chaur | 389 |
| 15.13 | Among the birds the following are important | 394 |
| 15.14 | The migratory birds coming to Telia Chaur | 398 |
| 15.15 | Among the creatures found in Mahbal Man | 400 |
| 15.16 | Species of fishes found in Kuleshra Chaur | 402 |
| 15.16a | Migratory birds of Kuleshra Chaur | 402 |
| 15.17 | Birds and their weight in Kharudah Lake | 404 |
| 15.18 | The crops grown in the surrounding area of Sowa lake | 405 |
| 15.19 | Production of Nardang Wetland | 412 |
| 15.20 | The Birds, Plants and Creatures found in Dighi Wetland | 413 |
| 15.21 | Plants found in Lake Finglas | 424 |
| 16.1 | Sensors: High Resolution Visible (HRV) | 443 |
| 17.1 | Area Under Wetlands in Darbhanga Division | 456 |
| 17.2 | Wetlands of Darbhanga Division, 1997 | 456 |
| 21.1 | One Important Wetland in each district of North Bihar | 495 |

# 1

# INTRODUCTION

The Management of Wetlands Environment is considered essential because it is neglected since millennium but now the time has come to think about them. It provides food, medicinal plants, fishes, Makhana and acts as pollution filter besides reserves of plants and game birds as well. Wetlands help in beautifying the environment, attracting more rainfall and it has great potentiality in maintaining the ecological balance and resource generation.

Wetlands are among the most productive and most threatened ecosystem. On marshes, swamps and flood plains the great civilizations of Nile valley, Mesopotamia and Indo-china have flourished which continue to support rural and urban communities throughout the world. All these are in jeopardy by drainage reclamation and used as dumping ground of refuge water. Some of the wetlands have been damaged and destroyed in search of short term profit and many have already been lost their existence and character as well.[1]

In North Bihar the rivers coming to the plain from the Himalaya in the north are the Budhi Gandak, the Ghaghra, the Balan the Lakhandei, the Kareh, the Kamla, the Bhutahi Balan, the Jibachh[2], the Bagmati and the Kosi and its tributaries. These rivers deposit sand and silt, bring devastating floods, goads the process of alluviation and deluviation in the wetlands of North Bihar.

Recently, with minute observation it has been found that even in wetland areas some high mounds are found here and there due to Neo-tectonic Earth Movement going on in the sub-stratum of North

Bihar. This is also responsible for the formation of wetlands in the region under study.

In North Bihar the wetlands are mostly concentrated in the same area. The geographical factors responsible for this pattern are the gentle slope of the land, meandering courses of the river, high water table and relatively high amount of rainfall. This could be exemplified with the availability of wetlands in the course of Jibachh and Kareh rivers in Samastipur and Darbhanga districts, the Kamla, Balan, Bhutahi Balan and Jibachh in Madhubani and Darbhanga Districts. This situation is more or less the same in the catchment area of the Kosi river in Saharsa and Purnea districts. Sometimes, wetlands occur due to unequal deposition of sand and silt and sometimes sheet wash erosion.

## Model of Wetland Linkage

According to Fig.1.1 the linkage of wetlands on the earth surface is covered by Physical environment of water bodies and vegetation every where. The types of birds in the wetlands are representative of the depth of water and the availability of food chain in the habitat. The livestock in the area are also closely linked with the types of wetland for example the wetlands of Tanzania, Africa (especially lake Maniyara - Hippopotamus and water buffaloes are found) where as in wetland area of Darbhanga Nilgai is quite often found because it is accustomed with the grasslands found near wetlands. The crops of wetlands are Makhana, Singarhara, Bhent, Saurkha and various types of medicinal plants. The availability and production of crops depend on the duration of waterlogging in the wetland along with its depth.

Human being has the prime concern with the wetland because the value of wetlands in terms of social, economic and ecological, are due to the presence of human being; and only those wetlands are considered as resource which are approachable to man and utilized by man.

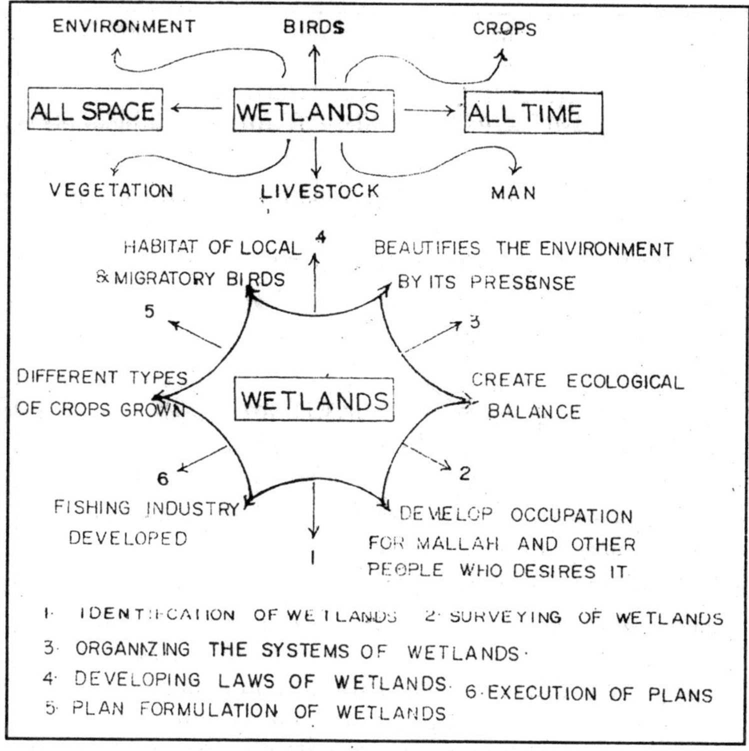


**Fig. 1.1 :** Model of Wetland Linkage

## Dimensions of Wetland

1. The wetlands have mainly, six dimensions which provide occupations to fishermen and other people who wants to catch fish, keep the wetlands clean, develop wetland plantations and bird sanctuary, etc.
2. Wetland is the vast inland fishing ground not only in the division of Kosi but in the entire North Bihar. The types of fishes and the amount of their catch vary according to the technical abilities of Mallah, the area of fish catch covered and the types of fishes for which the fishermen are desirous.
3. The protection and conservation of wetland environment in North Bihar is quite essential to maintain ecological environment.

Recently, the overwhelming growth of population has harnessing the resources of wetlands indiscriminately besides its filling, cutting of trees, killing of rare birds, etc.

4. The presence of wetlands has the capacity to beautify the environment for example the desert of Rajashan has several lakes of sweet water and salty water but their presence is really decorative in order to make the environment beautiful.
5. The wetland is a habitat for both local and the migratory birds; because some birds have a habit to wade in the water such as duck while others have a tendency to make nests on the trees found in the near-bye-area. For example, in Junglee Tal English of Amdabad anchal Katihar and Jalai-malai in the course of the Kosi river west of Nawhatta are wetlands where millions of migratory birds visit each and every year from Himalaya and Siberia and the wetlands of Darbhanga and champaran are not very different from these areas.
6. In wetlands different types of crops are grown which are of three varieties-

   (a) Edible crops e.g., *makhana* and *singarhara.*
   (b) Medicinal crops e.g., Litchen, Kai and Shewar.
   (c) Ornamental crops e.g., different types of flowers which are found in wetland environment e.g., Rodendron, Lotus and water hyacinth.

**Meaning of Wetlands**

1. Wetland is a marshy or waterlogged area formed naturally or artificially.
2. Wetlands are inland fishing ground on he land in the form of lakes, tals and rivers.
3. Wetlands are pollution filters in terms of absorbing the dirty soil and obnoxious gases present in the environment.
4. Wetlands are ecologically more desirous as place of birds sanctuary, as places of beautiful scenery and as recreational places for boating and walking on its embankment.

5. Wetlands are reserve pool for varieties of acquatic products, as food, fodder and plant of medicinal value.

## Statement of the Research Problem

1. The fragile wetland environment of North Bihar is suffering from agricultural extension and encroachment besides the threat of its reclamation due to fast increasing population in the area.
2. The real problem could emerge only after wetlands survey and assessing the number and amount of problem.
3. The assessment of types and pattern areas, their extent, flora, fauna and the amount of siltation could be measured through this study.
4. The proper management of wetland is essential in order to save ecological balance as the wetlands are the saviour from soil, water and air pollution besides providing sustenance to varieties of game birds and plant life too.
5. The value of wetlands could be determined in terms of ecology, economy and society as the art, culture and religion of Mithila region is dominated by fish culture found in wetland and the economy is dominated by wetland products namely — makhana, singarhara, rice, mothi, saurkha, vent, mothi and purain leaves.
6. This study also highlights the problem and planning measures of wetlands as the area is often visited by floods and flood ravages are so severe that they are increasing and sustaining the presence of wetlands. Wetlands are not always beneficial but sometimes they are harmful as they deteriorates the environment.

## Theme of Research Coverage

The management of wetland environment is considered essential because it has been found to be neglected since millennium.

But now the time has come to think about them. Wetlands provide food, medicinal plants, fishes, makhana and act as pollution filter. They are the reserves of plants and game birds as well.

Wetlands help in beautifying the environment, attract more rainfall and it has great potential in maintaining the ecological balance and resource generation.

In North Bihar there is no forest cover but there is a lot of chaur lands. In Chhotanagpur plateau there is an abundance of forest cover but the presence of chaur land is negligible. It is a natural area of forest cover and wetlands which controls their ecological conditions of the area. In this way, there is a close relationship of biogeo-chemical cycle adjustment in between forest land and the chaur land.

### Parameters to be Considered

1. Spatial distribution of wetlands.
2. Floral and faunal distribution in wetlands,
3. Ecology of wetlands
4. Economic grains from wetlands
5. Social value of wetlands
6. Soil characteristics of wetlands
7. Physico-chemical composition of water in the wetlands
8. Wetlands environmental studies

### The Study Area

The North Bihar is located in Bihar in between the Ganges river in the south and the border of Nepal in the North. In western side of this area the districts of Champaran and Gopalganj are found where as on its eastern side the districts of Purnea and Katihar are located. On southern side the Ganges river makes its sway. Total area of North Bihar is 52,000 km$^2$ and the total population in 1991 is 36 million. The average population density is 948 and the total Number of important wetlands are 840.

The latitudnal extent of North Bihar is 25° 30′N to 26°45′N and the longitudinal Extent is 85°30′E to 86°40′E. In this way, the geographical personality of North Bihar has been redressed by he falling of the remnants of the last phase of Tethys sea south of the Himalaya mountain. This has been filled by the river coming from the Himalaya in the north e.g. the Kamla, the Kosi, the Mahananda, the Balan, the Jibacch, the Bhuthibalan, the Bagmati, the Kareh, the Budhi Gandak and the Ganges in the extreme south

**Objectives of Study**

The objectives of this research is to search the evolutionary process of the growth and decline of wetlands in North Bihar as this area is rich in marsh and waterlogged chaurs. For this fact, it is known as Tirhut which means that the land distributed along the rivers. These objective is to search the types and patterns of wetlands, in North Bihar so that the planning procedures feasible the environmental situations could be adopted.

The third objective is to search the value of wetlands in terms of environmental quality, economic gains and judging the social values of wetlands even the marginal area's of marshy and waterlogged could be spared for the economic emancipation of people as only poors are living in North Bihar who sustain their life on fishes, Singarhara, Makhana, Mothi, Purain leaves and lotus flower. Through sample study and planning procedures the author will try to show that how even shallow water bodies could be utilised in a better way in order to have sound ecological balance and environmental adjustment with various parameters of economic development.

**The Scope of Wetlands Study**

Wetlands are swamy ground in low lying areas. The term wetland has been applied to a broad range of shallow water, periodically flooded and high groundwater environments with special functions and values. These shallow water surface systems are characterized by certain type of vegetation adapted to periodic flooding or saturation and soils that reflect an aerobic conditions. Wetland functions vary but include food storage and means of pollution control. It controls sediment load, food chain support, ground water replenishment and habitats for waterfowl, fishes and many rare and endangered species.

A variety of more specific terms, such as marsh: bog, fen, mudflat, slough and swamp have been used to characterise lands with various frequencies, depths and velocities of wetness and various types of vegetation and soils. Several years ago, Don Willard of Indiana University collected more than 50 different wetland definitions. This abundance of wetland definition has been offered as proof that the definition of wetlands is a policy question that should be decided by politicians and administrators rather than by scientists. Although the definition of a wetland has and should involve certain discretionary elements related to the purpose of the definition, most of the 50 definitions were scientifically quite similar and they are different primarily with regard to the waterbound boundary of the system and the drier land boundary.

Some scientists and politicians have argued that all lands that are periodically wet are therefore, "Wetland" and should be considered as wetlands. Unfortunately, this delineation is not so simple. Wetness is a relative term. Practically all the land on the Earth, including desert lands are subject to periodic rain and flooding. Wetness varies in terms of frequency, duration, depth and velocity of inundation, water quality and other parameters. What is considered wet in one area of the nation, such as in the arid south-west of the United states, may be relatively dry for another area, such as Louisiana.

The function and values of the areas that may be considered wetland and the natural hazards posed by these areas- such as flooding, drainage, structural bearing capacity, problems, and unsuitability for septic tanks-depend upon a broad range of factors, including location, morphology, vegetation and the use of adjacent areas. The annual number of days of wetness is only one factor contributing to wetland values.

In some cases, certain lands that are only very rarely wet can be viewed as wetlands. For example, to characterize as wetland that may only be subject to flooding once in every 100 years may be a stretching concept. However, under certain conditions such as the construction of a nuclear power plant or a chemical factory, even infrequent wetness may seriously threaten public safety. The states of Massachusetts and Rhode Island characterize the entire

100 years, flood plain as wetland for some regulatory purposes. Although the number of days of inundation or saturation is a poor basis for characterizing an area as a. wetland, such quantitative measures of, wetness have come to dominate the dialogue on wetland definition.

Wetlands located in the marginal areas of human interaction of tourism, fishing and creating ecological balance between men and biosphere. Wetland is the area where the availability of varieties of fishes, birds and medicinal plants are available from shallow and deep waters. Wetlands act as the highway, beautification of environment, source of irrigation, recreation, bridging the gap of protein supply and increasing the selectivity of men in different types of resources.

## Review of Past Literature

In the year 1971 at Ramser, Iran a conference was hosted on wetlands[3] which is the beginning of identifying wetland throughout the world. In India in 1971 First of all wetlands conference was organised in New Delhi.[4]

K. D. Choudhary in his field study report (1973-75)[5] highlighted the Fisheries Biology and Fisheries Technology and Fisheries economics in terms of Wetlands of India.

H.R. Singh & Badola (1978)[6] described the location of lakes of the Nainital area, followed by a discussion of the problems being faced by the lakes. The problem related to land slides resulting from the instability of the north-eastern slope, soil erosion, silting of lakes, pollution of lakes from local drainage, evaporation and lowering of water level of the lakes during lean season and remedial measures for each of the problems have also been suggested. The author also suggests the development of Bhim Tal and Sat Tal area as tourist sites in order to diffuse the tourist flow to Nainital, thereby preventing heavy traffic and increased water consumption both of which lead to ecological imbalances. The major factors responsible for the depletion of the rich fish wealth of the rivers of Garhwal, namely over exploitation and pollution have been discussed in the article. The author stress the position that the declining fisheries of the region can only be saved through proper management and balanced exploitation of the resources on the basis of sound ecological principles. They put forth certain concrete suggestions in this direction.

The dangers to the sensitive ecosystem of the beautiful flowering valley of Bhyunder, posed by the tourist boom resulting from machanization of road system and adhoc planning have been discussed in detail by the authors. They pleaded that the valley should be declared restricted area till the time of effective measures for its protection could be planned and enforced.[7]

Again in September, 1980, "The National Institute of Ecology and the Indian Nation Science Academy" in New Delhi hosted a conference on wetlands on behalf of "International Association of Ecology."[8] In this symposium both tropical and temperate wetlands were discussed in an ecosystem perspective. Besides discussing the present state of knowledge, this symposium also identified gaps, recommended areas of further investigation and tried to develop guidelines, for conservation and management of a wide variety of wetlands, e.g. mangroves, coastal wetlands, flood plains, shallow tanks, ponds, marshes, forested wetlands and chaurs as cultivated wetlands.

In June 1984 the Czechoslovak National, MAB Committee SCOPE UNESCO-MAB and the Czechoslovak National Academy of Science jointly organised the second international wetlands symposia.[9]

Recently, in April 1994[10] a conference on wetland archaeology and nature conservation has been convened in the University of Bristol U.K. by Margaret Cox, and her motto was to manage the wetland environment of Summerset Levels and Moors as well as the Developing countries of neighbouring areas. So far as the study area is concerned U.P.Chaudhary[11] has presented his thesis on the problems and prospects of wetlands in North Bihar in Tilka Manjhi Bhagalpur University in the year 1993 and his study was a general survey of wetland problems and not in depth study of, Wetlands Environment Management.

U.P. Sharma & J.S. Dutta Munshi (1995)[12] in their book "Ecology, conservation and Management of Kabar Lake: A Major Tropical Wetland of South East Asia" highlighted the

Physicochemical and biological quality of sample water from wetlands and analysed their environmental scenario. They also suggested management strategies for the development of Wetlands.

R.B. Mandal (1995)[13] in his paper on "Management of Wetlands in North Bihar" discussed planning prospects through development of conceptual view and stages of the growth of wetlands. He also discussed spatial variations and suggested proper measures for wetland management. Again in 1996 R. B. Mandal[14] discussed about Wetland Environment of North Bihar, and analysed wetland linkages, current situations of wetlands and suggested that wetlands are the productive eco-systems in Bihar.

Shamin Ahmad (1993) studied about the ecology and wetland of Milkichak, Darbhanga. He considered wetland as the kidney of nature by analysing Physico-chemical nature of water in different seasons.[15]

## Contribution of the Research Work

1. Due to neglect of wetlands as they are the marginal lands both the government and the public considered them as problem area (*Jhanjhatia mahal*) but this study will show that how wetlands are beneficial for the human society by judging its value at ecological, economic and social levels.
2. The study about wetlands will create environmental awareness which is a must as the people are always trying to cut trees, catch fishes and prey rare birds.
3. The geographical distribution of wetlands has never been studied and hence this study will open a new front in the field of geography to consider about wetland environment seriously.
4. This study will present detailed sample study of wetlands in order to highlight the real problem and suggest planning measures.

## Methods of Study

In this study of wetlands largely systematic approach based on firm quantitative techniques has been applied to analyse and illustrate the relevant aspects of wetlands studies under different sub heads. An analytical view has been taken so that form and description of each element could be examined with a bird's eye view and its relationship with other elements in space and time could be determined. Finally, resource measurement, method & conservation of land and wetlands planning have been suggested for the integrated development of wetlands economy.

Recently, the applications of dynamic production function and probability theory are changing the geographer's attitude towards quantitative interpretation of wetlands studies.

In this study, following methods have been used to explain the problems of wetlands and its relationship with physical features:

1. It has been tried to complete this work through field study and analysing the physical conditions of wetlands in terms of the availability of flora, fauna and other products of marginal lands.
2. The data has been collected through fieldwork and cartographic analysis of toposheets and Geological memoirs available for North Bihar.
3. Regional analysis of wetlands cannot be ruled out in terms of spatio-temporal dimensions because the area was covered with a lot of wetlands during ancient period, but nowadays most of them have lost their characteristics due to siltation of lakes, waterbodies, courses of rivers, tank land other lowlying areas.
4. At some places the use of statistical techniques may be adopted to draw inferences for the formation of wetlands in North Bihar.
5. The impact studies which explain variations of wetlands in terms of population density, agricultural development, transport network, level of industrialisation and the urban development.

**Sources of Data**

In this project data have been collected from census handbook of different Districts of North Bihar besides literature collected from various sources about wetlands. Marshy areas have been depicted from topographical sheets, satellite imageries, fieldwork and cartographic analysis of the available data.

Hypotheses determine the relationship of two variables and is accepted or rejected after empirical verification. Friedman defines "hypothesis as it explains and abstracts the common and crucial elements from the mass of complex and detailed circumstances." The level of significance must be known before the hypothesis is verified for acceptance or rejection.

## Hypothesis Formulation

1. The growth of wetland is a result of filling of Tethysian foredeep found south of the Himalaya by the rivers coming from the north. Hence, they are the remnants of vast lacustrine Gangetic trough called Indo-Braham river by Krishnan and Ayangar.
2. The decline and ecological degradation of wetland is a result of continuous increase in population density of the area, besides dump of garbage and accumulation of refuse water.
3. The wetlands are prolific due to high flood, high rainfall and the plain land having less variations of relief.
4. Structural wetlands are found in area of tectonic disturbances and extremely meandering courses of rivers.
5. Wetlands are dumping ground of waste material and hence they are facing the challenge of environmental degradation.
6. Wetlands should be conserved as they are the shelter of flora and fauna wealth and act as the filter of environmental pollution.
7. Wetlands should be preserved as they are the habitat of varieties of birds, sources of protein, herbs and raw materials for mat industry.
8. Although wetlands are marginal area but they act as saviour of human life by protecting the environment from pollution.
9. It has been found that in North Bihar the number of tanks in each district is closely related with the number of orchards found in the area because the farmers of the locality marry tanks and wells with the orchards planted recently.

**Example of the Test of Hypothesis**

The test of hypothesis is as follows:

By field investigation it has been found that in North Bihar the number of tanks in each district is closely related with the number of orchards found in the area because the farmers of the locality marry tanks and wells with the orchard planted recently. Hence, the hypothesis may be stated that the number of tanks (independent variable) in 1996 is dependent on the number of orchards (dependent variable) found in the area.

In order to know the distribution and magnitude of one variable with the other variables comparisons may be made so that their coincidence can be measured. (Table 1.1) (Fig. 1.2)

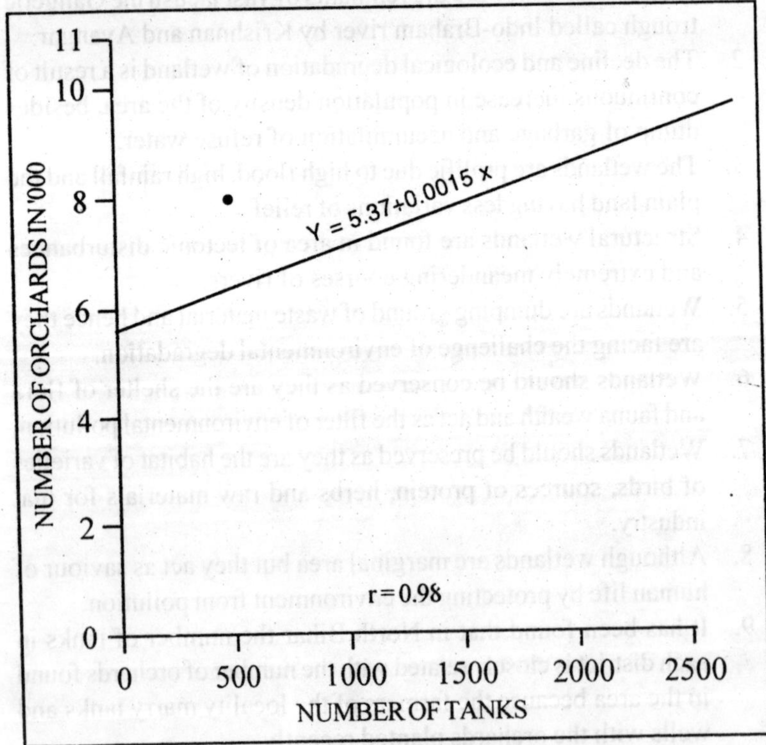


**Fig. 1.2 :** Relationship between Tanks and Orchards in Darbhanga Division.

**Table 1.1 :** Relationship between Tanks and Orchards in Darbhanga Division

| *Districts* | *Tanks (X)* | *Orchards in .000 (Y)* | *XY* | $X^2$ | $Y^2$ |
|---|---|---|---|---|---|
| Darbhanga | 1435 | 9 | 12,915 | 20,59,225 | 81 |
| Samastipur | 508 | 8 | 4,064 | 2,58,064 | 64 |
| Madhubani | 2425 | 11 | 26,675 | 58,80,625 | 121 |
| Total | 4368 | 28 | 43,654 | 81,97914 | 266 |

$$r = \frac{\Sigma XY - \dfrac{\Sigma X \Sigma Y}{N}}{\sqrt{\left(\Sigma X^2 - \dfrac{(\Sigma X^2)}{N}\right)\left(\Sigma Y^2 - \dfrac{(\Sigma Y^2)}{N}\right)}}$$

where $r$ is Pearsonian correlation coefficient

$\Sigma x$ is sum of all values of independent variables.

$\Sigma X^2$ is sum of squares of all independent variables.

$\Sigma Y$ is sum of all values of dependent variables.

$\Sigma Y^2$ is sum of squares of all dependent variables.

$\Sigma XY$ is sum of products of all X and Y values, and N is number of units.

With the help of Table 1.1 the product moment correlation coefficient has been calculated which is as follows:

$$r = \frac{43654 - \dfrac{4368 \times 28}{3}}{\sqrt{\left(8197914 - \dfrac{(4368)^2}{3}\right)\left(266 - \dfrac{(28)^2}{3}\right)}}$$

$$r = \frac{43654 - \dfrac{122304}{3}}{\sqrt{\left(8197914 - \dfrac{19079424}{3}\right)\left(266 - \dfrac{784}{3}\right)}}$$

$$r = \frac{43654 - 40768}{\sqrt{(8197914 - 6359808)\ (266 - 261.33)}}$$

$$r = \frac{2886}{\sqrt{(1838106)\ (4.67)}}$$

$$r = \frac{2886}{1355.77 \times 2.16}$$

$$r = \frac{2886}{2928.46}$$

0.985 (r)

**Calculating from the above, we get the value of *r*=O. 985 (r). This shows that the relationship is very close. The result has been tested by student 't' test by the formula:**

$$t = \sqrt{\frac{r^2 (N - 2)}{1 - r^2}}$$

$$= \sqrt{\frac{(0.985)^2 (3 - 2)}{1 - (0.985)^2}}$$

$$= \sqrt{\frac{0.970225}{0.02975}}$$

$$= \sqrt{32.58}$$

$$= 5.707$$

HO : According to null hypothesis (Ho) there is no correlation between number of tanks and number of orchards in Darbhanga Division in 1996.

HI : According to research hypothesis ($H_1$) there is positive correlation between the number of tanks with the number of orchards in Darbhanga Division in 1996.

The table value of "t" at N-2 Degree of freedom for 5 per cent and 1 per cent level of significance are 3.27 and 1.95 respectively, where as the calculated value of "t" is 5.707. As the calculated value of "t" is significant at n-2 degree of freedom therefore, Ho (null hypothesis) is rejected in favour of $H_1$ (research hypothesis).

The regression of X upon Y has been calculated by the method of least squares according to the formula

$$Y = a + bx \pm Sey$$

Where *Y* is the dependent variable and *X* is the independent variable.

The value of *a* and *b* are given by the following formula:

$$b = \frac{\Sigma XY - \frac{(\Sigma X).(\Sigma Y)}{N}}{(\Sigma X^2) - \frac{(\Sigma X^2)}{N}}$$

$$b = \frac{2886}{1838106} = 0.00157$$

$a = \bar{y} - \bar{x}.b$

$= z - 1092 \times 0.0015$

$= z - 1.63$

$= 5.37(9)$

$y = 5.37 + 0.00157\text{X}$

The accuracy of this estimate of Y can be tested by calculating the standard error of estimate. It is a measure of the error to be expected in estimating the value of Y from a given value of X by means of the computed value of Y. The formula is as follows

$$\text{Standard error (Sey)} = \frac{1 - r^2}{N}$$

$$= \frac{1 - (0.985)^2}{3}$$

$$= \frac{0.02975}{3}$$

$$= 0.009925$$

The standard error of estimate gives the probability of error for two-third of all cases on both sides of regression line Fig. 1.2. Thus the final equation takes the formula:

$$Y = 9331 + 0.00157 \pm 0.0099$$

Fortunately, the standard error of estimate is very low.

## NOTES

1. Ramsar Convention, UNESCO, Ramsar, Iran,Feb., 1971.
2. R.B. Mandal, The Value of Wetlands in North East India, Wetlands (Edt. M. Cox. *et al.*) p. 30.

3. K.D. Choudhary, The Fisheries Biology, Fisheries Technology and Fisheries Economics, Central Institute of Fisheries Education, Bombay, 1975, pp. 274-315.
4. H.R. Singh and S.P. Badola, ''The Location of lakes of the Nainital Area'', *Himalayan Studies and Regional Development*, Vol.II, 1978, pp. 29-32.
5. Tejvir Singh & Jagdish Kaur, The Valley of flowers in Garhwal : A case study for a Biosphere Reserve, *Journal of Himalayan Studies and Regional Development*, 1978, pp. 63-71.
6. Gopal, B. Thakur *et al.*, Wetlands Ecology and Management; National Institute of Ecology and International Scientific Publications, Jaipur, 1982.
7. Wetlands conference in Czechoslovakia strategy and Trends, Washington, D.C.; U.S. 1984, p. 22.
8. Margaret Cox *et al.*, Wetlands Archaeology and Nature Conservation; London HMSO: 1994.
9 U. P. Choudhary, Geographic Aspects of Wetlands in North Bihar; Unpublished Ph.D. Thesis, Bhagalpur University, 1993.
10. U.P. Sharma and J.S. Datta Munshi, *Ecology, Conservation and Management of Kawar Lake: A Major Tropical Wetland of South East Asia*, NEO-PRINTS, Calcutta, 1995.
11. R.B. Mandal, 'Management of Wetlands in North Bihar, *East West Geographer*; Vol.6, No.1, March, 1995.
12. R.B. Mandal, Wetland Environment of North Bihar", *East West Geographer*; Vol.7, No.1, March, 1996.
13. Ahmad, Shamim, Ecology of Wetland of Melkichak, Darbhanga Unpublished Ph.D.Thesis, L.N. Mithila University, Darbhanga, 1993.
14. *Ibid.*
15. *Ibid.*

# 2

# GEOGRAPHICAL BACKGROUND

It is necessary to make an assessment of the physical, economic and cultural level of the region before going into the details of wetlands investigation. This is because the types and patterns of wetlands and the location and site of chaurs have close connection with the physical landscape of the region and this in turn controls the environmental setting, economic resources and the cultural heritage of the people. Physical planning of wetlands and chaurs have taken place within the geographical background of the region. It is, thus, essential to deal with some of these aspects of geography of North Bihar.

North Bihar is situated north of the Ganges river in the State of Bihar (Fig.2.1). It extends from latitude 25°18'N to 27°37'N and from longitude 83°48'E to 88°17'E. The region consists of alluvial deposits of rivers coming down from the Himalayas in the north. It covers an area of 51,814 square kilometres with 32 million people living in 20,262 inhabited villages (1991). In this way, North Bihar is bounded by Nepal in the north, Uttar Pradesh on the West, river Ganges in the south and West Bengal in the east (Fig. 2.1).

In Table 2.1 certain relevant data on district level of North Bihar is given which represents the name of new districts, the date of creation and area, population and the number of wetlands.

## Geology

North Bihar Plain forms a part of the Indo-Gangetic Plain, the origin of which has been a subject matter of controversy and conjecture.

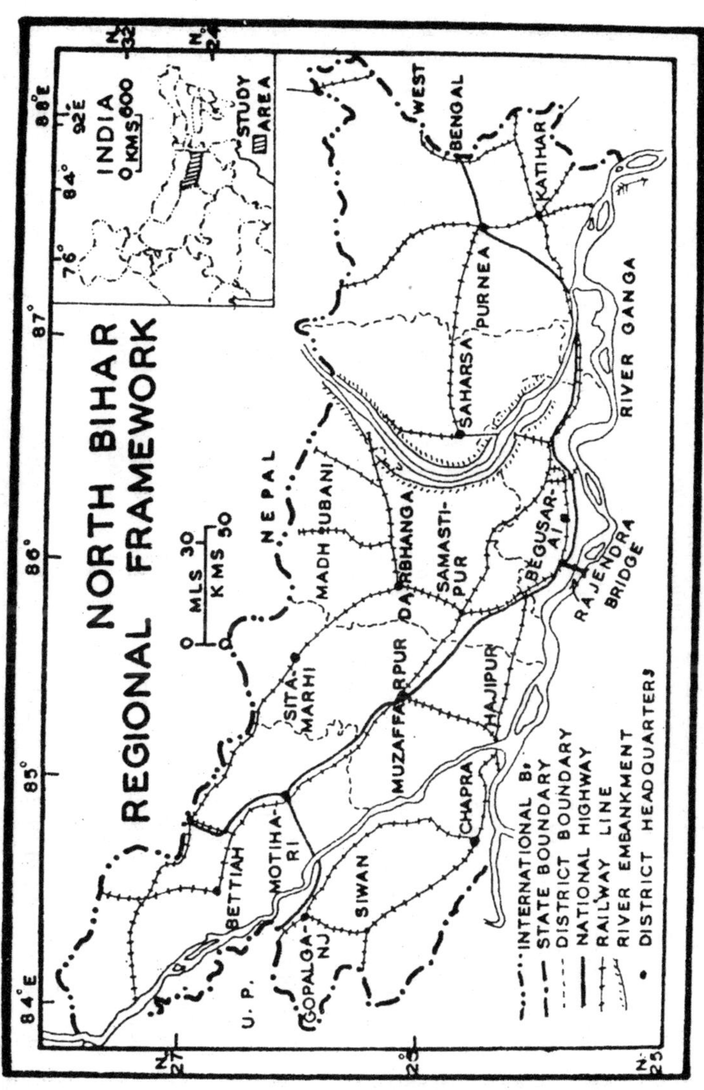


Fig. 2.1 : North Bihar : Regional Framework

**Table 2.1** : Certain Relevant Data on District Level of North Bihar (1991)

| *District* | *Headquarters* | *Date of Creation* | *Area in 000 sq. km.* | *Population in Lakhs* | *Density of Population per sq. km. (1971)* | *Density of Population per sq. km. (1991)* | *Number of Wetlands* | *Sub-division* |
|---|---|---|---|---|---|---|---|---|
| Begusarai | Begusarai | 2.10.1972 | 1.90 | 11.47 | 604 | 945 | 6 | Begusarai |
| Gopalganj | Gopalganj | 2.10.1973 | 1.40 | 11.17 | 610 | 837 | 4 | Gopalganj |
| North Bhagalpur | Bhagalpur | 1774 | .86 | 3.30 | 378 | 572 | 3 | Bhagalpur Sadar |
| Katihar | Katihar | 2.10.1973 | 4.0 | 9.42 | 360 | 596 | 115 | Katihar |
| Darbhanga | Laheriasarai | 1875 | 2.4 | 15.17 | 661 | 1101 | 218 | Darbhanga |
| East Champaran | Motihari | 1873 | 4.3 | 19.24 | 449 | 767 | 160 | Motihari, Sikarhria |
| West Champaran | Bettiah | 8.11.1972 | 4.9 | 15.87 | 326 | 446 | 152 | Bettiah, Bagaha |
| Madhubani | Madhubani | 1.12.1972 | 3.5 | 18.92 | 536 | 808 | 145 | Madhubani, Jhanjharpur |
| Khagaria | Monghyr | 1870-71 | 0.79 | 7.45 | 346 | 664 | 3 | Khagaria |
| Muzaffarpur | Muzaffarpur | 1875 | 3.2 | 19.09 | 604 | 929 | 4 | East and West Muzaffarpur |
| Kishanganj | Kishanganj | 1994 | | 10.00 | — | 524 | 75 | |
| Purnea | Purnea | 1813 | 7.0 | 30.00 | 358 | 581 | 245 | Purnea, Sadar, Araria, Kishanganj |
| Araria | Araria | 1994 | | 16.00 | — | 569 | 26 | |
| Saharsa | Saharsa | 1954 | 5.9 | 20.50 | 399 | 612 | 201 | Saharsa Sadar |
| Madhepura | Madhepura | 1994 | | 12.00 | — | 659 | 20 | Madhepura, Birpur, Supaul |
| Samastipur | Samastipur | 04.11.1972 | 2.9 | 18.85 | 639 | 935 | 5 | Samastipur Sadar, Rosera |
| Saran | Chapra | 1866 | 3.2 | 20.35 | 628 | 970 | 3 | Chapra |
| Sitamarhi | Sitamarhi | 11.12.1973 | 2.7 | 15.83 | 595 | 904 | 3 | East and West Sitamarhi |
| Siwan | Siwan | 03.12.1972 | 2.3 | 11.27 | 605 | 973 | 2 | Siwan |
| Vaishali | Vaishali | 12.10.1972 | 2.00 | 13.49 | 668 | 1053 | 5 | Hajipur |

*Source* : Directorate of Census Operations, Bihar, Census of India, 1991, Bihar, Primary Census Abstracts, March, 1991

Austrian geologist Edward Suess considered it a "foredeep" (Wadia, 1961), which seems to be of the nature of "synclinorium". On physical and geodetic considerations, Sir S. Burrard viewed it "a deep rift or fracture in the subcrust" with parallel faults on either side with a maximum down throw of 32 kilometres (Burrard, 1912). The third and more recent view regarding this is a sag in the crust formed between the northward drift of the Indian peninsula and the comparatively soft sediments accumulated in the Tethyan basin when the latter were crumpled and lifted up into a mountain system (Krishnan). The generally accepted view at present is that it has been formed by buckling down of the northern border of the Peninsular shield beneath the sediments thrust over it from the north. The formulation of this plain commenced after the final upheaval of the mountains in the Tethys sea and since then the alluviation has uninterruptedly continued up to the present. Naturally, the solid geology of the North Bihar plain has been obscured underneah the thick alluvial mantle.

The Gangetic plains of North Bihar consist extensively of alluvium deposits which is variable in extent and has a maximum depth of 1829 metres (Dunn, 1949). Only a small portion in the north-west of champaran district consists of Siwalik rocks. The alluvium is of two categories, older and newer, while the Siwalik deposits include sandstone, limestone, conglomerate and clay of the Tertiary and older alluvium of Holocene Periods.

(a) The older alluvium (*Bhangar*) of Lower Pleistocene age occupies the higher ground areas not liable to flooding, which covers the entire *Terai* region of North Bihar, West of Maharajganj in Saran district and north-east of Saharsa and Purnea. It is characterised by the presence of *'Kankar'*, sandy loam, nodular limestone, and has ofen Yellowish in Colour (Majid, 1951).

(b) The newer alluvium (*Khadar*) of Upper Pleistocene to recent Age is confined to areas annually covered by floods and consists of silt, clay and fine sand deposited on eitherside of river channels, especially in North Bihar. As the youngest deposit, it is characterised by absence of *'Kankar'* and is often dark in colour. (Fig. 2.4)

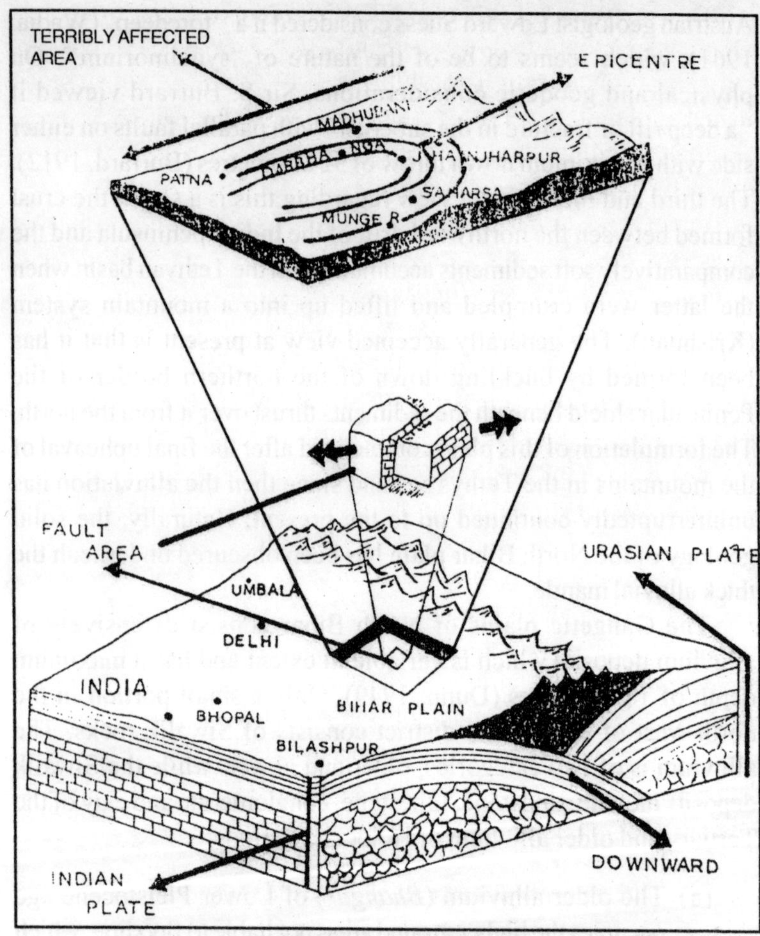


**Fig. 2.2 :** Effect of 1988 Earthquake on Darbhanga Division

(c) The Siwalik represents foothills of the Himalayas in a small portion of Champaran district, where different types of rocks are found. They contain folded sedimentary rocks of micaceous sandstone, variegated shales and different types of clays are found in the Dun and Sumeshwar ranges. The alluvium deposits of this area is youngest in age while Sumeshwar stage is the oldest of all the formations. The alluvium contains sandy soil, loose pebbles and boulders.

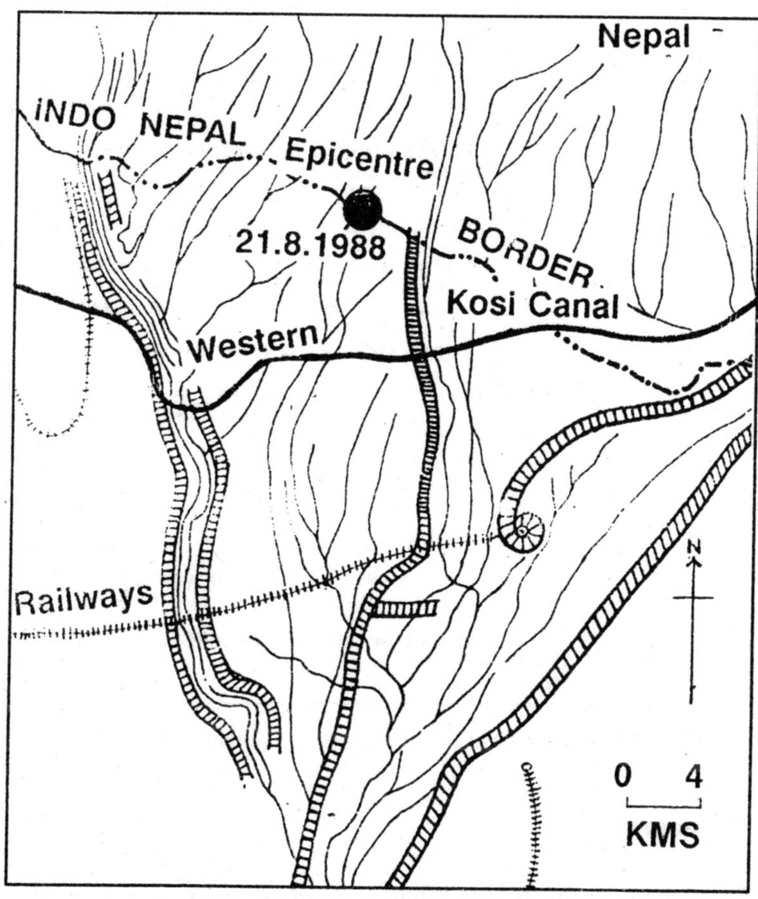


**Fig. 2.3 :** North Bihar : Epicentre of 1988 Earthquakes

Below this, boulder conglomerate stage dominate successively. The older alluvium of Holoiene is found from Valmikinagar towards east for a distance of 33 kms.

So far as the deposit of different sedimentary layers of rocks of North Bihar is concerned Fig. 2.2 shows the succession of beds, their thickness and the characteristics of soil deposited in the region. This clearly reveals that the silty loam, fine sand, yellow sand and clay dominate as different layers of soil deposits in North Bihar.

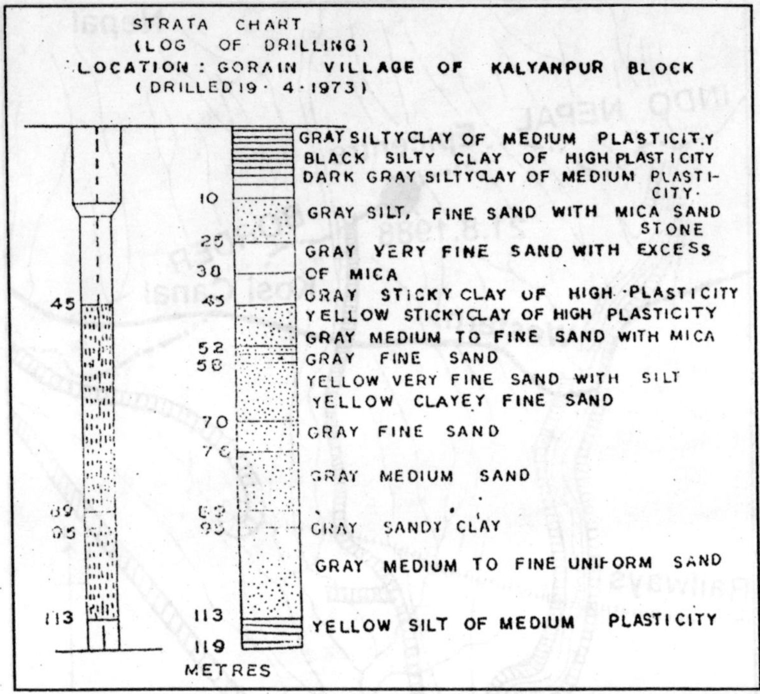


**Fig. 2.4 :** Strata Chart (Log of Drilling) Location : Gorain Village of Kalyanpur Block.

## Physiography

Physiogaphically, North Bihar is divided into two-parts (a)The Himalayan Foothills and (b) the North Ganga Plain (Fig. 2.5).

The foothill zone covers an area of 932 square kilometres and is distinguished by 76 metres contour line on the south. It consists of two distinct lines of hills and valleys along the border of Nepal which run from north-west to south-east. The southern range of Ramnagar Dun has an average width of 6-8 kilometres and extends for about 32 kilometres. Its highest point is 242 metres near Santpur. This area has been dissected by numerous small rivers. The valley of the Harha river, which is 22 kilometres long and whose average height is below 152 metres from mean sea-level, is known as Dun Valley, lying north-east of the Ramnagar Dun.

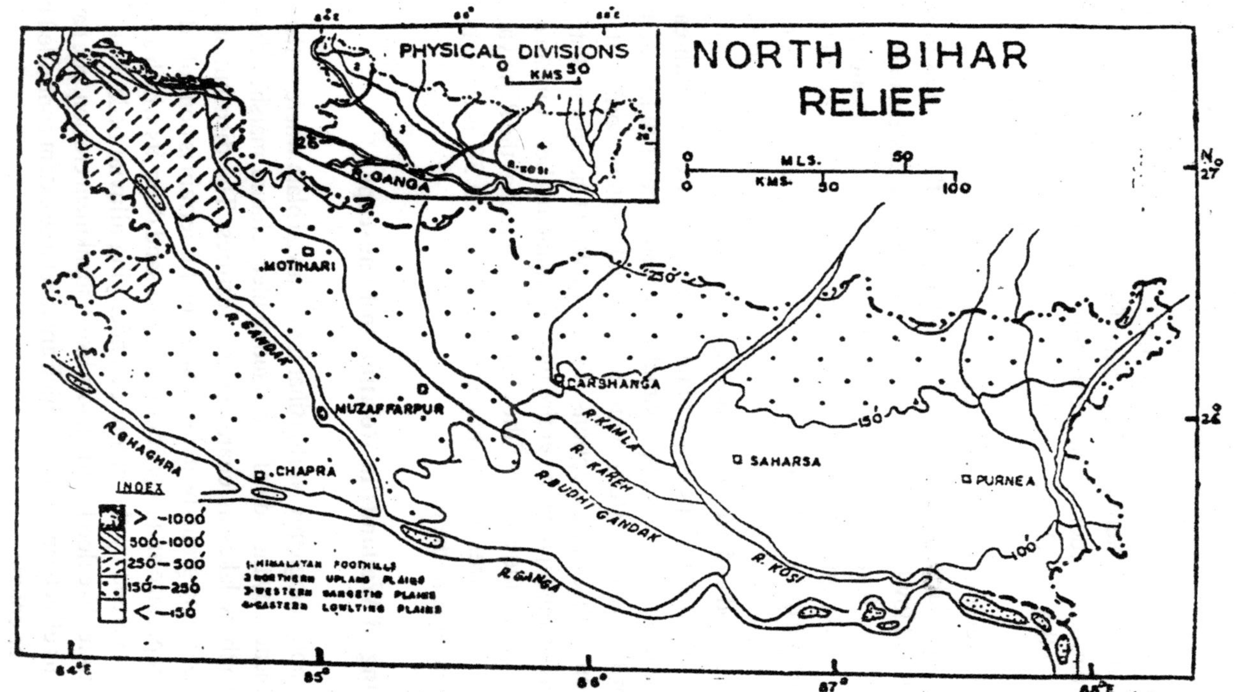


**Fig. 2.5 :** North Bihar : Relief Feature

North of the Harha Valley the Sumeshwar range extends over 74 kilometres from the head of the Tribeni canal in the west to Bhikhnathori gap in he east. The highest point is Fort Sumeshwar (880 metres). There are some gaps formed by streams along the international border. These are the Sumeshwar pass along the Harha river valley which are used for inter-communication with Nepal. (Fig. 2.6)

The entire North Bihar Plain which lies north of the river Ganges is an alluvial plain with minor slopes towards the Ganges in the south and lowlands of the Kosi Belt in the middle eastern part. The significant features are the levee deposits and sand bars along the river banks and marshy depressions known as '*chaurs*'. These chaurs are quite often old abandoned courses of the streams (oxbow lakes) and some of them have formed due to sheet-wash erosion during flood and irregular deposition of silts.

The general slope of the plain is from north-west to south-east. The average slope is approximately 8 metres per 100 kilometres from the north-western point to the south-eastern corner of the region. With some exceptions of a part of West Champaran district, and Kishanganj area the entire plain is 76 metres below mean sea-level. Along the course of the Ganges, the height of the Plain varies from 43 metres near Chapra in the west to 30 metres near Naugachhia in the east.

## Sitting of Wetlands in Relation to Landscape

Geomorphologically North Bihar is an alluvial plain where wetlands are located by the side of rivers and rivulets, chaurs, marshes, diaras and oxbow lakes as characteristic features. The distribution of wetlands and groundwater resources in this terrain is controlled by the shape, size and inter-relationship of sand deposits which are in turn governed by the nature of underlying alluvial beds. Natural calamities like floods and factors like embankment erosion, etc. have various effects on wetland which are to a large extent controlled by the river courses.

The change in the site of wetlands is due to large scale alluviation, meandering of rivers and excessive floods resulting in the filling of

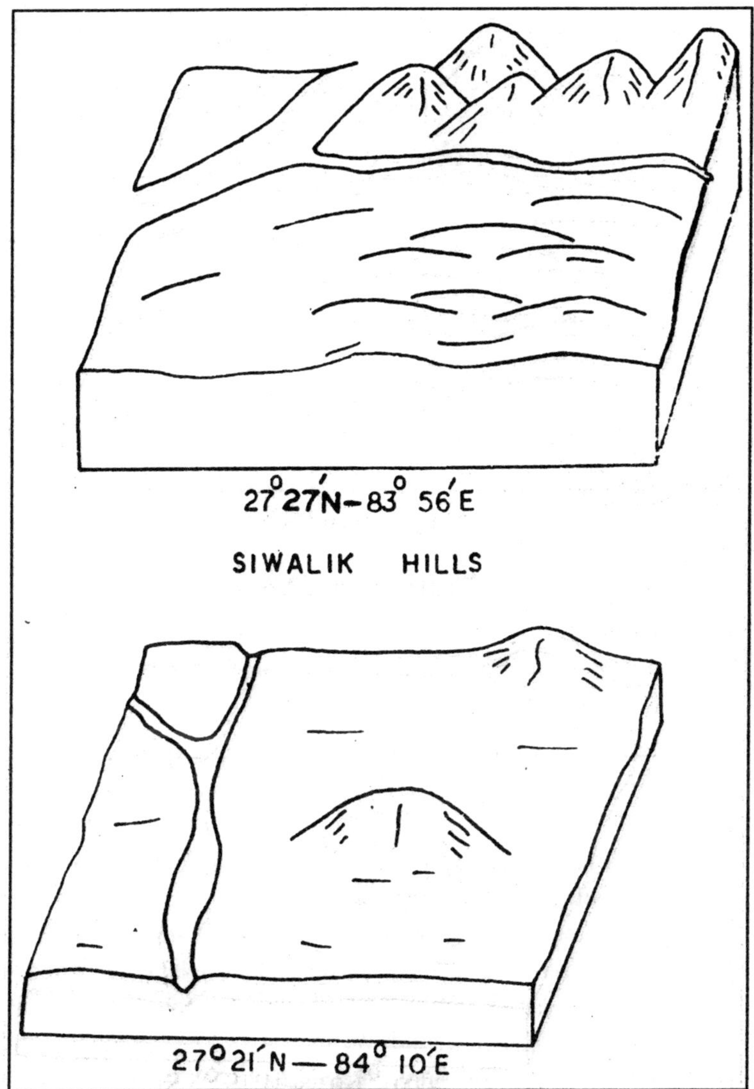


**Fig. 2.6 :** Siwalik Hills of Champaran

wetlands, cultural features, and crops and the development of waterlogging, marshy lands, formation of alluvial fans, cones and intercones. This has happened due to unequal. deposition of sand bodies and sheet wash erosion. These are some of the geomorphic

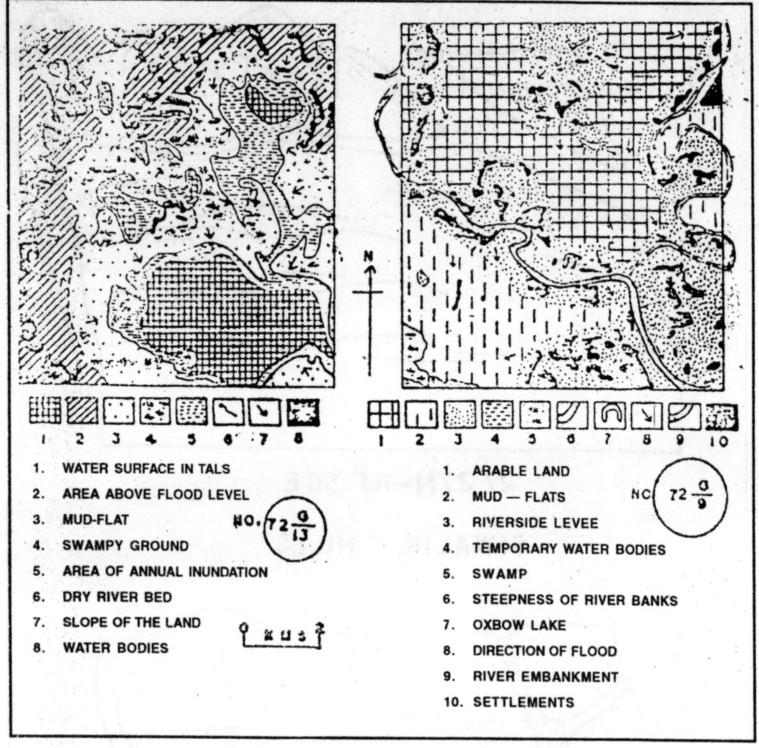


**Fig. 2.7 :** North Bihar : Alluvial Geomorphology, Samastipur District

aspects which have an overriding importance for a geographer studying the sitting of wetland in North Bihar.

In Fig. 2.7 the alluvial geomorphic features of Samastipur district represents the following features: water surface in lakes, area above flood level, mud-flat, swampy ground, area of annual inundation, dry river bed, slope of the land, water bodies, river embankment, direction of flood, oxbow lake, steepness of river banks, riverside levee and arable land.

In regional planning the chief aim of the author is to analyse, classify and to map the various topographical features in their correct position and examine the mutual relationship for assessing their physical properties and economic potentialities (Singh and Kaith, 1971) in relation to landscape and wetland.

(a) This region is an alluvial plain. The diversities seen on the surface are those due to river action and series of raised riverside uplands known as levee dotted with wetland and alternating deprecations or *chaurs* of the streams.

(b) The weathering process on higher lands are strengthened by the action of gullies and rills, particularly in the Terai areas of North Bihar. This erosion produces shifting position of wetlands and formation of alluvial cones. At the base of mountains the boulder strewn debris roll down under gravity in the fashion of an apron (Despande & Bhat, 1954), especially in the Siwalik hill region of north western Champaran district.

(c) A narrow moist Terai belt in Champaran at the foot-hill formed by re-emergence of water soaked underground in the upper foot-hill gravel zone of Nepal which has given rise to smaller chaurs.

(d) A Sub-Terai belt of marshy land in the north with intervening tracts of uplands along rivers is successed in the south by a wide belt of marshy lowlands, characterised by permanent depressions and lakes which help in evolving medium size wetlands.

(e) In the riparian tracts of the Ganges the land is high due to which wetlands cling with a few intervening depressions and lakes. Due to the presence of river bluffs on the northern bank of the Ganges, all rivers flowing along the gravity of slope from north to south, turn towards east and run parallel along the Ganges river for a few kilometres before they finally meet together.

## Alluvial Landscape and Wetland Features

### *Alluvial Cones*

North Bihar Plain consists of the alluvial cones or fans of the Gandak, the Kosi and the Mahananda-Tista with two intervening slopes or intercones (Geddes, 1960) lying between them. The cones exhibit a radial pattern of distributaries, and the intercones generally have lower gradients than the cones. Because of the large quantities of silt which they deposit, the rivers flow at a higher level than the surrounding country. In case of the Kosi and the Gandak, annual shift of wetland and river channels form several new types of wetland and spill patterns respectively. These are distinctly seen together with traces of earlier patterns. The availability of underground lenticular beds of sand, loams and consolidated clays must embody the successive overlay of old spill patterns and the changing character of wetland, because the pybst-rata of the intercones are less irregular than those of the cones. Several layers of underground water in the clayey intercones help in boring tubewells. Alluvial cones and river terraces (Davis, 1954) are numerous especially along the riparian tracts of the Kosi, the Kareh, the Baghmati, the Ehuthi-Balan, the Gandak and the Mahananda.

Fig. 2.8 : Gandak Alluvial Cone

Fig. 2.8 represents the formation of alluvial cone in the course of river Kosi. As this river enters into the plain it is marked with 76 metres of contour height but slowly and slowly in a semi-circular fashion it has attained a height of 30 metres from mean sea level at the confluence of the river Ganges.

The expanse of the Kosi alluvial cone covers areas of Saharsa, and parts of Purnea, Darbhanga, Katihar, Khagaria, Bhagalpur, Madhubani and Samastipur districts. It is traversed by numerous rivers all of which are branches of the Kosi, which flow in the name of old courses of the Kosi. From its source to straight south up to the Ganges the apron of the alluvial cone projecting towards south while in the present course of the Kosi it tapers towards north due to lower level of the flood plains of the Kosi.

### *Flood Plains*

Flood plains or flood terraces which are formed by the rivers are the deposition of alluvium in meandering river basins of North Bihar. These are always of low relief as compared to the rugged terrain of north-western Champaran. In the Southern half of the region the characteristic topographic features, viz., flat plains, alluvial cones, stream neanders, oxbow lakes, marshes, irregular temporary lakes which occupy small depressions including sand bars, natural levees, spill cones, spill hollows and other minor relief features formed by flood or shifting of channels are important. Over these landscape features the wetlands of varying forms i.e. circular, square, rectangular, hollow square, fan pattern and several others are emerging slowly according to the shape and size of the landscape units.

### *Meanders*

The streams which cut their basins at base level and graded streams of flat plains before meeting the Ganges tend to flow in broad sweeping curves. This is due to the low velocity of the current and the deposition of alluvium which divert the stream courses

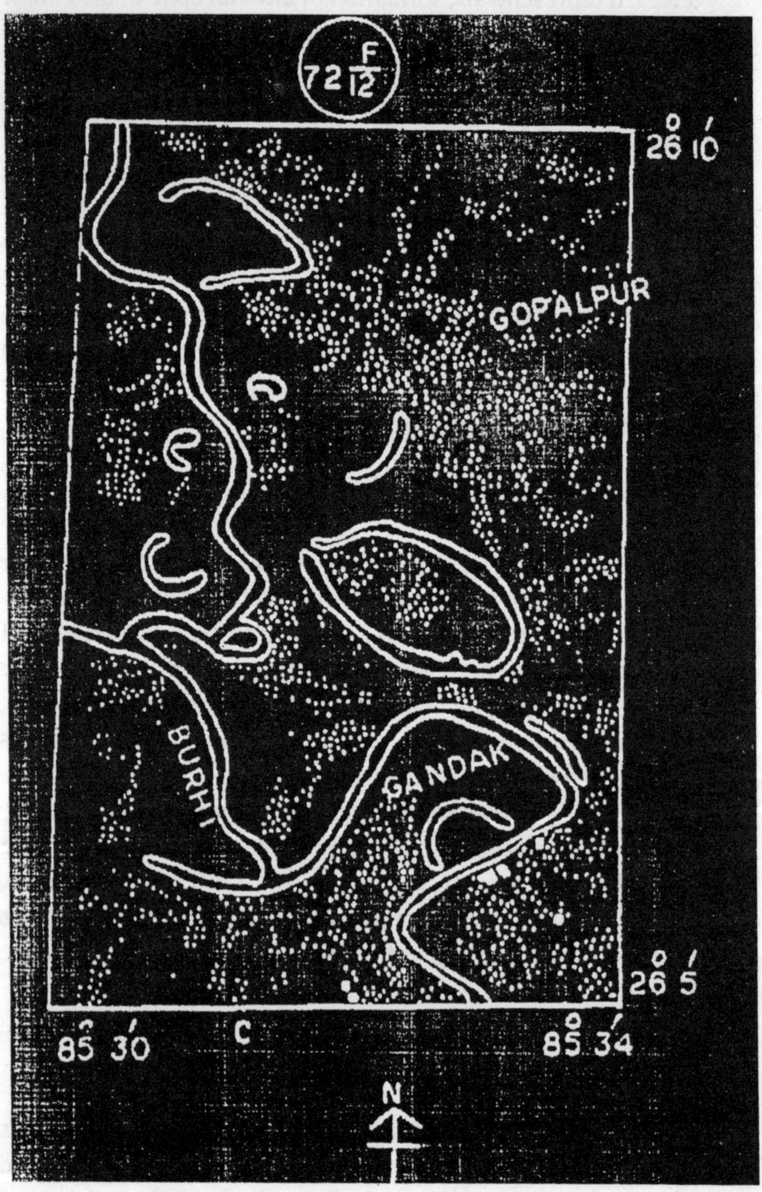


Fig. 2.9 : Oxbow Lake in Vaishali District.

(Worcester, 1967). As the current is directed against the outer bank of a meander (Fig. 2.9) it cuts further in this direction and at the same time builds up a bar of sand on the inner side. Swings of current around one curve tends to cross the channel and develop another curve in the opposite bank. The meanders grow and shift down streams. In this way, the eroding bank of a river represents old and large size of the meander where as the wetland are new, small and fragmented in nature which is directly controlled by the volume and speed of water.

The development of length in meandering stream is apparent from a study of a few representative villages given below:

**Table 2.2 :** Meandering of River Kareh

| *Actual Place* | *Straight Length of river in kms.* | *Length of River with meander in kms.* | *Name of river* |
|---|---|---|---|
| Cheria-Bariarpur to Khagaria | 38.40 | 88.00 | Budhi Gandak |
| Samho to Latipur | 75.20 | 105.60 | Ganges |
| Chapki to Chautham | 73.60 | 134.40 | Kareh |

*Source :* Calculated from Quarter Inch Toposheet No. 72K, Survey of India, Dehradun, 1950.

The Ganges, the Burhi-Gandak, the Kareh and other rivers have a meandering channels in North Bihar. The presence of oxbow lakes on single side of the arcute bend of a river suggests that it is flowing under, second cycle of erosion but still further the availability of oxbow lakes on anti-podal side suggests that the landscape is passing under third cycle of erosion. The severence of such meandering oxbow lakes clearly show phases of degradational and agradational topographic features (Fig. 2.10C). As a consequence of the flat gradient of country, the rivers that flow southwards tend to take pronounced meandering courses. Strabo, described the river as "so exceedingly winding that everything winding is called meandering (Russel, 1954)". The Kosi frequently changes its course and within 214 years this mighty river has shifted 115 kilometres

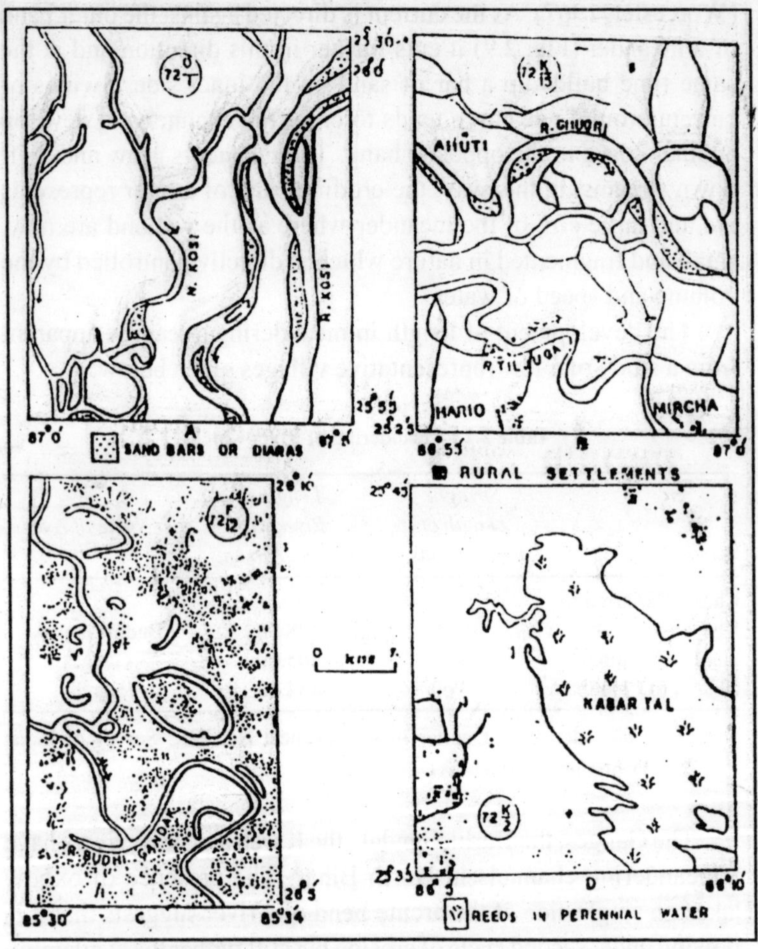


**Fig. 2.10 :** Topographic Features of North Bihar

west of its original 1736 AD. course. The shift was not by gradual cutting of its embankment but by the flowing of a number of distributaries. As such this river presents a braided channel topography (Fig. 2.10 A-B) in Saharsa, Purnea and Katihar districts of north-eastern of Bihar.

In the Kosi basin some of the older alluvial deposits have been removed and redistributed down stream. The presence of hard and consolidated blocks of Siwalik clay as buried topography having

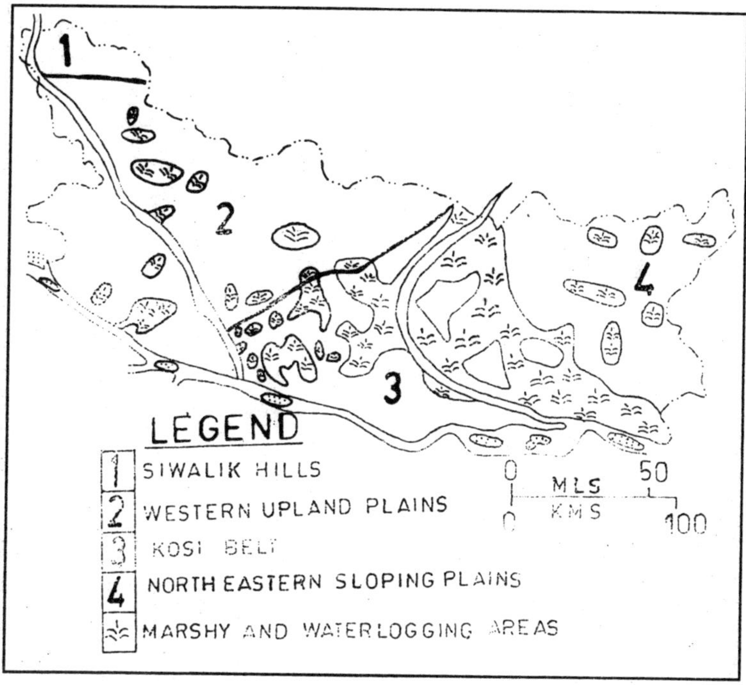


**Fig. 2.11 :** North Bihar : Geomorphic Regions

marks of fossils on the banks of most of the rivers have led to the development of meandering courses in this riverine plain. For example, near Dubepur, Parbana, Kharsam and Ghibahi villages of Samastipur district, the river Kareh makes four bends within a distance of three kilometres. Due to the flat and low level of the country the meandering of river channel is the chief feature in the lower reaches of the Burhi Gandak river where the serpentine course of the stream has given rise to excessive flood during the rainy season. It also helps in the formation of oxbow lakes and marshy lowlands along the river banks.

### *Oxbow Lakes and Bayous*

As meanders grow, it frequently happens that a narrow neck of land is cut through from two sides (Fig.2.9) thus allowing the stream to straighten its course. The two ends of the meander so separated from the channel, are likely to be filled up by sand. Fig.2.9 presents the best example of an oxbow lake on the bank of river Burhi-Gandak in Vaishali district. These water bodies form excellent wetland sites. The whole face of the country is dotted with wetlands besides small oxbow or elongated water bodies and chaurs (long semi-circular marshes) which lie in between the rivers marking the old abandoned courses of the streams. Though found extensively in all parts of this region, the abandoned courses are more prolific in Madhubani, Champaran Sitamarhi and Begusarai districs of North Bihar, Hardia Chaur in Saran extends up to nearly 32 kilometres along the Gandak embankment and has a breadth of 3 to 8 kilometres.

### *Marshes*

The abandoned channel of a stream on a flood plain may become partially filled with vegetation, thus forming a marsh. They may also occur in any depression on the flood plains especially in areas of waterlogging. Marshes are numerous towards the south-eastern part of North Bihar.

Some of these marshy lands dry up during the hot season. There are some marshes which exist throughout the year like a tank (Fig.2.11). Marshes are also found in the beds of rivers like the Mahananda, the Panar, the Kosi, the old Kosi, the Bhuthi-Balan, the Kamla, the Jibachh, the Kareh, the Burhi Gandak, and the Gandak during the hot weather season but during rainy months the river establishes its normal course.. The marshes are utilised by the peasants for irrigation, rearing fishes, for growing mothi and makhana and for washing animals in the summer season. wetlands in the marshy areas are dotted here and there.

### *Natural Levees and Bluffs*

These are commonly found on the banks of rivers in North Bihar, which help in protecting the wetlands from the furry of floods in most cases. Due to the growth of levees and infilling of the side of water course with alluvium, all streams raise their beds and f low in normal conditions well above their flood plain. During the rainy season almost all the rivers of the region overflow their natural levees and cause extensive floods. Artificial embankments of 2240 kilometres have been constructed on either side of most of the rivers of North Bihar as a flood protection device. This serves as an artificial levee and prevents the river from inundating the side area.

Sandy flat diaras, smaller alluvial cones and river terraces are found on the bank of every perennial river in North Bihar, because these are the common topographic features of the riverine plains.

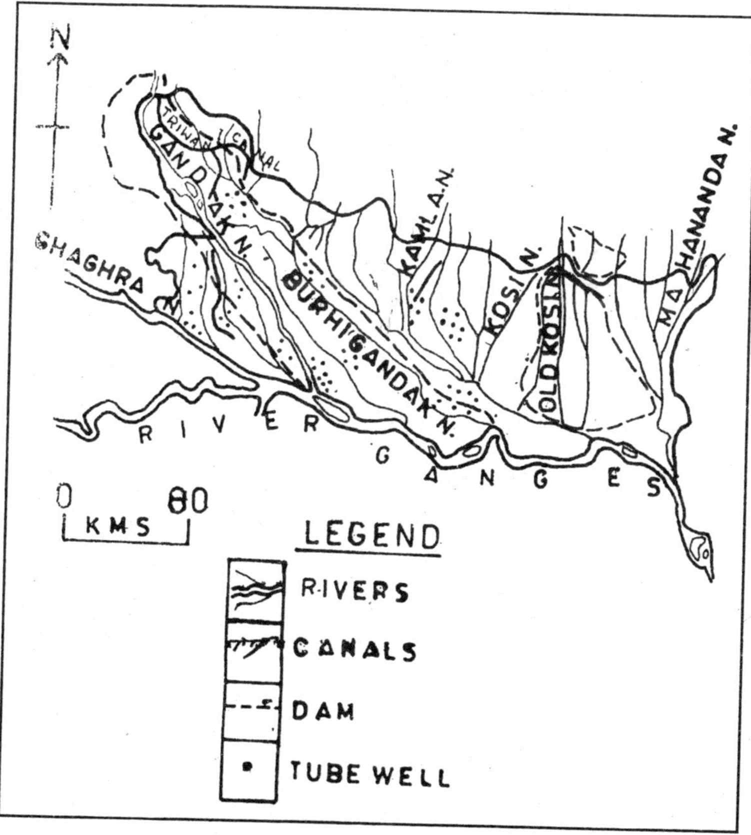


**Fig. 2.12 :** North Bihar : Sources of Irrigation

In most cases the sandy unproductive flood prone diara's discourage the location of wetlands. Sandy diaras are very common, especially on the banks of the Gandak in Saran, Champaran, Muzaffarpur and Vaishali districts.

On the northern side of the Ganges the sandy flats are so extensive that it is difficult to cross them on foot. No tract of man is seen there. Every where sand and silt deposited in different patterns form a number of topographic features. Raghopur diara of 160 square kilometres and Saintia Diara of 8 square kilometres opposite Fatwah and Barh towns north of the Ganges respectively are the best examples of diara topography marked by smaller wetlands.

Fresh water lakes are also found in the southern part of the region. Tal Baraila of 15 square kilometres in Vaishali district, (Fig. 2.12) presents the best example of fresh water lakes.

**Table 2.3 :** Approximate Rate of Shifting of The River Kosi (1736 to 1950 A.D.)

| *Years* | *(Years Interval)* | *Distance Moved in Kilometres* |
|---|---|---|
| 1736-170 | 34 | 10.72 |
| 1770-1823 | 53 | 9.28 |
| 1823-1856 | 33 | 6.08 |
| 1856-1883 | 27 | 12.80 |
| 1883-1907 | 24 | 18.40 |
| 1907-1923 | 15 | 10.88 |
| 1922-1933 | 11 | 28.80 |
| 1933-1950 | 17 | 17.60 |

*Source :* Aids, R.N. and Mukherjee, D., "Sedimentation in the Kosi : A Unique Problem", *Journal of C.B.I. & P, Calcutta*, July, 1963, p. 266.

## Drainage

The heavy rainfall and the shape and slope of the region have given rise to dendritic pattern of drainage in the upper reaches and parallel drainage in the middle and lower parts of rivers in North Bihar. There are a number of major rivers such as the Gandak, the Baghmati, the Kamla-Balan, the Kosi, the Mahananda and a host of smaller streams which come down from the Himalaya make, their way to the Ganges in frequently changing (Dayal, 1968) and mendering courses. The occurrence of floods is a common feature in the Kosi basin and has earned bad name "the river of sorrow". The completion of the Gandak and the Kosi projects have not made significant change in this part of the State, and large scale damage to crops and wetland from floods occur annually.

The presence of marshy depressions in the southern part of Saharsa, Begusarai, Purnea and Katihar districts and Khagaria district of Munger Division have formed permanent shallow sheets of water expanding during the rains and contracting during the dry season. Some of them represent the deeper portions of abandoned river channels e.g., the 'Kabar Tal' in Begusarai district, 'Baraila Tal' in Vaishali district and a chain of 43 lakes with an aggregate area of 356 square kilometres in Champaran district.

Hence, North Bihar lies on a low level, in many places, indented with chains of shallow marshes, marking the lines of drainage by which the local rainfall and overflow of the hill streams which intersect the districts find their way south-wards into the Ganges. The rivers flow on raised beds, which they have gradually constructed for themselves out of the silt brought down from mountains in Nepal (Fig. 2.13).

The *Brha Vishnu-Purana* gives the name of several other rivers that are sometimes difficult to be identified today. The names of the ancient rivers as given in the Mithilamahatmyakhanda are: Kausiki, Kamla, Vilvavati, Vyashravati, Viraga, Madana, Ichamati, Lakshmana, Vagmati, Saligrami, Tiljuga, Jivayika, Yamauni, Haridra, Panu Amaya, Arddhavara Vanaghoss, Dhemura, Ghosavati, etc. All the important places of ancient India were situated on the banks of the little Gandaka, the smaller offshoot of the Great Gandaka until the seventh Century B.C.

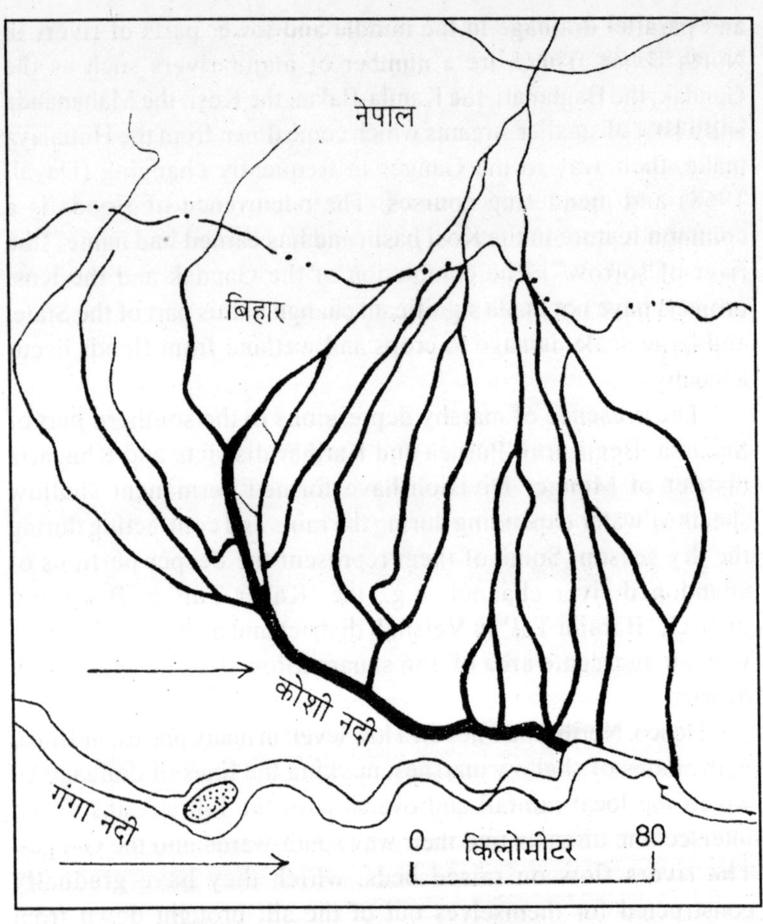


**Fig. 2.13 :** Kosi Basin : Drainage Lines

The *Mahabharata* also called North Bihar *Jalodbhava* (land reclaimed from swamp). Besides rivers, there are several lakes and ponds which formed either by the heavy rains or by the floods or independently being dug by religious Purposes by Mithila kings and inhabitant , which have created a vast lowlying plain. It has been rightly said that Mithila is mainly a vast chain of temporary lakes, joined together by the numerous beds of the hill-streams which pass on their way from Nepal to the Ganges. Larger tracts in this area do not dry up till the end of cold weather and for this fact in some places communication lines are open for only three to four months of the year (Mishra, 1949)

## Climate

North Bihar has a moderated climate in between the humid West Bengal in the east to that of drier Uttar Pradesh in the West. The summer heat is neither so intense as in the drier west, nor so moist and enervating as in the Ganges delta. Hot westerly winds start in March and last until May. Light damp easterly wind blow intermittently and afternoon storms accompanied by rain (Norwester) take the place of the rainless dust storms of Uttar Pradesh. The monsoon rains begin a little later than in West Bengal in mid-June. The rainfall is much less than in Bengal but is considerably higher than in Uttar Pradesh (Fig.2.14).

### *Winter Season*

The cold weather sets in during November when the morning and the evening are pleasant and cool. In December and January the weather is delightful during the day, while the nights are distinctly cold. The average dry-bulb-temperature in this season is 18.6°C. In some years the bitter cold wind continues throughout the day and night for some days. The sky is, as a rule, cloudless and the average seasonal rainfall is 38.7 mm which is only per cent of the total rainfall of the year. It is, however, of considerable importance for Rabi crops.

In the month of February, the nights are still cold but the days become progressively warmer until the hot weather sets in by the end of March.

### *Summer Season*

It commences by mid-March and continues till mid-June. During this season the westerly winds bring high temperature and reduce humidity in the region. The average dry-bulb-temperature is 28.4°C which is 100C more than the temperature in the winter season.

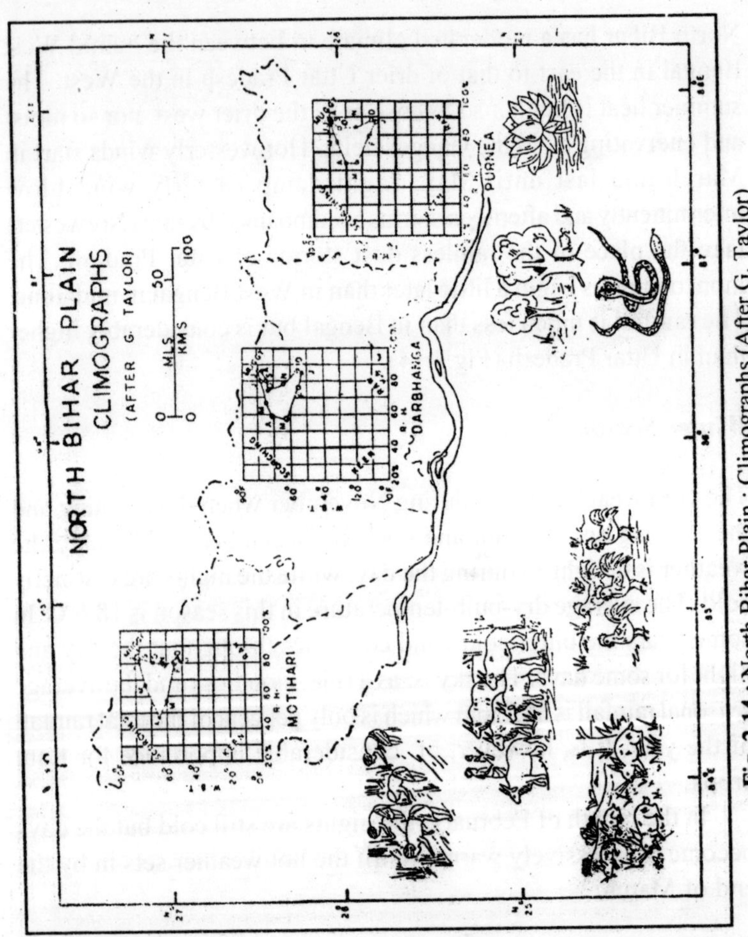


**Fig. 2.14 : North Bihar Plain : Climographs (After G. Taylor)**

There are occasionally strong gales and storms during this season which may either result in thunder storms or may give rise to blinding clouds of dust. The average rainfall in this season is only 25.3 mm.

### *Rainy Season*

Soon after the burst of monsoon in the month of June, the percentage of humidity becomes very high and the scorching heat of the sun rays gives place to an oppressive muggy heat. The average dry bulb-temperature in this season is 28.80°C, which is similar to that in the summer. But the relative humidity becomes as high as 86 per cent. Above 1200 mm or over 90 per cent of the total annual rainfall occurs in this season. Average monthly rainfall is around 250 mm, with a peak in July and August. Considering the annual rainfall, Purnea district enjoys a comparatively heavier shower than the entire region under study. In Purnea, rainfall increases ratidly towards the north-east rising to over 200 cms in the Terai area near Thakurganj and Pothia, while the districts of Saran, Siwan, Gopalganj, Vaishali, Samastipur and Begusarai are the areas of low rainfall, varying from 90 to 125 cms.

In Fig.2.15 the mean annual distribution of rainfall is represented with isohyt lines. The area of highest rainfall over 200 cms lies in the north-eastern part of Purnea district. Similarly, the smallest zone of 175 to 200 cms rainfall and 150 to 175 cms rainfall lie in the districts of Purnea and mountainous area of the West Champaran.The zone of 125 to 150 cms rainfall cover a wider zone in northern part of North Bihar. The South-western part of the region has below 125 cms of rainfall.

This shows that the distribution of rainfall is quite uneven in the region which we receive in the rainy season of July to September except 10 to 15 cms rainfall of the winter season through westerlies coupled with sub-tropical Jet Stream.

After careful consideration of relevant data for the three meteorological stations in North Bihar, two climographs have been drawn to illustrate the conditions in Bihar Plain. The first have been developed by G. Taylor (Fig. 2.14) to show the effect of humidity

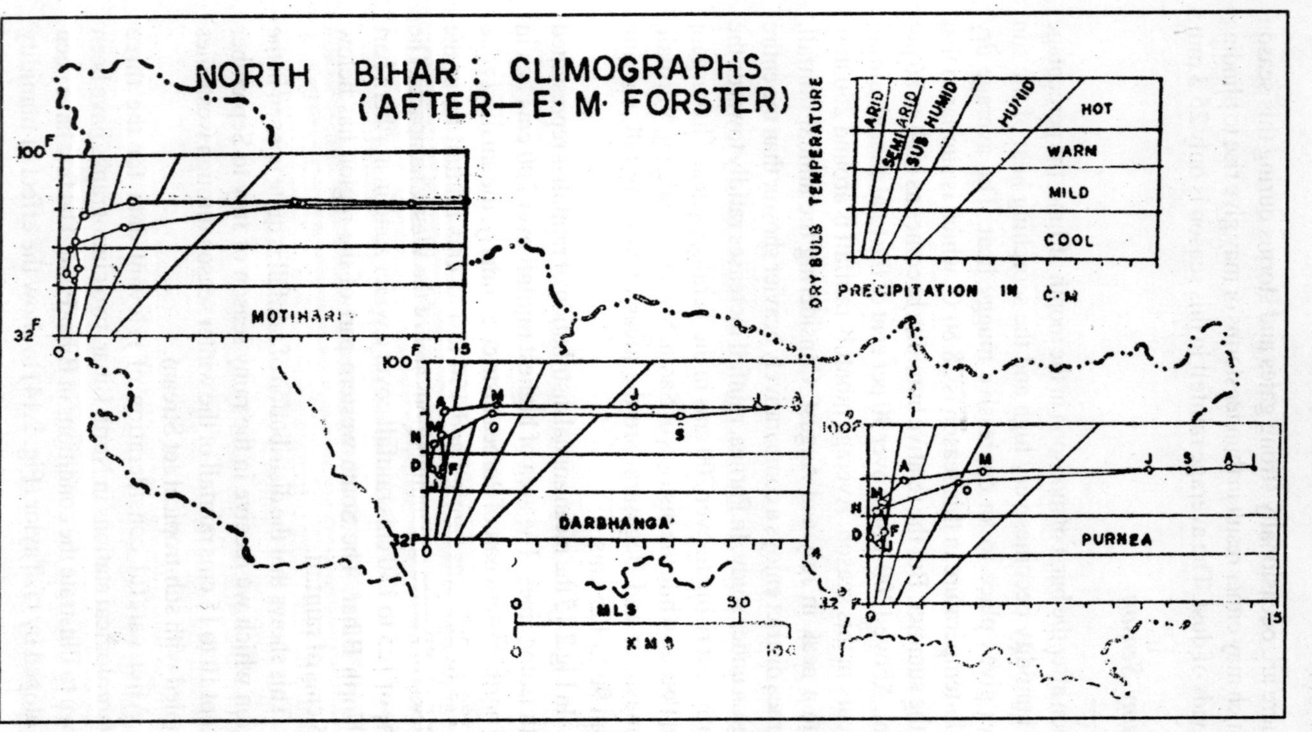


Fig. 2.15 : North Bihar : Climographs (After E.M. Forster)

and temperature upon wetland of the region. The second is based on Thornthwait's formula was developed by E.M. Forster, (Fig. 2.15) and takes into account temperature and precipitation (Monkhouse, 1952). The conclusion from this study are given below:

(a) The Wet-bulb-temperature in the region ranges between 50°F to 42°C throughout the year, but in general 15°C is the value lower over the eastern lowlying plains than in the western Gangatic Plains. In most part of the year humidity is high (88%) in Purnea and relatively low (50%) in Saran and Champaran.This leads to the larger number of wetlands in Saharsa, Purnea and Katihar districts, and the shallow chaurs over the rest of the Plain of Saran, Siwan and Gopalganj.

(b) The climographs occupy an elongated central position in the upper half of the graph. Thus summer month (March to May) are nearer 'scorching' and the rainy season (June to October) nearer 'muggy' in character. This difference is more marked in the South-West (Motihari) than in the north-east (Purnea).

(c) Examining the climograph based on Thornthwait's formula we find that the winter season can be classed as mild and cool, the summer as semi-arid to arid and the rainy season as hot and humid. The entire plain is distinguished by the hot and humid rainy season, which has greatly affected the types of wetlands and chaurs, in the region under study.

(d) The Dry-bulb-temperature ranges from 50°C to 45°C and the rainfall ranges from 7 cms to 40 cms in the year, for any one month. The range of temperature, however, is least in Purnea and highest in Gopalganj. Peak rainfall has been received in July and August for the entire region, each of these months contributing approximately 25 per cent of the total annual rainfall. The contrast of summer and winter season is less than 5 per cent of the total annual rainfall in any one month. The extreme range of rainfall, particularly the peak rain falls in July and August which have a profound impact on the types and patterns of wetlands.

## Effect of Climate on Wetland

Air and light are primary requirements in a wetland and as such in chaurs, the ditches have no definite shape and size. Among other factors, wind, temperature and rainfall have profound influence over the wetlands found in the area.

The heavy showers in monsoon season causes inundation especially in the rivers of North Bihar. This occurs almost every year. Due to this people have to build their tanks a little away from the river banks, above the annual flood-level. Secondly, heavy rainfall and coarse texture of steams flowing sluggishly on flat plains have created marshy areas due to waterlogging. At the same time poor drainage also causes formation of alkaline and saline soils. These have resulted in the formation of smaller ditches which are frequent in the northern part of the Kosi basin and Saran district respectively.

Thirdly, heavy rainfall in Purnea and Saharsa forces to have larger and widespread wetlands. In the drier parts of North-West Bihar, shallow chaurs are more common. (Fig. 2.16)

## Soils

The soils of North Bihar is formed by a thick alluvial mantle of drift origin deeply underlain for the most part of Siwalik and older Tertiary rocks of the surface deposits; silty loam, silty sand and sandy silt are found near the stream bank. Sandy loam is generally found on the young flood plain and loamy sand and sandy loam soils are the characteristic features of the old flood plain.

North Bihar has generally soils of light textured, comparatively low amount of clay but higher amount of silt and sand (Dayal, 1954). These have been deposited by numerous rivers and streams which flow from the Himalaya north to the Ganges in the south. These alluvial soils of the north have been further grouped into seven broad soil associations the important ones being, the recent alluvium non-saline, non-calarecus soils of the Kosi-Mahananda system; young alluvium non-saline, non-calcareous soils of the Adhwar system (Baghmati, Kamla-Balan, etc.) and young alluvium calareous soils of the Gandak system.

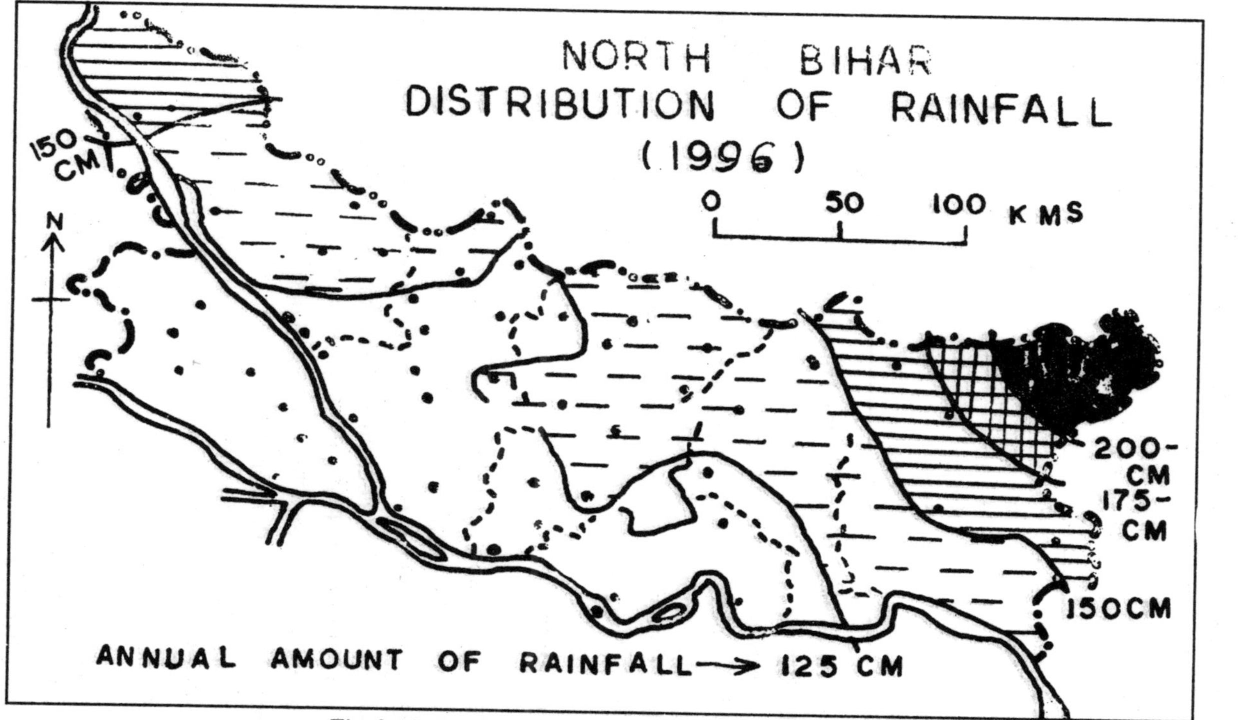


**Fig. 2.16 :** North Bihar : Distribution of Rainfall (1996)

So far as the underground conditions of soil is concerned sand content prevails on others which is shown in Table 2.5 given below:

**Table 2.4 :** North Bihar : Conditions of Soil in percentage

| *Name of the Village* | *Anchal* | *Sand* | *Clay* | *Sand and Clay* |
|---|---|---|---|---|
| Basuwanal | Bagaha | 85.86 | 9.14 | 5.00 |
| Panchrukhia | Ramnagar | 77.74 | 19.92 | 7.33 |
| Basmanpur | Motihari | 61.41 | 32.58 | 5.92 |
| Kargahies Purab | Bettiah | 60.00 | 37.00 | 3.00 |
| Kharsam | Rosera | 59.00 | 30.100 | 11.00 |
| Pokharbhinda | Jhanjharpur | 42.05 | 40.95 | 177.00 |

This clearly shows that the Himalayan rivers are depositing a huge amount of sand throughout North Bihar.

The main crops grown on these soils are paddy under unirrigated conditions and paddy, wheat, barley, sugarcane, potato and other vegetables under irrigated conditions. Paddy cultivated on soils are able to support dense population and hence waterlogged areas are found in North Bihar. (Fig. 2.17)

## Vegetation

The region has mostly deciduous type of vegetation, with patches of agricultural fields in very limited areas. Much of the original vegetation cover has been destroyed by the extension of cultivation, reckless and wasteful cutting and unrestricted grazing by animals.

In North Bihar Plain, there are only 912 square kilometres of forests in North-west Champaran and only 10 square kilometres of planted forests in Purnea district.

The districts of Saran, Muzaffarpur, Darbhanga and Saharsa are altogether devoid of forests. The types of forests found in North Bihar are as follows:

(a) Valley Sal Forest,
(b) Hill Sal Forest,
(c) Mixed Forest,
(d) Grass,

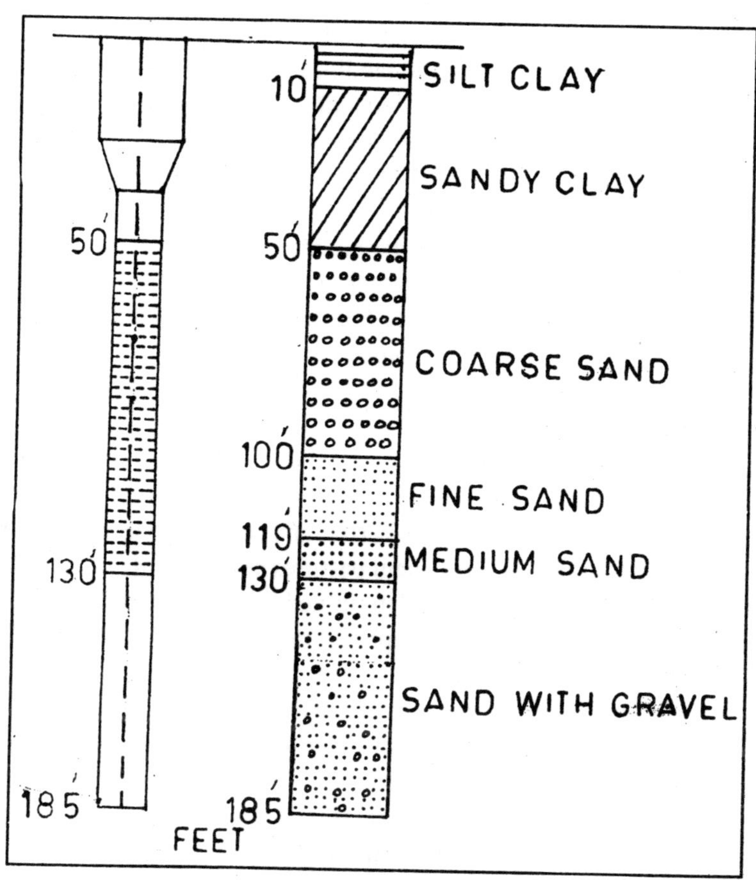


**Fig. 2.17 :** Strata Chart of Singhara Village, Mahua Anchal

(a) Valley Sal forest occurs in the valley of Sonha, Bhopsa, Harha, Baghia and Pandsi. Very good sal occurs in Massan and Sonha valley where natural tress of Sal of 25 mtrs to 35 mtrs in height are found on flat ridges and gently sloping areas of the Sumeshwar Range. Further east the quality is poor.

(b) Hill Sal forest occurs throughout the hilly region. The quality of the tree is poor and the natural Sal trees attain a height of 25 to 30 mtrs only. These forests are not as important for direct yield of timber as for their indirect effect of protection against soil erosion.

(c) Sal is the predominant tree found in mixed forest. Other trees are khair, semal, jamun and banjhi. The exploitable diameter of these trees is 35 to 60 cms depending on the species. Khair and Semal are common in Madanpur and Tribeni Blocks of West Champaran. Semal occurs in riverine tracts and is mainly used for matchwood.

(d) Two types of grass are encountered in the area: low level Savanah and high level Savanah. They occur on the river banks and hill slopes respectively. The area is small, and the yield is used for manufacture of paper.

## General Land Use

Land is classified into six classes according to use as net sown area, current and old fallows, barren and uncultivable waste and non-agricultural uses, permanent pastures and orchards, forest and others. Pattern of land use is determined by two sets of factors (a) the physical factors like topography, climate and. soil which broadly determine the capabilities of the land, and (b) the human factors like the length of occurrence, density of population, social and economic institutions, etc. Which determine the extent to which the resources of the land are utilized.

Taking the net sown area and fallow lands together, cultivation is found to be extended to the farthest limits. There are considerable amount of forests in the Sub-Himalayan zone of extreme north-west in Champaran where the percentage rises to about 10. All other districts are marked by flat alluvial plains. The land under forest is less than 0.5 per cent. Similarly, the barren and unculturable wastelands constitute 5 per cent or less of the total area. So far as the non-agricultural uses of land are concerned, built up area, roads and water bodies are major constituents under this head and the picture is practically the same all over North Bihar (Fig. 2.18).

Orchards and pastures occupy 2 to 3 per cent of total land in North Bihar. It is only in basins of the river Kosi in Saharsa and the Adhwara group of rivers in Mazaffarpur and Darbhanga districts, that the land under orchards and pastures reach more than 3 per cent.

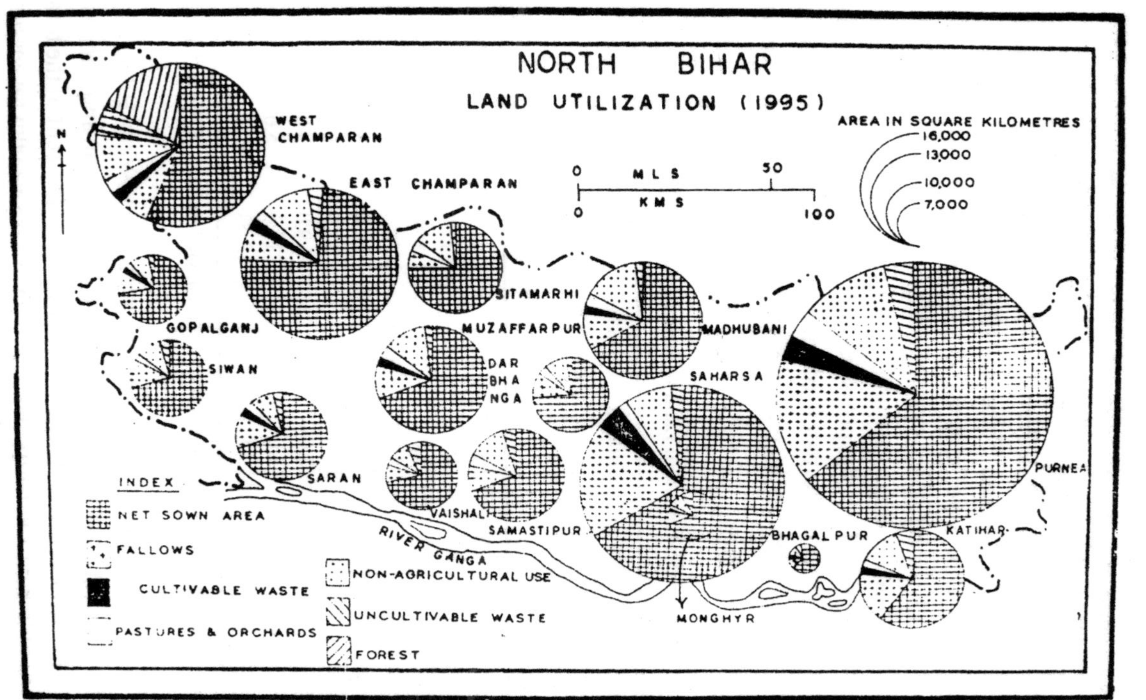


**Fig. 2.18 :** North Bihar : Land Utilization, 1995.

Fallows include two types of land, namely, old fallow (for 2 to 5 years) and current fallows. These are cultivated lands which have been left fallow because of rainfall deficiency or economic reasons in one year or other.

According to rainfall conditions in different years, fallow are highest in Saharsa (17%), Purnea (14%) and Khagaria (16%) where the land is relatively poor. Saran has 10 per cent fallow land, probably because of extensive sugarcane cultivation in which land has necessarily to be left fallow periodically.

The net sown area is around 70 per cent or more in Tirhut and Kosi Divisions. Here, the pressure of population is so intense that nearly every available patch of land is cultivated. Extension of cultivation is often at the expense of mango orchards and pasture lands.

**Table 2.5 :** Pattern of Land Utilization in North Bihar (1995)

| *Districts* | *Net sown area* | *Fallows* | *Permanent Pastures and Orchards* | *Barren & Unculti-vable Waste* | *Non-agricul-tural uses* | *Forests* |
|---|---|---|---|---|---|---|
| Saran | 71.0 | 10.0 | 3.0 | 11.0 | 5.0 | X |
| Champaran | 68.0 | 6.0 | 2.0 | 12.0 | 2.0 | 10.0 |
| Muzaffarpur | 74.0 | 6.0 | 2.0 | 16.0 | 2.0 | X |
| Darbhanga | 69.0 | 8.0 | 3.0 | 18.0 | 2.0 | X |
| Begusarai | 59.0 | 16.0 | 4.0 | 13.0 | 8.0 | X |
| Saharsa | 60.0 | 17.0 | 6.0 | 11.0 | 6.0 | X |
| Bhagalpur | 61.0 | 12.0 | 15.0 | 9.0 | 13.0 | X |
| Purnea | 66.0 | 14.0 | 4.0 | 11.0 | 5.0 | X |
| Khagaria | 66.0 | 11.13 | 3.63 | 12.63 | 5.38 | 1.25 |

*Source :* Department of Statistics and Evaluation, Government of Bihar, Patna.

When we consider the land-use pattern in North Bihar as a whole the net sown area constitutes 66 per cent and fallows 11.13 per cent of the total land. Thus almost 77 per cent of the total land is cultivated. Orchards and cultivable wastes account for another 5 per cent of the total land. Uncultivable land is about a fifth of the total area, which is shared almost equally by the built up area and

**Table 2.6 :** Area under Different Crops in '000 hectares of North Bihar (1995-1996)

| *Districts* | *Rice* | *Wheat* | *Barley* | *Maize* | *Gram* | *Masoor* | *Arhar* | *Khesari* | *Sugarcane* | *Potato* | *Total* |
|---|---|---|---|---|---|---|---|---|---|---|---|
| Saran | 82 | 94 | 5 | 51 | 4 | 2 | 5 | 2 | 3 | 9 | 257 |
| Siwan | 82 | 75 | 9 | 36 | 3 | 1 | 8 | 2 | 9 | 3 | 228 |
| Gopalganj | 79 | 72 | 4 | 27 | 1 | 1 | 5 | 2 | 16 | 3 | 210 |
| East Champaran | 208 | 86 | 18 | 26 | 2 | 10 | 4 | 9 | 13 | 5 | 381 |
| West Champaran | 211 | 82 | 11 | 11 | 1 | 6 | 2 | 9 | 41 | 3 | 377 |
| Muzaffarpur | 188 | 66 | 10 | 30 | 1 | 2 | 2 | 10 | 5 | 5 | 239 |
| Vaishali | 58 | 40 | 6 | 33 | 1 | 1 | 2 | 1 | 1 | 4 | 147 |
| Sitamarhi | 152 | 97 | 4 | 6 | 1 | 5 | 1 | 24 | 5 | 3 | 248 |
| Darbhanga | 76 | 43 | 3 | 8 | 3 | 3 | 1 | 10 | 2 | 3 | 152 |
| Madhubani | 207 | 46 | 3 | 5 | 4 | 6 | 1 | 18 | 4 | 4 | 299 |
| Samastipur | 66 | 60 | 4 | 51 | 2 | 1 | 4 | 7 | 4 | 5 | 204 |
| Begusarai | 11 | 60 | 2 | 66 | 3 | 1 | 4 | 2 | 2 | 1 | 157 |
| Khagria | 66 | 25 | 2 | 22 | 5 | 3 | 2 | 8 | 1 | 2 | 136 |
| Bhagalpur | 15 | 11 | 3 | 7 | 3 | 1 | 1 | 3 | 1 | 1 | 46 |
| Saharsa | 195 | 94 | 5 | 69 | 1 | 2 | 1 | 24 | 1 | 4 | 387 |
| Purnea | 400 | 79 | 6 | 37 | 4 | 6 | 1 | 21 | 1 | 7 | 569 |
| Katihar | 118 | 32 | 6 | 19 | 3 | 2 | 1 | 5 | 1 | 2 | 189 |

*Source :* Department of Statistics and Evaluation, Government of Bihar, Patna.

water bodies on the one hand, and forests and barren lands on the other. The former is distributed almost uniformly over the region, the latter is confined in the extreme north. The intensity of cultivation is highest in the Ganges riparian tract of North Bihar.

## Agriculture

On account of over dependence on rainfall Indian agriculture is said to be a 'gamble in monsoon'. But agriculture is the predominent occupation of the people of the region. Nearly 77 per cent of the total population derives sustenance from agriculture as compared to 69.50 per cent in India as a whole. North Bihar forms one of the richest and most fertile agricultural tracts in India and grows a variety of crops.

The alluvial plain of North Bihar which intervened with rivers and ridges is rich in all sorts of crops. In some tracts nothing but an enormous stretch of rich fields meet the eye, but in others the level plain is dotted with numerous clusters of bamboos and groves of mango and also trees.

Rice is a principal *Aghani* crop and its greatest concentration lies in a triangular belt between the Burhi-Gandak and the Kosi river in North Bihar. Maize and millets are the main *Bhadai* crops. They are predominent to the south and west of the Burhi-Gandak in the districts of Saran, Siwan, Gopalganj, southern part of East and West Champaran, Vaishali, Samastipur, Begusari, Khagaria and along the Gandak and the Ganges diaras.

Wheat, Barley, Gram, Oilseeds and other Rabi crops become more and more important as we move from east to west. In North Bihar wheat cultivation is found south-west of the Baghmati in Samastipur, Begusarai and Khagaria districts, where the loamy soil is annually fertilized by fresh deposits of silt.

Chillies and tobacco are cash crops, dominant in the well-drained sandy soils of the Gangetic riparian tract throughout sandy soils of North Bihar. Sugarcane is by far the most important cash crop of the region having higher percentage (33) of calcium in the soil, Saran, Champaran, Sitamarhi and Darbhanga districts produce large quantities of sugarcane.

Under favourable climatic conditions, Jute covers relatively larger areas to the east of the Kosi river in Saharsa, Purnea and Katihar districts. There are four Jute mills in North Bihar: one each at Muktapur (near Samastipur) and Purnea, while two others are at Katihar.

A new method has been devised here for crop combination on regional level. The formula is as follows :

$$\frac{HA}{1} - 1 = \text{Ist ranking crop.}$$

$$C.C \left[ \begin{array}{l} \frac{HA}{2} - 2 = \text{IInd ranking crop.} \\ \\ \frac{HA}{3} - 3 = \text{IIIrd ranking crop.} \\ \\ \frac{HA}{4} - 4 = \text{IVth ranking crop.} \end{array} \right.$$

Lower Limit of Crop Diversification for good combination = TA/N where C.C. is crop combination.

HA is highest hectares of crop in the study area. 1,2,3, and 4 are denominators for crops of a particular rank, and 1,-2,-3, and -4 are diversification index in order to relegate lower hectares of crop. (Fig. 2.19)

TA is total hectares of all crops and N is the number of crops.

The computation of crop combination on the basis of above formula is as follows:

**Saran District**

Rice-82, Wheat-94, Barley-5, Maize-51, Gram-4, Masoor-2, Arhar-5, Khesari-2, Sugarcane-3 and Potato-9.

Thus according to TA/N in case of Saran district the total hectares is 257 for 10 crops. Hence, the lower limit of a crop to enter into the combination is 257 thousand hectares of land under

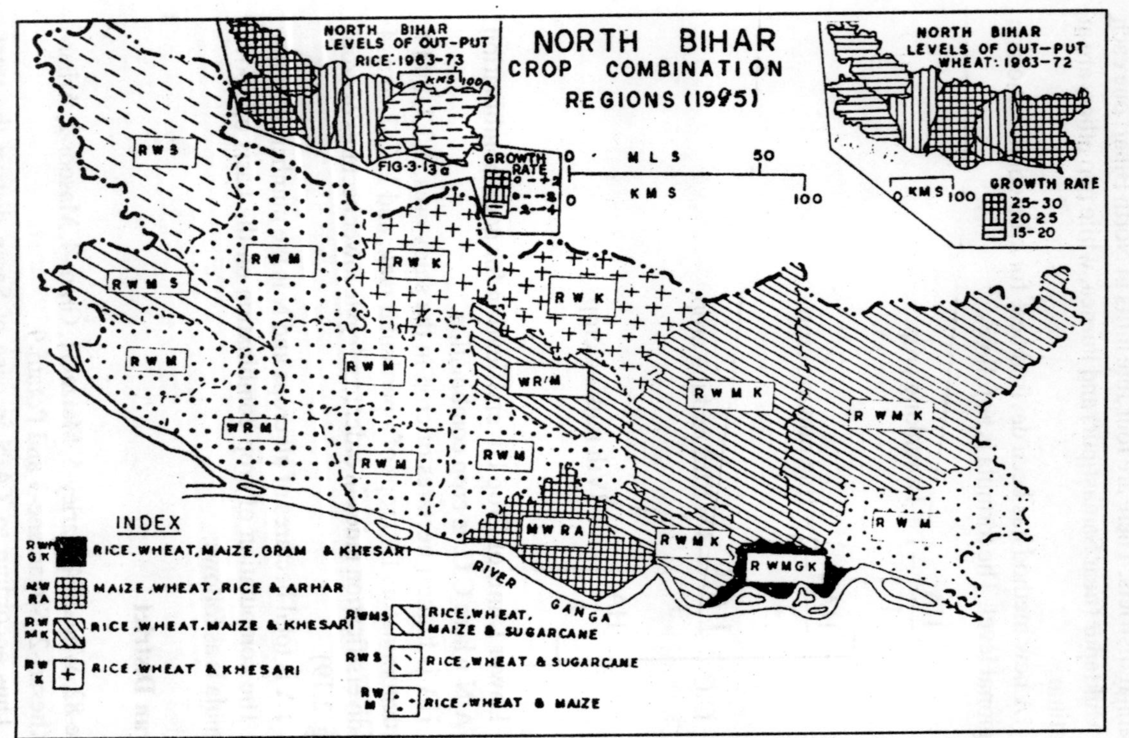


Fig. 2.19 : North Bihar : Crop Combination Regions, 1995.

particular crop. In such a situation only Wheat, Rice and Maize will enter into the combination.

$$\frac{94}{1} - 1 = 93 \text{ Ist ranking crop Wheat.}$$

$$\frac{94}{2} - 2 = 45 \text{ IInd ranking crop Rice and Maize.}$$

A case of three crop combintion. According to Table 2.6 and Fig. 2.19.

Fig. 2.20 shows the levels of output of the growth of rice in 1992 to 1993 in North Bihar. This clearly represents that districts of Saran, Siwan, Gopalganj, East Champaran and West Champaran which have plus one to plus two per cent of growth. The districts of Vaishali, Muzaffarpur, Sitamarhi, Samastipur, Darbhanga and Madhubani have medium level of growth of rice during the same period, where as the district of Saharsa has 1 to 2 per cent of the level of growth in rice production. The districts of Purnea and Katihar have recorded the lowest growth rate of 2 to 4 per cent during the same period,

So far as the level of out-put of wheat is concerned old. Darbhanga and Purnea districts have recorded 25 to 30 per cent of growth rate from 1992 to 1993, where as old Saran and Champaran districts have a growth rate of 20 to 25 per cent only. The districts of Saharsa and Muzaffarpur have an equal growth rate of just 15 to 20 per cent during the same period.

## Irrigation

Due to uncertainty of rainfall, Bihar's agriculture has been described as a gamble in the hands monsoon. This places agriculture on a sound economic footing. It is necessary to provide better irrigational facilities throughout the region. Steps have been taken in this direction and 1,227,000 hectares of land or about a quarter of the total cropped area in the region was irrigated from different sources in 1995-96. Table 2.7 shows the total irrigated land in which wells, tubewells

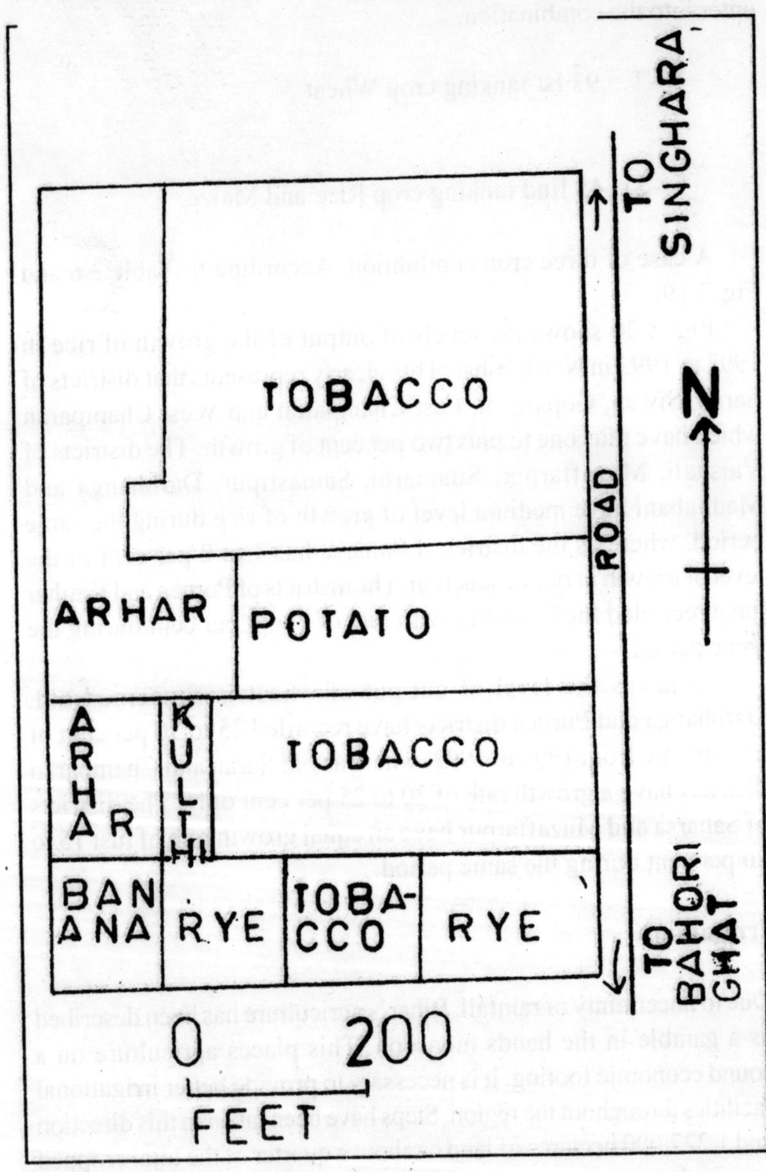


Fig. 2.20 : Field and Cropping Pattern of Singhara Village (Mahua Anchal)

and tanks together account for another 30 per cent. The balance 28 per cent of the irrigation is provided by other sources, like ahars, chaurs and smaller ditches, etc.

In North Bihar the average rainfall is coupled with the overspill of rivers which normally ensures an adequate water supply and hence the irrigated area is meagre except in the two westernmost districts of Saran and Champaran, where on account of the lower rainfall about 25 per cent of the total cropped area is irrigated.

Nowadays in most of the districts of North Bihar, the condition is more or less the same. The least irrigated districts are Katihar, Madhubani and Vaishali where only about 30, 000 hectares of land is irrigated. In Champaran district, about 90 per cent of the irrigation is from Dhaka (Lal Bakya) and Tribeni (from the Gandak) canals which together irrigate about 150 hectares of land. Throughout North Bihar tubewell is the chief source of irrigation nowadays, but in Saran, Siwan and Gopalganj well is the cheap source of irrigation which irrigate over 100 hectares of land. (Fig. 2.21)

Two important irrigation schemes which have recently started irrigating large areas are the Kosi Project and the Gandak Project in North Bihar. The Kosi Project is designed to protect.

**Table 2.7 :** Total Irrigated Area in '000 hectares (1995-96)

| *District* | *Area* | *District* | *Area* |
|---|---|---|---|
| Saran | 96 | Darbhanga | 32 |
| Siwan | 91 | Samastipur | 64 |
| Gopalganj | 89 | Madhubani | 33 |
| East Champaran | 85 | Begusarai | 39 |
| West Champaran | 85 | Khagaria | 144 |
| Muzaffarpur | 57 | Bhagalpur | 144 |
| Vaishali | 33 | Saharsa | 121 |
| Sitamarhi | 38 | Purnea | 56 |
| | | Katihar | 20 |

*Source :* Department of Statistics and Evaluation, Government of Bihar, Patna.

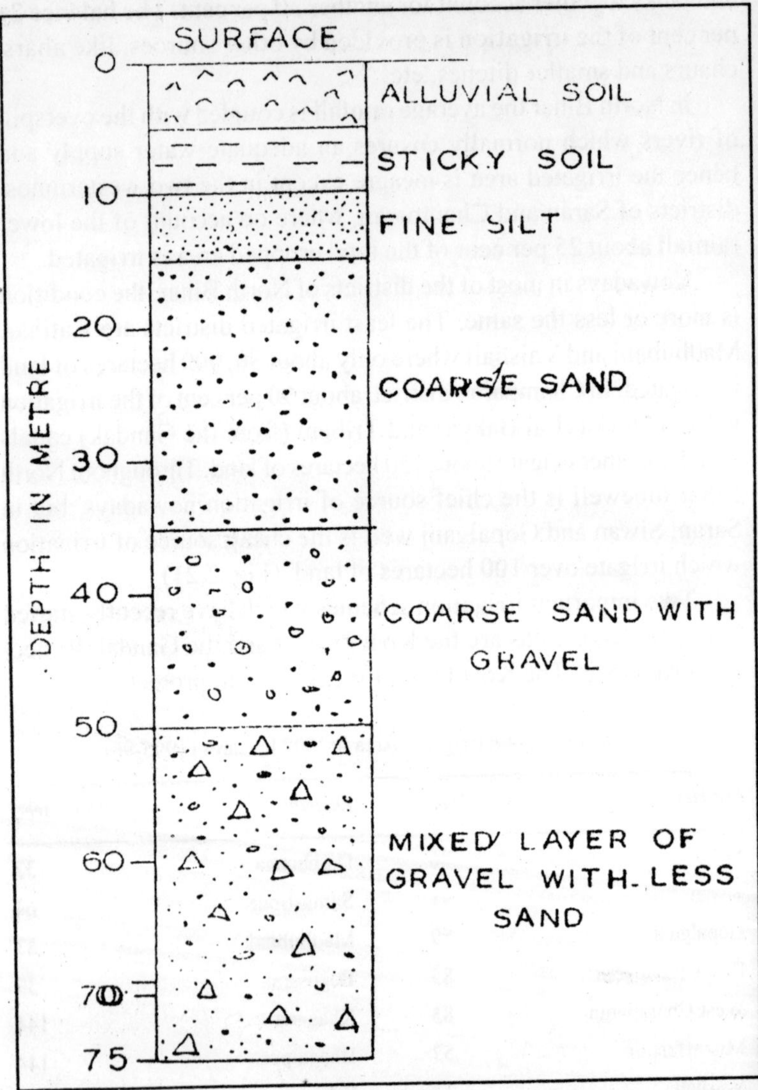


**Fig. 2.21 :** Strata Chart of Tubewell in Majarahia Village (Samastipur District)

About 3 lakh hectares of land in North Bihar have to save from devastating floods and to irrigate 12 lakh hectares in Purnea Saharsa, Katihar, Munger, Madhubani, Darbhanga and Samastipur districts and the Terai region of Nepal. The five distributaries of

Eastern Kosi canal are Murliganj branch canal, Jankinagar branch canal, Purnea branch canal, Araria branch canal and Rajpur branch canal. The eastern canal of the Kosi includes five main canals, five branch canals, several tributary and distributary channels. It has been assumed that eastern canal releases 15,000 cubic feet of water per second. Its total length is 45 kilometres and irrigated area is 10 lakh hectares (Fig. 2.22).

The Gandak Project is designed to irrigate 13 lakh hectares in Bihar, 3.24 lakh hectares in Uttar Pradesh and more than 40 thousand hectares in Nepal. Area mainly benefited would be East and West Champaran, Gopalganj, Siwan, Saran, Sitamarhi, Muzaffarpur, Vaishali and Samastipur districts. The Gandak Project includes Tirhut main canal, western main canal, Saran canal, Eastern Nepal canal and western Nepal canal, besides generating hydro-electricity and providing the facility of navigation (Fig. 2.23).

**Industries**

The Chief source of industrial raw material in North Bihar is agriculture. Naturally agro-based industries have developed to a great extent here. These include the sugar industry, rice-flour mills, *dal* (pulses) oil, and textile and tobacco factories, which have a direct concern with agriculture. These industries first developed in the larger settlements which had better road and market connections. Therefore, such settlements may be designated as 'pre-industrial settlements'. Some centres have selective locations, such as the centres of sugar industry in North Bihar, and Barauni with Petro-chemical and fertilizer industries. These may be known as 'Post industrial settlements'. Because they have developed consequent upon the installation of industrial units.

Sugar factories employ 20,000 persons in 31 mills in North Bihar Plain. Besides this, Jaggery is also prepared on cottage basis. The large sugar factories are distributed as given below:

The two main problems of the industry are firstly, the relatively poor quality of cane grown by small holders and secondly, the inadequacy of quick transport resulting in the loss of sucrose content in transit.

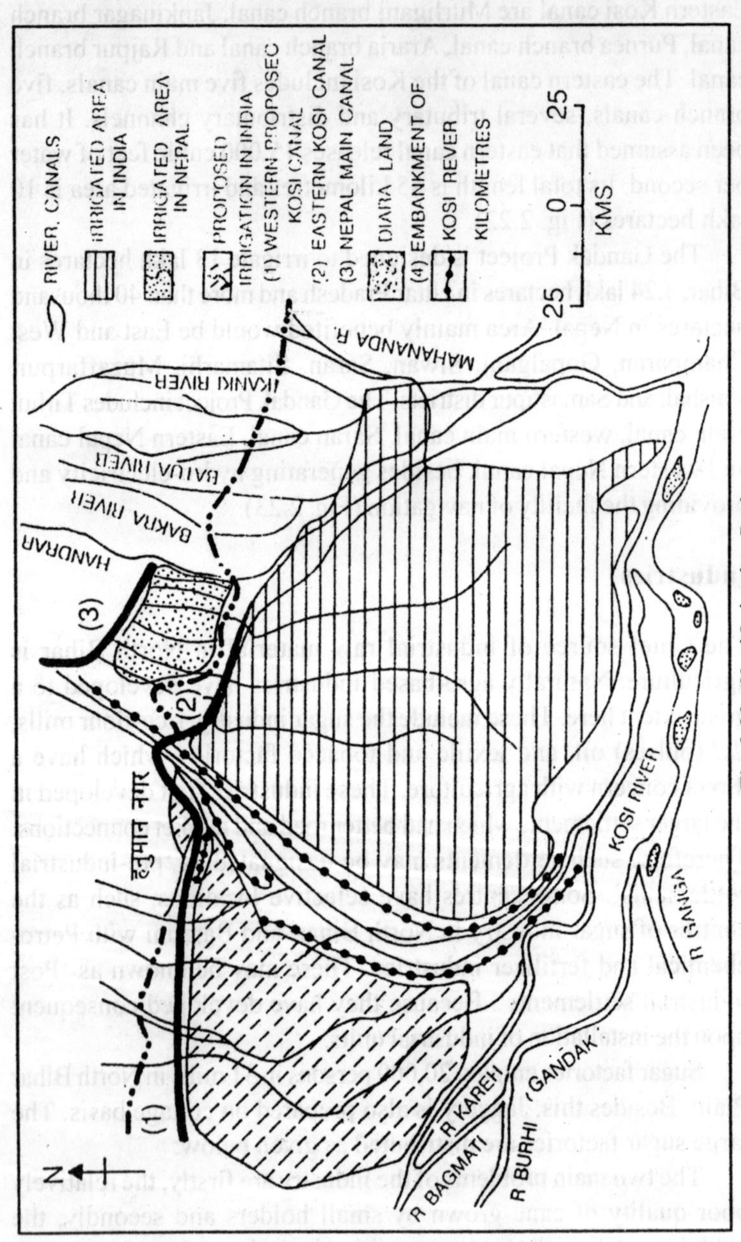


Fig. 2.22 : Kosi Irrigation Project

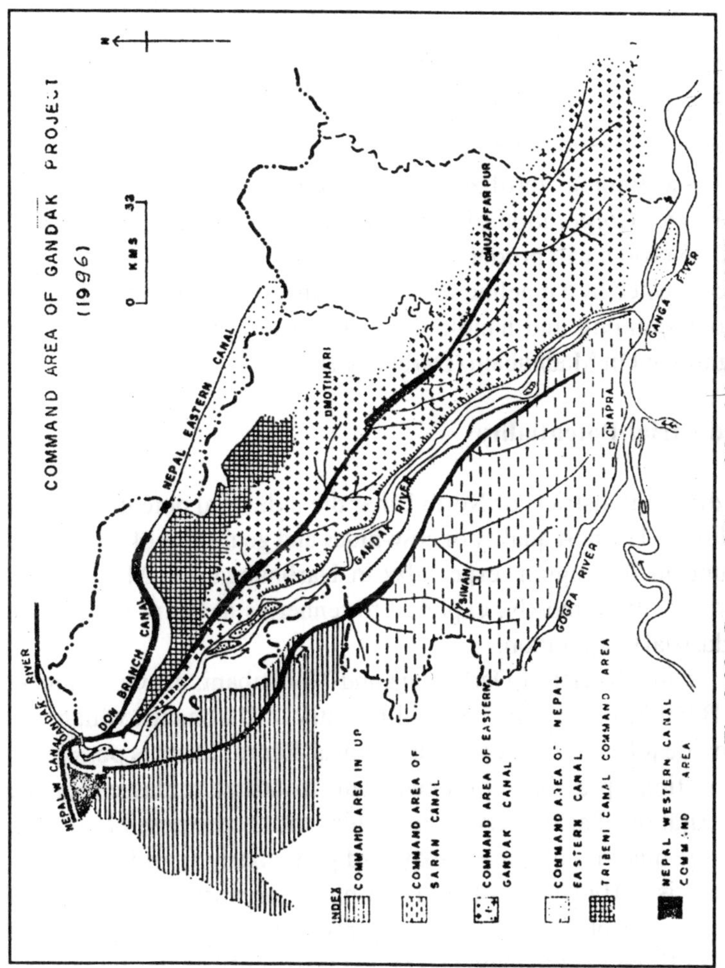


**Fig. 2.23 :** Command Area of Gandak Project (1996)

**Table 2.8** : Sugar Mills of North Bihar, 1998.

| *Districts* | *Important Centres* |
|---|---|
| Darbhanga | Sakri, Lohat Darbhanga, Hasanpur Road and Samastipur. |
| Muzaffarpur | Motipur, Riga, Goraul. |
| Champaran | Bara-Chakia, Motihari, Sugauli, Majhaulia, Chanpatia, Lauriya, Narkatiaganj, Harinagar, Naraipur. |
| Saran | Sitalpur, Marhaura, Maharajganj, Pachrukhi, Siwan, Sidhwalia, Sasamusa, Gopalganj and Hathwa |
| Purnea | Barinmankhi. |

The Barauni fertilizer project, under implementation by the Fertilizer Corporation of India Ltd. at an estimated cost of about Rs. 45 crores will produce 330,000 tonnes per annum of urea, and is connected by a pipeline with the Assam oil fields and Haldia port. Hand spinning and handloom weaving of cotton are, however, significant in Madhubani (Darbhanga).

**Industrial Potentiality**

In different districts of North Bihar the industrial potentiality is as follows: The best quality of cow-hides and goat skins of the State is found in the region, especially in Darbhanga and Muzaffarpur districts. It is, mostly, exported to tenneries at Sakri and Bettiah Industrial Corporation.

In the district of Darbhanga and Madhubani, the Government of Bihar has sanctioned a wool industry in Darbhanga which will provide job to 2500 weavers in the near future. There is possibility of setting up a well equipped plant to utilize molasses for the preparation of alcohol. A bone crushing mill is also possible as quite a large quantity of bone is exported particularly from Darbhanga. There is sufficient availability of hides for starting a large-scale tennery. At present, there is no large scale tennery anywhere in North Bihar. There may also be the possibility of starting a large and well equipped unit for the treatment of timber and its utilization on the border of Nepal. Cold storage could probably be a good investment in order to help the potato growers. The possibility of starting a fruit tanning industry is also under the active consideration of the State Government.

The State government (1973) approved the scheme for the establishment of an industrial area at Darbhanga. About 42 hectares of land has been acquired for this purpose at a total cost of Rs.8 lakhs. In this area the Mithila Woollen Mills, the Darbhanga Roller Flour Mills, a unit for the manufacture of concrete poles, a steel foundry and several other industrial units in the small scale sector will be set up by the entrepreneurs with financial support of the Government. Darbhanga has already an Industrial Estate which was established in 1958. Another Industrial Estate has been constructed under the special employment programme (1973) at a total cost of Rs.22 lakhs.

In East and West Champaran districts, there is a good scope for the development of drug industry because of the availability of all kinds of herbs and chemicals. Many of the herbs grown here and in the nearby Himalayan region of Nepal, yield valuable alcoloids and glucosides which form the raw materials for a number of drugs. In 1974 the Government of India have agreed to establish a basic drug manufacturing unit at Bettiah at a capital outlay of Rs. 10 crores.

Gopalganj district has great potentiality to become an agro-industrial district, wood based industries, flour and oil mills, match factory and cigarette factory could be established. Virginia quality of tobacco is grown here over 15,000 hectares of land. Saran and Siwan districts have saveral sugar mills which could encourage the establishment of large industries of alcohal, alcohlic beverage and toffee.

In Muzaffarpur district the State Government has planned to establish a manure factory at village Kanti to produce 20,000 tonnes of manure per year. This will be the first of its kind in this State and in a backward industrial district of Bihar. The unit has proposed to reserve the State's entire collections of raw materials for the production.

The district of Purnea grows a large quantity of Jute much of which is sent out for feeding Jute Mills in West Bengal. There are schemes to start one Jute mill, one paper mill, one tennery, one bone mill, one tile manufacturing unit at Raniganj including a brick manufacturing unit on mechanised methods. In private and cooperative sectors there are also possibility of starting one weaving mill, a tennery, a cycle assembly unit, card-board manufacturing unit utilising paddy straw, and Jute carpet, etc. The State Government has planned to set up a Jute factory at Purnea or Forbesganj at a total cost of Rs. 3 crores.

In Samastipur district one card-board factory has already started at Shambhupatti 5 kms. west of Samastipur town in this district 102,400 million tonnes of maize has been grown over 80,162 hectares of land. The quality and quantity of production is enough to support an industry which may be opened for preparing cornflakes. Tobacco industry has also large prospect.

There is also good prospect of ancillary industries in and around Samastipur for feeding the North Eastern Railway workshop with small stereotyped spares. There is good scope for pharmaceutical, plastic and chemical units based on alcohal which is manufactured by molasses. The State Government of Bihar also decided to start big sophisticated industrial plants, such as graphite, electrodes, polyster fibre, etc. at Samastipur which will shape the future industrial structure of the district.

There are two Jute mills at Katihar and one at Samastipur. The rice mills are located in a narrow belt in the Terai Region of North Bihar, where Adapur, Raxaul, Narkatiaganj, Nirmali, Jainagar, Sitamarhi, Madhubani and Forbesganj, etc. are important centres. Flour mills are fairly and widely distributed over the entire North Bihar.

## Transportation Lines

In any region the pattern of transportation line is determined by the physical and economic factors which in turn influence the growth and development of economic and industrial locations. Hence, for regional development, the growth of transportation line is as essential as agriculture and industry.

According to the modality and difference in providing the service, there is a great variations in the network of railways, roads, waterways and airways in North Bihar. In transportation lines railways work as the important arteries along with road and waterways. In rural areas of North Bihar where 95 per cent people resides, metalled and unmetalled roadways and rail networks are helpful in relegating unaccessibility. The rivers of North Bihar are not suitable for the movement of goods and people from one place to another due to its meandering courses and tortuous routes.

## Railways

The total length of railways in North Bihar is 1795 kilometres. It comes under the command of North Eastern and North Eastern Frontier Railways. Before April, 1952 it was known as Awadh Tirhut Railway which later on renamed as North Eastern Railway. In this North Eastern part one branch connect Gorakhpur, Sonepur and Katihar, second branch connect Narkatiaganj and Samastipur, and the third branch connect Narkatiaganj with Muzaffarpur. With the formation of sub-branches from the above branch lines the efficiency of railways have increased a lot.

North Eastern Frontier Railway served a small part of North Bihar in between Katihar and Barsoi. The capacity of Railways, depends on the types, density, formation of sub-branch, speed and size of trains, management of good signalling and the number of trains running on a particular route. There are metre gauge and broad gauge rail lines in North Bihar. Broad gauge has recently introduced from Barauni to Katihar, Barauni to Siwan and Katihar to Kumedpur. The Government of India has also approved the conversion of metre gauge into broad gauge from Samastipur to Jainagar and Motihari to Raxaul. Except north-western part of North Bihar the entire area is a plain land where the physical variations are very low. But due to inummerable rivers the rail lines have too many joints which lessens the carrying capacity of goods. In case we draw a straight line in between Katihar and Bachhwara, it can be quite evident how rail lines are built in a zig-zag fashion which abnormally increased distance in between the above places.

High slope, tunnel, cutting, etc. problems are lesser in North Bihar but the construction of bridges and the reclamation of lowlying areas require a greater amount of maintenance cost. In between Samastipur and Narkatiaganj over a distance of 160 kilometres there are 23 bridges where as in between Darbhanga and Nirmali over a distance of 40 kilometres there are only ten crossings of rivers and bridges. Due to wider expanse of the courses of rivers it is needed to construct a long bridge which is expensive. In flood affected areas the rail lines should have a flood protective embankment. In rainy season due to breaches of embankments quite often communication lines have been badly, disrupted over North Bihar Plains.

## Density and Distribution of Rail Lines

In order to measure the accessibility of railways in North Bihar a distance of 6 kilometres from a rail line is designated as highly accessible areas, 6 to 12 kilometres as low accessible areas and other than the above as unaccessible areas. On this basis the entire flood affected areas of the Gandak, the Burhi Gandak, the Adhwara group of rivers e.g.; the Lakhandei, the Dhaus, the Kareh, the Baghmati, the Kosi and the Panar are unaccessible. The highest accessible areas are found in the environs of Katihar, Samastipur, Narkatiaganj, Siwan, Chapra, Darbhanga, Muzaffarpur, Purnea and Barauni.

In North Bihar the highest density of railway is found near Katihar, Raxaul, Siwan and Samastipur, and slowly this is decreasing towards the Ganges in the south. Rajendra Bridge which connects Mokameh with Simariaghat also linked North Bihar with South Bihar Plains but in other places due to lack of bridge people generally crosses the Ganges on boat and ferry ships. The higher number of rivers in Saharsa and Purnea districts are the main hurdle in the expansion of railways and economic development of the area.

In North Bihar there are one railway station in 15 square kilometres of area which is higher in comparison with the all India average where per 19 square kilometres have one railway station. In Western part of North Bihar due to high density of population and late development of road network the density of rail line is high.

There is a great difference in the growth and expansion of railways in the east and west of the river Kosi. Especially in the Western part in between Kamla-Balan to Gandak and Gandak to Ghaghra plain agro-based industrial locations and higher density of population have boosted the development of railways. Due to low density of railways in the Kosi basin it has poor economic base in the region.

Due to the devastating flood of 1987 the railway connection between Darbhanga and Supaul have disrupted to a granding halt. In between Supaul to Bhaptiahi it has again started functioning.

In North Bihar the construction of bridge is necessary over rivers especially on the Ghagra, the Gandak and the Baghmati, which have a wider flood affected basins. The main hurdle is the flowing of rivers from north to south and the extension of railway lines from east to west. In the entire riparian tracts of the Ganges the land is high and fertile which favours higher density of railway network just north of the Ganges river. The highest density of railway lines are found in Saran and Bhagalpur districts where it is 0.16 kilometres per square kilometre and the lowest density is found in Supaul, and Sitamarhi districts including Kishanganj and Araria districts. This clearly shows that the Ganges helps in the development of grain collecting centres while in Western part of North Bihar the transport of sugarcane up to sugar mills and the cultivation of indigo have highly helped in the development of railway. In north frontier region due to the problem of bridge construction over so many rivers, the problems of flood, changing courses of rivers, the problem of the construction of embankment, the presence of big swampy land and waterlogging areas, the close relationship of the forest environment of Terai region and the dearth of big cities have retarded the higher density of railway network in North Bihar.

In Western section where per square kilometre the density of population is over 1,000 persons and for this fact there is a huge rush in almost all trains which depart from Darbhanga, Muzaffarpur, Chapra, Siwan, Motihari and Samastipur.

## Road Transport

In North Bihar the important road is National Highway Number-28 which runs from Sameshwar to Barauni, and again National Highway) Number-31 which runs from Barauni to Thakurganj and this act as the life line in North Bihar. There are so many branch roads which radiate from the National Highway such as Barauni to Hajipur, and Chapra to Siwan which serve in the river basins of both the Ghaghra and the Gandak. Similarly, the branch roads which run from Thana Bihpur to Madhepura, Pipra to Jogbani via Bhimnagar, Manihari, Katihar and Purnea are the major roadways of the Kosi basin. There are another set of roads which connect Hajipur to Muzaffarpur, Sitamarhi to Sonbarsa, Bachhwara to Samastipur and Darbhanga to Jainagar.

Beyond this, there are several smaller roads which connect one urban centre with the other including various rural chaurs and wetlands.

## Characteristic of Roadways

In North Bihar both metalled and unmetalled roads are found. Metalled roads are mainly State Highways and National Highways. The roads which connect different wetlands are also metalled owing to the planned development of roads by the Rural Engineering Organization (REO), Government of Bihar. National Highways have a breadth of 12 metres in which 7 metres is metalled. State Highway have a breadth of 7 metres in which only 4 metres is metalled. The other roads have a breadth of just 3 metres (Fig. 2.24).

The National Highway connects one State with the other. In North Bihar it has a length of 478 kilometres. In 1991 the total length of roads and railways available in North Bihar is given in Table 2.9.

In Saran, Muzaffarpur and Darbhanga districts most of the roads are metalled but in Khagaria and Saharsa there are still prevalence of unmetalled roads. In Champaran district due to access up to mountainous areas, and in Saharsa and Purnea due to flood relief measures of the government the metalled roads are constructed. Inspite of this, the condition of roads are not good in North Bihar which is quite evident both in the summer and rainy seasons. The breaches of road in rainy season and the formation of Pot holes on them are the common problems with the area.

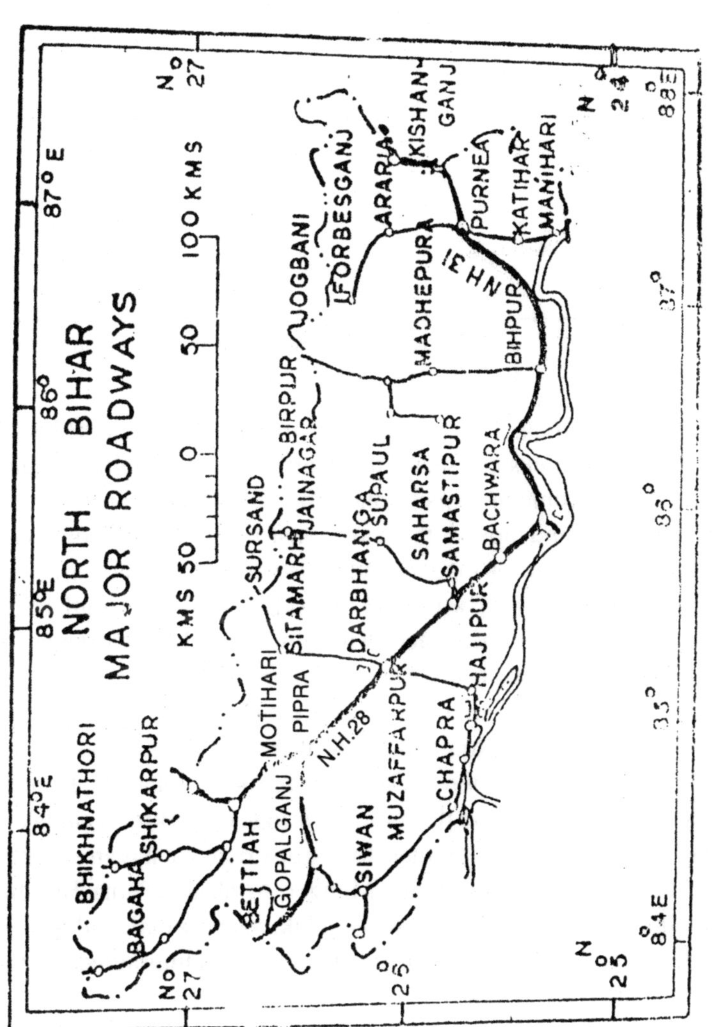


**Fig. 2.24 :** North Bihar : Major Roadways

**Table 2.9 :** Length of Roads and Railways in North Bihar in kms.

| *Name of District* | *Length of Roads* | *Length of Railways* |
|---|---|---|
| Saran | 712 | 325 |
| Champaran | 770 | 288 |
| Muzaffarpur | 712 | 176 |
| Darbhanga | 941 | 354 |
| Saharsa | 314 | 88 |
| Purnea | 514 | 368 |
| Khagaria | 315 | 157 |
| North Bhagalpur | 98 | 38 |
| Total | 4376 | 1794 |

*Source :* Calculated from the map available from the Department of Statistics and Evaluation, Government of Bihar, Patna, 1991.

In North Bihar 25 per cent road network of entire Bihar is located. In north-eastern sector the dearth of road is highly felt due to number of problems as mentioned above. In this region roads run in straight line and most of them are constructed above flood level. In the construction of longer road, it is necessary to construct so many bridges. As on Assam road 58 bridges having a length of 30 metres have been constructed. Thus for overall development of road the construction of strong and wider bridge seem to be essential. Due to lack of bridge so many areas are disconnected by the Kosi, the Gandak, the Ghaghra and the Mahananda rivers. There is no doubt that the construction of Ganga bridge near Mokameh, Kursela bridge over the Kosi and the national bridge over Burhi Gandak in Khagaria have eased the problem to a large extent but it is an essential over the Ganges near Bhagalpur, Munger, Arrah, and Patna, Bagaha, Gopalganj and Rewaghat on the Gandak; near Nirmali and Supaul on the Kosi; Bariahighat on the Kareh and Dingraghat on the Mahananda river.

For the planned development of road in North Bihar the abstract of the programme which has submitted to the government is as follows:

1. To connect the villages and towns having 2000 of population.
2. To connect all the industrial, religious and historical places by road.

3. To keep all the villages up to a maximum distance of four kilometres from the road.

**Density and Accessibility of Road**

In south-western side of North Bihar due to productive land, high density of population, number of major towns and having a chequerred historical background the density of road is 0.18 kms per square kilometre in Siwan, 0.17 in East Champaran, 0.15 in Bhagalpur, 0.14 in West Champaran and Muzaffarpur districts. But in North-eastern part of the region due to the presence of number of rivers, waterlogging in lowlands and problems of floods are the causes of low density as for example 0.04. km in Kishanganj, l0.07 in Supaul and Araria, and 0.08 in Madhubani district., The highest accessibility of road is observed near Purnea, Chapra, Muzaffarpur, Hajipur, Darbhanga, Bettiah, Chanpatia, Siwan, Motihari and Sitamarhi.

**Inland Waterways**

This constitutes an important highways in North Bihar, especially in Ancient and Medieval periods. But these days it's importance has decreased due to growth and expansion of road and railways and the use of river water for irrigation purposes. The total length of waterways is 1600 kilometres in North Bihar including length of the Ganges, the Gandak, the Kosi, the Kamla., the Balan, the Bhuthi Balan and the Mahananda-Panar group of rivers.

**Rural Settlements and Urban Centres**

Rural settlements are the product of man for its self-satisfaction, shelter against the rigours of climate, and are generally made at the access of roads, drinking water, defensible higher site, and productive land, for the purpose of human living, storing of foodgrains and hay and tethering of domestic livestock. A settlement having a higher percentage of population engaged in tertiary services and with the facility of a municipality or notified area committee may be regarded as a town. A town has also the facilities of permanent shops, professional services and recreation facilities while a village has to content itself with the agricultural fields and orchards or pastures.

A village thus is marked by primary occupations without any complexities of life. But now the fertility of soil has been utilized to the utmost and gives diminishing return to the peasants, while the population is constantly increasing. This has led to the creation of congested slums in rural and urban areas both. In rural areas, the condition is so alarming that barefoot children, swarming with dust and dirt having no clothes on their body are found moving with begging bowls or digging rat holes in the fields with small spades in search of food. A large percentage of the people of North Bihar are living under slum conditions and cannot aspire for desent living for want of resources. (Fig. 2.25)

North Bihar has 19,252 inhabited revenue villages where as 2886 are uninhabited revenue villages (1991). It has been found that flood affected areas have higher number of uninhabited villages in comparison with flood free areas. Actual number of inhabited and uninhabited villages are given in Table 2.10.

**Table 2.10 :** North Bihar : Number of Inhabited and Uninhabited Rural Settlements (1991)

| *District* | *Number of Villages* | |
|---|---|---|
| | *Inhabited* | *Unihabited* |
| East Champaran | 1187 | 42 |
| West Charnparan | 1337 | 195 |
| Gopalganj | 1410 | 156 |
| Siwan | 1439 | 90 |
| Saran | 1504 | 177 |
| Darbhanga | 935 | 271 |
| Madhubani | 1015 | 101 |
| Samastipur | 1211 | 150 |
| Saharsa | 1304 | 149 |
| Purnea | 1487 | 359 |
| Katihar | 1233 | 318 |
| Bhagalpur North | 105 | 73 |
| Khagaria | 352 | 70 |
| Vaishali | 1390 | 179 |
| Muzaffarpur | 1635 | 89 |
| Sitamarhi | 992 | 52 |
| Begusarai | 716 | 475 |
| Total | 19,252 | 2886 |

*Source :* District Census Handbook of All Districts of North Bihar, 1991.

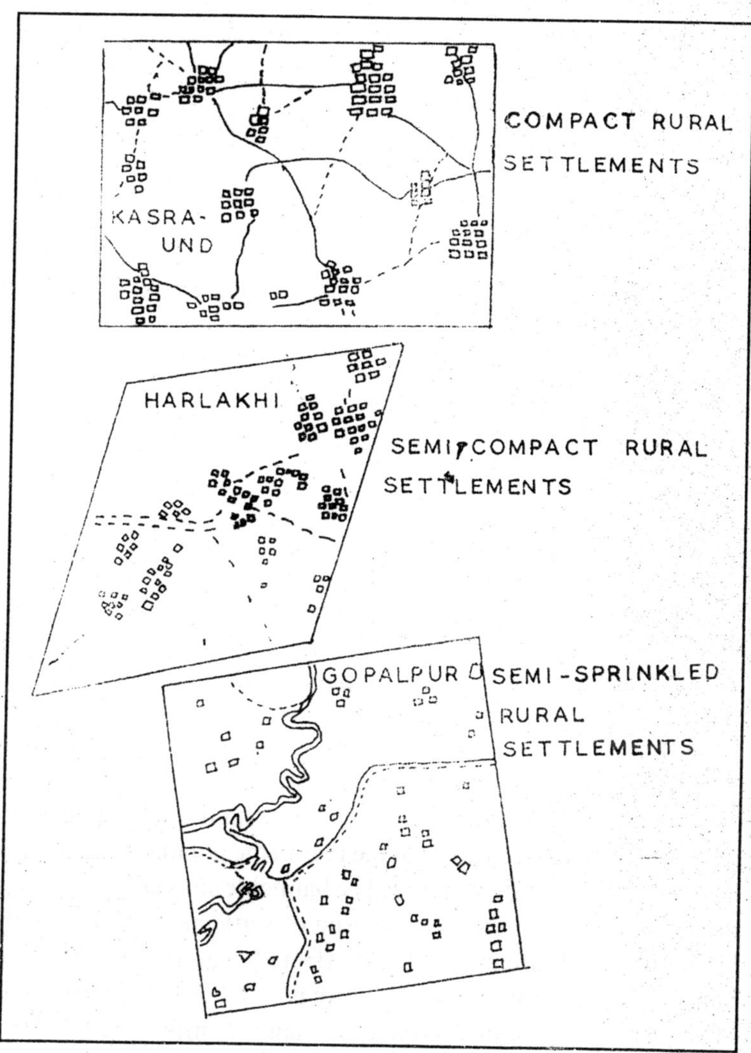


**Fig. 2.25 :** North Bihar : Types of Rural Settlements

North Bihar is a land of large villages and small towns, (Tallents, 1921) while medium sized villages are abundant and smaller rural settlements comprise only a little over 40 per cent of this region (Table 2.11).

**Table 2.11** : North Bihar : Size Class of Rural Settlements, 1991

| *Name of the District* | *Less than 200* | *200/ 499* | *500/ 999* | *1000/ 1999* | *2000/ 4999* | *5000/ 9999* | *10,000 and above* |
|---|---|---|---|---|---|---|---|
| Saran | 164 | 352 | 524 | 374 | 259 | 16 | 2 |
| Siwan | 140 | 368 | 433 | 344 | 139 | 12 | 0 |
| Gopalganj | 2377 | 441 | 385 | 233 | 96 | 6 | 0 |
| East Champaran | 93 | 218 | 357 | 352 | 212 | 49 | 6 |
| West Champaran | 159 | 331 | 415 | 263 | 164 | 20 | 5 |
| Muzaffarpur | 193 | 445 | 520 | 369 | 174 | 22 | 3 |
| Vaishali | 268 | 318 | 392 | 274 | 124 | 14 | 1 |
| Sitamarhi | 49 | 136 | 2.64 | 316 | 189 | 34 | 5 |
| Darbhanga | 104 | 164 | 240 | 234 | 156 | 40 | 5 |
| Samastipur | 139 | 213 | 298 | 263 | 248 | 47 | 5 |
| Madhubani | 70 | 151 | 232 | 278 | 230 | 61 | 6 |
| Begusarai | 116 | 105 | 154 | 154 | 130 | 25 | 8 |
| Khagaria | 5 | 16 | 43 | 48 | 91 | 23 | 3 |
| Bhagalpur | 5 | 9 | 14 | 19 | 41 | 10 | 5 |
| Saharsa | 107 | 183 | 288 | 362 | 287 | 66 | 9 |
| Purnea | 466 | 563 | 604 | 508 | 336 | 40 | 6 |
| Katihar | 286 | 348 | 305 | 196 | 83 | 19 | 2 |

*Source :* District Census Handbook of All the Districts of North Bihar, 1991.

The high density of population, settlements of smaller size and closer spacing have a direct relationship with the flood free zone, while in flood affected areas of the region the population density is low and settlement size is large. The habitable sites are spread over the entire space but the inter-spacing of settlement is abnormally high. Such areas are mostly flood affected, e.g., in the districts of Saharsa, Munger, Bhagalpur, Western part of Purnea and the whole of Darbhanga division. On the other hand, in hilly areas of West Champaran district owing to stony waste and forest clad rugged terrain the density of rural settlement is low, the population size is also low,where as spacing is high and the area is free from floods. In the central and eastern parts of the region, the districts of Purnea, Katihar and the whole of Muzaffarpur division (except West Champaran) have a high density (2, 3, 4) of rural settlements and closer spacing (1.04 kms) but the population size is low and these areas are less frequently visited by floods.

On the basis of per square kilometre density of rural settlements, North Bihar has been divided into four sub-regions on the basis of Quartile and Median values. The anchals of high density of rural settlements above 0.64 are found in Saran, Gopalganj, Siwan, Vaishali, Muzaffarpur, Begusarai and some of the south-eastern anchals of Katihar district. The areas of low density of rural settlements are found in the flood affected zones of Saharsa, Purnea, Katihar, Madhubani, Sitamarhi, East Champaran and forest covered areas of Ram Nagar and Gaunaha anchals in West Champaran district. (Fig. 2.29)

There are 53 urban centres in North Bihar (1991). But the process of urbanization is rather slow due to poor infrastructure facilities and lesser development of industries. Hence, urbanization deals with the land as well as the machine production and is closely linked with the concentration of people at one place through migration from the fringe and surrounding areas with an ambitious hope for future materialistic self-development. But due to limited resource, the polarization of transportation networks are found just near urban centres which helps in urban development on multi-level whether the same may be an urban expansion in a zig-zag crab like fashion or enlargement of the zone of influence by administrative set up and commercial development, especially in North Bihar (Fig. 2.28).

In the study area the distribution of urban centres is sparse account for 21 per cent of the region's urban population and the balance is found in dispersed urban centres of smaller sizes. In North Bihar urban centres are components of regional economic development because urban centres provide, inter-alia, a variety of centralized services for the surrounding zone of influence, e.g.; marketing of agricultural surplus, products of cottage industries, including the supply of fertilizer, engineering goods, pumping set, medicines and specialized skills in a wide variety of situations which are necessary for regional development.

So far as the density of urban centres in North Bihar is concerned some old towns show a high density e.g; Siwarn (8547 per km$^2$), Darbhanga (6797), Muzaffarpur (61777), Jainagar (6160) and

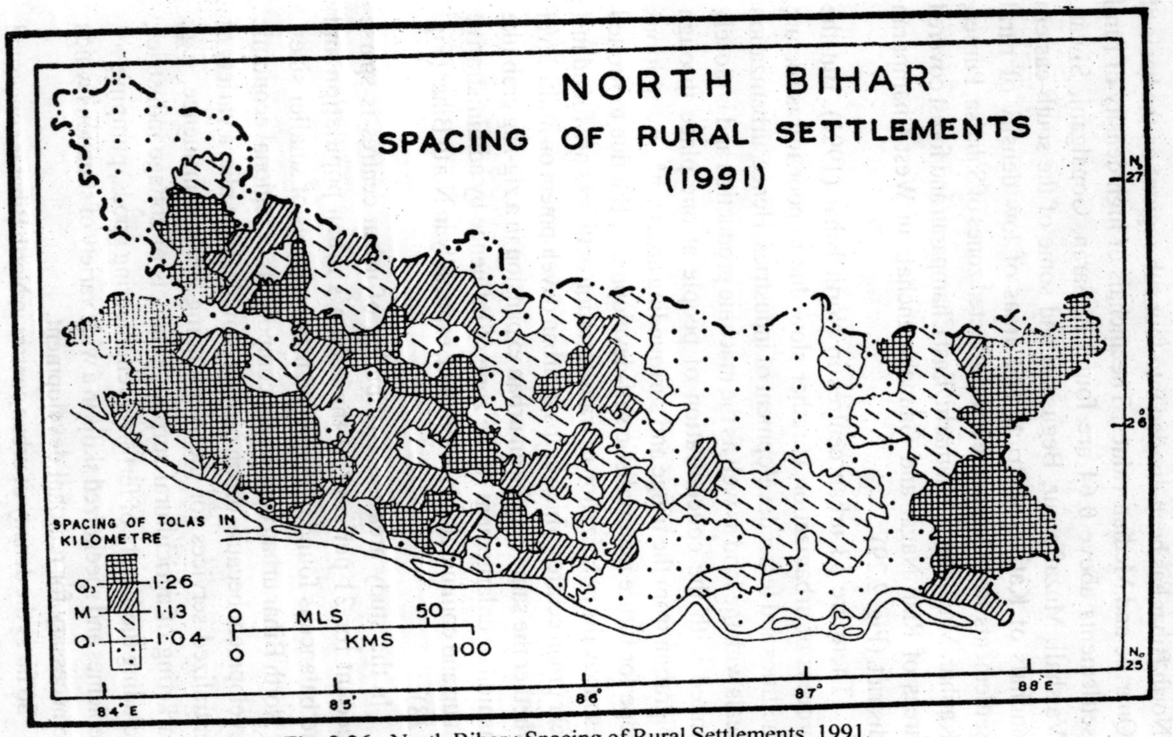


Fig. 2.26 : North Bihar : Spacing of Rural Settlements, 1991.

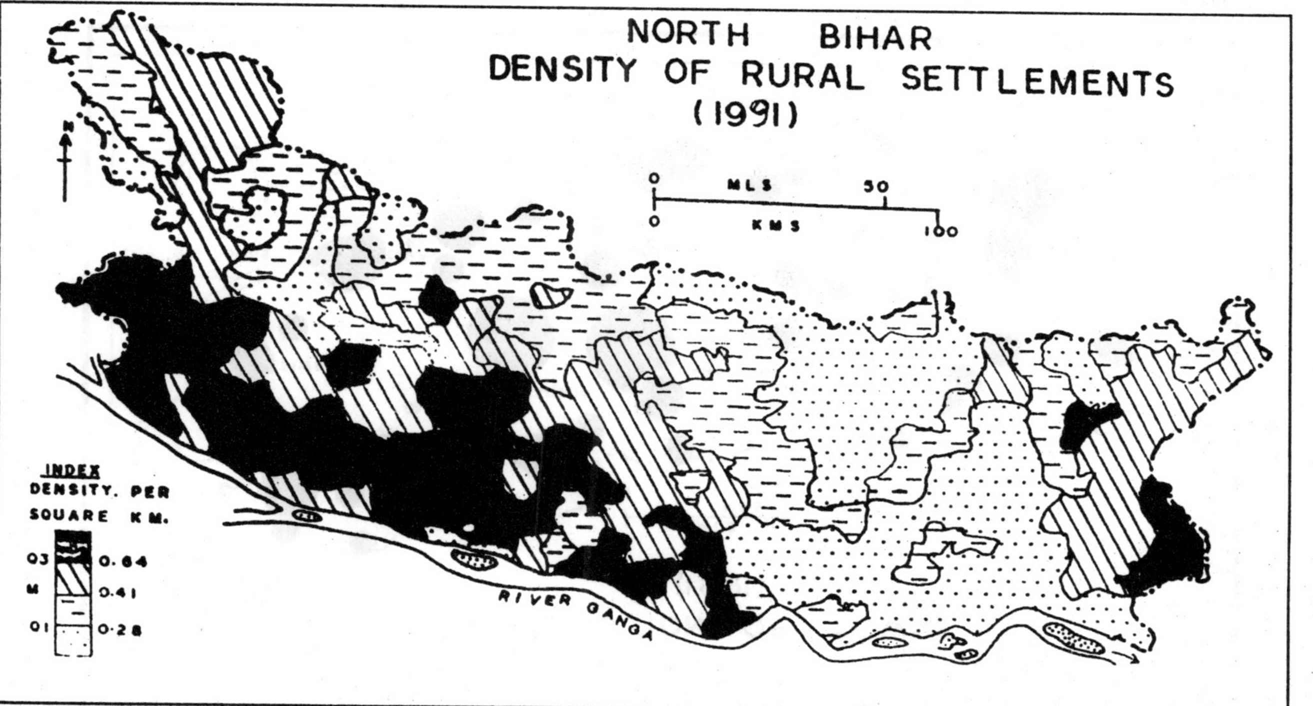


**Fig. 2.27 :** North Bihar : Density of Rural Settlements, 1991.

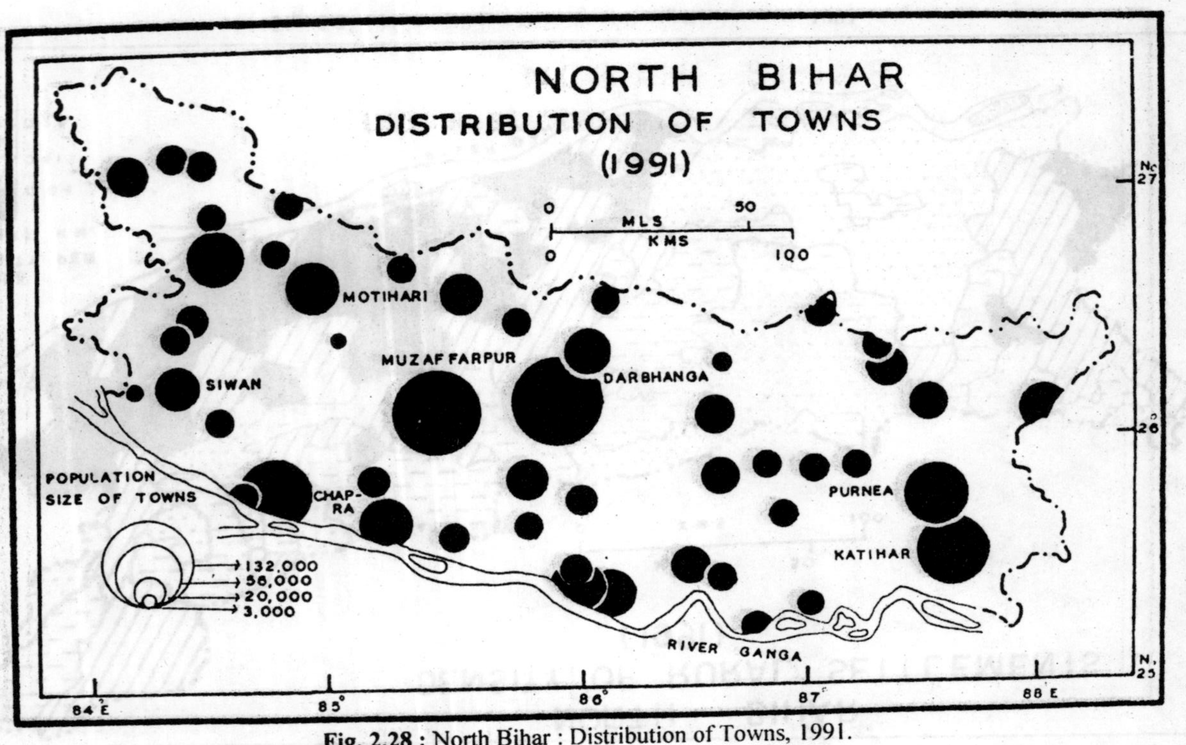


**Fig. 2.28** : North Bihar : Distribution of Towns, 1991.

Katihar (6148), where as in some of the smaller and newer towns per square kilometre the density of population is very low) e.g.; 305 in Banmankhi Bazar, 389 in Chakia, 275 in Barauni and 700 in Birpur (Table 2.12).

**Table 2.12 :** Population Density of Urban Places in North Bihar (1991)

*(Per Square Kilometre)*

| *Name of the Urban Centre* | *Area in $km^2$* | *Population Density* | *Name of the Urban Centre* | *Area in $km^2$* | *Population Density* |
|---|---|---|---|---|---|
| Chapra | 19.42 | 4279 | Samastipur | 4.53 | 528 |
| Revelganj | 3.84 | 4722 | Roseraj | 5.18 | 2855 |
| Maharajganj | 7.61 | 1563 | Dalsinghsara | 4.87 | 2207 |
| Siwan | 3.88 | 8547 | Khagaria | 11.91 | 1440 |
| Mirganj | 5.49 | 2196 | Barauni | 30.33 | 275 |
| Gopalganj | 9.32 | 1851 | Begusarai | 7.56 | 472 |
| Motihari | 20.07 | 1845 | Naugachhia | 8.39 | 1138 |
| Sugauli | 11.47 | 1060 | Saharsa | 14.06 | 1651 |
| Raxaul | 13.67 | 952 | Suapul | 22.02 | 1024 |
| Chakia | 7.64 | 389 | Nirmali | 5.28 | 131 |
| Bettiah | 8.68 | 5878 | Birpur | 13.44 | 700 |
| Chanpatia | 16.11 | 7577 | Madhepura | 7.93 | 1943 |
| Shikarpur | 7.28 | 2203 | Murliganj | 12.79 | 992 |
| Muzaffarpur | 20.46 | 6177 | Purnea | 37.56 | 1504 |
| Sitamarhi | 12.95 | 1713 | Kasba | 17.09 | 868 |
| Lalganj | 9.07 | 932 | Banmankhi | 30.43 | 305 |
| Hajipur | 25.90 | 1617 | Araria | 28.49 | 789 |
| Mahnar | 6.92 | 2883 | Forbesganj | 9.09 | 2332 |
| Darbhanga | 19.43 | 6797 | Jogbani | 5.18 | 17703 |
| Jainagar | 1.61 | 6160 | Kishanganj | 30.04 | 1228 |
| Madhubani | 9.07 | 3629 | Katihar | 10.90 | 6148 |

*Source :* Census of India, 1991.

The growth of urban centres in North Bihar is very low for the period 1901 to 1941, as this rose 0 per cent in 1911 to 26.67 per cent in 1921 and from 0 per cent in 1931 to just 10.53 per cent in 1941. In North Bihar the, maximum growth has been observed in 1951 which is 52.38 per cent. Further, this shows a declining trend of 31.25 per cent in 1961 and again it is just 26.19 per cent in 1971. Form 1981 to 1991 the growth is 30 per cent.

## City of Muzaffarpur : A Case Study

The city of Muzaffarpur is a district headquarter and leading trade mart of North Bihar. It is situated on the southern bank of Burhi Gandak river and National Highway No. 28, Since 1901 population of the city is as follows:

| 1901— | 1921— | 1941— | 1961— | 1981— |
|---|---|---|---|---|
| 45,617 | 32,755 | 54,139 | 109,048 | 175,892 |
| 1911— | 1931— | 1951— | 1971— | 1991— |
| 43,668 | 43,049 | 73,594 | 126,379 | 240,450 |

**Table 2.13** : Growth of Urban Places in North Bihar (1901-1991)

| *Census Year* | *Total Number of Towns* | *% Growth* |
|---|---|---|
| 1901 | 15 | 0 |
| 1911 | 15 | 0 |
| 1921 | 19 | 26.67 |
| 1931 | 19 | 0 |
| 1941 | 21 | 10.53 |
| 1951 | 32 | 52.38 |
| 1961 | 42 | 31.25 |
| 1971 | 53 | 26.19 |
| 1981 | 60 | 29.03 |
| 1991 | 72 | 30.00 |

*Source* : Census of India 1961 and 1991.

In Muzaffarpur business zone is located in the central part which is surrounded by the residential belt. Administrative, educational and medical functions represent a sectoral growth where as industrial and transport zones lie in the outer zone (Fig. 2.29).

The chief commercial area Saraiyaganj is located in the inner core of the city. It is a populous area and its nodal chapter has helped the wholesale and the retail trades to develop in the nearby areas. The residential areas found throughout the city. The central part has highly congested housing arrangement. The lake side has modern houses of double and treble storeyed, whereas industrial zone has different type of structures, usually single storeyed houses with modest modern amenities. Muzaffarpur has only one large scale industry namely Arthur Butler and Co. Private Limited which

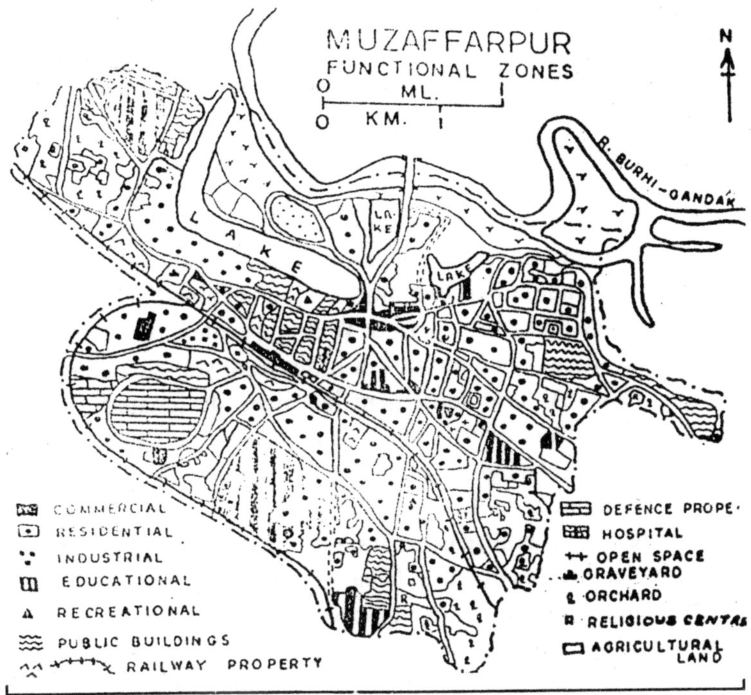


**Fig. 2.29 :** Muzaffarpur : Functional Zones.

manufacture rail wagon, sugar mill spare and agricultural implements. Besides, there are dozens of oil crushing, flour mills, hosiery works and engineering industries located in different parts of the city.

Among the educational institutions the important higher centres of learning are L.S. College, R.D.S. College, M.D.D.M.College, C.M. Science College, Anugrah Narayan College, Evening College, Law College, Medical College, Homeopathic College and the location of Bihar University Office, besides 76 primary municipal schools and ten secondary schools.

Administrative areas include State administrative units such as Commissioner's Office, the district courts, police lines, hospital and Ganda Project office beside several others. Among the central government properties cantonment, railways, post offices, defence property, barracks, rifle-range, parade ground and sport grounds are notable.

Muzaffarpur has number of play grounds, open spaces besides dairy farming, nursery and lichi gardens which help in changing the monotony of urban living in favour of creating a sound ecological balance.

## The Territorial Basis of Village Organisation

Village organizations (Palakshappa, 1967) with their neighbouring small settlements have changed their boundary several times with the change in administrative units of the region. This process is going on since Prehistoric period. Within their territorial limits the traditional village communities in India were self-sufficient units (Singh, 1968) A rural settlement has been designated as 'little kingdom, by Cohn (1959); 'interlocking mesh' of villages by Smith (1960); network of neighbouring villages' by Dube (1958); and 'large systems of villages, by Karve (1961).

There are several reasons for self-sufficiency or interdependence in the villages of North Bihar and their appraisal would help in analysing the histogenesis of the territorial functional systems as they have affected the growth of rural settlements in the region during different periods. But now the population increase and consciousness of people are making the rural folk more dependent on nearby central places for oil, cloth, salt, soap, sugar, paper, cement and so many other items of consumption.

During Prehistoric period the clearing of forests induced different clan groups and warriors to separately demarcate fields, which developed a sense of well integrated territorial limit of community life comprising several families (Singh, 1955). This ultimately coalesced into the village communities.

## Kingdoms and Republics of Ancient Period

According to the Upanisads, ancient literature and religious books, i.e. the *Mahabharata*, the *Puranas* and the *Ramayana*, there were four Kingdoms namely Videha, Vaishali, Mallad and Angutarap in North Bihar. They were called *Mahajanpadas* during the Buddhist period.

### *Mithila and Videha*

As mentioned in the *Jatakas* and epics Mithila was bounded by the Kauski in the east, the Gandak in the West, the Ganges in the south and the Himalayas in the north. Thus the kingdom of Videha extended over most parts of North Bihar throughout historic and Pre-historic periods comprising a large number of wetlands.

During the past Mithila was called from several names such as: Mithila, Tirabhukti, Videha, Nemikanan, Gyanshila, Kripapith, Swarnlalangalpadhati, Janki Janmabhumi, Nirapeksha, Vikalmasa, Ramanand Kuti, Vishwabhamini and Nityanangla.

Videha was originated from Nemi, the son of Ichhbaku. This clan is regarded as Suryabanshi branch. It was established in 1314 B.C. In Mithila before the king of Siradhwaj 15 kings had administered, where as 61 in Ayodhya. After Janaka up to *Mahabharat* war 29 kings had administered the kingdom of Videha.

### *Vaishali*

It has been identified with the present village Bania Basarh lying on the east of the Gandak in Vaishali district. There were 7707 ruling families amongst the Lichhavis of those times who ruled turn by turn over the western part of North Bihar.

Vaishali was a powerful state from the beginning of Indian Culture. Its boundary was fixed by the Gandak in the West, the Burhi Gandak in the east, the Ganges in the south and the Himalaya in the north.

Vaishali lies in Vaishali district of Hajipur Pargana. There were a lot of archaeological remains in Vaishali. Besides, the excavation site of houses one can see the entire excavated materials of Vaishali in Vaishali-Museum which lies north of the Lotus lake. There also lies a Ashoka pillar on which the treble mouth statue of lions head looks marvellous.

Vaishali was divided into three parts. There were 7,000 houses in the first part which had golden minarates standing in. the middle upper part. In the second part there were 14,000 houses with silver minarates in the upper part, and in the third quarter there were 21,000 houses having copper minarates in their upper part. In these types of houses people lived according to the level of their income and caste e.g., upper class, middle class and lower class people respectively. In the religious books of *Tibet Vaishali* was regarded as the heaven on the earth. This is because the houses, garden and ponds look very romantic. The melodius songs of birds and the non-stop recreational festivals and the dancing of girls had made the environment joyful.

### *Anguttarap*

There was a small kingdom or *Janapada* named Apana in Anguttarap which included a portion of Saharsa and the whole of Purnea and Katihar districts.

In Anguttarap the materials of houses were that of wattle and daub and settlements were situated in a planned way of linear fashion along the river embankment.

### *Mall*

The country of Mall lies west of Videha and north-west of Magadha. Modern Saran and parts of Champaran districts were included in Mall. Its Western neighbouring States were Vatsyakaushal and Kapilvastu and it extend up to Himalaya in the north. According to Huentsang it was situated West of Sakyasland in the Terai and the north of Vrijian confederacy.

Mall was the name of a people of one caste and the country too. It was one of the important *Janapadas* of the country besides fifteen others. *Panini* had called the capital of Mall as Mallagram. In *Mahabharata* it was known as Mallarashtra. This clearly shows that before 1234 B.C. at the time of *Mahabharat war* Mall was a democratic State and up to the time of Kautilya (400 B.C.) it was remains a democratic one.

In Mallagram there were seven rows of houses before reaching into the central part up to the kings house. The names were Swarn, Rajat, Vaidarys, Asfatic, Lohitkan, Abhrak and Ratanmei from central part to outerside of the capital city respectively. In Pawa and Kushinagar there were assembly houses of Mall. But at the time of Budha these areas were filled with forests.

### *Territorial Limit by Fortification*

During the ancient period, it seems that the wetlands had a well integrated territorial limit of forts (Havell, 1915)

According to Kautilya a fort defending 200 villages was called Sthaniya, 400 villages Dronamukha, 20 villages Kharvata and 10 villages Sangrahana. Thus Kautilya gave a description of well evolved stages of military fortification of rural settlements in North Bihar for strategic purposes. This may still be observed in the relics of fortifications with well developed moats and rampart walls at Vaishali, Lauriya Nandangarh, Balirajgarh, Jaimanglagarh and Chechar (Swetpur) the capital of Tirabhuktil near Lalganj in Vaishali district and at several other places.

### Bhukti, Visaya, Naya and Gaon

During Gupta period (320 to 1097 A.D.) the administrative units of North Bihar were divided into *Bhukti* (Province), *Visaya* (district) and *Naya* (anchal) which comprised several rural settlements. The names of only two *Bhuktis* of ancient North Bihar have come to light through inscriptions. These were Pundravardhan Bhukti (including portions of Saharsa, Purnea and North Bengal); and Tirabhukti (practically whole of western North Bihar). The Bangaon Copper Plate (12th Century A.D.) refers to a Mardeya Visaya in Tirabhukti. Thus it is apparent that the eastern limit of Tirabhukti extended up to Saharsa district. Similarly, near Darbhanga the Panchob Copper Plate (12th Century A.D.) records the Jambubani Visaya, but it does not mention the Bhukti in which it was situated (Pandey, 1954). An image inscription of Nowagadha in Begusarai district mentions Kruila Visaya. A seal from Baniya Basarh records the Vaishali Visaya. Vaishali (Choudhary, 1960) was definitely an important place during the Gupta kings. This Visaya should have occupied the area now under the jurisdiction of Vaishali district.

## Sarkar, Pargana, Tappa and Gaon

Shershah made a memorable contribution to the administrative and territorial history of North Bihar by demarcating Sarkar, Pargana, Tappa (Fig.2.30) and Goan (Survey and Settlement, 1922) as the basic administrative units of his empire. As a result of these divisions, there evolved a hierarchy of settlements. The original chief settlements at the Sarkar level have become the urban centres of the present day, while Parganas and Tappas have developed as rurban centres, because of their respective territorial and sub-territorial command of resources. The gaon has evolved as the basic rural unit of settlement today.

A brief description of the constituent Sarkars and Parganas of North Bihar is given below:

The Tappa is represented by the present day large villages with their component hamlets, evolved as the most basic local unit, rural in origin and function (Table 2.15).

## Gulma, Rastra, Gramapatti or Gramadhipatti

Similar to the Mansabdari system as introduced by Moghal Emperor Akbar about 200 years later, the village heads were earlier appointed in order of merit and efficiency. We have references of Gulma, consisting of 3 to 5 villages, 'Rastra' consisting of hundreds of villages, "Gramapatti" or 'Gramadhipatti, (i.e. village head), "Dasa Gramapatti" (head of ten villages), 'Vimsatimsa Gramapatti" (head of twenty or thirty villages), and "Saharsa Gramapatti" (head of one thousand villages)—(Survey and Settlement, 1908). The head quarters of these leaders naturally became large villages in size.

## Division, District, Sub-division and *Anchals*

During British regime the State of Bihar was divided into administrative units of division, district, subdivision and *thanas*. After independence in 1947 the revenue thanas were spilt up into *anchals* which comprise roughly 100 to 150 villages in as many square kilometres of area. This five tier segmentation of administrative units resulted in the

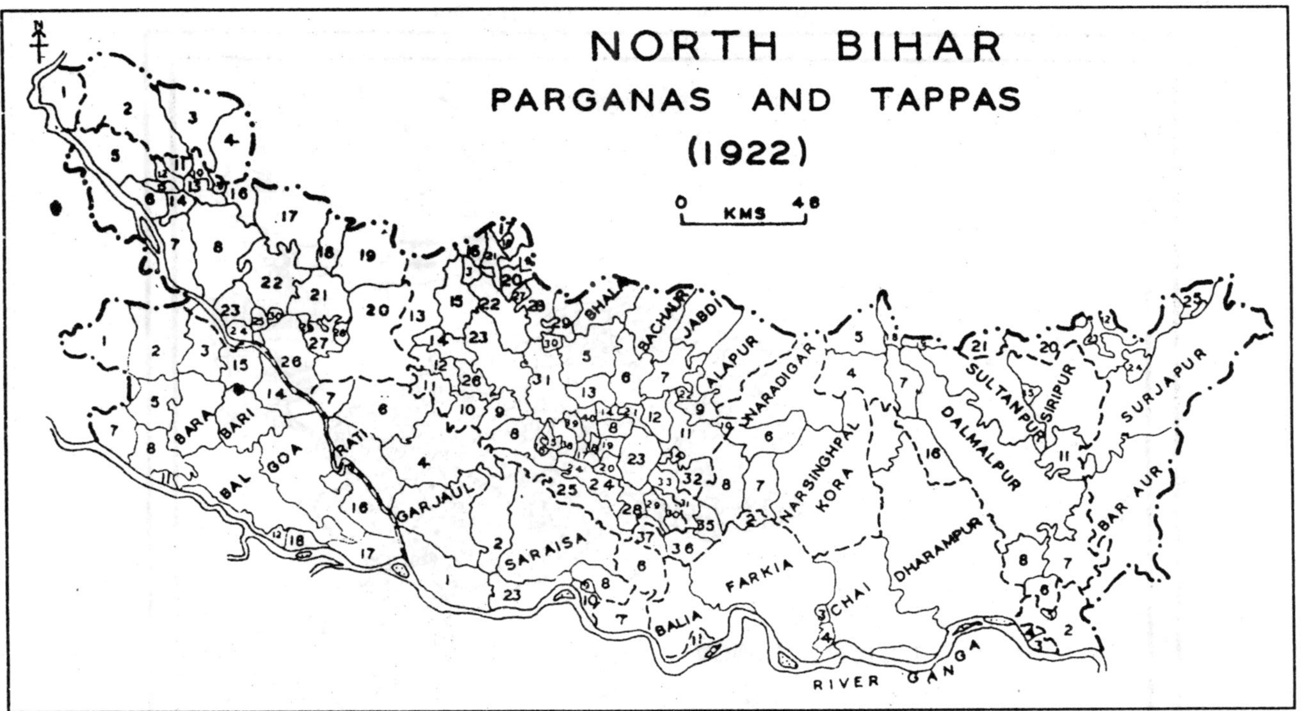


**Fig. 2.30 :** North Bihar : Parganas and Tappas, 1992.

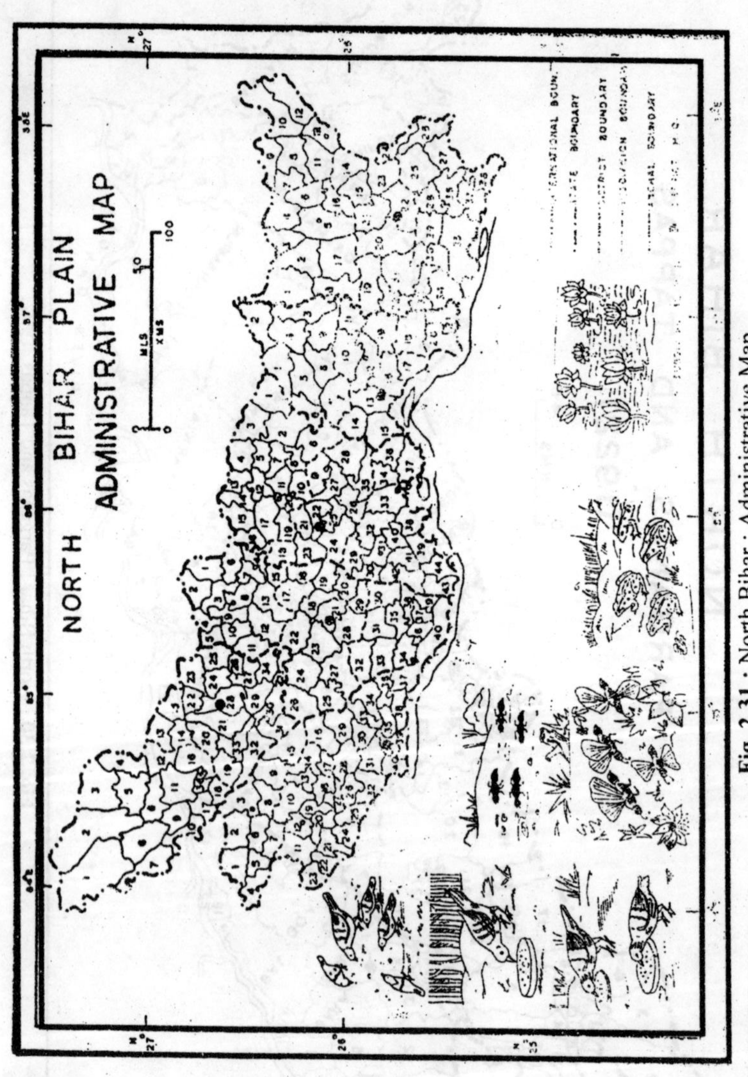


Fig. 2.31 : North Bihar : Administrative Map.

development of a hierarchy administrative units resulted in the development of hierarchy of settlements including cities, towns, rurban centres and rural settlements.

At present there are three divisions in North Bihar, i.e., Muzaffarpur, Kosi and Darbhanga with their headquarters at Muzaffarpur, Saharsa and Darbhanga respectively. The jurisdiction of Muzaf f arpur Division includes Sitamarhi, Muzaffarpur, Vaishali, West Champaran, East Champaran, Saran, Siwan and Gopalganj districts covering an area of 23073 sq. kms. with a population of 22.6 millions. The Darbhanga division consists of Darbhanga, Madhubani, Samastipur and Begusarai districts covering an area of 10383 sq. kms and 1.38 milions people (1991) The Kosi Division comprises Purnea, Katihar and Saharsa districts covering an area of 11000 sq. kilometres and a population of 10.93 millions. The study area also includes Khagaria district comes under Munger Division, while Bihpur, Naugachia and Gopalpur anchals lies under the jurisdiction of Bhagalpur district. All district and subdivisional headquarters have become towns. (Fig. 2.31)

## REFERENCES


Chaudhary, R.K., *Early History of Vaishali,* Vaishali Visesank, Muzaffarpur, 1960.

Cohn, B.S., "Some Notes on Law and Change in North India", *Economic Development and Cultural Change*, Vol. 8,1959, pp. 79-93.

Davis, W.M., "River Terraces in New England", *Geographical Essays,* Harward, University, U.S.A., 1954, 1 p. 514.

Dayal, P., 'The Bihar Plain : A Regional Study, *Transactions of the Council of Indian Geographers*, Vol. V, 1968, p. 2.

Dayal, P., *Bihar in Maps;* Kusum Prakashan, Patna, 1954.

Despande, C.D. and Bhat, L.S., "The Upper Panch Ganga Basin: A Study in the Geomorphology of the Deccan Traps' *The Indian Geograpical Journal*, Vol. XXIX, 19 54, Nos. 2 & 3, pp. 35-47.

Dube, S.C., *India is Changing Villages: Human Factors in Community Development*, Cornell University Press, 1958, pp. 26-27.

"Final Report on the Survey and Settlement Operations in Muzaffarpur District", Patna, 1922.

Geddes, A, "The Alluvial Morphology of the Indo-Gangetic Plain", *Transactions and Papers*, 1960, No.28, p. 262.

Havell, E.B., *The History of Aryan Rule in India*, George G. Harrap, London, 19151)

Karve, L., *"Some Aspects of the Organization of Caste System of the Hindus"*, Changing India (Edts. Socani Dandekar), London : Asia Publishing House, 1961, p. 147.

Lata, S., "Changes in the Built-up Area of Muzaffarpur" *Applied Geography*, (Ed. R..L., Singh). National Geographical Society of India, Varanasi, 1968, pp. 79-84.

Mishra, Jayakanta, *A History of Maithili Literature*, Vol.1, Allahabad, 1949, pp. 10-14.

Palakshappa, T.C., "Village Organization in India", *Quarterly Journal of India Studies in Social Sciences*, Vol.1, No. 4, 1967- 68, pp. 175-178.

Pandey, M.S., *Historical Geography and Topography of Bihar*, Patna, 1954.

Russel, J.R., 'Alluvial Morphology of Anatolian Rivers, *Annals of the Association of American Geographers*, Vol. XLIV, 1954, p. 370.

Singh, K.N., "The Territorial Basis of Medieval Town and Village Settlement in Eastern U.P. India", *Annalyst of the Association of American Geographers*, Vol. 58-62, 1968, p. 203.

Singh, S. and Kaith, D.S., "Geomorphological Analysis of Land form Features of Pali Development Block, from Aerial Photographs" *The Indian Geographical Journal*, Vol. XLVI, Nos. 3 & 4, 1971, p. 50.

Singh, R.L., "Evolution of Settlements in the Middle Ganga Valley" *The National Geographical Journal of India*, Vol.1, Part-2, 1955.

Sinha, P., "Urban Functions: A Case Study of Muzaffarpur", *Indian Geographical Studies*, R.B. No.1, Sept.,1973, pp. 1-11.

Smith, M.W., *Social Structure in the Punjab, Indian Villages*, (Edt.M.N. Sriniwas), London, Asia Publishing House, 1960, pp. 21- 35.

Survey and Settlement Operations, Purnea (190,1-1908), Calcutta, 1908.

Tallents, P.C., Census Report of Bihar and Orissa, 1921.

Trived, D.S., *Prehistoric Maurya Bihar*, Rashtra Bhasha Parishad, Patna, 1954, pp. 2,12,33.

Worcester, R.G., *A Text Book of Geomorphology*, Von Nostrand East-West Press, Bombay, 1967, p. 200.

# 3

# FACTORS CONTROLLING WETLANDS

The planned development of wetlands is essential in order to safeguard our environment and maintain ecological balance. It may not be proper to left our marshy lands, waterlogged areas, *tals* and ponds uncared because they have a great potentiality to produce many items which have great utility for human being besides resource generation. The wetlands are also 'pollution, filters along with beautifying the environment, attracting more rainfall and provide living abode for many species of birds, fishes, insects and plants which have very high medicinal value in our day to day life.

Wetlands are the shallow waterbodies found on the earth surface either permanently or temporarily in the form of waterlogging. In North Bihar most of the wetlands are remnants of Indo-Gangetic foredeep formed due to rise of Himalaya as the remains of Tethys sea.[1] Now with the rise in devastating floods during pleistocenes period with the melt of snow most of the wetlands have been filled and they are found only in the form of chaurs and marshy lands. (Fig.3.1).

In North Bihar bigger lakes are not found except Jalai-Malai, Kabar lake and Kusheshwar Asthan but there is no dearth of man made tanks as people are digging it for religious purposes.

## Research Design

In this chapter it has been tried to search the problems in hand for most of the bigger wetlands which have an area of upto 25 hectares

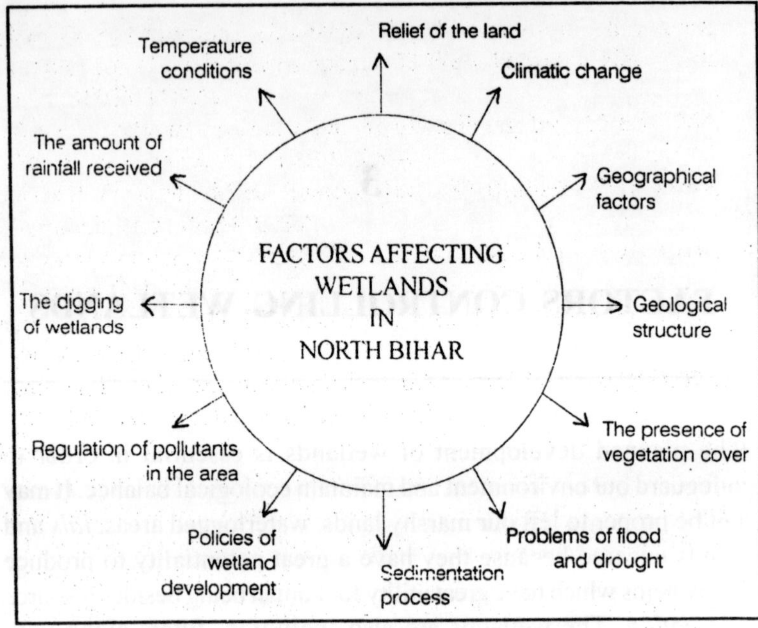


**Fig. 3.1** : Factors Affecting Wetlands in North Bihar.

in North Bihar following the stratified random sampling in the selection of wetlands. The sample study of the bigger wetlands namely Simri Chaur and Kusheshwar Asthan Chaur would be considered for detail analysis.

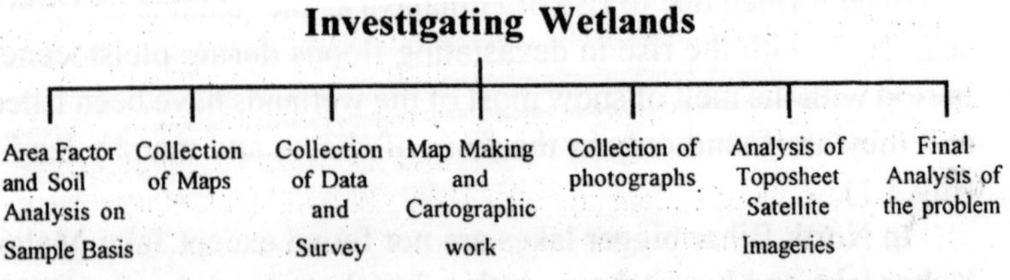


## The Concept of Wetland

Wetland has been applied to a broad range of shallow water, periodically flooded and wetland environment with special functions and values. These shallow water (surface or ground) systems are characterized by certain type of vegetation adapted to periodic flooding or saturation and soils that reflect anaerobic conditions. Wetland functions vary but include water reservoir and transport attenuation, pollution control, sediment control, food chain support, groundwater replenishment, habitat for waterfowl, fish and many rare and endangered species[2].

A variety of more specific terms, such as marsh, bog, fen, mudflat, slough and swamp have been used to characterise wetlands with various frequencies, depths, and velocities of wetness and various types of vegetation and soils. Several years ago, Dan Willard of Indiana University collected more than 50 different wetland definitions. The abundance of wetland definitions has been offered as proof that the definition of wetlands is a policy question that should be decided by politicians and administrators rather than by scientists[3].

The Table 3.1 shows the variations of some of the wetlands embankment and sometime the heavy down pour filled all the lowlying areas and the water crosses even the railway lines and made the people homeless. The continuation of this process for some years favour the formation of wetlands even in those areas where it was non-existent before.[4] Thus the encoming of flood is a positive factor for the formation of wetlands.

**Table 3.1 :** Some of the Important Wetlands of Darbhanga Division

| *Wetland* | *District* | *Lat.* | *Long* | *Area in Hectare* |
|---|---|---|---|---|
| Kanail chaur | Darbhanga | 26°10' | 85°54' | 12141 |
| Phulhara | Darbhanga | 26° | 85° | 1000 |
| Jina | Sarnastipur | 25° | 85° | 60 |
| Meghulia | Samastipur | 25° | 85° | 105 |
| Simardah | Darbhanga | 25° | 85° | 250 |
| Sirnri Chaur | Samastipur | 25° | 85° | 500 |

*Source :* Collected by Manju Kumari.

## Drought

The prevailing drought is a negative factor for the formation of wetlands. In the years of drought the flora and fauna of wetlands

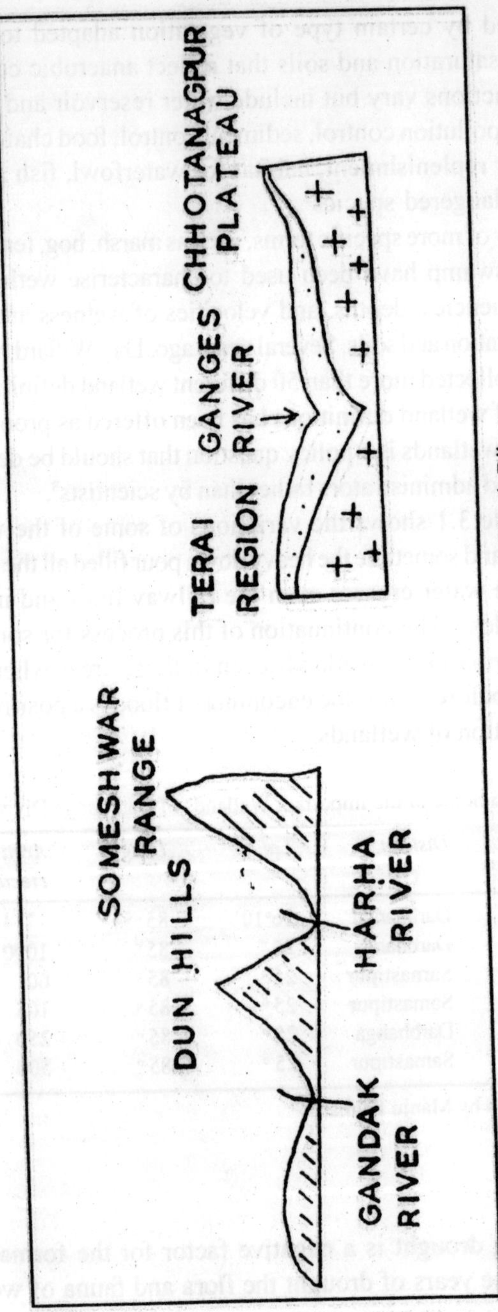


Fig. 3.2 : Patterns of Landforms in North Bihar

die. But in bigger wetland the drying effect is just partial. Sometimes wells, tanks, lakes, rivers and chaur as wetland also got dry and hence the entire wetland environment is getting disrupted.[5] But with the beginning of first shower of monsoonal rain, the process of wetland environment get a new Shy of relief by the big-bang song of frogs.

## The Process of Alluviation

Prior to Pleistocene, period the entire area was covered by discontinuous lakes, but due to melt of snow in the Himalaya and Chhotanagpur Plateau have filled most of the discontinuous lakes during Pleistocene period. During flood of rainy season this process of alluviation is still continuing. This helps in dismantling older wetlands and formation of some newer wetlands. Although Chaurs are numerously found in the form of filled wetlands and some new one's get formed at the time of flood. Hence, the process of alluviation and diluviation have helped in, the formation of wetlands.[6]

## Change in Climate

From year to year the climatic conditions are changing. During Pleistocene period of Gunj, Mindel, Riss and Wurm, the climate changes three times and this freeze and thaw conditions have helped in the formation — and filling of wetlands. Even in the normal year of flooding several new wetland: formed and in the year of drought several wetlands withered away.

## Vegetation Cover

The vegetation cover both inside and outside wetlands have their definite impact in the surrounding area. For example, the vegetations in the wetlands of North Bihar are Sewar, Litchen, Kai, Mothi, Makhana, Singarhara and several others. In Goga beel some medicinal plants are also found just like Narail Chaur of Kusheshwar Asthan. In some tanks of North Bihar the water has digestive value due to plantation of black berry trees around the lake e.g. in Belhi of Narayanpur and Udaipur West of Bettiah. Without vegetation the wetland may be a desert and hence wetlands must have some sort of flora and fauna. The businessmen come from Calcutta and collect most of the medicinal plants, fishes and frogs of the wetlands of North Bihar.

### Temperature and Rainfall

Wetlands as saviour of ecology cools down the temperature of surrounding area. It has been found that surface temperature of water of wetland is slightly higher in comparison with the ground level inside the water (0.50°C). In areas and season of high temperature the wetlands get dry whereas at the time of low temperature the wetlands are full of water[7].

The high amount of rainfall is beneficial for the survival of wetland environment whereas low rainfall is detrimental. The encoming of flood is the disturbing element because it washes away the plants or sedimentation cover the plants among which micro-organisms suffer a lot. The micro-organisms are Ghonghari, Ship, fishes, snails, frogs, tortoise and several varieties of reptiles.

### Digging of Wetlands

Due to religious point of view digging of tank as wetland is a must for the higher income group people in North Bihar. By digging tank people wants to marry tank with mango, orchard.[8] This is because people have a belief that the above action has the same religious value as marrying a daughter. Besides this, some people dig wetland for rearing fishes and cultivating makhana while others do the same for irrigating the land. The accumulation of water also favour washing cattle wealth, washing utensils besides bathing and emersion of statues of Goddess.

### Desires of Local People

Peoples participation is quite necessary in keeping the wetlands of smaller nature. Because some people like to reclaim wetland for agricultural extension whereas others wanted to use it for odds and errands. In bigger wetlands fish rearing is the only alternative left because in North Bihar crocodile and tortoise farming are not practised by the farmers. Some people left wetland uncared while others wanted to cultivate Bhent and lotus flower along with the rearing of ducks.[9]

**National Policies**

In case the national policy is to save wetlands no one has the power to reclaim it. Both for high national income and in order to make the environment beautiful the survival, protection and conservation of wetland environment is highly desirous. Recently, the state and the central government are trying to save wetland for the stabilization of birds, maintain stability in the level of water and beautifying the environment.

**The Determinants of Wetland**

Wetlands can be divided into many types based on the conditions of water availability on the ground, namely-man made ditches, chaurs (temporary waterlogged area of a wider dimension), *tals* (Permanent, waterlogged area of a smaller dimension), cultivated rice fields, Jute lands, alluvial fans, waterlogged areas, diara land (sand bars on the side of rivers), shallow lakes, coastal tracts, delta, managrove areas, swampy ground, forested wetlandsj of terai zone, riverine tracts, flood plains, irrigation channels, ponds and spill ways of diara lands or riverine coastal tracts (Fig. 3.3).

The intensity of wetlands could be determined on the basis of following formula which has been devised by R.B. Mandal (1992) in course of the present study.

$$IW = \sqrt{12AX\frac{TW}{RF} + \frac{DNL}{LEP} + - - - - - - - + N}$$

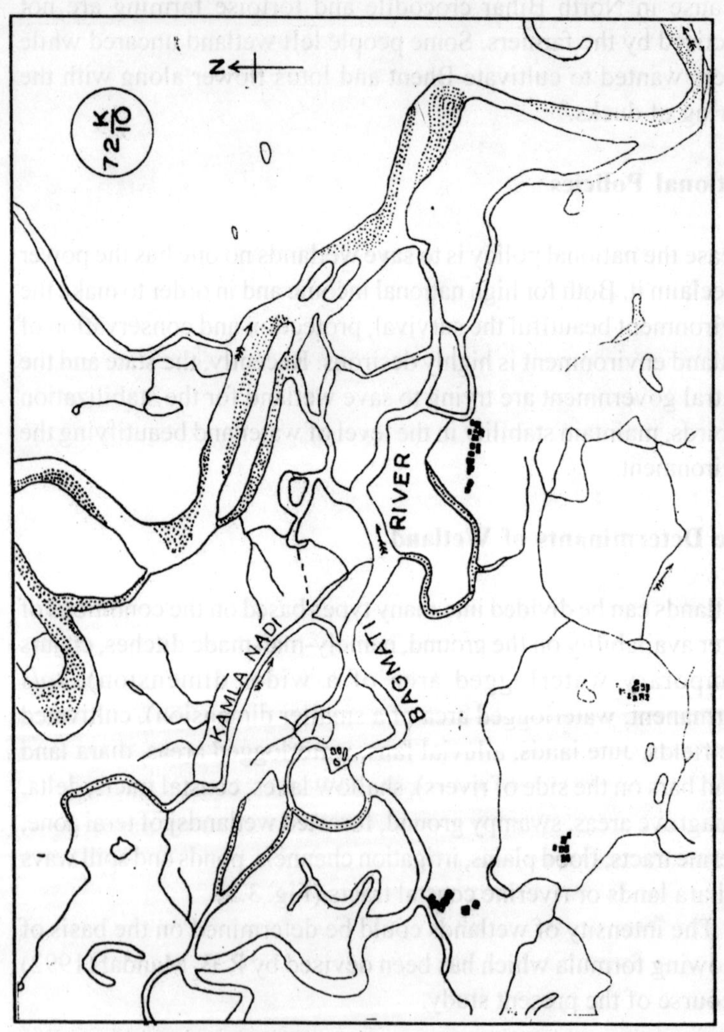


Fig. 3.3 : Meandering Courses of Rivers and Diara lands in Samastipur District

Where,

IW = Index of Wetland
A = Total area
TW = Total Area of Wetland
RF = Total Rainfall
DNL = Total Destruction of Natural Lakes
LEP = Level of Environmental Pollution

$$= \sqrt{10 \times \frac{500}{1500} \times \frac{30}{20} + - - - - - + N}$$

$$= \sqrt{3.33 + 1.50} \quad \sqrt{=4.83}$$

$$= 2.19(\text{I.W.})$$

**Conclusion**

On the basis of above discussion it could be said that in North Bihar the presence of wetlands are controlled by the interplay of several factors among which the physical and cultural factors are more dominant. The role of physical factor could be observed in the formation of oxbous lakes, chaurs, tals and marshy depressions. The presence of wetlands create barner for direct movement besides it helpful in the spread of asthama and the stagnant water provide breeding ground for mosquitoes. Recently, it has been observed that due to sedimentation the wetlands are dwindling but on the other hand the growth of population need enhanced life of lakes and tals.

The factors affecting wetlands are the features of terrain. The volume of water received by the area besides alluviation and diluviation forces of the floods brought by river in North Bihar. Recently, it has been observed that due to increased human interactions with the wetland man tries to reclaim it for the expansion of agriculture, establishment of industries as well as routes of transportation and human settlements. All these have dwindled the wetlands in North Bihar extensively. During the ancient period there were 41 lakes around Motihari but nowadays only three lakes e.g. Motijheel, Suhagman lake and Kararia lakes are found. Thus the favouring and disfavouring factors are both help in the expansion and dieing out of wetlands in North Bihar.

## NOTES

1. Skalar, F.H., *et al.,* "Development in Regional Scale Simulation and Analysis: Case Studies from coastal Wetland Eco-system", in *Environmental Monitoring Application of Remote Sensing and GIS*, Edited by R.B. Singh, Geocarto International Centre, Hong Kong, 1991, p. 47.
2. Dale, P. E. R., *et al.*, "Image Subtraction of Digitised Large-Scale colour Infrared Aerial photographs to Monitor the Impact of Habitat Modification on a Subtropical coastal wetland", *op.cit.*; p. 63.
3. Mandal, R.B.; "Geophysical Aspects of Wetlands in North Bihar", Paper presented in the Wetland Seminar of Forest Department, Government of Bihar, Purnea, 1988.
4. Das, K.N., "Population and Land Use Changes in the Kosi Region, Bihar", Unpublished Ph.D. Thesis, Bhagalpur University, 1969.
5. Gopal, B., *et al.*, "*Wetland Ecology and Management*", National Institute of Ecology and International Scientific Publications, Jaipur, 1982.
6. "Wetlands Conference in Czechoslovakia", *Nature and Resources*, UNESCO, Vol. XX; No.2., 1984, p. 22.
7. Mandal, R.B., *The Geography of Rural Settlements in Bihar Plain*; Patna University, 1971.
8. Choudhary, U. P., *Geographical Aspects of Wetlands in North Bihar Plain*; Patna University, 1971.
9. Margaret, Cox, *Wetland Ecology and Conservation*; Facts on File; New York, 1995.

# 4

# THEORETICAL BACKGROUND

Nowadays wetlands become the central theme in physical as well as social science because it is related with the physical as well as social phenomenon of the region. Under physical phenomena the wetlands may be the result of tectonic processes inside the earth surface besides the formation of rivers, lakes, chaurs, marshes and the man made lakes, ponds, ditches and reservoirs.

The location of wetlands has immense value in terms of purifying and modifying the environment, keeping the water level up, production of various crops of economic value, and provides fishes, snails, birds, insects and variety of plants species which are diverse in utility and nature but complementary to each other in terms of food habit.

Wetlands are marginal areas for human being but economically important as they have immense value in bridging the supply of protein and collection of plants of medicinal value. In North Bihar the wetlands are mainly riverine origin whose taxonomy could be seen below.[1] (Fig. 4.1)

## Swamps

Swamps are basins partially filled with water of fresh or decayed vegetation and muddy soil. They vary greatly in different cases. The term swamp will be used here to include such similar form as swamp, marsh (except tidal marsh), bog, marsh, and muskeg, although the vegetation of swamps and marshes may include many trees and even forests, while in marshes, swales and bogs the

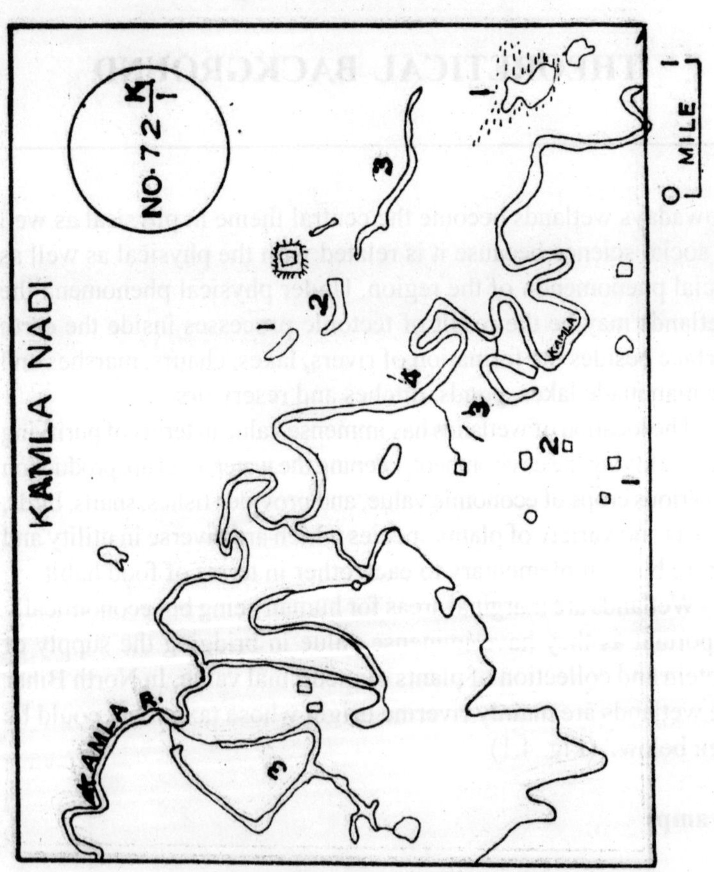


Fig. 4.1 : Stages of Wetlands Formation Along Kamla River

vegetation consists of grasses, mosses, litchens, etc. The water of swamps may be fresh, brackish or salty. The distribution of swamp is essentially the same as that of lakes. They are most numerous in recently glaciated regions, but they are abundant in humid regions, coastal plains, flood plains and deltas. Although they are less common in arid regions.

## Peat Bogs

Many shallow lakes in humid regions and in high latitudes become filled with various species of vegetation, particularly sphagnum moss. The growth of these in basins and on the boarders completely filled. The lower layers of vegetation decompose under water which because of its anticeptic properties, prevents complete decay. The partially decomposed vegetable matter, which may be many feet thick, turns brown in colour and becomes peat. This is the first stage of the formation of coal.[2]

## Muskegs

Over vast areas in North Bihar for similar reasons ancient glacial lake basins have become largely filled with vegetations, muskeg, which in some places is so mixed water that it is practically liquid but in others it is firm enough to support the growth of grass, mosses and even trees. In many cases the grass and mosses have formed a crust — like cover over the muskeg which trembles when one steps on it, giving rise to the name quaking bogs. The underlying *mick* is so deep and often in such a liquid condition that if persons break through the crust they may have difficulty in getting out, while without human aid cattle, horses and other large animals that break through usually became hopelessly bogged down.

## Tidal Marshes

Along many sea coasts there are lagoons and shallow bays fringed and more or less filled with grasses and other vegetable matters that grow in saline water. They flow on the ebb tides alternately,

Birds in Kabar Tal

covers and uncovers tidal marshes which is quite different in composition from ordinary fresh water swamp growth. These marshes are almost flat but slope gently seaward while others are channeled by tidal currents.

## The Origin of Swamps

Swamps form in different ways, but the great majority of them are glacial basins that have been filled or covered by vegetation. Another large group of swamps, are found on the margins of coastal plains. These are the result of a slight uplift of to design at sea shore or the filling of lagoons by silt and vegetation. A third major group of swamps are those on flood plain and deltas where abandoned river channels have been filled with vegetation.[3]

In arid and semi-arid regions many swamps, which support vegetation that grows in salt and brackish water, brings play lakes or other types of salt lakes. When the lakes have a maximum volume of water the swamp may be entirely covered. When the water level drops the swamp disappears. Other minor types of swamps are correlated with different types of lake basins.

## Topography of Swamp

Most swamps are relatively small and like lakes suggest youthful topography. However, swamp on flood-plains and some coastal plains are indicators of old topography.

In North Bihar there are thousands of swamps that vary from less then one acre to many square kilometres on the surface. The surface of the swamps themselves are quite flat, although many small elevations and depressions are likely to occur, but associated with them are numerous larger hills and depressions, the hummocks and kettle of ground moraines. Naturally, where large shallow basins have been filled with vegetation, the flattish surfaces of the swamps are less broken and interrupted by plains.[4]

The Everglades of Florida and the Dismal swamp of Virginia are good examples of the marginal swamps of coastal plains. Both these lie practically at sea level and they are essentially flat.

**The Everglades**

This great region has half lake and half swamp which occupies a shallow rock walled basin some 160 kms long and 64 kms wide between lake okeechobee, and the southerntip of Florida in USA. The Everglades are fed by water from heavy rains and from the overflow of lake okeechbee, which is the second largest body of fresh water wholly within the United States of America. The water cover is on 10, 240 square kilometres and the swamp is fresh. When high, it stands barely above sea-level and moves with a distinct current into rivers and canals which partially drain it.

Although the land is clothed with varieties of tropical vegetation including cypress, palms, bay, live oak, papayas, wild rubber, giant ferns and with orchids., abound in the Everglades. Saw grass grows under water and above water to a height of 2 to 3 metres. Decayed vegetation and muck underlie the whole area. Where properly drained, the fertile soil yields fabulous crops of sugarcane and vegetables. Similar, but less extensive swamps of our coast lines offers interesting possibilities for reclamation of the extremely fertile swampy land.

## PRINCIPLES OF WETLAND FORMATION

Geographers try to study Wetlands at different levels. At the lowest levels they have been interested in the characteristics and qualities in terms of there make up of site, situations, levels of flood, qualities of birds visiting the place, general ecological conditions, and highways which connect wetlands with the living world. Wetlands could be classified into four component parts water surface (fishing ground), sub-water surface, cultivation of *Makhana* and *mothi*) and deep water surface (Recreation by navigation) and marginal tracks along with rivulets. The rivulets are quite essential to make a closer link between wetland and the cultural environment around.

The principles of wetland formation that emerge out of fieldwork are as follows:

(a) Minimization of potential contact.

(b) Maximization of production.

(c) Optimization of the beautification of cultural world.
(d) Optimization of qualities of mans relationship with the wetland ecology.
(e) Optimization of the synthesis of all the above principles.
(f) Generally people in urban and rural areas don't want to live close to the wetlands, because it is dangerous for the small child who may sink inside the water or die by droning.

For example, every year dozens of people die due to drowning in most of the anchals of North Bihar. Similarly, a residential site near wetlands develop as *asthama* disease or hopping cough which are dangerous for human being. Some of the wetlands also act as the breeding ground of variety of mosquitoes, snakes and lizards which do not provide congenial atmosphere for the human being to reside close to the wetlands.

(b) People living close to wetland wants maximization of the production of fish, mothi, Makhana, and Singarhara from wetlands. These days, it has been felt that wetlands are potential areas for the production of varieties of crops even if they are considered as marginal land. Wetlands favour preying of migratory birds, recreation by boating, intensive production of rice and collection of varieties of herbs which are so lucarative that wetlands have really proved to be worthy of attention to conserve and protect and not too disturb the ecolozy of wetland.

(c) For optimization of the beautification of cultural world wetlands are considered as modifier of the environment because they act as pollution filters and the plantation of tree in the surrounding areas in order to beautify the environment to a substantial degree. This beautification does not only enhance the environment for cleaning the environment with the supply of oxygen but they have a capacity to absorb more and more carbondioxide present in the atmosphere.

(d) Optimization of the qualities of man's relations with the wetland ecology shows that human being wants closer relationship with the wetlands because they are the bathing place for men and beasts, cleaning of clothes, worship of different goddesses, ancestors besides water sites present favourable place for the performance of marriage ceremony, establishment of brick factor in the proximity and they are the centres of cremation ground for dead body of human being and animals. In this way, it is quite clear that human being has close relationship with the wetland ecology because they tide together in an unifying bound for cultural enhancement and the production of various types of foodgrains, fishes, plants, herbs, and preparing a sound environment for physical and cultural appraisal of the wetland in two dimensional space.

(e) Optimization of the synthesis of all the above principles shows the optimization of production and minimize the effort in maintaining the present ecology of wetlands. For proper management of wetland the potential contact of human being is quite essential so that the wetland could be more meaningful in ameliorating the environment for better human living.

**Table 4.1** : Taxonomy of Wetland as Riverine Origin

| Oxbow Lakes | Meandring Channels | Unusual Deposition of sand | Sheet Wash Erosion | Man made Tanks | Man made Lakes& Ditches | Torrential rain in the mountains & plains | Breach of Embank-ment |
|---|---|---|---|---|---|---|---|

## Location and Stages of Wetlands

In North Bihar most of the wetlands are located in lowlying areas in comparison with local topographic features besides they are the areas of annual flooding where the deposition of sand during flood is the common feature. The North Bihar was primarily known as part of Tethys sea after the upheaval of Himalayas during Eocene, Miocene and Pliocene periods about 10 to 5 crore years ago. The remaining part of Tethys sea become a vast wetlands known as Indo-Gangetic trough. But slowly and slowly the vast amount of detritous annually comes to North Bihar and fill the Indo-Gangetic plain. This process of formation and filling of wetlands is a common feature in North Bihar giving rise to multistage of wetlands. For example, in 1700 AD around Motihari there were 42 lakes but at present most of them have filled up except 3 and we call them the wetlands of second category because the first stage of wetlands may be the chaurs or bigger lowlying riverine basin (Fig.4.1). The third stage wetlands may be the present oxbow lakes such as the Gogabeel of Katihar district on the Kankhar river and the oxbow lake of Gandaki river in Vaishali district. The fourth stage wetlands may be regarded as rivers and places of sheet wash erosion nor the Butahibalan, the Kosi, the Kareh, the Burhi Gandak, the Lakhandei, the Dhaus, and the Jibachh rivers of North Bihar.[5]

The fifth stage wetlands are man made ponds which are transitory physical features because without reexcavation their life cannot be regarded more than 20 to 25 years at one place. With this the decreasing slope in plain land especially in the flood plains the chances of the location and occurring of wetlands is greater in comparison with upland plains. This clearly signifies that in river basins the wetland has better locational condition than uplands but sometimes the location of wetlands in mountainous areas are closely associated with the diastrophic conditions during geological past. For example, in Bihar the Kharagpur lake, Kukurjhap Project and Naktidam Project in the district and Munger are the oldest formations of wetlands.

The present site and situation of wetland in North Bihar present a cyclic character especially the meandering channel of the rivers. For example, near Gandaki river in Vaishali district, the five generations of oxbow lake clearly gives a cyclic character of the landscape as well as wetlands because the remnants of oxbow lakes testify various stages of the evolution of wetlands by the way of straightening of its course.

In the plains of North Bihar the digging of tanks is a common feature in each and every village for four purposes namely bathing, place for men and beasts, rearing of fishes, raising of Makhana and mothi as bumper crops besides it beautifies the surrounding environment and provide beautiful sites for the location of human settlements. North Bihar is a land of rice and fish culture and for this fact in Pokharbhinda village there and 75 tanks and in Narayanpur village there are 35 tanks. These tanks are the major source of fish and makhana production in the area. Throughout its length the rivers of North Bihar have smaller or bigger wetlands on both sides of the flood plain and there is a chain of wetlands because the changing and meandering courses of rivers sometimes cut its meandering bend of course as oxbow lakes and this feature favours the formation of a chain of wetlands throughout its basin whether the river is the Ganges, the Kareh, the Kosi, the Mahananda, the Kamla, the Balan, the Bhuthi Balan, the Jibachh, the Lakhandei, the Burhi Gandak and the Dhaus.

The flood affected areas (Fig.4.2) of these rivers are covered with several wetlands.

The valley location of wetlands indicate the first stage of normal cycle of erosion as discussed by Davis. This concept of landscape erosion and sculpturing started with the rise of landscape from the sea level and the on going rainfall on such a landscape create small channels in the form of resequent and insequent streams. Hence, the origin of wetlands took place in the course of river valleys and around. This type of valley development and meandering of river courses help in the formation of wetlands of various stages in the form of oxbowlakes, byous and left portion of rivers in the form of ditches and others. In flood plain areas wetlands formed due to alluviation and diluviation of sand bodies disproportionately here and there. (Fig. 4.3).

The socio-economic model of wetlands development comes in the direct measurement. In this method, the perception of wetlands development means ultimate development of the society through wetlands because natures laws are fixed and any change in the natural system than by people comes under the purview of wetlands development not for the sake of nature but for the human being. In this regard, the flow of labour and items produce in wetlands to the well being of people like Brahmans and Rajputs produced a vicious circle because resources, entreprenuers and infrastructure facilities for wetlands development come to fishermen, Chamar and Dushadh who are closely associated with wetlands developments from so called higher strata of people in the society or higher income group people like Rajput and Brahmans. In this way, we can say that socio-economic model for wetlands gives us an idea for wetlands measurements in a caste ridden Indian society like North Bihar. Here most of the social, religious and economic developments took place on caste line. (Fig. 4.4).

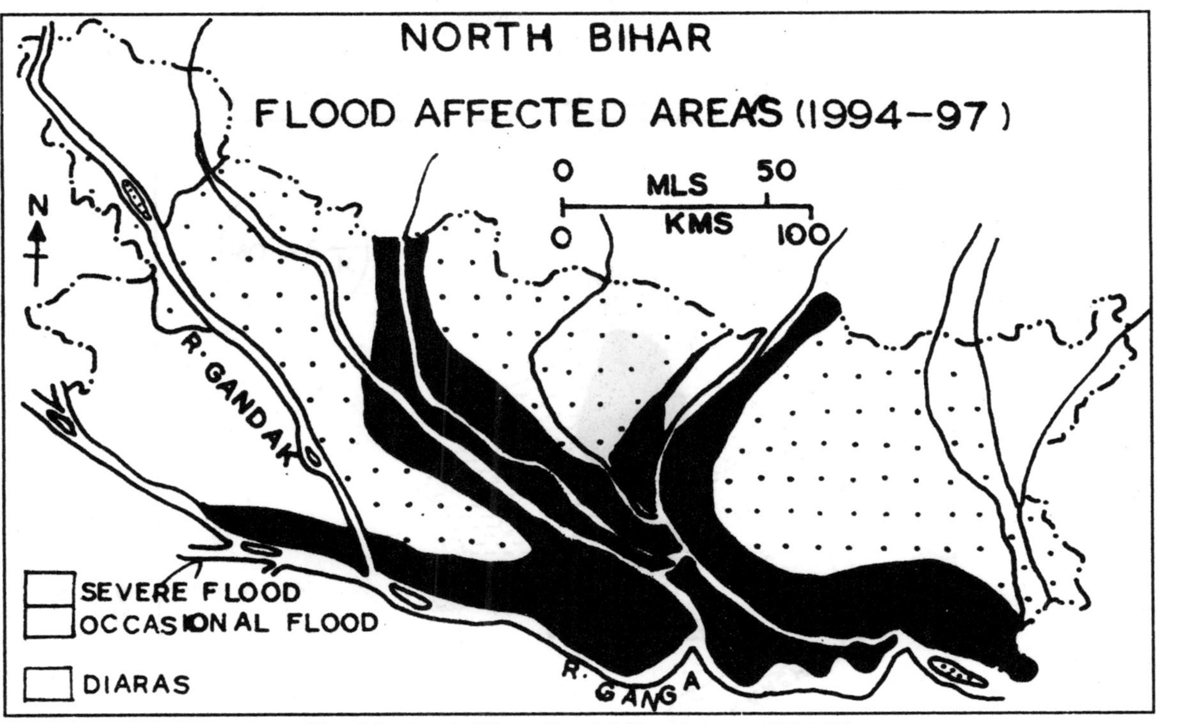


**Fig. 4.2 :** North Bihar : Flood Affected Areas, 1994-97.

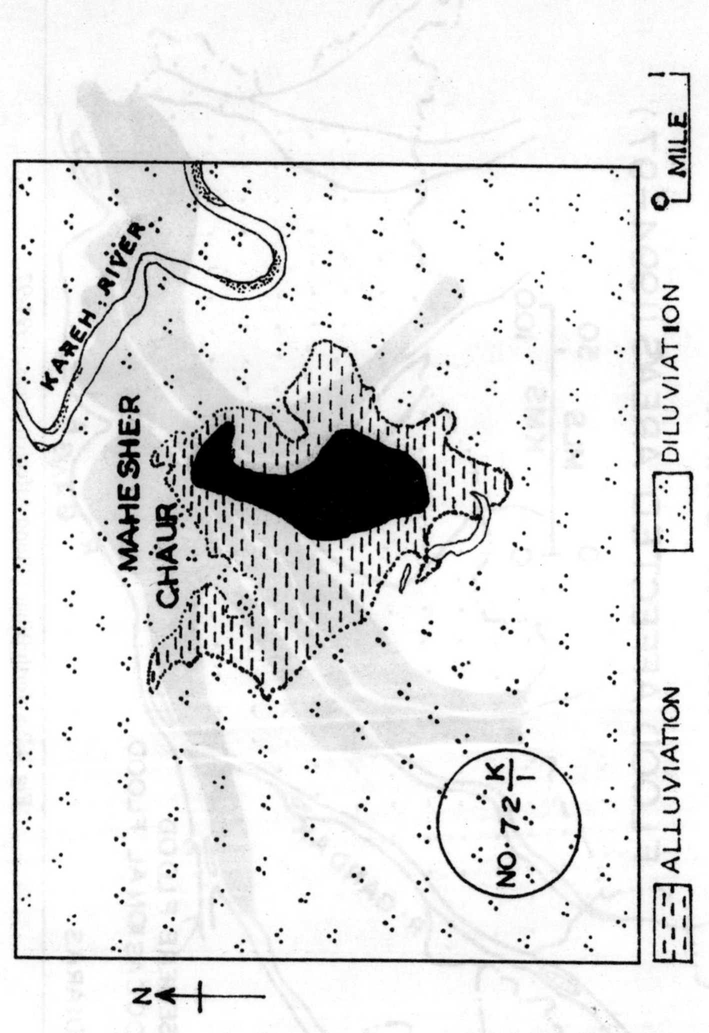


**Fig. 4.3 :** Alluviation and Diluviation as Forces of Wetland Formation

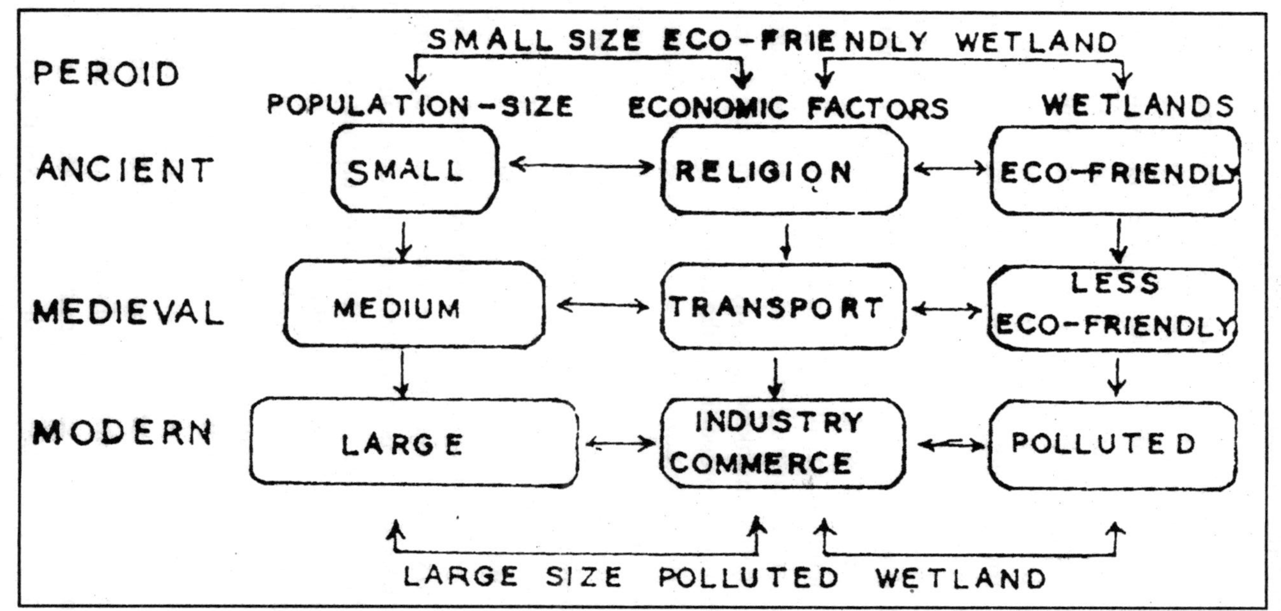


**Fig. 4.4 :** Socio-economic Diversities and Wetland

## Conserving Wetlands for the Future

Wetlands have been identified as one of the most useful natural resource system, which essentially support life systems and playing a vital role in controlling water cycles and waterlogged wealth. Unfortunately, wetlands are fast disappearing all over the world, including North Bihar, and the time has come to make a coordinated effort to halt this trend and optimise the use of wetlands. Wetlands can earn ten times more money in comparison with agricultural operations.

In India, apart from a few surveys and study programmes which are fragmentary and region specific, little has been done to conserve our wetlands. At the third meeting of the conference of the contracting parties of the Ramsar convention in June 1987, it was said that the "wise use of wetlands is their sustainable utilisation for the benefit of mankind in a way compatible with the maintenance of the natural properties of the ecosystem."

Sustainable utilisation was defined as the "human use of a wetland so that it may yield the greatest continuous benefit to present generations while maintaining its potential to meet the needs and aspirations of future generations".

One unique characteristic of wetland is the presence of water and a water-saturated soil. This may be either a permanent feature or occurring for a part of year. This ecosystem is a zone between the dry terrestrial and the wet acquatic systems, having characteristics of both besides some unique use in itself. Diversity of character, size, type and mode of occurrence of wetlands have given rise to different ways of describing them and wetlands have been defined from time to time to suit a particular location, scholar and orientation of the problem.

According to Mitesh and Gosselins, wetlands often include three main components; water, unique soil differing from those of uplands and the presence of vegetation adapted to wet conditions. The Ramsar convention of which India is a signatory, defines wetlands as areas of marsh, salt Pan, peatland or water, natural or artificial, permanent or temporary, with water that is static or flowing, fresh, brackish or saline, including areas of marine water, the depth of which at low tide does not exceed six metres with the amount of scientific thinking and research that is now going into the study of this ecosystem and its management, more appropriate definitions are likely to emerge.

Common people in this country understand easily marshes and swamps, or lakes and mud flats. A vast multitude, in fact, draws sustenance from wetland resources. The wetlands are always evaluated from and anthropogenic approach. The usefulness of wetlands can be determined from the point of view of the flora and fauna they sustain, their ecosystem values, and the contribution in maintaining global air and water cycles.

Man uses wetlands in a number of ways; from gathering food to disposal of wastes. Wetlands are habitat for endangered and rare species of birds and animals and are especially important for migratory birds and waders. They are the habitat for a number of endemic relict, regional/varieties of sub-species of plants, insects and invertebrates.

As an ecosystem, wetlands are useful for nutrient recovery and cycling, releasing excess nitrogen, deactivating phosphates, removing toxins, chemicals and heavy metals through absorption by plant and also in the treatment of waste water. Retention of sediments by wetlands also reduces siltation of river. Wetlands also help in mitigating floods, recharging aquifers and reducing the surface run-off and the consequent erosion. Mangrove wetlands of India and Bangladesh act as buffers against the devastating storms of the Bay of Bengal. Wetlands also influence the Microclimate of a locality besides checking underground salt water intrusion of an adjacent brackish water environment through interface pressure.

On a global scale, wetlands maintain air and water quality including nitrogen, sulphur, methane and carbondioxide cycles. Not all uses of wetland's become definite 'opportunities' in development planning. Resource opportunities are location specific and can be defined as socially feasible use of resource system or service.

Social and economic perceptions help in perfecting the choice of technology options and design. Educated people's effort in planning for rural development technology meet with success no more than that is due to these native efforts. The scenario becomes so dismal that it falls contingent upon-introducing the concept of appropriate technology to distinguish, the useless ones and also to give a direction to what is needed in the field of technology design and development. Today, a major criterion of appropriate technology is to ensure sustainable change. Use of these advanced perception of planning need and planning process is particularly important while dealing with the problems of marginal area development. Yet, it will be proper to remember that fundamental understanding of the process and appropriate methods to bring change remain far from being achieved.

To assist the task of planning for natural resource systems a set of ground rules has been developed. But previous work has been revised and modified to suit the subjective dimension of the specific area of developing untilised and under-utilised wetlands. These postulates are tentative and are based on the author's direct experience in wetland ecosystems. The seven postulates are:

(1) Wetlands, in most cases, will have conflicting land-use interests and any change contemplated by universally good to all the contending interests. Therefore, the designer will have to take sides.

(2) In land-use study no observation is independent of the, observer-object relationship and the observer, for that matter, becomes a part of the object. This is why participatory action research is the strongest methodological tool for understanding the use of land and design of wiser use.

(3) The culture of conserving resources and using them in as many ways as possible has been found to thrive among the poor. There is prima-facie and inverse relationship between affluence and the affinity to recycling or reuse.

(4) Information about natural resource system particularly about those of developing countries is meagre. Taking decisions on "wise use", therefore, will use cybernetic models in place of any exercise in pretentious optimisation.

(5) All public decisions are political decisions; and any misuse of natural, biological systems will have its social, economic and environmental backlash. However, such reactions are not instant and this time-lag provides opportunities to the manipulators and speculators to inflict permanent damage to the ecosystems by forcing wrong land use changes on society.

(6) Environmental damage is identified not by observing the quality of the environment or measuring the external stresses alone but also by evaluating the internal strength and metabolic resistance of the particular group of people inflicted by that external stress.

(7) It is easily agreed that the above postulates are of preliminary nature. Subjective ability to handle the challenge of sustainable development is still amateurish. This maturity will only come through the experiments going on all over the world. These experiments are either in the form of a movement to preserve a biosphere or to design 'wise use' of an ecosystem for achieving sustainable development.

Major concerns in developing rural technology in general and wastelands in particular can be summarised as; Beneficiaries are externalities in the process of planning; social feasibility of the proposed changes are ignored; and the search for alternative technologies is not rooted on the strength and weakness of the existing technologies. It is, therefore, considered imperative to reorient the search for development options through benchmark studies of existing technology and use of land.

There are large areas of land which fail to drain the water they collect during rainy season. Some of them are shallow basins with wide shores. These waterlogged areas in the flood plains have almost imperceptible slope of the fringe and the shore lines fluctuate appreciably in different seasons.

These reasoanally flooded regimes, with a few pockets of permanent waterlogging are some of the least productive lands. In most of such areas, local villagers can at best grow a crop of paddy or jute. An interesting phenomenon of 'oscillation' takes place with respect to the cropping pattern with one year interval. Villagers take advantage of the receding shoreline and keep on extending the area under cropping till the whole area gets flooded.

Most, if not all, of the development efforts of these wetland regions are based on the premise that the land will have to be drained properly. The actions suggested include; modification of the regimes to introduce more efficient resource systems, mainly involving agriculture and fisheries and developing location specific schemes on the basis of study of existing practices.

Under one group of wetlands, in North Bihar and West Bengal there is a classified list of derelict and semi-derelict water bodies prepared by the Directorate of Fisheries giving police station wise estimates under various size classes.

Since 1986, two projects have been initiated to augment fish productivity. First, a World Bank aided project for which each district took up some of such water bodies through the Fish Development Agencies (FDA). The second, a similar project using financial support from the Rural Landless Employment Guarantee Programme (RLEGP). However, the efforts do not as yet match the opportunities and, therefore, have to be strengthened.

By strengthening the existing activity linking them with the National Mission on Wetland Development; introducing highly effective system to oversee the technical and financial management of on-going project and to ensure similar facilities to new projects; by exploring the possibilities of growing blue-green algae in some waterbodies; and ensuring institutional supports to strengthening the project infrastructures and the opportunities can be exploited to the full.

At many places wetlands act as municipal sewage receptacles to high without any formal design. The idea is to develop appropriate pond system in such wetlands that will handle a definite range of sewage application rate to obtain the desirable effluent quality and a good harvest of fish to make the system self-sustaining. Using wetlands, lying mostly derelict, cities for sanitation and resource recovery does, in fact, open up a new vista for low-cost sanitation technology where the state of the art, is critically deficient in providing a viable and dependable alternative.

Using wetlands for water quality improvement has been tried in cold climates in Canada and in the United States. Though in its experimental stage, wetland disposal system has been found quite effective in reducing appreciably most of the pollution load, both natural and artificial marshes ape effective to purify waste water.

To the east of Calcutta, the oldest practice, incidentally also the largest in the world, of using a backswamp for water disposal flourishes. It has been possible to draw initial engineering lessons for developing a pond system on the basis of the studies carried out on the wetlands of Darbhanga. In principle, the pond system should be designed on the basis of stabilisation tank to obtain a desired effluent quality for given waste water loading features. It has also become customary to discuss opportunities of rearing fish in the third pond in series, also termed as maturation pond. In the wetlands of Calcuta ponds directly ingress raw sewage which has a Biochemical Oxygen Demand (BOD) value between 120-160 ppm. Experiments have shown that fish grown in village ponds and not fed with sewage. This is concerned with hacterial contamination. Incidentally, Calcutta sewage has low metalion concentration to give rise to the possibility of contamination.

Untreated municipal sewage contributes a major pollution load to the rivers of India. Cost of installation and maintenance of conventional treatment plants be disproportionately high relative to the amount of funds available and this makes the conventional treatment plants non-viable disorders in conventional sewage treatment plants are frequent. Wetlands in urban periphery are natural receptacles for waste water and can harness nutrients available in the waste through fisheries and agriculture.

Planning for municipal effluent sanitation, therefore, can be more effective if it can follow three basic lessons which have become apparant. Sewage treatment plants are essentially non-viable because of the high plant cost, prohibitive operational cost and repeated plant breakdowns. Municipal effluent is a nutrient pool which is exploited effectively to grow fish and also for irrigational purposes and Indian cities occasionally have contiguous back swamps for waste water disposal.

These lessons corroborate the observation made in a World Bank/IDRC report on 'Low-cost sanitation technology' options, which has summarised the experiences in developing countries. It has stated inter alia; ''Universal solution of sewage and treatment plants does not reach more than 6.5 per cent of the people in developing countries, reuses of excreta in fish culture, algae production and adequatic plants/energy production is new and promissing technology that radically changes the context of urban sanitation".

In fact, the publication of the report in 1978 caused waste water fisheries to gain a quantum jump. The report provides a dedicated pointer towards a 'new approach' which appreciates the role of reuse of human excreta. It is heartening to note that under-utilised marshes around a number of municipalities in Bihar and West Bengal have been identified for being transformed into resource-efficient stabilisation tank systems under the Ganga Action Plan.

The National Committee on the Development of Backward Areas has, in a report to the Planning Commission in 1981, identified coastal areas affected by salinity as a backward area. The Committee identified coastal saline areas as places with saline top soil or where the water strata is saline even at great depths. The Committee has appreciated the efforts to develop brackish water fisheries in mud flats.

A 'big swing' has taken place in using the land for brackish-water fish culture independently or along with paddy cultivation over a large area in the estuarine region of West Bengal, since the flooding of about 40 hectares of Ranigachhi Mauza in South 24-Parganas. A favourable ecological condition and unattractive export market have combined to influence the decision. Although profitable, brackishwater fishery is technically inefficient and comparatively low-yielding. Existing social and institutional structures are inadequate to handle the phenomenal surge earnings. This generated discernible inequality in wealth distribution and related disorders.[6]

Suggested action includes giving effect to the recommendations in the National Committee on the Development of Backward Areas in relation to coastal saline areas, removing the policy uncertainly over land use to introduce brackishwater fishery in such areas that will be considered as ecologically feasible and taking care to see that the rivers in this region do not loose the opportunity to deposit their silt on the plains to the extent that the phenomenon of heaving up takes place on the bed of the river itself and the river looses its conservancy.

The extent of wetland loss in the country become apparent when a comparison is made by the Survey of India topographical maps brought out at intervals of 20 years. This phenomenon is particularly pure of urban and semi-urban areas where wetlands have the strongest possibility of conversion. Such fragile areas are in critical need of wetland management, for a few more years of inaction will inflict perpetual damage to this system.

It is also true that the wetlands are complex ecosystems and their detailed evaluation is a time-consuming process requiring the attention of socialists, the minimum working time is enough for large areas of wetlands to be lost in the meantime, Therefore, a thorough inventory of the existing wetlands, identification of their potential and existing uses, and comparative evaluation using a list of simpler criteria should serve the purpose of deciding on land use options.

In these circumstances it is suggested that the task of wetland preservation begin by using a modified technique to achieve workable information in the least possible time and this is where 'rapid appraisal survey' comes in which involved collection of baseline information. But, in a few cases detailed evaluation becomes necessary depending on the resources potential and the ecosystem of the subject wetland. Further, the appraisal will have to be reviewed from time to time to guide the changes necessary in planning for contingencies.

The programme of developing wetlands will have to begin by solving two handicaps. First, weak research support and second, shortage of trained wetland managers and technical assistants. A sustained effort will be necessary to build these support systems.

The general trend is unscientific research which still remains confined to laboratories and the tendency of safe research is largely predominant amongst most researchers. The challenge of creating additional wealth out of a difficult area of land fails to attract budding scientists and in most cases teachers as well. The most serious gap here is the inability of the scientific community to appreciate the significance of traditional practices in the use of land. There is very little curriculum opportunity to learn the use of land. No formal training is available to study the nature of land use conflicts — a knowledge which constitutes the basis of many alternative suggestion for more efficient use of land. These defects will have to be rectified before expecting anything big to happen in the effort of the National Mission on Wasteland Development.

It is not surprising that many of the creative practices innovated by the people do not reach other areas where this know how could have been easily utilises. There is little opportunity to exchange the experience of those who, in so many separate ways, waive the constraints of the land to generate wealth. The net loss for the absence of these networking facilities is incurred by the poorest who do not have good plot of land to sustain them. For any successful programme on better land use, gaps of the same will be self-defeating.

The problem areas should be studied on existing resource systems and traditional uses of wetlands; benefit estimates and impact assessment of developmental projects and actions relating to the use of wetlands; preparation of classified inventory of unutilised and under-utilised wetlands and training the participants in wasteland development efforts through ecosystems management on a micro-level.

## Conservation Problems

Land and people are two basic resources of North Bihar. The types of land is different from one area to another area besides the people because land and its use have always been the main factor in determining the way of living and the way of earning food for the people of the area. Now, 'wetlands' are found every where be it the terai of the north and diaras of the south or the flood plains of

North Bihar. However, the types and extent of damage to the 'wetland' of different areas is also varied due to differences in spatio-temporal dimensions.

The North Bihar has four types of wetlands, as mentioned below, and their conservation problems differ from each other.

The wetlands of small marshylands along the Indo-Nepal border in the Terai region of Himalayas lie in the district of East Champaran, West Champaran, Saharsa and a very small part of Purnea. The wetlands of these areas are fast-declining forest area, which are succumbing to the tremendous pressure of civilization and development in road and rail-communication. It is rather ironic that we are encroaching into this nature's treasure without fully realising the consequences of short-term profits. What needs to be done is to get these wetlands in the Terai region thoroughly surveyed. The effort should be made to ensure that no human encroachment is done in this territory in any way be it for farming, or for housing or for industrialisation. Since almost all of these wetlands are in the Terai forest region. The Department of Forest and Environment can chalk out plans and take up the necessary work on the basis of the survey-reports. The idea here would be to try to restore the original natural state of the land in the area in general.

The second category of wetlands in North Bihar are the flood plains, where there is water mostly in the rainy season only, and people manage to get at least one crop of Rabi annually. These are usually lowlying areas, and the damage done to them is mostly due to soil-erosion and the deposition of silt carried from elsewhere by the flood-waters. This can be checked at least to some extent if we follow only those cultural practices which will not favour soil-erosion. Effort should be to ensure that there is sufficient grass and weed-cover especially during rainy season. In this way, erosion by run-off water will greatly be checked in flood-plains, if managed well because there lies one of the most productive lands. Therefore, the target should be to save the top 10-20 cms. of the soil layer at least.

In third category are the wetlands which come under perennial water, and are old river-beds. These are formed by change in the course of rivers and streams. These are now cut-off from the main river and hence, they are big reservoirs of fresh water fish catch. These usually get connected to the rivers in rainy season, so their water gets replaced annually. Such wetlands are mostly used for fish-farming alongwith farming of water loving crops. Wetlands of this category are potentially and economically rich. But since these are also getting shallower progressively, some soil-erosion-checking practices must be followed for them too. These should include afforestation, strip-cropping, introducing contour-bunding of the banks of these wetlands. However, there are difficulties in the implementation of these practices; like the owners of the land on the banks would not always agree to these practices for saving a wetland belonging to somebody else. They cannot be forced to do so on legal points. Now, in a situation like this the only thing that can be done is to try to explain to people the importance and the necessity of saving the natural environment for a balanced ecological system because no project could be successful without proper public-participation.

The fourth of wetland consists of lakes of big and small size on landscape resulting into the accumulation of water. Since these in normal circumstances do not get connected with rivers in rainy season, these are very much favoured for fish-farming. The conservation-problems and their solutions are almost the same as for the third category of wetlands mentioned before. The bigger among these wetlands are mostly owned by the Government, and are settled for 1 to 10 years by the Government with private parties fishermen's co-operatives. There is one such lake by the name in Manigachhi Block of Darbhanga district. The water area of the lake is around 100 acres or more in December, but the deepest area in which there is water round the year is 60 acres. Now, as this 60 acres land belong to the Government and the rest to private parties, the settled area is 60 acres only. In a situation like this, conservation-projects are very difficult to be carried out without the consent and active participation of the people concerned which is quite essential.

There is another lake named Kabar Tal near Begusarai. This spreads out in a very large area. Part of the original lake has been drained, and the rest has been developed as a sanctuary for migratory birds-cum-recreation sport. In this case, the draining was not a very wise step, but its other development was certainly a positive thing to do. Planting of erosion resistant trees, shrubs and grasses have been taken up on the embankment of Kuseshwar Asthan.

Here the delineations have been made about the theoretical background of wetlands found in North Bihar. Although there is a lack of sufficient data and literature on wetlands. The wetlands are remenats of former Indo-Gangetic trough found in pleistocene period in North Bihar. At this period due to deglaciation the wetlands have been filled up and their remnants are still found here and there in the form of lakes, tals and pynes in North Bihar.

## NOTES

1. Choudhary, P.C.Roy, *Inside Bihar*; Bookland Private Ltd., Calcutta, 1956.
2. Diwakar, R.R. (Editor), *Bihar Through the Ages*, 1954, p.
3. Ahmad, Enayat, *Bihar, Physical, Economic and Regional Geography,* Ranchi University, Ranchi, 1965.
4. Dunn, J. A. and Dey, A. K., The Geology and Petrology of Eastern Singhbhum and the Surrounding Areas. *Mem.G.S.T.*,Vol. IXIX, Pt, II, 1942.
5. Dunn, J.A., The Economic Geology and Mineral Resources of Bihar Province, *Mem. G.S.I.*,Vol. LXXVIII, 1942.
6. Singh, R.P., *Geomorphological Evolution of the Highlands of Chhotanagpur and the Adjoining Districts in Bihar,* Ph. D. Thesis, London, University, 1956. Micro Methods Ltd., East Ardslay, Wakefield, Yorkshire.

# 5

# DISTRIBUTION OF WETLANDS

Wetlands may be defined as submerged areas in saturated lands, which includes both natural and artificial, permanent or temporary, with water, i.e., static or flowing, fresh, brackish or saltish, including areas of marine water, the depth of which at low tide does not exceed six metres, for the major portion of the year. Such areas include swamps, marshes, deltas, palaya, lagoon, lakes, etc. Wetlands serve as suitable nitche for fish and other acquatic animals as breeding and nursery ground for water fowls and as filter for sediments and pollutants. The country is loosing its wetlands rapidly due to biotic interference and anthropogenic pressure.[1]

Considering the importance of wetlands, measures have been initiated for their conservation and management to educate the public on the need for their conservation as well as economic utility and to commence scientific and application oriented research studies on their productivity. A National Wetland Committee has been constituted comprising of experts in various wetland disciplines.[2]

The Committee has identified the Nineteen (10 during 1987-88 and another 9 during 1988-89) and onwards in India as a whole wetlands for preparation of Management Action Plan. The nodal academic research institutions for each of the area have also been identified as given in Table. 5.1.

**Table 5.1** : Wetlands under Environmental Study

| *Wetland* | *State* | *Nodal Academic Institutions* |
|---|---|---|
| Kolleru | Andhra Pradesh | Osmania University<br>Nagarjuna University |
| Wullar | Jammu & Kasmir | Jammu & Kashmir University |
| Chilka | Orissa | Utkal University |
| Loktak | Manipur | Manipur University |
| Bhoj (Lower, and upper lakes) | Madhya Pradesh | Bhopal University |
| Sambhar | Rajasthan | Jodhpur University and Central Arid Zone Research Institute, Jaipur, |
| Pichola | Rajasthan | Udaipur University |
| Ashtamudi | Kerala | Kerala University |
| Harike | Punjab | Punjab Agricultural University, Ludhiana |
| Ujni | Maharashtra | Pune University |
| Sukhna | Chandigarh | Punjab University |
| Sasthankota | Kerala | Kerala University |
| Renuka | Himachal Pradesh | Himachal University |
| Kabar Lake | Bihar | Bhagalpur University |
| Nalsarovar Lake | Gujarat | Gujarat University |
| Kanjli | Punjab | Punjab Agricultural University |

*Source :* Ministry of Environment and Forests, Government of India, Annual Reports, 1987-88 and 1988-89.

## Mangroves

Mangroves are the salt-tolerant forest eco-systems found mainly in tropical and sub-tropical inter-tidal regions. They consist of swamps, forest and water spread areas. The total area of Mangroves in India is estimated to be 6,740 sq.km. which is 7 per cent of the world's mangroves. The mangroves areas of Sundarbans, West Bengal and Andaman and Nicobar Islands constitute over 80 per cent of the mangroves in India. This ecosystem is a reservoir of a host of plant and animal species. Mangroves in India have been subjected to reckless exploitation due to biotic interference and other factors.

Considering, the importance of mangroves steps have been initiated to conserve the mangroves, to educate the public on the need for their conservation as well as their economic utility and to commence scientific and application oriented research on their productivity, flora and fauna, etc. The National Mangrove Committee was constituted to recommend policies and actions.

The Committee has identified the following first batch of 15 areas for the preparation of Management Action Plan: Northern Andaman Nicobar; Sundarbans (West Bengal); Bhitarkanika (Orissa); Coringa (Andhra Pradesh); Mahanadi Delta (Orissa); Pichavaram (Tamil Nadu); Goa; Godavari Delta (Andhra Pradesh): Gulf of Kutch (Gujarat) ; Coondapur (Karnataka), Achre Ratnagiri (Maharashtra) ; Vembanad (Kerala); Point Calimare (Tamil Nadu); and Krishna Estuary (Andhra Pradesh).

The Action Plans have been drawn up by the steering committees set up in the states concerned with the Chief Secretary as the Chairman and consisting of representatives from various subject matter departments, Universities, non-official organisations, etc.

The components of the Action Plan include natural regeneration in selected areas, afforestation and protective measures.

## Situations Available in North Bihar

The entire North Bihar plain which lies north of the river Ganges is an alluvial plain with minor slope towards the Ganges in the south and lowlands of the Kosi Belt in the middle eastern part. The significant features are the levee deposits and sand bars along the river banks and marshy depressions known as '*Chaurs*'. These *chaurs* are the oxbow lakes of meandering streams and some of them have formed due to sheet wash erosion during flood and irregular deposition of silt and sand bodies.

The general slope of the plain is from north-west to south-east. The average slope is approximately 8 metres per 100 kilometres from the north-western point to the south-eastern corner of the region with some exceptions of a part of west Champaran district and Kishanganj area, the entire plain is 76 metres below mean sea level. Along the course of the Ganges, the height of the plain varies from 43 metres near Chapra in the west to 30 metres near Naugachhia in the East.[3]

Geo-physically North Bihar is an alluvial-plain where wetlands are located by the side of rivers, rivulets, chaurs, diaras and oxbow lakes as characteristic features. The distribution of wetlands are controlled by water resources in North Bihar besides the shape, size and interrelationship of sand bodies which are in turn governed by the nature of the underlying alluvial beds. Natural calamities like floods, embankment erosion, sheet-wash erosion, etc. have various effects on wetlands which are to a large extent controlled by the river courses.

A change in the site of wetlands is due to large scale alluviation, meadering of rivers and excessive floods resulting in destruction and sometimes enlargement of waterlogged areas, marshy lands, alluvial fans, change in the river courses besides the formation of cones and inter-cones due to unequeal deposition of sand, silt and erosional hazards. These are some of the important geo-physical aspects which should be considered for the location and siting of wetlands in North Bihar. Fig. 5.1 shows the alluvial geomorphic features in Samastipur District namely water surface in lakes, area above flood level, mud flat, swampy ground, areas of annual inundation, dry river beds, slope of the land, river embankment, human settlement, direction of floods, ox-bow lake, steepness of river banks, riverside levee and arable land.

In order to maintain ecological balance the chief aim of the author is to analyse, classify and to map the various landscape features in their correct position and examine the mutual relationship for assessing their physical properties and economic importance.

(a) North Bihar is an alluvial plain. Most of the diversities seen on the surface are those due to river action and a series of raised river side uplands known as levees, dotted with wetlands in the form of alternating depressions or chaurs on the line of streams.

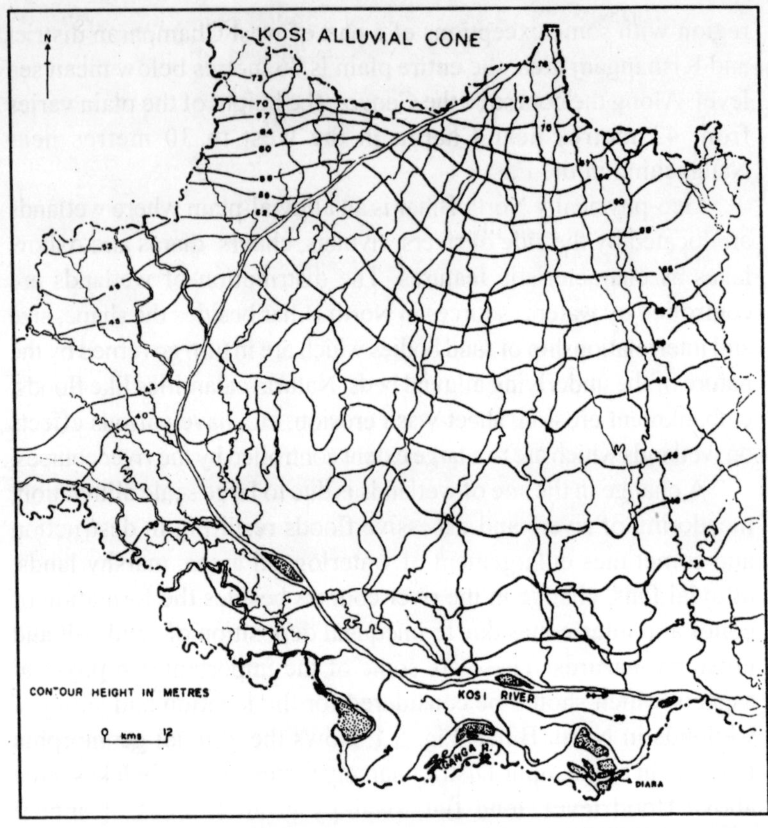


**Fig. 5.1 :** Kosi Alluvial Cone

(b) A sub-terai belt of marshy land in the north with intervening tracts of uplands along rivers is succeeded in the south by a wide belt of marshy lowlands, characterised by permanent depressions and lakes besides tanks which are man made features of wetlands.

(c) In the riparian tracts of the Ganges, the land is high due to which wetlands are found a slight away from levee in the form of intervening depressions. Due to the presence of river bluffs on the northern bank of the Ganges all rivers flowing along the gravity of slope from north to south turn towards east and run parallel along the Ganges river for a few kilometres before they finally meet together.

North Bihar plain consists of alluvial cones in courses of the Gandak, the Kosi and the Mahananda-Tista rivers. The cones exhibit a radial drainage pattern and spill patterns. Several layers of underground water found in clayey intercones which help digging tubewells in the riparian tracts and flood plains of North Bihar.

Fig. 5.1 represents the formation of alluvial cone in course of the Kosi river. On the northern part of this cone the height is 76 metres but on the south near the Ganges the contour height is only 30 metres.

Flood plains are formed by floods which are the deposition of alluvium in meandering river basins of North Bihar. They are always of low relief as compared to the rugged areas of North-estern Champaran. In southern half of the region the characteristic topographic features, viz; flat plain, alluvial cones, stream meanders, oxbow lakes, marshes, irregular temporary lakes which occupy small depressions including sand bars, natural levees, spill cones, spill hollows and other minor relief features formed by the flood or shift of channels. Over these landscape features the wetlands of varying forms i.e. circular, square, rectangular, hollow square, fan pattern and several others are emerging slowly according to the shape and size of the landscape units.

The streams which cut their basins at base level are graded streams of flat plains, and before meeting with the Ganges they tend to flow in broad sweeping curves. This is due to the low velocity of the current and the deposition of alluvium which divert the stream courses (Worcester, 1976). As the current is directed against the outer bank of a meander it cuts further in this direction and at the same time builds up a bar of sand on the inner side. Swings of current around one curve tends to cross the channel and development another curve in the opposite bank. The meanders grow and shift down streams. In this way, the eroding bank of a river represents old and large size of the meander where as the wetlands are new, small and fragmented in nature are found which directly controlled by the volume and speed of water.

The Ganges, the Burhi-Gandak, the Kareh and other rivers have a meandering channels in North Bihar. The presence of oxbow lakes on single side of the acute bend of a river suggests that it is flowing under second cycle of erosion but still further the availability of oxbow lakes on anti-podal side suggests that the landscape is passing under third cycle of erosion. The severence of such meandering oxbow lakes clearly show phases of degradational and agradational topographic features. As a consequence of the flat gradient of country, the rivers that flow southwards tend to take pronounced meandering courses, Strabo described the river as "So exceedingly winding that everything winding is called meandering (Russel, 1954). The Kosi frequently changes its course and within 214 years this mighty river has shifted 115 kilometres west of its original course. The shift was not by gradual cutting of its embankment but by the flowing of a number of distributaries. As such, this river presents a braided channel topography in Saharsa, Purnea and Katihar districts of north- eastern parts of Bihar.

In the Kosi basin some of the older alluvial deposits have been removed and redistributed down stream. The presence of hard and consolidated blocks of Siwalik clays as burried topography having marks of fossils on the banks of most of the rivers have led to the development of meandering courses in this riverine plain. For example, near Dubepur, Parbana, Kharsam and Ghaibahi villages of Samastipur district, the river Kareh makes four bends within a distance of three kilometres. Due to the flat and low level of the country the meandering of river channel is the chief feature in the lower reaches of the Burhi Gandak where the serpentine course of the stream has given rise to excessive flood during the rainy season. It also helps in the formation of ox-bow lakes and marshy lowlands along the river banks.

As meanders grow, it frequently happens that a narrow neck of land is cut through from two sides thus allowing the stream to straighten its course. The two ends of the meander so separated from the channel that they are likely to be filled up by sand. The best examples of oxbow lake on the bank of river Burhi Gandak are found in Vaishali district. The side of these water-bodies provide excellent settlement sites on its embankment. The whole face of the country is dotted with rural settlements besides small oxbow or elongated water bodies and chaurs (long semi-circular marshes) which lie in between the rivers making the old abandoned courses of the streams. Though found extensively in all parts of this region, the abandoned courses are more prolific in Madhubani, Sitamarhi and Begusarai districts of North Bihar. Hardia chaur in Saran extends upto nearly 32 kilometres along the Gandak embankment and has a breadth of 3 to 8 kilometres.

The abandoned channel of a stream on a flood plain may become partially filled with vegetation, thus forming a marsh. They may also occur in any depression on the flood plains especially in areas of waterlogging. Marshes are numerous towards the south-eastern part of North Bihar.

Some of these marshy lands dry up during the hot season. There are some marshes which exist throughout the year like a tank. Marshes are also found in the beds of rivers like the Mahananda, the Paimar, the Kosi, the old Kosi, the Bhutahi Balan, the Kamla, the Jibachh, the Kareh, the Budhi Gandak and the Gandak during the hot weather season, but during the rainy months the river establishes its normal course. The marshes are utilised by the peasants for irrigation, rearing of fish, for growing *mothi* and *makhana* and for washing animals in the summar season, wetlands in the marshy areas are dispersed type.

**Tanks as Wetlands**

In North Bihar the total number of tanks are distributed unevenly in different parts of the area and determined by the presence and absence of river in the area. It is quite discernible that river embankments of the Ganges, the Kosi, the Mahananda, the Gandak, and others have very few number of tanks near them but away from river banks their number increases. In the districts of Saharsa, Madhubani, Darbhanga and the northern parts of Samastipur, Sitamarhi and Muzaffarpur, the number of tanks are very high because the areas of rice and fish culture? The highest number of tanks are available in Madhubani district (2,421) and Darbhanga district (1,435) in 1991 (Fig.5.2).

In Pokharbhinda village of Manigachhi anchal there are 75 tanks and in Narayanpur village of the same anchal there are 32 tanks which are not only a lowlying wetlands but economically they are highly potential. For example, Rajokhar of Narayanpur which has a expanse of over 21 hectares of land is annually producing *makhana*

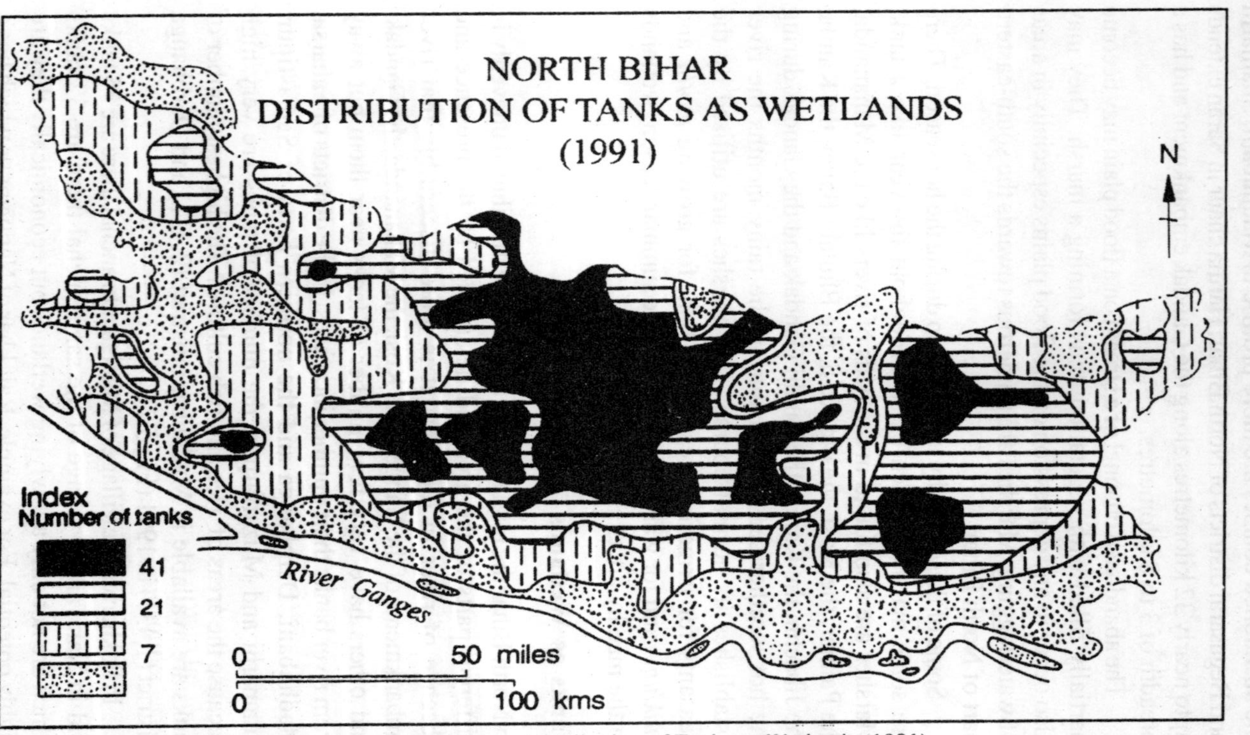


**Fig. 5.2 :** North Bihar : Distribution of Tanks as Wetlands (1991).

of Rs.3 Lakhs and fish of Rs.3 lakhs respectively. It has a powerful tool to make ecological balance, beautify the environment, providing recreation ground on boats, bathing place for human being and cattle besides irrigating the land through, pumping sets over more than 5000 hectares of land in the surrounding area.

In North Bihar there is a close correlation in between ponds as artificial wetlands and planted mango orchards as vegetation cover, because people have a belief to marry tank with mango orchard and hence, these two are the assets for making the ecological balance, checking flood hazards besides increasing the water holding capacity of the land in tank to use it for irrigation and provide a bathing place for buffaloes in each and every village.

Table 5.3 and Fig.5.3 shows that the distributional patterns of wetlands in North Bihar is quite uneven because the relief and clamatic conditions are not equal throughout the region. The location quotient value for wetlands differ substantially. For example, the highest percentage of wetlands 21 is found in Wast Champaran district where the area around Motihari was famous for the chain of 42 lakes followed by 10 per cent in West Champaran, 9 per cent in Katihar, 8 per cent in Madhubani, and 7 per cent in Purnea districts respectively. The lowest percentage of wetlands in North Bihar are in Vaishali, Siwan, Gopalganj, Samastipur and Begusarai districts. In these areas bigger wetlands are found in the form of oxbow lakes and chaur lands formed due to unequal deposition of sand bodies. The actual distribution of wetlands is very closely related with the line of equal distribution. Hence, it could be said that North Bihar on the whole has flooded farm land and the distribution of wetlands is more or less equal in almost all the districts. Table 5.3 and Fig.5.4 shows the distribution of wetlands in North Bihar on Lorenz curve. The actual distribution deviates abnormally from the line of equal distribution. These deviations are some how closer in case of Madhubani, Khagaria, Katihar, Purnea and Saharsa districts. But differences are quite large, in case of Gopalganj, East Champaran and West Champaran districts. (Fig. 5.4)

This chapter relates to the distribution of wetlands in North Bihar. Geographically this area is known as 'Trihut' which means the riparian tracts or flood plains of the rivers where alluvial deposits

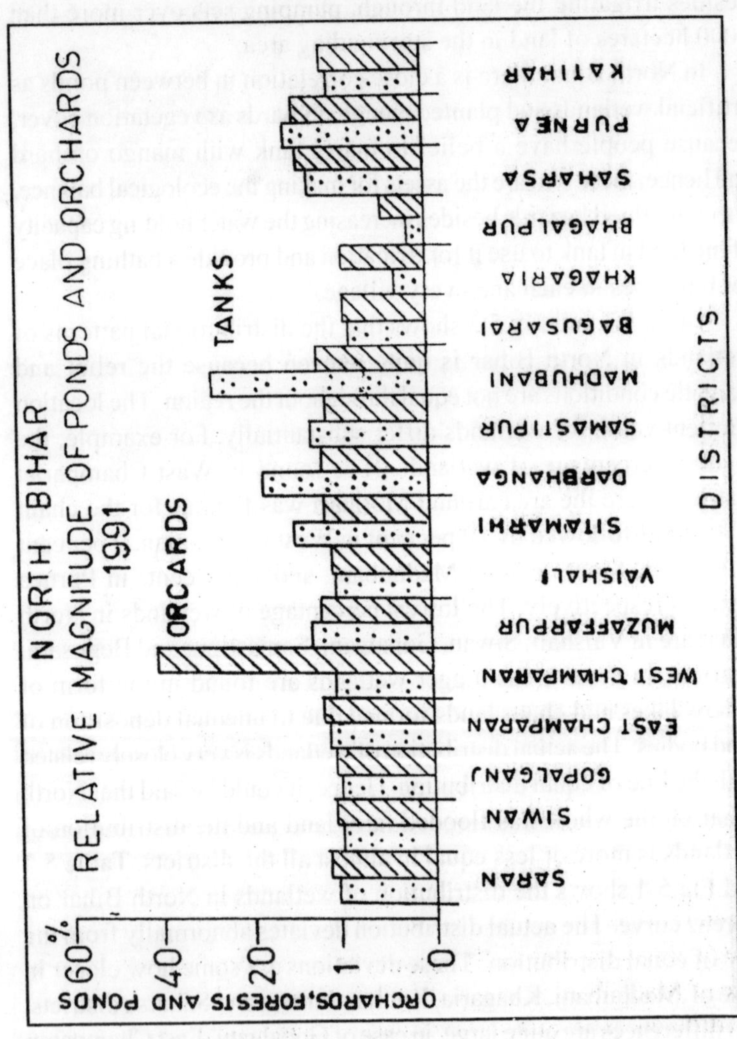


**Fig. 5.3 :** North Bihar : Relative Magnitude of Ponds and Orchards, 1991.

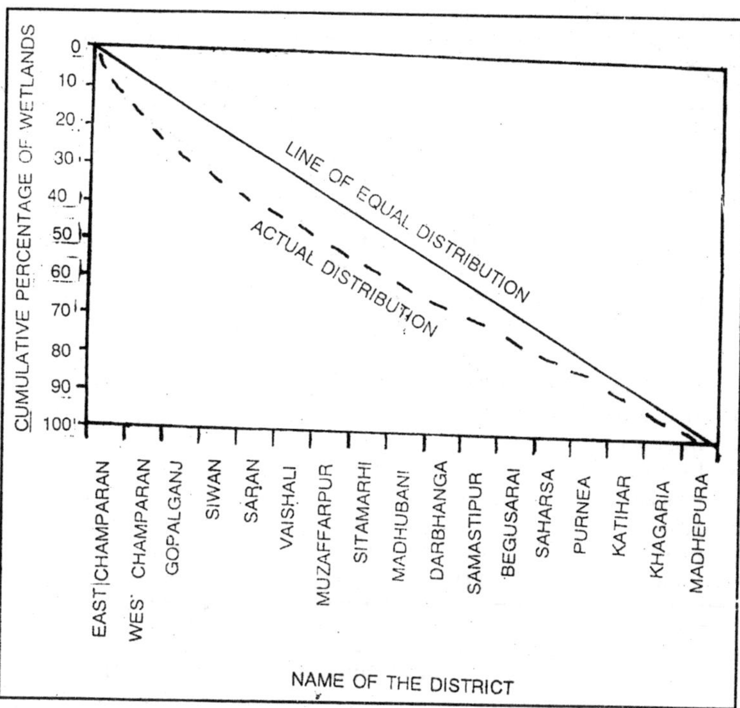


**Fig. 5.4 :** North Bihar : Lorenz Curve showing Distributional Patterns of Wetlands (1991)

**Table 5.2 :** Characteristics of the Distribution of Wetlands in North Bihar

| *District* | *Characteristics of Wetland* |
|---|---|
| 1. Saran | Chaurs and Tank |
| 2. Siwan | Chaurs and Tank |
| 3. Gopalganj | Chaurs and Canals |
| 4. East Champaran | Oxbow Lakes |
| 5. West Champaran | Chaurs and Ditches |
| 6. Muzaffarpur | Tanks, Chaurs |
| 7. Vaishali | Oxbow Lakes |
| 8. Sitamarhi | Chaurs |
| 9. Darbhanga | Tanks and Chaurs |
| 10. Samastipur | Tanks, Chaurs and Oxbow Lakes |
| 11. Madhubani | Chaurs and Tanks |
| 12. Begusarai | Natural Lakes |
| 13. Khagaria | Ditches, Chaurs |
| 14. Bhagalpur | Ditches, Chaurs |
| 15. Saharsa | Chaurs, Lakes |
| 16. Purnea | Chaurs, Lakes |
| 17. Katihar | Chaurs, Ditches Oxbow Lakes |

*Source :* Prepared by R. B. Mandal.

**Table 5.3 :** Distribution of Tanks and Forests/Orchards in North Bihar (1991)

| *District* | | *No. of Tanks* | *%* | *No. of Orchards* | *%* |
|---|---|---|---|---|---|
| 1. | Saran | 197 | 2.31 | 8 | 3.55 |
| 2. | Siwan | 139 | 1.63 | 5 | 2.22 |
| 3. | Gopalganj | 115 | 1.35 | 5 | 2.22 |
| 4. | East Champaran | 331 | 3.88 | 9 | 4.00 |
| 5. | West Champaran | 144 | 1.69 | 92 | 40-88 |
| 6. | Muzaffarpur | 524 | 6.15 | 11 | 4.88 |
| 7. | Vaishali | 196 | 2.39 | 6 | 2.67 |
| 8. | Sitamarhi | 787 | 9.24 | 9 | 4.00 |
| 9. | Darbhanga | 1435 | 16.86 | 9 | 4.00 |
| 10. | Samastipur | 508 | 5.97 | 8 | 3.57 |
| 11. | Madhubani | 2425 | 28.49 | 11 | 4.88 |
| 12. | Begusarai | 73 | 0.85 | 2 | 0.88 |
| 13. | Khagaria | 26 | 0.30 | 2 | 0.88 |
| 14. | Bhagalpur | 16 | 0.17 | 1 | 0.46 |
| 15. | Saharsa | 526 | 6.18 | 20 | 8.88 |
| 16. | Purnea | 937 | 11.01 | 22 | 9.79 |
| 17. | Katihar | 131 | 1.53 | 5 | 2.24 |
| | Total | 8510 | 100 | 297 | 100 |

*Source :* District Census Handbook of Different Districts of North Bihar, 1991.

are found here and there. In the riverine plain of North Bihar varieties of wetlands are found due to unequal filling of Indo-Gangetic foredeep at the later state of Pleistocene period when deglaciation took place not only in Himalaya or North Bihar but in the mid latitudinal areas of Alps in Europe to Indiana, Illinois, Nebraska and Kansas area of North America which cover the great plains of U.S.A.

In North Bihar wetlands are found in the form of natural lakes, rivers, chaurs, marshy lands, temporary marshy land and diteches of different sizes here and there and even in the near by area of human settlements where there is a myth that the marriage of Mango orchard should held either with tank or with a drinking water well as essential and this favours the digging of more and more ponds as wetlands in North Bihar.

But with the spurt of higher education and cultural preferment in North Bihar this area needs proper reclamation and management of wetlands in order to improve our national environment.

**Table 5.4 :** North Bihar : Lorenz Curve showing Distributional Patterns of Wetlands (1991)

| *Sl. No.* | *Name of the District* | *Total Area in Hectare* | *Percentage* | *C.P.* |
|---|---|---|---|---|
| 1. | West Champaran | 4,602 | 9.99 | 9.99 |
| 2. | East Champaran | 9,906 | 21.33 | 31.32 |
| 3. | Gopalganj | 997 | 2.14 | 33.46 |
| 4. | Siwan | 812 | 1.74 | 35.20 |
| 5. | Saran | 948 | 2.04 | 37.24 |
| 6. | Vaishali | 871 | 1.87 | 33.11 |
| 7. | Muzaffarpur | 2,232 | 4.80 | 43.91 |
| 8. | Sitamarhi | 2,570 | 5.53 | 49.44 |
| 9. | Madhubani | 3,743 | 8.05 | 57.49 |
| 10. | Darbhanga | 3,490 | 7.51 | 65.00 |
| 11. | Samastipur | 1,216 | 2.61 | 67.61 |
| 12. | Begusarai | 1,034 | 2.22 | 69.83 |
| 13. | Saharsa | 1,057 | 2.27 | 72.10 |
| 14. | Purnea | 3,448 | 7.42 | 79.52 |
| 15. | Katihar | 4,176 | 8.99 | 88.51 |
| 16. | Khagaria | 3,163 | 6.81 | 95.32 |
| 17. | Madhepura | 2,176 | 4.68 | 100.00 |
| | Total | 46,441 | 100.00 | 100.00 |

*Source :* Calculaed by U.P. Choudhary, 1991.

## Conclusion

The distribution of wetlands in the form of swampy ground and lakes are more prolific in the Kosi-Mahananda Basin and the Gandak and Burhi Gandak Basins of North Bihar. In these areas the lowlying ground, the replication of annual flood and the excessive meandering courses of rivers help in the formation of oxbow lakes. The wetlands are more and more near the southern end of North Bihar near the lower reaches of the Ganga river but it is rare near the Terai Belt of Nepal. This happens because it is a higher ground where the formation of wetland is notl conducive.

### NOTES

1. Singh, R.B., "Environmental Monitoring of Remote Sensing and GIS-Geocarto International Centre, Hong Kong, 1991.
2. Choudhary, U.P., Wetlands in North Bihar, *East-West Geographer*, Vol.1, No.1, 1990.
3. Mandal, R.B., Geo-Physical Aspects of Wetlands in North Bihar, Conference on Wetlands, Organised by Forest Department, Government of Bihar, 1988.
4. Singh, R.P. and Kumar, A., *Monograph of Bihar*, Bharti Bhawan, Patna-4, 1971.

# 6

# TYPES AND PATTERNS OF WETLANDS

The taxomy of wetlands considers various parameters for determining wetland. It may be varying in extent and locational dimensions. The wetlands also vary in spatio-temporal dimensions. It may be saturated or submerged lands, natural or artificial, permanent or temporary, static or flowing, fresh or brackish; marine or riverine origin; and may be swamp, marshes, delta, palya, lagoon, lakes, pond or ditches. The depth of water may not exceed 3 metres. It is fit for rearing fishes, ducks and act as pollution filter for sediments and pollutants. North Bihar is loosing its wetlands rapidly due to ecological imbalances and increasing population pressure.[1]

Recently, measures have been initiated for the conservation and management of wetlands in order to educate the public regarding economic utility and commence scientific and application oriented research on the productivity of wetland. A National Wetland Committee has been constituted comprising of experts in various disciplines of wetland studies.

The Committee has identified 19 public institutions in India for the preparation and management of wetlands in India. These nodal academic research institutions in different parts of India has been identified as follows (Table 6.1).

There are large varieties of habitats whose environment is predominantly characterized by excess of water. They are chiefly divided into two categories: the marine and the fresh water. Marine environment is practically the same everywhere except for variations mainly in temperature and light. The plant life is also fairly similar widely.

The common fresh water bodies are pools, ponds, lakes, rivulets, river and marshy lands. Although a lake or a river is separated from other such aquatic bodies yet on account of uniform similarity in environmental conditions, the plants are also very much the same. In fact, the hydrophytes of even different continents are nearly the same everywhere.

**Table 6.1 :** General Conditions of Wetlands in North Bihar

| *Sl. No.* | *Name of Wetlands* | *Area in km²* | *Percentage* |
|---|---|---|---|
| 1. | Ditches | 65,987 | 25.80 |
| 2. | Tanks | 37,459 | 14.70 |
| 4. | Rivers | 3,772 | 1.50 |
| 5. | Oxbow lakes | 1,22,225 | 4.80 |
| 6. | Moat | 5,000 | 1.95 |
| 7. | Warn Areas | 25,000 | 9.80 |
| 8. | Chaurs | 1,00,500 | 39.35 |
| | Total | 2,55,535 | 100 |

*Source :* Fishery Department, Government of Bihar, Patna, 1991.

## Typology

Wetlands include swamps, marshes, ponds, peatlands, lagoon, lakes, etc.

There are varieties of natural habitats whose environment is predominantly characterised by excess of water. They are chiefly divided into two categories; the marine and the fresh water. Marine environment is practically the same everywhere except far variations mainly in temperature and light.

The common fresh water bodies are pools, ponds, lakes, small streams, rivers and swampy lands. Although a lake or a river is separated from other such acquatic bodies yet on account of uniform similarity in environmental conditions, the plants are also very much the same. In fact, the hydrophytes of even different continents are nearly the same everywhere.

**Types of Wetlands**

The aquatic environment has been classified in a number of ways (Fig. 6.1). The standing water bodies are called lentic (like lakes and ponds) and running water bodies are called lotic (like rivers and streams) . The stationary and fast running conditions influence plant growth profoundly. In the latter condition only such forms survive which develop a very effective attaching mechanism, extremely flexible tissues, the escape injury from physical force of water current and have streamlined external morphology to offer least resistance. Depending upon the temperature factor the upper warmer region of lakes is called 'epilimnion' which is rich in plants and the deep cold almost plantless zone is called 'hypolimnion'. The intermediate zone is diagrammtic representation of types of fresh water bodies and their zonations. The lower view gives a section of profile with respect to depth of a shallow and very deep water body[2] which is called 'thermocline'. On the basis of productivity and fertility, the lake may be eutrophic or highly productive and rich in plants. They are shallow and rich in nutrients. The other type is oligotrophis in which lakes are deep, poor in productivity and low in nutrient concentration. The zones of aquatic bodies are also classified on the basis of availability of light. The marginal shallow region where abundant light is available for plant growth is called 'littoral' zone'. The deeper layer where light condition is just sufficient for plant growth or say at compensation point is called 'limnetic zone'. Deeper than this, where plant life is not possible due to paucity of light is called 'profoundal zone'. In shallow ponds and lakes the entire area is of littoral type.

In margine environment, the classification is somewhat different. The shallow share region is called 'neritic zone'. This region is visited by tides that periodically wash the shore and, therefore neritic zone is further divided into outed up land or supratidal zone, the intermediate region where high tides reach or intertidal zone and the lower subtidal regions.

The portion of sea away from land is called 'oceanic zone'. The deeper slopes in continuation of the shore upto a depth of two thousand metres is called 'bathyal zone' while still deeper zone of aquatic belt is called 'abyssal zone'.[3]

## CLASSIFICATION OF HYDROPHYTES

On the basis of life forms hydrophytes are broadly classified into phytoplanktons and the macrophytes. Macrophytes are predominantly vascular plants. They are further divided usually on the basis of their habitat and location in ponds or lakes. They may be : (1) the marginal emergent plants, (2) the submerged rooted hydrophytes, (3) the rooted hydrophytes with floating leaves, and (4) the free surface floating hydrophytes.

### The Marginal Emergent Hydrophytes

These are found around the ponds and lakes where the level of water has gone down considerably and only 2 to 15 cms. of basal part of plant is immersed and the rest lies straight up emerging in the air. Such plants keep on extending down as the pond water recedes on deriving. The common Indian species of this category are — (1) *Eteocharis plantaginea*, (2) *E.pallustries, Isoetes coromanelina* and other *Isoetes spp.* (3) *Typhasp* (4) *Cyperus spp.* (5) *Fimbristylis sp.*, (6) *Polygonum sp.* (7) Some *Wild Oryma* (8) *Zizania*, etc.

## The Submerged Rooted Hydrophytes

From periphery next to marsh zone, depending upon the size and depth of the pond, different life forms and communities get distributed in different regions. The rooted hydrophytes which remain submerged are restricted to shallow regions where light is abundantly available right upto the bottom. The submerged hydrophytes are divided into:

(a) Plants with long stem covered with leaves and roots arising from nodes. The examples are *Hydrilla sp.*; *Lagarosiphon sp.*; *Potamogeton pectinatus, Najas*, etc.
(b) Tuberous stem with cauline leaves e.g. *Vallisneria*, some species of submerged *Aponogeton*, etc. In these plants the leaves are ribbon shaped, thin and filmy. In general the submerged leaves do not bear any stomate.

## The Rooted Hydrophytes with Floating Leaves

This type is also restricted to more or less shallow region of ponds or lakes say upto three metres depth. The leaves emerge up and keep floating. This group of plants may be fixed in mud. (i) by rhizomatious structures with floating leaves on long flexible petiole e.g. *Nymphea stellata*, *Nelumbo nucifera*, (*Nelumbium speciosum*), *Aponogeton sp.* etc. or (ii) by trailing type of stoloniferous structure where leaves are fixed on short *petioles* e.g. *Nymphoides* and *potamogeton natans*.

## The Free Surface Floating Hydrophytes

These occur scattered everywhere in ponds and lakes and keep on changing their position due to water or wind currents. Usually in small ponds such species are aggregated more in the centre where other categories of hydrophytes are very little. In form and structure free floating hydrophytes may be — (i) larger with rosettes or big leaves either floating or rising above in the air as in *Trape bispinosa* (water chestnut) and *Eichorniacras-sipes* (water hyacinth) respectively. The roots are also abundant and long with prominent root pockets, (ii) Slightly smaller forms are pistia and salvinia with spongy floating leaves (iii) The other variety is of very small surface floating plant with the body reduced to thalluslike structures e.g. *Lumna, Wolffia, Spirodela* and *Azolla.* Some species may remain just below the surface water or come up periodically and sink down for perennation e.g. *Utricularia.* Wetlands are marginal areas filled with water in different form. But there modalities are quite different from one another because the difference in rain and other physical conditions available in different parts of North Bihar are different from each other (Fig. 6.1).

Wetlands have been formed due to physical factors and human activities. For example, rivers, lakes and swampy areas are wetlands made by nature where as tanks, canals, ditches and moat are the outcome of human activities. All these have been regarded as wetlands which have close affiliation with the human being but the waterlogged areas with varied dimensions are really problematic as in these the ecological conditions are not favourable for crop production and permanent occupation for continuation of a particular land use. For this fact, the wetland only set up a particular dimension either for bird sanctuaries, and fish production ground place for aquatic plants. For the purpose of recreation the shallow waterlogged area should be reclaimed for the meaningful utilisation. For example, in North Bihar the problem of waterlogging have been widely felt in and around Kesaria chaur in East Champaran where the waterlogging has spread in almost 60 thousand hectares of land due to leaking of water through Tribeni canal. In this way, it is quite apparent that only the correct and timely management of wetlands and the repairing of Tribeni canal will irrigate the agricultural land for growing crops. The Government of Bihar should pay a proper attention in this regard.[5]

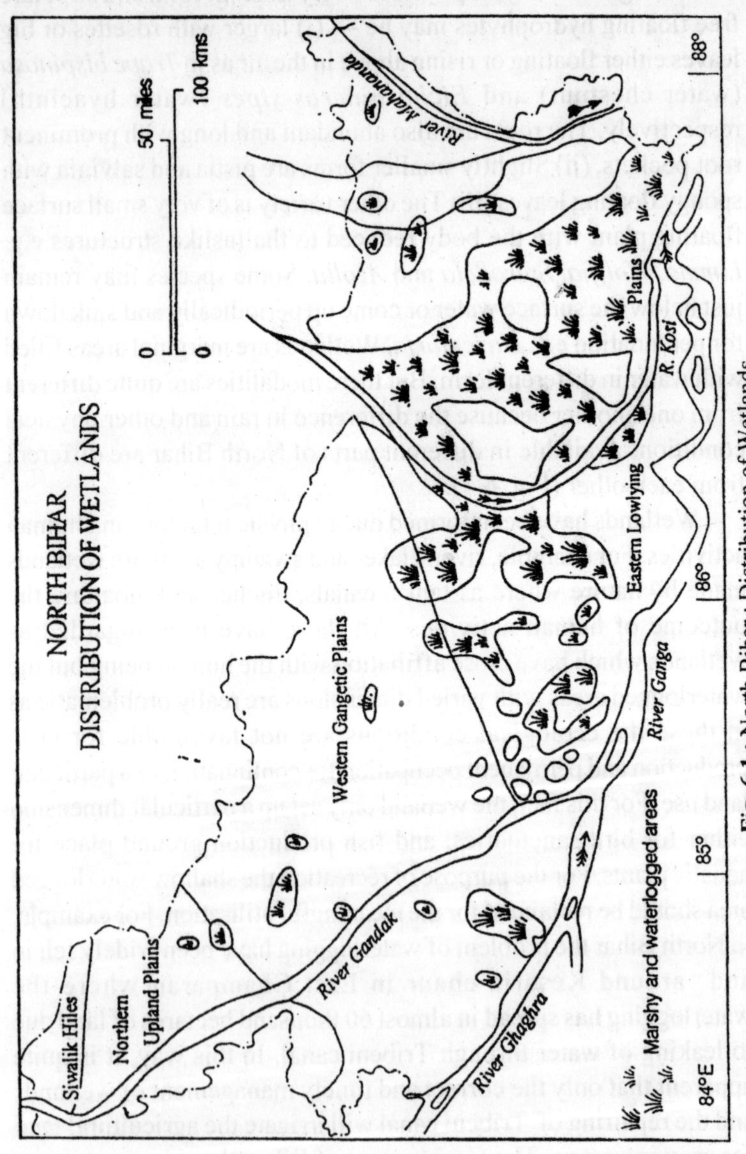


**Fig. 6.1 : North Bihar : Distribution of Wetlands.**

On the other hand, the canals in North Bihar are another form of wetlands which are problematic to some extent due to over siltation, and leaking of water in unwanted fields. This has made a good chunk of land unproductive near irrigation canals specially in case of Eastern Kosi canals, Eastern extension of Tribeni canals, Saran canals and Trihut canals. The work on these canals finished 15 years ago but unfortunately they are not irrigating the land as yet.

The man made ditches which have formed due to digging of soil for the construction of houses are basically meant for fulfilling the irrigation purposes of field around and in some cases in North Bihar, it is troublesome, where the abundance of wetlands create flood around human habitations in lowlying areas and does damage to crops each and every year.

Oxbow lakes are the remnants of meandering courses of rivers since historic times in North Bihar. Oxbow lakes are abundantly found in the river basin of Burhi Gandak, in Vaishali district and the Kankhar river in Katihar district. Oxbow lakes are best source of irrigational water supply, rearing of fishes and controlling the environment for pollution besides the cultivation of Makhana and several other aquatic plants which are used as medicinal herb oxbow lakes are also found in East Champaran and Madhubani districts but their size vary according to the slope of the ground and intensity of flood in lowlying areas.

Moat is commonly found around forts and garh sites especially in Vaishali which is known as Puskarni, Vaitarni and others. Similar type of fort has been recognised around Baghauni Kothi, Ilmasnagar Kothi, and around the campus of Darbhanga Maharaj, Laurianandan Garh and others. It is almost a permanent feature but it lacks proper maintenance so that so that it could help human being in the upkeep of environment and better sanitation of the area. Swampy areas are abundantly found in almost all parts of North Bihar, where due to the over growth of unwanted vegetation cover the degradation of environment took place as the area is infested with Malaria and Kalazar.

The steep side of embankment, and the neglect of the place due to dump of garbage and others have immensely made the place unhygienic both for the production of an item and proper utilisation of the wetland. These area may be regarded as wasteland in the form of wetlands. The pattern of wetlands also covers chaur lands which are abundantly found in different parts of North Bihar. Among these chaurs the Kanail of Darbhanga district, Kabartal of Begusarai district, Mehsar Chaur of Samastipur district, Kosban Jalker in Katihar district, Kesaria Chaur in East Champaran district and Hardia Chaur in Saran are some of the best example of wetlands in North Bihar. They have originated due to unequal deposition of sand and silt specially during flood besides the sheet wash erosion and neo-tectonic earth movement going on in the area. The chaur lands are utilised for the production of rice, besides fishes, snails and crabs found in the area. On the basis of these discussions it could be concluded that in North Bihar varieties of wetlands are found. Their origin and occurrences varies from place to place. All wetlands are not equally likely important for the human being. It depends upon the depth of water, quality of water, maintenance of the area around wetlands besides laws of the Government. The ignorance of people living around wetland does not know that what actually they want from such a marginal land.[3]

This chapter mainly relates to the of pattern formation of fresh water wetlands which are closely associated with typology of wetlands. This clearly shows the difference between ponds, ditches, lakes, streams, rivulets, rivers and Marshy lands which are found in various environmental conditions and closely associated with the landscape features of North Bihar.

In North Bihar the different patterns of wetlands occur due to differential rates and amounts of land degradation by running water. This clearly denote that in any scheme of planning one has to plan different types of wetlands differently in accordance with the need of people and the availability of resources for the development of a particular fresh water ecology. It may be developed for rearing of fishes and cultivation of medicinal plants besides making birds sanctuary and as place of pollution filters, attraction of tourist, bridging the gap of protein supply besides the place of recreation through navigation, etc.

**Chaurs of Mithilanchal as the Dominant Part of Nature**

There is a possibility of ecological imbalances due to the reduction of wetland area in North Bihar. Due to the reclamation of chaurs for other uses the area of wetlands has been reduced considerably which leads to environmental problems. No measures have been taken uptill now to ameliorate the environmental situation of the area.

There is no forest cover in Darbhanga division but there is a lot of chaur lands. In South Bihar there is an abundance of forest cover but, negligible amount of Chaur lands. It is a natural division of forest cover and the wetlands which control is the ecological conditions of the area. In this way, there is a close relationship of Bio-Geochemical cycle adjustment in between forest land and the Chaur land.[4] In North Bihar forest is found only in West Champaran and Kishanganj districts.

Currently, due to pollution of Chaur the situation is most pitiable. In the nearby towns and villages the household refuge gets dumped into the wetlands along with solid wastes, affluent chemicals from the industries, gases of different types and solid particles dampense the situation of pollution of water in chaurs.

Generally, people understand that chaurs are not so valuable in terms of economic gains, but this help people in many ways. The people should be educated to understand the use of wetlands. In order to maintain ecological balance, acquatic and chemical cycle receiving of solid wastes in a natural way should be channelised by human being, cleaning of polluted water, protection from flood, protection of rivers and increasing the level of water under wetland are some of the important functions of wetland. Hence, it is known as the kidney of nature.[5]

So far as the economic aspect is concerned the vegetation is necessary for living creatures and birds which are highly important as they have close relationship with the social and economic conditions of the society where the wetlands are found. In the wetland a huge amount of plants of medicinal value are found besides; providing raw materials like mothi, sikki and banshi to make mat, dalia, basket and whistle. All these have immense economic value. This could help in the establishment of Small Scale Cottage Industries. Some areas also produce *singhara* and *makhaana* besides catching of snail which are highly used as delicious food item in different districts of North Bihar. Once in a year food crop is also grown in a better way because its production level is very high.

The number of natural wetlands in Darbhanga Division are 462 which coverse an area of 224,787 hectare. The man made chaurs are 233 in number which have an area of 48,607 hectare. The Ministry of Environment has selected 19 wetlands in India for production among which the 'Kabar Lake' of North Bihar is one of them. There is a proposal to protect the Kusheshwar Asthan lake of Darbhanga District also whose position is not less than Kabar.

So far as the situation of Darbhanga is concerned there are altogether 118 chaurs which could be seen blockwise in the Table 6.2 given below:

**Table 6.2 :** Number of Chaurs in Darbhanga District, 1998

| *S. No.* | *Block* | *Number of Chaurs* |
|---|---|---|
| 1. | Jale | 8 |
| 2. | Singwara | 17 |
| 3. | Hayaghat | 8 |
| 4. | Keotiranway | 15 |
| 5. | Darbhanga | 3 |
| 6. | Bahadurpur | 12 |
| 7. | Baheri | 10 |
| 8. | Biraul | 14 |
| 9. | Kusheshwar Asthan | 8 |
| 10. | Manigachhi | 8 |
| 11. | Benipur | 9 |
| 12 | Ghaynshyampur | 8 |
| | Total | 118 |

On the basis of fieldwork it has been observed that some of the wetlands are very big in areal extent. Darbhanga District has a total area's of 250 sq.km$^2$ out of, which 23.8 sq. km$^2$ is under wetland which comes about 9.5 per cent of the total wetland area.

Considering the country as a whole there are four per cent land under wetland where as the world as a whole there is 6 per cent land under wetlands (Fig. 6.1).

As an important part of the nature the wetland should be conserved immediately. On this matter there is a tug of war in between the government officials and the environmental scientists. Due to increasing population, the private organisation, agencies and the social workers should come forward to reclaim, wetland for residential quarters, but according to environmental scientists wetland is an important ecosystem which should be conserved and protected.

Nowdays, its importance has been understood at the global level for its protection and several researches are going on to think about its utility.

So, far as the conservation of wetland in Kusheshwar Asthan block is concerned the late done by the Government of Bihar to make it a birds sanctuary is highly lamented because migratory birds are coming after crossing Himalaya to this wetland. It is not proper to prey the migratory birds coming from distant places as they are highly helpful in making the ecological balance. It could be hoped that the state and the Central Governments should come forward to protect the cause of wetlands.[6]

**Table 6.3 :** Some of the Important Chaur as Wetlands of Darbhanga District

| **Hayaghat Anchal** | **Singhia Anchal** |
|---|---|
| Bhama | Ashraha |
| Kanail | Pindaruch |
| Bhima | Andma |
| Bachti | Dubraha |
| Maknahi | Rasalpur |
| Chatauna | Chatlapatti |
| Keoti | Dobgawa |
| **Jale Anchal** | Chandapur |
| Gari | Barhi |
| Debra | Kharma |
| Badhauli | Latolia |
| Samdhinia | Patli |
| Prasadi Tola | Gangi |
| Ratanpura | Bishunpur |

Table 6.3 (*Contd.*)

| **Singhwara Anchal** | **Ghanshyampur Anchal** |
|---|---|
| Kodha | Turaul |
| Dholha | Aghma |
| Khanur | Dulauri |
| Sinia | Ishunpur |
| Sefrodih | Chanan |
| Kishoria | Lohnari |
| Chatrauli | Urmaha |
| Pipra | Putai |
| **Singhwara Anchal** | **Benipur Anchal** |
| Kachka | Jatiani |
| Gorgama | Aansar |
| Patori | Fuhar |
| Fultha | Meha |
| Manjai | Kawa |
| Dirha | Narma |
| Sarbara | Gahat |
| Barhulia | Sahri |
| **Manigachhi Anchal** | Barban |
| Ghora | **Baheri Anchal** |
| Chandaura | Pathrahi |
| Kata | Lakshmipur |
| Maha | Jaria |
| Sajaur | Simardah |
| Mahda | Bithaulia |
| Bajipur | Chamna |
| Katra | Balane |
| **Kusheswar Asthan Anchal** | Mani |
| Sonapur | Atma |
| Nadiyami | Narsar |
| Palwar | **Biraul Anchal** |
| Mehrala | Mohiuddinpur |
| Mehri | Saho |
| Singhalia | Rampur |
| Mahra | Lalpur |
| Sauta | Sadubha |
| **Darbhanga Anchal** | Basupur |
| Sundarpur | Baruara |
| Lakshmipur | Kharkharia |
| Bahadurpur | **Biraul Anchal** |
| Milkichak | Pokhram |
| Dekuli | Katia |

Table 6.3 (*Contd.*)

| | |
|---|---|
| Gopati | Bora |
| Jarkhane | Supaul |
| Sahla | Balia |
| Kadne | Bek |
| **Basantpur** | **Bhanpur** |
| Kaudulia | Pagri |
| Khaira | Lothra |

## LOCATIONAL

The entire North Bihar which lies north of the river Ganges is an alluvial plain with minor slope towards the Ganges in the south and lowlands of the Kosi Belt in the middle eastern part. The significant features are the alluvial deposits and sand bars along the river banks and marshy depressions known as '*Chaurs*'. These chaurs are the oxbow lakes of meandering streams and some of them have formed due to sheet wash erosion during flood and irregular deposition of silt and sand bodies.

The general slope of the plain is from north-west to south-east. The average slope is approximately 8 metres per 100 kilometres from the north-western point to the south-eastern corner of the region with some exceptions of a part of west Madhubani district and Kuseshwar Asthan area. The entire plain is 76 metres above mean sea level. Along the course of the Ganges, the height is just 30 meters near Moniharighat in Katihar.

In order to maintain ecological balance the chief aim is to analyse, classify and to map the various landscape features in their correct position and examine the mutual relationship for assessing their physical properties and economic importance.

(a) North Bihar is an alluvial plain. Most of the diversities seen on the surface are those due to river action and a series of raised river side uplands known as levees, dotted with wetlands in the form of alternating depressions or chaurs on the line of streams.

(b) A sub-terai belt of marshy land in the north with intervening tracts of uplands along rivers is succeeded in the south by a wide belt of marshy lowlands, characterised by permanent depressions and lakes besides tanks which are man made features of wetlands.

(c) In the riparian tracts of the Ganges the land is high due to which wetlands are found slight away from levee in the form of intervening depressions. Due to presence of river bluffs on the northern bank of the Ganges, all rivers flowing along the gravity of slope from north to south turn towards east and run parallel along the Ganges river for a few kilometres before they finally meet together.

As meanders grow, it frequently happens that a narrow neck of land is cut through from two sides thus allowing the stream to straighten its course. The two ends of the meander so separated from the channel, are likely to be filled up by sand. The best example of an oxbow lake on the bank of river Baghmati in Samastipur district could be seen. These water bodies from excellent settlement sites. The whole face of the country is dotted with ditches besides small oxbow or elongated water bodies and chaurs (long semi-circular marshes) which lies in between the rivers making the old abandoned courses of the streams. Though found extensively in all parts of this region, the abandoned courses are more prolific in Madhubani, Darbhanga, Vaishali, Champaran, Saharsa and Samastipur districts of North Bihar.[7]

The abandoned channel of a stream on a flood plain may become partially filled with vegetation, thus forming a marsh. They may also occur in any depression on the flood plains especially in areas of waterlogging. Marshes are numerous towards the south-eastern part of North Bihar.

Some of these marshy lands dry up during the hot weather season. There are some marshes which exist throughout the year like a tank. Marshes are also found in the beds of rivers like, the Kosi, the Bhuthi-Balan, the Kamla, the Jibacch, the Kareh, the Burhi Gandak, and the Gandak during the hot weather season but during rainy months the river establishes its normally course. The marshes are utilised by the peasants for irrigation, rearing of fish, for growing mothi and makhana and for washing animals in he summer season. Settlements near the marshy, areas are dispersed type.

## Distribution of Tanks

In North Bihar the total number of tanks are 8509 which are distributed unevenly in different parts of the area and determined by the presence and absence of river in the area. It is quite discernible that river embankments of the Ganges, the Kosi, the Mahananda, the Gandak, and others have very few number of tanks near them but away from river banks the number increases. In the districts of Saharsa, Madhubani, Darbhanga and the northern parts of Samastipur, Sitamarhi and Muzaffarpur, the number of tanks are very high because these are the areas of "rice and fish culture". The highest number of tanks are available in Madhubani district (2421) and Darbhanga district (1435) in 1991 (Fig. 6.3) (Table 6.4).

**Table 6.4** : Distribution of Tanks and Forests/Orchards in North Bihar (1991)

| *District* | *No. of Tanks* | *%* | *'000 Orchards* | *%* |
|---|---|---|---|---|
| 1. Saran | 197 | 2.31 | 8 | 3.55 |
| 2. Siwan | 139 | 1.63 | 5 | 2.22 |
| 3. Gopalganj | 115 | 1.35 | 5 | 2.22 |
| 4. East Champaran | 331 | 3.88 | 9 | 4.00 |
| 5. West Champaran | 144 | 1.69 | 92 | 40.88 |
| 6. Muzaffarpur | 524 | 6.15 | 11 | 4.88 |
| 7. Vaishali | 196 | 2.39 | 6 | 2.67 |
| 8. Sitamarhi | 787 | 9.24 | 9 | 4.00 |
| 9. Darbhanga | 1435 | 16.86 | 9 | 4.00 |
| 10. Samastipur | 508 | 5.97 | 8 | 3.57 |
| 11. Madhubani | 2425 | 28.49 | 11 | 4.88 |
| 12. Begusarai | 73 | 0.85 | 2 | 0.88 |
| 13. Khagaria | 26 | 0.30 | 2 | 0.88 |
| 14. Bhagalpur | 16 | 0.17 | 1 | 0.46 |
| 15. Saharsa | 526 | 6.18 | 20 | 8.88 |
| 16. Purnea | 937 | 11.01 | 22 | 9.79 |
| 17. Katihar | 131 | 1.53 | 5 | 2.24 |
| Total | 8509 | 100 | 225 | 100 |

*Source :* District Census Handbook of Different Districts of North Bihar, 1991.

In Pokharbhinda village of Manigachhi anchal there are 75 tanks and in Narayanpur village of the same anchal there are 35 tanks which are not only a lowlying wetlands but economically they are

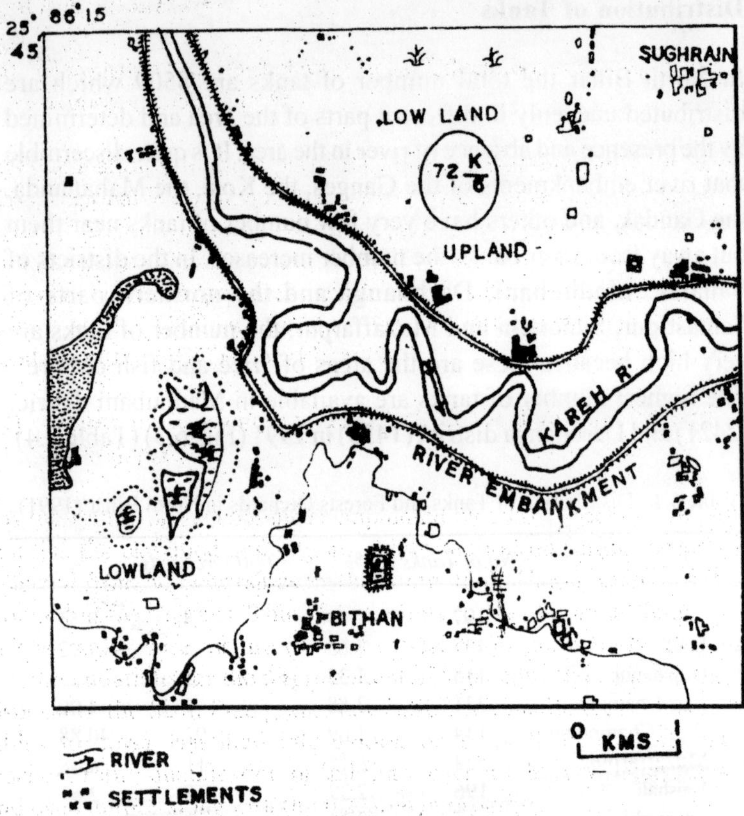


**Fig. 6.2 :** Role of Rivers in Economic Development of an Area.

highly potential. For example, Rajokhar pond of Narayanpur which has a expanse of over 21 hectares of land is annually producing makhana of Rs.3 lakhs and fish of Rs. 3 lakhs respectively. It has a powerful tool to make ecological balance, beautify the environment, provide recreation ground on boats, bathing place for human being and cattle besides irrigating the land through pumping sets over more than 5000 hectares of land in the surrounding area.

In North Bihar there is a close correlation in between ponds as artificial wetlands and planted mango orchards as vegetation cover, because people have a belief to marry tank with mango orchard and hence, these two are the assets for making the highest suspended

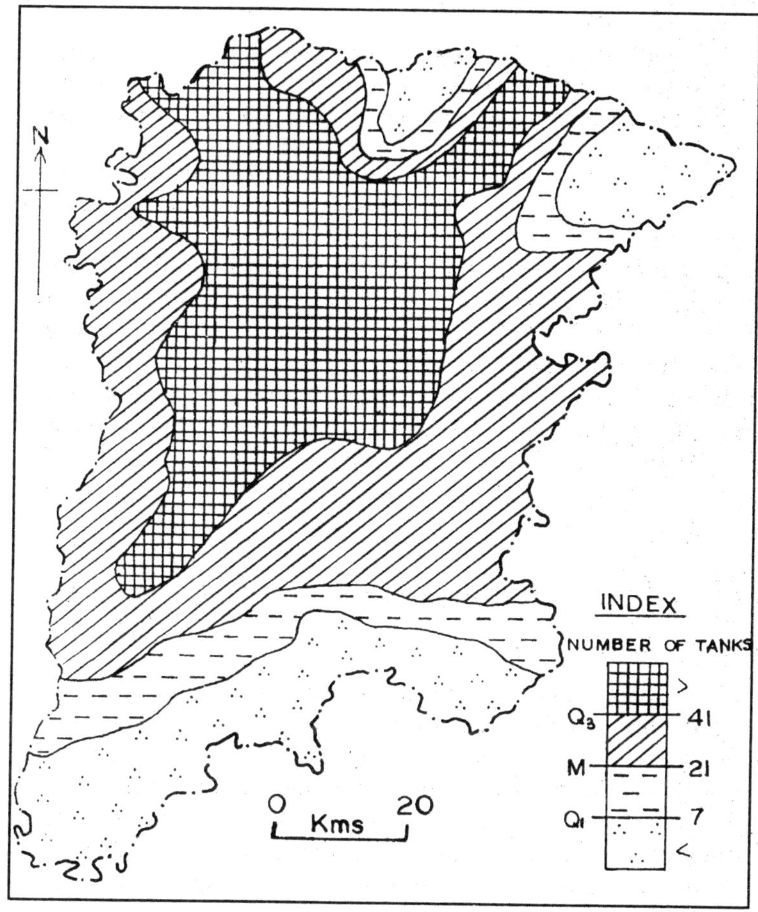


**Fig. 6.3 :** Distribution of Tanks in the Division of Darbhanga (1971)

particles is found in Krishnaraj Sagar 1065. The highest turbidity is in lake Kathara 7.7 followed by Narail chaur of Kuseshwar Asthan 6.6. The highest Alkali value is 49 in Dighi, Hardness is 825 in Belhi, calcium is highest 792.5 in Belhi, the highest S04 is 22.4 in Ganga Sagar followed by 17.2 in Narail chaur.

## Rennovation of Wetlands in North Bihar

It has been learnt that with the expense of 6 billions of rupees, the rennovation of Darbhanga Forbesganj latteral road could not be

**Table 6.5 :** Chemical Analysis of the water of sampled wetlands

| *Sr. No.* | *Wetlands* | *TS* | *Turb* | *pH* | *A/K* | *Hardness* | *CL* | $SO_4$ | $NO_2$ | $NO_3$ | *F* |
|---|---|---|---|---|---|---|---|---|---|---|---|
| 1. | Ghordur | 280 | 3.4 | 7.38 | 260 | 265 | 37.5 | 9.8 | 0.03 | 0.023 | 0.24 |
| 2. | Simardah | — | 4.3 | 7.80 | 335 | 265 | 7.5 | 7.2 | — | 0.020 | 0.34 |
| 3. | Daihara | 848 | 2.7 | 6.79 | 348 | 300 | 77.6 | 9.8 | — | 0.010 | 0.54 |
| 4. | Mehsar Chaur | 294 | 4.0 | 7.05 | 430 | 235 | 92.5 | 12.4 | 0.0 | 0.020 | 0.34 |
| 5. | Kanail Chaur | 256 | 4.0 | 6.06 | 168 | 239 | 65.4 | 14.3 | — | 0.017 | 0.49 |
| 6. | Phulhara Chaur | 390 | 4.9 | 6.03 | 278 | 120 | 38.2 | 18.7 | 6.1 | 0.018 | 0.37 |
| 7. | Keotiranway | 290 | 3.9 | 7.02 | 169 | 130 | 48.2 | 15.6 | 5.2 | 0.026 | 0.42 |
| 8. | Ballipur | 190 | 2.9 | 7.01 | 170 | 230 | 58.2 | 14.5 | 4.2 | 0.016 | 0.45 |
| 9. | Krishnaraj Sagar | 1065 | 3.9 | 7.01 | 230 | 179 | — | 5.5 | 4.9 | 0.018 | 0.47 |
| 10. | Madhwapur Chaur | 451 | 2.8 | 7.53 | 3.75 | — | 12.6 | 14.8 | 0 | 0.031 | 0.24 |
| 11. | Hirni Chaur | 561 | 2.9 | 6.96 | 45 | 365 | 57.5 | 7.2 | 0.004 | 0.024 | 0.00 |
| 12. | Ahiya | 1276 | 6.7 | 7.23 | 335 | 296 | 160 | 7.3 | 0.005 | 0.07 | 0.85 |
| 13. | Naimalia Chaur | 1115 | 7.8 | 7.83 | 276 | 279 | 170 | 12.5 | 0.003 | 0.06 | 0.89 |
| 14. | Raghopur diara | 360 | 6.9 | 5.90 | 390 | 270 | 172 | 13.6 | 0.001 | 0.02 | 0.78 |
| 15. | Bora Chaur | 1130 | 5.9 | 8.09 | 550 | 170 | 259 | 3.8 | — | 0.28 | 0.38 |
| 16. | Kulesra Chaur | 290 | 3.0 | 7.54 | 271 | 285 | 25.0 | 7.3 | — | 0.39 | 0.96 |
| 17. | Telia Chaur | 270 | 1.8 | 6.9 | 390 | 140 | 16.0 | 7.5 | 0.003 | 0.93 | 0.87 |

*Contd.*

*Table 6.5 (Contd.)*

| *Sr. No.* | *Wetlands* | *TS* | *Turb* | *pH* | *A/K* | *Hardness* | *CL* | *SO⁴* | $NO_2$ | $NO_3$ | *F* |
|---|---|---|---|---|---|---|---|---|---|---|---|
| 18. | Mahwal Maun | 270 | 7.1 | 8.04 | 415 | 305 | 32.5 | 9.8 | 0.150 | 0.75 | — |
| 19. | Kanti Lake | 1015 | 7.3 | 9.04 | 416 | 340 | 12.4 | 9.3 | 0.139 | — | 0.39 |
| 20. | Muradpur Chaur | 4.0 | 5.0 | 4.30 | 150 | 190 | 40.0 | 5.9 | 0.029 | 0.230 | 7.20 |
| 21. | Bhagwa Chaur | 5.8 | 3.0 | 5.70 | 390 | 290 | 50.0 | 7.9 | 0.030 | 0.127 | 5.39 |
| 22. | Khetar | 409 | 4.0 | 0.20 | 139 | 250 | 38.0 | 8.3 | 0.002 | 0.280 | 0.39 |

*Source* : Department of Soil, Agriculture College, Pusa, Bihar.

**Table 6.6 : North Bihar : Lorenz Curve showing Distributional Patterns of Wetlands (1991)**

| *Sr. No.* | *Name of the District* | *Water Bodies Area in Hectare* | *Percentage* | *C.P.* |
|---|---|---|---|---|
| 1. | West Champaan | 4,602 | 9.99 | 9.99 |
| 2. | East Champaran | 9,906 | 21.33 | 31.32 |
| 3. | Gopalganj | 997 | 2.14 | 34.46 |
| 4. | Siwan | 812 | 1.74 | 35.20 |
| 5. | Saran | 948 | 2.04 | 37.24 |
| 6. | Vaishali | 871 | 1.87 | 33.11 |
| 7. | Muzaffarpur | 2,232 | 4.80 | 43.91 |
| 8. | Sitamarhi | 2,570 | 5.53 | 49.44 |
| 9. | Madhubani | 3,743 | 8.05 | 57.49 |
| 10. | Darbhanga | 3,490 | 7.51 | 65.00 |
| 11. | Samastipur | 1,216 | 2.61 | 67.61 |
| 12. | Begusarai | 1,034 | 2.22 | 69.83 |
| 13. | Saharsa | 1,057 | 2.27 | 72.10 |

made with doubling of Sakhri-Hasanpur rail line, construction of underground drainage lines in North Bihar with the expense of Rupees 30 crore, two crores has been kept to rennovate tank in the city of Darbhanga. One crore will be expend for the construction of Bus stand and vegetable market and one crore will be expend in making sports complex in Darbhanga. All these expenses have come from the Central Government. The work has already been started in November, 1996. It has been hoped that the city of Darbhanga will certainly get benefit in comparison with Samastipur and Madhubani for which three crores Rupees have been given for the development work.

This was announced by Food and Supply Minister Sri D.P.Yadav in his meeting in Jhanjharpur, Phulparas and Madhubani. According to Sri Yadav the Planning Commission, the Ministry of Railway and Defence Ministry have already given their consent to start work on the above mentioned projects. This project will also help in the construction of 5 kilometres long road in between Mahadevmath and Bhaptiyahi (Supaul) on the Kosi river.

For the construction of Darbhanga-Forbesganj lateral road several scholars have tried to see the problem but unfortunately this has not been completed as yet. The then Railway Minister Sri Ram Vilash Paswan had inaugrated the construction of Sakari-Hasanpur rail line over a distance of 76 kilometres for which Rs. one billion will be spent. The foundation has been laid in Kusheswar Asthan also. The approval for the construction of this line has been given by the formal Minister Lalit Narayan Mishra on 22nd February, 1974. But later on due to paucity of fund this Project has been kept in awayance. In 1974, the cost of the Project was Rs.6.88 crore but now due to inflation of Rupee the cost has gone up to Rs. 1 billion. In between Sakri and Hasanpur the railway station selected are- Bithan, Kusheswar Asthan, Harinagar, Jibachh ghat, Biraul, Neori, Benipur and Jagdishpur.

Darbhanga is also considered as the capital of Mithilanchal but the condition of Darbhanga is so diplorable that Rs.34 crore has been given as grant out of this several Projects have been started in November 1996 in which the construction of underground drainage channel was considered quite essential in order to make the area free from pollution.

## NOTES

1. Cow, M. and *et al.*, *Wetlands: Archaeology and Nature Conservation*, HMSO, London, 1994.
2. Finlayson, M. and Moser, Michael, *Wetlands, Facts on File*, Oxford, 1994.
3. Singh, R.B., *Environmental Monitoring of Remote Sensing and GIS*. Geocarto International Centre, Hong Kong, 1991.
4. Choudhry, U.P., Wetlands in North Bihar, *East-West Geographer*, Vol.1, No.1, 1990.
5. Mandal, R.B., "Geo-Physical Aspects of Wetlands in North) Bihar", Conference on Wetlands, Organised by Forest Department, Government of Bihar, 1988.
6. Ahmad, S.S., *Ecology of Wetlands of Milkichak Darbhanga*, Ph.D. Thesis, L.N. Mithila University, Darbhanga, 1993.
7. Singh, R.P. and Kumar, A., *Monograph of Bihar*, Bharti Bhawan, Patna, 1975.

# 7

# ECONOMIC GAINS FROM WETLANDS

## Introduction

Water is an important resource on which all living being depend. Wetland increases the human activity, consequent upon population and industrial growth, intensive agriculture, river basin development, recreational use of water and domestic and industrial exploitation of littoral properties. These are contributing to excessive nutrient enrichment of lakes and streams as wetlands (Cox, 1974).[1] Aquatic plants and animals function as components of a diversified community. Aquatic plants may block or clog rivers and canals, with hydroelectric generation, promote water borne diseases, with fish culture and fishing, hinder boat traffic and causes floods in rivers.

The excessive growth of blue algae and acquatic plants choke the open water drains, render the water turbidityless and nonpotable. The algae and aquatic plant die and rot and produce repugnant odour and the organic matter obtained there from sinks and consumes the deep water oxygen which is vital for fish and other animal lives.

The stagnant water, with its dissolved nutrients and gases, is a wonderful medium for the growth of plants. Aquatic plants often provide shelter and breeding grounds for many animals in water bodies and import ethics to them. Some microscopic plants (*Anabaena Spp*) fix atmospheric Nitrogen which is of great agricultural significance while others absorb tons of pollutants created by man. There are still others that are sources of food and feed materials for humans. In fact, without aquatic plants, and animals, most waterbodies would look like wet deserts. But for some reasons, the natural balance among numerous components of an aquatic ecosystem is disturbed, leading to over growth of one or more of its plant components. This is a negative factor in the production potential and energy resources of water. Thus, over-growth of aquatic plants is, no doubt, a matter of serious concern.

Recently, it has been recognised that aquatic plants constitute a free crop with potential values. They do not require tillage, irrigation, fertilization, weeding, protection from pests and diseases and maintenance in general. Efforts, towards exploring the potential uses of aquatic plants, exhibits to publicise their potentials, evaluation of the public responsed and the socio-cultural aspects of the society.

**Situations in North Bihar**

The economic gains of wetlands are manifold which starts from production of mothi, *makhana*, Purain leaves and *Jalkumbhi* to check environmental pollution, beautify the environment, maintain ecological balance, and provide place for cattle bathing, locational place for towns, place of ritual performance and others.

In this chapter an appraisal has been made regarding the economic gains of wetlands because wetlands are not only bridging the gap of ecological balance. Wetlands are mostly situated in marginal areas where no food crops could be raised that is considered as a negative zone for the construction of human habitation. Very recently, the Government of India started paying attention on our wetlands because they are not only negative areas but they are rich in flora and fauna besides beauifying the environment and they are recreation grounds especially for North Bihar and the preying of fishes and birds as well. The wetlands have great economic potential in terms of rearing fishes, cultivation of Makhana, collection of medicinal plants and giving employment opportunity to millions of people specially in the management of wetlands. The recruitment of labourers for the collection of Mothi, Singarhara, Frogs, Tortoise, Crab, varieties of cranes, snails, situa shells and bathing place for men and beasts as well. With the help of Table 7.1 and Figure 7.1

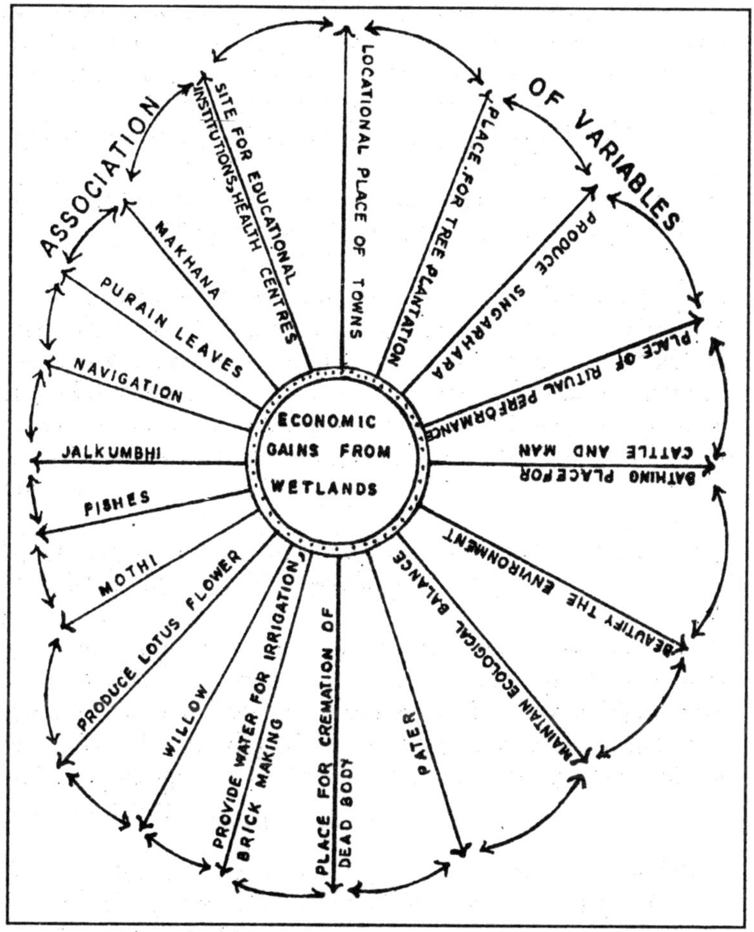


**Fig. 7.1 :** Economic Gains from Wetlands

the fish production and economic achievement in North Bihar have been shown in order to measure the viability of wetlands like ponds, chaurs, rivers and tals, in different districts of the area. It has been found that the highest amount of fish production (23,000 MT) comes from Darbhanga District and the lowest amount of 1025 tonnes comes from Northern part of Bhagalpur district. Most of the districts of North Bihar have sufficient amount of wetlands and hence the amount of fish produce may be increased manifold with scientific management and digging of waterbodies because, nowadays due to the process of sedimentation at the time of flood the problems have been deteriorated to a substantial degree which need urgent attention of plants and administration to amelioratel our physical environment. The prices gained from fish production is not so high in comparison with the total revenue earned in a district but it could be raised with the adoption of proper managerial procedure.

This is the call of the day to preserve our natural environment (Fig.7.2).

**Table 7.1 :** Fish Production in the Wetlands of North Bihar, 1987

| *Sl. No.* | *District* | *Fish production in M.T.* | *Average price in Rs. per M.T.* |
|---|---|---|---|
| 1. | Darbhanga | 23000 | 13,000 |
| 2. | Muzaffarpur | 12495 | 12,000 |
| 3. | Champaran | 7500 | 12,000 |
| 4. | Purnea | 6390 | 10,000 |
| 5. | Saharsa | 4592 | 10,000 |
| 6. | Saran | 4100 | 10,000 |
| 7. | Munger | 1700 | 6,000 |
| 8. | Bhagalpur | 1025 | 4,000 |

*Source :* Fisheries Department, Government of Bihar, Patna (1986-87).

## Plant Resources of Wetlands of Kosi Division

Wetlands are areas of submerged or water soaked lands, both natural or man made, permanent or temporary, freshwater or marine. Ecologically wetland ecosystem is intermediate between aquatic and terrestrial ecosystems and has specialised vegetation and floristic composition. Extensive areas are often inaccessible to large predatory mammals including man and so provide a refuse for diversity of beautiful wildlife. In recent years due to their economic, ecological and biological importance fairly understood, wetland have attracted attention world over and more and more people working in various fields of knowledge are trying to explore their potentialities for the benefit of mankind together with their role in environment protection and conservation of rare plant and animal species. This

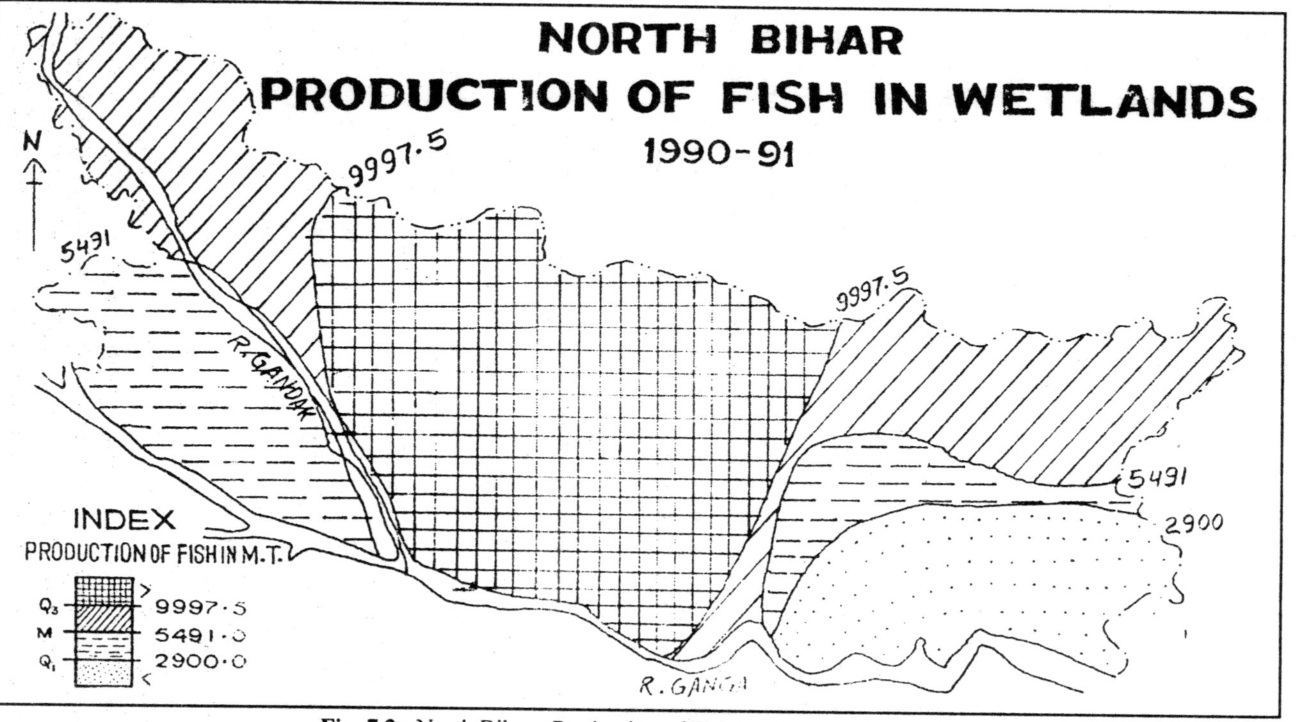


**Fig. 7.2 :** North Bihar : Production of Fish in Wetlands, 1990-91.

chapter deals with the plant resources of the wetlands of Kosi Division of Bihar. The data presented here are based on extensive fieldwork carried out between the year 1980-87. More than 200 species of vascular plants have been collected, identified, documented and deposited in the Herbarium of University Department of Botany and Bhagalpur University. The analysis of floristic data revealed that wetland plants constitute about 25 per cent of the total plant species recorded from this area. Except for few species like *Eichhornia crassipes*, *Chenopodium ambrosioides*, *Solvia anthemifolia*, majority of those species are inhabitants of this area and grow in wild condition.

The Kosi Division was purposely selected as it is the area through which the main, channels of Kosi and Mahananda river flow at present. With frequent change in courses of the river Kosi flood become the usual features every year. The large amount of detritus during flood results in a number of temporary ponds, ditches, swamps and marshes throughout the area. All these provide an ideal habitats for the growth and development of plants specific to such types of habitats.[2]

**Plant Resources of Wetlands of Kosi Division**

Vascular Flora of the Kosi Division

| *Plant Group* | *Pterrido-phyta.* | *Gymnos-perms* | *Angiosperms* | | *Total* |
|---|---|---|---|---|---|
| | | | *Dicot* | *Monocot* | |
| Families | 10 | 2 | 90 | 30 | 132 |
| Genera | 25 | 4 | 360 | 120 | 509 |
| Species | 30 | 5 | 530 | 170 | 735 |

**Wetland Flora of the Kosi Division**

| | | | | |
|---|---|---|---|---|
| Families | 10 | 37 | 18 | 55 |
| Genera | 20 | 75 | 55 | 150 |
| Species | 25 | 106 | 75 | 206 |

Five Dominant Families of the Wetlands with Number of Species

| | |
|---|---|
| *Poaceal* | 35 |
| *Cyperaceae* | 20 |
| *Asteraceae* | 13 |
| *Scrophulariaceae* | 11 |
| *Polygonaceae* | 10 |

## Food for Human Use

| *Botanical Name* | *Local name* | *Frequency* | *Distribution in Kosi Div.* | *Cultivated Wild* | *Edible parts* |
|---|---|---|---|---|---|
| *Certopteris thalictroides* | — | +++ | throughout | wild w/o cultiva-ted in some parts of the World | Leaves |
| *Colocasia* | Kachu | +++ | throughout | wild / cultivated | Rhizome Leaves |
| *Commeling Bengalensis* | Kena | +++ | throughout | wild | Leaves |
| *Elaeocharis* | Kachu-mar | +++ | " | wild cultivated in other part of the world | Tubers |
| *Euryale Ferox* | Makhana | +++ | " | Cultivated | secds edible after reasting leaves |
| *Ipomea aquatic* | Karmisag | +++ | " | Wild | Hecoptocle |
| *Nelumpo nucifera* | Kamal | +++ | " | " | Seeds and Rhizome |
| *Nymphaea nouchali* | Bhent | +++ | " | " | Seeds and rhizome |
| *Nymphaea nouchali* | Kokka | +++ | " | " | Receptacle seeds and rhizome |

| | | | | | |
|---|---|---|---|---|---|
| *Nymphaides hydrophylla* | | +++ | " | " | Tubers |
| *Marsilea Minute* | Charpatia | +++ | " | " | Sporocarp |
| *Monocharia Hostata* | | | | | Leaves |
| *Potamogeton Nodosus* | | +++ | " | " | Tubers and rhizome |

*Source :* Department of Botany, Bhagalpur University, 1986.

## Food for Fishes

| *Botanical Name* | *Frequency* | *Distribution in Kosi Div.* | *Cultivated / Wild* |
|---|---|---|---|
| *A ponogeton notans* | +++ | " | " |
| *Ceratophyllum demursurn* | +++ | " | " |
| *Hydrilla, Variticillata,* | +++ | " | " |
| *Lemna Perpusiha* | +++ | " | " |
| *Ottelia Alismoides* | +++ | " | " |
| *Naja graminea* | +++ | " | " |
| *Potamogeton crispus* | +++ | " | " |
| *Potamogeton nodosus* | +++ | " | " |
| *Sagittaria quayanensis* | +++ | " | " |
| *Spirodella Polyrhiza* | +++ | " | " |

*Source :* Department of Botany, Bhagalpur University, 1986.

## Fodder

| *Botanical Name* | *Frequency* | *Distribution in Kosi Division* | *Cultivated/ Wild* |
|---|---|---|---|
| *Amischophacelus* | + + + | Throughout | Wild |
| *Augallis arvensis* | + + + | Throughout | Wild |
| *Bracharia reptans* | + + + | Throughout | Wild |
| *Branchiaria mutica* | + + + | Throughout | Wild |
| *Commelina bengalensis* | + + + | Throughout | Wild |
| *Coix lecrymajobi* | + + + | Throughout | Wild |
| *Cyperus iria* | + + + | Throughout | Wild |
| *Cyperus difformis* | + + + | Throughout | Wild |
| *Echinochla Colonum* | + + + | Throughout | Wild |
| *Echinochloa crusgalli* | + + + | Throughout | Wild |

| *Botanical Name* | *Frequency* | *Distribution in Kosi Division* | *Cultivated/ Wild* |
|---|---|---|---|
| *Elaeochasis dulcis* | + + + | Throughout | Wild |
| *Eriochloa procera* | + + + | Throughout | Wild |
| *Fimbristylis littoralis* | + + + | Throughout | Wild |
| *Fimbristylis millacea* | + + + | Throughout | Wild |
| *Finbristylis tetragena* | + + + | Throughout | Wild |
| *Furena ciliaris* | + + + | Throughout | Wild |
| *Hackelochloa granuleris* | + + + | Throughout | Wild |
| *Medicago lupulina* | + + + | Throughout | Wild |
| *Medicago denticulata* | + + + | Throughout | Wild |
| *Melitotus alba* | + + + | Throughout | Wild |
| *Melilotus indica* | + + + | Throughout | Wild |
| *Murdania nudiflora* | + + + | Throughout | Wild |
| *Panicum repens* | + + + | Throughout | Wild |
| *Paspatidium punctaturn* | + + + | Throughout | Wild |
| *Paspalidium serobiculatum* | + + + | Throughout | Wild |
| *Saccharurn spontaneurn "Kash"* | + + + | Throughout | Wild |
| *Setaria glouca* | + + + | Throughout | Wild |
| *Setaria intermedia* | + + + | Throughout | Wild |
| *Setaria verticillata* | + + + | Throughout | Wild |
| *Sporopdus diander* | + + + | Throughout | Wild |
| *Scri scirpus maritimus* | + + + | Throughout | Wild |

*Source :* Department of Botany, Bhagalpur University, 1986.

## Biofertilizer/Biogas

| *Botanical name* | *Frequency* | *Distribution in Kosi River* | *Cultivated/ Wild* |
|---|---|---|---|
| *Azolla, pinnata* | + + + | Throughout | Wild |
| *Ceratophyllurn demursum* | + + + | Throughout | Wild |
| *Eichhornia crassipes* | + + + | Throughout | Wild |
| *Ipomoea aquatica* | + + + | Throughout | Wild |
| *Ipomoea cornea subsp* | + + + | Throughout | Wild |
| *Marsilea minuta* | + + + | Throughout | Wild |
| *Melilotus alba* | + + + | Throughout | Wild |
| *Meliliturn indica* | + + + | Throughout | Wild |
| *Melicego denticulaton* | + + + | Throughout | Wild |
| *Medicage lupulina* | + + + | Throughout | Wild |
| *Pistia stratiotes* | + + + | Throughout | Wild |
| *Postamogeton crispus* | + + + | Throughout | Wild |
| *Potamogeton nodosus* | + + + | Throughout | Wild |
| *Salvinia sp.* | + + + | Throughout | Wild |
| *Sosbania sesban* | + + + | Throughout | Wild |

*Source :* Department of Botany, Bhagalpur University, 1986 and Fieldwork.

## Fuel

| *Botanical Name* | *Frequency* | *Distribution in Kosi Div.* | *Wild/ Cultivated* |
|---|---|---|---|
| *Eichhornia crassipes* | + + + | Throughout | Wild |
| *Ipomoea carnea subsp.* | + + + | Throughout | Wild |
| *Panianus Fascicularis* | + + + | Throughout | Wild |
| *Pistia stratioites* | + + + | Throughout | Wild |
| *Tamarix dioica* | + + + | Throughout | Wild |

## Fibre

| *Botanical Name* | *Frequency* | *Distribution in Kosi Div.* | *Wild/ cultivated* |
|---|---|---|---|
| *Corchorus capsularis* | + + + | Throughout | Cultivated |
| *Corchorus olitorius* | + + + | Throughout | Cultivated |
| *Hibiscus cannabinus* | + + + | Throughout | Cultivated |
| *Connabis sativa Wild* | + + + | Throughout | Wild |
| *Melochia corchorifolia* | + + + | Throughout | Wild |

## Wild Plants with Ornamental Value

| *Botanical Name* | *Frequency* | *Distribution in Kosi Div.* | *Wild/ cultivated* |
|---|---|---|---|
| *Celsia chinensis* | + + + | Throughout | Wild |
| *Centaurium centaurioides* | + + + | Throughout | Wild |
| *Exacum tetragenum* | + + + | Throughout | Wild |
| *Gnaphalium Luteo-alnum* | + + + | Throughout | Wild |
| *Hydrolea zeylanica* | + + + | Throughout | Wild |
| *Ludwigia abscendens* | + + + | Throughout | Wilu |
| *Melastoma malasathricurn* | + + + | Throughout | Wild |
| *Rosa involucrata* | + + + | Throughout | Wild |

*Source :* Sample Figure, 1986.

## Utilization and Management of Aquatic Plants

An aquatic weed management programme is based on certain principles. The foremost amongst these are the identification of the weed problem and estimation of the extent of damage incurred by the water body in question. The selection of the method of attack on aquatic weeds should be based on this information and the local economics and feasibilities. By and large, an integrated approach to weed control is to be preferred over individual aquatic weed control methods. Choosing the right time of employing each control measure depending upon the weed age, climate of the area and other factors. Any aquatic weed control plan should be flexible, capable of accommodating need-based changes in the strategy.

In fact, man has to live with the aquatic plants. Destruction of aquatic plants to improve the quality of water bodies is financially an uneconomic proposition particularly in North Bihar. In the U.S.A. there has been both extensive and intensive attempt to destroy the water hyacinth with herbicides and in Florida along with the annual expenditure in this programme has been 10 to 15 million dollars. But, in spite of all these efforts to destroy it, Florida still has 40,000 ha of water bodies covered with water hyacinth. Consequently, our attempt should be to harvest and utilize the aquatic plants, accepting themas nature's gift rather than curse (BRANCH, PAA; 1976, pp. 353-360).[3]

Several years of investigation has proved that aquatic plants, particularly water hyacinth can be utilized as cattle feed, base material for mushroom culture, biogas and fertilizer production and for making several items of handicrafts.

Removal of these plants, which contribute significant quantities of phosphorous and nitrogen, will lead to improving the water. It will also improve the asthetic quality of water bodies, facilitating boarding and swimming, and creating better shoreline sanitation. Development of new and more effective harvesting machines are needed and research is also called for to find out a commercial outlet for the harvested vegetation. Eutrophicated lakes produce large crops of fish which has to be harvested more intensively by commercial fishermen, if necessary, because the unharvested fish die and decompose, adding nutrients to the already over-rich environment.

Research funds have to be directed towards finding new methods of processing aquatic weeds into economic products that aquatic weeds may be purposefully harvested by manual or mechanical methods. Already certain aquatic weeds are converted, on small scale, into animal feed, manure, medicine, peasant crafts, paper pulp, etc. Use of aquatic weeds as an energy, resource, through their anacrobic decomposition, and as source of edible leaf proteins being developed. There are also some herbivorous fish like the grass carp, that can be made to graze aquatic weeds and fatten for human consumption. Use of aquatic weeds for pollution control including radioactive waste abatement, is another feasibility.

The current emphasis is on formulating a programme of relieving the sick water bodies of their weeds and finding commercial use for them in order to over come the present negative economics of harvesting aquatic weeds. This particularly is true of North Bihar which can still afford fantastic expenditure on herbicides in foreign exchange. With usually adequate manpower to harvest aquatic weeds, utilization of aquatic weeds is a method of their control. It should be given serious consideration. Government incentive to develop and practice, the utilization of aquatic weeds which will go a long way in controlling aquatic weeds cheaply and restoring our water bodies to their required use.

In parts of tropics and sub-tropics, in summer vegetation is found rarely on ground but it is abundant in water. A complete mat of water-hyacinth, has been found to produce 350-1700 tonne green vegetation, growing at a fantastic rate of 50/ha day (Westlake, D.F., 1963, pp. 385-425) . A standing crop of an emerged weed like — cattail, can yield up to 500 tonnes per ha of vegetation (Steward, K.K., 1970, pp. 34-35)[4].

## Utilization of Aquatic Plants

The harvested aquatic weeds may be utilized for industrial uses. Certain aquatic weeds are converted on a small scale into animal feeds manure, medicine, handicraft goods, paper pulp, etc. Aquatic weeds are utilised as source of energy after their anaerobic decomposition and their use as source of edible leaf proteins is being examined. Use of aquatic weeds for depollution including radio active factory wastes statement is another great possibility.

In fact, the current emphasis on formulating a programme of relieving the 'sick water bodies' of their weeds, and finding their commercial uses to away with the present negative economics of harvesting these.

**Utilization as Cattle Feeds**

Water-hyacinth can be used as cattle feed, but it cannot be directly consumed by the cattle. Consequently, ways and means have to be found out for making it acceptable to the cattle. Dried and powdered water-hyacinth can be used as a source of forage for broilers, ducks and pigs. Other aquatic weeds of varying fibre contents can also be used as feed for different kinds of animals. Although low fibre content is desirable, as in the case of submerged weeds, but high fibre content weeds like water-hyacinth and cattlaits can also be used as roughage fodder for the ruminants. Non-ruminants, like pigs can also be fed on high fibre weeds, after softening by boiling and mixing them with vegetable waste, rice bran, salt, etc. Aquatic weeds when dried contain 10-20 per cent crude protein, though the fresh water-hyacinth and the duck weed contain 25-35 per cent crude protein in their leaves. Most aquatic weeds are low in lysine, but in water-hyacinth the lysine content is adequate (Gupta, 1979, p. 71)[5]. Lack of sufficient information on the nutritive value of aquatic weeds creates a need for their systematic bio-testing and analysis as animal feed.

In the U.S.A. sophisticated solar drying of aquatic weeds is being developed. In energy rich countries like the U.S.A. and Canada, complete artificial drying of aquatic weeds, followed by its pelleting has been experimented with, but not much success has been achieved. Aquatic weeds from polluted water may harm animals that feed on them. The water-hyacinth growing in clean nutrient rich water have long petioles and is of low ash content. It makes better animal feed than the short petioted growth of water-hyacinth which commonly occurs, in polluted refuse water.

**Fish Feed**

Several edible fish and similar aquatic fauna are herbivorous. Making these animals to graze on aquatic weeds and fattening them for meat combines biological control and utilization of aquatic weeds. Tilapia, silver, dollar fish and the silver carp are a few important herbivorous fish which could be raised on aquatic weeds and plants. Besides carp, curry fish, ducks, geese, and swam could also be raised on aquatic plants.

## Bedding Material for Mushroom Culture

Dried and powdered water-hyacinth can replace the commonly used rice straw to grow tropical mushroom. The water hyacinth beddings are arranged in a mushroom compartment made out of bamboo.

## Soil Amendment and Culture Medla

Water-hyacinth is often used as potash rich (4.5% d.w.) manure and source of organic matter (3.5% f.w.) for cropped-yields by some farmers in North Bihar as also in other developing countries. Hyacinth compost is very good for this purpose, as well as for fertilizing flowerbeds and vegetable gardens. It is good for being put in low fertility fish ponds to induce planktonic growth (Mishra, 1976, pp. 103 -106)[6]. The use of several species of aquatic weeds as soil amendments deserves our attention. Only a few studies have been made on this subject. In Ceylon and India, water-hyacinth is turned into good compost. The bacterial concentrates to expedite serobic decomposition of chipped raw material have been developed, comprising three species of bacillius of aquatic weeds for use as soil conditioners has been attempted. However, high transportation cost of the fresh weeds to the drying and grinding factories has acted as a great impediment to its success.

## Source of Paper Pulp

The aquatic weeds utilized as a source of paper and rayon pulp is another possibility. For his purpose, we need aquatic weed species with high fibre strength, and a high drainage rate of moisture. A few species of aquatic weeds, especially reeds are used on a large scale to make printing paper and card-boards. The air-dry reed plant yields 60 per cent pulp. Reed paper forms a good insultating material.

The cattail pulp makes good and strong wrapping paper. Its fibre is very long like the jute fibre, and the yield is 30-40 per cent of the air dry plant weight. Cyperus papyrus is another aquatic weed that is used for making paper. Its large pith, although difficult to separate, can be used for making card boards. Other aquatic plants also need to be examined for their paper making specialities.

## Source of Protein and Carotene

Certain freshwater algae (*Chlore la sp*. Synthesis) are very rich in protein which accounts for 40-60 per cent of their body weight (d.w.). In China and Japan, these are consumed up to 50 *g*. per head each day. High amounts of algae food may cause gastro-intestinal disorders. The consumption of algae as food is also limited by its disagreeable flavour. Possibilities of extracting digestible protein and carotene from leaves of certain macrophytic aquatic vegetation are being explored (Pirie, 1970, pp. 20-22)[7]. This needs to be further developed, particularly for the protein deficient areas of the world, especially North Bihar.

## Supplement Food

Many aquatic plants grow in fresh water that bear either edible foliage, fruits and seeds of starch rich roots, rhizomes and tubers. These can be used to supplement food in many countries. Aquatic wild rice grains are harvested as food, particularly for people suffering from gastic trouble. But the wild rice grain takes longer time to cook. Aquatic wild rice (*Zigania aquatica*), known at 'Taro', 'Swamp' 'Taro' and arrow-head, is used as edible food in various forms. In Kashmir (India) and Indonesia, floating vegetable gardens are made with aquatic weeds in Dal and Wullar Wetlands.

## Biogas Production

Sufficient progress has been made in the U.S.A. in the use of water-hyacinth for biogas production (Casf Bow, 1967, pp. 243-244).[8]Anagobic methane-producing bacteria can convert water-hyacinth mass into 70 per cent methane and 30 per cent carbon dioxide. One of the most important advantages in using water-hyacinth for bio-gas production is that the mass does not require dewatering. On the other hand, the high moisture content is needed for its fermentation. The gas can be used for cooking, heating and as a source of power, water-hyacinth chopped into pieces and mixed with 1/10 fresh animal dung is kept for one week in a fermentation tank for biogas production. The remaining liquid sludge can be used as an organic fertilizer and soil condition. Research is still in progress to further concentrate the biogas in its CH3 content especially the plants found in wetlands.

**Pollution Abatement**

Some kind of aquatic plants are especially efficient in absorbing nutrients from water. These can be used for adecontrophying the effluent resulting from anerobic decomposition of raw sewage before it is let into pollute a fresh water body. Aquatic plants thus grown on the effluent can be used for making manure waste water from households, food preservation factories and even radio-thermal plants, can be purified by growing aquatic weeds. Common pollution abatement aquatic plant are water-hyacinth, common reed, bolrush, duckweeds, elodeahydrilla, cootail, etc. (Steward, 1970, pp. 34-35; Haller & Sutton, 1973, pp. 59-61)[9].

**Fertilizers**

The varieties of water-hyacinth and aquatic plants could be utilized as soil conditioners by directly incorporating the bio- mass into the soil, to be planted 1-2 months later. It can be used as a mulching material primarily to condition the temperature and soil moisture. A better method is the preparation of compost from water-hyacinth. This compost can be properly used for growing food, horticultural and industrial crops, e.g. maize, peanuts, orchids, clove, rubber, cacao, etc. The reeds, rushes, 'Cattails' and sedges can be used for peasant crafts, traditional boats, weavers spools, fishing rods, writing pens mouth pieces of musical instruments, roof thatching, crack fillers, insulators, floats, etc. cattail mats, coated with plastic resins, are very strong like fibre-glass. Some other important uses of water hyacinth are production of handicrafts like bags, carpets, vasel and decoration pieces. The water-hyacinth can also be used as a proper material to absorb pollutants from water, particularly N.P. and heavy metals, e.g. Ca, Cr, Ni, Hg, etc. However, its over-growth can create problems in water resource management, consequently efforts have to be made to utilize the plantation for beneficial uses, e.g. animal feed, bio-gas and fertilizers production, mushroom culture and manufacture of handicraft items.

It has been felt that a total annihilation of aquatic weeds and plants is almost impossible inspite of large sums spent over their eradication in some developed countries. Their over-growth can be curtailed by finding economic uses for the same wherever possible. Processing of aquatic weeds and plants into beneficial products will need the services of semi-skilled and skilled labour. Consequently, it has great employment possibilities especially in North Bihar.

Removal of aquatic weeds and plants at the one hand will lead to improvement in the quality of water-bodies and their planting in polluted water-bodies will absorb pollutants but they require great managerial skill and advance planning. Nonetheless the betterment of the human habitation and the environment greatly depend on the efficient and planned use of aquatic plants and weeds, their socio-economic impact are very many.

The wetlands of North Bihar are endowed with beautiful aquatic and water resources but lack of expertize and managerial skill has either led to their under-utilization and some times misuse or sevre wastage. The ponds and shallow lakes of these areas are used for cultivating water-chestnut, 'makhana' and some water lily which yield nominal returns only. Fish culture, in the area, is also of the traditional type. In Bangladesh, Assam, West-Bengal and the deltaic region of Orissa, cultivation of jute in shallow water lakes and depressions also brings a poor return to the farmers.

Consequently, the socio-economic impact of under-use or misuse or sevre wastage of the aquatic and water resources of these areas have resulted in perpetuating poverty which is large on the faces of their inhabitants. In contrast, the farmers of North Bihar have shown keen interest in the scientific management of their scarce water resources, resulting in their comparative affluence, which is a matter of envy for other countrymen.[11]

## Wetland Resources and Ecology

Considering the ecology of wetlands in North Bihar, the number of tanks and orchard in thousands could easily be correlated because according to a religious mythology, the rich people of the area generally plant mango orchard and favour digging of a tank and well in order to marry orchard with the tank or well. Orchards provide farmers varieties of food where as tanks provide water for irrigation, bathing and washing place for domestic animals.

This shows that in North Bihar the environmental situation could be well managed with the help of plantation of orchard and digging of tanks. The tanks are source of huge amount of inland fisheries in North Bihar, where as orchards are source of mango, Jack fruit, black berry, Mahuwa Kernal and varieties of items of economic importance.

**Table 7.2 :** Distribution of Tanks and Forests/Orchards in North Bihar (1991)

| *District* | *No. of Tanks* | *%* | *Orchards in 000 Ha* | *%* |
|---|---|---|---|---|
| 1. Saran | 197 | 2.31 | 8 | 3.55 |
| 2. Siwan | 139 | 1.63 | 5 | 2.22 |
| 3. Gopalganj | 115 | 1.35 | 5 | 2.22 |
| 4. East Chanparan | 331 | 3.88 | 9 | 4.00 |
| 5. West Champaran | 144 | 1.69 | 92 | 40.88 |
| 6. Muzaffarpur | 524 | 6.15 | 11 | 4.88 |
| 7. Vaishali | 196 | 2.39 | 6 | 2.67 |
| 8. Sitamarhi | 787 | 9.24 | 9 | 4.00 |
| 9. Darbhanga | 1435 | 16.86 | 9 | 4.00 |
| 10. Samastipur | 508 | 5.97 | 8 | 3.57 |
| 11. Madhubani | 2425 | 28.49 | 11 | 4.88 |
| 12. Begusarai | 73 | 0.85 | 2 | 0.88 |
| 13. Khagaria | 26 | 0.30 | 2 | 0.88 |
| 14. Bhagalpur | 15 | 0.17 | 1 | 0.46 |
| 15. Saharsa | 526 | 6.18 | 20 | 8.88 |
| 16. Purnea | 937 | 11.01 | 22 | 9.79 |
| 17. Katihar | 131 | 1.53 | 5 | 2.24 |
| Total | 8509 | 100% | 225 | 100% |

*Source :* District Census Handbook of Different District of North Bihar, 1991.

The items of economic value are fishes, snails, crabs, tortoise, prawns, snake-skin, frog, mothi, makhana, situa snail, medicinal plants, birds meat, etc. The people of the area are, engaged in collecting the wetlands resources because it offer agricultural produce. These are the only options for them to engage themselves in some gainful employment as most of the farmers and fishermen of the area are partially unemployed after agricultural operations (Table 7.3).

**Table 7.3 :** Production of various resources from Wetlands in North Bihar Production in M.T. (1991)

| *Sl. No.* | *Districts* | *Fishes* | *Snails* | *Crabs* | *Tortoise* |
|---|---|---|---|---|---|
| 1. | Saran | 4100 | 330 | 115 | 450 |
| 2. | Siwan | 3600 | 290 | 105 | 425 |
| 3. | Gopalganj | 3800 | 310 | 109 | 430 |
| 4. | East Champaran | 7500 | 490 | 125 | 705 |
| 5. | West Champaran | 6825 | 470 | 120 | 690 |
| 6. | Muzaffarpur | 12495 | 900 | 215 | 1100 |
| 7. | Vaishali | 2600 | 240 | 90 | 350 |
| 8. | Sitamarhi | 2800 | 250 | 95 | 360 |
| 9. | Darbhanga | 23000 | 1100 | 295 | 1650 |
| 10. | Samastipur | 3300 | 320 | 105 | 451 |
| 11. | Madhubani | 3100 | 295 | 102 | 405 |
| 12. | Begusarai | 3400 | 280 | 95 | 390' |
| 13. | Khagaria | 980 | 260 | 85 | 370 |
| 14. | Bhagalpur | 1025 | 90 | 35 | 130 |
| 15. | Saharsa | 4592 | 340 | 117 | 455 |
| 16. | Purnea | 6390 | 445 | 130 | 605 |
| 17. | Katihar | 2700 | 230 | 85 | 315 |
| 18. | Madhepura | 800 | — | — | — |

*Source :* Fisheries Department, Government of Bihar, Patna (1990- 91) and Estimates made by the author, 1991.

Table 7.3 (*Contd.*)

| *Prawns* | *Snake* | *Frogs* | *Mothi* | *Makhana* | *Situa Snells* | *Medicinal Plants* | *Birds Meat* | *Total* |
|---|---|---|---|---|---|---|---|---|
| 335 | 95 | 117 | 105 | 125 | 110 | 55 | 85 | 6022 |
| 305 | 90 | 110 | 100 | 115 | 107 | 53 | 80 | 5380 |
| 315 | 92 | 112 | 105 | 117 | 108 | 52 | 8 | 5631 |
| 495 | 97 | 130 | 120 | 135 | 122 | 60 | 90 | 10069 |
| 480 | 98 | 125 | 115 | 125 | 120 | 60 | 90 | 9323 |
| 915 | 170 | 205 | 195 | 205 | 205 | 102 | 150 | 16837 |
| 235 | 75 | 95 | 85 | 100 | 80 | 45 | 62 | 4057 |
| 260 | 77 | 97 | 90 | 95 | 82 | 41 | 65 | 4312 |
| 1200 | 190 | 270 | 205 | 220 | 275 | 145 | 205 | 28755 |
| 315 | 85 | 101 | 95 | 110 | 100 | 51 | 75 | 5108 |
| 285 | 75 | 100 | 92 | 105 | 95 | 45 | 65 | 4764 |
| 270 | 60 | 90 | 80 | 95 | 90 | 43 | 60 | 4953 |
| 255 | 70 | 80 | 75 | 85 | 85 | 40 | 55 | 2440 |
| 85 | 25 | 30 | 25 | 35 | 30 | 15 | 25 | 1550 |
| 345 | 95 | 105 | 95 | 105 | 100 | 52 | 75 | 6476 |
| 455 | 101 | 120 | 100 | 110 | 125 | 60 | 85 | 8726 |
| 235 | 70 | 75 | 65 | 75 | 65 | 32 | 40 | 3987 |
| — | — | 45 | — | — | — | — | 32 | 877 |

## The Management of Aquatic Plants

Many factors led to the menace of aquatic weeds as a problem. These may be (i) easy dispersal of weeds with a greatly invigorated transport system, (ii) increasing enrichment of natural water from farm run-off and city wastes, (iii) erosion and silting, and (iv) various other causes. Under tropical conditions, high temperature, eutrophication from fertilizer run-off and nutrients from human and agricultural wastes enhance aquatic plant growth in irrigation channels and reservoirs.

In North Bihar paddy farmers face disaster almost every year when rafts of water hyacinth float on to their paddy fields during floods. Several large fishery lakes have been rendered unproductive by aquatic weeds. As aquatic weeds spread, they disperse the water snail, e.g. Bellamva Javonica, that cause enchinostomiasist: they foster malaria, encephalitis and other mosquito-borne diseases, and schisto-somians — the Insidi, 1980's debilitating diseases prevalent especially in Saharsa and Purnea districts.

The serious negative implications of the presence of aquatic weeds are becoming more widely recognized, scientists, engineers and administrators have beginning to take action. Unfortunately, there is no simple way to reduce the aquatic weed infestations. Herbicides, mechanical devices, biological enemies of aquatic weeds, harnessing weeds for their economic utilization, and proper designing of water bodies, all must be used in a judiciously interwoven manner to tackle the problem of aquatic weed infestation.

In Africa, aquatic weeds are notorious chiefly for hindering smooth navigation. Even large ships are obstructed by the dense mats of floating weeds in the upper Nile river and lakes like Volta, Naviasha and Kariba. In the upper Nile, water-hyacinth is the most problematic weed while in lakes Naviasha and Kariba water-fern covers 10-25 per cent of their surface area. In Australia, algae blooms, water-hyacinth and water fern infest the water reservoirs. In Bangladesh and West Bengal, water-hyacinth is the chief aquatic weed, particularly devastating the paddy fields and fishery ponds. In Cambodia and Laos too, water-hyacinth is definitely a major weed, but reports on other aquatic weeds are wanting. In Indonesia, water-hyacinth is again the most-noxious aquatic weed, and in Philippines and Vietnam irrigation channels are plagued with water-hyacinth and water lettuce.

Lakes used for hydro-electric generation in Thailand but they are threatened with water-hyacinth, water fern and water lettuce. These weeds already cover 10 per cent of the surface area of the vast papong reservoir.

In the U.S.A., aquatic weeds are a menace, in the South-east where water-hyacinth, hydrilla and alligator weeds infest the lakes, flood control channels and rivers. Thus, they interfere with their navigational and recreational utilities. In Hawaii, aquatic weeds pose a great problem to the irrigation system of sugarcane plantations.

## NOTES

1. Mandal, R.B., *The Value of Wetlands in North-east India in Wetlands Archeology and Nature Conservation* (Ed.M.Cox *et.al*), HMSO, London, 1995, p.30
2. Sharma, U.P. and Munshi, J.S.D., *Ecology, Conservation and Management of Kabar Lake*; NEO Print, Calcutta, 1995;
3. Steward, K.K., Nutrient Removal Potentials of various aquatic plants. *J.C.* (2): pp. 24-35.
4. Joklik, O.F., Preparation of an Organic Biofertilizer from agricultural waste and weeds Residue, UNIDO Report, 1976.
5. Gupta, O.P., *Aquatic Weeds : Their Menace and Controls*. Today and Tommorow, Printers and Publishers, New Delhi, 1979, p.71.
6. Mishra, R, Seasonal Dynamics and Aquatic Weeds of the Lowlying Lands of the Mid-Ganga Plains in South-East Asia, in (Ed.) W.Clunk, *The Hague*, 1970, pp.103-106.
7. Kig.G. Ann., *Geomorphoology for Geogrphers*, London, 1962.
8. Fish Rev, 30, 1963.
9. Cash Bow, A.J., *Convert water-hyacinth to methane*, Pans C-13-2, 1967, pp. 34-244.
10. Frank, P.A., Distribution and utilization research on tropical and sub-tropical aquatic weeds, W. Junk B.V. Publishers, *The Hague*, 1976, pp. 353-360.
11. *Fish Rev.* 30(15-18) 1968, PE.

# 8

# THE VALUE OF WETLANDS

## Introduction

Wetlands are submerged areas of water bodies which include both natural and artificial, permanent or temporary, static or flowing; fresh, brackish, saltish lake, ditches and shallow marine for the major portion of the year.

The value of wetland is immense in order to safeguard our environment and maintain ecological balance. It may not be proper to leave out marshy lands, waterlogged areas, tals and ponds uncared as they have a great potentiality to produce many items which have great utility for human being besides resource generation. The wetlands are also pollution filters along with beautifying the environment, attracting more rainfall and provide living abode for many species of birds, fishes, insects and plants which have very high medicinal value in our day to day life.

Wetlands are among the most productive and most threatened ecosystem. On marshes, swamps and flood plains, the great civilizations of Chechar, Ganga valley, Egypt, Mesopotamia and Indo-China have flourished which continue to support rural and urban communities throughout the world.[1] All these are in jeopardy by drainage reclamation and used as dumping ground of refuse water. Some of the wetlands have been damaged and destroyed in search for short term profit. Many have already been lost their existence.

Most of the wetlands are natures gift at a place which is neglected but most of them are endowed with an environment of scenic beauty. Since long human being have not cared about wetlands as they are treated as marginal lands. But with the recent spurt of population in most countries of the world the wetlands need special attention for the imancipation of people from economic ills. This could be possible as the shallow wetlands are productive areas in terms of fishes, makhana, mothi and varieties of medicinal plants. Wetlands are areas where the pollutants get precipitated on the ground. Wetlands are the source of oxygen supply, develop places of scenic beauty and they are the habitat for local as well as migratory birds. Wetlands serve as suitable niche for fish and aquatic animals, breeding and nursery ground for water fowls and as filter for sediments and other pollutants. Most countries are loosing the wetlands rapidly due to biotic interference and anthropogenic pressure[2].

Considering the value of wetlands, measures have been initiated for their conservation and management. It is essential to educate people regarding the need for the conservation of wetland as well as their economic utility besides the commencement of scientific and application oriented research on their productivity.

## Dimensions of Wetland Development

Wetlands located in the marginal areas of human interactions of tourism, fishing and creating ecological balance between man and the biosphere. Wetland is an area where the availability of varieties of fishes, birds and medicinal plants could be acquired from shallow and deep waters. Wetlands act as the highway, beautification of environment, source of irrigation, recreation, bridging the gap of protein supply and increasing the selectivity of man in different types of resources (Fig. 8.1)

## Origin and Evolution of Wetland

Wetlands are remnants of the Gangetic trough or the Indo-Brahm river formed in course of the rise of Himalayas in three successive periods of Eocene, Miocene and Pliocene. At the end of pleistocene period when deglaciation had taken place in the entire northern

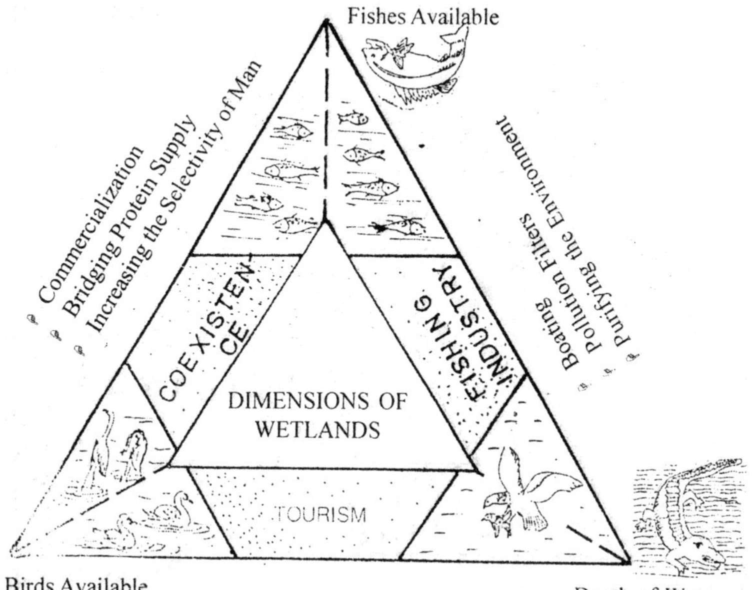


**Fig. 8.1 :** Dimensions of Wetlands

hemisphere, a vast amount of sand and silt have been deposited by the Himalayan rivers in North Bihar. Since then due to annual flooding both severe and occasional by the south flowing rivers the Gangetic trough gets filled, in the form of plain land of North Bihar (Fig. 8.2). The rivers coming to this plain from the Himalayas in the north are the Gandak, the Burhi-Gandak, the Ghaghara, the Balan, the Lakhandei the Kareh, the Kamla, the Bhutahi Balan, the Jibachh, the Bagmati, the Kosi, the Panar and the Mahananda. These rivers deposit sand and silt, bring destructive floods, and enhance the process of alluviation and deluviation in the wetlands of North Bihar plain.

Recently, with minute observation it has been found that even in wetland areas some high mounds are found here and there due to Neotectonic Earth movement going on in the sub-stratum of North

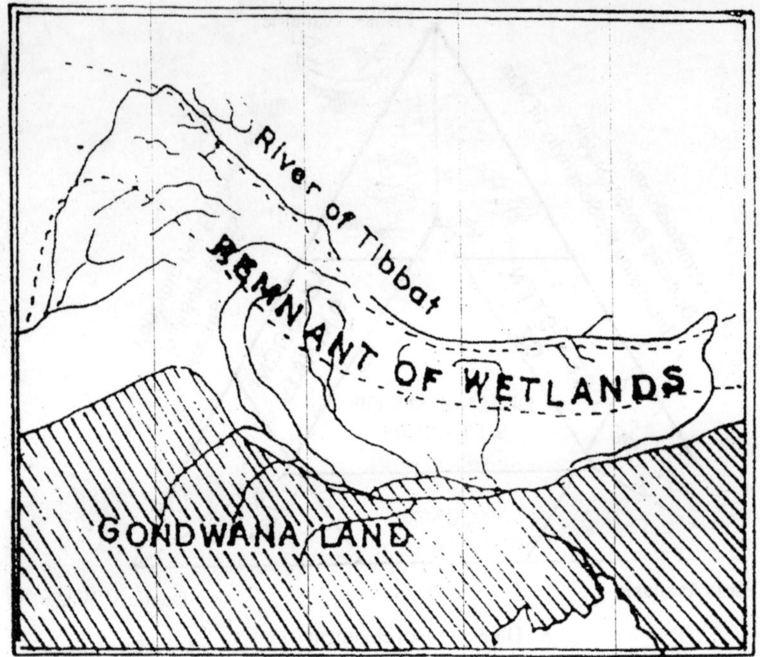


**Fig. 8.2 :** North Bihar : Origin and Evolution of Wetland in the Division of Darbhanga

Bihar. This is also a factor responsible for the formation of wetlands in North Bihar.

## The Concept of Wetland

Wetland has been applied to a broad range of shallow water, periodically flooded and wetland environment with special functions and values. These shallow water (surface or ground) system are characterized by certain type of vegetation adapted to periodic flooding or saturation and soils that reflect anaerobic conditions. Wetland functions very but include water reservoir and transport attenuation, pollution control, sediment control, food chain support, groundwater replenishment, habitat for waterfowl, fish and many rare and endangered species.

A variety of more specific terms, such as marsh, bog, fen,

mudflat, slough and swamp have been used to characterise wetlands with various frequencies, depths, and velocities of wetness and various types of vegetation and soils. Several years ago, Dan Willard of Indiana University collected more than 50 different wetland definitions. This abundance of wetland definitions has been offered as proof that the definition of wetlands is a policy question that should be decided by politicians and administratore rather than by scientists[3].

## Objectives of Study

This chapter intends to highlight the economic, cultural and ecological values of wetlands in North Bihar. Recently, with the rapid increase

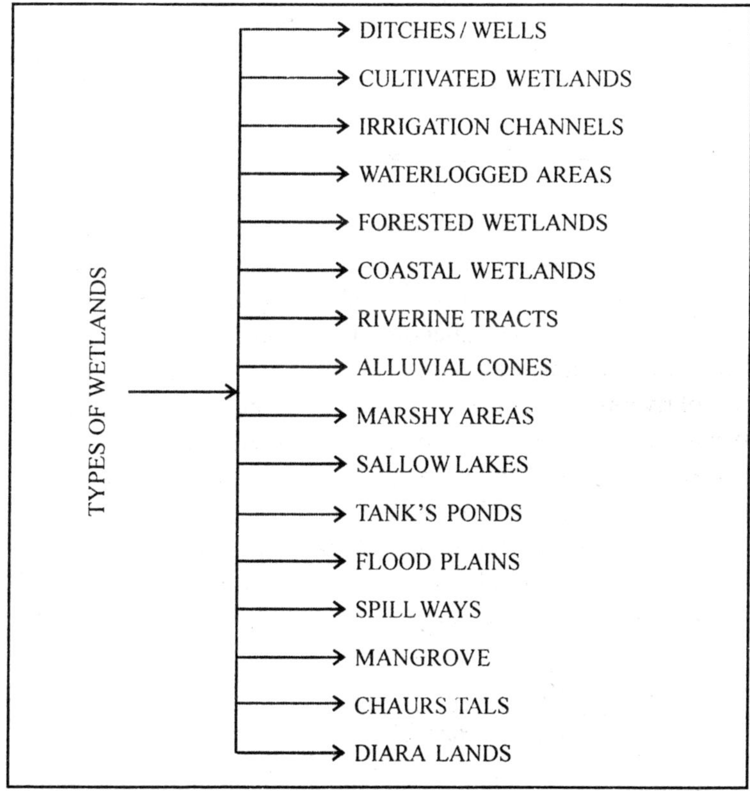


**Fig. 8.3 :** Types of Wetlands

of population, and reckless cutting of forests the formation of wetlands is limited. This chapter will also show how the marshy and waterlogged areas can be utilized in a better way in order to have sound ecological balance and environmental adjustment with various parameters of economic development. Even marginal lands like marshy land.

Waterlogged areas produce a vast amount of fish, singahara, Makhana, Mothi, Purain-leaves, Lotus flower and Jalkumbhi which contains a high amount of nitrogen and is highly suitable for nitrogen fixation in the soil.

## Sources of Data

Data has been collected from census Handbook of various districts of North Bihar besides published literature collected from various sources about wetlands.

## The Determinats of Wetlands

Wetlands can be divided into many types based on the conditions of water availability on the ground, namely — manmade ditches, *chaurs* (temporary waterlogged area of a wider dimension), *tals* (Permanent waterlogged area of a smaller dimension) cultivated rice fields, Jute lands, alluvial fans, waterlogged areas, *diara land* (sand bars in the side of rivers) , shallow lakes, coastal tracts, delta, menaqrove areas, swampy ground, forested wetlands of tera zone, riverine tracts, flood plains, irrigation channels, pond and spill ways of diara lands or riverine coastal tracts (Fig. 8.3).

The intensity of wetlands could be determined on the basis of following formula which has been devised by R. B. Mandal (1991) in course of the present study.

$$IW = \sqrt{A \times \frac{TW}{RF} + \frac{DNL}{LEP} + .. + N}$$

Where,

IW = Index of wetland,

A = Total area.
TW = Total wetland.
RF = Total Destruction of Natural Lakes
LEP = Level of Environmental Pollution.

$$= \sqrt{10 \times \frac{500}{1500} \times \frac{30}{20} + +N}$$

$$= \sqrt{3.33 + 1.50}$$

$$= \sqrt{4.83}$$

$$= 2.19 \text{ (I.W.)}$$

## Research Design

In this chapter it has been tried to search the problems in hand for most of the bigger wetlands which have an areas of upto 25 hectares in North Bihar following the stratified random sampling in the selection of wetlands. The sample study of the bigger wetlands namely Kabartal, Gogabeel, Simri Chaur, Kusheshwar Asthan Chaur and Tal Baraila of Vaishali would be considered for detail analysis.

## Investigating Wetlands

| Area Factor and Soil Analysis on sample basis | Collection of Maps | Collection of Data and Survey | Map Making and Cartographic work | Collection or photographs | Analysis of Toposheet, Satellite Imageries | Final Analysis of the problem |
|---|---|---|---|---|---|---|

## Location and Stages of Wetlands

In North Bihar most of the wetlands are located in lowlying areas in comparison with local topographic features besides the areas of annual flooding where the deposition of sand during floods are the common feature. The North Bihar was primarily known as *Tethys* sea prior to the upheaval of Himalayas during Eocene, Miocene and Pliocene periods about 10 to 5 crore years ago. The remaining part of *Tethys* sea become a vast wetlands known as Indo-Gangetic trough. But slowly and slowly the vast amount of detritous annully comes to North Bihar and fill the Indo-Gangetic plain. This process of formation and filling of wetlands is a common feature in North Bihar giving rise to multistage of wetlands. For example, in 1700 AD around Motihari there were 42 lakes but at present most of them have filled up except 3 and we call them the wetlands of second category because the first stage of wetlands may be the chaurs or bigger dimension lowlying riverine basin. The third stage of wetlands may be the present oxbow lakes such as the Gogabeel of Katihar district on Kankhar river and the oxbow lake of Gandak river in Vaishali district. The fourth stage wetlands may be regarded as rivers and places of sheet wash erosion near the Butahibalan, the Kosi, the Kareh, the Gandak, the Lakhandei, the Dhaus, and the Narayani rivers of North Bihar.

The fifth stage wetlands are man made tanks and ponds which are transitory physical features because without re-excavation their life cannot be regarded more than 20 to 25 years at one place. With the increasing downward slope in plain land especially in the flood plains near the rivers the chances of the location and occurring of wetlands is greater in comparison with upland plains. This clearly signifies that in river basins the wetland has better locational condition than uplands but some times the location of wetlands in mountainous areas are closely associated with valleys and structural basins. Sometimes cut its meandering band of its course as oxbow lakes and this feature favours the formation of a chain of wetlands throughout its basin whether the river is the Ganges, the Kareh, the Kosi, the Mahananda, the Kamla, the Balan, the Bhuthi Balan, the Gibachh, the Lakhandei, the Budhi Gandak and the Narayani.

As per Table 8.1 wetlands have been formed due to physical factors and cultural factors, e.g. shallow river beds, lakes and swampy areas are wetlands made by nature whereas tanks, canals, ditches and most are the outcome of human activities. All these are known as wetlands which have close affiliation with the human being but the waterlogged areas with varied dimensions are really

**Table 8.1** : List of Wetlands in Bihar

| *Sr. No.* | *District* | *Wetland* | *Village/Town* | *Latitude (N)* | *Longitude* | *Area in ha.* | *Ecological Condition* |
|---|---|---|---|---|---|---|---|
| 1. | Begusarai | Kanwar Lake | Majhaul | 25°30′ | 87°40′ | 7000 | Freshwater |
| 2. | Chaibasa | Roro Lake | — | 22°34′ | 85°34′ | 240 | Freshwater |
| 3. | Champaran (East) | Kasaria Chaur | Motihari | 25°45′ | 85°00′ | 500 | Freshwater |
| 4. | Champaran (West) | Khetar | Sarotar | 26°45′ | 84°45′ | 350 | Freshwater |
| 5. | Champaran (West) | Chatia Chaur | Pipara Pakaria | N.A. | N.A. | 100 | Freshwater |
| 6. | Champaran (West) | Manshi Dubey Chaur | Phulia Khar | N.A. | N.A. | 125 | Freshwater |
| 7. | Darbhanga | Khara, Dhuseshwar, Kanail, Arai, Anismigia Chaura | Darbhanga | 26°10′ | 85°54′ | 12,141 | Freshwater |
| 8. | Dhanbad | Top Chanchi | Dhanbad | 23°50′ to 23°56′ | 86°06′ to 23°56′ | 12,823 | Freshwater |
| 9. | Katihar | Goga-Beel | Ausdabad | 25°30′ | 88°10′ | 150 | Freshwater |
| | | Koshan Jalkar | Manihari | 23°56′ | 88°0′ | 100 | Freshwater |
| 10. | Muzaffarpur | Bharthua Chaur | Bhathua | 26°15′ | 85°30′ | 125 | Freshwater |
| 11. | Muzaffarpur | Bhusara Mann | Bhusara | 26°08′ | 85°30′ | 125 | Freshwater |
| 12. | Muzaffarpur | Brahampura | Muzaffarpur | 26°05′ | 85°22′ | 130 | Freshwater |
| 13. | Muzaffarpur | Tal Baraila | Mahnar | 26°35′ | 85°25′ | 300 | Freshwater |
| 14. | Palamau | Kanhar Bandh | Baradih | 24°20′ | 83°40′ | 5000 | Freshwater |

*Table 8.1 (Contd.)*

| *Sr. No.* | *District* | *Wetland* | *Village/Town* | *Latitude (N)* | *Longitude* | *Area in ha.* | *Ecological Condition* |
|---|---|---|---|---|---|---|---|
| 15. | Rohtas | Kaimur Sanctuary | Sasaram | 24°03′ to 25°00′ | 85°00′ 85°25′ | 1,34,222 | Freshwater |
| 16. | Saharsa | Bhagwa Chaur | Balua Bazar | 26°20′ | 85°25′ | 200 | Freshwater |
| 17. | Saharsa | Bora Chaur | Kharka Talwa | 25°50′ | 86°30′ | 500 | Freshwater |
| 18. | Saharsa | Ekpira Dhar | ishanpur | 25°25′ | 85°50′ | 200 | Freshwater |
| 19. | Saharsa | Kauda Lauhr & Bangoon Tachar | Kauda Lauhar | 25°50′ | 86°25′ | 200 | Brakishwater |
| 20. | Saharsa | Murdapur Chapur | Murdapur | 25°45′ | 86°00′ | 125 | Brakishwaster |
| 21. | Saharsa | Parbamurli Chaur | Kumar Ganj | 25°45′ | 86°45′ | 100 | Brakishwaster |
| 22. | Saharsa | Ratanpura Phulkaha Chaur | Kumar Ganj | 25°45′ | 87°00′ | 100 | Brakishwaster |
| 23. | Saran | Hardia Chaur | Ailpur | 25°45′ | 85°00′ | 10,000 | Brakishwaster |
| 24. | Vaishali | Ahiya | Ronna | 25°55′ | 85°10′ | 150 | Freshwater |
| 25. | Vaishali | Raghupur Diara | Hazipur | 25°30′ | 85°20′ | 2,000 | Freshwater |
| 26. | Vaishali | Fatehpur, Naimallia & Paintia Chaurs | Hazipur | 25°40′ to 25°50′ | 85°10′ to 85°40′ | 11,400 | Freshwater |
| 27. | West Champaran | Udaipur Lae | — | 25°50′ to | 84°30′ | 657 | Freshwaterh |

*Source* : Fishery Department, Government of Bihar, Patna, 1991.

problematic as in all these the ecological conditions are not favourable for crop production and human living. Table 8.2 represents the list of oxbow - lakes and marshy ground in the form of wetlands in North Bihar.

1. Total Geographical Area : 1, 73, 877 sq. km[3]
2. Wetland Area
   A. Natural Wetlands (Bakes, Bog, Marshes, Mangroves, etc.) : 2, 24, 788 ha.
   B. Man made Wetlands (Tanks, Reservoirs etc.) : 48, 607 ha.

At present in the state of Bihar all the above wetlands are considered as marginal areas filled with water in different forms. But their modalities are quite different from one another due to variations in rain and other environmental conditions found in different parts of North Bihar are quite different from one another.

**Table 8.2 :** General Conditions of Wetlands in North Bihar

| *Sl. No.* | *Type of wetland* | *Area in km²* | *Percentage* |
|---|---|---|---|
| 1. | Ditches | 65,987 | 25.80 |
| 2. | Tank | 57,459 | 22.48 |
| 3. | Canal | 5,592 | 2.10 |
| 4. | Rivers | 3,772 | 1.50 |
| 5. | Oxbow Lake | 122,225 | 47.83 |
| 6. | Moat | 5,000 | 1.36 |
| 7. | Swampy Areas | 25,000 | 6.83 |
| 8. | Chaurs | 100,500 | 27.49 |
| | Total | 365,535 | 100 |

*Source :* Fishery Department, Government of Bihar, Patna, 1991.

Wetlands are numerously found in almost all districts of North Bihar. But it is prolific in Saharsa, Purnea, Katihar, Begusarai, Madhubani, Sitamarhi, Vaishali districts of North Bihar.

## Wetlands in Saharsa and Purnea

In Saharsa, Supaul, Udakishanganj and Banmankhi drainage division there are several *chaurs* which have an areal extent of 400 to 4000 hectares. In Supaul water drainage division Kusumi-Karjhail Balan Chaur 1350 hectares, Chainpur Bhagwanpur 800 hectares, Bhagwanpur Bochaha 700 hectares, Hasanpur Sonbarsa 600 hectare, Gopalpur-Musharhia 600 hectares and Sadanandpur Kalyanpur 500 hectares to name a few. There are 65 chaurs (Wetland) in Saharsa out of which Barsam, Hanumannagar - Kothaila, Lao, Dasin, Bhon-Goriahi and Dhahali Chaur have an area of 400 to 4200 hectares each.

In Udakishanganj drainage division, the bigger *chaurs* (wetland) are Lasma-Baghauna, Bela, Ramnagar, Tilhar, Mahmudin Topra and Baghangama. In Banmankhi drainage division the bigger chaurs are Bhawanipur, Dhima-Makhana, Haripur-Aurahi-Laukhi, Jankinagar-Ekraha-Rikabganj, Lakshmipur, Askaties Tilangawa and Dhanesar. Out of these wetlands Dhima-Makhnaha of Banmankhi is the biggest as it has an area of 4000 hectares.

## Wetlands in Champaran

Wetlands are chiefly confined to the riparian tracks of the Gandak and Burhi Gandak rivers specially in their lower reaches. One-third of the waterlogged areas are found in the six Gandak riparian anchals viz. Madhubani, Thakrahan, Baina, Nautan, Gobindganj and Kesaria which spread in a ribbon pattern. On the other hand, one-fifth of it occurs in another six *anchals* viz. Sugauli, Turkaulia, Motihari, Chiraiya, Harsidhi and Patehi — These two combined together account for 5.56 per cent of the total area of the plain. Wetland areas are not found in the Terai and Anchals of Kalyanpur and Mehsi. Good conditions of drainage underlie such a situation. As much as 23.42 per cent in Sikta and 17.48 per cent of Raxual is reportedly permanently waterlogged. The famous marshes of Tappas Bahas and Balthar are situated in these anchals. The vast areas of wetland formed due to seismic subsidence occurred in 1934. West and east of Bettiah town Sarea Man and Amua Man are very famous wetlands located. The wetland areas falling under different river systems are as follows.

**Table 8.3 :** Excessively Waterlogged Areas of Champaran Districts

| *Sl. No.* | *Wetland Areas* | *Permanently Submerged Land in Hectere* |
|---|---|---|
| 1. | Harha | 284.90 |
| 2. | Chandrawat | 2260.22 |
| 3. | Utter Bahini | 77.70 |
| 4. | Dhanauti | 4144.07 |
| 5. | Mekhawa | 3569.40 |
| 6. | Konbara | 484.42 |
| | Total Land | 10820.71 (1.29% the Total) |

*Source :* Gandak Command Area Development Authority, Muzaffarpur, p. 6.

The Table 8.3 clearly shows that Dhanauti and Mekhawa riparian tracts are worst-hit by waterlogging. Together they account for 59.17 per cent and 63 per cent of the inundated areas in Kharif and Rabi seasons respectively. Waterlogging damages the standing Kharif crops, delays the sowing of Rabi, marsh the prospect of double cropping and makes the harvest of Kharif paddy costly.

## The Value of Wetlands

The economic value of wetlands are diverse including the production of mothi, makhana, purain leaves and Jalkumbi, by checking environmental pollution wetlands beautify the environment, maintain ecological balance, provide places for human and cattle bathing, serve as foci of towns and as places of ritual performance.

## The Economic Value of Wetlands

Some caution is, however, needed in rank-ordering of different wetlands. This exercise should, in principle, be based on a full appreciation of the total economic value of wetlands. While measurement and valuation of wetland expressed in terms of environmental commodities and amenities of direct benefit to human being have been undertaken, indirect use value has remained difficult to quantify. Not enough is known about wetland functions such as, life-support and pollution assimilation. Equally, the non-use value of wetlands has not been quantified, but environmental resources suggest that their existence values are positive and significant. It can, therefore, be argued that all the remaining wetlands stock ought to be protected, even though not all individual wetlands are considered to be uniformly valuable for the present.[4]

**Table 8.4 :** Location and Threats to Wetland Resources in North Bihar

| | | |
|---|---|---|
| 1. | Flood Plains | Interference with hydrology, dams; river walls; rehabilitation of flood plains. |
| 2. | Rivers and Lakes | Land reclamation; pollution; industrial development; abstraction of water for irrigation; reduction of aquaifer supply and surface waterflow; recreation pressure; hunting activities. |
| 3. | Wet meadows (Grasslands) | Drainage schemes (On-and off-site). |
| 4. | Terai lands | Drainage schemes and agricultural reclamation; resource extraction (energy and non-energy); forestry. |

Table 8.4 lists a number of threats to the main wetland types. In terms of market failure there is evidence in the wetlands as there is a lack of incentive to the disclosure of information on wetlands. Clearly, the use and non-use value of wetlands is not widely known. In some cases, the precise location and extent of wetlands are not known to public agencies or owners who may be unaware of management programmes that are officially available.[5]

Externalities are also relevant to wetlands. They have suffered external cost damage due to pollution generated by agricultural and industrial activities located outside the wetland boundaries. The economic value of wetland has been summarised in Fig 8.4 and the corresponding chart.

— Bhent, Lotus, Kumudii, Production of Mothi, Makhana and Singarhara

**Fig. 8.4 :** The Concept of Wetland

— Varieties of Fish catch
— Water Reservoir as Fund Resource
— Flow Resource
— Irrigational value
— Herb Farming
— Washermen's work Place.
— Source of salt
— Navigation / Transport
— Ports and Harbours
— Promote Boat Making
— Ferry Point
— Source of Drinking Water
— Hunting Place of Birds
— Promote Farming of Parwal and Watermelon on Sandy Diara.
— Source of Purain leaves
— Source of Organic Nutrients to the Fields.
— Crabs, snails, shells
— Promote Tourism.
— Favours Regional Economic Development
— Medicinal value of water
— Source of employment to Fishermen and Cultivators.

For Wetlands that yield recreation opportunities, there is the danger that utilisation levels will result in congestion and subsequent decline in resource quality, as the wetlands carrying capacity is exceeded.

The development of wetlands can in a number of circumstances involve the irreversible loss of wetland preservation/conservation value. It may be that wetlands option value is a significant factor for many people and this would be lost in the presence of irreversibility. The desie to keep one's options on possible use of the wetland open will be partly individual, but may also involve bequest motivations towards one's children or future generation. Individual may also place existence value on wetlands, i.e. the knowledge that the stock of wetlands will continue to be conserved, even though no individual current or future use is anticipated, may itself generate utility. The in-filling of wetlands may represent permanent removal and therefore a denial of opportunity for future generations to benefit from them (i.e. a failure to met the intergenerational efficiency objective).

Because of the general absence of integrated resource management policies, inter-sectoral policy inconsistency frequently occurs and results in intervention failure.

The interface between agricultural development policy and wetland conservation is an appropriate context in which to analyse such intervention failure. Examples can be drawn from North Bihar. (e.g. Saline soil marshes in the Kosi river basin of Saharsa and Purnea) and from North America (e.g. northern prairie pot-holes and southern bottom-land forested wetlands).[6] In all these cases, high-value wetlands have suffered considerable losses due to conversion to intensive agriculture. The agricultural conversion processes have been artificially stimulated by a range of subsidies, price guarantees and tax incentives given to farmers.

In this way, it could be said that the economic value of wetlands are very many and on any cost it should be saved from dwindling.

## Ecological Value of Wetlands

In order to maintain ecological balance the chief aim is to analyse, classify and to map the various types of wetlands in their correct position and examine the mutual relationship for assessing their physical properties and economic potentialities in relation to wetlands.

(a) North Bihar is an alluvial plain. Most of the diversities seen oil the surface are those due to river action and a series of raised riverside uplands known as levees, dotted with wetlands in the form of alternating depressions (chaurs) of streams (Fig. 8.5).

(b) A Sub-Terai belt of marshy land in the north with intervening tracts of uplands along rivers is succeeded in the south by a wide belt of marshy lowlands, characterised by permentnt depressions and lakes besides Lanks which are manmade features of wetlands.

(c) In the riparian tracts of the Ganges the land is high due to which wetlands are found slight away from levee in the form of intervening depressions. Due to the presence of

**Table 8.5 :** Production of various resources from Wetlands in North Bihar

*Production in M.T. (1991)*

| Sl. No. | Districts | Fishes | Snails | Crabs | Tortoise | Prawns | Snake | Frogs | Mothi | Makhana | Situasnells | Medicinal Plant | Birds Meat | Total |
|---|---|---|---|---|---|---|---|---|---|---|---|---|---|---|
| 1. | Chhapra | 4100 | 330 | 115 | 450 | 335 | 95 | 117 | 105 | 125 | 110 | 55 | 85 | 6022 |
| 2. | Siwan | 3600 | 290 | 105 | 425 | 305 | 90 | 110 | 100 | 115 | 107 | 53 | 80 | 5380 |
| 3. | Gopalganj | 3800 | 310 | 109 | 430 | 315 | 92 | 112 | 105 | 117 | 108 | 52 | 81 | 5631 |
| 4. | East Champaran | 7500 | 490 | 125 | 705 | 495 | 97 | 130 | 120 | 135 | 122 | 60 | 90 | 10069 |
| 5. | West Champaran | 6825 | 470 | 120 | 690 | 480 | 98 | 125 | 115 | 125 | 120 | 60 | 95 | 9323 |
| 6. | Muzaffarpur | 12495 | 900 | 215 | 1100 | 915 | 170 | 205 | 195 | 205 | 205 | 102 | 150 | 16837 |
| 7. | Vaishali | 2600 | 240 | 90 | 350 | 235 | 75 | 95 | 85 | 100 | 80 | 45 | 62 | 4057 |
| 8. | Sitarnarhi | 2800 | 250 | 95 | 360 | 260 | 77 | 97 | 90 | 95 | 82 | 41 | 65 | 4312 |
| 9. | Darbhanga | 23000 | 1100 | 295 | 1650 | 1200 | 190 | 270 | 205 | 220 | 275 | 145 | 205 | 28755 |
| 10. | Samastipur | 3300 | 320 | 105 | 451 | 315 | 85 | 101 | 95 | 110 | 100 | 51 | 75 | 5108 |
| 11. | Madhubani | 3100 | 295 | 102 | 405 | 285 | 75 | 100 | 92 | 105 | 95 | 45 | 65 | 4764 |
| 12. | Begusarai | 3400 | 280 | 95 | 390 | 270 | 60 | 90 | 80 | 95 | 90 | 43 | 60 | 4953 |
| 13. | Khagaria | 980 | 260 | 85 | 370 | 255 | 70 | 80 | 75 | 85 | 85 | 40 | 55 | 2440 |
| 14. | Bhagalpur | 1025 | 90 | 35 | 130 | 85 | 25 | 30 | 25 | 35 | 30 | 15 | 25 | 1550 |
| 15. | Saharsa | 4592 | 340 | 117 | 455 | 345 | 95 | 105 | 95 | 105 | 100 | 52 | 75 | 6476 |
| 16. | Purnea | 6390 | 445 | 130 | 605 | 455 | 101 | 120 | 100 | 110 | 125 | 60 | 85 | 8726 |
| 17. | Katihar | 2700 | 230 | 85 | 315 | 235 | 70 | 75 | 65 | 75 | 65 | 32 | 40 | 3987 |
| 18. | Madhepura | 800 | — | — | — | — | — | 45 | — | — | — | — | 32 | 877 |

*Source* : Fisheries Department, Government of Bihar, Patna (1990-91) and Estimates made by the author, 1991.

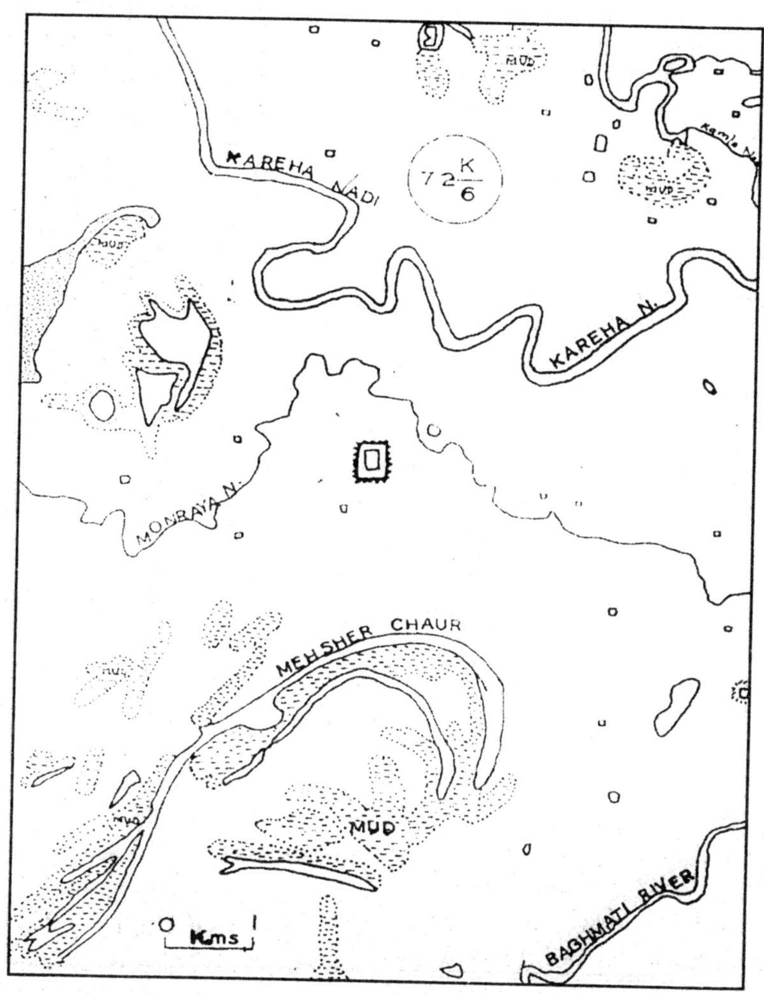


**Fig. 8.5 :** Meandering Courses of the Kareha River

natural levee on the northern bank of the Ganges, all rivers flowing along the gravity of slope from north to South turn towards east and run parallel along the Ganges river for a few kilometres before they finally make confluence.

The conservation of wetlands focuses attention on the ecological disturbance caused by the impoundment of waters in dams and reservoirs. The ecological effects of water impoundment have been summarized and certain measures for the conservation of fish, flora, vertebrate and invertebrate fauna in the affected areas have been suggested.

The development of Kawar lake Goga Beel as Birds sanctuary in order to diffuse the tourist flow to Nainital, thereby preventing heavy traffic and increased water consumption both of which lead to ecological imbalances. The major factors responsible for the depletion of the rich fish wealth of the rivers of Ganges, namely over exploitation and pollution should be stopped. The declining management and balanced exploitation of the resource on the basis of sound ecological principles.

The dangers to the sensitive ecosystem of the beautiful flowering valley of the Gandak near Balmikinagar posed by the tourist boon resulting from mechanization of road system and adhoc planning may be considered although the area is infested with criminals. They plead that the valley should be declared restricted area till the time of effective measures for its protection could be planned and enforced.

**Oxbow Lakes and Bayons**

As meanders grow, it frequently happens that a narrow neck of land is cut through from two sides thus allowing the stream to straighten its course. The two ends of the meander so separated from the channel, are likely to be filled up by sand. Presents, the best example of an oxbow lake on the bank of river Burhi-Gandak in Vaishali district. These water bodies form excellent settlement sites. The whole face of the country is dotted with rural settlements besides small oxbow lakes or elongated water bodies and chaurs (long semi-circular marshes) which lie in between the rivers making the old abandoned courses of the streams. Though found extensively in all parts of this region, the abandoned courses are more prolific in Madhubani, Sitamarhi and Begusarai districts of North Bihar. Hardia Chaur in Chhapra district extends up to nearly 32 kilometers along the Gandak river embankment and has a breadth of 3 to 8 kilometers.

## Marshes

The abandoned channel of a stream on a flood plain may become partially filled with vegetation, thus forming a marsh. They may also occur in any depression on the flood plains especially in areas of waterlogging. Marshes are numerous towards the south-eastern part of North Bihar.

## List of Ecological Factors

— Disfavour Desertification
— Dumping Ground of Industrial and Urban Wastes
— Breeding Ground of Mosquitoe and Ducks.
— Abode of Migratory Birds
— Arrangement of Birds Binding station
— Increases Hunting spot of Birds
— Haven of Insects and Pests
— Keeps water level of the surrounding Area High
— Favours Waterlogging and Humid Climatic Conditions
— Favours luxurious Growth of Vegetation.
— Maintain Ecological Balance.
— Saviours of Flora and Fauna Wealth

Some of these marshy lands dry up during the summer season. There are some marshes which exists throughout the year like a tank (man made; square shapped wetland). Marshes are also found in the beds of rivers like the Mahananda, the Panar, the Kosi, the old Kosi, the Bhutahi-Balan, the Kamla, the Jibachh, the Kareh, the Burhi Gandak, and during hot weather season but during rainy months the river establishes its normal course. The marshes are utilised by the peasants for irrigation, rearing fish, for growing mothi and makhana and for washing animals in the summer season. Settlements in the marshy areas are of dispersed type.

The ecological value of wetland has been summarised in a Table 8.5. But it is quite unfortunate that during the recent furry of floods many wetlands of North Bihar suffer from sedimentation and some of them have completely lossed their existence especially in Manigachhi Anchal of Darbhanga district.

**Cultural Value of Wetlands**

The cultural value of wetlands include religious performance along its shores, recreation by navigation, craddle land for civilizations, cremation ground for dead bodies and provide beautiful site for human settlements.

**Distribution of Tanks**

Tank is an artificial square shaped water body constructed near settlement site for bathing of human being and animals. Its construction also attaches religious sentiments due to welfare of people.

In North Bihar the total number of tanks are 8509 which are distributed unevenly in different parts of the area and determined by the presence and absence of river in the area. It is quite discernible that river embankments of the Ganges, the Kosi, the Mahananda, the Gandak and others have very few number of tanks near them but away from river banks their number increases. In the districts of Saharsa, Madhubani, Darbhanga and the northern parts of Samastipur, Sitamarhi and Muzaffarpur, the number of tanks are very high because these are the areas of "rice and fish culture". The highest number of tanks are available in Madhubani district (2421) and Darbhanga district (1435) in 1996 (Fig. 8.6).

In Pokharbhinda village of Manigachhi anchal there are 75 tanks (Fig. 8.7) and in Narayanpur village of the same anchal tanks which are not only a lowlying wetlands but there are 32 economically they are highly potential. For example, Rajokhar pond of Narayanpur which has an expanse of over 21 hectares of land is annually producing makhana of Rs. 3 lakh and fish of Rs. 3 lakhs respectively. It has a powerful tool to make ecological balance, beautify the environment, providing recreation ground of boats, bathing place for human being and cattle besides irrigating

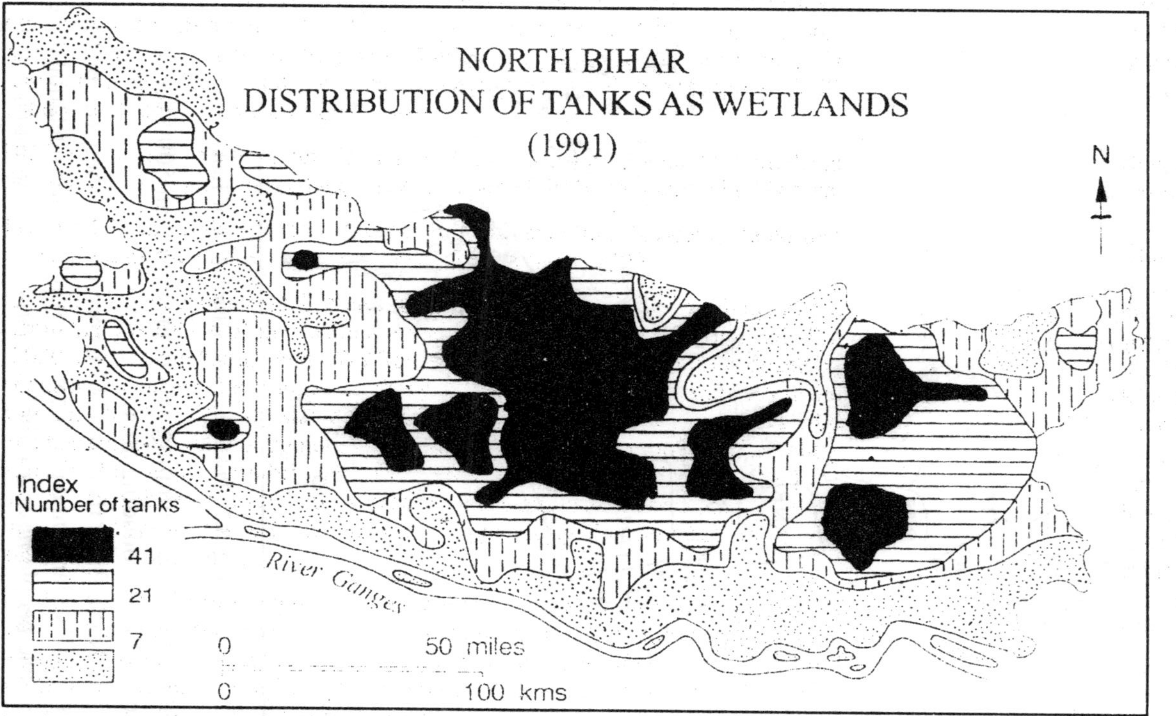


**Fig. 8.6 :** North Bihar : Distribution of Tanks as Wetlands, 1991.

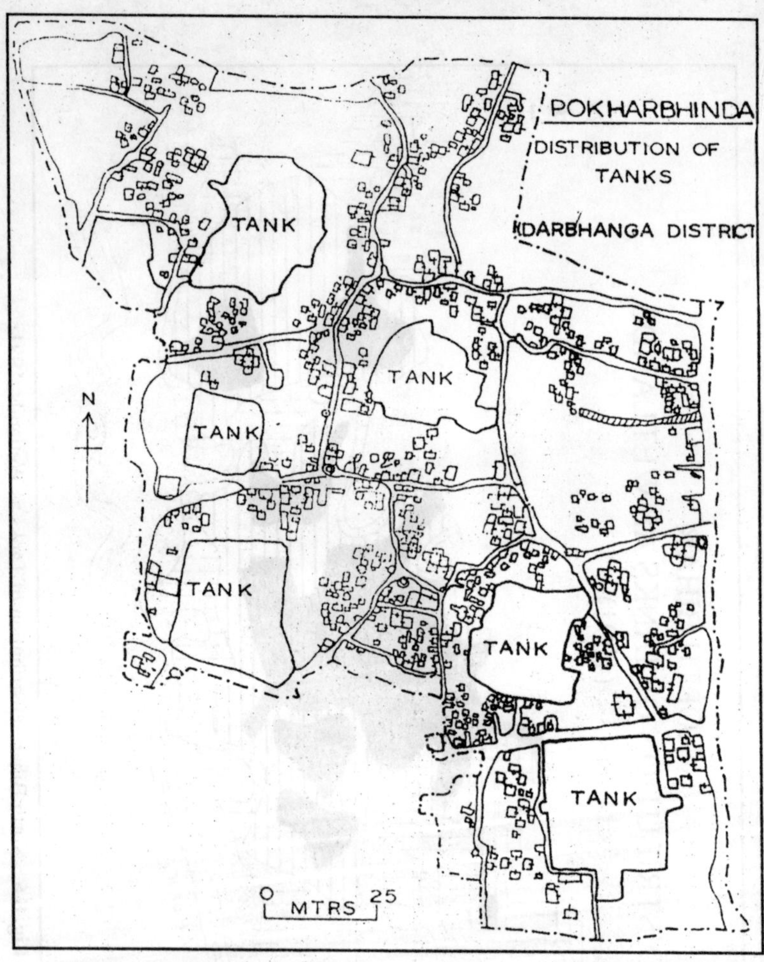


**Fig. 8.7 :** Pokharbhinda : Distribution of Tanks

the land through pumping sets over more than 5000 hectares of land in the surrounding area.

In North Bihar there is a close correlation in between ponds as artificial wetlands and planted mango orchards as vegetation cover, because people have a belief to marry tank with mango orchard and hence these two are the assets for making the ecological balance, checking flood hazards besides increasing the water holding capacity of the land in tank to use it for irrigation and provide a bathing place for buffalow in each and every village.

**Table 8.6 :** Distribution of Tanks and Mango Orchards in North Bihar, 1991.

| *Sl. No.* | *District* | *No. of Tanks* | *%* | *Orchards* | *%* |
|---|---|---|---|---|---|
| 1. | Chhapra | 197 | 2.31 | 8 | 3.55 |
| 2. | Siwan | 139 | 1.63 | 5 | 2.22 |
| 3. | Gopalganj | 115 | 1.35 | 5 | 2.22 |
| 4. | East Champaran | 331 | 3.88 | 9 | 4.00 |
| 5. | West Champaran | 144 | 1.69 | 92 | 40.88 |
| 6. | Muzaffarpur | 594 | 6.15 | 11 | 4.88 |
| 7. | Vaishali | 196 | 2.39 | 6 | 2.67 |
| 8. | Sitamarhi | 787 | 9.24 | 9 | 4.00 |
| 9. | Darbhanga | 1435 | 16.86 | 9 | 4.00 |
| 10. | Samastipur | 508 | 5.97 | 8 | 3.57 |
| 11. | Madhubani | 2425 | 28.49 | 11 | 4.88 |
| 12. | Begusarai | 73 | 0.85 | 2 | 0.88 |
| 13. | Khagaria | 26 | 0.30 | 2 | 0.88 |
| 14. | Bhagalpur | 15 | 0.17 | 1 | 0.46 |
| 15. | Saharsa | 526 | 6.18 | 20 | 8.88 |
| 16. | Purnea | 937 | 11.01 | 22 | 9.79 |
| 17. | Katihar | 131 | 1.53 | 5 | 2.24 |

*Source :* District Census Handbood of Different Districts of North Bihar, 1991.

— Bathing place for Men and Beasts.
— Marriage Ritual
— Den of criminals
— Shradh/Tarpan/Nagpanchmi
— Emersion of Goddess Saraswati, Bihula, Durga and Kali
— Bathing on Purnimas, Shankranti and Sun and the Moon Eclipses
— Natural Boundary
— Quarrel Ground
— Embankment provide site for Human Settlements
— Abode of Goddess Kamla (Goddess of Water)
— Sama-Chakewa

Ecologically the tanks are very significant as they beautifies the environment, provide place for bathing and religious performance along with the washing of utensils, rearing fishes and ducks besides they are place of pride for a human settlement. Because, the owners of tanks are relatively rich people as the poor cannot afford so much of land and capital in the construction of a tank for the community as a whole. Although most of the tanks are treated as a personal property but their use is common except fish rearing and production of makhana.

**Socio-Economic Model of Wetland Development**

The socio-economic model of wetlands developments come in the direct measurement. In this method, the perception of wetlands developments means ultimate development of the society through wetlands because natures laws are fixed and any change in the natural system than by people comes under the purview of wetlands developments not for the sake of nature but for the human being. In this regard the flow of labour and items produce in wetlands to the well-being of people like Brahmans and Rajputs produced a vicious circle because resources, entreprenuers and infrastructure facilities for wetlands development come to Mattah, Chamar and Dushadh who are closely associated with wetlands developments from so-called higher in the society or higher income group people like Rajput and Brahmans. In this way, we can say that socio-economic model for wetlands estimate idea for wetlands measurements in a caste ridden Indian society like North Bihar. Here most of the social, religious and economic developments took place on caste line (Fig. 8.8).

## SAMPLE STUDIES

**Kabar Lake**

*Location*

Kabar lake or Kawar Tall is located in Manjhaul village of Begusarai district. It is 18 km North of Begusarai town and is situated in

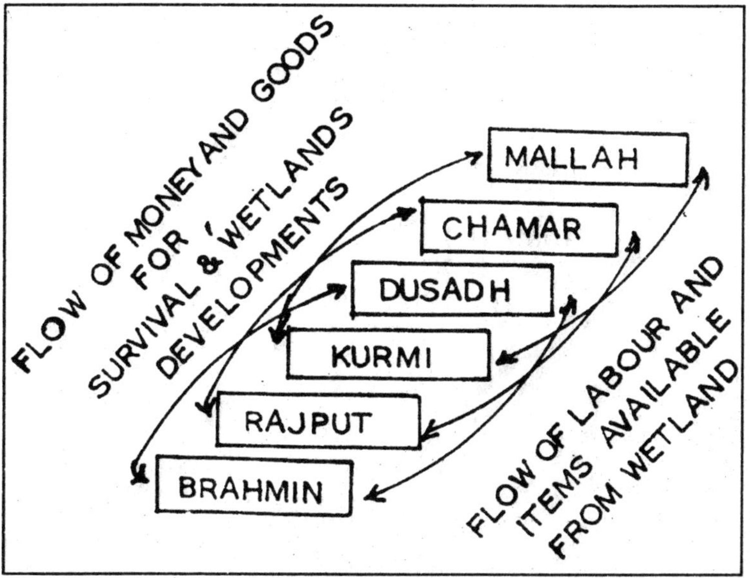


**Fig. 8.8 :** Socio-economic Model for Wetlands Development

between the two railway tracts lying about 30 kilometres apart. On the south the rail runs from Barauni to Katihar while on north rail runs from Samastipur to Mansi. The river Budhi Gandak flows quite close to the lake and the overflow of water from the lake falls into this river which ultimately meets with the Ganges river near Mansi (Fig 8.9)

Jaimangala Garh is an Island in the Kabar Lake. It is a land-mass having an area of about 500 acres and is about 20ft. higher than the adjoining land. This is located in the south east corner of the lake and is connected to the mainland by the road. The north-eastern fringe of the land is occupied by about 50 houses of Harijan families in a colony built by the Government. There is a temple of Jaimangala Devi on the land mass which is the focal point of the area. There is another small temple located at about 200 fts. south of main Devi Temple. *Mela* is held on every Tuesday in which local people participate.

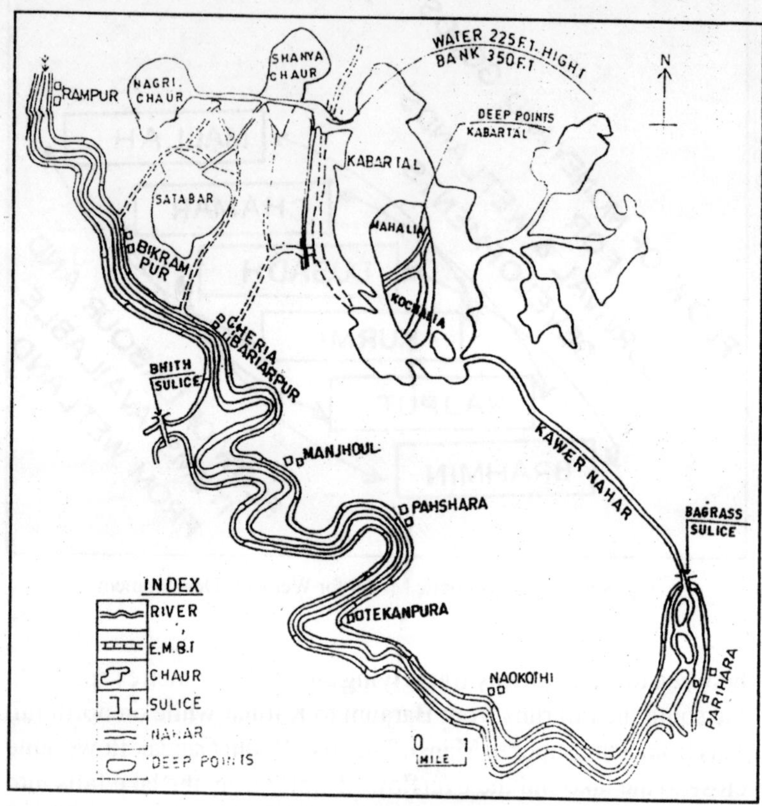


**Fig. 8.9 :** The Environs of Kabar Tal

## Goga Beel or Goga Chaur

The Goga Chaur is another big lake of North Bihar in Katihar District. It falls in Manihari Block, 32 km. South-East of Katihar. Some parts of Goga Beel come under the jurisdiction of Amdabad Block (Fig. 8.10).

Begharbeel stream and Kankhar river through their meanders have brought new channels and abandon old courses and thus resulted Gogabeel an oxbow lake. The river Ganges which flows at a close distance to the south of this lake, also add flood water and silt. During the mansoon, floods fill the oxbow, stream marshes and river and they look contiguous stretch of the lake. The character of

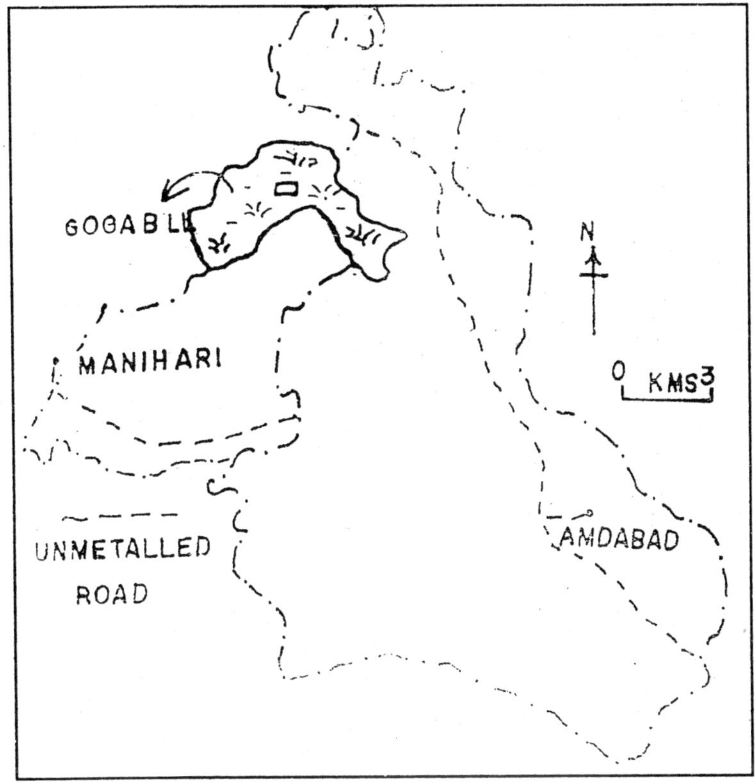


**Fig. 8.10 :** Regional Location of Goga-Beel

the plant and animal species is influenced by flooding and the resultant siltation. Although such flooding resupplies nutrient annually, species of perennial plants that will not tolerate periodic flooding are reduced or eliminated. Plants that are well adapted to this unstable system, such as animals or perennials that estabiish easily by seed, are highly productive and become dominant.

Gogabeel is valuable in providing unique type of landscape and plays crucial roles in maintaining water quality, water retention, enhancement of water-tables, erosion-control and soil and nutrient trapping.

It is of paramount importance to birds when the lakes of northern and Central Asia freeze in winter, millions of birds migrate to the south of feeding grounds in the Indian Peninsula. Here, they face persecution by commercial netting and shooting and habitat disturbance through intensive fish netting and reed cutting and even such valuable wetlands have been reclaimed for agricultural use.

Gogabeel which lies in the extreme south-east corner of block of Katihar district previously Katihar was a Sub-Division under Purnea District a sportsman paradise. At one time there was an abundance of big game birds for the *Shikar*. Rhino used to be shot in the district about half a century before. Tigers were quite common. The ordinary hog deers were so abundant and the Raja Krityanand Sinha of Baneli Raj had remarked (1916) that one could get a hundred hog deer a day if he wishes, though it would be cruelty to shoot so many.

## Tal-Baraila Wetlands

Tal-Baraila is closely associated with the people of 200 villages of the Anchals of Mahua, Patepur, Jandaha and Tajpur in Vaishali district. With the proper management of wetland of the Tal-Baraila, the prosperity could be brought. The people of surrounding area felt that the area around Tal-Baraila once upon a time was known as the grainery of Tirhut division but unfortunately it has not been included in the major irrigation project of the district of Vaishali.

Tal-Baraila may be converted into a big reservoir of water with the help of construction of dam around the lake and with the establishment of hydel power station at least 50 Megawat electricity could be generated.

## The Wetland of Kusheshwar Asthan

In different chaurs and lakes of Kusheshwar Asthan are migratary birds come from China, Japan, Korea, Siberia and Mangolia which lie north of Himalaya. The birds come every year from October to December. The main cause of migration is to save from excessive cold besides getting food, shelter and search of abode for giving birth to younger ones. The food of these birds are paddy and varieties of insects found in North Indian plains specially after the harvest of paddy crops in November. Kusheshwar Asthan is surrounded by wetland from North, South and East and hence the area is highly potential for birds sanctuary and the rearing of variety of fishes.

The stagnation of water around Kusheshwar Asthan for a longer period creates such an environment that the local people depend on fishes, anails, saduk, Bhent and Situwa. For the purpose of rearing fishes-Rehu, Katla, Mirgal, common carp, silver carp and grass carp are important. Besides these some rare fishes Kawai, Garai, Singhi and Mangur produces in large quantity without any expense.

The lake of Kusheshwar Asthan is very famous for its beauty. The Red Lotus flower, among green leaves around, the white flower of Kumudani and herds of varieties of birds amidst flower beautify the environment manifold. All these prey of birds has been prohibited by the Government of Bihar. But even than the Deputy Collector of Kusheshwar Asthan gives order to prey birds on some payment of rupees which is quite illegal on part of the Government machinery in terms of saving our ecology. The birds which caught here is lalsar, Sarachar, Arum, Andhigi, Makta and dighouch. These migratory birds come every year in October and goes back in the respective country upto March, keeping these aspect under the conservation projet. The preying of birds in the lakes of Kusheshwar Asthan should be immediately checked in order to ameliorate the environment for better human living conditions. We also noted a large number of Brahmini Duck, large flock of sponbill nad several Gangetic Dolfin in the Kosi river. Another population of Lesser Adjutant stork was recorded at Simri Jheel.

**Simri Bakhtly Arpur Jheel**

Several adjoining Jheels form a large chunk of wetlands at Simri Bakhtiyarpur Block. This Blokck is situated 25 kms South to Saharsa. The notable Jheels are Jamunia, Sardiha, Kumihi and Gobraha. These Jheels have been the traditional Bird shooting reserve of the then Nawab of Simri. The Jheels form a horse-shaped big lake and in the south-west joins the tributeries of Kaber and in the North-West continues upto Kusheshwar Asthan. In fact, during Monsoon one can travel by boat from Kabar to Kusheshwar via Simri Jheel and thus during winter season Simri Jheels provide alternate habitat for visiting birds. The crwfly distance between Kabar, Simri and Kusheshwar Asthan being not more than 10 kilometers.

The composition of vertebrate fauna and other features of these lakes are similar to Kabar and Gogabeel. However, the cultivation around these lakes is mostly paddy whereas around Kabar mostly wheat is grown. Apart from many other birds we noted several nests of white-backed vulture and two nests of ring tailed fishing eagle at the Bank of Gobraha lake. As reported by adjoining villagers the number of birds visiting this lake is reducing year after year.

**Wetland of Simardah**

Simardah is a natural wetland formed due to subsidence of land at the time of earthquake sometimes in the 16th century. It is a vast area south of Dhanauli in Baheri Anchal. It covers an area of more than 200 hectares especially during the rainy season, but in summer the water area comes down to 50 hectare only. The water comes through Juria bridge in the west. Sometimes in the reign of Raja Shivai Singh of the estate of Darbhanga who went to Bhent which is a road material to make Ramdana Ladoo.

**Rajokhar Wetlands**

Rajokhar is a man made tank constructed at the reign of Raja Shivai Singh of Darbhanga estate about 1650 A.D. It is really a very big man made wetland surrounded by human settlements. The western and southern side of the tank are occupied by villagers residential houses whereas the northern side covered by High English School and Basic Middle School. The Eastern side of the tank is vacant but some part is occupied by mango orchards.

The source of water is Kamla river which flows just 2 km. south of this tank and attached with it through small canal. The quality of water is not palatable but it is fit- for washing cloths, animals, raising fishes, and producing Makhana and provide habitat for several birds.

Rajokhar is the habitat of water birds especially Lalsar, Hen, Bagula besides Pansilli and several others. Some of these birds came to this wetlands especially during the winter season.

Rajokhar produces 700 munds of Makhana guri each and every year. Rajokhar is so big that it really aids a new life and culture to the villagers because most of the functions like *chhat*, Samachakewa and others performed on its embankment. Rajokhar cools down the temperature of its surrounding area and it has a soothing effect on the vegetation and people of the area. It serves the purpose of irrigation and its fringe provides place for making bricks and tiles beside it provides soil to raise village and house sites.

## Wetlands Management

The management of wetlands for better use of the limited land could be possible by removing sand deposites from river courses each and every year, plantation of forests under social forestry scheme. Intensive repair of river embankments at breach point, checking of sheet wash and gully erosion by creating artificial barriers and most important is guarding the river embankment during flood from rowday elements.

It seems that there would be a fight between various aspects of wetlands development and environment, but it is not a reality as they are just making an adjustment with one another.

## Evaluation and Monitoring

The monitoring of wetlands development is quite essential in order to :

(a) Safeguard our wetlands from filling and extinction.
(b) The migratory birds coming to North Indian Plains seasonally are vanishing and slowly due to local prey which needs protection and conservation through proper guidance.
(c) With the rapid increase of population the trees and forest wealth are facing extinction which should be properly monitored for

the survival because vegetation has a great power to purify the environment for the survival of wetlands. The annual flood is a menace in managing the affairs of wetlands because it hampers afforestation work, plugging the breach points, scare away the fishes, birds and disrupts the whole economy of the area.

(d) Monitoring of wetlands are essential because most of the polluted water from towns, villages, industrial establishments and agricultural fields with excess of pesticides and insecticides have a disastrous effect on the living things in lakes, ponds and rivers found in the area.

## Conclusion

Wetlands are waterlogged and flood affected marshy lowlying areas of North Bihar whose investigation is rightly directed because the rapid increase of population and livestock wealth have endangered the ecological balance due to over exploitation of forest by reckless cutting for fuel and building materials since ancient period. In Bihar most of the lakes, old tanks and dried river beds are almost filled up by the agent of weathering and erosion due to human activity and floods in North Bihar. For example, Motihari was surrounded by 42 lakes in 1800 A. D. but most of them have filled up by detritous and silt from the surrounding area and nowadays only the remnants of some of them have lift. This clarified the point that wetlands should be saved to beautify the environment, maintain the ecological balance producing Singarhara (a fruit produce in shallow water) and Makhana (a black bead produce in throny plant of shallow water) rearing varieties of fishes and providing place surrouding higher embankment of ponds, canals and river embankment for the plantation of trees. A national and internatioanl wetland development committee should be constituted comprising the experts of various disciplines related to wetlands.

Wetlands are not wastelands rather they are among the most fertile and productive ecosystems in the world. They are essential life support systems and play a vital role in controlling water-cycles, and help to clean up our environment. They make many commercial fisheries possible and protect coasts from floods and storm surges.

Wetlands are pollution filter, water reservoirs, offering homes for endangered plants, birds and animals and hence we have an obligation to maintain and preserve them.

## NOTES

1. Gopal, B., Turner, R. E., Wetzel, R. G. and Whigham, D. F. *Wetlands Ecology and Management*; National Institute of Ecology and International Scientific Publications, Jaipur, 1982.
2. Wetlands conference in Czechoslovakia, *Nature and Resources, UNESCO*, Vol. XX, No.2, 1984, p. 22.
3. U. S. Fish and Wildlife Service, Wetlands Strategies and Trends, Washington, D. C. ; U. S. Department of the Interior, Fish and Wildlife Service, 1991.
4. White House Press Release, "President 15th Plan for Wetlands", 9th August, 1991.
5. The Conservation Foundation, "Protecting America's Wetlands, An Action Agenda (Washington D. C.; The Conservation Foundation, 1988).
6. Sklar, F.H., Costanze, R. and Dayj . W. Dynamic, Spatial Simulation Modelling of coastal wetland – Habitat Succession; *Ecology Mod*; 1985, 29, pp. 261-281.

# 9

# ENDANGERED WETLANDS ECOLOGY

All the water bodies whether lakes, rivers, tanks, ditches, shallow marshes, swamps and delta area come under wetlands. Recently, due to increased human interference both the flora and fauna wealth of wetlands are facing the danger of their disappearance. Our aim should be to protect them for the safe survival of humanity and maintaining the ecological balance.[1]

The reckless cutting of forests in the environs of these wetlands have created problems of over siltation, acts as dumping ground of waste material from human settlements and cremation ground of dead bodies on its embankment which lead to rise of Biochemical Oxygen Demand (BOD) in water.[2] Although wetlands act as pollution filter. The problem is more or less the same in almost all wetlands of India such as the Dal lake of Jammu & Kashmir, Loktak lake of Manipur, Nainital of Kumaon, Kabar lake of Begusarai (Bihar), Ghana Birds Sanctuary in Bharatpur, Rajasthan, Chilka lake of Orissa and the Ganges delta of West Bengal, etc.

Although the Directorate of Wetlands, Government of India has entrusted the task of investigating the ecological problems of these wetland to different scientific bodies[3] (Universities and Research Organizations) but due to the non-execution of findings and their research and lack of coordination among these research groups and the government, the plans are not being implemented to fulfil people's desire. Hence, the ecological situations have aggravated to a substantial degree threatening the very existence of the wetland eco-system. We should protect them as they are the savioures of clean environment and source of our food and protein supply.

Considering the importance of Wetlands, measures have been initiated for their conservation and management to educate the public on the need for their conservation as well as their economic utility and to commence scientific and application oriented research studies on their productivity. A National Wetland Committee has been constituted comprising of experts in various wetland disciplines.

## Mangroves

Mangroves are the salt-tolerant forest eco-systems found mainly in tropical and sub-tropical inter-tidal regions. They consist of swamps, forest land within and its water spread areas. The total area of Mangroves in India is estimated to be 6,740 sq.km., which is 7 per cent of the world's mangroves. The mangroves areas of Sundarbans, West Bengal and Andaman and Nicobar Islands constitute over 80 per cent of the mangroves in India. This ecosystem is a reservoir of a host of plant and animal species in India have been subjected to reckless exploitation due to biotic interference and other factors.

Considering the importance of mangroves steps have been initiated to conserve the mangroves, to educate the public on the need for their conservation as well as their economic utility and to commence scientific and application oriented research on their productivity, flora and fauna, etc. The National Mangrove Committee was constituted to recommend policies and actions.

The Committee has identified the following first batch of 15 wetlands for preparation of Management Action Plan : Northern Andaman Nicobar, Sundarbans (West Bengal), Bhitarkanikal (Orissa), Coringa (Andhra Pradesh), Mahanadi Delta (Orissa), Pichavaram (Tamil Nadu), Goa, Godavari Delta (Andhra Pradesh), Gulf of Kutch (Gujarat), Coondapur, (Karnataka) Achre Ratnagiri (Maharashtra) Vemband (Kerala), Point Calimare (Tamil Nadu) Krishna Estuary (Andhra Pradesh).

The Action Plans have been drawn up by the steering committees set up in the states concerned with the Chief Secretary as the Chairman and consisting of representatives from various subject matter departments, Universities, non-official organisations, etc.

The components of the Action Plan include natural regeneration in selected areas, afforestation and protective measures.

## Environment Impact

Wetlands are waterlogged areas which may be temporary or permanent in nature. They have multifacets impact on the society in terms of relief, production of various crops, acquatic animals besides the places of religious importance and tourist attraction.

In terms of ecological and environmental protection, wetlands may be regarded as green spots in the ocean of desertification and degradation of land due to decreasing amount of rainfall annually. The breakdown of ozon layer in the upper atmosphere and carbondioxide build up developed green house effect on the earth surface. The upward shrinkage of snow-line in the mountainous areas resulted into excessive flow of water in the rivers in the form of flood besides the ongoing alluviation of riverine plains where most of the wetlands are located.

## Lakes and Rivers : A Running Problem

The "International Decade of Drinking Water and Sanitation" ended last year and it is a good time to review the situation on the supply of clean drinking water to everyone."

India relies for drinking water largely on the southwest monsoon, though northeast winds (not 'monsoon', according to many climatologists) and the snow from the Himalayan ranges do contribute their mite. The country gets some 1900 billion cubic metres of water every year, 86 per cent of which is surface runoff in rivers and lakes. Rivers such as the Ganga, the Yamuna, the Ghaghra, the Gomati, the Kosi, the Sone and the Brahmaputra in the north; the Narmada and the Tapti in central India; and the Godavari, the Krishna and the Cauvery in the south are the main channels for runoff. There are several small coastal rivers.

While the rivers rising in the Himalayas are perennial, those in peninsular India, dependent completely on the monsoon, appear as trickles in summer. These rivers, with variable flow, are the lifeline of the people, satisfying all their needs of drinking, bathing and washing, irrigation and power generation.

If water quantity in rivers and water bodies is inherently uncertain, its quality has been perennially suspect. From the Dal lake in Srinagar to the Hussaina Sagar lake in Hyderabad or from the Pichhola lake in Udaipur to the lake in Udhagamandalam, all have turned eutrophic (with high nitrogen and phosphorous content), due to community wastes and drainage, made worse by tourism. The condition of rivers is even worse as is evident from the Ganga in the north to the Periyar in the south and from the Hooghly in the east to the Ulhas in the west. The polluted water is responsible for two-thirds of all illnesses and at times the incidence of typhoid, cholera, malaria, diarrhoea and dysentery reaches epidemic proportions. Examples 40,000 cases of jaundice in 1955-56 in Delhi, 2,000 cases in Bombay in 1978 and some 310 fatalities in West Bengal in July 1990. Reasons for contamination of water are not far to seek. Few settlements near lakes or rivers have systems to treat their wastes. The ability of the water-body to clean itself has been affected because of the sheer quantity of water generated by the ever increasing population of the 3119 towns and cities in the country, only 209 have partial and just eight have full sewage treatment facility.

Coliform bacteria harbouring viruses, measured in MPN (most probable number) per unit volume, are the indicator of the water quality. Indian standards permit up to 5000 MPN per 100 ml. water. When the Yamuna leaves Delhi, it contains 24 million coliforms per 100 ml. The Mutha river in Pune is highly eutrophic and causes the growth of water hyacinth. Srinagar lakes are progressively getting more eutrophic thanks to wastes from the large number of house-boats. The Kodaikanal lake is likely to be similarly affected as more tourist amenities are developed around it.

Diverse industrial wastes have aggravated the problem of water pollution. This problem becomes complex because of the qualitative differences in pollution according to the industries involved, and due to the non-degradability of many of the effluents. Though industrial wastes, discharged into water-bodies, are just a fourth of the community wastes, the treatment of the polluted water becomes more complex and expensive.

Which increasing industrialisation, the problem of water pollution is no longer confined to a few places. Thus talk of water pollution is heard from all over in the Chambal at Kota, the Gomati at Lucknow, the Damodar at Bokaro, the Godavari at Rajahmundry, the Narmada at Hoshangabad, the Tungabhadra at Harihar and the Chaliyar at Mavoor (Kerala). The list seems endless the extent of pollution near the highly-industrialised and densely-populated Bombay is such that satellite photographs show the Arabian sea contaminted for a hundred kilometres northward.

The identification of the pollutants of a water body is not too difficult where a few units are located. For example, the Indian Rare Earths causing pollution of the Periyar in Kerala, agro-chemicals spoiling the Zuari river in Goa, tanneries affecting the Palar in Tamil Nadu, and so on. But industrial estates and large complexes pose problems because of the number of pollutants, their interaction and the generation of secondary products. An average water testing laboratory is not likely to have facilities for sophisticated analytical procedures. But the water quality can be assessed from some routine tests of the Biochemical Oxygen Demand (BOD) and Suspended Solids (SS) Water samples give BOD and SS values in milligrams per litre; the permissible values are 3 and 100 respectively.

While numerous studies report about chemical and biological pollution of water bodies and their effects on organisms, two aspects of physical pollution have rarely been quantified methodically.

1. Suspended solids, especially near open cast mines. Red-earth colouration of sea water for nearly a kilometre from the coast of Sindhudurg and Goa where iron ore mines are located and a rise in the sea-bed level in the Goa harbour and the loss of paddy due to runoff from mines have been reported by scientists

of the National Institute of Oceanography. These deserve more investigation. The recent announcement by the Bombay Port Trust that the hull depth of ships entering the harbour should be less compared to earlier limits speaks volumes of the sedimentation in the harbour receiving runoff and drainage from the surrounding landmass.

2. The other problem is that of thermal pollution caused by waste heat emitted into water bodies by nuclear and thermal power plants as well as industrial units. Though the receiving waters are monitored for dispersal effects, the chemical reactions and the reaction on the biota are yet to be understood.

Much of the information available on water pollution in the country is scattered, and period specific. Pollution prevention measures have also been correspondingly localised. Gauging the gravity of the problem the Planning Commission launched a programme called 'Sky to Sea' for continuous monitoring of the Ganga involving hundreds of research organisations and universities along' the river course. The programme was later adopted by the Department of Environment. An Action Plan for improving the river ecosystem was prepared in 1984. For implementation, the Central Ganga Authority was set-up. It has undertaken the task of determintion of policies and programmes, allocation of resources and mobilisation of public support.

As it was found that 75 per cent of pollution of the Ganga could be controlled by stopping the discharge of sewage sullage into the river, the work of improving/installing sewage treatment plants, covering 27 major cities along the river, has been taken up in the first phase at an estimated cost of Rs.250 crores. The integrated sewage treatment and utilization system envisages not only cleaning of the river water but also biogas, sludge as fertilizer, algal slurry for poultry and pisciculture and talwater for irrigation.

A similar programme is on the anvil for the Cauvery. The Madras Science Foundation is coordinating an intensive, multidisciplinary research and data generation effort to determine the river water quality, in the first phase, since late 1989. It is expected that a massive programme for improvement of the river ecosystem will emerge along the Ganga Action Plan lines.

Efforts to control water pollution by legislation are old. One of the old laws against discharging industrial wastes into rivers was promulgated in 1898. The Calcutta Municipal Act of 1951 aimed at preventing the fouling of water. The most comprehensive Act was drafted in 1970 by Maharashtra called the Water Pollution Control Act, which was the draft for a similar legislation by the Union Government in 1974.

The water pollution episodes, enactment of laws and the functioning of pollution control boards notwithstanding, it is the people who are important in the ultimate analysis. There is, thus a need to educate the masses about personal and community hygiene, and their rights and duties vis-a-vis society in this regard. Without adequate education, laws and action plans will remain limited in success.

**The Ganga at a Glance**

This river originates from the Gangotri glacier in the Himalayas as the Bhagirathi. Meeting the Alaknanda, originating in the Sapta Tal glacier, at Devaprayag, the Ganga enters the plains at Haridwar. After traversing 2525 km., it reaches the Bay of Bengal through the world's largest delta region — the Sunderbans. The major distributary is include the Yamuna, the Ghagra, the Gandala, the Gomati, the Kosi, the Chambal, the Betwa, the Tons, the Ken, and the Sone.

Basin area — 8,61,404 sq.km.

Runoff water — 4,93,400 million cumpa, or 30 per cent of the total water resource of the country.

Sown area — 58 million hectares.

Population (in 1981) — 199,930,634 or 464 per sq.km.

Urban population — 36,858,508.

Cities — Class I (population above 1,00,000) — 27 Class

II (Pop.between 50,000 and 1,00,000) — 23 Town (Pop. below 50,000) — 48.

Hydropower potential — 5000 MW; installed capacity-1899 MW.

Number of dams of 30m height and above — 25.

Flood situation between 1953 and 1981 Average of 22.6 lakh ha affected every year.

Major places of industrial pollution: Allahabad, Kanpur, Lucknow, Varanasi, Monghyr, Sultanganj, Bhagalpur, Farakka, Nadia and the Howrah-Calcutta region.

Other causes of pollution: The lakhs of devotees taking a dip all along the course mating the river water dirty. Some 30,000 dead bodies are burnt on its banks every year. Ashes and partly burnt or unburnt bodies are released into the river.

**The Cauvery**

Eighth largest river in the country, the Cauvery originates 1355 m above the mean sea level in the Western Ghats (Sahyadris) at Talaikaveri in Brahmagiri hills, Karnataka. The 765 km river joins the Bay of Bengal at Poompuhar in Tamil Nadu.

Water comes mainly from the South-West monsoon besides small contributions from the north-east winds. Tributaries include the Hanagi, the Hemavati, the Laxmanateertham, the Kabini, the Arakavati and the Suvarnati in Karnataka and the Bhavani, the Noyyal and the Amaravathi in Tamil Nadu. Distributaries are the Coleroon, the Uyyakondan, the Vennar and the Grand Anicut canal and several smaller canals.

Basin — 90,000 sq.km. Water discharge — 20,950 million cumpa. Major dams across the river — Four.

*Major urban areas — Eight.*

Water flow control practised from the time of the Chola dynasty in the second century A.D. Almost 95 per cent of water of the river utilised.

Major industrial establishments at Mettur, Pallipalayam, Erode, Sirumugai and Tiruchi, discharging about 5082 lakh lpd of effluents into the river. Untreated sewage discharged into the river - 80 lakh pounds.

## The Bhatsa River Episode

A small river, the Bhatsa has been dammed to augment drinking water supply to Bombay. Water from the artificial lake is allowed to flow for some distance before it is piped. In this open stream region, a few industrial units were permitted while many were planned. At this stage the people realised the folly of locating polluting industrial units in the river basin. The move was opposed so emphatically that the Department of Industries had to set up an expert committee to study the problem. Based on its suggestions the types of non-polluting, small-scale units and their locations with reference to the local drainage pattern were redefined and a major source of drinking water was saved from pollution.

Intensive investigations, cleaning and regular monitoring of the Kalu and the Ulhas rivers, as also the Thane creek in Bombay, were undertaken by the Maharashtra Government in the face of findings of studies by students and voluntary organisations. An a result, the villages along the Kalu were saved

## Distribution of Wetlands

India has innumerable wetland ecosystems distributed in different geographical regions ranging from cold and zone of Ladakh to wet humed climate of Imphal; warm arid zone of Rajasthan and Tropical Monsoon of Central India, besides the wet and humid zone of southern Peninsula. Most of the wetlands in India are directly or indirectly linked with the mazor river systems like the Ganga, Brahmaputra, Narmada, Tapti, Godavari, Krishna, Cauvery, etc.

Several significant steps have been initiated for conservation and management of wetlands. A National Wetland Management

Committee has been constituted for advising the Government on appropriate policies and measures to be taken for conservation and management. This committee has identified 16 wetlands on priority basis for conservation and management. A directory on wetlands of India has been published which gives information on location, area and ecological categorisation of wetlands in different parts of the country.

## The Plan of Kabar Lake

The Kabar lake situated in Begusarai district of North Bihar. It attracts a lot of Himalayan birds each and every year especially during the winter season. The area of Kabar lake is two times bigger than the Bharatpur lake situated in Rajasthan where the migratory birds come especially in the month of November from U.S.S.R., Afghanisthan, China, Siberia and Himalayas. A famous bird specialist Salim Ali from Bombay Natural history society served the Kabar lake and he announced that 59 varieties of migratory birds are coming to this lake each year. Almost 106 types of birds reside in this lake permanently. Only Siberian crane visits the Bharatpur Bird sanctuary. The Government of Bihar has prepared a plan of Rs.5.78 crore in the Eighth Five Year Plan. There are 16 protected wetlands in India, out of which Kabar lake is one of them. It is situated 20 km. North of Begusarai near Jaimangla Garh, where waterlogging is found since 1976, when the Government of India is completely banned the catch of fishes and trapping of birds in Kabar lake. The birds like, Adhinga, Sarair and Dighaunch are in heavy demand in the local market. But now these birds are not trapped at all and hence the fishermen and farmers of the area are facing problems of unemployment, which is not a social justice as done by the Government.

## Loktak Lake of Manipur

The Loktak lake, the biggest in eastern India, is sick and if preventive measures are not taken it will dry up. For generations its fish has been the source of income for thousands of villages surrounding it. Located 40 km. from Imphal, the lake also houses the Keibul Lamjao National Park, the world's only floating sanctuary, the natural habitat of the endangered brow antlered deer.

The Loktak or Logtak lake is a large wetland located near Imphal, Manipur. It consists of a large lake and is surrounded by a number of swamps and marshes. The lake is the home of the famous Thamin of Dancing deer (Cervus, *eldi*) which were once nearly extinct and were confined to the swamps of the Keibul Lamjao are of the lake. However, after the area was converted into a national park, the population of this deer is slowly increasing. The principal factors responsible for the ecological degradation of this lake are:

— siltation from the adjoining slopes
— influx of sewage and waste products.

All rivers in Manipur discharge into this lake. Unchecked denudation around this water body is causing soil erosion resulting in heavy silt formation. Experts say that if the lake bed is not dredged, it will soon become a playground. Without caring for the future of this lake, the National Hydroelectric Power Corporation was allowed to put up a 150 MW power project at a cost of Rs.120 crores by taking water from the lake through a tunnel. Heavy siltation and continuous draining of water, without its recycling, have almost dried up the lake.

During dry season, the Ithai barrage is closed so that there is no shortage of water for generating power. There have been numerous artificial floods after heavy rain as project officials fail to open the shutters. The State Government has approached the Centre to permit it to operate the barrage.

Experts have been warning that in case the lake dries up the ecological balance of Manipur will be seriously upset. The first casualty will be the brow antlered deer. Millions of migratory birds, which used to come here every season, are already looking elsewhere because of the receding water levels and poaching.

Realising that the threat is real, the Manipur Government has set up the Loktak Development Authority with the objective of saving this sick lake. But what was surprising was the appointment of the Authority's chairman: a retired IAS officer whose name was closely linked with poaching of birds and animals. Not surprisingly, nothing was done during his tenure though the State and Central Governments pumped in several crores of rupees.

The Authority has been charged with planting of saplings in the hills and plains around the lake, to check the heavy soil erosion during rain; dredging the lake bed; and clearing of water hyacinth and "*phums*" (floating particles of putrid water, plants which pollute the water and kill the fish). But till date nothing has been done though the Authority faces no shortage of funds. There is no fish in this lake, which once used to supply the entire area. The only silver lining is that as north-eastern States have refused to pay for the power from the Loktak project and moves are foot to stop power generation.

**Keoladeo Ghana National Park**

There is one paradise that is dear to the hearts of birds from all over the world, Keoladeo Ghana National Park, Bharatpur. In Rajasthan twenty-nine square kilometres of marshy land that was once the hunting reserve of the Bharatpur rulers. Here, the rare Siberian crane flies thousands of kilometres to rub shoulde with the myriad species of its avian brethren. Egrets, darters, cormorants, grey heron and storks hatch their chicks here. Other migratory birds like the rosy pelican, the Spanish sparrow, the Chinese bar-headed goose and the grey-lag goose-distinguished Russian guest-mingle with a host of native feathered friends. For the number and variety of birds, this park is matchless. One of the largest bird sanctuaries in the world. Keoladeo Park, Bharatpur also plays host to a variety of wildlife species. Spotted Deer, Sambar, Nilgai, Wild Boar, Python, and Porcupine. To cross the marshylands there are Jeepable roads and for close-up viewing, boats are punted through weeds and water rushes.

**The Dying Lake Renuka (Himachal Pradesh)**

Among Himachal Pradesh's picturesque lakes, Renuka is closest to the plains of Punjab-Haryana. Located 125 km from Chandigarh, the lake, with a water spread of 670 hectares, abounds in fish, tortoises and crocodiles. Though this natural lake has perennial water supply, it is dying. The lake has been shrinking due to the growth of elephant-gross on its banks and the heavy siltation during rains. The region was rich in forest wealth and criss-crossed by streams and dotted by lakes. The Giri river, which has been dammed for power supply, flows close by. During monsoons, the Renuka lake discharges excess water into the Giri.

For environmentalists the forest wealth, the wide variety of animals and the large number of water birds, especially migratory ones, are of interest. The Ministry of Environment and Forests in 1989 designated Renuka as the State's only "natural wetland" and accorded a national status to the lake. But, to the great dismay of environmentalists the State Government has done precious little to conserve-much less improve the area.

To retain the lake's health the first thing to be done is to stop its siltation. The Government has done nothing in this direction. But some educated youth of the surrounding areas have formed a social group — the People's Action for People in Need (PAPN) — and organised a vigorous desiltation campaign through "*kar seva*" and "*Shramdan*" last December. The group also organised a "*padayatra*" through several villages to explain the environmental issues and problems in the region.

A memorandum, listing several steps to control effectively environmental degradation such as a blanket ban on tree felling and a ban on mining activities in the area, was presented to the Chief Minister.

As mining involves blasting, it is having an adverse impact on the people and the wildlife. To check soil erosion tree planting has to be taken up on a war footing. The memorandum pleaded for special efforts to protect the wildlife, especially the musk deer; it suggested the creation of a musk deer sanctuary in the forest ranges of Choordhar, Haripurdhar and Shillai.

Besides mining, construction of Kutcha roads in the area is

causing the maximum damage. The loose soil silts up the lake further. The Forest Department has been objecting to the new road. Environmentalists claim that road construction has been taken up without assessing its environmental impact. They feel the road would disturb the ecology of the area as it passes through the wildlife sanctuary. No study has been done on the wildlife habitat requirement nor its effect on the wildlife assessed. They say the road will have extremely adverse effects such as destruction of the productive ecosystems, soil erosion, siltation and pollution of the Renuka lake. The State Tourism Development Corporation's hotel on the lake bank also disturbs the ecology.

## Sunderbans (West Bengal)

The Sunderbans delta is the largest delta in the world. It is the home of a unique combination of plants, birds, animals, reptiles, fishes and amphibians. However, the mangrove forests of this tract have come under severe ecological strain due to :

— demographic pressure in the adjoining areas
— increase in the population of undesirable plant species
— unprecedented floods have washed away many islands in the Sunderbans delta and created new ones which are devoid of all vegetation. These floods are the result of the degradation of forests in the uplands.
— conversion of parts of the wetland into fields for raising paddy and other crops.

## Chilka Project not to Hit Eco-system

The Chilka aquatic farm project of the Tatas would have no adverse impact on the eco-system of the Chilka lake and its environs as the 6 sq.kms of land being used for the project was a part of uninhabited wasteland.

A study undertaken by the Water and Power Consultancy Services (WAPCOS), a Government of India undertaking, investigated all areas of concern like displacement of people, cattle, air, noise and water pollution and possible adverse impact on vegetation and aquatic fauna.

A press release issued by the Tatas said that the WAPCOS in its revised interim report has stated that there would be no displacement of people and cattle and that there would be no adverse effect on migratory birds coming from the northern Himalayas and the Caspian Sea to the Nalaban Island, 35 km. away from the proposed farm site.

The report pointed out that the quality of the discharged water from ponds was rich in nutrients with no industrial chemicals and the effluent quality was well within the standards specified by the Bureau of Indian Standards.

The report also clarified that the water, in any case, would be discharged into a nallah flowing into the sea and would at no point interact with the water in the Chilka lake.

The press release said that extension services would be an integral part of the project and dissemination of technology information and on-the-job training would be given to local farmers.

The release said that about 15 million post-larval shrimps; would be distributed to the local small prawn farmers and the fair-priced outlets of the Tatas would buy back their fully grown prawns. This would result in an increase of the per capita income by about 35 per cent and help the farmers in attaining economic independence.

The Tata project proposes to use a semi-intensive technology which would result in an annual acquaculture yield of 6 tonnes per hectare as against the current yield of 0.4 tonnes per hectare.

The project, in which the Orissa Government would hold a 49 per cent stake, the Tata Steel 30 per cent, Tata Oil Mills 18 per cent and Otto India 3 per cent, would yield 1500 tonnes of shrimps annually, fetching an income of Rs.225 million.

## WETLANDS OF RAJASTHAN

There are more than 15 bigger wetlands found in different part of Rajasthan. Characteristically the lakes found in east of Aravalli mountain are of sweet water e.g. Pushkar, Rajsaman and Sambhar where as lakes found west of Aravalli are salt water lakes due to desert environment e.g. Umeghsagar, Didwana and Rawat Bhata, etc. Table 9.1.

**Table 9.1 :** Some of the important Wetlands of Rajasthan (1993)

| *Name of the Wetland* | *Area in which it Lies* | |
|---|---|---|
| Puskar | Ajmer | |
| Ramgarh | Jaipur | |
| Jaisaman | Udaipur | |
| Fatehsagar | Udaipur city | |
| Pichhola Lake | Udaipur city | Sweet |
| Lake Palace | Udaipur | Water |
| Udai Sagar | Udaipur | Lakes |
| Rajasaman | Lankroli | |
| Sambhar Lake | Jaipur | |
| Ghana Bird Sanctuary | Bharatpur | |
| Umeghsagar | Shahpura | |
| Didwana | Nagore | |
| Panch Bhadra | West Rajasthan | Salt |
| Rawat Bhata | Chitorgarh | Water |
| Jawahar Sagar | Kota | Lakes |
| Gandhi Sagar | Madhya Pradesh | |

*Source :* Prahalad Viyas of Udaipur, 1993.

## Udaipur Lake (Rajasthan)

It is situated about 48 kms away from the Udaipur in Rajasthan. It was constructed by Late Maharaja of Udaipur named Jaisingh, on the river Gomati in 1939 AD. The waste wair joins the Gangetic river system.

### *Physical Features*

The dam is an old one being 1100 ft. in length and 120 ft. in height. The length of the waste wair is 150 ft. and consist a water spread area of 28 sq. miles (7200 f.). The average rainfall in the region is 62 cms. This dam was constructed mainly for irrigational purposes.

### *Biological Features*

Detailed biological studies of the reservoir has not been done. The available informations indicate that the predominant Plankters include cladecera, copepods, Desmids and other blue a l gue. No developmental efforts was made for fisheries in this reservoir. The well known each of this lake was and still is from natural stock. The fish fauna of this lake is represented by the following species, *Catla, Rehu, Mrigal, Calhasly, L. jonices, Meor, M.Seenghala, Tortor, Nootopterus, C.Maralices, C.Striaths, W.atter, S.Silondia, Om Pok Pileda* etc. Catla has shown such depletion in the stock due to irrigation.

### *Fish Production*

Reliable catch statistics is not given by the contractor. The parcel booking figures of the railway show the following weight in quintals. The fish is generally transported in bamboo basket in sufficient ice.

| *Year* | *Wt. of fish booked* |
|---|---|
| 1994 | 10608.8 Quentals |
| 1995 | 10528.52 Quentals |
| 1996 | 11086.33 Quentals |
| 1997 | 10907.98 Quentals |

The Statistic war collectial in 1998 for catch per man from November to June. The fisheries obtained are as follows:-

| | |
|---|---|
| November | 3.13 kg. |
| December | 3.04 kg. |
| January | 6.03 kg. |
| February | 6.98 kg. |
| March | 6.45 kg. |
| April | 8.10 kg. |
| May | 6.55 kg. |
| June | 7.38 kg. |

As reported during our study tour, the average production is 400 tons per year and the catch per ha. comes to 60 kg./year.

### *Exploitation*

In 1949 the reservoir was based out for Rs. 30,000 to the contractor are in the next year the last value was increased to Rs. 50,000 per year to the same contractor. His main aim was to fish out maximum fish to get maximum profit. It is reported that not even single fishing was stocked by him. Fishing was done throughout the year. Now, from 1999 the reservoir has been taken up by the state department completely.

### Present Management and Method of Fishing

The department has given the reservoir to the same contractor for seven years i.e. from 1969-1987 on the minimum royality of Rs. 1,25,000 per year with the increase of 10.1201 per year. The amount is deposited in advance and the fishing is done by gill-nets, drag-nets, Hook and Lines. The arrangement of fishing parties and payment to the fishermen is managed by him. The entire catch is brought at one place where it is fished and given to the contractor by the following royalty rates. The adjustment of every day landings is made to the advance deposited by the contractor.

1. Major carp about 2 kg. Rs. 110
2. Major carp below 2 kg. Rs.40
3. Caf fishes about 2 kg. Rs.40
4. Caf fishes below 2 kg. Rs.35

The minimum least value has to be deposited by the contractor every year and if the fish exceeds the least value then according to the rates given above the contractor will agaii. deposit that amount to the Govt. he has told that the fishermen have paid for their catches as given below.

1. Major carp about 2 kg. Rs. 50 per Quintals.
2. Scale less fish Rs. 45 per Quintals.
3. Minor carps and miscellaneous Rs.36 per Quintals.

### Gandhi Sagar Reservoir (M.P.)

Gandhi Sagar is the second man made lake in India and is situated in District Mandasaur in Madhya Pradesh 50 kms by road from Halawar Road railway station. It is constructed on river Chambal.

It is a multipurpose river valley project. The Chambal river valley project started in 1949 and on completion it was inaugurated in 1960. Bu the fisheries development work started in 1958-59.

**Leading Details**

| | | | |
|---|---|---|---|
| 1. | Water spread area | — | 265.9 sq.miles or 655 sq.km. |
| | Dead storage area | — | 50 sq.miles |
| | Total water storage capacity | — | 5.345 million ft. |
| | Dam length | — | 514 metres |
| | Height | — | 65 M. |
| | Crust gate | — | 10 Nd. |
| | Sluice gate | — | 9 Nd. |
| | Discharge capacity | — | 13705 Cu. M./Se |
| | Max-length of the reservoir | — | 112 kilo metre |
| | 11 Breadth of the reservoir | — | 32 km. |
| | Catchment area | — | 22,533 sq. km. |
| | Basin | — | Rocky |
| | Rate of silting | — | 0.0857 la/sqm. |

Gandhi Sagar has an important place in fish culture nearly 34,000 acres of water area is available for fish culture. Preliminary survey shows that the dam was having 39 varieties of fish fauna including some of the economically important spp. According to 1948-49 fisheries survey the following spp. were recorded which are farming the fishery of the lake.

1. Tortoise
2. Carps both Major and Minor carps
3. Om Pokoima Calatus
4. Wattu
5. M. Seenghala
6. Maor
7. Rita rita
8. Bagariles
9. Silonia silohia

10. Channispp
11. Liza corsula, etc.

About 200 families were living around the dam. Most of them have originated from Calcutta and Bangladesh. They are using cast nets, a cotton twines to catch fishes. The reservoir is the combined property of the Rajasthan and M. P. Govt. these are the dams and one barrage named Rana Pratap Sagar, Jawahar Sagar and Kotla barrage respectively. Both the Governments have equal rights of electricity and irrigation. One bank of the reservoir comes in M.P., and other in Rajasthan. The entire Chambal valley project was estimated to cost Rs.100 crores. The cost of construction of Gandhi Sagar reservoir is 35 crores. After completion of the reservoir 59 villages were completely submerged and 169 villages, partially under water.

### *Stocking*

The fisheries development programme was started in 1958-59 on scientific pattern in this reservoir. The seed of the quick growing and economically profitable fishes have stocked in the reservoir every year. Total 48, 03953 lakhs major carp fingerlings and 1,80,000 common carp fingerlings have been stocked till 1973-74. The Govt. has constructed a fish farm called 'Nauther'. The total area of the farm is 8.74 acre. There are 57 nurseries and rearing ponds. The collection of seed is done from joining area mostly from dry bundh, previously it was brought from Calcutta.

Yearwise stocking figures of Fingerlings.

| Year | Fingerlings stocked |
|---|---|
| M. Carp | |
| 69.70 | 161,130 |
| 70.71 | 8,327 |
| 71.72 | 585406 |
| 72.73 | 320040 |
| 73.74 | 200000 |
| Common carp | 1,80,000 |

## Fateh Sagar Lake

Fateh Sagar lake is situated at the southern point of Udaipur city near Sahelion-ki Bari. It is situated at 1983 ft. above mean sea level. It was constructed in 1678 but the remodelling was done in 1890. The water spread area of the lake is 639 acres which is the mean water spread area. As the sides are hilly the depts does not affect the water spread during the summer and the rainy season. The total catchment area is about 8 sq. miles. The length of the dam is 2,600 ft. and height is 50 ft. on the sides of the dam is the waste wair through which the surplus water is passed out.

The soil of the lake is loamy clay.

### *Fish Production*

A number of different species of fishes are available in the lake. The presence of *labco rohita*, *C.Mrigla* are of special significants in view of its economic importance. Another featues of great importance is the availability of Marheseer, cat fishes, Mlerrels are seldom caught. Catla is absent in the lake.

It has been observed during 1966 that advanced fingerlings of Rehu, Mahaseer, were caught when small side caste nets were operated which indicated that natural jereeding is taking place in the lake. The lake has been stocked with fish seed. During monsoon fishes with ripe gonads were observed ascending against the current in the bud channel for breeding.

But in order to increase the production of the lake it has been decided to stock advanced fingerlings of major carps at the rate of 500 fingerlings per acre. The total requirement for stocking the lake is about 3 lakhs. For establishing catla in the lake about 5001 of the total stocking would comprise catla only.

About 8 acres of land have been alloted for the construction of fish farm in the south-west side of the lake. The object of such farm is to produce fingerlings for stocking.

**Exploitation**

Gill nets are used for catching the fishes, since the main water spread area of he lake is about 600 acres. This can be easily controlled. Moreover, due to self stocking and presence of rich food organises, a high productive of 200 kg./hectare is anticipated by the Fisheries Department. Thus the revenue will be Rs.2 Lakhs per year at the roughly rate of Rs.1,500.00 per tonne.

**Rihand Reservoir (U.P.)**

This reservoir has come up after the construction of dam over the river Rend near Pipari village in Mirzapur district of U.P. 46 kms miles upstream of its confluence vide river sone at Chopan. The artificial lake thus created in 1962 is spread over an average of 180 sq. miles and is primarily a hydro electric project.

***Physical Features of the Reservoir***

The width of the dam is 3000 ft. and height is 294 ft which gives Maximum water depth of 250 ft. The area submerged in mostly hilly terrains dense forest which were not cleared before impoundment. Rarely at some places, sandy bottom is observed. The average rainfall in this area is 56"/year.

***Physico-chemical Conditions***

In the course of post impoundment survey the physico-chemical and Hydro-biological data were also collected, which reveal that plankton density per litre of water at the surface ranged between 11 to 22 organisers per litre as compared to 2-5 organisers/litre at 16 metres and 1-4 organisers/litre at 32 metre below the surface. It was obvious that the primary productivity of Rihand Reservoir was extremely poor. Amongst the 300 plankton, Rotifers and copeponds were mainly.

### *Fish Farm*

Since rearing facilities were not available in the area, a fish farm comprising of 150 nurseries of 20.70 acres, 16 rearing ponds of 9.61 acres and 10 breed ponds of 3.72 acres were provided and has been completed close to the breeding areas. Only 7,000 fingerlings of carpio have been socked so far.

### *Exploitation*

The fishing is conducted in the reservoir only for nine months during the year. The period from June to August is observed as closed season. The vastness of the area and presence of submerged stumps and hillocks did not permit large scale departmental exploitation. In such a situation the fishing was envisaged through the agency of contractors given for 3 years. The catch is given to the contractor who aids the highest price. Tenders for lifting the fish catch from the landing centre are initiated every year for different varieties of fishes.

## Keeham Reservoir, Agra (U.P.)

Keeham is an artificial reservoir having an area of 640 acres (1 sq.mile). It is situated on Agra Delhi stational Highway at a distance of 20 km. from Agra.

The reservoir was constructed in 1923 to serve as reserved stock of water for drinking purposes in case of emergency.

The scientific development of fisheries in this reservoir was taken up by the fisheries department in the year 1952-53. Prior to this, the exploitation of fish in the reservoir was being managed by the Irrigation department and an average revenue of Rs.8,000 was being earned by leasing to the contractor.

### Fish Fauna

No special scientific study of the fish fauna, of the reservoir have been undertaken so far by the Department. But from day today fishing the following species have been collected:

1. L. Rohita 2. C.Catla 3. C. Mrigala 4. L. Calbasa 5. L.Gonias 6. L. Bata 7. L. Pongusia 8. C.Reba 9. Punctiles Sarona 10.W. Attu 11. M. Seenghala 12.M.Aor 13. Rita rita 14. P.Pangasiles 15. N. Chitola 16. N. hotop ferns, etc.

## Stocking

The stocking in reservoir with major carps fingerlings at the rate of 2, 000 per acre was reported since 1952-53 stocking of this lake is wholly dependent upon natural collection from Keethm rola which connect river Jamuna. This is done very easily because of peculiar topography of the reservoir.

Yearwise and species wise stocking figures are given below for nine years (1965-1974).

| *Year* | *Total No. of fingerlings stocked* | *Size* | *Species composition* | | | | *Expenditure on stocking* |
|---|---|---|---|---|---|---|---|
| | | | *Rehu* | *Mrigal* | *Catla* | *Cal.* | |
| 1965-66 | 7,50,000 | 2"-3" | 24.1% | 31.6% | 20.6% | 23.7% | Rs. 24.00 |
| 1966-67 | 10,06,000 | 2"-3" | 20.3% | 36.1% | 26.7% | 16.9% | Rs. 130.00 |
| 1967-68 | 12,80,000 | 2"-3" | 44.1% | 30.7% | 20% | 5.1% | Rs. 273.00 |
| 1968-69 | 12,90,000 | 4½"-11" | 38.8% | 41.2% | 16.7% | 4.3% | Rs. 270.00 |
| 1969-70 | 13,10,000 | 5"-3" | 38.5% | 26% | 28.5% | 7.5% | Rs. 336.00 |
| 1970-71 | 9,83,500 | 2"-6pp | 32.0% | 22.0% | 17.0% | 29% | Rs. 234.00 |
| 1971-72 | 12,85,000 | 2"-6" | 29.36% | 28.17% | 39.75% | 2.12% | Rs. 225.00 |
| 1972-73 | 2,00,350 | 3.30cm. | 49.0% | 41.2% | 5.8% | 4% | Rs. 63.00 |
| 1973-74 | 7,05,180 | 5.28cm. | 16.0% | 52.3% | 17.6% | — | Rs. 261.00 |

## Production and Revenue

The reservoir is very productive. The production has touched a new high peak of 232.25 kg./acre which is perhaps one of the highest productions per acre in India.

**Pollution of Lakes in India**

It has been claimed by the environment study group that more than 50, 000 big and small lakes in the world are either dead or they are in the process of dying. In India, except Kodai Kanal and Mukerti lakes of Nilgiri, all 18 other lakes situated above 2000 metres from sea level are badly affected by pollutants. The endangered Indian lakes are Nainital and Bhimtal in Uttar Pradesh, Dal, and Wular in Kashmir, Pushkar in Rjasthan, Loktak in Manipur, Khichipiri in Sikkim and Udhagamandalam in Tamil Nadu.

While in western countries the lakes have been polluted by acid rains, in a developing country like India they are in danger due to eutrophication — excessive plant growth caused by pesticides, sewage, fertilizer runoffs and open air pollution. The total area of lakes in India cover 0.2 million hectares. Most of the lakes near big urban places are found to be heavily polluted. The Ahmedabad lake is totally eutrophied. The famous Hussain Sagar of Hyderabad is in the process of dying by massive killing of fishes.

In some cases the lack of oxygen also endangered the species in the lake. In an eutrophic lake, the oxygen content varies from sufficient at the surface to very low at the bottom. In case of Nainital lake the bottom is anoxiototally without oxygen. The causes for the slow death of the Dal lake in Kashmir are attributed to the creation of gardens and planting of trees around the lake to feed the wood industries of Pahalgam besides increasing amount of wood and population pressure. But most alarming is due to the rapid spread of floating gardens, encroachment on fringes of the lake by willow planters and construction of a take shore road under the World Bank supported Dal development programme. Another sewage system is highly needed for Srinagar to prevent the lake from pollution by the city sewer.

1. Effect of domestic sewage on aquatic ecosystem and human health,
2. Effect of agricultural and forestry practices,
3. Effect of industrial wastes,
4. Effect of engineering works,

5. Effect of exotic biota
6. Effect of recreational activities.

On the above six areas, at least first three are involved with biology of pollution. The subject and organic pollution, eutrophication, toxic pollution, thermal and mine pollution etc. have now become specialized of works.

The organic pollution largely originates from domestic sewage (raw or treated), urban runoff, industrial runoff, industrial effluents and waste from farmland. Effluent from sewage can be considered as the major source of organic pollution of wetlands.

A new international organisation "Wetland International" has been launched in October 1996 to meet the challanges of arresting the loss of degradation of wetlands requires new way of working and a significant increase in level of activity has been noticed.

## REFERENCES

Ahmad, S.S., *Ecology of Wetlands of Milkichak*, Darbhanga, Ph. D. thesis, L.N. Mithila University, Darbhanga, 1993.

Cowardin, L.M., V.Carter, F.C. Colet, and E.T. La Roe, *Classification of Wetlands and deep water habitats of United States*, U.S. Fish and Wildlife Service Pub., FWS/OBS- 79/31, Washington, D.C., 1979, p. 103.

Mitch, W.J. and J.G. Gosselink, *Wetlands*, Van Nostrand Reinhold Company, New York, 1986, p. 537.

Moore, P.D.(ed.), *European Mires*, Academic Press, London, 1984, p. 367.

Moore, P. D. and D. J. Bellamy, *Peatlands Springer,* Verlag, New York, 1974. p. 221.

Shaw, S.P., and C.G. Fredine, *Wetlands of the United States, Their extent and other wild life*, U.S. Dept. of Interior, Fish and Wild Life Service, Circular 39, Washington, D.C. 1956, p. 67.

Smith, R.L., *Ecology and Field Biology*, (3rd. ed.) Harper and Row, New York, 1980, p. 835.

Steward, R. E. and H.A. Kantrud, *Classification of natural ponds and lake in the glaciated Praise region*, U. S. Fish and Wild Life Service Research Pub. 92, 1971, p. 57.

Trishal, C.L. and D.P. Zutshi, *Ecology and Management of Wetland Ecosystem in India*, MAB, Department of Environment, Govt. of India, 1985, p. 27.

Wetlands, The newsletter of Wetlands International, Institute of Advanced Studies, University of Malaya, 50603, Kuala Lampur, Malaysia, 1995. p.1.

Zinn, J.A. and C. Copeland, *Wetland Management*, Congressional Research Service, The Library of Congress, Washington, D.C., 1982, p. 149.

# 10

# SOIL AND WATER OF WETLANDS

Soil and Water are the composite form of mineral constituent (45%) organic matter (5%), air (25%) and water (25%) and they form the upper layer of the earth surface. In wetland soil the presence of organic matter is relatively high. The organic matter of soil is an active state of decomposition caused by micro-organisms. Thus it is a transient soil constituent which must be renewed by the addition of organic residues. The amount of organic matter in the soil represents a balance between the addition of plant residue and the destructive decomposition by soil micro-organism. In a representative wetland soil, the organic matter in the top soil is about 3 to 5 per cent by weight. It is low but it has a great influence in setting productive properties of the soil.

## Soil Water

The presence of water in the soil is quite essential for all the physical, chemical, and biological activities in soils. The moisture retaining capacity in soils is of varying nature which depend on the porocity of soil. It acts as a medicine for the transport of nutrient from soil to plant roots. Plants absorb water from soil through their roots which is necessary for metabolic processes, mainly, photosynthesis, maintaining soil turbidity and regulating plant temperature. The soil water also influences the activities of soil organisms, matter decomposition and the transformation of nutrients. The soil water also acts as a solvent and hastens the weathering of roots and minerals in soils. The biological properties of soil components would enable man to manage the soil environment in a manner conducive to optimum crop production. In the wetlands of North Bihar the soil association regions are as follows :

(a) The recent alluvium-non saline.
(b) Non-calcareous soils of the Kosi Mahananda System.
(c) Young alluvium non-saline, non-calcareous soils of the Kosi Mahananda System.
(d) Young alluvium non-saline, non-calcareous soils of the Adhwara System (Baghmati, Kumla-Balan) and young alluvium calcareous soils of the Gandak System.

**Table 10.1 :** Surveyed Wetlands of North Bihar

| *Sl. No.* | *Name of wetlands* | *Name of Anchal* | *District survey* | *Date of survey* |
|---|---|---|---|---|
| 1. | Narha | Raghopur | Supaul | 03.10.94 |
| 2. | Tilabayman | Supaul | Supaul | 07.10.94 |
| 3. | Chauri | Kahara | Saharsa | 16.10.94 |
| 4. | Lasahar | Supaul | Supaul | 17.10.94 |
| 5. | Dighi | Basantpur | Supaul | 29.10.94 |
| 6. | Balapatti | Basantpur | Supaul | 20.10.94 |
| 7. | Bhagwatpur | Chhatapur | Supaul | 27.10.94 |
| 8. | Cenia | Chhatapur | Supaul | 10.10.94 |
| 9. | Dhasundha | Tribeniganj | Supaul | 25.10.94 |
| 10. | Terrha | Tribeniganj | Supaul | 25.10.94 |
| 11. | Ketara | Tribeniganj | Supaul | 25.10.94 |
| 12. | Finglesh | Raghopur | Supaul | 01.11.94 |
| 13. | Paraharma | Raghopur | Supaul | 01.11.94 |
| 14. | Dehla | Raghopur | Supaul | 01.11.94 |
| 15. | Nardang | Raghopur | Supaul | 31.10.94 |
| 16. | Gordah | Simri-Bakhtiarpur | Supaul | 11.11.94 |
| 17. | Khagma | Saikhua | Supaul | 08.11.94 |
| 18. | Tinmuha | Sour Bazar | Supaul | 16.11.94 |
| 19. | Rareba | Salkhua | Supaul | 07.11.94 |
| 20. | Laib | Sonbarsa | Supaul | 14.1.94 |
| 21. | Marghati | Simri-Bakhtiarpur | Supaul | 12.11.94 |
| 22. | Chakmaka | Barhara | Supaul | 08.02.95 |

*(Contd.)*

*Table 10.1 (Contd.)*

| | | | | |
|---|---|---|---|---|
| 23. | Kumarkhad | Barhara | Purnea | 13.62.95 |
| 24. | Bhangha chap | Barhara | Purnea | 11.02.95 |
| 25. | Bargaon Kateens | Nauhatta | Sharsa | 16.02.95 |
| 26. | Chauri | Nauhatta | Saharsa | 19.02.95 |
| 27. | Bagaghesan | Pipra | Supaul | 22.02.95 |
| 28. | Hezar Panch | Barari | Katihar | 06.03.95 |
| 29. | Maikayan | Mansahi | Katihar | 14.03.95 |
| 30. | Sonakhal | Mansahi | Katihar | 11.03.95 |
| 31. | Jhauedhab | Barari | Katihar | 13.03.95 |
| 32. | Motijheel | Motihari | East Chemparan | 26.10.94 |
| 33. | Ratahari | Bairia | East Chemparan | 30.10.94 |
| 34. | Gangaram | Nautan | W. Champaran | 31.10.94 |
| 35. | Maniyari | Bairia | W. Champaran | 30.10.94 |
| 36. | Gangaram | Bairia | W. Champaran | 30.10.94 |
| 37. | Saraiyaman | Bairia | W. Champartri | 29.10.54 |
| 38. | Karariaman | Motihari | W. Champaran | 28.10.94 |
| 39. | Gehiri | Nautan | W. Champaran | 31.10.94 |
| 40. | Dhanauti | Motihari | W. Champaran | 27.10.94 |
| 41. | Chanmari Chaur | Nautan | W. Champaran | 06.11.94 |
| 42. | Bardie Chaur | Sonepur | Saran | 04.12.94 |
| 43. | Baraila Tal | Jandaha | Vaishali | 21.11.94 |
| 44. | Kesaria Chaur | Kesaria | E. Champaran | 28.11.94 |
| 45. | Chamara Chaur | Patepur | Vaishali | 23.11.94 |
| 46. | Kachudhua | Thakurganj | Kishanganj | 04.01.95 |
| 47. | Ghogha | Kishanganj | Kishanganj | 12.01.95 |
| 48. | Dahichal Chaur | Kishanganj | Kishanganj | 22.12.95 |
| 49. | Shitala | Kochadhamin | Kishanganj | 31.12.94 |
| 50. | Tengarmari | Kishanganj | Kishanganj | 10.02.95 |
| 51. | Sodha | Kishanganj | Kishanganj | 12.02.95 |
| 52. | Goga-Beel | Amebad | Katihar | 16.02.95 |
| 53. | Baghar Beel | Manihari | Katihar | 18.02.95 |
| 54. | Koshban | Manihari | Katihar | 20.02.95 |
| 55. | Sowa | Manihari | Katihar | 22.02.95 |
| 56. | Fulbhasa | Thakurganj | Kishanganj | 25.02.95 |
| 57. | Ruidhasa | Thakurganj | Kishanganj | 27.02.95 |
| 58. | Khemdah | Thakurganj | Kishanganj | 01.03.95 |
| 59. | Ruidhas | Thakurganj | Kishanganj | 03.03.95 |
| 60. | Gothara-Kanakpur | Thakurganj | Kishanganj | 05.03.95 |
| 61. | Kabar | Khodabandpur | Bagusarai | 27.10.94 |
| 62. | Bororit lake | Bagusarai | Begusarai | 20.02.95 |

(*Contd.*)

*Table 10.1 (Contd.)*

| | | | | |
|---|---|---|---|---|
| 63. | Merda | Balia | Begusarai | 20.02.95 |
| 64. | Moin Lake | Majhaul | Begusarai | 20.02.95 |
| 65. | Jeewaya Lake | Majhaul | Begusarai | 20.02.95 |
| 66. | Narail Chaur | Kusheshwar Asthan | Darbhanga | 30.10.94 |
| 67. | Baheri | Darbhanga | Darbhanga | 01.12.94 |
| 68. | Dighi | Darbhanga | Darbhanga | 23.11.94 |
| 69. | Rajokhar | Manigachhi | Darbhanga | 10.11.94 |
| 70. | Ganga Sagar | Darbhanga | Darbhanga | 22.11.94 |
| 71. | Mahadev Tank | Manigachhi | Darbhanga | 16.11.94 |
| 72. | Kathara | Manigachhi | Darbhanga | 11.11.95 |
| 73. | Pachkurwa Sahra | Manigachhi | Darbhanga | 14.01.95 |
| 74. | Shisulia | Manigachhi | Darbhanga | 21.01.95 |
| 75. | Masbasi | Manigachhi | Darbhanga | 13.02.95 |
| 76. | Belhi | Manigachhi | Darbhanga | 18.02.95 |
| 77. | Ghordaur | Manigachhi | Darbhanga | 25.02.95 |
| 78. | Simardah | Baheri | Darbhanga | 06.03.95 |
| 79. | Deihara | Baheri | Darbhanga | 10.03.95 |
| 80. | Mahsar Chaur | Baheri | Darbhanga | 13.03.95 |
| 81. | Simri Maun | Jogapatti | W. Champaran | 08.01.96 |
| 82. | Chatia Chaur | Bettiah | W. Champaran | 12.01.96 |
| 83. | Lal Saraiya Maun | Majhaulia | W. Champaran | 16.01.96 |
| 84. | Amua Maun | Majhaulia | W. Champaran | 21.01.96 |
| 85. | Brahampura Maun | Musahri | Muzaffarpur | 24.01.96 |
| 86. | Manika Maun | Musahri | Muzaffarpur | 28.01.96 |
| 87. | Bharthua Chaur | Aurai | Muzaffarpur | 09.01.96 |
| 88. | Sora Jheel | Purnea Sadar | Purnea | 04.02.96 |
| 89. | Kajha Kothi Tank | Purnea Sadar | Purnea | 30.01.96 |
| 90. | Banbhag Jheel | Krityanand Nagar | Purnea | 29.01.96 |
| 91. | Dhima Makhnaha | Banmankhi | Purnea | 03.02.96 |
| 92. | Rambag | Banmankhi | Purnea | 05.02.96 |
| 93. | Dasyn Chaur | Bakhri | Begusarai | 15.01.96 |
| 94. | Mahsar Chaur | Rosra | Samastipur | 16.06.96 |
| 95. | Kanail Chaur | Manigachhi | Darbhanga | 17.06.96 |
| 96. | Phulhara Chaur | Biraul | Darbhanga | 05.07.95 |
| 97. | Ghordaur | Keoti | Darbhanga | 08.07.95 |
| 98. | Ballipur Moin | Rosra | Samastipur | 10.07.95 |
| 99. | Krishnaraj Sagar | Madhubani | Madhubani | 12.07.95 |
| 100. | Madhwapur Chaur | Madhwapur | Darbhanga | 16.07.95 |
| 101. | Hirni Chaur | Birau-1 | Darbhanga | 16.07.95 |
| 102. | Benua-Fharkia | Koparia | Saharsa | 19.07.95 |

*(Contd.)*

*Table 10.1 (Contd.)*

| | | | | |
|---|---|---|---|---|
| 103. | Khetar | Kesaria | E.Champaran | 22.07.95 |
| 104. | Manshi | Phuljakhar | W.Champaran | 24.07.95 |
| 105. | Bhagwa Chaur | Balna Bazar | Saharsa | 28.07.95 |
| 106. | Murdapur Chaur | Murdapur | Saharsa | 05.08.95 |
| 107. | Ratanpura Chaur | Kumarganj | Saharsa | 07.08.95 |
| 108. | Ahiya | Mahna | Vaishali | 10.08.95 |
| 109. | Naimelia Chaur | Hajipur | Vaishali | 12.08.95 |
| 110. | Raghopur Diara | Hajipur | Vaishali | 14.08.95 |
| 111. | Bora Chaur | Kharka Talwa | Saharsa | 20.08.95 |
| 112. | Kulesra Chaur | Turki | Muzaffarpur. | 20.03.96 |
| 113. | Telia Chaur | Kudhni | Muzaffarpur | 21.03.96 |
| 114. | Mahwal Maun | Motipur | Muzaffarpur | 22.03.96 |
| 115. | Kanti Lake | Kanti | Mazaffarpur | 24.03.96 |

**Physico-Chemical Analysis of Water**

*Temperature* : Surface water temperature was recorded with the help of mercury thermometer while bottom water temperature was recorded by a reversible thermometer.

*Hydrogen ion I concentration (pH)* : The pH of the water was recorded by griph pH meter (Systronics).

*Conductivity*: It was recorded with the help of conductivity bridge and the value was expressed as micro Siemens/cm.

*Dissolved Oxygen ($DO_2$)* : It was analysed by the Winkler's volumetric method with azide modification. The sample was collected in BOD bottle without bubbling and was fixed with 2ml of Mn $SO_4$ followed by 2ml of alkaline iodide. The resultant brown precipitate was dissolved by the addition of 2 ml of conc. $H_2SO_4$. 50ml of the above solution was titrated against N/40$Na_2S_2O_3$ using starch as an indicator.

The $DO_2$ content is calculated by the following formula:

$$DO_2\,(mg/I) = \frac{8 \times 1000 \times N \times V_1}{V_2}$$

**Table 10.2 :** Pooled Mean Soil Analysis of some of Wetlands in North Bihar

| *Sl.* | *Wetland* | *Taxture* | *pH* | *T.S.S.* | $P_2O_5$ *A.V.* | *Organic Carbon %* | *N* | *P* | *K* | *F.Y.M.* |
|---|---|---|---|---|---|---|---|---|---|---|
| 1. | Simri Maun | Medium Light | 6.8 | 0.129 | 15 | 0.48 | 110 | 55 | 35 | 8.5 |
| 2. | Lal Saraiya Maun | Medium Light | 7.1 | 0.200 | 72 | 0.54 | 43 | 32 | 22 | 8.00 |
| 3. | Amua Maun | Light | 7.6 | 0.764 | 60 | 0.18 | 100 | 50 | 25 | 10.0 |
| 4. | Chatia Chaur | Medium Light | 6.7 | 0.300 | 41 | 0.41 | 100 | 55 | 37 | 9.0 |
| 5. | Brahmpura Maun | Medium Light | 7.1 | 0.190 | 42 | 0.48 | 75 | 40 | 27 | 8.5 |
| 6. | Mania Maun | Medium Light | 7.1 | 0.350 | 11 | 0.47 | 95 | 80 | 35 | 8.5 |
| 7. | Bharthua Chaur | Medium | 7.0 | 0.250 | 13 | 0.46 | 100 | 80 | 20 | 10.0 |
| 8. | Sora Jheel | Light | 7.2 | 0.250 | 18 | 1.09 | 75 | 65 | 30 | 5.0 |
| 9. | Banbhag Jheel | Medium Light | 7.3 | 0.260 | 31 | 0.69 | 100 | 67 | 25 | 6.0 |
| 10. | Dhima Mahnaha Chaur | Medium | 7.1 | 0.160 | 28 | 0.65 | 30 | 22 | 20 | 7.5 |
| 11. | Rambag | Medium | 7.1 | 0.400 | 29 | 0.65 | 90 | 67 | 35 | 7.5 |

*Source :* Tested in the Laboratory, 1996.

where, $V_1$ = Volume of titrant
$V_2$ = Volume of sample titrated
N = Normality of $Na_2S_20_3$

*Free Carbon Dioxide ($FCO_2$)* : It was estimated with the help of phenolphthalein as an indicator and titrated against standard alkali (N/44 NaOH) solution. To 50 ml of sample water, 2 drops of above indicator was added. Solution remained colourless which indicated the presence of $FCO_2$ in the sample. Now it was titrated against N/ 44 NaOH. End point was slight pink in colour. Calculation was made as follows:

$$FCO_2\ (mg/1) = \frac{\text{ml. Titrated x 1000}}{\text{ml. of sample water}}$$

**Alkalinity**

*Carbonate*

It was determined using phepolphthalein as an indicator and N/50 $H_2SO_4$ as titrant. To 50 ml of sample water, 2 drops of indicator was added. Pink colour indicates the presence of carbonate. End point is colourless. Calculation was made as follows:

$$CO_3\ (mg/I) = \frac{\text{ml. Titrated x 1000}}{\text{ml. of Sample water}}$$

*Bicarbonate ($HCO_3$)*

It was estimated by titrating the sample water against N/5OH$_2$SO$_4$ using Methyl Orange as an indicator. End point was pink colour. Calculation was made as follows:

$$\text{Biocarbonate (mg/I)} = \frac{\text{ml. of Titrant x 1000}}{\text{ml. of sample water}}$$

*Total Hardness*

It was determined by titrimetric method using EDTA as titrant and Eriochrome Black 'T' as indicator (APHA, 1989)

In 50 ml of sample water, half tablet of Eriochrome Black 'T' indicator was added and shaked to dissolve. To it lml of Ammonia buffer followed by 1/2 ml. of 4N NaOH was added, which developed wine red colour. The above solution was titrated against N/50 EDTA solution. End point was blue colour. Calculation was made as follows:

$$\text{Total hardness (mg/l)} = \frac{\text{ml. of Titrant x 1000}}{\text{ml. of sample water}}$$

*Calcium hardness*

It was determined by calcium hardness indicator tablet and N/50 EDTA solution as titrant (APHA, 1989) In 50 ml of sample water, 1/2 tablet of calcium hardness indicator was added and shaked. 1/2 ml of 4N NaOH was added to the above solution. Pink colour develops. Now the above solution was titrated against N/50 EDTA solution. End point was violet colour. Calculation was made as follows:

$$\text{Calcium hardness (mg/l)} = \frac{\text{ml. of Titrant x 1000}}{\text{ml. of sample water}}$$

*Calcium :* It was calculated as follows (APHA, 1989):

$$Ca^{++} \text{ (mg/l)} = \frac{\text{Ca Hardness x 4}}{10}$$

*Magnesium :* It was calculated as follows (APHA, 1989):

$$Mg^{++} \text{ (mg/l)} = \text{TH — CaH) x 0.244}$$

*Chloride :* It was estimated by argentotitrimetric method (APHA, 1989) using 0.0141 N $AgNO_3$ as titrant and potassium chromate as indicator. Calculation was made as follows:

$$Cl^{-1}\ (mg/l) = \frac{\text{ml. of Titrant x N x 35.46 x 1000}}{\text{ml of sample water}}$$

*Sodium ($Na^+$) :* It was determined by the 'Flame Photometric Method (APHA'1989). The instructions for sodium estimation were followed as supplied by the manufacturer of ''Flame Photometer", using sodium filter and standard curve.

*Potassium ($K^+$) :* It was also determined by the "Flame Photometric Method" (APHA,1989) instead of sodium here potassium filter was used.

*Silicate :* Silicate in sample was determined according to the method described by Jhingran *et al.* (1969). Standard potassium chromate (248mgL-1), 10 per cent Ammonium molybdate and 25 per cent Sulphuric acid were used as reagents. The value was expressed in mgl-l.

*Phosphate Phosphorus ($PO_4$-P) :* It was determined spectrophotometrically. 50 ml of sample water was filtered. 2ml of ammonium molybdate reagent was added followed by 5 drops of $SnCl_2$ solution. Blue colour developed of this which was determined at 690 nm on a spectrophotometer using distilled water as a blank. The value was compared with the standard curve and expressed as mg/I.

***Nitrate Nitrogen ($NO_3$-N)***

It was determined by phenol di-sulphonic acid method spectrophotometrically. 50 ml of sample water was filtered and heated to dryness. 2ml of phenol di-sulphonic acid was added and the final volume was made upto 50ml. With distilled water. 6ml of liquid ammonia was added which developed yellow colour. The reading was taken at 410 nm on a spectrophotometer with distilled water as blank. The value was compared with the standard curve and expressed as mg/I.

## Physico-Chemical analysis of Soil

### *Conductivity*

It was determined according to Trivedy and Goel (1984). Soil solution was prepared in 1:5 ratio and the conductivity value was recorded immediately with the help of conductivity bridge. The values were expressed as micro-mhos $cm^{-1}$.

### Hydrogen ion Concentration (pH)

Hydrogen, ion concentration (pH) of soil suspension (1:5) was determined with the help of griph pH meter according to Trivedy and Goel, (1984) method.

### Alkalinity

Total alkalinity was determined by the titration of soil solution (1:5) with strong acid (0.1N HCL) (Trivedy and Goel, 1984) using phenolphthalein and methyl orange as indicators. Phenolphthalein alkalinity denotes the value of carbonate. If the solution remained colourless on adding phenolphthalein then carbonate alkalinity is zero. Now methyl orange alkalinity was determined which gives the value of total alkalinity.

$$\text{Total alkalinity (mg/10-g)} = \frac{\text{(ml x N) of HCl x 500}}{\text{ml of soil solution.}}$$

### *Organic Matter*

Organic matter of soil was determined by the modified Walkley and Black method (Trivedy and Goel, 1984).

The organic matter of the soil was digested with excess of $K_2Cr_2$ O7 $SO_4$. The residual unutilized $K_2$Cr207 was then titrated against ferrous ammonium sulphate. Calculation was made as follows:

$$\% \text{ organic matter} = \frac{3.951}{g} (1\text{-}T/S) \times 1.724$$

where, g = Wt. of sample in gm.

S = ml of ferrous solution with blank titration

T = ml of ferrous solution with sample solution.

***Organic carbon :*** It was calculated as follows:

% Carbon = % Organic matter/1.724

### *Chloride*

It was estimated titrimetrically using Potassium chromate as indicator and $AgNO_3$ as titrant (Trivedy and Goel, 1984) of the soil suspension (1:5). Calculation was made as follows:

$$Cl^{-1} \text{ (mg/100g)} = \frac{\text{ml. x N of } AgNO_3 \times 35.5 \times 1000}{\text{ml. soil solution} \times 2}$$

### *Total Calcium and Total Magnesium*

It was determined by titrimetric method using EDTA as titrant and Ca hardness tablet as indicator (Trivedy and Goel, 1984).

50g of air dried soil sample was mixed with 100 ml ammonium acetate solution. The suspension was kept over night and then filtered through Whatman filter paper (No.50). The filtrate was titrated against EDTA solution.

For total Magnesium, first total hardness was determined and from it the value of Ca hardness was subtracted. Calculation was made as follows:

$$\text{Ca (mg/100g)} = \frac{\text{A x 400.8V}}{\text{V x S x 10}}$$

$$\text{Mg (mg/100g)} = \frac{\text{(B-A) x 400.8 x V}}{\text{V x 1.645 x S x 10}}$$

Where, A = Volume of EDTA used for calcium determination
B = Volume of EDTA used for Ca and Mg determination
V = Total Vol. of soil extract prepared (500ml)
S = Weight of soil (50g)
V = Vol. of soil extract titrated

***Total Sodium and Total Potassium***

For this estimation the ammonium acetate leachate was used. The level of Na and K in ammonium lachate was obtained by flame photometer as described in the case of water analysis.

$$\text{Total Sodium (mg/100g)} = \frac{\text{mg Na/1 of Soil extract x V}}{\text{10 x S}}$$

$$\text{Total Potassium (mg/100g)} = \frac{\text{mg K/1 of soil extract x V}}{\text{10 x S}}$$

where V = Total volume of Soil extract prepared
S = Weight of Soil taken (g)

**Nitrate**

For estimation of nitrate, 50g of dry soil was taken in a flask and to which 25ml of nitrate extraction reagent was added. The solution was mixed for 15 minutes. Then 0.5 of calcium hydroxide was added to the mixture and the solution was mixed further for 5 minutes. To this solution lg of magnesium carbonate was added and mixed thoroughly. The contents was filtered through a Whatman No. 50

filter paper and the total volume of filtrate was measured. The nitrate content of the filtrate was determined spectrophotometrically as described earlier for water analysis.

$$\text{Nitrate (mg/100g)} = \frac{F \times V}{10 \times S}$$

where, F = Nitrate determined in filtrate (mg/1)
V = Total volume of filtrate (ml)
S = Weight of soil taken (g)

**Ammonical Nitrogen**

For estimation of ammonical nitrogen l00g of fresh soil sample was taken in a 500 ml conical flask and mixed with 200 ml of acidified $NaC_l$ solution. After 30 minutes the suspension was filtered through Whatman No. 42 filter paper. The conical flask was rinsed with 500 ml of NaCkkl solution and rinsings was poured into the soil.

Soil was also leached with additional 200 ml of sodium chloride. The volume of leachate was raised to 500 ml with acidified sodium chloride solution. Now calibration curve was prepared by placing aliquots of diluted standard (ranging between 3 to 30 ml) in a series of 100 ml voiumetric flas. 2ml of sodium tartrate solution and 50ml of acidified sodium chloride was added to it and final volume was raised to 90 ml with distilled water. Now 5ml of Nessler reagent was mixed thoroughly and again volume of the content was raised to 100 ml. Finally, percentage transmission was observed at 41onm. Calibration curve was prepared by plotting percentage transmission against concentration on a linear scale. Soil extract was also prepared for estimation of ammonium as descrived above except acidified sodium chloride was not added.

Ammonical Nitrogen (mg/100g)= 10 x (mg NH4 from curve).

**Available Phosphorus**

For estimation of available phosphorus lg of air dried soil was taken in a flask and to it 200 ml of 0.002N $H_2SO_4$ was mixed. The

**Table 10.3 :** Chemical Analysis of some of the Water Sample of North Bihar

| *Sl. No.* | *Wetland* | *P.H. Value* | *Cloride* | *Sulphate* | *Quality of Water* | *Oxidizing Agent* | *Reducing Agent* |
|---|---|---|---|---|---|---|---|
| 1. | Maikayan Lake Katihar | 7.00 | Present | Negligible | Crystal Clear | Absent | Absent |
| 2. | Marda, Bagusarai | 7.00 | Present | Absent | Crystal Clear | Absent | Absent |
| 3. | Kewar, Begusarai | 7.00 | Heavily Present | Absent | Crystal Clear | Absent | Absent |
| 4. | Dhaneuti, E. Champaran | 7.00 | Present | Absent | Fungi in Water | Absent | Absent |
| 5. | Brahamputra, Muzaffarpur | 6.00 | Present | Absent | Muddy | Absent | Absent |
| 6. | Mania Lake, Muzaffarpur | 7.00 | Negligibly Present | Absent | Crystal Clear | Absent | Absent |
| 7. | Bharthua Chaur, Muzaffarpur | 7.00 | Present | Present family | Crystal Clear | Absent | Absent |
| 8. | Chatia Chaur, Champaran | 7.00 | Present | Absent | Crystal Clear | Absent | Absent |
| 9. | Amua Maun, W. Champaran | 7.00 | Present | Absent | Crystal Clear | Absent | Absent |
| 10. | Lal Saraiya, Champaran | 7.00 | Present | Absent | Crystal Clear | Absent | Absent |
| 11. | Simri Maun, Champaran | 7.00 | Present | Absent | Crystal Clear | Absent | Absent |
| 12. | Marghati | 7.00 | Present | Absent | Crystal Clear | Absent | Absent |
| 13. | Gordah Lake, Saharsa | 7.00 | Faintly present | Negligible Present | Crystal Clear | Absent (Hydrilla is found) | Absent |

*(Contd.)*

*Table 10.3 (Contd.)*

| *Sl. No.* | *Wetland* | *P.H. Value* | *Cloride* | *Sulphate* | *Quality of Water* | *Oxidizing Agent* | *Reducing Agent* |
|---|---|---|---|---|---|---|---|
| 14. | Dhima Mukhnaha, Purnea | 7.00 | Heavily Present | Absent | Crystal Clear | Absent | Absent |
| 15. | Kajha Kothi, Purnea | 7.00 | Faintly Present | Absent | Water Muddy | Absent | Absent |
| 16. | Saura | 7.00 | Faintly Present | Absent | Crystal Clear | Absent | Absent |
| 17. | Banbhag Chaur | 7.00 | Faintly Present | Absent | Crystal Clear | Absent | Absent |
| 18. | Rambag | 7.00 | Present | Absent | Crystal Clear | Absent | Absent |

*Source* : R.B. Mandal, 1996

**Table 10.4 :** Physico-chemical Parametres of Wetlands Soil in North Bihar

| Sl. No. | Name of Wetlands | TS | Turb | pH | Alk. | Hard | $Cl^-$ | $SO_4$ | $NO^-$ | $NO_3^-$ | $F^-$ |
|---|---|---|---|---|---|---|---|---|---|---|---|
| 1. | Narha | 1275 | 6.6 | 7.23 | 335 | 295 | 150 | 7.2 | 0.007 | 0.06 | 0.84 |
| 2. | Tilabayman | 1115 | 7.8 | 7.83 | 285 | 285 | 27.5 | 12.4 | 0.003 | 0.03 | 1.04 |
| 3. | Chauri | 745 | 4.8 | 7.66 | 310 | 310 | 35.0 | 4.8 | 0.003 | 0.02 | 1.04 |
| 4. | Lasahar | 130 | 5.3 | 7.60 | 310 | 310 | 12.5 | 4.8 | 0.007 | 0.06 | 0.74 |
| 5. | Dighi | 582 | 5.3 | 7.28 | 388 | 388 | 23.0 | 17.2 | — | 0.01 | 0.24 |
| 6. | Balapatti | 416 | 4.3 | 7.24 | 400 | 400 | 11.0 | 7.2 | — | 0.02 | 0.24 |
| 7. | Bhagwatpur | 402 | 5.3 | 7.18 | 376 | 376 | 29.0 | 9.8 | 0.003 | 0.01 | 0.24 |
| 8. | Ganda | 498 | 4.0 | 7.12 | 488 | 488 | 57.0 | 19.8 | — | 0.03 | 0.14 |
| 9. | Dhasundha | 404 | 2.7 | 7.18 | 420 | 420 | 88.0 | 17.2 | 0.003 | 0.02 | ND |
| 10. | Terrha | 226 | 0.54 | 7.04 | 435 | 435 | 12.5 | 14.8 | 0.003 | 0.02 | 0.54 |
| 11. | Katara | 202 | 0.24 | 7.03 | 310 | 310 | 17.6 | 7.2 | 0.003 | 0.01 | 0.24 |
| 12. | Finglash | 192 | 0.34 | 9.07 | 405 | 405 | 12.5 | 9.8 | — | 0.01 | 0.34 |
| 13. | Parshama | 128 | 0.44 | 8.75 | 370 | 370 | 05.0 | 4.4 | — | 0.02 | 0.44 |
| 14. | Dahia | 1065 | 0.74 | 7.93 | — | 335 | 32.5 | 9.8 | 0.003 | 0.01 | 0.74 |
| 15. | Nardang | 188 | 4.0 | 6.40 | — | 250 | 10.0 | 14.8 | — | 0.02 | 1.04 |
| 16. | Gordah | 188 | 2.7 | 6.98 | 210 | 215 | 7.5 | 12.4 | 0.003 | 0.02 | 0.93 |
| 17. | Khagma | 232 | 2.7 | — | 355 | 95 | 27.5 | 7.2 | 0.003 | 0.03 | 0.24 |
| 18. | Tinmuhe | 18 | 3.4 | 7.70 | 120 | 115 | 5.0 | 7.2 | — | 0.04 | 0.64 |
| 19. | Hareba | 191 | 2.6 | 7.50 | 360 | 290 | 22.5 | 7.2 | 0.003 | 0.023 | 1.04 |
| 20. | Laib | 414 | 3.4 | 7.42 | 285 | 305 | 22.5 | 9.8 | 0.007 | 0.059 | 0.24 |
| 21. | Marghati | 400 | 3.0 | 7.08 | 585 | 295 | 10.0 | 7.2 | 0.000 | 0.020 | 1.04 |
| 22. | Chakmaka | 1084 | 3.4 | 7.05 | 410 | 510 | 547.5 | 4.8 | 0.000 | 0.020 | 0.74 |

(Contd.)

(Table 10.4 Contd.)

| Sl. No. | Name of Wetlands | TS | Turb | pH | Alk. | Hard | $Cl^-$ | $SO_4$ | $NO^-$ | $NO_3^-$ | $F^-$ |
|---|---|---|---|---|---|---|---|---|---|---|---|
| 23. | Kumarkhand | 990 | 3.4 | 7.82 | 710 | 500 | 102.5 | 7.2 | 0.003 | 0.033 | 0.68 |
| 24. | Bhangha Chap | 586 | 4.3 | 7.60 | 430 | 330 | 32.5 | 7.2 | 0.003 | 0.033 | 0.24 |
| 25. | Bargaon Kateen | 650 | 4.0 | 7.73 | 335 | 295 | 42.5 | 4.8 | 0.000 | 0.020 | 0.24 |
| 26. | Cheuri | — | 4.8 | 7.74 | 500 | 355 | 52.5 | 7.2 | 0.007 | 0.059 | 0.77 |
| 27. | Bengaghasan | 1055 | 3.4 | 7.75 | 275 | 250 | 25.90 | 9.8 | 0.007 | 0.069 | 0.93 |
| 28. | Hazar Panch | 60 | 3.0 | 7.53 | 270 | 285 | 25.0 | 7.2 | 0.003 | 0.013 | 0.84 |
| 29. | Malkayan | 755 | 4.8 | 7.90 | 500 | 355 | 12.5 | 4.8 | 0.003 | 0.053 | 1.14 |
| 30. | Sonakhal | 1795 | 4.3 | 7.81 | 425 | 350 | 40.0 | 7.2 | 0.007 | 0.069 | 1.14 |
| 31. | Jhauadhab | 1265 | 7.1 | 8.05 | 415 | 305 | 32.5 | 9.8 | 0.003 | 0.023 | — |
| 32. | Moti | 650 | 8.5 | 8.03 | 295 | 325 | 22.5 | 7.2 | 0.003 | 0.023 | 0.74 |
| 33. | Ratahari | 580 | 5.3 | 7.87 | 410 | 300 | 17.5 | 4.8 | 0.007 | 0.069 | 0.74 |
| 34. | Gamharia | 885 | 7.1 | 7.31 | 310 | 290 | 82.5 | 7.2 | 0.007 | 0.059 | 0.84 |
| 35. | Maniyari | 505 | 5.3 | 7.35 | 285 | 235 | 22.5 | 7.2 | 0.003 | 0.033 | 0.84 |
| 36. | Gangaram | 1465 | 3.4 | 7.06 | 310 | 280 | 467.5 | 4.8 | 0.007 | 0.059 | 0.74 |
| 37. | Sariyaman | 460 | 4.8 | 7.50 | 280 | 245 | 55.0 | 7.2 | 0.003 | 0.033 | 1.14 |
| 38. | Karariaman | — | 7.00 | 7.35 | 355 | 260 | — | 9.8 | 0.007 | 0.059 | 0.74 |
| 39. | Gahiri | 515 | 3.4 | 7.55 | 270 | 250 | 15.0 | 4.8 | 0.003 | 0.003 | 1.14 |
| 40. | Dahnauti | 380 | 6.2 | 7.70 | 445 | 325 | 85.0 | 9.8 | — | 0.020 | 0.74 |
| 41. | Chanmari Chaur | 116 | 1.6 | 7.70 | 355 | 290 | 40.0 | 7.2 | 0.003 | 0.013 | 0.84 |
| 42. | Hardia Chaur | 102 | 9.7 | 7.60 | 115 | 95 | 12.5 | 17.2 | 0.003 | 0.033 | — |
| 43. | Baraila Tal | 30 | 4.3 | 7.72 | 45 | 95 | 5.0 | 7.2 | 0.003 | 0.033 | 0.24 |
| 44. | Kesaria Chaur | 282 | 4.0 | 7.28 | 295 | 240 | 40.0 | 12.4 | — | 0.030 | 0.19 |

(Table 10.4 Contd.)

| Sl. No. | Name of Wetlands | TS | Turb | pH | Alk. | Hard | $Cl^-$ | $SO_4$ | $NO^-$ | $NO_3^-$ | $F^-$ |
|---|---|---|---|---|---|---|---|---|---|---|---|
| 45. | Chamra Chaur | 212 | 6.2 | 7.35 | 460 | 235 | 10.0 | 12.4 | 0.003 | .023 | 0.74 |
| 46. | Kachudhua | 228 | 4.0 | 7.70 | 325 | 210 | 12.5 | 12.4 | — | .020 | 0.74 |
| 47. | Ghogha | 170 | 3.4 | 7.60 | 365 | 255 | 12.5 | 4.8 | — | .030 | — |
| 48. | Dehichal Chaur | 30 | 4.6 | 7.50 | 450 | 325 | 10.0 | 7.2 | — | .030 | .93 |
| 49. | Shitala | 314 | 3.4 | 7.60 | 280 | 1880 | 20.0 | 7.8 | — | .040 | .54 |
| 50. | Tengarmari | 1082 | 4.3 | 8.10 | 125 | 130 | 5.0 | 12.4 | .003 | 0.033 | .24 |
| 51. | Sodha | 108 | 4.8 | 7.90 | 55 | 75 | 10.0 | 7 | .003 | .033 | .24 |
| 52. | Goga Beel | 462 | 3.0 | — | 385 | 330 | 15.0 | 7.2 | — | .030 | .64 |
| 53. | Baghar Beel | 352 | 4.0 | 7.78 | 310 | 260 | 7.5 | 9.8 | .003 | .058 | 1.14 |
| 54. | Koswan | 215 | 4.3 | 7.60 | 385 | 300 | 10.0 | 9.8 | .003 | .043 | .93 |
| 55. | Sowa | 215 | 4.0 | 7.57 | 385 | 300 | 17.5 | 9.8 | .003 | .033 | .24 |
| 56. | Fulbasa | 920 | 4.8 | 7.42 | 520 | 215 | 70.0 | 12.4 | — | 0.20 | .64 |
| 57. | Khamdah | 200 | 4.0 | 7.09 | 250 | — | 25.0 | 9.8 | .007 | .068 | .23 |
| 58. | Khamdah | 215 | 3.0 | 7.41 | 575 | 390 | 177.5 | 9.8 | .007 | .058 | 1.04 |
| 59. | Ruidhas | 665 | 3.4 | 7.14 | 575 | 390 | 177.5 | 9.8 | .007 | .058 | 1.04 |
| 60. | Cothara-Kanapur | 208 | 6.2 | 6.88 | — | 280 | 15.0 | 9.8 | — | .020 | 0.74 |
| 61. | Kaber | 32 | 6.6 | 7.03 | — | 125 | 25.0 | 12.4 | .007 | .009 | 0.64 |
| 62. | Borofit lake | 34 | .2 | 6.20 | — | 160 | 52.5 | 17.6 | .003 | .053 | 0.54 |
| 63. | Marda | 128 | — | 6.70 | 155 | 105 | 22.5 | 12.4 | .007 | .069 | 0.24 |
| 64. | Moin Lake | 2404 | 5.3 | 6.56 | 510 | 900 | 592.5 | 4.8 | — | .030 | 0.44 |
| 65. | Jeewaya Lae | 122 | 6.2 | 7.02 | 300 | 280 | 30.0 | 2.4 | — | .020 | 0.54 |
| 66. | Narail Chaur | 454 | 6.6 | 7.07 | 288 | 285 | 56.0 | 17.2 | — | 0.20 | 0.54 |

*(Table 10.4 Contd.)*

| Sl. No. | Name of Wetlands | TS | Turb | pH | Alk. | Hard | $Cl^-$ | $SO_4$ | $NO^-$ | $NO_3^-$ | $F^-$ |
|---|---|---|---|---|---|---|---|---|---|---|---|
| 67. | Harahi | 202 | 3.4 | 9.33 | 400 | 340 | 67.5 | 14.8 | — | .010 | 1.04 |
| 68. | Dighi | 118 | 3.0 | 9.36 | 490 | 255 | 5.0 | 7.2 | — | .030 | 0.54 |
| 69. | Rajokhar | 82 | 3.4 | 9.86 | 458 | 345 | 7.5 | 12.4 | — | 0.20 | 0.64 |
| 70. | Ganga Sagar | 220 | 6.6 | 7.65 | — | 330 | 3.0 | 22.4 | — | .20 | 0.54 |
| 71. | Mahadev Tank | — | 4.8 | 7.83 | 165 | 185 | 1.5 | 7.2 | — | .020 | 0.24 |
| 72. | Kathara | — | 7.7 | 7.62 | 370 | 300 | 27.5 | 9.8 | — | .030 | 0.64 |
| 73. | Pachkhurwa Saharsa | — | 5.3 | 7.35 | 545 | 115 | 17.5 | 4.8 | — | .020 | 0.74 |
| 74. | Shisulia | 390 | 6.2 | 6.82 | — | 300 | 7.5 | 12.4 | .003 | .023 | 0.44 |
| 75. | Mashbasi | 202 | 4.8 | 7.20 | 280 | 245 | 12.5 | 9.8 | .003 | .013 | 0.34 |
| 76. | Belhi | 782 | 4.3 | 6.82 | 260 | 285 | 792.5 | 12.4 | .003 | .013 | 0.23 |
| 77. | Ghordaur | 280 | 3.4 | 7.38 | 260 | 265 | 37.5 | 9.8 | 0.003 | 0.23 | 0.24 |
| 78. | Simardah | — | 4.3 | 7.80 | 355 | 265 | 17.5 | 7.2 | — | 0.20 | 0.34 |
| 79. | Daihara | 848 | 2.7 | 6.7 | 348 | 300 | 77.6 | 9.8 | — | .010 | 0.54 |
| 80. | Mehsar Chaur | 516 | 3.4 | 6.9 | 304 | 230 | 37.5 | 14.8 | — | .020 | 0.24 |
| 81. | Simri Maun | 384 | 3.0 | 7.08 | 385 | 250 | 5.0 | 9.8 | — | .030 | 0.64 |
| 82. | Chatia Chaur | 450 | 2.7 | 7.52 | 375 | — | 12.5 | 14.8 | — | .030 | 0.24 |
| 83. | Lel Saraiya Maun | 238 | 3.0 | 7.50 | 224 | 235 | 2.5 | 9.8 | — | .020 | 0.24 |
| 84. | Amua Maun | 1374 | 2.2 | 6.50 | 284 | 525 | 227.5 | 12.4 | — | .010 | 1.04 |
| 85. | Brahampur Maun | 850 | 2.7 | 6.67 | 284 | 445 | 215.0 | 17.2 | — | .003 | 1.34 |
| 86. | Manika Maun | 186 | 3.4 | 7.55 | 284 | 230 | 25.0 | 9.8 | — | .020 | 0.24 |
| 87. | Bharthua Chaur | 402 | 2.4 | 7.60 | 276 | 355 | 60.0 | 7.2 | .003 | .003 | 1.14 |
| 88. | Sora Jheel | 324 | 3.4 | 7.54 | 168 | 305 | 40.0 | 4.8 | — | .020 | 1.44 |

(Table 10.4 (Contd.)

| Sl. No. | Name of Wetlands | TS | Turb | pH | Alk. | Hard | $Cl^-$ | $SO_4$ | $NO^-$ | $NO_3^-$ | $F^-$ |
|---|---|---|---|---|---|---|---|---|---|---|---|
| 89. | Kajha Kothi Tank | 626 | 3.4 | 7.20 | 250 | — | 12.5 | 9.8 | — | .020 | 1.04 |
| 90. | Banbhag Jheel | 1512 | 4.00 | 8.70 | 470 | 355 | 102.5 | 4.8 | 0.000 | .030 | 0.74 |
| 91. | Dhima Mekhnaha Chaur | 330 | 4.3 | 6.95 | 45 | 365 | 57.5 | 7.2 | .003 | .023 | — |
| 92. | Rembag | ,06 | 3.0 | 7.12 | 364 | 335 | 190.0 | 12.4 | — | .030 | — |
| 93. | Dasyn Chaur | — | 3.4 | 7.73 | 155 | 115 | 12.5 | 9.8 | .003 | .003 | 0.26 |
| 94. | Mehsar Chaur | 294 | 4.0 | 7.05 | 430 | 235 | 92.5 | 12.4 | 0.000 | .020 | 0.34 |
| 95. | Kanail Chaur | 256 | 4.0 | 6.06 | 168 | 239 | 65.4 | 14.3 | — | .017 | 0.49 |
| 96. | Phulhara Chaur | 390 | 4.9 | 6.03 | 278 | 120 | 38.2 | 18.7 | 6.1 | 0.180 | 0.37 |
| 97. | Ghordaur | 290 | 3.9 | 7.02 | 169 | 130 | 48.2 | 15.6 | 5.2 | .026 | 0.42 |
| 98. | Ballipur Moin | 190 | 2.9 | 7.01 | 170 | 230 | 58.2 | 14.5 | 4.2 | .016 | 0.45 |
| 99. | Krishna Raj Sagar | 1065 | 3.9 | 7.01 | 230 | 179 | — | 5.5 | 4.9 | .018 | 0.47 |
| 100. | Madhwapur | 451 | 2.8 | 7.55 | 375 | — | 12.6 | 14.8 | — | .031 | 0.24 |
| 101. | Hirni Chaur | 561 | 2.9 | 6.96 | 45 | 365 | 57.5 | 7.2 | .004 | .024 | — |
| 102. | Benua-Fharkea | 707 | 3.5 | 8.2 | 138 | 249 | 27.6 | 8.2 | .003 | .290 | 0.37 |
| 103. | Khatar | 409 | 4.0 | 0.2 | 139 | 250 | 38.0 | 8.3 | .002 | .280 | 0.39 |
| 104. | Manshi Dubey Chaur | 503 | 4.9 | 0.3 | 259 | 390 | 39.0 | 7.3 | .003 | .560 | .080 |
| 105. | Bhagwa Chaur | 5.8 | 3.0 | 5.7 | 390 | 290 | 50.0 | 7.9 | 0.030 | .127 | 8.39 |
| 106. | Murdapur Chaur | 4.0 | 5.0 | 4.3 | 150 | 390 | 40.0 | 5.9 | 0.029 | .029 | 7.20 |
| 107. | Ratanpur Chaur | 232 | 2.7 | — | 356 | 96 | 28.5 | 7.2 | 0.003 | .04 | 0.23 |
| 108. | Ahiya | 1276 | 6.7 | 7.23 | 335 | 296 | 160.0 | 7.3 | 0.006 | 0.07 | 0.85 |
| 109. | Naimalie Chaur | 1115 | 7.8 | 7.83 | 276 | 279 | 170 | 12.5 | 0.003 | 0.06 | 0.89 |

*Table 10.4 (Contd.)*

| Sl. No. | Name of Wetlands | TS | Turb | pH | Alk. | Hard | $Cl^-$ | $SO_4$ | $NO^-$ | $NO_3^-$ | $F^-$ |
|---|---|---|---|---|---|---|---|---|---|---|---|
| 110. | Raghopur Diara | 360 | 6.9 | 5.90 | 390 | 270 | 172 | 13.6 | 0.001 | 0.02 | 0.78 |
| 111. | Bora Chaur | 1130 | 5.9 | 8.09 | 550 | 170 | 259 | 3.8 | — | 0.28 | 0.38 |
| 112. | Kulesra Chaur | 290 | 3.0 | 7.54 | 271 | 285 | 25.0 | 7.3 | — | 0.39 | 0.95 |
| 113. | Telia Chaur | 270 | 1.8 | 6.90 | 390 | 140 | 16.0 | 7.5 | 0.003 | 0.93 | 0.87 |
| 114. | Mahwal Maun | 270 | 7.1 | 8.04 | 415 | 305 | 32.5 | 9.8 | .0150 | 0.75 | — |
| 115. | Kanti Lake | 1015 | 7.3 | 9.04 | 416 | 340 | 12.4 | 9.3 | 0.139 | — | 0.39 |

*Source* : Fieldwork by Field Investigators

**Table 10.5 :** Results available from Sampled Water Test in the Wetlands of North Bihar (1995-96)

| *Sl. No.* | *Lab. No.* | *Sample* | *pH* | *Ec. MOhm⁻¹ cm²* | *% Org. C.* | *Avail. $P_2O_5$ kg/ha* | *Avail. $k_2O$ kg/ha* |
|---|---|---|---|---|---|---|---|
| 1. | 682 | Dhasundhar Supal | 8.7 | 0.26 | 0.73 | 59.24 | 187.95 |
| 2. | 683 | Ghogha Lake, Kishanganj | 7.5 | 0.20 | 1.22 | 113.10 | 171.84 |
| 3. | 684 | Nathatta, Lake | 8.2 | 0.50 | 1.18 | 48.48 | 413.49 |
| 4. | 685 | Amuaman, Hamparan | 8.3 | 0.68 | 1.89 | 42.08 | 247.02 |
| 5. | 686 | Sisulya | 7.9 | 0.24 | 1.08 | 59.24 | 467.19 |
| 6. | 687 | Simri, Champaran | 8.3 | 0.16 | 0.91 | 16.16 | 64.44 |
| 7. | 688 | Bhagwatpur Paribaha | 8.0 | 0.28 | 1.59 | 21.54 | 107.4 |
| 8. | 699 | Rambag | 8.1 | 0.11 | 0.82 | 236.98 | 42.96 |
| 9. | 690 | Magha | 7.5 | 0.23 | 2.57 | 290.84 | 118.14 |
| 10. | 691 | Lakshmipur | 7.8 | 0.16 | 0.18 | 37.70 | 53.7 |
| 11. | 692 | Kharun Ruighasa | 7.3 | 0.16 | 0.81 | 75.40 | 187.95 |
| 12. | 693 | Brahampur | 7.6 | 0.17 | 0.46 | 37.70 | 139.62 |
| 13. | 694 | Khama Lake | 8.0 | 0.12 | 0.45 | 16.16 | 42.96 |
| 14. | 695 | Borofit Lake Baraum | 7.2 | 0.22 | 1.13 | 64.63 | 365.16 |
| 15. | 696 | Sital Lake, Kishanganj | 7.0 | 0.23 | 1.06 | 183.13 | 295.35 |
| 16. | 697 | Kanti Lake | 7.2 | 0.15 | 0.060 | 70.02 | 139.62 |
| 17. | 698 | Gahiri Lake | 7.5 | 0.18 | 0.52 | 5.38 | 48.33 |
| 18. | 699 | Chatia Chaur, Champaran | 7.6 | 0.34 | 0.69 | 26.93 | 59.07 |
| 19. | 700 | Mahshar Chaur | 7.6 | 0.17 | 0.58 | 32.32 | 105.36 |
| 20. | 701 | Mahlabman, Motipur | 8.0 | 0.14 | 0.34 | 5.38 | 85.92 |

*Table 10.5 (Contd.)*

| Sl. No. | Lab. No. | Sample | pH | Ec. $MOhm^{-1}$ $cm^{1}$ | % Org. C. kg/ha | Avail. $P_2O_5$ kg/ha | Avail. $k_2O$ |
|---|---|---|---|---|---|---|---|
| 21. | 702 | Kanti, Muzaffarpur | 7.8 | 0.22 | 0.35 | 5.38 | 75.18 |
| 22. | 703 | Kurlaha | 7.5 | 0.36 | 1.03 | 118.49 | 279.24 |
| 23. | 704 | Lala Saraiya, Champaran | 7.8 | 0.25 | 1.22 | 26.93 | 257.76 |
| 24. | 705 | Raghopur Nahta Lake | 7.8 | 0.28 | 0.19 | 16.16 | 118.14 |
| 25. | 706 | Dauhara Lake | 7.9 | 0.10 | 0.95 | 64.63 | 182.58 |
| 26. | 707 | Loha Lake | 7.4 | 0.15 | 0.34 | 16.16 | 59.07 |
| 27. | 708 | Tedha Lake | 7.2 | 0.30 | 1.06 | 86.18 | 214.8 |
| 28. | 709 | Ghordhaur Lake | 7.5 | 0.21 | 1.18 | 107.72 | 204.06 |
| 29. | 710 | Simardhah Lake | 7.5 | 0.21 | 1.20 | 134.65 | 134.25 |
| 30. | 711 | Chauri Lake | 6.4 | 0.20 | 0.37 | 70.02 | 139.62 |
| 31. | 712 | Tilabai Moin | 7.0 | 0.13 | 0.08 | 8.08 | 91.29 |
| 32. | 713 | Nardang Lake | 6.8 | 0.14 | 0.68 | 75.40 | 402.75 |
| 33. | 714 | Dahilchal Chaur | 6.9 | 0.09 | 1.58 | 16.16 | 107.40 |
| 34. | 715 | Katra Talauna | 6.6 | 0.32 | 0.46 | 16.16 | 85.92 |
| 35. | 716 | Dhanauti Lake | 6.6 | 0.20 | 0.55 | 21.54 | 161.10 |
| 36. | 717 | Dighi Tal, Darbhanga | 6.5 | 0.26 | 0.90 | 70.02 | 386.64 |
| 37. | 718 | Lahar, Supaul | 7.0 | 0.32 | 0.16 | 13.46 | 214.80 |
| 38. | 719 | Katra | 7.7 | 0.10 | 0.53 | 5.38 | 187.95 |
| 39. | 720 | Pipra Kodhasan Lake | 7.3 | 0.39 | 0.49 | 64.63 | 483.30 |
| 40. | 721 | Mahadev Tank | 7.8 | 0.09 | 0.31 | 13.46 | 161.10 |
| 41. | 722 | Nagda Nadiar, Muzaffarpur | 7.6 | 0.25 | 0.78 | 16.16 | 241.69 |

*Table 10.5 (Contd.)*

| Sl. No. | Lab. No. | Sample | pH | Ec. $MOhm^{-1} cm^{1}$ | % Org. C. kg/ha | Avail. $P_2O_5$ kg/ha | Avail. $k_2O$ |
|---|---|---|---|---|---|---|---|
| 42. | 723 | Gordah | 7.6 | 0.47 | 1.60 | 59.24 | 510.15 |
| 43. | 724 | Manikaman, Muzaffarpur | 7.2 | 0.85 | 2.32 | 26.93 | 1075.20 |
| 44. | 725 | Godda Lake | 8.3 | 0.18 | 0.20 | 5.38 | 107.40 |
| 45. | 726 | Bhagbatpur, Supaul | 8.5 | 0.13 | 0.45 | 16.16 | 161.10 |
| 46. | 727 | Pinglas Hariraha | 7.8 | 0.39 | 0.96 | 64.63 | 375.90 |
| 47. | 728 | Charnauria Chaur Muzaffarpur | 8.0 | 0.34 | 0.7 | 37.70 | 322.20 |
| 48. | 729 | Haldia Chaur | 8.6 | 0.16 | 0.30 | 10.77 | 306.09 |
| 49. | 730 | Banbhag Lake | 8.3 | 0.44 | 0.73 | 96.95 | 134.25 |
| 50. | 731 | Moin Lake | 7.7 | 0.60 | 2.58 | 215.44 | 504.78 |
| 51. | 732 | Balapatti, Basantpur | 8.6 | 0.15 | 0.61 | 10.77 | 123.51 |
| 52. | 734 | Dhima Makhanaha | 8.5 | 0.12 | 0.15 | 21.54 | 80.55 |
| 53. | 735 | Kajha Kothi | 8.4 | 0.23 | 0.20 | 53.80 | 134.25 |
| 54. | 736 | Jibaya Lake | 8.6 | 0.16 | 0.42 | 21.54 | 429.60 |
| 55. | 737 | Saura City | 8.5 | 0.32 | 0.88 | 102.33 | 295.35 |
| 56. | 738 | Kharudah | 6.5 | 0.29 | 1.16 | 182.12 | 510.72 |
| 57. | 739 | Rambag | 7.1 | 0.18 | 0.91 | 32.32 | 161.10 |
| 58. | 740 | Bharthua | 7.7 | 0.12 | 0.23 | 8.07 | 69.81 |
| 59. | 741 | Dighi Basantpur Supaul | 7.5 | 0.55 | 0.97 | 161.58 | 618.24 |
| 60. | 742 | Dahla Lake, Dumri | 8.4 | 0.15 | 0.14 | 16.16 | 64.44 |
| 61. | 743 | Baghi Chaur | 8.5 | 0.20 | 0.45 | 10.77 | 134.25 |
| 62. | 744 | Gobra | 6.6 | 0.60 | 0.61 | 96.95 | 483.30 |

*Source :* Pusa Agriculture College Laboratory.

suspension was shaked for 40 minutes and it was finally filtered through Whatman No.50 filter paper. The concentration of phosphorus in filtrate was obtained as described for water.

$$\text{Available P (mg/100g)} = \frac{\text{mgP/1 in soil extract x 100}}{50}$$

Fig. 10.1 and Table 10.5 show the distribution of wetlands in the district of Saharsa. The highest area of wetland is found in Chhatapur Anchal (532.67ha) and the highest number is 51 found in Raghopur Anchal.

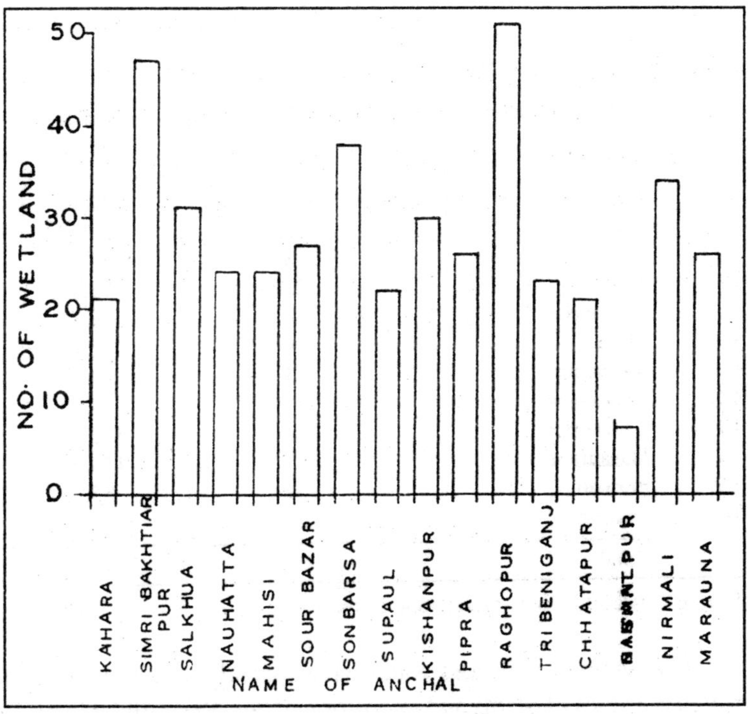


**Fig. 10.1 :** Number of Wetland in Saharsa District

## Conclusions

In North Bihar Silty-loam or alluvied Tal land soil is found in wetlands.

The character of water change during flood when the percentage of Turbidity is high. In the North in the month of December when the turbidity is lows the water in most of the wetlands become crystal clear but it is not palatable. Due to presence of micro-organisms and unwanted chemical elements come to the water from the nearby fields where the farmers have used chemical fertilizers in the field. Although, the water of wetland acts as pollution filter but sometimes the wetland water itself fall to the prey of pollution especially near urban and industrial areas like, Kanti Thermal Power and others.

**Table 10.6 :** Water Area of Wetland in Saharsa District (1994-95)

| *Sl. No.* | *Anchal* | *No. of Wetland* | *Water Area (in Hectare)* |
|---|---|---|---|
| 1. | Kahara | 21 | 24.66 |
| 2. | Simri-Bakhitiarpur | 47 | 373.30 |
| 3. | Salkhua | 31 | 398.90 |
| 4. | Nauhatta | 24 | 250.00 |
| 5. | Mahisi | 24 | 37.30 |
| 6. | Sour-Bazar | 27 | 167.90 |
| 7. | Sonbarsa | 38 | 1-07.85 |
| 8. | Supaul | 22 | 15.85 |
| 9. | Kishanpur | 30 | 46.34 |
| 10. | Pipra | 26 | 22.25 |
| 11. | Raghopur | 51 | 40.11 |
| 12. | Tribeniganj | 23 | 79.90 |
| 13. | Chhatapur | 21 | 532.67 |
| 14. | Basantpur | 7 | 150.00 |
| 15. | Nirmali | 34 | 85.36 |
| 16. | Marauna | 26 | 13.67 |
| | Total | 452 | 2783.06 |

*Source :* District Fishery Department Saharsa.

The wetland soils and water have specially due to mix of the rotten particles of plants and micro-organisms. Recently, it has been felt that the acid rain affects the character of wetland water too much. In the district Saharsa, the water of Manuadhar was polluted so much that most of animals drinking water of this river died in the year, 1994.

## REFERENCES

Aquatech, 1988, *Developing World Water*. Grosvenor Press International, Hongkong, 1988.

Aquatic Conservation, Marine and Fresh Water, *Ecosystems*, Vol. 3, No. 3 1993.

Mononova, M. M., *Organic Matter of Soils*, Moscow, 1963.

Pearce, D.W., *et al.*; *Economic of Natural Resourcs and the Environment*; The Joints Hopkins University Press, Ballimore, 1990.

Prasad, S.D., *Census of India*. 1961, Vol. VI Bihar, Par I (A) General Reports on the Census.

Uriyo, A.P. *et. al; Introductory Soil Science*, Tanzania Publishing House, Dar es Salaam, 1979, p. 2.5.

Zonn, S.V., *Tropical and sub-tropical soil science*, Mir Publishers, Moscow, 1986.

# 11

# EUTROPHICATION OF WETLANDS

## Eutrophication means Ecological Degradation

India's wetlands include lakes, reservoirs, mangroves and vast stretches of waterlogged areas which are the home of pests and diseases such as malaria and jaundice. These include the placid waters of Dal lake in Kashmir; the Udaipur lake in Rajasthan, the Chilka lake in Orissa and the Vast delta of the river Ganges — the Sunderbans. Wetlands represent a transition between open waters and land endowed with clear cut structural and functional roles and having a specific ecological function.

In India there occur a large variety of wetlands. These are inclusive of both natural and man-made, permanent or semipermanent fresh water of marine habitats. A number of definitions have been put forward to explain and delineate wetlands. These include:

## IUCN (1971)

Submerged or water-saturated lands, both natural and man-made, permanent or temporary, with water that is static or flowing, fresh, brackish or salty, including areas of marine water, the depth of which at low tide does not exceed 6 meters.

**International Biosphere Programme (1972)**

Areas dominated by herbaceous macrophytes the production of which takes place predominantly in the aerial environment above the water level while the plants are supplied with amounts of water that would be excessive for most other higher plants.

**Cowardin *et al.* (1979)**

Lands transitional between terrestrial and aquatic systems where the water level is usually at or near the surface or the land is covered by shallow water.

Broadly speaking, wetlands are areas which are wholly submerged by water on a permanent or temporary basis. The following are the salient features of wetlands:

(a) An area which supports plant communities dominated by hydrophytes. These grow for a major part of the year.
(b) The substrata is predominantly comprised of the drained by hydric soil.
(c) The substrata is non-soil in the true sense of the terms. It is saturated, submerged or covered by water for a major part of the growing season each year.
(d) Areas without a soil cover but covered by hydrophytes such as rocky lake shores covered by variety of weeds.

Mahajan (1988) has defined wetlands in the following words, "areas of submerged or water-saturated lands, natural or artificial, permanent or temporary, existing forest for at least 6 months during the year, confined or open including shore areas with depth not exceeding 6 meters at low tide".

**Ecology**

Wetlands are complex hydrological and biogeochemical systems with specific structural and, functional roles. They perform a definite task in the biosphere. There are three main ecological attributes of a wetland ecosystem.

— The ecosystem supports a vegetative community dominated by hydrophytes for a major part of each year.
— The substrata consists primarily of undrained hydric soil.
— The substrata is essentially non-soil and saturated with water.

It may be submerged for a considerable period each year.

Studies carried out by the International Biosphere, IUCN and other agencies during the previous decades have concluded that wetlands are amongst the highly productive ecosystems of the world.

Wetlands in India perform the following ecological and environmental functions:

(a) They serve as a habitat for wildlife including migratory birds. A large number of wetlands of India are the home of fishes, reptiles, emphibians and birds. Migratory birds from places as far away as Siberia come to spend the winter months in these wetlands e.g. Bharatpur Bird Santuary.
(b) They help in controlling floods.
(c) Wetlands richarge aquifers: regulate the quality of water and serve to treat waste waters.
(d) They help to reduce the sediment load of the surface run off by creating conditions suited to deposition.
(e) Wetlands are producers of organic matter at rates which are equalled by few other eco-systems.
(f) They provide water for agriculture and for cattle during the lean summer months.
(g) Wetlands help in the conservation of rare and endangered species.

**Distribution of Wetlands**

Wetland eco-systems are very well distributed in India. Wetlands are formed in areas where the potential evapotranspiration is less than the total annual precipitation. This leaves a large surplus of water which if undrained accumulates on the land surface and forms a wetland ecosystem. The following conditions may lead to the formation of wetlands in India.

— Poor drainage of the surface run off
— Natural depressions such as glacial lakes
— Geo-tectonic causes viz; faulting which may lead to the formation of lakes.
— Impeded drainage
— Deltas and estuaries
— Inundation of low-lying areas by tidal waves
— Construction of dams across the flow of a river or stream
— Formation of natural dams by landslides and other forms of mass movement.

Wetlands may be classified into the following :

(a) Natural Formed by physical process. This includes waterlogged areas, flood plains, deltas, estuaries and lakes.
(b) Man-made: Formed by man. This class includes reservoirs of multipurpose projects, ponds and shallow depressions that are used for storing water and which support a marshy vegetation.

Wetland ecosystems of India are located in diverse climatic, geographic and geological zones ranging from the cold, dry trans - Himalayan tracts of Ladakh and Lahul Spiti to the of Kashmir valley; the arid areas of Rajasthan and to the moist, high rainfall region of Manipur.

**Eutrophication of Indian Wetlands**

Eutrophication is a term given to explain the ecological degradation of a wetland. A number of Indian wetlands are under various stages of eutrophication. Such as waterbodies are :

### *1. Dal Lake (Kashmir)*

The Dal lake, situated in the beautiful Kashmir valley is the destination of thousands of tourists each year. With an area of 11.35 sq. kms, this waterbody is one of the main tourist attraction of Kashmir. However, during the previous three decades, eutrophication has begun to set in. This has quickly turned the once serane waters into a major environmental problem.

#### *Causes*

The major causes responsible for the ecological degradation of the Dal lake are:

***Tourists :*** Thousands of tourists visit the Dal lake each year. They pollute the water by dropping wrappers and dicans. A large number of hotels and restaurants have come up along the periphary of the lake. The part of the lake lying towards Shankaracharya hill is most affected by tourist activity.

***Outwash :*** Outwash from the agricultural fields around the lake, vegetables gardens and floating gardens that have come up both in and around the periphery of the lake are polluting the once crystal clear water.

***Houseboats and Shikaras :*** There are over 2000 houseboats and 5000 *shikaras* (Negi, 1982) in this lake. Houseboats are small boats capable of accommodating upto 15 persons. These are anchored along the periphery of the lake and rented out to tourists. The sewage from these houseboats is flushed into the lake waters.

Shikaras are small pleasure boats rowed by one or two persons. They are used for pleasure trips around the lake. At times *shikaras* are also used for other purposes such as business or transporting goods from one part of the lake to the other. Service or business *shikaras* ply to and fro landen with fruits, vegetables, carpets and handicrafts.

Houseboats and *shikaras* are contributing to the eutrophication of this once crystal clear lake by adding to the rising levels of pollution in the Dal lake. These boats are also responsible for many environmental problems that have beseiged the river Jhelum which drains Srinagar city and the surrounding valley.

***Floating Gardens :*** Floating gardens are small islands made from weeds which virtually float on the water. They cover a fairly large area along the periphery of the lake. Such floating gardens are used for two purposes — for raising vegetables, and as a source of entertainment for tourists. Thus, these floating gardens or islands have become an acute problem for the ecology of the lake.

***Siltation :*** A vast quantity of silt is flowing into the Dal lake each year. This silt comes from the following sources:

— Run off from the nearby slopes having a poor vegetative cover.
— Debris of road construction along the periphery of the lake.
— Streams bringing water to the lake.

V. Kaul of the Botany Department, Srinagar University estimated the annual deposition of silt into the lake at 80 thousand tonnes. About 25 years back, a large quantity of sediment was coming into the Dal lake from the Shankaracharya hill. However, a massive afforestation drive has helped to bring down the inflow of silt from this hill.

***Sewage :*** Sewage and other waste is unceremoniously dumped into the Dal lake and its surrounding wetlands. This comes from parts of Srinagar city adjoining the lake.

**Adverse Effects**

The following are the adverse effects of the eutrophication of the Dal lake:

**1. Recession**

The area of the Dal lake has been steadily going down during the past 60 years. Negi (1982) has given the following table:

**Reduction in the Area of Dal Loke**

| *Year* | *Area of lake and wetlands (in sq. kms)* |
|---|---|
| 1940 | 22.5 |
| 1950 | 21.0 |
| 1960 | 17.5 |
| 1970 | 14.0 |
| 1980 | 12.7 |
| 1985 | 11.4 |
| 1995 | 10.2 |
| 2000 | 8.0 |

**2. Chemicals**

Over the past three decades there has been a distinct change in the level of various chemicals in the waters of the lake. This has been brought out in the following text:

***Dissolved Oxygen***

In spring, the level of disolved oxygen is around 7 mg/litre. This level falls to about 5 or even 4 mg/ litres during the summer season which coincides with the peak tourist season.

***Nitrogen Compounds***

The Dal lake is deficient in nitrogen compounds. The $NH_3$ ¾ N level is about 7 mg/litre during the summer season and rised to about 15 mg/litre in winter. The level of $NH_3$-N fluctuates between 5 to 15 mg/litre in different seasons. The concentration of $NO_2$-N is moderate, varying between 120 and 440 mg/litres.

***Other Chemical***

The level of other chemical compounds in the Dal lake varies from season to season as shown in the following table (after Kaul and Pandit, 1979).

## 3. Biological Organisms

The Dal lake is the home of a large variety of biological organisms, both plants and animals. These includes fishes, moulds and planktons. A number of aquatic birds, also live in the marshes around the Dal lake. Eutrophication has affected the habitat of these biological organisms.

**Biological Organisms of Dal Lake**

| *Chemicals* | *Level of Concentration (in $mg^l$ per litre)* |
|---|---|
| Ca | 25 to 45 |
| Na | 4.2 to 8.4 |
| K | 0.80 to 1.74 |
| Mg | 10 to 16 |
| $PO_4$-P | 214 to 450 |
| Si | 1.9 to to 8.0 |
| $CO_2$ | 10 to 15 |
| $SO_2$ | 1.0 to 1.7 |

***Fishes***

The Dal lake is rich in fish life. These include the following fishes:

Cyprinus carpio communis C.C. specularis
Labeo rohuta Schzothorax sp.

In the past, the population of fish in the Dal lake appears to have gone down. Each year, a large number of fishes die. The spawning and breeding grounds of carp fishes has been adversely affected by the disposal of sewage and due to the intake of unusual quantities of silt. The periphery of the lake which is the breeding grounds of these fish is the worst affected.

***Zooplanktons***

Some of the zooplanktons which have been adversely affected are:

| | |
|---|---|
| Bosmina coregoni | Caphalodalla sp. |
| Cyclops sp. | Dephnia midden |
| Diaptrhus sp | Diorffiana |
| Keretalla sp. | Pseudoside bidentata |
| Sida | Crystalliana |

***Phytoplanktons***

The habitat of the following phytoplanktons has been disturbed by the process of eutrophication:

| | |
|---|---|
| Astronella formosa | Caratium sp. |
| Ceratoneis sp. | Coconeis sp. |
| Cymatopheura sp. | Cryosigms sp. |
| Dinobryon divergens | D.sertularia |
| D. sociala | Syndera acus |
| Tabellaria sp. | |

***Other Organisms***

Other biological organisms whose habitat has been adversely affected include certain varieties of duck weeds (*Gammarus sp.*) and the snail (*Lymnaea sp.*).

Kaul (Rai, 1982) has estimated that the debris due to profuse weed growth is to the tune of 40 to 50 thousand tonnes per year.

The sewage and outwash bring in about 16 tonnes of phosphorous and 365 tonnes of nitrogen per year into the lake system.

## Nainital and Bhimtal Lakes

Nainital is a popular mountain resort in the lower hills of Kumaon. There are a number of major lakes and wetlands in this area. Each year, thousands of tourists flock to this town to escape from the scorching summer heat of the plains of India. Small townships have sprung up around these lakes. Amongst them, Nainital is by far the largest, followed by Bhimtal. During the summer months the population of the Nainital may temporarily increase upto 15 times of its normal size. This results in an increase in the biotic pressure on the Nainital lake. The pressure on Bhimtal lake is of a relatively lower magnitude because of the lesser number of tourists going there. In the past two decades, eutrophication has begun to set in the Nainital lake and in some of the neighbouring wetlands.

### *Causes*

The following factors are responsible for the ecological degradation of these wetlands:

#### *Sewage Disposal*

The Nainital lake and other wetlands in the region are a vast dump of sewage including human excreta. The quantity of sewage emptied into the Nainital and Bhimtal lakes goes up in the summer season due to the influx of tourists. Wrappers and tin cans are also thrown into these wetlands by picnickers and tourists.

#### *Siltation*

The vegetative cover on the slopes surrounding these wetlands has been degraded due to the construction of hotels, restaurants, houses and roads. Thus, the surface flow coming into the wetlands is carrying more silt with it.

*Boating*

Boating is very popular with the tourists visiting these mountain resorts. A rapidly increasing number of rowing boats, sail boats and motor boats have disturbed the bird and fish life of these waterbodies.

**Adverse Effects**

Various stages of degradation or eutrophication are evident in the Nainital and Bhimtal lakes. This effect is more pronounced along the periphery of these wetlands of the two waterbodies, the Nainital lake is in a worse condition, probably due to the heavy influx of tourists to this town. The main aspects of the eutrophication of these lakes are:

*Chemicals*

There has been a distinct change in the level of various chemicals in the waters of these wetlands during the past three decades.

*Dissolved Oxygens*

The level of dissolved oxygen in the surface layers of the waters of Nainital and Bhimtal lakes is around 100 per cent saturation. In Nainital, the level of dissolved oxygen during the spring season is 5 mg/per litre. In summer which is the main tourist season, this level falls to below 2.5 mg/per litre. This condition has been found to be very dangerous for freshwater fishes (Ellis, *et al* 1946). There are coldwater carps in the Nainital lake. They are extremely sensitive to low oxygen concentration and find it difficult to live under these conditions. A substantial number of coldwater carps die each year when the concentration of dissolved oxygen drops to below the, critical level of 0.9 mg per litre (Pant and Sharma, 1980) Pant and Bisht (1981) have expressed the opinion that the deficiency of oxygen in the hypolimmion waters and the entire body of water during winters in the Nainital lake can be related to the decomposition of accumulated organic matter in the lake bottom and decaying of large quantities of algae (planktonic, algae and mat algae) which blooms frequently, then die and finally sink to the bottom.

*Level of Nitrogen and Phosphorous*

The levels of nitrogen and phosphorous have a significant bearing on the biological activity of aquatic systems. Studying the levels of these two elements in the Nainital and Bhimtal lakes, Pant and Bisht (1981) reported the following results:

"In Nainital lake, the $NO_3$-N reaches its peak value of 499 mg/litre during autumn and decrease to a lowest value of 76.25 mg/litre in spring in this lake, the value of $PO_4$ was found to be 35.3 mg/litre. In Bhimtal lake the $NO_3$-N varies from 0 mg/litre in spring and late summer to 40 mg/litre in winter. $PO_4$-P was 24 mg/litre..."

Negi (1982 b) states, "that there was a rapid increase in the level of $NO_3$-N and $NH_2$-N in Nainital lake between 1960 and present. On the basis of nitrogen and phosphorous levels the Nainital lake can be said to be in a fairly advanced level of eutrophication while the Bhimtal lake is in a pre-eutrophication stage".

*Other Chemical*

The levels of pH, free $CO_2$ and organic matter have also been changing during the past 20 years. At the surface, the pH of both the Nainital and Bhimtal lakes varies from 5 to 7. However, there is a difference in the pH levels at various depths. In Nainital lake, the water at a depth of about 3 mts is acidic. The concentration of free carbon dioxide in the Nainital lake varies from 27 mg/per litre in summer and winter to 21 mg/per litre in the monsoon season. This level is about 10 mg/per litre is Bhimtal lake during the summer months. The organic matter in the Nainital lake ranges from 1000 to 1500 parts per million. It varies from season to season.

There are many harmful substances in the Nainital lake primarily due to the disposal of sewage and other waste products into the once crystal clear waters. Ammonia, hydrogen sulphide, methane and other toxic substances have formed at the bottom of the lake. This has adversely affected the physiology of biotic organisms in the lake.

*Biological Organisms*

Several plant and animal species are found in the Nainital and Bhimtal lakes. This include planktons, moulds and fishes. The degradation of these lakes has affected their life and habitat in the following manner:

*Fishes :* A large population of fishes are found in these waterbodies. The main fishes inhabiting the Nainital and Bhimtal lake include:

Asala (*Schizothorax sp.*) Catla (*Catla cata*)
Mrigal (*Cirrhins mrigala*) and Rohu (*Labeo rohuta*)

The advent of eutrophication in these lakes has brought about two major changes in fish life:

The fish mortality rate has increased steadily over the past 25 years. Each year, a large number of fish die and a rough estimate shows that about 40 to 50 kgs. of fish perish each year in the Nainital lake (Negi, 1982b) . Moreover, there has also been a decline in the fish catch from the Nainital lake (Das 1978; Das and Pande, 1978)

The spawning and breeding grounds of carp fishes are being destroyed by the inflow of sewage and a vast quantity of silt. The fishes in the Nainital lake breed in shallow water near the periphery of the lake.

*Water Moulds :* Water moulds are saprophytes and need organic matter to survive. Khulbe (1981) carried out a detailed study on the water moulds of Nainital lake and the Sariyatal lake located nearby. It is evident that there is an abundance of water moulds in the Nainital lake primarily because of a high intake of sewage. The occurrence of water, moulds is concentrated near zones of sewage inlets.

It was also observed by Khulbe (1981) that the addition of organic matter to the lake water reduces the quality of the drinking water due to the different pathogenic microorganisms which are directly or indirectly associated and are responsible for a number of water born diseases in animals and human population. The water of Sariyatal is more suited for human consumption.

*Zooplanktons :* Both the Nainital and Bhimtal lakes contains a large variety of zooplanktons. However, there are some zooplanktons which are found in abundance in the Bhimtal lake but are absent in the Nainital lake. These are :

*Cephaledella sp.*
*Dophnis sp.*
*Side sp.*

On the other hand, *Keretalla sp.* occurs in the Nainital lake but is absent in Bhimtal. This strange paradox is due to the different levels of pollution in these two waterbodies[3].

*Recession:* The Nainital lake has shrunk in size, The flat ground occurring along the northern shore of the lake (Mallital) was once part of the lake bottom. Recession of the lake has exposed this tract and today it is a playground called by the locals as the flat. The following causes have contributed to the recession of the lake:

— an inflow of a vast quantity of silt into the lake, due to degradation of the slopes around this waterbody.
— dumping of sewage into the waterbody.

**Hussain Sagar (Andhra Pradesh)**

This lake lies between Hyderabad and Secundrabad in Andhra Pradesh. It is situated in a small depression. The twin towns have come up around this lake. The main factors responsible for the ecological degradation of this lake are :

— A heavy influx of waste, sewage and industrial affluents into the lake waters..
— Abnormal levels of siltation
— Recession of the lake waters brought about by encroachments along its banks.

**Udaipur Lake (Rajasthan)**

This lake is located within the town of Udaipur in Rajasthan. A large hotel has been opened on a small island within the lake. The main factors responsible for the ecological degradation of this lake are:

— Dumping of waste sewage including human and animal excreta into the lake.
— Inflow of silt from the adjoining areas
— Invasion of weeds which have converted parts of this lake into swamps and marshes.

**Management of Wetlands**

Wetland ecosystems of India have been put under a severe strain due to the following principal reasons:

— Indiscriminate conversion of wetlands for agriculture, human habitation and industrial purpose. This produces a series of undesirable reactions such as the non-absorption of flood water, sealing the sources of groundwater discharge; loss of natural assimilative capacity and increasing the population levels of adjacent waters (Mahajan, 1988).
— Fertilizers used for boosting the production of foodgrains have an adverse influence on the primary productivity of wetlands.
— The free movement of water is hampered by the haphazard construction of earthen dams of local irrigation. Planting of weeds and other plants species to hold the earthen dam in place which may pose problems for the aquatic plants.
— Indiscriminate removal of the vegetation, channelisation and construction of earthen dams adversely affects the

hydrological cycle and sedimentation in the wetland. There are major changes in the biotic composition which may have long term effects on the ecology of wetlands.

— Disposal of sewage and industrial effluents into the lakes has upset its ecology and led to problems such as increased fish mortality and drop in the quality of the water.

A management plan for India's wetlands must take into account the following aspects:

(a) The magnitude of primary production. An understanding of the structure and functioning of wetland systems should be developed.
(b) Compilation of consumer inventories and ecological data sheets so that the most representative and economically important animals are identified and their conservation is ensured.
(c) The role played by different consumer organisms must also be taken into account.
(d) Correlation of morphological, physical, chemical and biological characters of wetlands.
(e) Identification of the threshold criteria or critical zones for the function and utility of wetlands for various levels.
(f) Geological characteristics, cycle of groundwater discharge and recharge needs to be taken into account.
(g) Effect of the hydrological regime.
(h) Impact of anthropogenic pressures on wetlands.
(i) Collection of basic data regarding wetlands.

The following are the main points along which India's wetlands should be managed:

— Diversion of sewage and industrial effluents away from the wetlands
— Afforestation of the slopes around the wetlands in the mountainous region so as to reduce the inflow of silt into the waterbodies.
— Proper land use management in the entire catchment areas.
— Immediate de-weeding and desilting operations in the

critically affected wetlands such as the Dal lake.
- — Minimising the level of irritants to the wetland ecosystem such as boating.
- — Conservation of the threatened flora and fauna.
- — Non-diversion of wetlands for other purposes such as agriculture or human settlements.
- — Regular monitoring and evaluation of the functioning of the wetland management programmes.

Mahajan 1988 states, ".... the overall management of wetlands should involve both short-term and long-term measures. Basic data is an essential ingredient for long-term management planning..".

The Ministry of Environment and Forest of the Government of India compiled certain basic information on the wetlands of India. This has been presented in the Table 11.1 (after Mahajan, 1988) below:

**Table 11.1 :** Basic Information of Wetlands in India

| *Origin Natural/Man-made* | *Number* | *Area (in hect.)* |
|---|---|---|
| 1 | 2 | 3 |
| **STATES** | | |
| **Andhra Pradesh** | | |
| Natural | 219 | 1,00,457 |
| Man-made | 19,020 | 4, 25, 892 |
| Total | 19,239 | 5,26,349 |
| **Arunachal Pradesh** | | |
| Natural | 2 | 20,200 |
| Man-made | — | — |
| Total | 2 | 20,200 |
| **Assam** | | |
| Natural | 1,394 | 86,355 |
| Man-made | — | — |
| Total | 11,394 | 86,355 |

(*Contd.*)

*Table 11.1 (Contd.)*

| | | |
|---|---|---|
| **Bihar** | | |
| Natural | 62 | 2,24,788 |
| Man-made | 8509 | 1,48,607 |
| Total | 8571 | 3,73,395 |
| **Goa** | | |
| Natural | 3 | 12,360 |
| Man-made | — | — |
| Total | 3 | 12,360 |
| **Gujarat** | | |
| Natural | 22 | 3,94,627 |
| Man-made | 57 | 1,29,600 |
| Total | 79 | 5,24,287 |
| **Haryana** | | |
| Natural | 14 | 2,691 |
| Man-made | 4 | 1,079 |
| Total | 18 | 3,770 |
| **Himachal Pradesh** | | |
| Natural | 5 | 702 |
| Man-made | 3 | 19,165 |
| Total | 8 | 19,867 |
| **Jammu & Kashmir** | | |
| Natural | 18 | 7,227 |
| Man-made | — | — |
| Total | 18 | 7,227 |
| **Karnataka** | | |
| Natural | 10 | 3,320 |
| Man-made | 22,758 | 5,39,515 |
| Total | 22,768 | 5,42,515 |
| **Kerala** | | |
| Natural | 32 | 24,329 |
| Man-made | 2,121 | 2,18,579 |
| Total | 2,153 | 2,42,908 |

*(Contd.)*

*Table 11.1* (*Contd.*)

| | | |
|---|---|---|
| **Madhya Pradesh** | | |
| Natural | 8 | 324 |
| Man-made | 53 | 1,88,818 |
| Total | 61 | 1,89,142 |
| **Maharashtra** | | |
| Natural | 49 | 21,675 |
| Man-made | 1,004 | 2,79,025 |
| Total | 1,053 | 3,00,700 |
| **Manipur** | | |
| Natural | 1 | 26,600 |
| Man-made | — | — |
| Total | 1 | 26,600 |
| **Maghalaya** | | |
| Natural | NA | NA |
| Man-made | NA | NA |
| **Mizoram** | | |
| Natural | 3 | 36.5 |
| Man-made | 1 | 0.5 |
| Total | 4 | 37.0 |
| **Nagaland** | | |
| Natural | 2 | 210 |
| Man-made | — | — |
| Total | 2 | 210 |
| **Orissa** | | |
| Natural | 20 | 1,377,022 |
| Man-made | 36 | 1,48,454 |
| Total | 56 | 2,85,476 |
| **Punjab** | | |
| Natual | 33 | 17,085 |
| Man-made | 06 | 5,391 |
| Total | 39 | 22,476 |

(*Contd.*)

*Table 11.1* (*Contd.*)

| | | |
|---|---|---|
| **Rajasthan** | | |
| Natural | 9 | 14, 027 |
| Man-made | 85 | 1,00,217 |
| Total | 94 | 1,14,244 |
| **Sikkim** | | |
| Natural | 42 | 1,101 |
| Man-made | 02 | 3 .5 |
| Total | 44 | 1,104.5 |
| **Tamil Nadu** | | |
| Natural | 31 | 58, 8 6 8 |
| Man-made | 20,030 | 2,01,132 |
| Total | 20,061 | 2,60,000 |
| **Tripura** | | |
| Natural | NA | NA |
| Man-made | NA | NA |
| **Uttar Pradesh** | | |
| Natural | 1 125 | 12,_832 |
| Man-made | 28 | 2,12,470 |
| Total | 1,153 | 2,25,302 |
| **West Bengal** | | |
| Natural | 54 | 2,91,963 |
| Man-made | 9 | 52,564 |
| Total | 63 | 3,44,530 |
| | **Union Territories** | |
| **Andaman & Nicobar Islands** | | |
| Natural | 4 | 71, 694 |
| Man-made | — | — |
| Total | 4 | 71, 694 |
| **Chandigarh** | | |
| Natural | — | — |
| Man-made | 1 | 1 |
| Total | 1 | 1 |

(*Contd.*)

*Table 11.1 (Contd.)*

| | | |
|---|---|---|
| **Dadar and Nagar Haveli** | | |
| Natural | NA | NA |
| Man-made | NA | NA |
| **Lakshdweep** | | |
| Natural | NA | NA |
| Man-made | NA | NA |
| **Pondichery** | | |
| Natural | 3 | 447 |
| Man-made | 2 | 1,131 |
| Total | 5 | 1,578 |

*Source :* Ministry of Environment and Forest, Government of India.

## Conclusion

On the basis of above discussion it could be said that due to increasing pressure of population, the ramification of establishments, the eutrophication of wetlands have been observed not only in Bihar and India but almost all parts of the globe. This is dangerous not only for the future generation but for the betterment of environment as well.

So far as, the eutrophication of wetland in North Bihar is concerned it has been affected by the input of dead body, dead animals, eutrophication by the dump of refuse water, industrial and urban wastes and sewage beside soil erosion in the periphery. Recently, it has been felt that acid rain from the NTPC, Kanti and Barauni Thermal Power Projects have polluted the nearby wetlands. Hence, environmental protection measures should be adopted by plantation of trees, checking of the dumping ground of urban refuse and so on.

## REFERENCES

Asthana, V. (1979) . *Limnological Studies of Lake Chilka*, Orissa, Tech. Rep. MAB Proj . DST. New Delhi.

Bhatia, B. (1979) . *Ecological Study of Loktak Lake*, Imphal, Tech. Rep. MAB Proj. DST., New Delhi.

Cowardian, L.M. *et at* (1979). *Classification of Wetlands and Deep Water Habitats of the United States*, U.S. Fish and WL. Serv., Washington D.C.

Das, S.M. (1978) . Pollution in High Altitude Lakes, *Sci. Cult.* 44 (4), 236.

Das, S.M. and Pande, J. (1978). Some Physio-chemical and Biological Indicators of Pollution in Nainital Lake, Kumaon, *U.P. Ind. Ecol.* 5(1), 7-16.

Gopal, B. (1973). A Survey of Indian Studies of Ecology and Production of Wetland and Shallow Water. *Communities, Pol., Arch. Hydrobiol.* 20, 21-29.

Handoo, J.K. (1978) . *Ecology and Production Studies of some Wetlands of Kashmir*, Ph.D. thesis, Kashmir Univ. Srinagar.

IUCN (1971). The Ramsar Conference: Final Act of the International Conference on the Conservation of Wetlands and Water *fowl. Spl. Suppl. IUCN Bull.* 2(19), 1-4.

Kaliyamurthy, M. (1974). Observations on the Environmental Characteristic of Pulicat Lake, *Jour. mar. Bio. Asson., India*, 16, 683-88.

Kaul, V. and Pandit, A.K. (1979). Is the Dal Lake Dying *Sci. Rep.* 16 (10).

Khulbe, R.D. (1981) . Frequency of Water Moulds as an Indicator of Water Pollution, *Sci. RD Mins.* 432-36.

Mahajan, K.K. (1988). Dangerously Threatened Habitats — The Wetlands: An Overview and suggestion for their Conservation as Harbours of Living Natural Resources Threat Hab., New Delhi, 241-68.

Negi, S. (1982a). Causes and Effects of the Deteriorating Himalayan Environment: A Preliminary Report, *Jour. Env. Sci*, 25(2), 47-50.

Nagi, S.S. (1982 b). *Environmental Problems in the Himalaya*, BSMPS Publ., Dehradun.

Pant, M. C. and Bisht, J.S. (1981) . Impact of the Changing Environment on the Lacustrine Fishes of Nainital, *Sci. R.D. Mtus.* 437-48.

Rai, U. (1982). A Dying Lake, *Times of India*, 14.3.82.

# 12

# WETLANDS AND AGRICULTURE

Wetlands have been arbitrarily defined as all areas of marsh and all stretches of water, including coastal water, less than six metres deep, temporary or permanent, static or flowing[1]. Such areas have been exploited and modified by man for many centuries. Some of them have been drained to establish network of roads and railways: install industrial complexes and develop housing colonies; some have been made free from water to eradicate the breeding grounds of malarial mosquitos and farmers attracted by the high fertility of the soil and hence they drained many wetland areas.

It is the demands for increased food production which continue to threaten the survival of many remaining wetlands. The nature reserves of many abandoned river courses, lakes and lowlying depressions will be fundamentally changed if crops such as rice are grown there. The conflict of interest between increase in production for the farmer, and, on the other, a biological interest with no economic gain means that many water meadows, will be gradually lost.

Paradoxically, the biological productivity of many wetland areas is considered to be as high as or even higher than the most intensively farmed arable land. A farmer converts the potential into crops which are more easily marketable but the management of wetlands, for livestock, ducks, fish, timber, reed, and for raising highly remunerative water berries like makhana, singhara, ramdana in the Kosi region, can allow these naturally productive areas to yield crops of greater benefit to man and with little modification of the environment. The amenity value of wetland areas is also being increasingly recognized, and although intensive recreation and man's interference could disrupt their scientific interests, there is now greater potential for their protection. Despite increased awareness of the need to retain and manage wetlands for economic and amenity purposes, such areas continue to be lost to meet the demands of agriculture.

**Wild Life Values**

The wetlands provide numerous habitats for wild life. All wetlands represent some stage in the active and directional process of plant succession. The major wetland habitats which are valued for their biological interest along with succession from open water, through fringing vegetation, marsh and fen to wetland will be looked at in the following discussion.

**Open Water**

Sheets of open water poor in nutrients (Oligotrophic) may remain unchanged for centuries, but habitats can become artificially enriched passing eventually to a nutrient-rich or eutrophic state. The main nutrients causing enrichment are nitrogen and phosphorus and these determine the level of plant growth and productivity of the water bodies. The input of external nutrients depends on land use within the catchment area: a mountain or moorland lake will generally be oligotrophic because the farmland surrounding it will be poor in nutrients. But modern fertilizers which enrich the runoff water may increase the nutrient status of water bodies; they can also change and aid lake into an alkaline one, thus causing a decline in acid loving plant communities. A lake in the lowland regions is likely to be mesotrophic, eutrophic or highly eutrophic according to the land use and the amount of fertilizer applied to the soil. Farming practice can, therefore, alter substantially the character of a water body, although urban activities also affect even the most remote rural areas and it is often difficult to separate the two causes of nutrient enrichment.

## Fringing Vegetation

Plant communities that develop in wetlands depend upon the nutrient balance in water, the degree of silting, the soil type, the shoreline pattern, and the distribution and flow of water. Open water becomes invaded by fringing vegetation as silting increases and a reed swamp may be produced which is the base upon which, according to soil type, marsh or fen vegetation develops. Swampy depressions and stagnant water bodies get over grown with water weeds, while reedy grasses, bulrushes and tamrisks (locally called *jhau*) grow on the margins.

Reed swamp is formed from the decay of common reeds (narkat) and tall grasses. A marsh can develop if the soil is either organic and mineral poor (leading to acid marsh) or inorganic and mineral rich (forming an alkaline marsh). In marsh-land,the water table is below the soil surface during the stimmer although water movement may be apparent. Fen will develop if the soil is organic in nature, composed of alkaline peat and mineral rich, and the water table is at the surface throughout the summer although there may be little water movement. Common marsh plants are sedges and rushes. Decay of sedges can lead to the formation of an organic peat characteristics of a fen, but the sedges peat may be acid. Continual cutting weakens the sedge and grass from the community. So, fen have obviously been considerably modified by man.

## Wood Land

Accumulation of fen peat effectively lower the water table, and if this remain just below the surface at the wet test time of year then woody plants can colonize, forming what is known as carr. If it is cleared a true 'mixed', fen develops which will contain rich and varied plant communities.

## The Fauna of Wetlands

White breasted water hen, bronze winged jacana, curlew stint black ibis, glossy ibis, white-necked stork, cattle egret pond heron, pink headed duck, silli or cotton teal, white fronted goose, large whistling teal, brahmny duck, eastern grey duck, marbled teal and eastern goosander are the different varieties of birds found in the wetland areas. The reclamation of many water pools and progressive conversion of the fringes into arable lands and indiscriminate shooting have led to the extinction of the pink-headed duck, marbled teai, copper breasted teal and floricans in this north-eastern part of Bihar which was once the marry land for the water birds. Various species of ducks, mallard, nakta, combed duck and geese are no longer found.

Many local or raremoths and butterflies are also found in wetlands but wide spread drainage has led to the complete extinction of some species.

## Wet Zones on Farm Land

Consequent upon man's interference water meadows have been gradually disappearing from the landscapes. Similarly, the intensification of agricultural management has been extinguishing the micro-wetlands once common on farms. Extension of field drainage, the ability to plough steeper and more uneven ground, and the wider use of pasture has meant the removal of many ponds and ditches once valuable for stock watering, together with patches of marshy ground which are themselves remnants of more extensive wetlands. In those areas where stock have been replaced by arable farming, or where the gazing system is based upon the permanent housing of animals fed on grass cropped from improved pastures, wetlands are no longer needed as they are considered wasteful of land and costly to retain. Even if they are not deliberately extinguished on a particular age, these micro-wetlands are difficult to maintain as the water table falls over surrounding agricultural land.

It is not easy to assess the wild-life values of these micro-wetland habitats of farmland. Some may contain valuable relict species of plant and animals once common on the fens and marshes of the region, while others may serve the purpose of ecological stepping stones between existing larger water bodies, but the habitats are ecologically untenable. Drainage and irrigation can mean a damaging fluctuation of the water table while if the areas escape drainage their values may be threatened in other ways. For example, nutrients, mainly nitrogen, from fertilizer applications to adjoining land will run off into ponds and water bodies, thus altering the nutrient balance; sewage, rich in phosphates from intensive dairy and pig farming, is often openly drained into farm water courses; gesticide and herbicide run-off could affect plant production and photosynthesis, dumping of pesticide containers and any consequent leakage could mean locally high and lethal level to many vertebrates, invertebrates and plants; the use of some molluscicides could affect plant growth on marsh systems; and direct applications of aquatic herbicides to keep drains free from "weeds" which reduce the chance of survival of any relict flora and fauna. Plants more able to adapt to the changing environment and increasing artificiality of the habitat could easily replace any surviving relict species.

## Forces for Change in Wetlands : Land Drainage

The drainage lines in Bihar is uneven in the sense that some parts are over-drained (i.e. water runs off too rapidly to allow the formation of extensive surface water bodies and to permit considerable soaking of water underground), some under-drained (i.e. the surface flow is very slow leading to the formation of extensive surface bodies of water and waterlogging conjunction with high water table) and others are well drained (characterized by features neither of over nor under drainage).

Drainage schemes to convert wetland into arable one can indirectly affect a large area. Even if an ecologically important area is not itself reclaimed, the 'sphene of influence' of drainage works can cause detrimental changes to water regimes.

But the main effect obviously occurs on those areas of marsh and open water which will be converted to farming land. The only wetland remaining will be drainage channels. Species richness as well as abundance of the aquatic flora will be affected, both will be reduced with the habitat effectively confirmed to the drainage channels and fewer species able to adjust to the new changed conditions. The drainage of wetlands poses the greatest direct threat to their wild life value but there are other indirect ways in which these areas can be damaged.

## Fertilizers and their Effects

Traditionally, farmers depends for improvements to silt fertility on the use of farm yard manure, leguminous crops. However, since last thirty years, artificial fertilizers, particularly those containing nitrogen, potash and phosphates, have been used in increasing quantities. Although potash and phosphate fertilizer use has grown only slightly over last 15 years, there has been marked increase in the use of nitrogenous fertilizers over the same period. Under-drainage has increased the rate of rainfall run-off into drainage channels and this is correlated with increased fertilizer applications. The nutrient balance of many water courses may have been drastically altered in this way.

## Nitrogen

Any nitrogen which has been applied to the land is subject to variable losses due to run-off. The amounts found in a drainage channel depend on several factors with soil type, land-use, varying rates of fertilizer application, rainfall, soil water content all affecting the rate of run-off. Furthermore, levels of nitrogen are affected by intensity of urban development and the amount of sewage effluent discharged into the rivers. In general fertilizer run-off seems less important as a source of nitrate pollution compared with the large amount released from industrial or urban sewage effluent.

## Nitrogen Levels in Groundwater

High use of nitrogen in modern farming may exceptionally high levels of nitrogen in the groundwater. Untreated water thus, in such ecological niches can bring on diseases such as methaemo-globinaemia. The source of this nitrogen pollution in rural areas is almost certainly due to modern agriculture. Increase in the level of fertilizer applications can be correlated with the increase in nitrogen in groundwater but a major source of excess nitrogen arises from the creation of arable land from grassland. The nitrogen in the soil becomes mineralized by aeration and inorganic nitrate leaches down into the groundwater. The exact contribution of artificial fertilizers have done to the groundwater levels has not been estimated.

## Phosphorus

Phosphate usage has also increased in the last few years, but phosphate unlike nitrogen, binds to the organic matter in the soil with only small amounts leaching out into water courses and the high phosphate levels in our rivers arise largely from urban sewage outfalls. Intensive animal husbandry effluents in non-urban areas, with their poor sewage disposal facilities, will make a significant contribution to the phosphate load in a river.

Again it seems that modern agricultural practice is not as detrimental to the biological interests of an area as are the effects of urban environment.

## Wetland Management Insecticide Effects

Pesticides and herbicides may enter rivers and water courses indirectly through rain, spray drift, surface runoff, and from sewage and industrial wastes. In agricultural areas surface run-off used to be considered the most important source of the DDT found in the water of many British rivers. But DDT is very volatile and the greater proportion left in the soil after application will be lost to the air so that, excluding industrial wastes and sewage, rainfall appears to be the major pathway for DDT and its breakdown products DDD and DDE to enter the water of a river system. In one study dieldrain could not be detected in the muds of many ponds (U.K.) even though adjacent fields had been treated with the compound[2].

Much greater contamination of rivers results from some industrial processes, such as moth-proofing, which can give concentrations of dieldrain or BHC in excess of 500 mg-litres[3]. In agricultural areas where the maximum level of 170 mg/litre for DDT, dieldrain and BHC has been detected, ecological effects on wetlands are likely to be minimal. It is only in areas where industry and agriculture mix pesticide residues could exert some ecological effect on wetland areas.

Organo phosphorus compounds do not persist in water for more than a few weeks. These compounds are likely to exert no permanent effect on aquatic plants and animals. Harmful environmental effects have been reported from the use of alkyl-mercury dressed seed from Sweden[4].

## Farming Practice and Wetland Conservation

Wetland conservation has always been relegated to second plan in agricultural development because farmers must put the economic needs of a thriving constryside before other interests. There is no doubt that we now face a multiplicity of often competing demands in rural areas and a scarcity of means to meet them. New vista of agricultural changes and gradual invasion of wetlands must concern all good people. In future, it will be difficult to produce more food from our own soil yet satisfy the increasing demands upon the countryside for leisure and recreation and for the conservation of landscape and wildlife.

Conservation can be seen as the management of habitats towards specific aim with the intention of maintaining their scientific interest or rehabilitating their physical, chemical and biological quality.

Conservation interests in wetlands are obviously affected by much in modern farming practice. Wetlands are one of the few groups of habitats where, with present agricultural methods, a compromise situation rarely exists. Wetlands require a high water table and waterlogged soil during one or more seasons; arable farming requires a low water table, and pasture land requires a water table at or below but never above the surface. For plant communities to remain unaltered, unpolluted water and nutrient stability (within acceptable limits) are necessary. It is not only farmers who cause water enrichment by their methods; areas such as industrial complexes around Barauni and so, and metropolis and surroundings thereof like Patna city-Patna-Dinapore thickly populous land stretch are probably affected more by industrial wastes and sewage effluent than by fertilizer run off. The ecological effects of wetlands of pesticides and herbicide residues are different to quantify mainly because the industrial rivers which carry levels of DDT, dieldrain, and BHC high enough to exert an effect, are also polluted with many other chemicals. These rivers are simply not clear enough to allow the effect of one pollutant to be identified. Direct applications of agricultural chemicals will have varying, but damaging ecological effects because of its applications to a wetland is the greatest threat.[5]

If the largest wetlands are to survive at all then farming practice in some areas must be verified to suit these habitats. Traditional crops may have to be forsaken, though cattle and sheep grazing could be tolerated in certain areas provided that the water table remained high and occasional flooding was not prevented, there are many breeds of cattle and sheep well adapted to produce high yields from the roughest-sedges. Other such larger, wetlands could produce controlled yields of climber, reed and even water berries.

On a smaller scale, farmers could help to conserve any relict flora and fauna of the modified and marginal wetlands remaining on agricultural land. Most dikes, ponds, ditches and even the persistent marsh probably contain some interesting plants and animals worth conserving. Preventing pollutants entering these habitats, keeping within the code of practice as set down by the government for pesticides. This will aid the survival of species in these artificial but nevertheless important habitats. Farmers could also play a more active part in recreating those small wetland habitats, such as pond and ditches which have dried up, and retaining, rather than filling in, those which have fallen into disuse. These areas should be managed by cutting their vegetation and leaving areas of open water, to maintain their interest as examples of previously common wetland types.

Conservation bodies cannot hope to purchase all the remaining wetlands before they disappear for ever. The retention of those which are more extensive as well as the micro wetland habitats of agricultural land, depends fundamentally upon the attitudes of the Water Boards/Drainage Authority and farmers. There may be a range of possibilities from persuasion to compulsion, from carrot to stick.

Incentives to farm in a particular way is a method much safer of success than more statutory controls. If a farmer is to be persuaded, for example, that draining a certain marsh will lead to an irreplaceable loss of plant and animal species, then society must make-up his economic loss in retaining the marsh. With all large schemes of land reclamation for food production, there should be much closer cooperation between the Ministry of Agriculture as the grant aiding agency and conservation bodies who can negotiate management of Wetlands.

The solution could be to devise an integrated policy, serving the needs of both the conservationist and the farmer, where by the farmer modifies his methods in areas of high scientific interest, but conservationists tolerate some commercial exploitation. Only by compromises the future of our remaining wetlands will be bright otherwise the things are setting worse due to reclaiming of most of the wetlands either for the purpose of dryland agriculture or the extension of housing colonies.

## NOTES

1. Hoffman, L., Project Mar. *Proceedings of Technical Meeting of the International Union for the consorvation of Nature and Natural Resources* No. 12, (1968) pp. 36-50.
2. Jefferies and French (Communication)
3. Croll, B.T. (1969); *Organochlorine Insecticides in Water*: Part I, Water Treatment and Examination, 18,225-214; and Lowden, G.F. Saunders C.L. and Edwards, R.W. (1969). *Organochlorine Insecticides in Water*: Part II, Water Treatment and Examination, 18, 1969, 275-287.
4. Bengf, W., Johnels, A., Siostrand, B. and Westermark, T. (1966).
5. Mercury contents in Feathers of Swedish Birds from the past 100 Oikos, 1975, 17.

# 13

# ECOLOGICAL DIVERSITIES OF KABAR TAL

## Introduction

The Kabartal of the district of Begusarai is a natural inland feature and its watershed spreading over an area of 12,500 hectare not only supports the ecosystem of the tal but also the human population as a part of complex and composite eco-system. Resources vary within the confines of the watershed both on terrestrial and acquatic environs and have defined the occupational structure of the population as well as specialized community classes with increasing population. The quality of resource utilization has become highly pressurized. The subsistant level of resources has to be evaluated in the light of sustenance they provide both at subsistant as well as economic levels.

## The Purpose of the Study

This chapter aims to measure the sustenance capability of economic resources when some of it are not only loosing their capacity but also because they are threatening the ecosystem for which the Kabar is famous.

## The Study Area

The Kabar is an inland fresh water lake on the north eastern side of Burhi-Gandak river spreading over Majhaul, Ekamba, Sakarbasa and Jamanglagarh villages of Begusarai district. It is located at 25°38'N latitude and 86°08'E longitude. The average elevation of the area is 35 metres near Jamanglagarh, 42 metres near Majhaul and 39 metres south of Kabartal. Its water reservoir area is about 24 $km^2$ which swells over 64 $km^2$ during the rainy season in flooded condition. The ephemeral land around the reservoir is marshy. The water body and its marshy approach provides ideal habitat to resident and migratory birds both national and international. The Kabar wetland is famous as it provides winter habitat for migratory water fowls.

The Kabar and its watershed which maintain this ecosystem are composed of feeder chaurs and fertile alluvial flood plains and perennial water body, where natural conditions in variations have been able to provide sufficient amount and number of resources. Its watershed is dominantly used as land resource and be able to support agricultural use as orchards and provides us horticultural products. The tal itself is resourceful and is able to support fishing (Fig.13.1) with the initiation of ex-Prime Minister Rajiv Gandhi Kabar Tal has been declared as closed area under Section 37 of the Wildlife Protection Act 1972 (Act 53). The Kabar is a rich habitat of micro and macro living organisms including millions of snails, fishes, crabs and water fowls. Among the other resources, the submergent and floating vegetations of Kabar is attracting thousands of resident water birds to nest each and every year during the winter. Among other birds ducks, teals, gees and varieties of waders could be seen. Some other birds e.g. Lalsar, Dighaunch and Cranes come from distant lands across the Himalayas. (Fig. 13.2)

## Geology

The area around Kabar Tal is Pleistocene unequal deposit of alluvium coming from the Himalaya by the Burhi-Gandak river. Due to annual flooding newer alluvium is found. The rate of siltation is 2 mm per year and its depth has drastically reduced in comparison with 1942 when it was 5 metres. The depth of acquifer is 5 metres, 8 metres, 12 metres and 25 metres with coarse to fine sand strata.

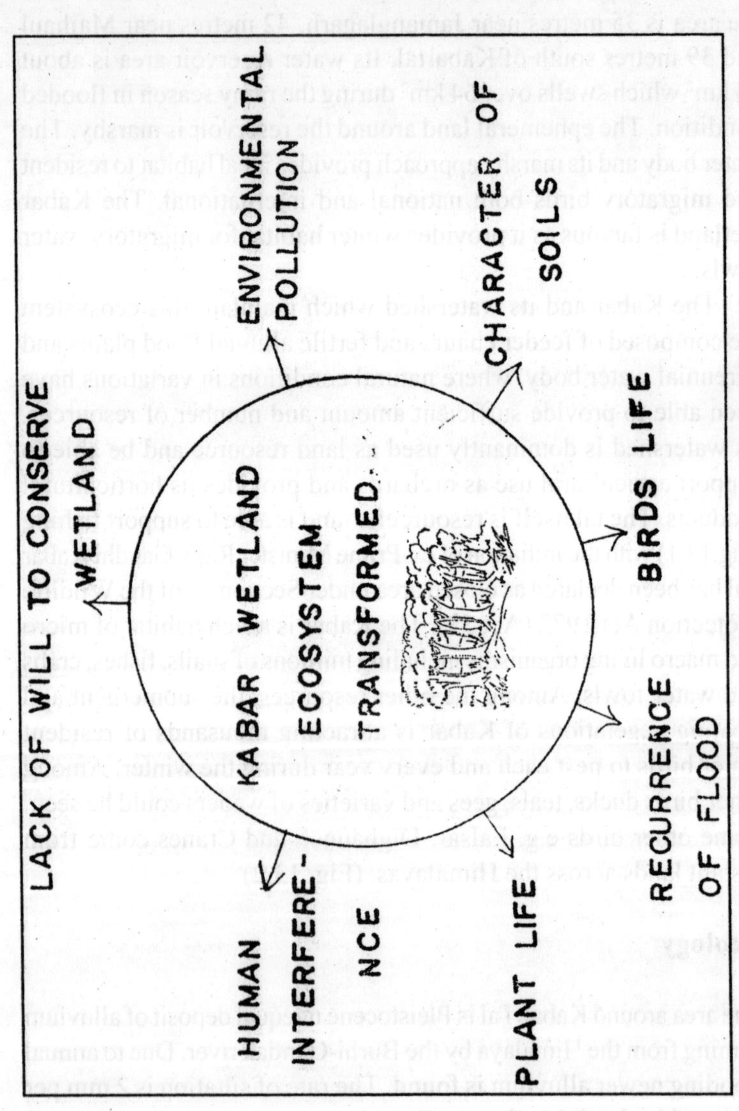


Fig. 13.1 : Kabar Tal Wetland Eco-system Transformed

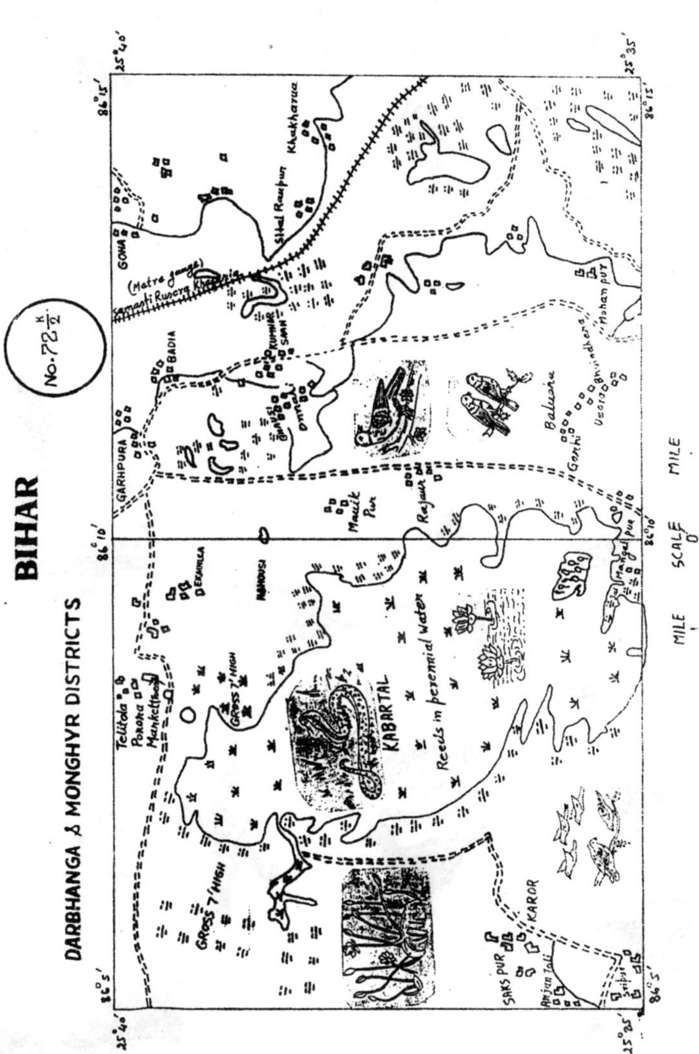


Fig. 13.1 (a) : Bihar — Darbhanga and Monghyr Districts

Fig. 13.2 : Check List of Kabar Tal

**Climatic Features**

The climatic condition around Kabar Tal is cooler where more extreme type of climate is found. The months of May and June are rather hot with 40°C temperature. The south-west monsoon usually breaks in the second half of June and lasts till September. The normal rainfall is 125 centimetres. Sometimes, frost occur during night hours in the winter season.

**Land Use Pattern**

In the environs of Kabar Tal about 80 per cent land is cultivated, 3 per cent is under human settlement, 7 per cent is under fallow and the rest 10 per cent is under orchard and waterbodies. Most of the net sown area is under rice cultivation during the rainy season, and almost all of them come under wheat, maize and gram cultivation during winter months.

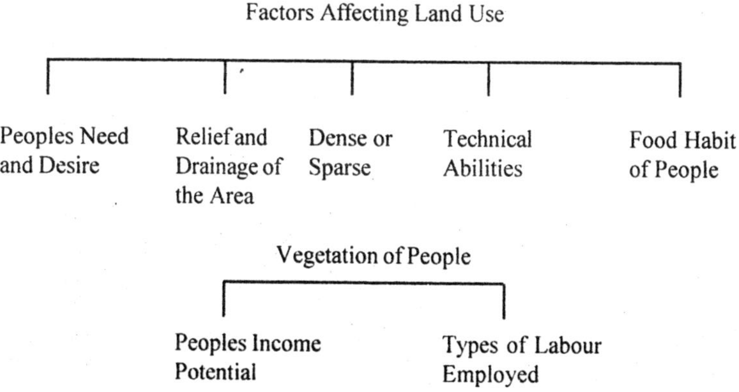


**Vegetation**

The vegetation of Kabar area could be divided into two parts, One is acquatic in water and the other found on the land in the form of planted orchard. Among acquatic lichen, kai, sewar, reeds and water-hyacinth are important. Here, it is important to note that some carnivorous plants are also found in Kabar. On the land mango orchard, Sisam, Sirith, Kansh and willow are found along the banana, palm tree and date tree.

## Human Settlements

Kabartal is surrounded by large size compact rural settlements which cling on higher site due to the effect of flood. Due to the presence of Kabar Tal most of the surrounding villages have Sahni population (10%). The average distance from one settlement to another is more than 1.50 km and the average population size is 2000 persons per village. Some of the important rural settlements of the area could be seen in the following Table. 13.1. (Fig. 13.3)

**Table 13.1 :** Area and Population of Rural Settlements in the Watershed of Kabar Tal

| *Sl. No.* | *Village* | *Area in Hectare* | *Sahni Population 1984* |
|---|---|---|---|
| 1. | Majhaul | 2,699 | 2,948 |
| 2. | Maheshwara | 456 | 134 |
| 3. | Pabsara | 1973 | 455 |
| 4. | Karore | 182 | 57 |
| 5. | Narayan Pipar | 583 | 938 |
| 6. | Parora | 262 | 719 |
| 7. | Sahpur | 210 | 661 |
| 8. | Ekamba | 2,948 | 923 |
| 9. | Khanjapur | 1,047 | 83 |
| 10. | Sakarbasa | 566 | 447 |
| 11. | Bariarpur | 124 | 940 |
| 12. | Kumbhi | 549 | 925 |
| 13. | Rajaur | 201 | 333 |
| 14. | Manikpur | 165 | 226 |
| 15. | Kanausi | 294 | 126 |
| | Total | 122,59 | 10,831 |

Among other villages which should be included in the list are Deora and Sakra of Bakhri, Jamangalagarh, Jaimangalpur and Dihi of Cheria Bariarpur.

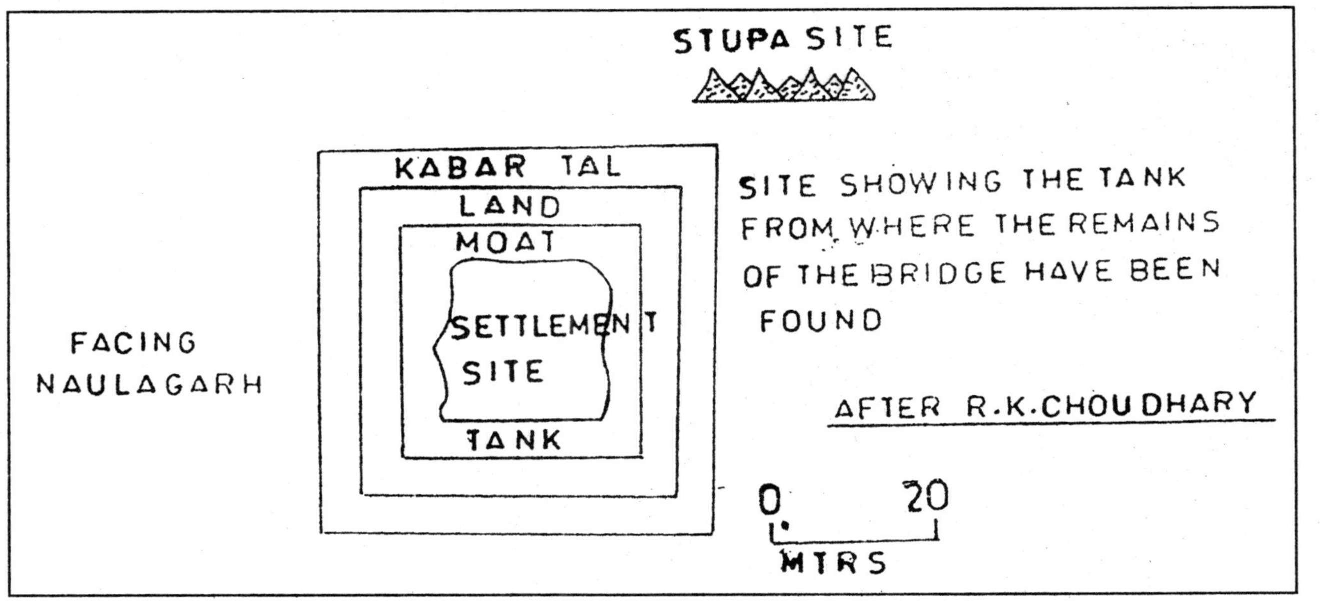


**Fig. 13.3 :** Plan of Jaimanglagarh

## Agriculture

In the environs of Kabar Tal rice, maize, wheat, pulse and oilseeds are grown. About 80 per cent land is net sown area. Due to alluvial plain and dense population in the surrounding area (900) the cultivation of land is done upto the farthest limit. During the rainy season flood is the only problem which the area is facing. It also disturb ecosystem of the Kabar wetland. It harms the fishes, tiny plants and deposition of sediments in the Tal.

## Industries

In the environs of Kabar Tal flour mill, saw mill, rice mill, boat making, net making and basket weaving industries are found in Majhaul. Major and small scale industries are completely absent from this area but brick kilns are seen here and there.

## Inflow and Outflow of Water

For the present the water comes into the Kabar from its catchment area. At the time of flood it comes through Chawara canal made amidst meandering courses of Chawara river. The depth of the canal is 3 metres only. Therefore, Chawara helps in the outflow of water from Kabar which rises slowly with the rise of water in the Burhi-Gandak and subsides slowly as the level of water in the Burhi-Gandak goes down. During flood the water comes into Kabar at the rate of 500 cusecs per second and it goes out at the same rate but during lean months it is not more than 25 cusecs and in May and June water does not go out.

Length of outlet channel - 39.20 kms, Width-14 metres, Depth-3.5 metres.

## Flora and Fauna

In the environs of Kabar Tal of Begusarai district mango orchards are common in most of the villages which are not subject to floods. The oak murtle is another common tree. Besides these pipal, banyan tree, Pakar and Gullar are frequently seen. Bamboo grooves, Palmyrra and date, Jamun, Kathal and Bel are commonly seen. Among microphytes sewar, lichen, kai and several medicinal plants e.g. reeds and water-hyacinth are found under aquatic condition.

Among the fauna varieties of ducks, teals, gees and dighaunch are found in acquatic condition along with fishes, Bagula and varieties of cranes. The migratory birds are also come from Siberia, Tibet and China in October and retires to their motherland sometimes in February and March. Kabar also provides habitat for snakes, earth worms, frogs and several types of insects, pests and ants as well.

## List of Fauna of Kabar

1. Rehu, 2. Katla, 3. Buari, 4. Mirgal, 5. Singhi, 6. Garai, 7. Dhalwa, 8. Pothia, 9. Chancla 10. Gaichi, 11.Bami, 12. Basrahi, 13. Chital, 14. Sauri, 15. Gajal, 16. Kurasi, 17. Mangur, 18. Kabai, 19. Lakwa, 20. Latahi, 21. Tengra, 22. Chenga, 23. Ghongha, 24. Kanker, 25. Tortoise, 26. Ichna, 27, Chalcla and 28. Kholosa.

## Population Dependent on Wetland Resources

Only Sahni a fishermen caste is wholly dependent on Kabartal for their livelihood. Villagewise population of Sahnis could be seen as: Majhaul 2,948, Maheshwara 134, Pahsara 455, Karore 57, Narayan Pipar 938, Parora 719, Sahpur 661, Ekamba 923, Klianjapiir 83, Sakarbasa 447, Bariarpur 940, Kumbhi 925, Rajpur 333, Manikpur 226 and Kanausi 126 only in1996.

| *Population* | *Sahnis on Fishing* | *Sahnis Not on Fishing* |
|---|---|---|
| Male | 2,001 | 873 |
| Female | 1,898 | 952 |
| Children | 3,500 | 1,552 |
| Total | 7,399 | 3,377 |

## Socio-economic Model of Human Occupation

The economy in the watershed of Kabar Tal is the product of its human occupations e.g. in areas of higher percentage of agricultural labourers, the economy will be poorest one. But in case of cultivators who are the land owners also, the economy will be slightly better. In case more and more people are engaged in mining and quarrying operations, the economy will be better than cultivators. In case more people are engaged in industrial and business activities, the economy will be much better. But increased human interactions in and around Kabartal will be detrimental for the ecosystem and its conservation according to the natures rule.

**Table 13.2 :** Subsidiary Occupational Structure of Workers

| | *Subsidiary Occupations* | *No. of Workers* |
|---|---|---|
| 1. | Bird Trapping | 490 |
| 2. | Paddy cutting | 444 |
| 3. | Farming | 63 |
| 4. | Businessmen | 45 |
| 5. | Others | 32 |
| | Total | 1,074 |

## Cultural and Indigenous Practices of Wetland Resource

Kabar provides space for the emersion of Goddess Durga, Kali, Bihula, Saraswati besides Chhat Barta, Sama Chakewaill Sradha, Tarpan, recreation and dance on boats along with Nagpanchmi and Kamla Puja.

In Jaimanglagarh of Kabar evidences of ancient settlements dating post Sunga period have been found on excavation. Coins of the Tughlak period were also discovered. The village name is derived from Jaimangla Devi whose temple is found on the garh.

## Existing Conservation Measures Taken

Long before the declaration of Kabar as birds sanctuary in the year

1954,Sri Krishna Singh has made Chawara channel with, the help of D.M., Munger. In 1990's after declaration of Kabar as birds sanctuary the USSR government has given Rs.12 crore for the conservation to Kabar so that their migratory birds may not be killed in the natural habitat of Kabar. But with the draining out of water from Kabar in December, the farmers of this area wants to cultivate the field for growing wheat and the fishermens society wants to catch fishes. But under Ramsar convention Kabar has been declared as closed area by Rajiv Gandhi the then Prime Minister in 1972. Therefore, illegal fishing should be immediately stopped along with netting of birds and in order to maintain water level and save this eco-system the draining out of water for the purpose of wheat sowing should also be stopped.

Instead of conservation due to ever increasing population in the area, the pressure of local people is increasing heavily on the existing Kabar Tal for fishing, boating, illegal netting and in the name of religious gathering.

## Conclusion

The eco-system found in the Kabar Tal and in its watershed should be preserved and protected for the future generation. This is the pride for the State of Bihar and the nation as it comes under the purview of Ramsar convention. It also attracts very high number of migratory birds, vast reserve of medicinal plants and micro-organisms for which this natural ecosystem needs conservation. It is sad that farmers of the area are trying to cultivate the land which comes under Kabar and Machhua society not only catch fishes but they also trap birds during night hours even if it has been considered as illegal. It is happy to note that only recently the Government of India is trying to survey the whole area for the nature conservation.

## REFERENCES

Ahmad, Shamim, "Ecology of the Wetlands of Milkichak, Darbhanga", Unpublished Ph.D. Thesis, L.N. Mithila University, Darbhanga, 1993.

Choudhary, U. P., 'Geographic Aspects of Wetlands in North Bihar', Unpublished Ph.D. Thesis, Bhagalpur University, 1993.

Gopal, B. Turner, *et al.*, *Wetlands Ecology and Management*, International Institute of Ecology and International Scientific Publications, Jaipur,1982.

Mandal, R.B., *The Value of Wetlands in North East India*, Wetlands Archaeology (Edt. & Nature Conservation; M. Cox, *et al.*), 1994, p. 30.

Margaret, Cox, *et. al*, *Wetlands Archaeology and Nature Conservation*, London, HMSO. 1994.

Ramsar Convention, UNESCO, Ramsar, Iran, Feb. 1971.

Wetlands Conference in Czechoslovakia; Strategy and Trends, Washington, D.C. U.S.,1984, p. 22.

# 14

# PRODUCTIVITY OF WETLANDS

The word productivity is currently one of the most used, misused abused word in our vocabulary. This is important since the concept of productivity lies at the very heart of agricultural geography, a subject which is, after all concerned with the allocation of resources and the maximization of goal relative to means. Thus the measurement and evaluation of agricultural productivity, however, continues to be the exclusive field of the geographers. And, therefore, it provides a very important and potential field of research in agricultural geography.

It is one of the essential pre-requisites of a sound statistical analysis that all terms involved in interpretation are precisely defined and their scopes delimited. The lack of such precision and clarity has often led to vague and faulty generalization, futile discussions, circular reasoning and considerable ambiguity, misunderstanding and confusion. In the case of different agricultural productivity measures the confusion which exists may be due to the multiplicity of terms entering into common every day parlance. The glib way in which terms are used often hides a cross ignorance of their exact implications and unfortunately there is a widespread disregard for detailed definitions. Therefore, the object of this study is to shed light on the concept, meaning and the measurement of productivity.

## The Concept and Meaning of Productivity

The word productivity is, unfortunately, one of those few words in agricultural geography that have aroused many different and conflicting interpretations. Indeed, the term productivity has been used in such a variety of senses, that it is exceedingly difficult to find out whether the term productivity is synonymous with "efficiency" or 'fertility' or 'over-all effectiveness' of a productive unit. It is generally used to express the power of agriculture to produce crops without taking into account the weather or the efforts of man. On the other hand, fertility denotes the ability of soil to provide all the essential plant nutrients in available form and in a suitable balance for the plant growth. In recent years several attempts have been made to define agricultural productivity, but even today opinions a differ regarding its concept, definition and methods of identification and deliniation.

Agricultural productivity is a measure of the efficiency with which inputs are used in agriculture to produce an output. When a given combination of inputs produces a maximum output, the productivity is said to be at its maximum. In fact, it is the ratio of output resources spent. It may be viewed as the overall effectiveness of a productive unit, be it a plant, farm or company, while some have considered productivity as to denote the ratio of output to the corresponding input of labour.

Sometimes productivity is misappropriately used as synonymous to production. But productivity is not production. Production may be defined as the values of output whereas the productivity is the continual improvement of the efficiency of an organisation resulting in increasing efficient use of the materials, labour, plants and machinery available. In other words, we may say that production merely connotes the volume of output, it can be increased without consideration of cost by increasing the input of labour, material and equipment. Duplication of a factory or an additional shift increases production but this may not increase productivity. Productivity is not merely volume of output in relation to resources employed. It may increase without increase in production, it increases when lesser quantities of inputs are employed for the same production. Productivity also increases when more input is turned out from the same resources.

A critical observer may, however, discover considerable degree of uniformity and consistency in all these apparently conflicting or different interpretations, for they all tend to portray one common characteristics i.e. some one's ability to produce more economically and efficiently. Thus agricultural productivity is defined as the ratio of output to input in relation to land, labour and capital and also in terms of the overall resources employed in agriculture. The scientific, validity and popularity of this definition, undoubtedly, rests on widespread interest in labour saving because such saving can affect costs, prices, profits, jobs, wages and even a nation's military security and level of living (Hiram, 1951). Another, but in no way less convincing argument in favour of the measure, that labour-time is more readily measurable than other input factors, and that it possesses a universal element common to all plants, processes and agriculture. This universality provides a common basis for measuring and comparing the relative productivity not only of different units but also of different sectors of country's economy.

In recent years, therefore, productivity is frequently used without qualification as ratio of output to the corresponding input of labour. It may be expressed either as output per unit of labour time spent, or in its reverse sense as labour time spent per unit of output. The latter is more widely applied for the measurement of productivity for the simple reason that whereas the unit labour requirements can be directly added or subtracted, the output data, if expressed in physical units, cannot be combined with similar figures unless they represent the same physical characteristics.

Thus, this definition, despite its simplicity and widespread usage, has not, however removed confusion either from analysis or interpretation, and the reasons are manifold. It is difficult to dislodge the deeprooted notion from the minds of the common man, experienced in the technique and methodology of productivity analysis that labour productivity data measures the productivity of labour and not the productivity of all the combined input factors.

It may be inferred from the above discussion that the yield per acre may be considered to represent the agricultural productivity in a particular region, and that other factors of production be considered as the possible causes for the variation, while comparing it with the other regions (Dandeker, 1964). Pandit (1965) has stated the connotation of productivity in these words. "Productivity is defined in economics as the output per unit of input ... the act of securing an increase in output from the same unit or of getting the same output from a smaller input." In fact, the productivity is generally the result of a more efficient use of some of all the factors of production, viz., land, labour and capital. According to Saxon (1965), productivity is a physical relationship between output and the input which gives, rise to that output. Horring (1965) defines productivity that it is generally used to denote the ratio of output to any or all associated inputs in real term.

The concept of agricultural productivity is even more controversial in geography and it has a different connotation in different part of the world. It could be measured in relation to land, labour and capital together with overall resources employed in it depending on the physical and socio-economic condition of the region. Obviously in a developing country where land is scarce and labour is in abundance, it is measured in per unit of area, whereas in a country of costly labour and abundant land, yield per man hour would be more appropriate yardstick to measure agricultural productivity and so on.

All over the world many scholars in the field of geography and economics have long been engaged in evolving methods to assess the agricultural productivity. (Buck, 1937; Kendall, 1939; Samp, 1960; Shafi, 1967; Sapre and Deshpande, 1964; Sharma, 1965; Bhatia, 1965; Sinha, 1968; Singh, 1972; and Husain, 1976). However, the main problem facing it are two-fold. Firstly, what should be the unit and nature of measurement of output, secondly output should be measured in relation to what?

Different units have been used to measure the output, the simplest and widely used one is to measure it in terms of weight which is possible only when a single commodity is produced otherwise it will create the problem of aggregation of different agricultural products. While food-grains could be added, fruit, vegetables, sugarcane, fibre, tea, and so on cannot be so added.

Even amount of foodgrains there is difference and all cannot be treated at par with one another. Therefore, Buck (1937) tried to solve this problem by converting all the foodgrains in unit of grain equivalence in relation to a staple food. But while all the foodgrains can be added after being converted into grain equivalence, other edibles like oilseeds, tea, coffee, fruits, vegetable, and so on cannot be added so. Thus, the concept of calories are unit of measurement of agricultural productivity is introduced in which all the edibles are converted into calories (Stamp, 1960). Consequent upon this the concept of Standard Nutrition Unit (SNU) was also developed by Stamp and later on used by several scholars all over the world. (Shafi, 1967; and Chakravorty, 1970). But this also does not solve the problem of the entire production of agricultural sector because agricultural products like jute, cotton, opium, and so on cannot be converted into calories. Therefore, the only common unit is value which involves pricing of different products, although it also poses the problem as to which price should be adopted for evaluation i.e. harvest price, wholesale price, price at the tail end or at the time of crisis and scarcity as each is having a definite significance and relevance (Sharma, 1965).

Another major problem concerned with agricultural productivity can be considered in relation to land, labour and capital together with overall resources employed in agriculture. However, if productivity is to be measured in per unit of land, the question is which area is to be considered? net sown area gross sown area, planted area or harvested area. Furthermore, whether intensity of cropping, irrigated land unirrigated area, quality of land should be taken into account while calculating and comparing the productivity of different regions or not. Although various studies have been done on different bases, they lack in one aspect or the other and are not comparable and perfect. Hence, it is necessary to evolve the concept of a standard hectare which takes into account all these various factors.

The measurement of productivity in relation to labour and consequent upon population density is also somewhat complicated. Generally, it is expressed as the ratio of output to labour input needed to produce that output. But there is a serious problem of working out the amount of labour employed in it especially in a subsistence economy. Moreover, the quality of labour and the level of mechanisation also poses several problems of comparability. Similarly, the total agricultural output may be taken as the value added by labour and other factors in agriculture. However, according to the purpose of study and the data available, the labour input may be expressed as the total number of labour force or as the number of man-hours worked in agriculture in order to account the intensity of labour.

The more refined system of measurement of productivity specially in case of labour, is value added per man-hour. In economically advanced countries where it is intended to compare labour productivity in agriculture with that of other occupations, it is necessary to compare the incomes and productivity of workers in agriculture. Moreover, they are of less importance in developing countries where there is abundance of farm labour and where farm workers are often seasonally employed or under employed except at times of peak labour demand i.e. at harvesting time. No such attempt has been made to measure agricultural productivity in India, perhaps, due to non-availability of data and complex nature of agriculture.

The measurement of capital productivity in agriculture is more complicated to compute and to interpret. It is due to the delivery of farms and the purpose for which capital may be utilized in agricultural production process. The capital is generally utilized for the purpose of land, land reclamation, land improvement, drainage, irrigation purposes, livestock purchase, feeds, seeds, fertilizers, agricultural implements and crop production chemicals. But the measurement depends upon consistent measures of aggregate agricultural output and input. Thus, the concept of inputs in productivity studies includes the resources committed to agriculture by the farmers. Although, these inputs are subjected to control by the decisions of the farmers under the framework of government's policies, they may be classified as labour and tangible capital. These tangible capitals are land, building, machinery, pesticide, livestock and purchased production services. Apart from that, there is a fixed capital, which is concerned with annual input for the use of capital stock. However, it is of minor importance as compared with the other major input groups, i.e. land, labour and working capital. Hence, working capital is most important aspect of capital in determining the productivity of agriculture. Agricultural productivity could also be measured with respect to all the resources used in agriculture. In this respect all inputs including labour, land, building machinery, fertilizer, seeds, etc. are aggregated and compared with gross output of the whole sector.

Since long, agricultural geographers have made a concerted efforts to bring out a viable definition and a measure of productivity. Accordingly, it has been defined as a function of the combined interplay of a variety of factors including physical, economic, social and technological, each acquiring its specificities as component in an interacting system over time. The combined effect of these factors manifest itself in per hectare productivity in any given area (Bhatia,1967). In other words agricultural productivity, as a concept, means the degree to which inputs are utilized and the degree to which economic, technical and organisational elements are able to exploit the physical resources of the area for agricultural production. Any clearcut definition of productivity, would necessarily be subject to regional bias and interpretation, nevertheless, these differ and conflicting views have a single fact in common, that is, the ability to produce more efficiently and economically with the minimum of loss and wastage. In fact, agricultural productivity is a relative concept and cannot be measured uniformly all over the world. In the developing countries where land is relatively scarce and labour abundant, yield per unit area is more important, while in countries where land is abundant and labour is scarce, the yield per man may constitute more suitable measure for the determination of agricultural productivity (Shafi, 1976). However, the land productivity is one of the most suitable production characteristics for the measurement of agricultural productivity in terms of yield of production (actual or monetary value) in the countries of subsistence economy.

**Measurement of Productivity**

On account of the multifarious utility, a number of scholars in the field of geography and economics have long been engaged in evolving methods to measure the agricultural productivity in various parts of the world. They are too numerous to be, listed here. Therefore, some of the important ones are mentioned here.

There are two basic problems in measuring agricultural productivity: Firstly, what should be the unit and nature of measurement of output? Secondly, output should be measured in relation to what ? Although various units have been used to measure the output, the simplest and widely used one is to measure it in terms of weight which is possible only when there is a single commodity, otherwise it will create the problem of aggregation of different agricultural products. While foodgrains could be added, fruit, vegetables, sugarcane, fibre, etc. cannot be so added. Even among foodgrains there is different and all cannot be treated at par with one another. Therefore, Buck (1937) tried to solve this problem by converting all the foodgrains in units of grain equivalence in relation to a staple food. He clubbed all grains grown in a region as equal to rice in food value, then distributed it per head of population, but other edibles like oilseeds, tea, coffee, fruit, vegetables, etc., cannot be added so. Therefore, the concept of calories as unit of measurement of agricultural productivity is introduced (Stamp, 1960).

Vries (1967), went a step further in improving the above method by giving it a uniform scale. Considering the fact that rice is the staple diet of the people in the Asian continent, the agricultural output in terms of 'husked rice equivalents', per head of population should be considered. This attempt was made to convert various grains into rice equivalent according to their local market value or price. Thus, the grain equivalent, and miled rice equivalent method enabled the use of a uniform scale.

Cohn Clarke and Margaret Haswell (1967), used the "kilogram of wheat equivalent per person", per annum as a scale of measurement. This new method did not prove very good as they could not prepare a composite index of productivity.

Kendall (1939) devised a method of measuring agricultural efficiency expressed in terms of output per unit area. He ranked various areal units according to the hectare-yields of different crops and obtained average rank called the ranking coefficient of each unit. The formula expressed as:

$$\frac{r_2 + r_2 + \ldots\ldots\ldots\ldots\ldots\ldots + r_n}{n}$$

where 'r' is the rank of yield of individual crops and 'n' is the number of crops. The procedure followed by Kendall in his ranking co-efficient method is as follows:

First, the enumeration units are ranked in the order of output per acre for each of the selected crops; second, the ranks (position) occupied by each unit in respect of the selected crops are added; third, the sum of ranks of each unit is divided by the number of selected crops to obtain ranking co-efficients.

Kendall evolved a measure of crop productivity by using index number technique. In this technique the yield of different crops should be expressed in terms of some common units. Kendall pointed out, that "there are two common units which can be taken note of; first, money value as expressed in price and second, energy as expressed in starch equivalent". But several difficulties arise in determining the money value index, e.g. there are many vegetables and beans which are grown mostly for the consumption on the farms and their price data are not recorded in contract to cereal crops whose data are adequate. With regard to the prices, which one should be adopted-prices prevailing in the area, or those prevailing in the region, or in the country as a whole. In this method, the crop production of each unit area is valued by multiplying the volume of production of a particular crop by the price, and then add the results for the selected number of crops together. The total is divided by the total acreage in the unit area under the total selected crops. The result gives for each unit area a figure of money value per acre/hectare under the crops considered. For energy co-efficient, an index based on nutritional factor ignores local variations because of the absence of data. Kendall, therefore, suggests starch equivalent as the most suitable unit and suggested that production of energy be preferred as the gross figures. The money value co-efficient does not take-into consideration the value of the by-products of the cross but a similar omission of any allowance would have a serious effect. Therefore, it becomes necessary to estimate the production by weight of by-products to the main products of wheat, barley, oats, beans, peas, etc.

The determination of productivity by the productivity coefficient method involves the use of higher mathematics, and the money value coefficient and starch equivalent or energy coefficient poses a practical difficulty. Therefore, Kendall looked for a coefficient which might lead to similar results in productivity and save a good deal of calculations. Kendall took the acre yields of ten leading crops in each, of the forty-eight administrative countries of England for four selected years. The places occupied by each country in respect to the selected crops were then averaged, and thus ranking coefficient of agricultural efficiency of each country was obtained. If a country was at the top of every list, it would have a ranking coefficient of one and if it were at bottom of every list, it would have a ranking coefficient equal to the number of countries divided by number of crops considered.

## Wetland Productivity

The biological yield of wetlands is enormous. They, are amongst the most productive eco-systems in the world, only by some tropical rainforests and the most intensively cultivated areas of land, such as prime corn fields in the Midwest of the United States. Table 14.1 lists the net primary productivity ranges and means for major global eco-systems (Leith, 1975) . The disproportionate contribution of wetlands to the global total is emphasized: 24 per cent from 6.4 per cent of the earth's surface. Variations of net primary productivity within different wetland types are not known globally, but Richardson (1979) has calculated the relative productivity of some North American wetlands on the basis of tonnes per hectare per year, all of which exceed grassland say by a factor of between 2 and 5 (Table 14.2).

Many wetland plants (autotrophs) are perennials and are nearly all leaf with little or no woody or thickened tissues. Therefore, they are constant and efficient converters of solar energy (photosynthesis) to fix carbon and create biomass. In addition, their root systems are specially adapted to take up inorganic nutrients and incorporate them into inorganic forms. Moreover, repeated flooding and/or tidal flux provides constant new supplies of nutrients and circulates others. There is no lack of moisture for plant growth.

**Table 14.1 :** Net Primary Product by Main Vegetation Units

| | *Net Primary Productivity* | |
|---|---|---|
| *Unit* | *Range ($g/m^2/yr$)* | *Approximate mean* |
| Forest | | 1290 |
| Tropical rain forest | 1000-3500 | 2000 |
| Raingreen forest | 600-3500 | 1500 |
| Summergreen forest | 400-2500 | 1000 |
| Chaparral | 250-1500 | 800 |
| Warm temperate mixed forest | 600-2500 | 1000 |
| Boreal forest | 200-1500 | 500 |
| Woodland | 200-1000 | 600 |
| Dwarf and open scrub | | 90 |
| Tundra | 100-400 | 140 |
| Desert scrub | 10-250 | 70 |
| Grassland | | 600 |
| Tropical Grassland | 200-2000 | 700 |
| Temperate Grassland | 100-1500 | 500 |
| Desert (extreme) | | 1 |
| Dry desert | 0-10 | 3 |
| Ice desert | 0-1 | 0 |
| Cultivated land | 100-4000 | 650 |
| Fresh water | 1250 | |
| Swamp and marsh | 800-4000 | 2000 |
| Lake and stream | 100-1500 | 500 |
| Total for continents | | 669 |

*Source* : Leith, 1975, p. 205.

Not much of the natural production is eaten directly, except perhaps for wild rice, cranberries and the like, although cattle, sheep and wild game graze on the herbaceous growth at low tide or in non-flooded periods. The greatest food value of wetland comes from the death of the plants to form detritus on which heterotrophic organisms such as larvae, fungi, bacteria and protozona thrive.

**Table 14.2 :** Productivity of some North American Wetlands

| | *Productivity (t/ha/yr)* |
|---|---|
| Cat-tail marshes | 27.4 |
| Reed marshes | 21.0 |
| Freshwater tidal | 16.2 |
| Swamp forests | 10'.5 |
| Sedge-dominated marshes | 10.4 |
| Bogs, fens, Muskegs | 9.1 |
| Grassland | 5.1 |

*Source :* Richardson, 1979.

This forms the basis for the aquatic food web of high-yielding animals and fish such as salmon, crabs, shrimps and worms (Crow and MacDonald, 1979, de La Cruz, 1979, Murkin and Wrubleski, 1988). Thus, the wetlands can be regarded as 'the farmlands of the aquatic environment' (Tiner, 1984, p.19) where large volumes of food are produced. Of course, there are other products, such as timber in river bottom-lands, reeds are thatching and, above all, the peat itself which is a valuable fuel in some economies.

Although the relationship between wetlands, net primary productivity and abundant invertebrate life, and hence fish and animal life, is beyond doubt, the mechanisms of the food chain are imperfectly understood. First, the process of decomposition on which the productivity depends, and how it relates to the food chain, is not fully known, and rates of decomposition will vary with a host of local physical factors including salinity, flow and above all, temperature. Secondly, the efficiency of the wider food chain depends on the export or flushing of the nutrients from the wetlands to other areas (e.g. estuaries or further out to sea) on the assumption that detritus is the main source of nutrients. However, the role of marshes in supporting fish and shelfish production is not convincing (OTA, 1984, p.60). Finally, the pathways whereby the nutrients are incorporated into food chains is not well established. It is done either by the grazing of living plants or by the consumption of dead material by lower-level heterotrophs, which in turn become the indirect source of wetland-derived nutrients to higher-level consumers. The grazing pathway is well authenticated; the detritus pathway is not (Sather and Smith, 1984, pp.24-8). Despite these uncertainties, however, the fact remains the wetlands have an abundant natural production that is most likely going to be lost if they are drained, although it could be replaced by higher yielding crops like corn or sugarcane.

**Table 14.3 :** Some of the important wetlands of Saharsa District. (1994-95)

| *Anchal* | *Wetland* | *Area in Acre* | *Settlement Amount in Rs.* |
|---|---|---|---|
| 1. Basantpur | Dighi | — | 4001 |
| | Kosi Bridge | — | 3301 |
| | Sitapur | — | 6251 |
| | Kataiya | — | 10,000 |
| 2. Nirmali | Satraha Tank | 7 | 2330 |
| | Bara Tank | 7 | 3025 |
| | Kamal Tank | 1 | 348 |
| | Dagmara Tank I | 1 | 460 |
| | Dagmara Tank II | 1.5 | 460 |
| | Nirmali Tank | 1.5 | 1014 |
| | Jaloly Tank I | 2 .5 | 575 |
| | Jaloly Tank II | 1.5 | 547 |
| | Lake Jalai Malai | 68 | — |
| 3. Simri Bakhtiarpur | Gordah Lake | 360 | 4,500,00 |
| | Kar Gail Lake | 60 | — |
| | Sardiha Lake | 68 | — |
| | Kusumi Lake | 95 | — |
| 4. Raghopur | Damamganj | 60 | — |
| | Pinglass Chaur | 950 | — |
| | Dehla Chaur | 60 | — |
| 5. Sour Bazar | Baruri Palel | 60 | — |
| 6. Mahisi | Manua Sahjahia | 50 | — |
| | Krishnawati | 50 | — |
| | Gorho Wetland | 52 | — |
| | Demra Wetland | 55 | — |

The average rate of production of fishes is 1000 kg. in a tank of one acre having input of compost, without compost it is 450 kg and in running water the production rate is 100 kg per acre only.

The Productivity of Wetland is so high that it never be so as any agricultural crops. For example, in Rajokhar Wetland of Narayanpur Rs. 2 lakhs come from makhana guri and Rs 3 lakhs from fish production. It has an area of 20 hectares of land. Hence, wetland is more beneficial in comparison with any agricultural crops.

## REFERENCES

Cash Bow, A. J. (1967). Convert water-hyacinth to methane, *PANS* (c) : 13(2): pp. 34 - 244.

Chapman, W.M. (1966) *Food Technol.* 20. (895).

*Fish Rev.* 30 (15), 18(1963), pp. Cal,

Fish, Rev., Editorial, *Comm.*, 30 (6) 1, (1968) P. J. E. Bardach and J. H. Ryther. The status and potential of Aquaculture particularly fish culture, Hindi prepared for national council on marine resources and Engineering Development 1967, PB 1977-78, (Clearing house Feb. Sel. Toch. Info.

Frank, P.A. (1976), Distribution and utilization research on tropical and sub-tropical aquatic weeds in United States. In Aquatic weeds in S.E. Asia Dr. W. Junk B.V. Publishers. *The Hague*, pp. 353 - 360.

*Fish, Rev. Editorial Comm.*, 30 (15), 18 (1968) P.J.E. Bardach and J.H. Pythey. The status and potential of aquaculture, particularly fish culture, prepared for national council on marine resources and Engineering Development 1967, PB. 1977 - 78 (clearing house Feb. Sci. *Tech. Info*, spring field, VA.1968).

*Fish Rev. Editorial Comm.* : 30 (15), 18 (1968) *op. cit.*

Gupta, O.P. (1979), *Aquatic weeds: Their Menace and control,* Today and Tomorrow's Printers and Publishers, New Delhi, 71.

Joklik, O. F. (1976), Preparation of an organic Bio-fertilizer from agricultural waste and weeds residue, UNIDO, Rept, RD/RAS/16/002.

Kig, G. Ann. *Oceanography for Geographer's*, London (1962), and Furon, R., *The problem of water : A World Study*, London, 1967, p. 22.

Mishra, R. (1970), Seasonal dynamics and aquatic weeds of the lowlying lands of the mid-Ganga plains. Aquatic weeds in S.E. Asia, Dr. W. Junk, b.V. pb. *The Hague*, pp. 103 - 106.

Steward, K. K. (1970), Nutrient removal potentials of various aquatic plants. Hyacinth contr. J.S. (2); pp. 24 - 35 Haller, W.T. and D.L. Sutton (1997); Effect of Ph and High phosphorus concentrations on growth of water hyacinth, *Hyscinth contr*. 7 - 11 (June) ; pp. 59 - 81.

Strahler, A.N. (1977), *Op. cit.*, pp. 331.

Yearb, Editorial, *Fish stet* 20, (1965).

# 15

# SAMPLE STUDIES

In this chapter the study has been done on the basis of purposive random sampling because in North Bihar, the wetlands are abound but their continuous study is not possible. Among the selected wetlands like Simardah of Baheri Anchaı in Darbhanga district, and Rajokhar of Manigachi Anchal in Darbhanga district are important. Some other important wetlands are Kusheshwar Asthan, Kanail Chaur, Lilhaul Chaur, Mehsar Chaur and Fulhara Chaur. Besides these, some other Chaurs are the product of meandering courses of the rivers and the formation of Oxbow lake besides the unequal deposition of sand bodies. The continuation of the processes of alluviation and deluviation in plain lands are some of the major factors[1] contributing to the formation of wetland (Fig.15.1).

Owing to its geographical location North Bihar is potentially rich in receiving adequate amount of rainfall and riverine waters. The greater part of North Bihar is in fact lowlands full of rivers. During the rainy season most parts appear as vast chain of temporary lakes, joined together by numerous beds of hill streams which flow from Nepal Himalaya up to the Ganges.[2] According to Choudhary (1976), between Himalaya and the Ganges the Terai region of North Bihar is intercepted by fifteen rivers beginning from the Kosi and running up to the Gandak. On account of the overflow of these rivers, during the rainy season water spreads over larger areas and at times the flood causes great damage to human lives and properties. However, when the rainy season is over, water recedes from the land except in the perennial *jheels* (lakes), deep Chaurs and lowlying areas surrounded by cultivated lands[3].

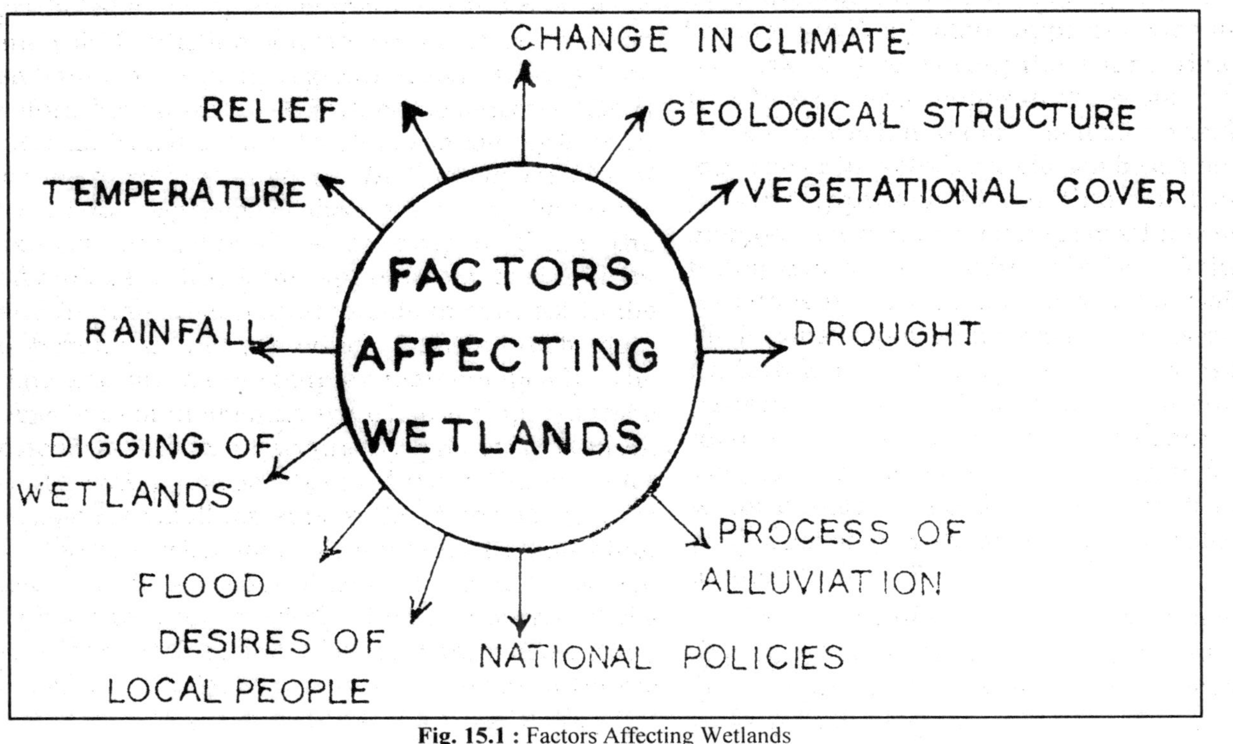


**Fig. 15.1 :** Factors Affecting Wetlands

Although most of the olden days *jheels* and *Chaurs* have already been vanished but some remains of wetlands in North Bihar have all the potential to be preserved.

The author has done intensive survey of North Bihar in relation to this project. Recently in December, 1995 Manju Kumari and the author did a survey of 3 districts of Darbhanga division. Although migratory birds were recorded from various places, we found the following lakes most ideal as prospective birds sanctuaries.

## Kathra Wetland

Kathra wetland formed due to flash flood in the Kamla river, about 70 years ago. The survey has been done on 4.1.1995 at 3 p.m. when the water temperature was 20.5°C. It has an area of 202 hectare. Kathra wetland comes under Kathra village of Kathra Panchayat, Manigachhi Anchal in Darbhanga district.

Currently, the waterlogged area of this wetland is found over 6 hectares of land. The depth of water varies from 3 feet in deepest part to 1 feet near shoreline. The width of the wetland is 15 metres and the length is 300 metres. It is surrounded by Putai in the west, the Kamla river in the east and north and Jaraul and Kumbhraval villages in the south.

### *Productivity of the Wetland*

The main crops produced in Kathra wetland are rice, wheat and mung. Rice is cultivated over 162 hectares of land without fail because flood water comes each year in this wetland. In the central part of this wetland about 25 metres river shaped lowland has been formed which remains full of water throughout the year. Ultimately, the water of this wetland goes to the Kamla river in the south.

In order to maintain fish and makhana production of Kathra wetland ring bund is needed from three sides and suilice gate towards the water discharge mouth of riverine chaur. This may help in increasing the productivity and ameliorating the standard of living of the people.

The local birds found are Bagula and Pandubi. Among migratory birds Silli and Ketchkerhar are important. They usually come in the month of November and retires to some distant land at the end of February. Other creatures found in the wetland are toad, snake, tortoise, snail, crab, sheeps, jonk and varieties of fishes.

The plants found in Kathra wetland are Semar, Chichor, Keshore, Bhent, water hyacinth and lotus.

The people near this wetland are associated with production of crops, work as labourer, fish rearing, livestock ranching, petty grocery shops and teaching. The rice and wheat crops near the chaur lands get water for irrigation from Kathra wetland. (Fig.15.2).

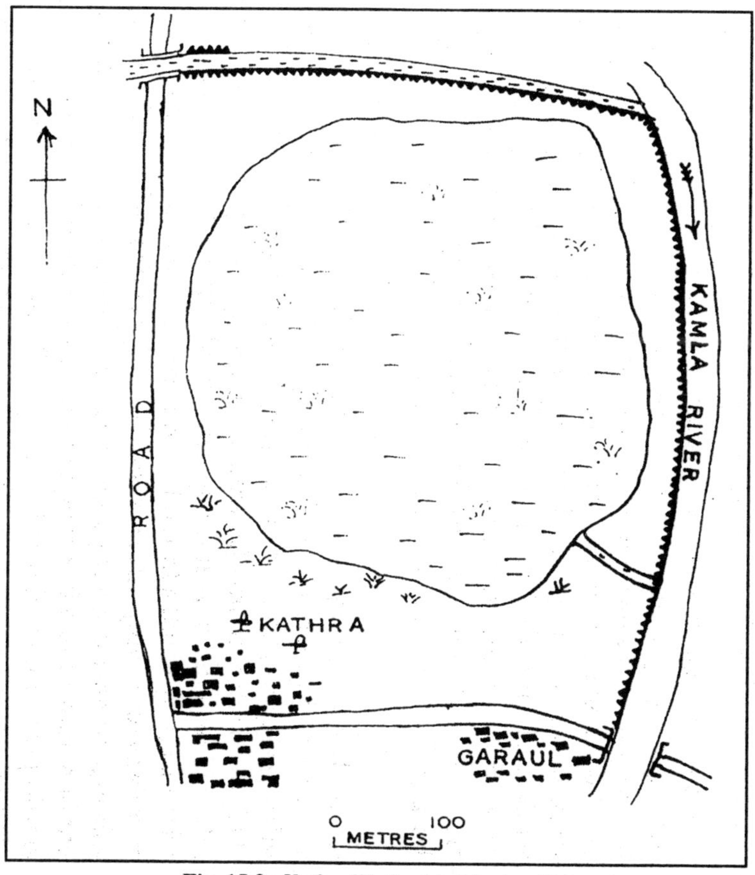


**Fig. 15.2 :** Kathra Wetland in Manigachhi

Currently, the land owners of Kathra wetland do not get any benefit out of their land as it is ravaged by flood each year. Hence, the wetland farmers have no satisfaction from their land.

The use of chemical fertilizer has no adverse effect on the water of wetlands. As yet the government has no planning for this wetland.

**Kusheshwar Asthan Wetland**

The wetland of Kusheshwar Asthan lies in Kusheshwar Asthan anchal. It is known as Narail chaur under the command area of Kamla-Balan river. Its area is 809 hectare. The eastern part of this anchal has an area of 525 hectare which always covered with water. The wetland of Kusheshwar Asthan is surrounded by Charkand and Ghoghepur in the east at a distance of 30 kms, Mangar in the north at a distance of 12 kms. Salha in the south at a distance of 15 kms. and Barhatta in the west at a distance of 10 kms. The water temperature on 15th June 1995 was 30.3°C.

The flora found in the lake are Semar, Bhushikhar, water hyacinth, Bhent, lotus flower, Sarukh, Banshi, Anchokair, Mirchaiya, Pulpul, Patti, Semar, Fulgodhair, Sarhauchi, Singhara and Karmi. In Kusheshwar wetland dolphin and tortoise are also found, because during flood it is connected with the Kosi river (Fig.15.3). The depth of water in the central part is 3 metres which reduces to zero towards the shore line. The areal extent during the normal period and flood time remains the same.

The digging of canal will help surrounding area for irrigation. The fishermen have a tendency to catch fishes and produce crops as well for better living conditions. The water upto one feet is used for the production of rice. Per hectare the production of rice is 15 quintal. The surrounding area also produces Mung as Garma crop whose production is 12.50 quintal per hectare.

The birds found in this wetland are Silli, Lalsar, Dighaunch, Haril, Sama-Chakeba (3 kg and above weight) Hasuadabi, Nakta, Karan, Mail, Duab, Sarayal, Chaiti, Chaha and Topra. The price of Lalsar is Rs.150 per set of two birds but the price for two Dighaunch is Rs.130 only.

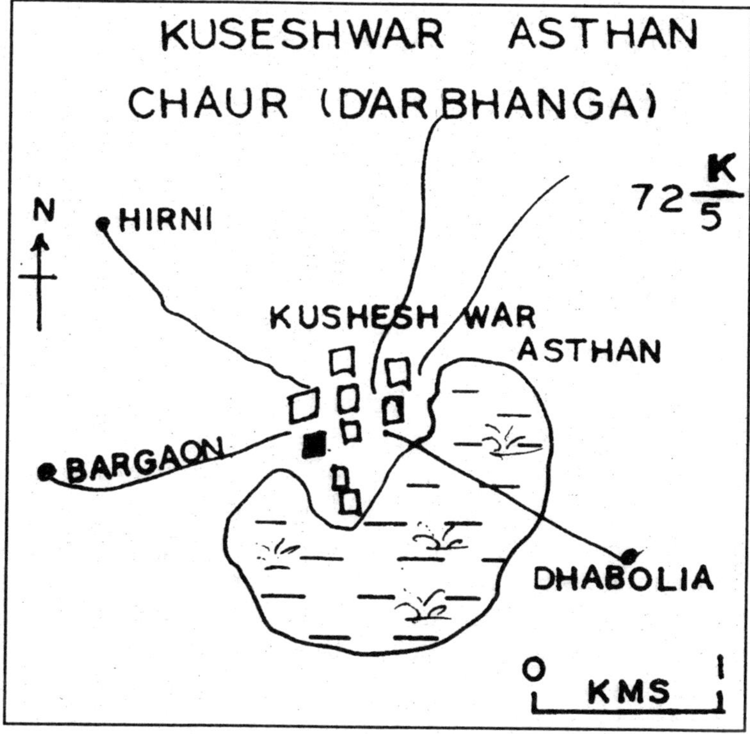


**Fig. 15.3 :** Kusheshwar Asthan Chaur (Darbhanga)

These birds start coming in the second week of November and retires to their native place sometimes in the first week of April. Legally, the preying of these birds are prohibited but due to weakness of the administration the poaching is still going on.

The fishes found in Kesheshwar Asthan are Bhuna, Buari, Gainchi, Rehu and Katla. Fish catch is the prime occupation of the people of this area.

In different Chaurs and Lakes of Kusheshwar Asthan the migratory birds come from China, Japan, Korea, Siberia and Mangolia which lie north of Himalaya. The birds come every year from October to December. The main cause of migration is to save from excessive cold besides getting food, shelter and search of abode for giving birth to younger ones. The food of these birds are paddy and varieties of insects found in North Indian plains specially after the harvest of paddy crop in November. Kusheshwar Asthan is surrounded by wetland from North, South and East and hence, the area is highly potential for birds sanctury and the rearing of variety of fishes.

The stagnation of water around Kusheshwar Asthan for a longer period creates such an environment that the local people have to depend on fishes, Snails, Saduk, Bhent and Situwa. For the purpose of rearing fishes — Rehu, Katla, Mirgal, common carp, silver carp and grass carp are important. Besides these, some rare fishes Kawai, Garai, Singhi and Mangur produces in large quantity without any expense.

The lake of Kusheshwar Asthan is very famous for its beauty. The Red Lotus flower, among green leaves around the white flower of Kumudani and herds of varieties of birds amidst flower beautify the environment manifold prey of all birds have been prohibited by the Government of Bihar. But even than the social elites of Kusheshwar Asthan gives order to prey birds on some lumpsum payment,which is quite illegal on part of the Government machinery in terms of saving our ecology. The birds which caught here is Lalsar, Sarachar, Arun, Andhigi, Nakta and Dighouch. These migratory birds come every year in October and goes back in the respective country up to March. Keeping these aspect under the conservation project. The preying of birds in the lakes of Kusheshwar Asthan should be immediately checked in order to ameliorate the environment for better human living conditions. We also noted a large number of Brahmini Duck, large flock of spoonbill and several Gangetic Dolfin in the Kosi River. Another population of Lesser Adjutant stork was recorded at Simri Jheel.

"Probably this is the best lake in North India so far as the area of water cover, aquatic vegetation and number of migratory birds are concerned." This was the comment of Mr. Hussain who visited the lake on 25th December 1986. George (1964) and Yahya (1982) have also emphasised the importance and potential of this lake. Unfortunately, nothing could be done till 1986, when a mild check on regular large scale trapping and selling of birds have been imposed by the D.F.O. Darbhanga.

### *Location*

Kusheshwar Asthan lake is located in the Kusheshwar Asthan Block of Darbhanga district. It is connected by a metallic road from the District headquarter. There is a regular bus service some being direct from Patna to Kusheshwar Asthan. The distance from Darbhanga to Kusheshwar Asthan is 80 kilometres.

### *Size*

There is a big depression at this point and during monsoon the area of water covers 100 sq.kms. During high flood of monsoonal rain this lake joins, with Simiri Jheels along with the Kabar lake by several tributaries. However, in winter season more than 20 sq.km. area is still under water providing good habitat to large number of resident and migratory birds. Rain and overflow of local rivers like the Kamla, Kareh are the main sources of water of this lake.

### *Geographical Features*

In vegetational composition and faunal representation of this lake is more or less similar to Kabar lake. However, in spite of large scale massacre, the overall population of migratory birds observed at this lake is far more than at any other lake. The population of Pintail duck, common Teal and Shoveller were also noted to be more, whereas coots outnumbered other species at Kabar.

Besides being a place of religious gathering, as is obvious from its name, Kusheshwar Asthan is also a big Centre for fish export. In addition to local marketing, there are special buses running from Patna to Kusheshwar Asthan to carry fish to the State Capital. According to an estimate this is the largest regular fishing centre in North Bihar.

Another interesting feature is that along with fish auction, the right for birds trapping is also auctioned by the private owners who claim to own a sizeable area of land in the lake. I do not think in India any where also the right of birds trapping are sold like this. This involves socio-economic problem of larger dimension.

### *Value of Wetlands*

Even the supreme creature human being proclaims that the wetlands have immense value. According to Sather *et al* (1984) the value of wetlands are not national and local but international. Besides affecting the water table the functions of wetlands are manifold. Robert (1984) enlists various functions ascribed to wetlands are groundwater recharge and discharge flood storage, desychronization, shoreline stabilization through dissipation of erosive forces, sediment trapping, nutrient retention and removal, food chain support habitat for fish and wildlife and active and passive recreation.

At places, wetlands also affect the regional climate, oxygen production, retention of heavy metals and other hazardous substances.

Owing to the fact that people of this area largely depend on agriculture and fishing, conservation of wetlands of North Bihar becomes imperative. Secondly, the forest coverage in this area is minimal which further necessitates the retention of wetlands.

### *Inclusions of Kusheshwar Asthan under Ramsar Convention*

The potential of Kabar and Kusheshwar Asthan as prospective bird Sanctuaries is very high. Those lakes are also very rich in floral and faunal composition. In species diversity of these lakes would be second to the Bharatpur but in other aspects they are far more rich than any lake of North India. Total population of waterfaul is also very high. Taking all these aspects into consideration Kabar and Kusheshwar Asthan should be listed under the Ramsar Convention as wetlands.

## Sisulia Chaur

The wetland of Sisulia Chaur has been surveyed on 21.1.1995 at 1 p.m. At that time the water temperature was 20.4°C. It is located in Narayanpur village and Panchayat under Manigachhi Block of Darbhanga district. The area of the wetland is 125 hectares out of which the waterlogged area is only 10 hecare. The depth of water is 2 metres in the central part and only one metre near the shorelines. One unmetalled road passes through eastern part of the wetland which connects Nadiyami, Narayanpur and Lagma through single transport route.

During flood of rainy season the extent of Sisulia wetland become 125 hectares. The occurrence of flood destroys the crops to an innumerable extent. In flood free year except 10 hectares of central waterlogged area the entire area produces bumper crops per hectare production of rice is 2480 kilograms. In the abnormal rainfall years the standing rice crop of 30 hectares of land gets destroyed (Fig.15.4).

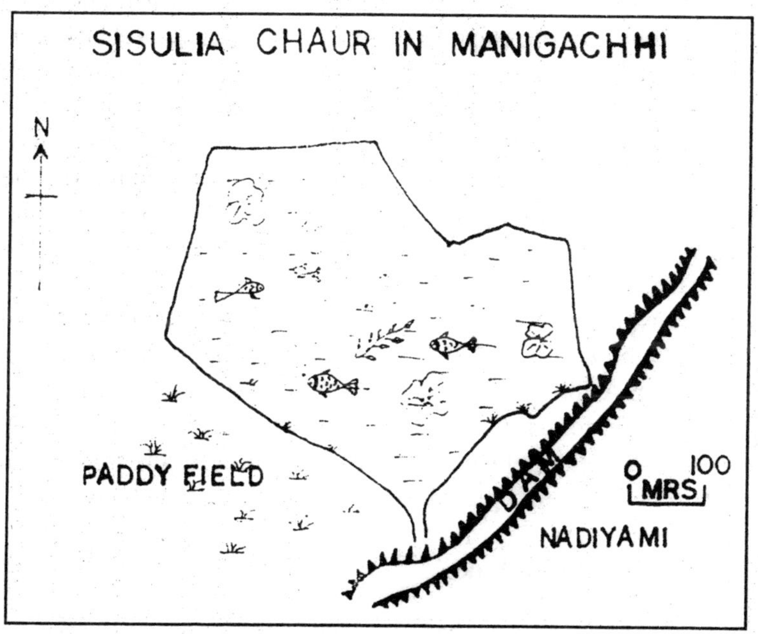


**Fig. 15.4 :** Sisulia Chaur in Manigachhi

Other important crops grown are mung, wheat and gram as rabi and summer crops. In Sisulia Chaur road, Garai, Buari, Jhinga, Pothi, Kabai and Mangur fishes are found. The local birds found in the wetland are Bagula, Dakhar and Pandubi. The migratory birds includes Pan Silli, Kentchkerhar and Lalsar.

**Table 15.1** : Birds and their weight

| *Name of Birds* | *Weight in Gram* | *Price in Rs. Per Bird* |
|---|---|---|
| Pan Silli | 400–500 | 25 to 30 |
| Kentchkerhar | 200–300 | 10 to 20 |
| Lalsar | 1000–2500 | 50 to 75 |

These migratory birds come at the end of October and goes back to their native place in the first week of February each year. In the permanent water cover the vegetation found are Semar, Chichor, Keshore, Bhent, Water hyacinth and Lotus. The people of surrounding area are engaged in cultivation, agricultural labourer, fish rearing, livestock ranching, trade and commerce, running brick kilns and teaching.

The surrounding area of Sisulia Chaur produces varieties of crops e.g. rice, wheat, sugarcane, gram, chickpeas and mung. The quarrel for fish catch is the common problem, because wetland knows no boundary and hence, the land owners fight for fish catch is but natural.

In case this wetland gets connection with the Kabila river which flows 1 km. west it will help in irrigation of the field in between these two. At present, the water of Sisulia is used for irrigating wheat crop's found in the surrounding area. The use of chemical fertilizer near the fields of wetlands is harmful for the insects and pests. The area needs plantation wherever the land is lying idle.

**Pachkurba Sahara Lake**

Pachkurba Sahara wetland has been located in Chanaur and Baghat village cum Panchayat of Manigachhi Block in Darbhanga district. The survey has been done on 14.9.1995. The water temperature was 20.5 degree celcius. Its area is 200 hectares which extends upto 400 hectares during peak hour of flood. In the month of January the water depth was 5 metre highest in the central part but during rainy season the depth of central part is maximum 2 metres. The living creatures found in this wetland are fishes, toad, snake, crab, snail, jonk and tortoise. The plants in this lake are Semar, Chichor, Chilmil, Keshore, Bhent, Sartikh, Kerhar, Ghenchul, Malkoka, Karmi, Faras, Emar and Hara, etc.

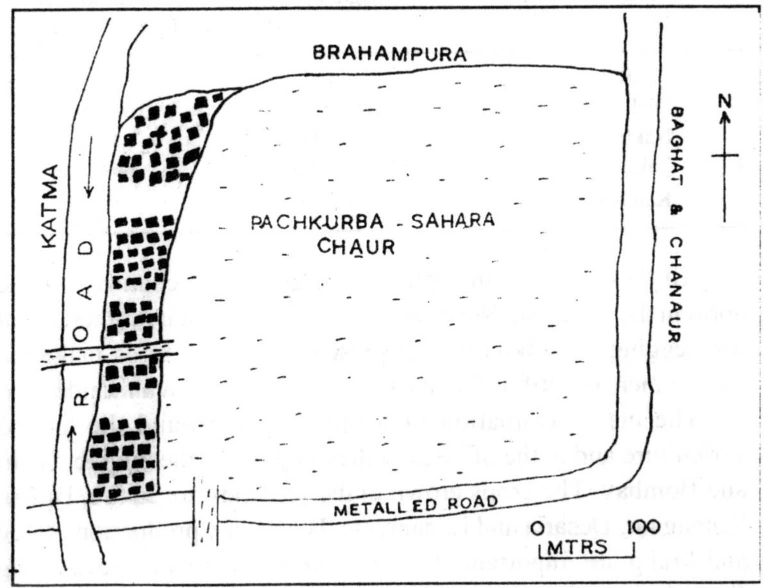


**Fig. 15.5 :** Location of Pachkurba — Sahara Chaur

The local birds found in this wetland are Bagula, Dakhar, Karan, Chaha which come in the months of November-December and ultimately migrate to their native place sometimes in February. These birds are generally caught in the night hours and its price is Rs.25 to 30 for two birds. The weight of a Chaha is about 200 grams. The person who catches Chaha is known as Alaibala. Alaibala make a fire in wooden pole in the night and beats a drum with big-bang. The birds understand, that lightening has taken a place and now the rain will occur. Hence, all Chaha get gathered in that direction from where the flash light comes and again gets down, and than Alaibala catches all the birds by throughing his net.

The migratory birds are named as Pan Silli, Dighaunch, Nakta, Lalsar and Ketchkarhar.

**Table 15.2 :** Birds and their weight in Sahara

| *Sl. No.* | *Name of Birds* | *Weight in Grams* | *Price in Rs. Per Bird* |
|---|---|---|---|
| 1. | Pan Silli | 400-500 | 46-50 |
| 2. | Dighaunch | 1000-1500 | 100-150 |
| 3. | Nakta | 400-500 | 40-50 |
| 4. | Lalsar | 100-200 | 60-120 |
| 5. | Ketchkarhar | 200-300 | 15-25 |

All these birds come from the neighbouring countries of the north in the month of November and go back to their motherland at the begging of February. The presence of these birds make the environment beautiful. The soil of the wetland is alluvium and black.

The main occupation of people living around the lake is agriculture and in the off season they migrate to the Punjab, Delhi and Bombay. The crops grown in the wetlands are Jamra, Dudhi, Kutchgaur, Desaria and Lodaur, etc. Hence, the production of rice and Mung are important. This wetland is the area of devastating flood during rainy season when the water enters into houses, but it also provides water for irrigation especially in the month of February when the standing crop of wheat needs irrigation at the interval of 19 days.

The use of chemical fertilizers make the fishes diseased as they have witnessed no cover on the body. With the construction of canal the water of the wetland may be used for irrigation purposes and the damming of Pachkurba wetland will help in the production of more fishes and Makhana. This wetland has been formed by the Kamla river about 90 years ago during the flash flood. (Fig. 15.5)

The fishes found in this wetland are Garai, Singhi, Momri, Buari, Katla, Pothi and Latha. After the land of this lake gets dry at the time of its ploughing the Latha fishes comes out dive from inside the earth. The area needs plantation of trees besides digging of old canal so that vast waterlogged area may be reclaimed for the production of rice. In case the Pachkurba wetland, gets covered by ring bundh from all side than it will produce vast amount of makhana.

**Belhi Wetland**

Belhi wetland lies in the western part of Narayanpur village of Manigachhi anchal in Darbhanga district. It's area is 10 hectare. The depth is 2 metres to 1 metre towards the shoreline. It's length and breadth is 120 squaremetres. It is surrounded by road coming from Lagma in the north-east in Tanti tola, mango garden in the west and the same in the south. The fauna found in this lake are toad, tortoise, snake, fishes, etc. Among the fishes Rehu, Katla, Naini, Pothia, Kabai and Jhinga are important. The local birds found in the lake are Bagula, Dakhar and Panduhi. The migratory birds which visit Belhi are Lalsar, Silli and Ketchkerhar. These birds come in November and retires in February, each and every year. The plants found in this wetland are Sewar, water hyacinth, lotus flower and mothi. The residents in the surrounding area are agriculturists, labourers and fishermen. The main products of the lake are fishes, Makhana, Gaddy, Wheat, Oilseeds and Pulses. The surroundings of Belhi gets flooded during the rainy season. The water of Belhi helps in irrigation, provides bathing place for men and animals besides emersion of Goddess Durga and Sama- Chakeba, etc. The annual revenue comes from Belhi is Rs.30,000 to the government for fish catch and makhana production but the contractors earn Rs.100,000 annually from this wetland.

This wetland help in the irrigation of paddy, wheat, mustard, sugarcane and ragi crops sown in the surrounding area. The area needs plantation of trees besides the construction of safety latrines so that Belhi wetland may not get polluted from the dump of night soil in the nearby areas (Fig. 15.6). The people living near Belhi wetland suffers from several diseases e.g. malaria, kalazar, cough and cold, tuberculosis, cancer, hooping cough, titnus, cytica, heart attack, dumb and deaf along with eye diseases.

**Lake Masbasi**

The survey has been done on 25.2.1995. The water temperature was 18.5°C at 1.00 p.m. It extends over 8 hectares of land. Masbasi lies on the south-western side of Kaithwar village. It comes under Manigachhi anchal of Darbhanga district. It's maximum depth is

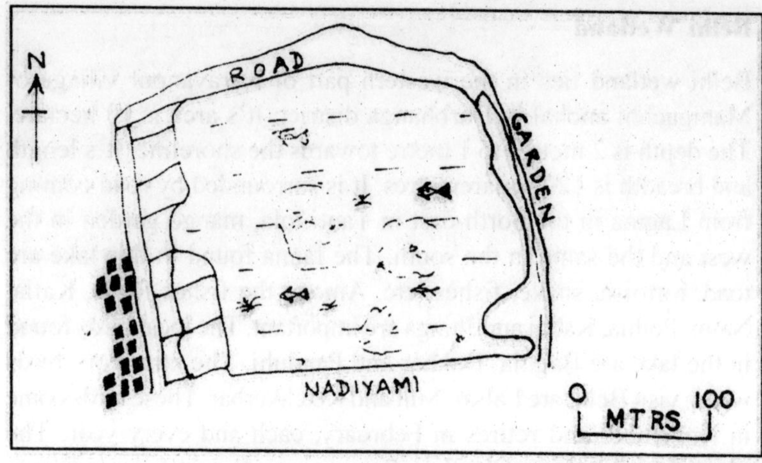


**Fig. 15.6 :** Belhi Wetland in Manigachhi

2 metres whereas length and breadth is 90 squaremetres.

The main faunas found are toad, tortoise, crab, snail and fishes. Among the floras found are Sewar, water hyacinth, mothi and lotus. Among the local birds Bagula and Pan-Silli are important.

The people of the surrounding area are mainly engaged in cultivation, fish rearing, cattle rearing and teaching. Some of the important products of the lake are fishes, makhana and mothi near the shoreline. The crops produced around the wetland are paddy, wheat, ragi, gram, mung, chick peas, lentil, khesari and sugarcane. (Fig. 15.7). The migratory birds of the wetland are Lalsar, Kechkerhar and Pan Silli.

The rotten tree leaves, the open vast latrine around the lake makes the environment polluted. During flood the rise in water level makes the peoples movement difficult from one house to another. The benefit from Masbasi wetland is :

— It helps in irrigation of Paddy and wheat crops.
— Provides bathing place for men and animal.
— It is a fishing ground for the local people.
— Produces fishes and makhana.

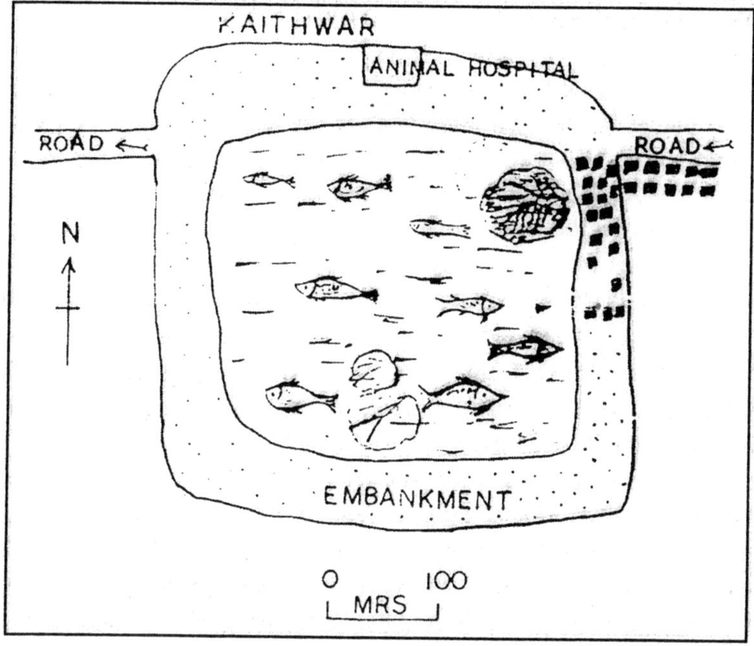


**Fig. 15.7 :** Masbasi Wetland, Darbhanga

***Planning Measures Suggested***

(a) Road should be constructed.
(b) Tree plantation should be done
(c) Digging of wetland should be done.
(d) Ring bundh should be developed along with the provision of suilice gate.

The people in the surrounding area suffer from cough, cold, kalazar, malaria and cancer. It provides place for *Chhath* festival and emersion of the statue of goddess. Masbasi has been formed due to soil erosion at the time of flash flood.

Masbasi is surrounded by veterinary hospital in the north, agricultural field in the south, human settlements of Tanti in the west and agricultural tract in the east.

**Wetland of Simardah**

Simardah is a natural wetland formed due to subsidence of land at the time of earthquake sometimes in the 16th century. It is a vast area south of Dhanauli and east of Dubauli villages. It covers an area of more than 200 hectares especially during the rainy season but in summer the water area comes down to 50 hectares only. The water comes through Juria bridge in the west. Sometimes, in the reign of Raja Shivai Singh of the estate of Darbhanga who went to worship Lord Shiva on the southern bank of Simardah felt the need of water to worship Lord Shiva and suddenly the subsidence took place and he got water to worship Lord Shiva. It lies in Dubauli village thana No.25 under Baheri Anchal.

In the fringe area of Simardah the crops grown are peddy, makhana, fishes, sorkha, mung and janera. The important birds which are found in Simardah wetland include Pansille, Lalsar, Dighauch and big cranes, especially during November and December most of these migratory birds which come to the area from Himalaya and Siberia and retires to the same especially in March, July and August are the months of flood especially during rainy season. Simardah gets water during rainy season from the west which flows to the east through lowlying channels especially through rice fields. Simardah does not produce too much of Makhana but it earns Rs.10 thousand each and every year from the sale of fishes. Simardah is also known as Jhanjhatia Mahal (Land of quarrels). It produces vast amount of Bhent which is a raw material to make Ramdana Ladoo. (Fig. 15.8).

**Rajokhar Wetland**

The wetland of Rajokhar lies in Narayanpur village of Manigachhi Anchal in Darbhanga district. It covers an area of 20 hectares (Fig. 15.9). Rajokhar is a man-made tank constructed at the reign of Raja Shivai Singh of Darbhanga estate about 1650 A.D. It is really a very big man made wetland surrounded by human settlements. The western and southern side of the tank are occupied by villagers residential houses where as the northern side covered

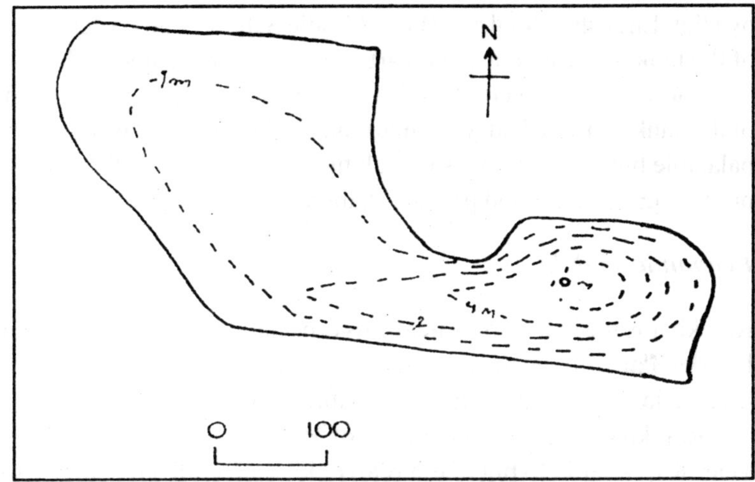


**Fig. 15.8 :** Simardah Wetland, Darbhanga.

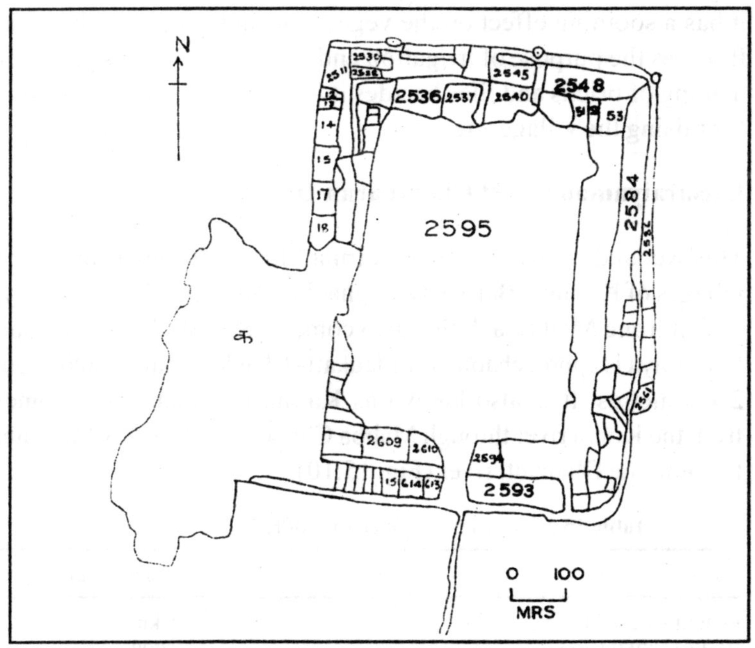


**Fig. 15.9 :** Rajokhar Wetland of Narayanpur, Manigachhi Anchal.

by High English School and Basic Middle School. The Eastern side of the tank is vacant but some part is occupied by mango orchards.

The source of water is Kamla river which flows just 2 kms south of this tank and attached with small canal. The quality of water is not palatable but it is fit for washing cloths, animals, raising fishes, and producing Makhana and provides habitat for several birds.

### *Economic Viability*

Rajokhar is the habitat of water birds especially Lalsar, Hen, Bagula besides Pansilli and several others. Some of these birds come to this wetlands specially during the winter season.

Rajokhar produces 700 munds of Makhana giri each and every year. Rajokhar is so big that it really aids a new life and culture to the villagers because most of the functions like Chhat, Samachakewa and others performed on its embankment. Rajokhar, cools down the temperature of its surrounding area and it has a soothing effect on the vegetation and people of the area. It serves the purpose of irrigation and its fringe provides place for making of bricks and tiles besides it is a place which provide soil for raising the village site.

## Lalsaraiyaman (West Champaran District)

This wetland is also known as Karma Man. Lalsaraiya covers the villages of Karmua, Bairya, Bhangha, Lalsaraiya Refugee coloney, Jaukatia and Majhriya. Lalsaraiya comes under Majhaulia Anchal. Lalsaraiya is approachable from Jaukatia Chauk towards south about 2 kilometres. It is also known as Karma in which water comes from the Kohra river through Mahba Chaur and ultimately the water fals into the Dhanauti river (Fig. 15.10).

**Table 15.3 :** General characteristics of Karma Man Wetland

| *No. Flood* | *During Flood* |
|---|---|
| Length — 5 kms. | 5 kms. |
| Width — 250 lietres | 1000 metres |
| Depth in the North 2.5 metres | 2 metres |
| Depth in the centre 5 metres | 3 metres |

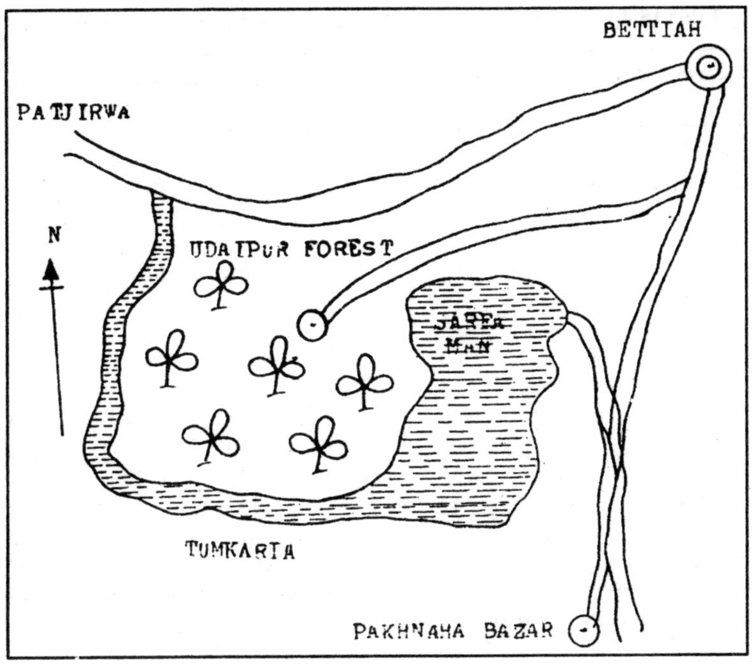


**Fig. 15.10 :** Udaipur Forest

### *Creatures*

In Karma Man varieties of fishes are found among which Rehu, Katla, Boari, Garai, Jhinga, Pothia, Kabari and Singhi are important. The weight and price of the fishes vary from one type to another along with their quality and quantity. The crabs and snails are also found in smaller quantity.

### *Vegetation*

In Karma Man the plants found are Shaibal, water-hycinth and other types of grasses through which green manure could be made.

On the basis of Table 15.4, it could be said that the economic conditions of villages in the environs of lake Lalsaraiya is pitiable. Fish catch is the only hope of people from this lake. Each year Jiora of Rs. 40,000 is given in this lake and its settlement is done with the people who are interested along with the local fisher men's society.

**Table 15.4 :** The Characteristics of Villages in the Environs of Karma Man

| *Villages* | *Bhangha* | *Karbhua* | *Bairya* | *Lals Saraiya* | *Jaukatia* | *Majhria* |
|---|---|---|---|---|---|---|
| Area in (Hec.) | 262 | 962 | 293 | 601 | 1011 | 866 |
| No. of Houses | 113 | 902 | 123 | 849 | 1414 | 766 |
| Total Population | 842 | 5560 | 944 | 5613 | 9624 | 4913 |
| Male | 498 | 2960 | 519 | 2974 | 5114 | 2595 |
| Female | 344 | 2600 | 425 | 2639 | 4520 | 2318 |
| Harijan | 365 | 735 | 120 | 489 | 1130 | 313 |
| Literate | 40 | 657 | 55 | 1152 | 1376 | 448 |
| Cultivator | 111 | 970 | 319 | 675 | 1068 | 765 |
| Unemployed | 394 | 3873 | 490 | 3967 | 6300 | 2985 |

*Source :* Collected Through Fieldwork.

## Tilabai Moin (Supaul)

The wetland of Tilabai Moin comes under, Ithari village of Supaul Anchal. It has an area of 1500 square metres. This wetland has been formed in the flash flood in Tilabai river which flows east of Ithari village from north to south. It is a Himalaya river (Fig. 15. 11) In old cadastral map of 1885 AD. The name of Tilabai river is known as Dalkhit river. Now most olden parts of this river has filled with sand and hence the farmers, have turned them agricultural plots. Some trees have also planted as Semal, Khair, Babol and Bamboo along with wattle and daub cultivated. Tilabai is an oxbow lake which formed due to changing courses of Tilabai river. This wetland never gets dry and in the rainy season it is full of water. The water of this Moin is crystal clear but in rainy season it is dirty. The Chief soil of this area is sand. Dighaunch is a migratory bird which come from Siberia in November to this lake and again they retires to their home in March each year. Its weight is 1 kg. to 2 kg. and the local price vary from Rs.100 to Rs.150 per bird. Besides this

Lalsar, Garur, Silli and duck are also available in this wetland. Some of these birds make nest on the trees found in the surrounding area of this lake. The vegetation found on the water of this lake are Makhana leaves, Koka, Lotus and Karmi. On the embankment of this lake Daib grass also grows which has been considered as the fodder of domestic animals. Among the fishes found in this lake are Garai, Pothi, Singhi, Ichna, Bami, etc. Crabs are also found on the shoreline.

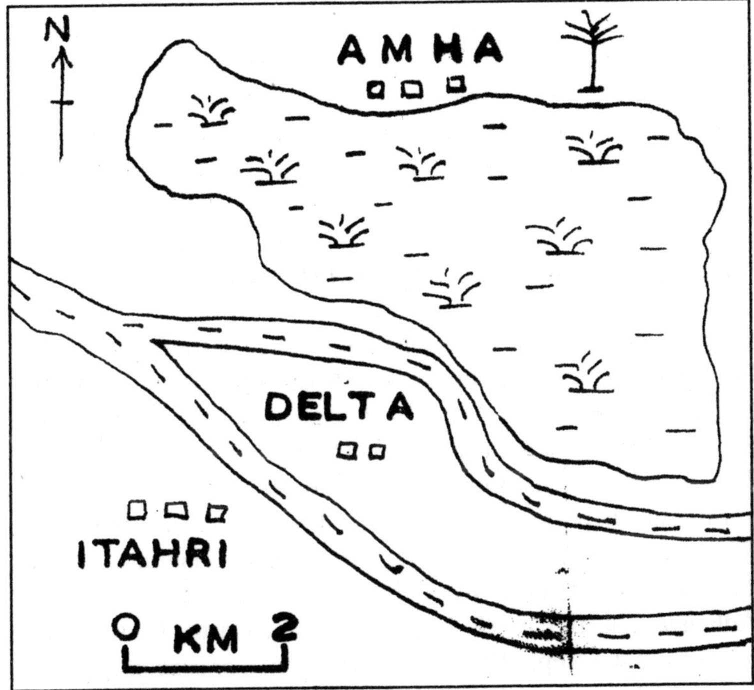


**Fig. 15.11 :** Tilabai Moin (Supaul)

Dhoria snake is also found in the water of this lake. The normal depth of this wetland is three metres. The shorelines are terraced but the depth increases with the increase of slope. There is no restriction from government side on this wetland and the people of Ithari, Hardi, Amta and Bhudura are getting benefit of all sort from this lake. The benefit is in the form of fish catch, getting grass for the animals, collect Purain leaves at the time of village feast besides the gathering of snails and Situa shells for making lime. Through lift irrigation it serves the purpose of irrigation as well.

With any obstruction the children will suffer from malnutrition. Cow ranching will be stopped and the fishing activities of Mallah will be stopped. The contract of this Jalkar provides benefit only to the rich, not poor.

This wetland keeps the local atmosphere cool. The plantation of Khair tree may be beneficial. The sandy soil also produces nice crops of Banana, Sugarcane, Potato and Sakarkand. The bamboo groves also develop very well. In order to have soil conservation on the embankment of Tilabai Moin the plantation of Shisham will be beneficial. This wetland comes in the way of Supaul- Singheshwar Asthan road and hence one bridge is necessary on this moin to cross its straight way.

## Lake Narha (Raghopur) of Supaul District

Narha Wetland comes under Dharhara village of Raghopur Anchal. Fig. 15.12. It has been surveyed by Roshan Kumar on 3.10.1994. Narha is surrounded by Mahadev Asthan in the east, Chiknapatti in the west, Dharhara in the north and Dhata Dharampur in the south. This lake has been formed due to intensive flow of flood water during ancient period but now the flood water from the north gushes from west of Raghopur through Nirmali and Kishanpur Anchals. The birds which visit Narlia during the winter season are Silli, Adhanga, Lalsar, Crench, Karan, Godil and Garur. All these birds come from the Nepal Himalaya and after winter season they again retires to their place of origin. The weight of these birds vary from 250 to 750 gram.

The vegetational cover is provided by Makhana, Purain leaves, Koka, Lotus and Kumudni flower. Sewar and water hyacinth dominate the scene as their growth is very fast in comparison with other plants. The depth of water is 3 metres in the months of July and August but it is only 1.25 metres in April and May each year. In Narha wetland black kewal soil is found. Local Kumhar people excavate and store this soil in their houses to make earthen jars.

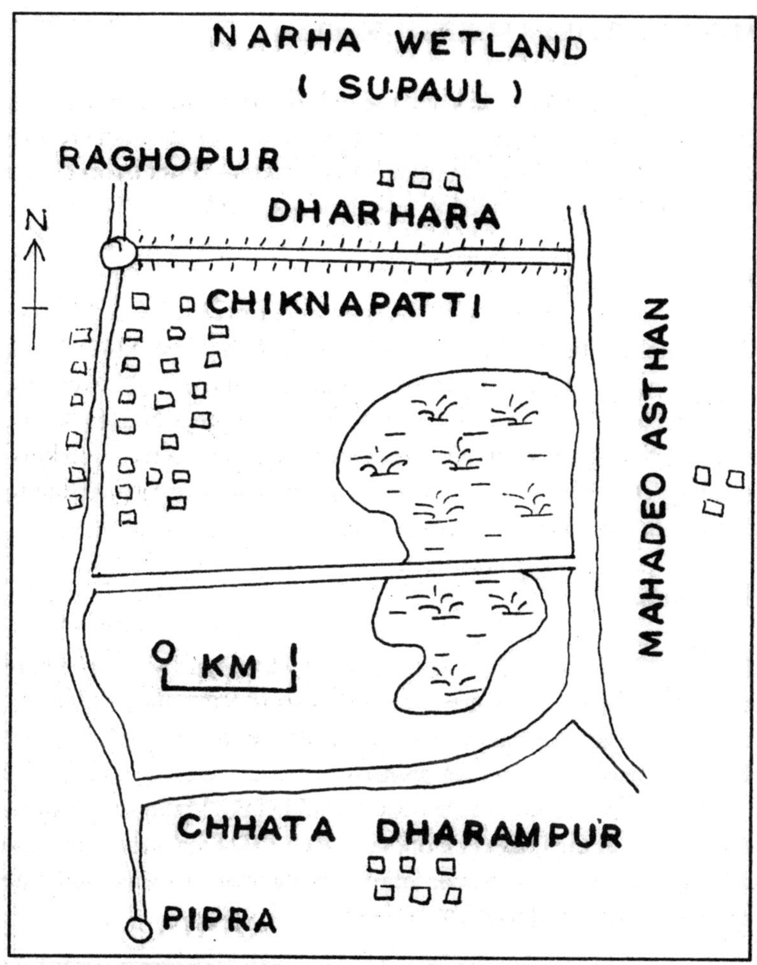


**Fig. 15.12 :** Lake Narha Wetland (Supaul)

The fishes found in Narha are Singhi, Momi, Saura, Garai, Buari, Pothi, Bami and Tengra. Among other creatures, tortoise, crab, snail and snakes are found. In Narha wetland the local people are allowed to catch fish and trap birds as there is no restriction from the government. During rainy season the area gets flooded but during summer season the water of Narha is used for the purpose of irrigation. The water remain clean for most parts of the year.

**Malkayan Wetland Manihari (Katihar)**

It is located in Madarichak village of Manihari Anchal in Katihar district. Its east-west length is 4 kilometres, and north-south breadth is 250 metres. The maximum depth is 6 metres in the central part but in the fringe it reduced to less than one metre.

***Location***

On the north side of lake Malkayan Bishunpur village, Madarichak in the south, Lakshmipur in the east and Dumaria in the west are the nieghbouring villages located. Lake Malkayan is located 8 kms. south of Manihari Block. The distance of the Ganges river is 5 kms. south of this lake. (Fig.15.13). It is an oxbow lake formed due to change in the course of Kankhar river.

***Vegetation***

Due to flow of water only little amount of vegetation is seen here and there e.g. Sewar, water-hyacinth, Karmi, Sami and Madhauna, etc. water-hyacinth has been used as fertilizer by the local farmers. Karmi is used as fodder for animals.

Several varieties of fishes are found in lake Malkavan. Among them some of the important ones are Rehu, Boari, Katla, Mara and Jhinga. Besides these Situa, Snail, Dhoria snake tortoise and crab are also found in Malkayan wetland.

**Table 15.5** : Fishes and their weight

| *Name of Fishes* | *Production* | *Price in Rs* |
|---|---|---|
| Rehu | 50 Quintal Per year | 20, 000 |
| Katla | 100 Quintal Per year | 30, 000 |
| Mara | 5 Quintal Per year | 12,500 |
| Jhinga | 5 Quintal Per year | 10,000 |

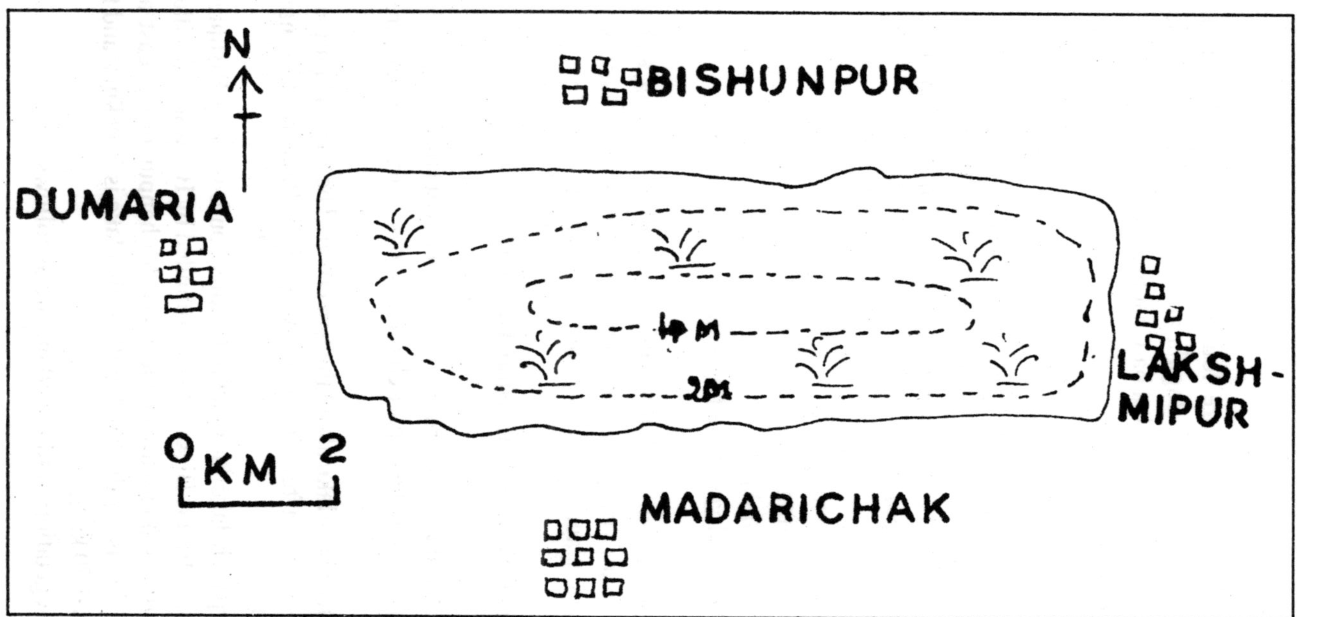


**Fig. 15.13 :** Malkayan Wetland, Katihar Anchal

***Birds***

The seasonal variations are found in the arrival of birds lake Malkayan. Here, Pansilli, Bagula and duck are commonly seen. During the winter season Chakba-Chakbai and Hansh-Hanshin also seen in Malkayan wetland.

***Planning***

As the surrounding area of Malkayan is flood affected and hence the construction of canal is quite impossible. This lake may be used for the following purposes.

(a) To prepare Jiora of fishes.
(b) To produce Singarhara
(c) To produce Makhana
(d) Provision of loan to the fishermen.

In the neighbourhood area of this lake Mallah, Gangota, Kabrath, Bind and Yadav's people reside. The main occupation of these people are cultivation, agricultural labourer and fish catch.

**Hajarpanch Wetland (Katihar District)**

Hajarpanch Lake comes under Barari Anchal of Bishanpur Village in Katihar district. The chief characteristics of this wetland are as follows:

It is an oxbow lake along the Kosi river. The name Hajarpanch has been given after the washed away village of this name (Fig.15.14).

Hajarpanch lake is located 18 kms south-west of Bishunpur Panchayat in Barari Block. It is surrounded by Bhawanipur village in the north, Kakiadiara in the west, Mohanpur in the east and Binodpur 2 kms south. The length of this lake is 2.50 kms. and the breadth is 0.50 kms,

The vegetation of this wetland are as follows:

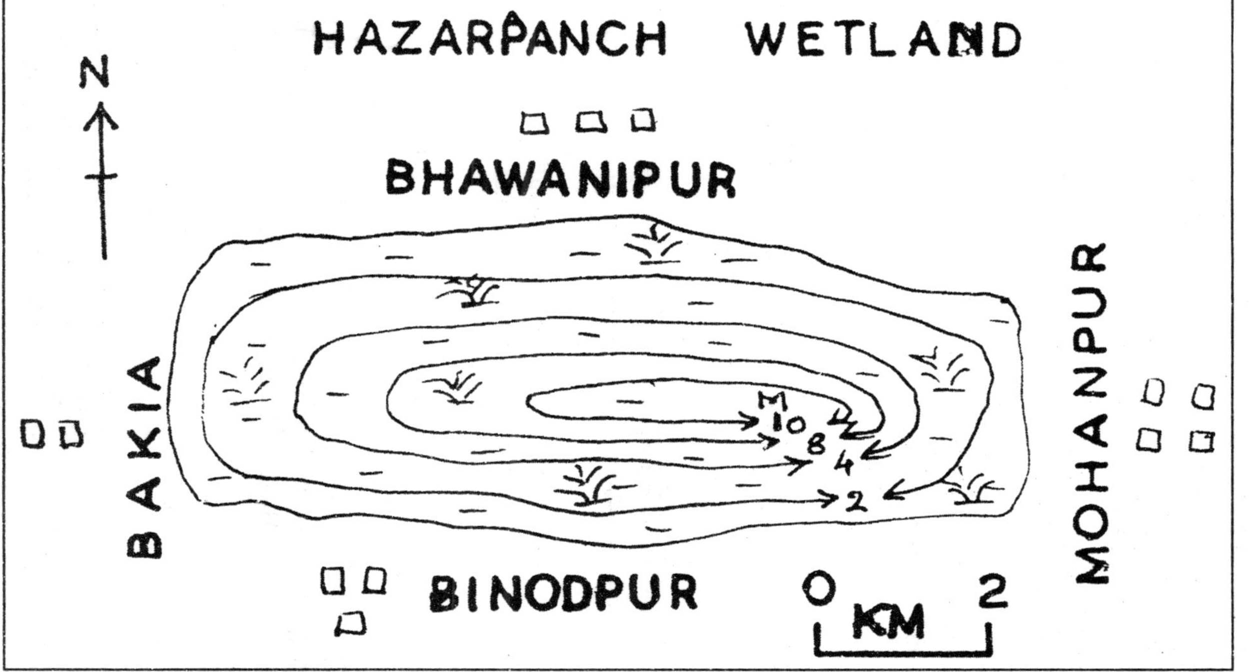


**Fig. 15.14 :** Hajarpanch Wetland

(a) Kash–Animals feed and raw material to construct house.
(b) Sew — used as fertilizer.
(c) Karmi – used as sag.
(d) Lotus flower root for vegetable and garland from beads.
(e) Dudhaili Grass — cows fodder.

The organisms found in this lake are fishes : Rehu 20 quintal Per year, Boari - 30 quintal per year, Katla - 50 quintal per year, Garai - 5 quintal per year, Tengra - 6 quintal per year, Tortoise - 50 only, Crab - 50 kg. only, Situa - 70 kg. only. Dhorna Snake - 50 only, Jonk - 1000 only

***Birds***

Pansilli - 500 per year, Duck – 50 only, Chakba – 50 only

***Crops Grown***

In the surrounding area of this lake the main crops grown are wheat, Maize, Matar, Urad, paddy, etc. per hectare production is as follows:

| | | |
|---|---|---|
| Paddy | 38 quintal, | Maize - 50 quintal |
| Urad | 10 quintal, | Matar - 12 quintal |
| Wheat | 38 quintal | |

***Irrigation***

Hajarpanch lake helps in irrigating 30 hectares of land in its surrounding area through pumping set. As this area is flood affected and hence the construction of canal is not possible.

***Planning***

Hajarpanch lake should be developed for rearing fishes. The better irrigational management is not possible. The Jeora of fishes is never used. The fishermens condition is quite pitiable. Quarrel is quite common in the name of fish catch. The land owners of the lake area are harrasing the fishermen.

In the surrounding area of this wetland the backward people reside e.g. Gorhi, Gangota, Yadav and Kharwar. The main occupation of these people are cultivation, agricultural labourers and fish catch. The literacy rate is very low and poverty is the rule.

**Wetlands of Simri-Bakhtiarpur**

In Simri-Bakhtiarpur Block of Saharsa district the important wetlands are Sardiha, Kusumi and Gordah having an area of (1 km and 150 metres). Kusumi lake having an area of 100 hectare located south of Sardiha. Sardiha Chaur 80 hectares north of Sardiha and lake Gordah, south of Kusumi (5 kms long and 200 metres wide) besides Knonmadhar located south of Gordah as tributary of the Kosi river. (Fig. 15.15).

In these wetlands the main migratory birds which resides from November to March every year are.

**Table 15.6 :** Birds and Weight in Sirdiha Chaur

| *Sr. No.* | *Name* | *Weight* | *Price in Rs.* |
|---|---|---|---|
| 1. | Dighaunch | 1 kg. | 35 |
| 2. | Khokhair | 3/4 kg. | 30 |
| 3. | Adhanga | 1/2 kg. | 15 |
| 4. | Toparia | 1/2 kg. | 15 |
| 5. | Lalsar | 11/2 kg. | 40 |
| 6. | Pansilli | 1/2 kg. | 24 |
| 7. | Duboo | 1/2 kg. | 24 |

*Source :* Available from fieldwork by R.B. Mandal, 1994.

1. It is a sad state of affairs that due to the complete negligence of government machinery the Gorh and Mushar people of the locality still use to kill and catch these birds during night. The netting of birds is still going on unchecked in these wetlands.
2. The fish catch from Sardiha has a characteristic that it does not give bad smell due to clean environment.
3. The wetlands are declared as land to the government even if it is a private land. But it is a sad state are getting the benefit of

these wetlands but society people give a poor royalty (10 times less) to the government and (5 times to) the public.

4. From the root of lotus flower and Purain Ponor long root is useful as poor mans food but due to these societies ownership people fails to get this benefit. Purain leaves could also be sold in the market in case the wetlands could be used by the private owner.
5. Although Jalkumbhi is a problem in all the wetlands but its collection on land from the wetlands makes it a good compost after 4 months rot and its price become Rs.200 per tonne in the market.

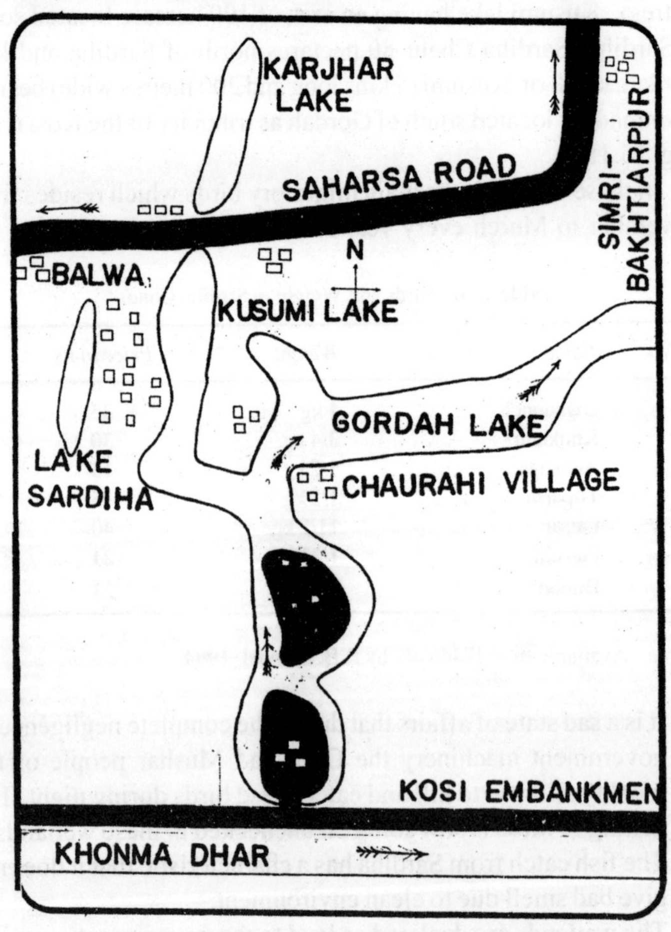


**Fig. 15.15 :** Wetlands of Simri-Bakhtiarpur Block

***Problems of these Wetlands both for the Public and in Management***

1. There is a lot of mud on the floor which creates a variety of insects which are harmful for the general health of the society e.g. jonk and others, but these insects are also bird's food for which they come to this area from far away places.
2. The wetlands have severely affected the private land around which should be reclaimed by draining water.
3. The netting of birds is quite rampant which is quite illegal but it is an un fortunate that there is no check on it.
4. The wetland keeps the surrounding land moist for a longer time and hence people have to sow their fields late either wheat or maize especially in January.
5. Due to annual flood, poor production of food crops and land falls in wetland is the only answer to the poors from where they tried to get their benefit whatever they can.
6. Proper management of these wetlands are quite essential either by the government, public or the foreign companies who could at least give 50 per cent return to the local people.

**Wetlands of Bangaon Mahisi**

Mahisi (105) is a village of 12,000 persons in Mahisi Block of Saharsa district, Bihar. This village is an emblem of Archaeological evidence and the junction of several wetlands. Ugra Tara Devi temple of this village is 5000 years old and it could be compared with Katanethan near Dhamhara Bridge of Kosi River, Jaimangla Devi of Kabar lake and Kamor-Kamrachha of Gauhati in Assam. All these archaeological places are of Aryan period where saints were found in a quite large number throughout North Indian Plains.

Some of the important wetlands in the surroundings of Mahisi are as follows:

1. Ganga Sagar Western side — 35 hectares but now it has been filled with silt.

2. Ghori Badh Western side — 35 hectares but now it has been filled with silt.
3. Osbadha - North 4 kms — 50 hectares during rainy season it expands up to Orebali.
4. Sonbarsa — 1/2 km. North-West near Sirsia — 100 hectares.
5. Dhimradhar — 1 km east of Sorho river — 200 hectares
6. Chanan — 1 km South — 50 hectares
7. East of Naharwar — 3 kms South-West — 100 hectares
8. East of Mahisi Block — 100 hectares.
9. Manuadhar — West of Mahisi — very long and Stable Wetland– it has a link with Nepal border in the north and Koparia 20 kms in the South.

As demand of the people of Manuadhar 100 feet bridge is on road number 17 District Board to connect Eastern Part of Mahisi with Bhagwatpur, Laraiya Tola and Kothia. Ara and Murli are located as human settlement on western part. (Fig. 15.16)

**Table 15.7** : Birds visiting the Area

| *Birds* | *Weight in kg.* | *Price in Rs.* |
|---|---|---|
| Karan (Blue) | 1/2 kg. | 20 |
| Pansilli (Block) | 1 kg. | 30 |
| Lalsar | 1 1/2 kg. | 50 |
| Adhni | 1/4 kg. | 10 |
| Dighaunch | 2 kg. | 60 |
| Bagula | 1/2 kg. | 10 |
| Wak | 3 kg. | 75 |
| Hasua Dabi | 1 1/4 kg. | 40 |
| Khurpi Dabi | 2 kg. | 60 |
| Dakhar | 2 kg. | 60 |
| Nakta | 3 kg. | 90 |

*Source :* Collected by R. B. Mandal on 15.3.1-994 by Fieldwork.

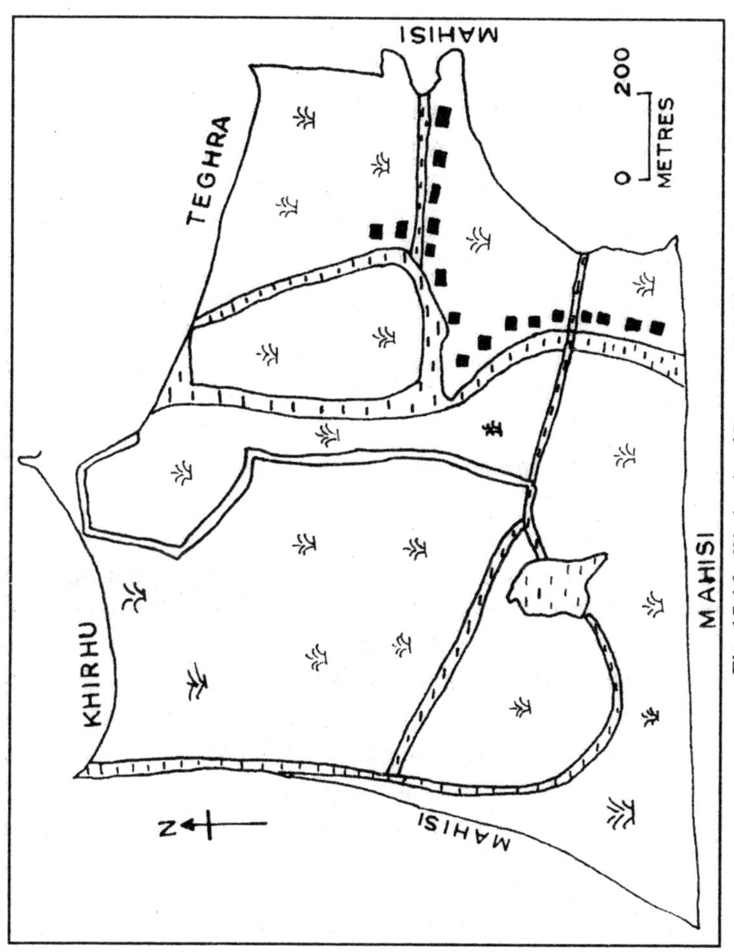


**Fig. 15.16 :** Wetlands of Bangaon Mahisi

***Problems to be Solved***

1. Plant trees on roadside.
2. Clean Manuadhar Jalkumbhi and debris of plants as these obstruct Makhana cultivation and obscure fishes inside.
3. In Manuadhar several people died due to drowning.
4. In case it could be converted into chain of tanks then Makhana cultivation is possible.
5. For the present the development of fishing industry is the only answer to develop the economic condition of people but unfortunately even private wetlands have been owned by the government. For this fact, neither with the government nor the public are beneficiaries but middlemen fishermen's society people gets benefit out of it. They have no mentality to conserve wetland nor provide facilities to the local people but with the help of big net (Mahajal) they extract fishes from the wetland whatever they can.

***Lakes in East Champaran to be Developed soon***

With the signing of a tripartite agreement among Fishermen's Co-operative Society, Central Co-operative Bank and the State Government through the district fishery officer recently, the ambitious World Bank sponsored project to develop different lakes in the district of East Champaran to rear fish on large scale has been cleared.

Giving this information to press the District Magistrate, Mr. Deepak Kumar, said that in the first phase three lakes namely famous Motijheel (Motihari lake), Kararia lake and Basman lake had been selected for development at the estimated cost of Rs. 18 lakh and Rs 12 lakh respectively. Mr Kumar said that with the implementation of this scheme, the long cherished desire of the people of Motihari to beautify the Motihari lake would also be fulfilled. He said that at the time of agreement, some top officials of the Fishery Department like Mr. Parma Nand Ram, Joint Director, Fishery (headquarters), Mr. R. N. Chaudhary, Joint Director of Fishery Project, Mr. Pancheo Singh, Deputy Director, Tirhut range, Mr. Rajiv Ranjan Prasad, assistant-director, Mr. Kavindra Nath Thakur, district co-operative officer and Mr. Dhirendra Kumar Singh, district fishery officer, were also present.

Earlier, the Fishermen's Co-operative Societies of Motihari Block and Basman Panchayat in the presence of these officers adopted the amended by laws of the society, paving the way of the agreement, Mr. Sheo Nandan Chaudhary, leader of the fishermen later, claimed the amendment to the laws was in the interest of the fishermen. Mr. Parmanand Ram said that with the development of these lakes in the district, some 250 families of fishermen would be benefited.

## Motijheel of Motihari

Ecology was defined as "physiology of the environment" and also as "the science of the economy of animals and plants". The organisms and their environment constitute the theoretical principle of modern ecology. The organism interacts and adapts with the surrounding environment for its relationship and existence. Ecological balance in population is maintained also by the quality and nature of food in an ecosystem.

Bihar in general and North Bihar in particular is very rich in water resources. It has a number of water bodies, such is lakes, ponds, ditches, rivers and streams, etc. Each water body has its own environment with interesting biotic populations and abotic factors. Among the animal population insects and fishes constitute the major part of the water body. The factors affecting the insect abundance are the best methods of utilizing beneficial species of controlling pest species.

## Turbidity of Water

Water turbidity was also regarded as a limiting factor. Ford (1882 to 1884) pointed out that turbid waters were warmer than the clean waters. Particles floating in the water absorbed heat more rapidly than did the water itself and these particles radiated this heat to the surrounding water. Ganapati (1955) found the high turbidity throughout the year of investigations, indicative of the presence of large amount of suspended materials. Oory and Mauman (1967) studies the turbidity of Patuxents surface water and found the variation of turbidity throughout the year and was influenced by tide, wind, fresh water and biological activities. Hussain (1967) studied the irregular turbidity and stated that the irregularity might be due to the plankton warms, flankton drifts and sudden contribution of wind blown materials. Michael (1969) did not observe the marked seasonal trends in trubidity. The highest values were in May and August and the lowest in March.

Turbidity = Depth of Disappearance + Depth of Reappearance

## Wetlands of East Champaran

Motihari, headquarter of East Champaran district of North Bihar lies between Lat 26°40' N to Long 84°17'E. The whole Champaran has 41 waterbodies (oxbow lakes or mans). They are a type of loop shaped and longitudinal lakes. They are defined as former river bends which were subsequently cut off from the main river when a change of its course took place. These lakes are perennial. They are generally shallow at their margins and have a depth even up to 9 metres at the centre. All these water bodies, by and large, are situated between Burhi-Gandak or Sikarhana on the east and Gandak river in the west. There is a rivulet, known as Dhanauti, flowing in between and connected to these rivers. This rivulet provide water connections to large number of mans during flood.

## Motijheel Lake

Motijheel lake is surrounded by the human settlements of Motihari town. On the southern bank of Motijheel there is a sugar factory and on the south western bank large trees are found. The leaves of tree fall in the water and decay. In such a situation, the physical and chemical nature of water and availability of organisms in the water change their character (Fig. 15.17).

Motijheel is a Ushaped lake which divides Motihari town into two halves. It is about 32 hectares in extent and connected by the Burhi-Gandak through channel on its north-western side while on its eastern side, it is connected to a bigger lake, Kararia by a canal.

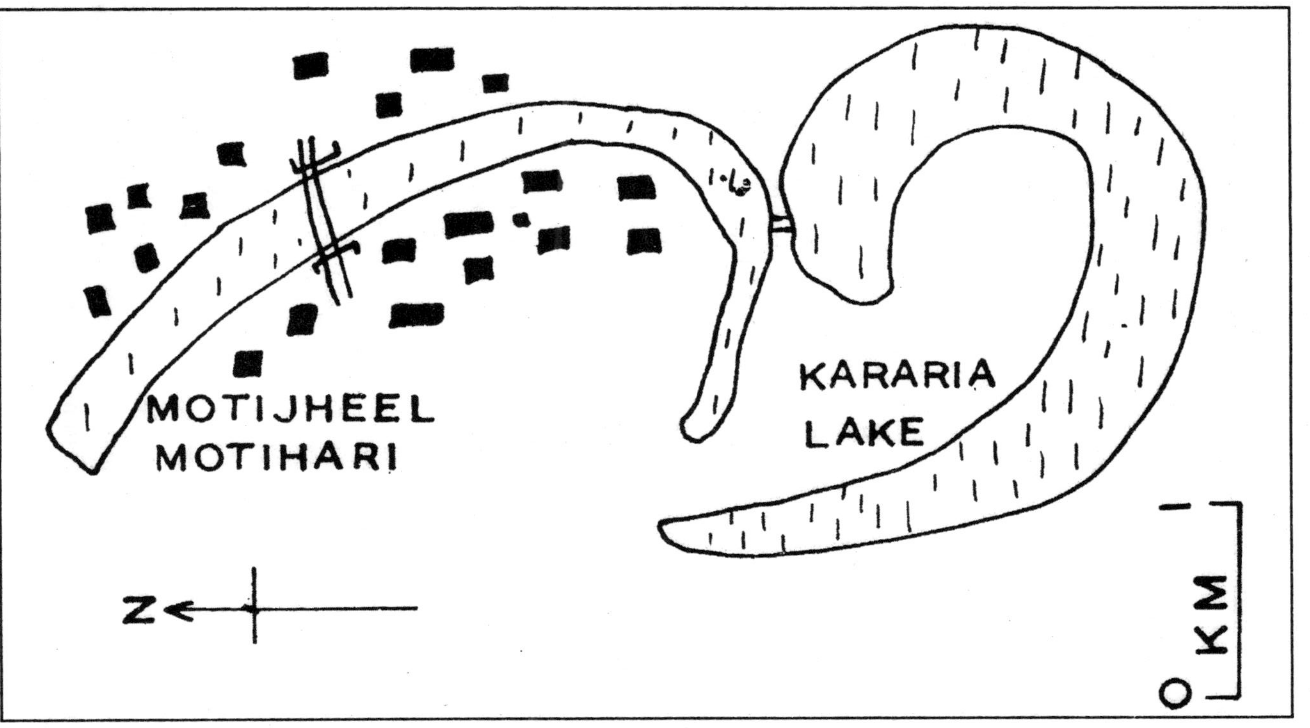


**Fig. 15.17 :** Motijheel and Kararia Lakes of East Champaran

The passage of this canal is controlled by a sluice gate. This connection was provided to divert the excess of flood water entering Motijheel lake into Kararia lake. A road divides the lake into two sections, except 10-12 metres continuity under a bridge in the middle.

Formerly Motijheel has a good flushing of flood water entering through linkage canal from Burhi-Gandak but nowadays this channel has been blocked by the irrigation canal constructed under the Gandak Project. However, at the time of flood, water overflows the 60 cms. height of the tributaries to reach the lake i.e. in 1975 and 1976 and 1987. These floods have disturbed the total populations of the lake both weeds and animals including insects.

The water of this lake is heavily polluted with the flow of untreated refuge and sewage from the town and the sugar factory's affluents. Sugar factory reportedly discharge affluents into the Dhananti river while hot water is discharged into the Motijheel lake. Even this has upsetted the ecology of the lake.

**Table 15.8 :** Chemical Factors of Motijheel Lake, 1995

| *Month* | *Date Time 8 a. m.* | *Dissolved 02 in ppm* | *Free Co² in ppm* | *ph* | *Phosp Gate mg/I* |
|---|---|---|---|---|---|
| J | 8.1.76 | 4.2 | 32.0 | 6.4 | 23.0 |
| F | 1.2.76 | 5.0 | .24.0 | 8.2 | 25.0 |
| M | 7.3.76 | 6.6 | 16.0 | 8.4 | 22.0 |
| A | 4.4.76 | 5.8 | 18.0 | 7.8 | 15.0 |
| M | 2.5.76 | 5.6 | 44.0 | 7.0 | 19.5 |
| J | 1.6.76 | 4.8 | 38.0 | 7.2 | 29.0 |
| J | 6.7.76 | 6.8 | 20.0 | 8.6 | 25.5 |
| A | 1.8.76 | 6.2 | 22.0 | 8.2 | 23.5 |
| S | 5.9.76 | 5.4 | 26.0 | 7.0 | 22.0 |
| O | 1.10.76 | 4.4 | 24.0 | 7.0 | 16.5 |
| N | 7.11.76 | 4.2 | 35.0 | 6.6 | 16.5 |
| D | 12.12.76 | 3.8 | 48.0 | 5.8 | 24.0 |

On the marginal lands of Motijheel cultivation is also done over 100 hectares in summer and 100 hectares during rainy season. The source of water is natural rain and tributaries of rivers. The weed infestation was about 60 per cent and depth varies from 0.90 metres to 2.10 metres.

The lake was infested with weeds which were present at the margins, at the surface and at the bottom with varying intensities. Due to rich soil, impregnated with organic matter, there is a thick growth of weeds. Following are the common weeds found in this lake :

1. Motijheel is heavily infested with water-hyacinth (Eiochornia) and Duck weeds. They were the floating weeds but on the margin polygonum, Antigonum and Phragmetes were found.
2. Bottom of the lake was covered by Olitella, Hydrill.., Nymphea, Nais, Ceratophyllus and Moriophyllum.

The bottom vegetation degenerated during December and January and again regenerated from February onwards. There was an abundant accumulation of decaying weeds at the bottom which maintained the basic productive qualities of water.

**Kararia Lake**

It is situated east of Motijheel lake and is larger in extent. This lake is less infested with Eidchornia. Its depth varies from 4.5 to 6.00 metres at some places. This lake has an outlet which got connected during monsoon months to the river Dhananti for the discharge of excess flood water. It provides good fishing ground for the local people.

The total area of this lake is 41 hectares. The source of water is rain and flood. The weed intestation was about 65 per cent. The depth of water varies from 6.30 m to 0.90 m.

***Weeds of Kararia Lakes***

The surface of this lake is almost open not covered by aquatic weeds some floating plants are found e.g. Eiochornia, Wolfia, Type, Agoma, Spirogyra, Chantophora and Dogonium. The bottom is composed of Vallienaria.

### *Turbidity*

In 1976 turbidity of the Motijheel lake ranged from 33 cm to 166 cm. Irregular fluctuations were observed in the turbidity. From January (128 cm) to April (65 cm), the turbidity showed a decreasing trend but from May to December this showed increase and decrease in alternate month. In October it was 33 cm. but in November it was 166 cm. Thus both maximum and minimum of the year was observed in the two consecutive months.

Kararia lake in 1995 gave different picture of the turbidity. It ranged from 76 cm. to 362 cm. The highest turbidity was recorded in the month of December and the lowest in the month of June. In this lake there was an increasing trend in the turbidity from August (76 cm.) to December (362 cm.) continuously. In November an increase in turbidity was abrupt from 140 cm. and October to 270 cm. in November. But from January to July there was fluctuation in each alternate month.

## Basman Lake

### *Shikrahara River*

Basman lake is an oxbow lake, located about 10 km. away from Motihari town. It is one of the 41 lakes of Champaran district. It is about 1/2 km. away on the left side of the Motihari to Patahi Road (Fig. 15.18).

The lake is a loop-shaped and narrow water stretch. It has geographical ordinates 26°40'N to 85°E longitude. It is a course of the Sikrahara river which was subsequently cut off from the main river when a change of its course took place.

The lake is "U" shaped, perennial with shallow margins. Total water area during the rainy and flood season was about 128100 hectares. But in the dry season, it became smaller in water area, about 50 hectares. The lake is deep in the central part some places 7 to 9 metres deep, which became 5 metres deep during the summer season. The margin is shallow and fishes were netted from 2 to 5

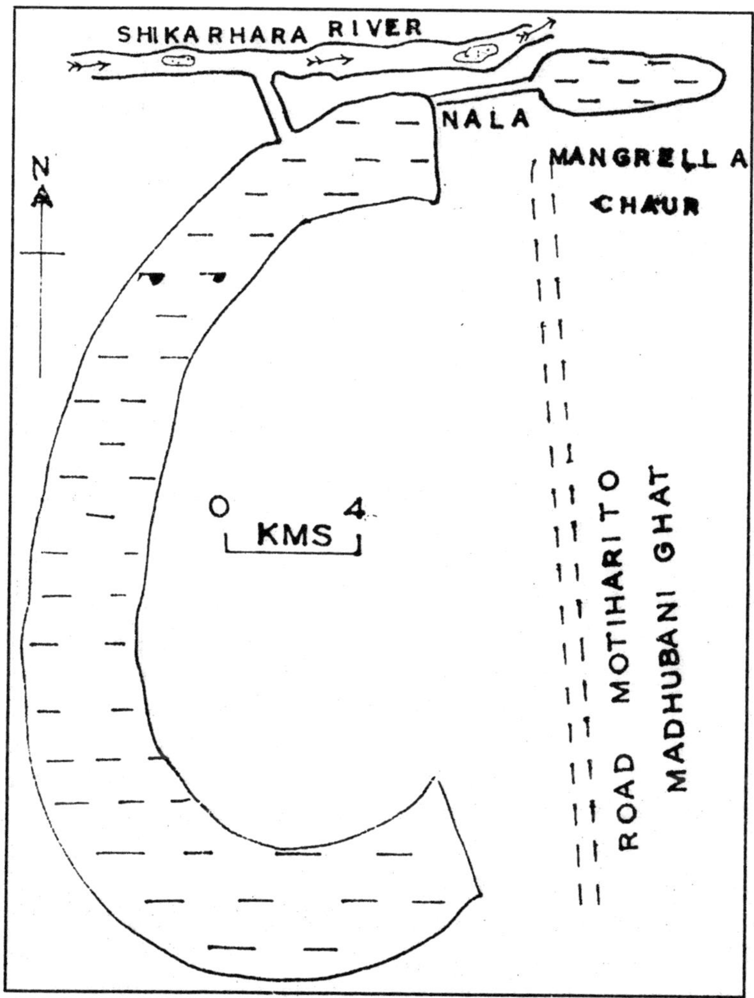


**Fig. 15.18 :** Basman Lake

metres deep water. In 1994-95 there were heavy flood and the whole area of the lake was completely flooded with water. It has caused mass destruction of flora and fauna.

The water from flooded chaur rushes towards the Suhagman lake. From Suhagman lake, water passes into the Dhanauti river and this river meets Sikarahara river again near Mehsi of East Champaran.

The Basman lake is large but smaller than Suhagman lake with bamboo grooves, sesam, etc. On the bank. Paddy fields are found on all sides of the lake. This lake is regarded less suitable for Pissicuture than Suhagman lake due to its location and connection with Sikarhara river.

**Khagma Wetland (Saharsa)**

Khagma is a wetland in Haripur village of Salkhua Anchal, in Saharsa district. Khagma is located 2 kms south of Salkhua Block. It has a length of 800 metres and breadth 500 metres. The water area is 4 hectare. During the rainy season its area increases three times even if it is surrounded by the Kosi embankment, roads and rail line. The water flows from north to south but now its suilice gate is in delapidated condition. Smaller fishes and snakes are found abundantly in this wetland. Shaibal is the vegetation found in the lake and Kichak, people residing in the surrounding area prey even Bagula for their food. Khagma is surrounded by Koparia in the north, Haripur in the south-railway line of Mansi to Saharsa in the east and Boharba village in the west. Jonk is normously found in this lake. Among the, other creatures snail, tortoise and fishes are important. Due to the dominance of rangdars the settlement of this wetland is in abeyance. The depth is 7 metres maximum and minimum 1 metre. Per acre production of crops are rice 880 kg, wheat 800 kg, maize 1480 kg and Mung 400 kg. water temperature was 21°C and village leaders were Panchanand Yadav and Basant Kumar. (Fig. 15.19)

**Chamra Chaur (Patepur)**

Chamra Chaur has been surveyed on 22-11-1994 at 12 noon. The water temperature was 24°C. It is located just 0.50 km north-west of Tal Baraila in Vaishali district. The latitudinal position is 25°40'N and 85°30'E longitude. It is located 6 kms from Dabhaich Chauk, Khalispur from eastern side gate No.13 and in the north 6 kms from Bijhrauli. (Fig. 15.20)

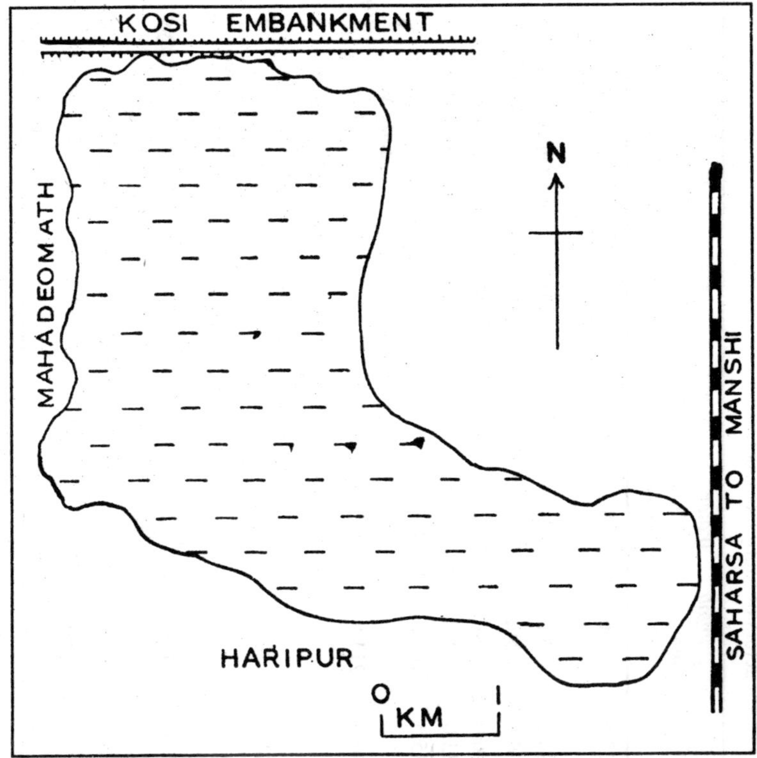


**Fig. 15.19 :** Khagma Wetland (Saharsa)

Chamra Chaur is connected with a small channel from Baraila Tal and during peak hours of flood it forms part of Baraila Tal. The surrounding rural settlements of the area are Mataiya, Eijhrauli, Indauta and Dih, etc.

The length of Chamra Chaur is 1.5 km and the breadth is I km. Its depth is 4 feet in the central part. The creatures found are crab and snail. The vegetation found are paddy, Sewar, Karmi and water-hyacinth. Agricultural operations and fishing are the main occupation of the people. The crops produced in the surrounding area are paddy, wheat, maize, janera, etc.

The government wants to reclaim the land by digging deep canal but due to its lesser depth for the present the water stagnates in the Chamra Chaur for a longer period.

**Table 15.9** : Physical Factors of Motijheel Lake, 1995

| *Month* | *Date of Collection at 8.a.m.* | *Air Min.* | *Temp. Max.* | *Water 0°C Min.* | *Max.* | *Rainfall mm.* | *Water Level Meters* | *Wind Velocity km/h* | *Turbidity cm.* | *Weather Condition* |
|---|---|---|---|---|---|---|---|---|---|---|
| Jan. | 4.1.96 | 15.0 | 25.5 | 12.5 | 23.0 | 5.0 | 0.98 | 0.6 | 128 | Clear and Cold Morning |
| Feb. | 1.2.96 | 14.8 | 23.0 | 19.0 | 24.0 | 5.0 | 0.93 | 0.2 | 116 | Clear Morning |
| March | 7.3.96 | 27.0 | 31.0 | 19.0 | 28.5 | Nil | 0.87 | 0.5 | 96 | Normal Cold |
| April | 4.4.96 | 29.0 | 37.0 | 25.0 | 26.0 | Nil | 0.62 | 3.3 | 65 | Clear Morning |
| May | 2.5.96 | 26.5 | 36.5 | 29.0 | 33.0 | 51.0 | 0.54 | 6.8 | 78 | Clear Morning |
| June | 1.6.96 | 30.0 | 36.0 | 28.0 | 35.5 | 106.8 | 0.91 | 5.2 | 63 | Clear Morning Easterly Wind |
| July | 6.7.96 | 31.0 | 41.0 | 29.0 | 36.0 | 211.8 | 1.42 | 6.7 | 67 | Clear Morning with previous night rain |
| Aug. | 1.8.96 | 33.0 | 34.5 | 36.05 | 34.0 | 180.1 | 1.72 | 5.2 | 55 | Penetrating sunrays closed morning |
| Sept. | 5.9.96 | 29.5 | 33.0 | 30.0 | 32.0 | 247.0 | 2.02 | 3.2 | 62 | Clear sky sunrays |
| Oct. | 1.10.96 | 31.5 | 36.0 | 29.5 | 33.5 | 28.2 | 0.91 | 1.8 | 33 | Clear sky |
| Nov. | 7.11.96 | 21.0 | 27.0 | 24.5 | 28.5 | — | 0.82 | 1.1 | 166 | Clear sky |
| Dec. | 12.12.96 | 14.0 | 18.5 | 16.5 | 18.5 | Nil | 0.70 | 0.6 | 140 | Colder Morning clear sky |

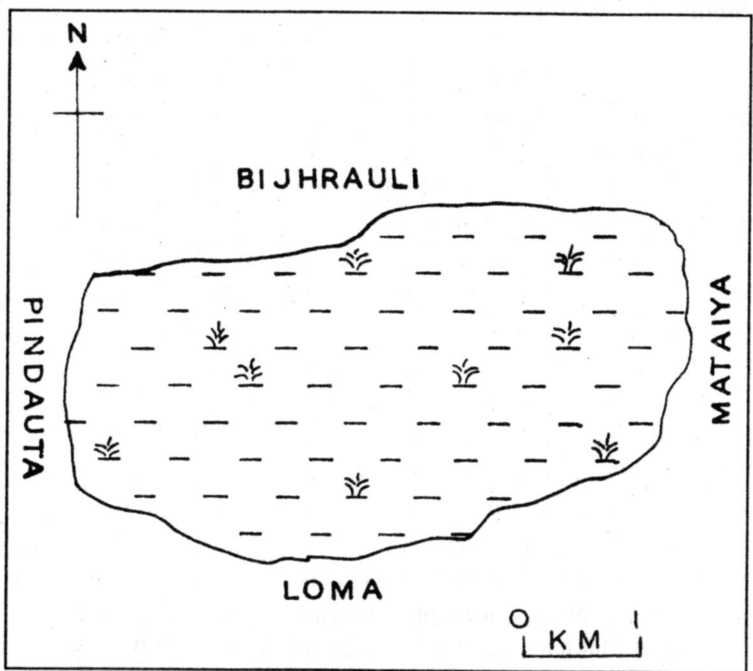


**Fig. 15.20 :** Chamra Chaur (Vaishali District)

**Table 15.10 :** Incoming of birds in Chamra Chaur

| *Birds* | *Weight in Kg.* | *Rice in Rs.* |
|---|---|---|
| Dumar | 1.000 | 100 |
| Dighauch | .500 | 60 |
| Maitha | .700 | 60 |
| Ghench | 1.000 | 85 |
| Khesrar | .500 | 30 |
| Adhena | .550 | 25 |
| Laklak | .400 | 30 |
| Dhodhil | .500 | 50 |
| Loha Astgar | .400 | 60 |
| Lalsar | .500 | 60 |
| Saras | 7.500 | — |

Among the local birds Bagula, Bodar and Pansilli are found. People in the surrounding area of lakes suffer from malaria, kalajar and cholera at times. Except some fishes the lake is quite unproductive.

## Phoolbhasa Wetland

The survey work has been done on 25.2.95 at 10.15 am. The water temperature was 19°C. It is located in Thakurganj Block of Kishanganj district. It is surrounded by Phoolbhasa village in the east, Ghantal in the west, Phoolbhasa Ghantal in the north and agricultural field in the south.

One can visit this wetland from Thakurganj 7 kms by rickshaw. Near this lake 13 houses of scheduled tribe, 10 houses of Anshari and some houses of refugees are found. The total number of residents are 225 and the literacy is only 5 per cent.

The length of Phoolbhasa wetland is 750 metres and breadth 150 metres. The depth of water is 2 metres but it expands during rainy season and subsides during summer season. Among the fishes found in the lake are Pothi, Buari, Gainchi, Momuri, Ichna, Garai, Bhuna and Rehu, etc. The average weight of the fish is 2.5 kg. Among the local birds Bagula and Pansilli are important. Migratory birds are not coming. The plants found are Sewar, Motha and Karmi. Fishes and Makhana are produced in this lake. In 1994 it gives a revenue of Rs.12052 to the government. The total annual makhana produce is about 40 quintal. The production of fishes and makhana earns more money in comparison with other crops. Bamboo is found as vegetation around the lake. It suffers from the flood of the Mahanadi river during the rainy season (Fig. 15.21).

## Kanti Wetland

Kanti lake has been surveyed on 24.3.1996 at 12 noon. The water temperature was 28°C. It is located in Kanti Block of Muzaffarpur district. National Highway No. 28 separates NTPC with Kanti lake. It is located 500 metres north of N.H. Road. It is semi-circular in shape. In between two rear end of the mouth of lake the distance is about, one km. On eastern of the lake Pakri and Madhuban villages are located, on the south NTPC and Kanti Bazar and on the north Kothia satellite settlement is located. One small channel of refuse water comes from Kanti NTPC to the eastern part of this lake

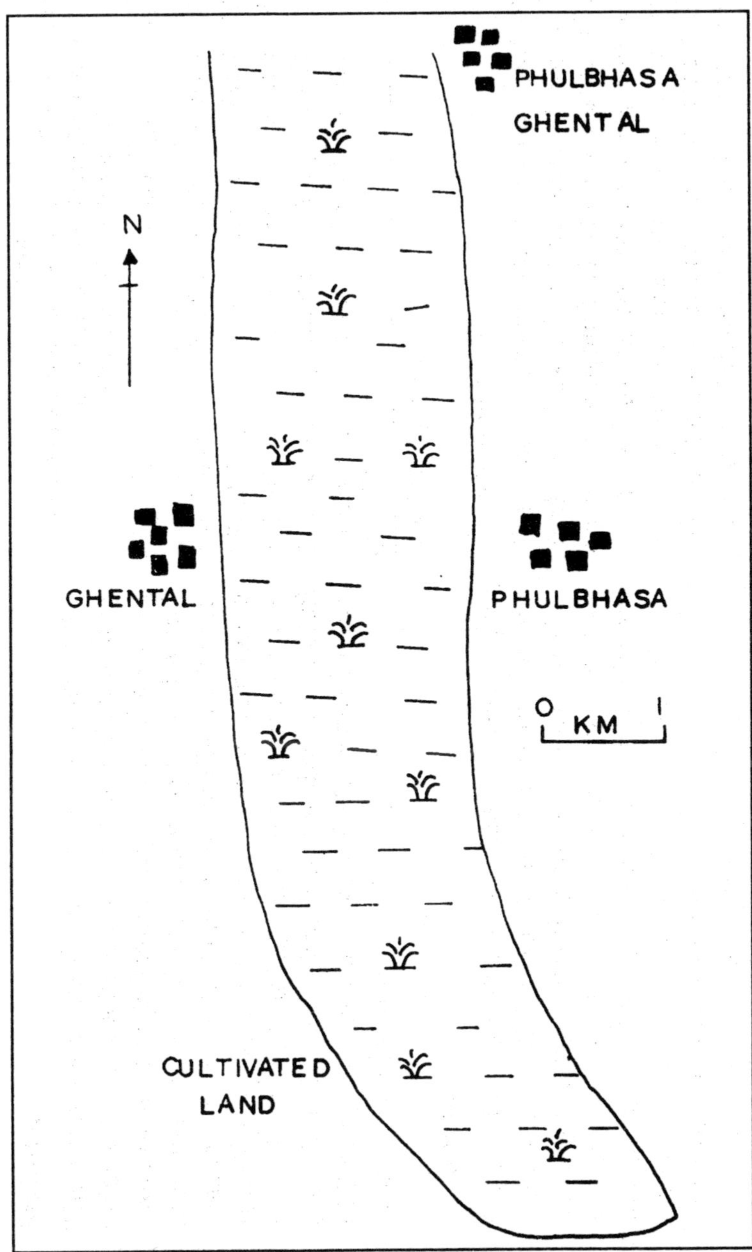


**Fig. 15.21 :** Phulbhasa Lake (Kishanganj)

**Table 15.11 :** Characteristics of Wetland in Muzaffarpur

| *Sl.No.* | *Characteristics of Area/ Population* | *Kanti Thana 77* | *Madhuban Thana 476* | *Pakri Thana 147* | *Kothia Thana 149* |
|---|---|---|---|---|---|
| 1. | Area of the village in Hectare | 112.50 | 103 – 15 | 258.88 | 138.17 |
| 2. | No. of residential House | 54 | 63 | 349 | 73 |
| 3. | Total Population | M/195–F/174 | M/209–F/191 | M/138–F/1082 | M/317–F/289 |
| 4. | Population below 6 years of Age | 41–41 | 46–33 | 293–260 | 62–59 |
| 5. | Harijan | – | 48–36 | 171–164 | 56–46 |
| 6. | Literate | 77–17 | 92–32 | 353–96 | 142–59 |
| 7. | Workers | 97–2 | 96–17 | 551–35 | 127–47 |
| 8. | Cuftiuations | 82–1 | 70 | 330–12 | 92–17 |
| 9. | Agricultural Labourers | 4 | 22–14 | 172–23 | 42–27 |
| 10. | Other Workers | 5–1 | 3 – | 14 – – | 7–16 |
| 11. | Unemployed | 95–159 | 108–174 | 617–1047 | 188–369 |

which has filled up 3 km$^2$ area of the lake by the deposit of ash. Shisam and Babool trees have been planted which are in good health. The depth of water in the lake is 5 to 6 metres. The water is dirty and polluted as it comes from the factory. Length of the lake is 3 kms and breadth 150 metres (Fig. 15.22.).

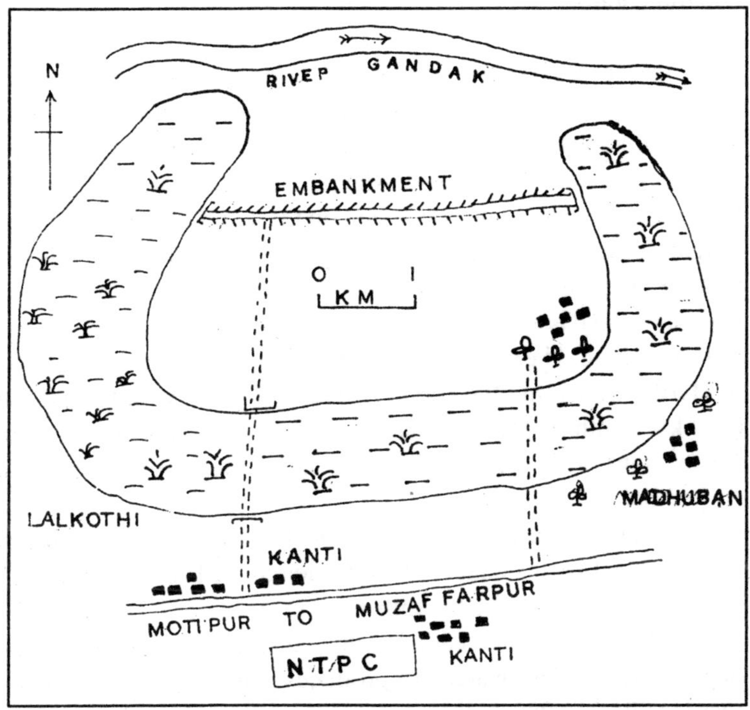


**Fig. 15.22 :** Kanti Wetland (Muzaffarpur)

Among the living creatures found in the lake are fishes, crab, among the fishes Garai 0.50 kg weight, Pothia 50 gram, Jhinga 10 grams, Naini 200 gram, Buari 1.50 kg and Sauri 1 kg. The land is of public and hence it has not been settled to the government. The annual sale of fish is at the tonne of Rs. 10,000. The snails collected is 150 kg, crab 160 kg. which has been used as food and protein supply for the poors.

Among the plants pater and water-hyacinth are important. The water of the lake looks black due to dump of refuse water from the factory but no bad effect is seen on the fishes.

Kanti lake is ultimately connected with the Burhi-Gandak river. Except fish rearing some areas are involved in cultivation of rice. In the western and northern side tube-well irrigation has been found.

**Hardia Chaur**

This has been surveyed on 4.12.94 at about 1 p.m. The water temperature was 24°C. It is located in Sonepur Block of Saran district. Its latitudinal and longitudinal position is 25°10'N and 85°10'E.

It is surrounded by Saraiya, Manpura and Darihara on the north; Hasanpur, Gopalpur and Nayagaon on the south; Darihara, Badua, Magarpal and Shikarpur in the east and Dumri on the west. Amidst Chaur Kankra in the east and Chilme villages in the west are situated. Hardia wetland is approachable after getting from train at Nayagaon railway station. The Gandak river is flowing just one kilometre north of Hardia Chaur and the Ganges river is flowing west to east just 0.75 km south of Hardia Chaur. Hence, Hardia Chaur is full of water right from July to October until the water recedes in November.

The land of this chaur is very productive. Both paddy and wheat are produced in this chaur. The total length of Hardia chaur is 12 km east to west and the breadth is 9 km from north to south. The longitudinal central part has a length of 2 km, width 150 metres and depth 2 metres. This water part produces fishes and the annual out-turn is of Rs.110,000. In the surrounding villages the male literacy is 85 per cent and the female literacy is just 25 per cent. Among these the fishermen are 25 per cent of the total population.

Among the fishes available in Hardia Chaur are Katla, Rehu, Garai, Pothia, Jhinga, Kabai, Bami, Chenga, Bhunna, Tengra, Singhi, Ichhna, Gaichi, etc. Besides, these the other creatures found are earthworm, frog, tortoise snail and crab. The average weight of the fish is 2.50 kg. The crab is of bigger in size and it is sold at the rate of Rs.5 per kg.

Among the local birds Bagula and Pansilli are very common. The weight and price of birds are as follows:

**Table 15.12 :** The Weight and Price of Birds in Hardia Chaur

| *Sl. No.* | *Birds* | *Weight* | *Price in Rs.* |
|---|---|---|---|
| 1. | Gohia | 400 gram | 45 |
| 2. | Dighounch | 500 gram | 25 |
| 3. | Lalsar | 500 gram | 35 |
| 4. | Chaha | 500 gram | 25 |
| 5. | Khokhar | 350 gram | 30 |
| 6. | Dhodhil | 500 gram | 45 |
| 7. | Laklak | 400 gram | 35 |
| 8. | Dumar | 1 kg. | 60 |
| 9. | Saras | 7.8 kg. | — |

*Source :* Available from fieldwork.

Although there are migratory birds coming to our country sometimes in October, November and retires to their original home sometimes in February each year. The people who illegally prey these birds are Nonia and Mallah who reside locally. The vegetations found in Hardia Chaur are Kash Makhana, Banpyaj and Sewar. As the surrounding area is higher in comparison with Hardia Chaur and hence it is not helpful in irrigation. The government has no plan to reclaim Hardia chaur and the tree plantation is not possible as the government land is covered with water. Malaria and Kalajar are common diseases from which the people suffers (Fig.15.23).

**Basman Lake (East Champaran)**

Basman lake is an oxbow lake located about 10 kms. away from Motihari town. It is one of the 41 lakes of Champaran district. It is about 50 km away located on the left side of the Motihari to Patahi road. Basman is loop shaped and the water stretch is very narrow. It has a geographical location of 26° 40'F and 85° E longitude. It is an abandoned former course of the Sikarhara river which was subsequently cut off from the main river when a change of its course took place.

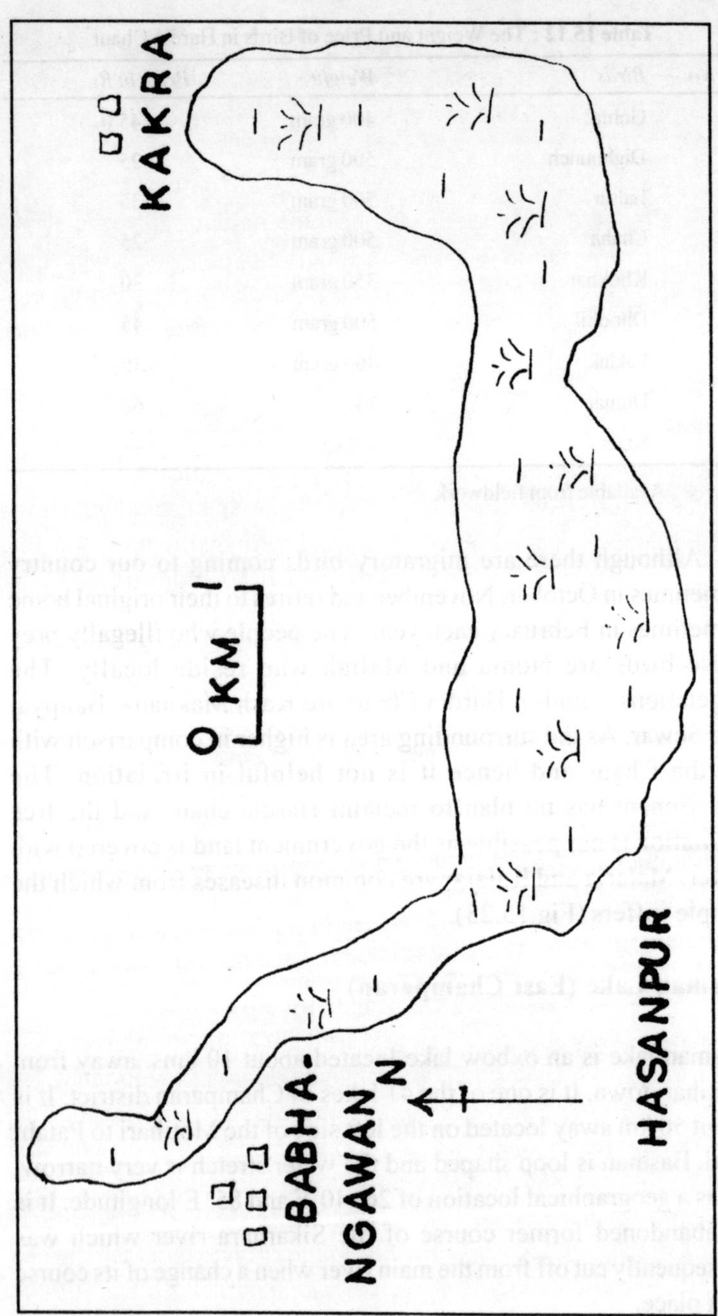


**Fig. 15.23 : Hardia Chaur Wetland (Saran)**

The lake is "U" shaped and perennial with shallow margins. Total water area during the rainy and flood season was about 52 hectare. But in the dry season it become smaller in water area, e.g. 40 hectare. The lake is deep in the central part 7 to 10 metres, but in the summer season it become 5 to 8 metres only. The margin is shallow and fishes are netted from one to two metres deep water. In 1998 there were heavy flood and the whole area of the lake was completely flooded with water. It has caused mass destruction of flora, fauna and the standing crops in the nearby area.

The water from the flooded chaur rushes towards the Suhagman lake. From Suhagman lake water passes into the Dhanauti river and this river meets Sikarhara river again near Mehsi of East Champaran.

The Basman lake is large but smaller than Suhagman lake with Bamboo, Groves, Shisam, etc., on its embankment. Paddy fields are found on all sides of the lake. This lake is regarded less suitable for Pissiculture, than Suhagman lake due to its local and linkage with Sikarhara river. (Fig. 15.24)

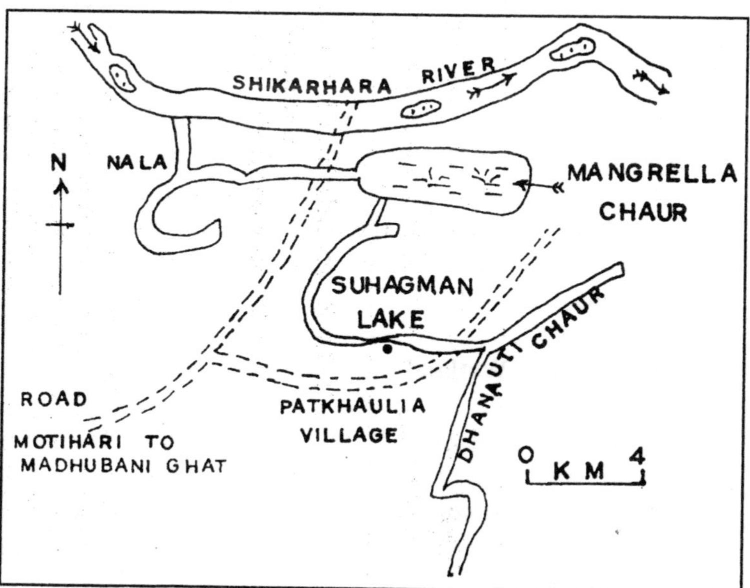


**Fig. 15.24 :** Suhagman and Basman Lake (Champaran)

**Bharthua Chaur (Muzaffarpur)**

Bharthua has been surveyed on 1.2.1996 at 1.05 m and the water temperature was 19°C. The lake area covers the Villages of Kalyanpur, Shankarpur, Kiratpur, Harthua and Besti. It comes under Aurai Block of Muzaffarpur district. The lake is surrounded by Shankarpur in the east, Besti on the west, Benipur on the north and Nayagaon on the south. Most of the villages of the area are surrounded by flood water at least for 10 months in a year. It is situated along Muzaffarpur-Sitamarhi road about 4 kms from Kataundha and 6 kms east of Saidpur. The flood water of this area goes to the Bagmati river on the south. Even at the time of survey about 2 to 3 feet deep water flow has been seen. At the time of flood people of the surrounding area moves on boat.

The water area of Bharthua Chaur is 150 to 200 metres and the depth is one metre. During rainy season the area become 10 km² and the depth is about 2 metres. (Fig. 15.25)

**Creatures**

Among the fishes Buari, Jhinga, Garai, Pothia, Kabai, Phunna and Singhi are important. In November the weight of the fish is around 1.5 to 2 kg. Among the birds Bagula besides snail, crab and bees are found. Some of these are the food for poors and fishermen. The plants of paddy, Sewar, Karmi, Chichore, Motha and varieties of other plants are found.

**Gothra Kanakpur Wetland**

It has been surveyed on 5.5.1995 at 11.00 am. The water temperature was 18°C. It is situated in Thakurganj block of Kishanganj district. It comes in the villages of Bahadurganj and Galgalia. In its south the village of Kanakpur, and north the village of Gothra are located.

This lake could be approachable from Thakurganj in the west at about 3 kms. The length is one kilometre, breadth is 750 metres

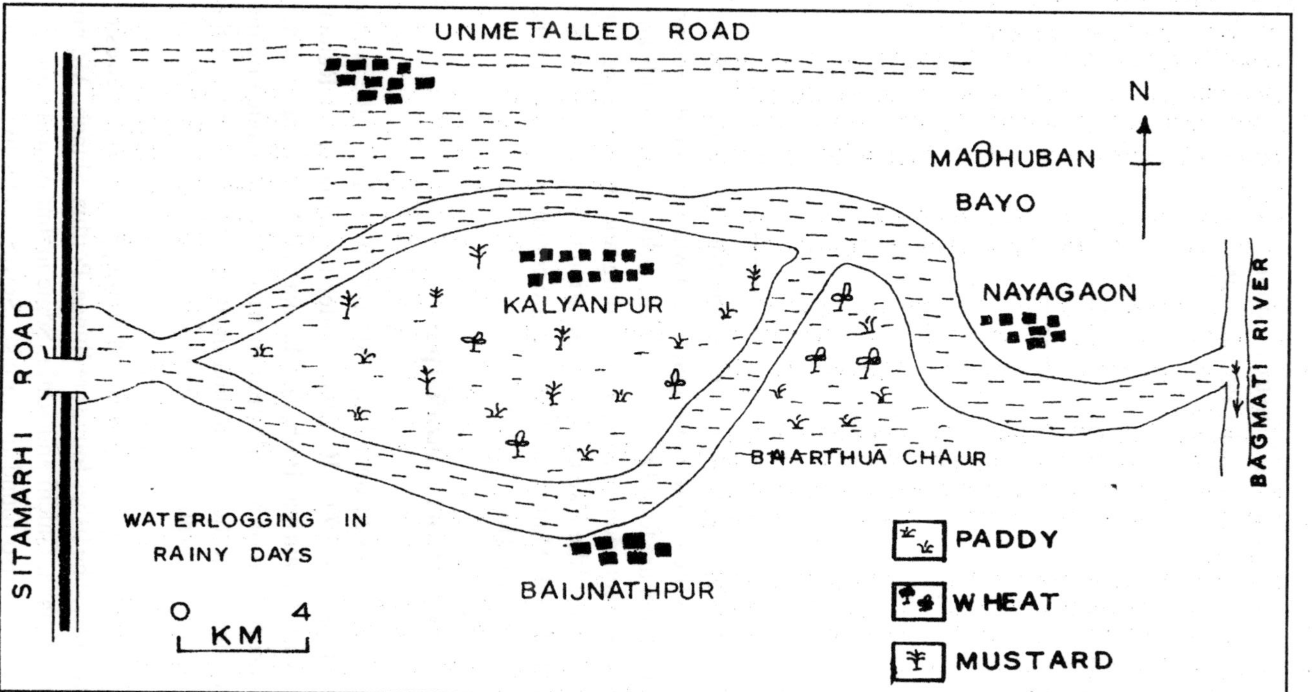


**Fig. 15.25 :** Bharthua Chaur (Muzaffarpur)

and the average depth is 2 metres. Among the water creatures Garai, Jhinga,Singhi, Momri, Pothia, Kabai and silver carp are important. Their weight vary from 1 to 1.5 kg.

**Table 15.13 :** Among the birds the following are important

| *Birds* | *Weight* | *Price in Rs.* |
|---|---|---|
| Duck | 0.50 to 3 kg. | 40 |
| Banmurgi | 0.50 to 1 kg | 40 |
| Chakba | 1 to 2 kg | 40 |
| Lalsar | 0.50 to 1 kg | 60 |
| Dighauch | 0.20 kg | 50 |
| Adhena | 0.30 to 2 kg | 30 |
| Gairi | 1 kg | 45 |
| Dumar | 0.70 kg | 55 |
| Mentha | 1 kg | 65 |

The migratory birds are preyed by the poor and gunned by the rich. So far as the vegetation is concerned water-hyacinth, Sewar, Lotus and pater are found abundantly. The cultivation of paddy and banana has been done in the surrounding area of this lake. On southern side of the lake coconut plantation has been done over 2 hectares of land. Malaria and Kalajar are common diseases of the people of the area (Fig. 15.26).

## Manikaman Wetland (Muzaffarpur)

It has been surveyed on 28.1.1996 at 1.30 p.m. and the water temperature was 19°C. It comes under the villages of Rehua, Mushhari, Bhadauriya, Bajbara, Manika and Narsinghpur under Mushhari Anchal of Muzaffarpur district. It is surrounded by the village Manika in the east, Rehua in the west, Bhadauriya in the north and Muzaffarpur-Samastipur road in the south (Fig. 15.27)

It has an area of 40 hectare on government record. The length is 5 kms, breadth is 750 metres and the depth is 1 to 3 metres of varying order. The fishes found are Jhinga, Porthia, Shinghi, Momri, Kabari, Bhunna, Gaichi and Katla. Some mount of snail, tortoise and crabs are also found in the lake. Sewar, water-hyacinth and

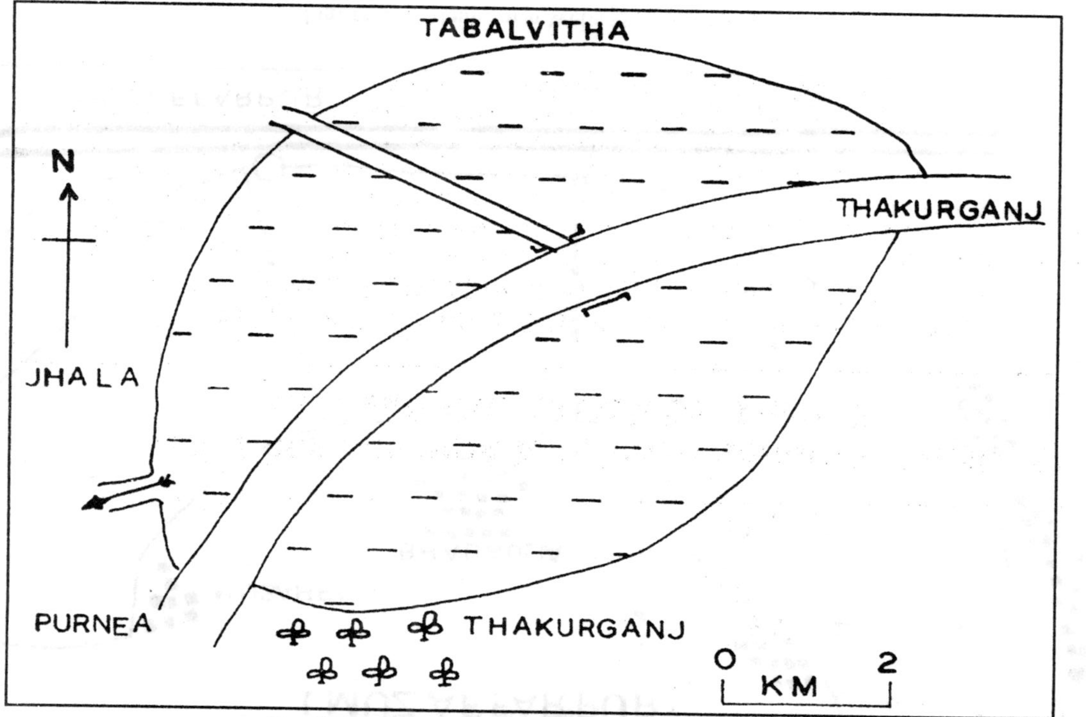


**Fig. 15.26 :** Gothara Kanakpur Wetland (Kishanganj)

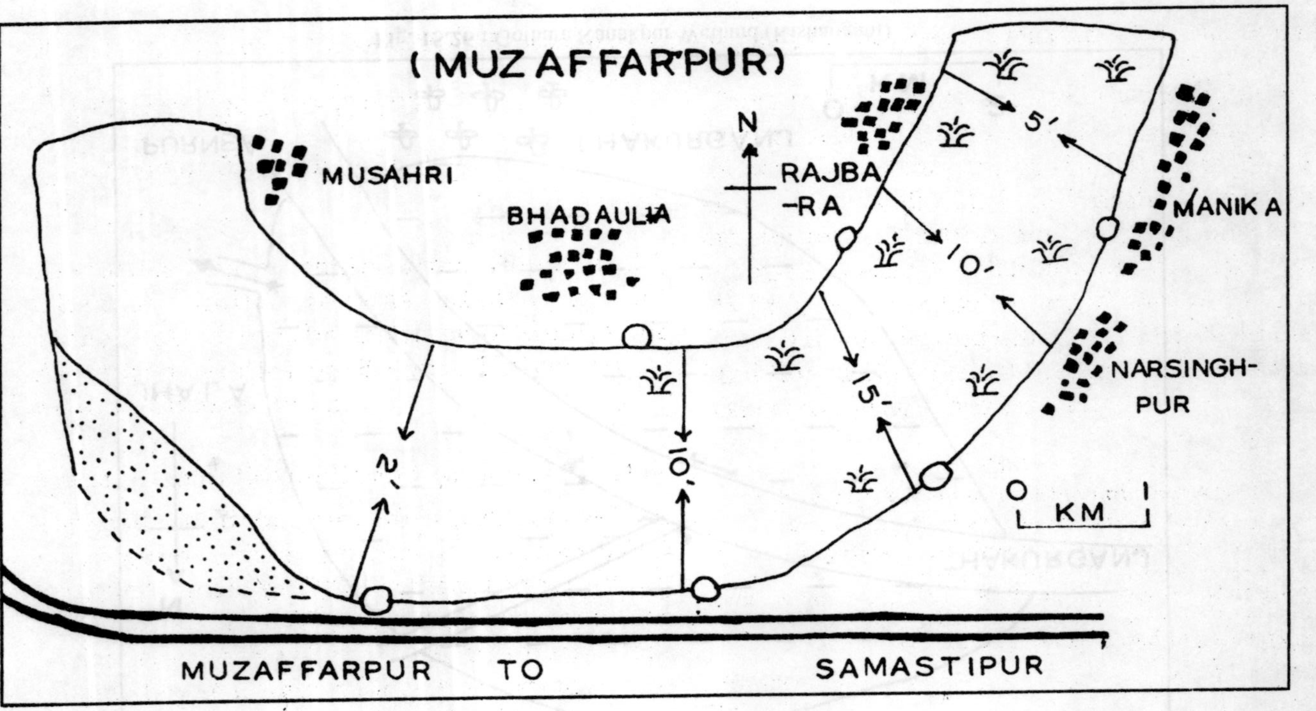


**Fig. 15.27 :** Manikaman Wetland (Muzaffarpur)

Karmi are the vegetation found in the lake. Among the birds Bagula and Pansilli are very common.

The crops produced in the surrounding area of the lake are paddy, wheat, maize, arhar, sweet potato, condiment, mustard, chickpeas and tisi. The flood in the lake damages crops in the surrounding area.

Manikaman helps in irrigation as it keeps the water level high in the tubewell. The impact of fertilizer has no adverse impact on people of the surrounding area. The development of fishing industry is the best utilization of this lake.

**Telia Chaur (Muzaffarpur)**

This chaur has been surveyed on 21.3.1996 at 1 p.m. The water temperature was 35°C. It is located in Sakri-Saraiya Panchayat of Kudhni Block in Muzaffarpur district. Two kilometres south Turki-Vaishali road runs and on north-western corner the flood protection embankment of the Gandak river is located. Here, the water comes from northern side of Nathnagar chaur (Fig. 15.28).

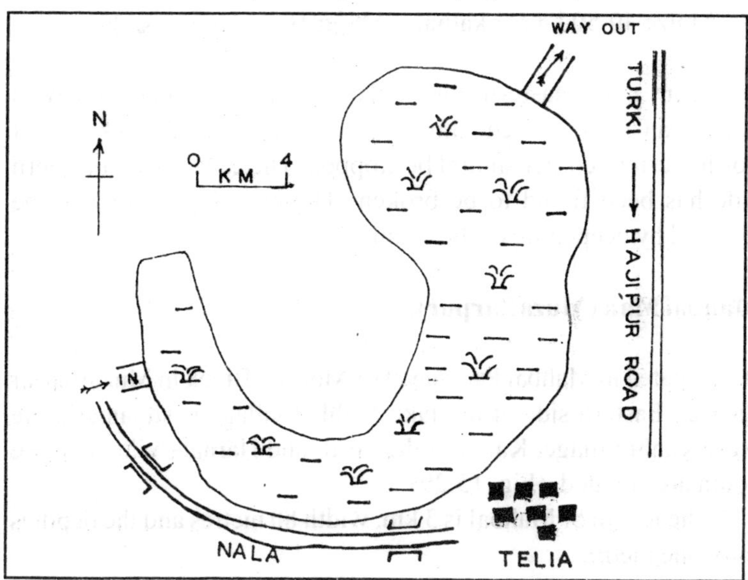


**Fig. 15.28 :** Telia Chaur (Muzaffarpur)

The length of Telia Chaur is 2 km., breadth 600 metres and depth 1 metre only. The fishes found in the lake are Jhinga 5 gram, Pothia 25 gram, Garai 250 gram, Kabai 250 gram, Katla 250 gram and Buari 500 grams. Among the aquatic plants Karmi and Makuna are important.

**Table 15.14 :** The migratory birds coming to Telia Chaur

| *Birds* | *Weight* | *Price in Rs. per bird* |
|---|---|---|
| Lalsar | 500 gram | 50 |
| Dighaunch | 500 gram | 50 |
| Garai | 1 kg. 1.50 kg. | 55 |
| Dumar | 1 kg. - 2 kg. | 50 |
| Adhena | 500 - 750 gram | 45 |

In the surrounding of Telia Chaur the crops produced are:

Paddy 50 kg. per katha, Wheat 30 kg per katha

Maize 40-50 kg per katha, Mung 10-15 kg. per katha

From north-eastern corner Telia Chaur is connected with Kuleshra Chaur. The encoming of water from the Gandak gate of north-western corner should be stopped. The canal in the northern side has been found to be broken. The outgoing water may be allowed by deepening of the channel.

**Mahbal Man (Muzaffarpur)**

It is situated in Mahbal Panchayat of Motipur Block in Muzaffarpur district. Eastern side of the lake Mahbal village is situated in the west Kuahi village, Kania in the north and Harnahi village in the south are situated. (Fig. 15.29)

The length of Mahbal is 3 km, width 80 metres and the depth is only one metre.

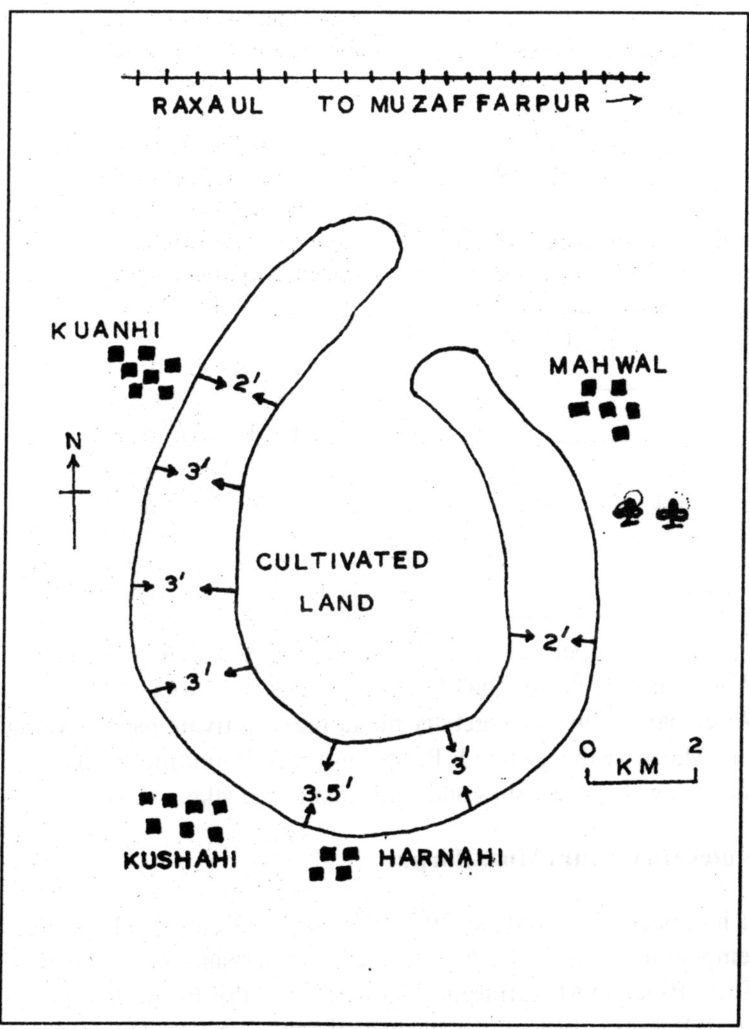


**Fig. 15.29 :** Mahbal Man Wetland (Muzaffarpur)

**Table 15.15 :** Among the creatures found in Mahbal Man

| *Birds* | *Weight (Gram)* |
|---|---|
| Sauri | 1 kg |
| Garai | 250 |
| Gaichi | 250 |
| Chenga | 200 |
| Othia | 30 |
| Ichna | 10 |

Buari and Momri species are found only when flood comes. snail, frog and crabs are found only during the rainy season.

Among the migratory birds coming to the Mahbal-Man are, threatened by the illegal poachers and hence only few birds are coming to this lake.

| *Birds* | *Weight in Gram* | *Price in Rs.* |
|---|---|---|
| Garai | 750-1000 | 50 |
| Dumar | 500-2000 | 60 |
| Gaichi | 1000 | 70 |
| Menth | 500-700 | 60 |
| Chakwa | 500-700 | 40 |

About 60 per cent area of the lake is covered with Karmi. Wattle and daub are found in the surrounding area of the lake. When part of the lakes get dry the farmers cultivate paddy, Mung and Maize in the wetland. People in the surrounding of lake are farmers who raise fishes and Makhana in the lake.

## Kuleshra Chaur (Muzaffarpur)

It has been surveyed on 20.3.1996 at 12 O'clock. The water' temperature was 35°C. It is located in Charkauria Panchayat of Turki Block in Muzaffarpur district. East of this Chaur Hajipur to Muzaffarpur road runs at a distance of one kilometre. The southern side is also traversed by a road going to Saraiya Kothi. On the south-eastern corner Turki railway station is located. In the west Charkauria village and on the north-western corner Telia village is situated (Fig. 15.30).

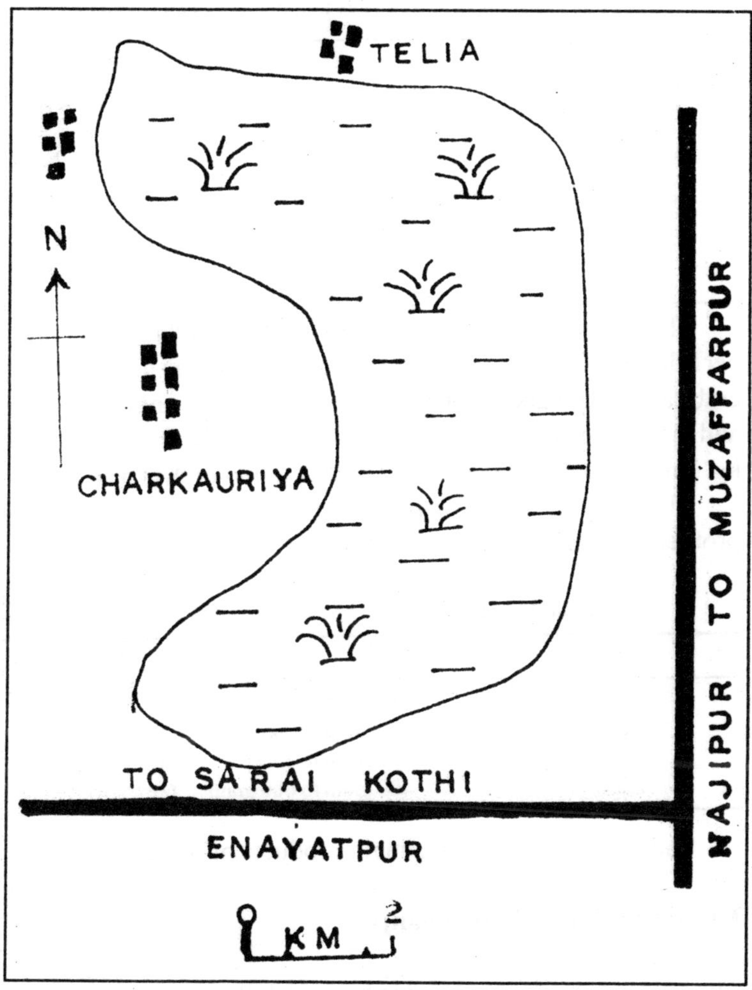


**Fig. 15.30 :** Kuleshra Chaur (Muzaffarpur)

Kuleshra Chaur is well connected with Telia Chaur during the rainy season. The water goes out through a culvert made on the road in the south. Even then water stagnates for a longer period. The length of this chaur is 150 km, breadth 0.50 km. and the depth is one metre.

Among the organisus fishes, snail, crab and situa are found. The following species of fishes are quite often found in this chaur:

**Table 15.16 :** Species of fishes found in Kuleshra Chaur

| *Species* | *Weight in Grams* |
|---|---|
| Garai | 250 |
| Pothia | 25 |
| Tengra | 100 |
| Gainchi | 50-75 |
| Singhi | 100 |
| Kabai | 200 |
| Katla | 200 |

The snails are available from 500 to 600 kg and its price is Rs. 5 per kilogram. Mostly, the hunters of crab use this as food. Similarly crabs are caught about 400 to 500 kgs per year during rainy season and it has been sold in the nearby villages at the rate of Rs. 6 per kg. karmi and daub are the vegetations found in the Chaur land.

The migratory birds come in large number to this lake but the problem of poachers remain lies there.

**Table 15.16a :** Migratory birds of Kuleshra Chaur

| *Birds* | *Weight* | *Price in Rs.* |
|---|---|---|
| Garai | 1 kg.-1.50 kg. | 50 |
| Dumar | 500 gram to 2 kg. | 60 |
| Dighounch | 500 gram to 1 kg. | 60 |
| Lalsar | 400 gram to 600 gram | 60 |

Paddy and fishes are the main products of this chaur.

## Kharudah Lake (Kishanganj)

The Lake Kharudah is located in Kharudah Panchayat of Thakuranj Block in Kishanganj district. In the eastern side of lake Mohantoli Nayabasti and Karuamani in the west, Bhatiabasti in the north and Kharudah village in the south are located. The lake has a distance of 4 km. from Khankhari, 10 km. from Pawakhali and 18 km from Thakurganj. At about 2 km west the Maichi river is flowing from where the water comes to the lake. The soil of this wetland is very fertile which can raise the production of crop three times. (Fig. 15.31)

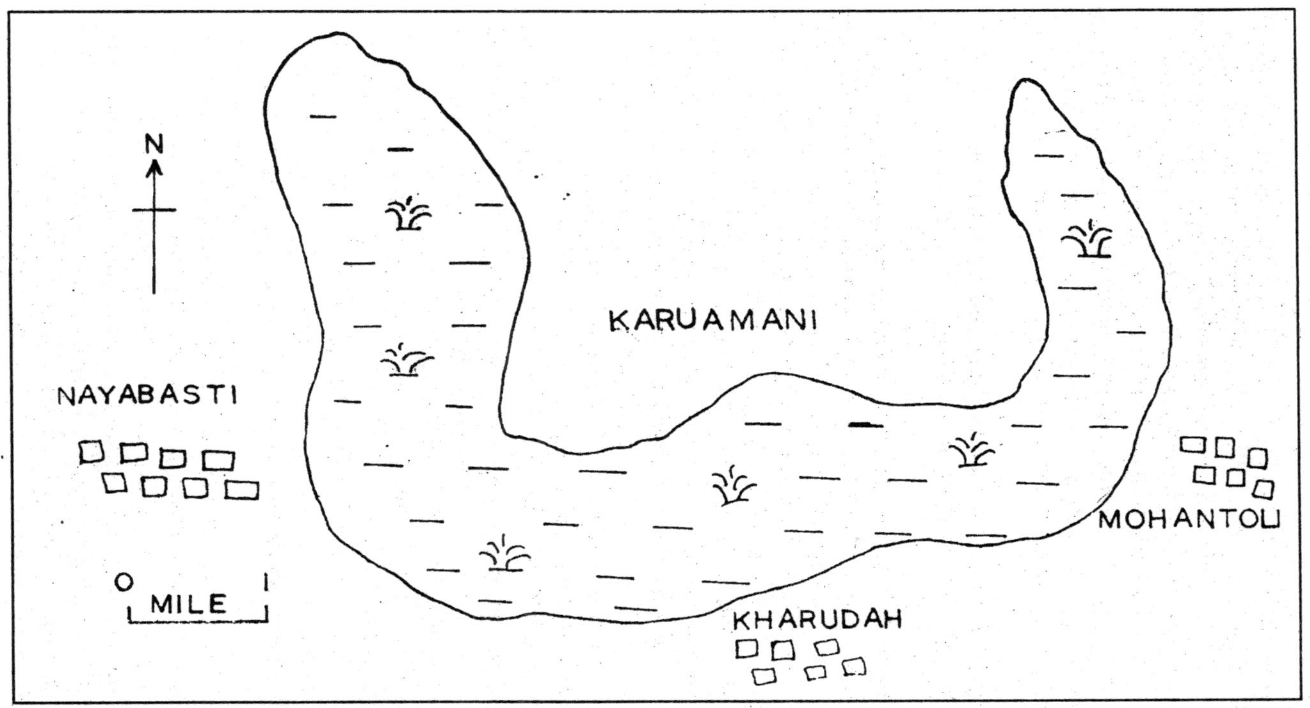


**Fig. 15.31 :** Kharudah Wetland (Kishanganj)

The length of Kharudah is 1.50 km, the width is 70 metres and depth only one metre. Among the species of fishes Singhi, Momri, Garai, Gaichi, Kabai, Ichna, Pothia and Tengra are important. varieties of worms are also found in lake Kharudah. The maximum weight of the fish in November is 250 grams. Although most parts of the lake is covered with water-hyacinth even then the migratory birds use to come to this lake.

**Table 15.17 :** Birds and their weight in Kharudah Lake

| *Birds* | *Weight* |
|---|---|
| Adhena | 500 gram to 2 kilogram |
| Sarali | 500 gram to 1.50 kg |
| Chakba | 1 kg. |
| Dighaunch | 500 gram to 1 kg |
| Lalsar | 1 kg |
| Kasrar | 500 gram |
| Garai | 300 gram to 2 kg |
| Dumar | 500 gram to 2.5 kg. |
| Khesrar | 500 gram to 2.0 kg |
| Mentha | 700 gram to 1.5 kg |
| Ghench | 1 kg. |
| Dhodhil | 500 gram to 2.00 kg. |

Those people in the society who own gun understand the killing of bird as their prestige. Water-hyacinth is the main vegetation found in the region. People in the surrounding area are farmers. Most important product of the lake is fish besides paddy. Malaria and Kalajar are the common diseases found in the area.

## Sowa Lake (Katihar)

Lake Sowa is situated in Nawabganj Panchayat, Manihari Block of Katihar district. On the easternside of lake Sowa Tinkauria, Bangri, Olipur, on the westernside Bolia and Narayanpur. On the northernside Sowapagalbari and on the south Nawabganj are situated. The lake Sowa is situated 10 km. west of Manihari, 20 km. east of Katihar. It is situated just one kilometre from Mahiarpur railway station. Its length is 2 km. width 100 metres and depth 2 metres.

Among the fishes Garai, Kabai, Ichna, Othia, Chenga Buari, and Rehu are important. The weight of the fish vary from 10 gram to 1000 grams. In Sewar lake water-hyacinth and Sewar are the vegetations mainly found along with Chichore. The migatory birds are not common to this lake due to heavy poaching. The availability of fishes is not much and the local fishermen are resort to do the work of labourers.

**Table 15.18 :** The crops grown in the surrounding area of Sowa lake

| *Crops* | *Weight in Man (One Man = 40 kg.)* |
|---|---|
| Garma paddy | 16 to 20 Man per acre |
| Ahani paddy | 8 to 10 Man per acre |
| Wheat | 8 to 10 Man per acre |
| Jute | 8 to 10 Man per acre |
| Mustard | 5.00 Man per acre |
| Tisi | 2.50 Man per acre |
| Groundnut | 4.00 Man per acre |
| Chickpeas | 2.50 Man per acre |
| Gram | 2.50 |
| Khesari | 5.00 |

In the lake the growth of water-hyacinth is so common that it has made the lake unapproachable. Its cleaning is quite essential. Flood is the major problem of the area. Summer paddy gets irrigated with the help of the lake. The impact of chemical fertilizer is not at all seen on the water of the lake. After due cleaning of the lake it could be used of fish rearing and makhana cultivation.

## There is no expected production of Fishes in Purnea

On 18th March 1996, it has been reported from Purnea that due to high demand of fishes, there are lakes of fishes in Purnea. The area is endowed with the biggest river of the Kosi, the Mahananda and the Panar.

Nowadays, this saying is wrong that due to several rivers and wetlands, Purnea has developed fishes where a greater number of work force is dependent on fish catch and the entire economy is dominated by fish. Recently, due to the said attitude of Government slowly and perceptibly the fish culture is diminishing.

According to the available sources each year there is a demand of five crore fish deora from the Government but the Government is giving 90 lakhs which covers, only tanks. Out of these 40 lakhs is coming from the government and 50 lakhs deora from the private fishermen.

The rest 410 deora is coming from West Bengal, whose prices is very high. Hence, when the size of the fishgets is bigger the fisherman have to catch fish in the hands of middlemen coming from West Bengal. They carry export fish in the bigger market of Calcutta, Gauhati, Sikkim, Siliguri and Darjeeling.

The Government of Bihar has been requested to establish mini hatchery but the government is not willing to work on this scheme and hence the problem is still the same.

In the district of Purnea 4592 hectares of land is covered with water out of which 780 hectare come under private tank, 630 hectare government tank and 3182 hectare under rivers. Due to lack of natural gullies the problem of flats is coming large throughout the year which is quite fit for the development of fish culture even then 250 metric tonne dried fishes has been sold to middleman. The annual production of fish in Purnea district is 3500 metric tonne according to a survey done by the Government of Bihar. There are 13750 persons engaged in fishing activities in the district of Purnea along with the lack of government help there migrating to other areas.

In order to develop fishing industry there is a fish farm development agency.

### The Development of Nine Panchayats of Keshariya Block in Champaran is still pending

On 22nd December 1995 it has been reported from Areraj, Champaran that 9 Panchayats of Keshariya wetland blocks are such where developments efforts have never been made by the administrators. These panchayats are named as Jasauli, Bhopatpur, Chandparsa, Bettia Basant, Sarotar, Shamuapur, Huseni and Khajuria panchayats. As these panchayat are flood area surrounded by wetland has neither roads, nor electricity, irrigation and other facilities. In this area only poor backward people are residing specially in Panchayat Jasauli and Sarotal and brick solling roads are not given to this area in Chandparsa, Bettiah Basant, Huseni, Khajuria and Shambhuapur Panchayats. Neither state boring nor canal, electricity and roads have reached.

In all these panchayats due to waterlogging the entire development work is standstill. Under water from Khetarwar Chaur canal has been constructed but due to lowland water never goes outside from Khetar Chaur and hence waterlogging is still continuing over thousands of hectares of land and it has caused substantial damage to standing crops.

**In Barhel and Pataura Lakes of Bhagalpur illegal fishing is continuing**

On 31st December 1995 it has been report from Bhagalpur that in reputed Birds Sanctuary of Barhel and Pataura lake the government official has given illegal permission to the fisherman to catch fishes in these to wetlands. Hundreds of fisherman move around these lakes to catch fish and kill migratory birds coming from distant lands in these two lakes wattle doub have developed besides Jalkhumbhi. The consultant of 'Mandar Nature Club', Sri Arvind Mishra has indicated that in these lakes along with Udhwa wetland of tourist attraction will be provided very soon by cleaning these lakes, along with the provision of cafeteria and the establishment of birds binding station.

Due to quarrying of stones from Mandar Hill the stones are continuously falling in the wetlands besides the falling of trees. In Barhail lakes where the number of birds are always very high is nowadays declined. The main caused is that the fisherman kill migratarge birds and the amount of unwanted vegetation. The canal in between Barhail and Kataura is really very deep but due to unwanted vegetation this canal has been completely filled.

In a raid one wounded bird has been collected from the illegal potcher besides 14 fishing nets have been collected in which fishes and crabs where in a possession to die.

## Development and Beautification of Manjhaul Trough of Begusarai

The development and beautification of Manjhaul trough scheme by the fisheries department is still hanging in balance. In 1995 it has been decided to develop four wetland of Bihar including this one. But due to non-execution the local fishermen and the public are very dissatisfied with the present government. On the other hand, squatter settlements and shops have been constructed illegally by some of the people in order to the moin land as wetland.

During the last two years after filling a big chunks of moin land, bus stand has been developed besides the market committee has also develop a fish and vegetable market on the illegally occupied land. They have also planned to construct cooperative Godaun and Khadi Gramo Udog Commission Office in the same area. For this purpose, they are filling another big chunk of land and the process of the construction has already been started.

Besides this, last year the local shopkeeper residing on the bank of moin and other *Goonda* elements have forcibly occupied and started permanent settlement of this land, so that the wetland area may be completely abolished and these process is going on with the involvement of Govt. officials in committing the Nefarrious Act.

The demarcation of moin area has never been done and no one has tried to remove this illegal occupation. In this surrounding area of bus stand this sort of illegal occupation is still going on and no one is trying to subvert this process.

## Katchudhua Wetland

Katchudhua was surveyed on 4. 1.1995. Its water temperature was 14°C at 11.45 a.m. It is located in Thakurganj Anchal of Kishanganj district. It could be approachable from Thakurganj towards south-east at a distance of 8 km. after traversing on unmetalled road. Katchudhua is surrounded by Hasanpur in the east. Dogachhi in the west, Kuridanga in the north and agricultural land of Hasanpur in the south.

Village Katchudhua is located like an island in the central part of the lake. The island is surrounded by a wide moat which looks like wetland. Its shape is circular. The moat is a protection to the village but it acts as a barrier in outside movement. It does not support 57 families of Mallah who are residing close to Katchudhua.

Its length is 2.5 km., breadth 200 metre and depth 2 metres. But during the winter season its size get reduced and expands enormously during the rainy season. Katchudhua is endowed with Prone, Katla, Rehu, Garai, Pothia, Enabas, Gainchi, Singhi, Bami, Tengra, Momri, Buari and Ichna fishes. Besides, these, Snail, Tortoise, Crab, Frog and varieties of earth worms are also found. Among the birds Salali, Baluhas, Ketna, Jatrasi and Bagula are important. In Katchudhua Echernia are found in huge quantity. At places sewar and lotus are also seen here and there. Occupation of people of the surrounding area are agriculture. Backward class people and tribals are mainly engaged in agricultural occupation. Among the crops grown Banana (1200 quintal per acre) and rice are the important ones. Banana and Ginger are sent to the markets of Calcutta, Dhanbad and Jamshedpur.

Karmi is the main product of Katchudhua, besides fishes and water-hyacinth. The annual revenue comes from this lake is Rs.14000. Irrigation is done through pumping set from this lake.

Cleaning of hyacinth is the only answer for better use of this lake fish production. Bamboo and Banana cultivation have been done on the side of this lake.

## Tengarmari Wetland

Tengarmari wetland is located in Kishanganj Anchal of Kishanganj district. Its latitudinal location is 26°N and longitudinal 88°E. It is surrounded by Bhatiatola in the east, Behrakola in the west, agricultural land on the north and Desitola on the south. Its another name is Tengarmari Dok. Tengarmari is approachable from Kishanganj to Thakurganj road. Through Galgalia road to Tengarmari chauk and 4 kms north from this chauk. The Mahananda river is situated 21 km west of Tengarmari. During the rainy season flood like situation is found over here. Its length is 2.5 km, width 200 metre and depth 2 metre. Among the creatures found in the lake are Ichna, Pothia, Garai, Kabai, Gaichi and Jhinga.Their weight varies from 1 kg to 1.50 kg. Some amount of crab and snails are also found in the lake. So far as the birds are concerned Bagula and Pansilli are important. Among the migratory birds Haril, Garur and Crentch are important. Haril comes in a herd of 100 and more and its weight is 1.50 kg. and more for one bird, Poor cannot prey these birds but only gunmen shot. Haril and Lalsar. Among the plants water-hyacinth, Sewar and lotus flower are important. In the entire lake the rotten detritus of Jalkumbhi is seen. The residents of the locality are cultivators of land who also do the work of fishermen and others.

The crops produced in the lake are Garma paddy, water hyacinth, makhana, fishes and onion during summer. Flood problem is quite common during the rainy season. Singhara and fishes are the common crop of this wetland. The size of fishes is so high in this lake that people are fearful in catching them. The cleaning of Tengarmari is quite essential in order to rearing of fishes and production of summer paddy. The effect of chemical fertilizer is negligible. The annual revenue which the Government earns from this lake is Rs.1500 only. Digging of this lake and Makhana cultivation may be the new hope of this lake. The lake was surveyed on 10.2.95 at 10 a.m. and the water temperature was 18ºC at the time of survey.

**Nardang Wetland**

***Raghopur (Supaul)***

This wetland is situated in Simrahi Panchayat of Raghopur Anchal in Supaul district.

***Location and Extent***

Nardang lake is situated 3 km. west from Birpur-Jihanpur road.

About 2 km North of Nardang lies Berdah, Sutrashahi is located 1 km south, and Pinglash-Chakla 2 km east. The length from west to east is 1 km and the breadth is 500 metre from north to south. During rainy season the size of the lake increases substantially.

### *Origin*

Nardang has been originated due to changing courses of the Kosi river about 50 years ago.

### *Toponyms*

During the historic period people have seen the dynamic faces of the Kosi river near Nardang and hence it is known as Nardang wetland. In the eastern part of Nardang the depth is just one metre while 2 metre in its western part. Nardang is a saucer shapped lake. Several creatures and organisms are found in the lake Nardang which are as follows: Rehu 5 to 6 kg; Katla 2 kg, Buari 4 kg, Singhi 1 kg, Bhaura 200 to 300 gram and Kabra 500 gram. Besides, these Jhinga, Kaua and Pothi are important. Among the snakes Dhoria is commonly found. Some amount of Snail, Situa, Crab, Lizzard, Tortoise and Jonk as earthworms found.

Among the birds found are :

| | | | |
|---|---|---|---|
| Lalsar | 1 to 2 kg. | Karan | 1 to 2 kg |
| Silli | 1/2 to 1 1/2 kg. | Dighaunch | 5 kg. |
| Banmurgi | 1/2 kg. | Bagula | 1 kg |
| Garur | 2 kg. | Dakhar | 3 kg |
| Garmaina | 1/4 kg. | Dhanchaha | 1/4 kg |

The vegetation of Nardang could be divided into two groups:

| *Beneficial Plants* | *Harmful Plants* |
|---|---|
| Makhana<br>Singhara<br>Lotus Flower<br>Koka<br>Purain | Karmi, Dhanuoir,<br>Chilmil, Lock<br>Motha, Sewar<br>Water hyacinth |

**Table 15.19 :** Production of Nardang Wetland

| *Sl. No.* | *Items* | *Weight* |
|---|---|---|
| 1. | Makhana | 1000 Quintal |
| 2. | Singhara | 10 Quintal |
| 3. | Fishes | 100 Quintal |
| 4. | Birds | 200 only |
| 5. | Crab | One Quintal |
| 6. | Tortoise | 30 only |

*Source :* Collected through field work.

In the surrounding area of Nardang lake Rice and Potato are mostly grown. Jute has been produced as a cash crop. Irrigation is done through pumping set from the lake. Most of the people in the surrounding area are either farmers or agricultural labourers as the poors are landless.

There is no effect of chemical fertilizer on water of Nardang lake. The smaller lakes found in the surrounding of Nardang are Milan Mandir tank, Bhular tank and Marshy tank. Linear settlements of semi-scattered type found in the lake side. So far as tile diseases are concerned those who enter into the water of Nardang suffer from skin diseases, snake bite, earthworm bite, and some people also suffer from asthma. The government has installed state boring on the embankment of lake Nardang but unfortunately that is not functioning.

The Machhua society pay annual rent to the individual landowner whose land come under the lake. The people are of the opinion that either it should be completely reclaimed for agricultural purposes or the lake should be digged for rearing of fishes in a better way. The plantation of Shisham and coconut could be done on the surrounding area of Nardang Lake as the land is lying vacant.

## Dighi Wetland (Basantpur) Supaul

The wetland of Dighi has been surveyed by Navin Kumar and Roshan Kumar on 29.10.1994.

### Location and Extent

The Wetland of Dighi is located north of Birpur-Bhimnagar road. It is situated at a distance of 3 km. west of Basantpur Block Development office. Dighi is surrounded by the Kosi College of Birpur in the north Birpur-Bhimnagar road on the south, L.N. Memorial College, Birpur in the east and cultivated land in the west. The length of lake Dighi is 1.25 km. and width is 250 to 500 metres. During rainy season Dighi expands in all directions. Dighi has been formed due to sheet wash erosion of the Kosi river. The local people called lowlying area as Dighi or lake. The depth of this lake is not more than 3 metres.

**Table 15.20 :** The Birds, Plants and Creatures found in Dighi Wetland

| *Birds* | *Plants* | *Other* | *Creatures* |
|---|---|---|---|
| Lalsar | Sewar | Pothi | Tortoise |
| Silli | Daun | Gainchi | Crab |
| Bagula | Jute | Latha | Earthworm |
| Garh Maina | Jalkumbhi | Garai | Frog |
| | Karmi | Saura | |
| | Talha | Buari | Dhorna |

### Benefit

1. It provides fishes to the local people.
2. Bird trapping by some people.

Dighi wetland is harmful for the local people as this is the breading ground of mosquitoes which is the source of diseases like Diahoria, Cholera and Kalazar. In Dighi one can see the flowers of Jalkumbhi, Karmi, Kash and Saina. The Machua society get harassed as they have to pay double taxes one to the government and the other to the private land owners. There is no tree on the side of the lake due to the problem of flood each and every year. Only the plantation on safer high site will solve the problem.

The other smaller wetlands around Dighi are Jichha Tank (6 hectare), Bhairwa, Tank (4.45 hectare) Hazari Tank (4.45 hectare) and Parshali lake (8 hectare). As the upkeep of the lake is not proper hence they are neither suitable for fish catch nor the production of Singhara and Makhana.The people have an opinion that the canal leading to different directions from this lake may open new vistas of crop up production.

**Ruighasa Wetland**

Lake Ruighasa has been surveyed by Kundan Kumar and Ajai Kumar on 27.2.1995 at 11.30 a.m. The water temperature was 20ºC. Lake Ruighasa lies in Thakurganj Block of Kishanganj district. It is surrounded by Kasewar village in the east, Ruighasa village on the west and agricultural land on the northern and southernside. It is located 8 kms east of Thakurganj Block Development office where one can reach on rickshaw. Except few most of the people in the surrounding villages are illiterate (Fig.15.32).

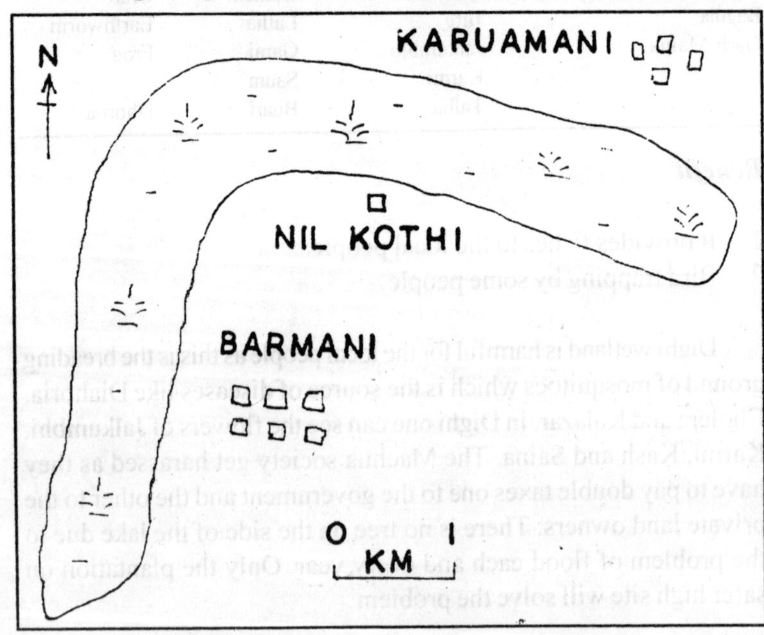


**Fig. 15.32 :** Ruighasa Wetland (Kishanganj)

The fishes found in Ruighasa are Ichna, Pothi, Garai, Kabai, Momri, Gaichi besides snails, situa, crab and earth worm. Only crentch could be seen in Ruighasa, as migratory birds never, visit this lake. The entire lake is full of water-hyacinth. Only Garma paddy is grown on fringe area of the lake. The presence of Jalkhumbi is the only problem of this lake. The lake is not beneficial neither for the Government nor public but only Machhua society gets some benefit out of the fish catch. There is no effect of the input of fertilizer in the fields of surrounding area on the water of this lake.

The residents of surrounding areas wants the digging of this lake for rearing of fishes. The government has no plan for improving the environment of this lake. On the surrounding area of this lake the trees of bamboo, banana, Guava, Sharita, Kadam and Munga are found. Sometimes, the people of the surrounding area suffer from Malaria and Kalajar. No other diseases have been reported.

**Chakmaka Wetland (Barhara) Purnea**

Chakmaka has been originated due to flash flood during the ancient period. Its length is 1 km. and the breadth is 500 metres. Chakmaka expands in all directions during the rainy season. In summer the depth of Chakmaka is only one metre while during the rainy season its depth is more than 2 metres. Step slope could be seen near the sidewall of Chakmaka wetland.

The depth of the lake is less than one metre near the embankment but more than two metres at a distance of 5 metres from the shore line.

The living organisms found in this lake are Snail, Situwa, Tortoise, small fishes, Dhoria snake, Harhara snake, etc. Among the birds Silli and Adhanga are important. Their weight vary from 250 grams to one kg and its price is Rs.100 for one pair.

**Vegetation**

Makhana cultivation is done in Chakmaka. Purain leaves are also found.

***Turbidity***

Turbidity in lake water is found during the rainy season. In all other months the water of lake remains crystal clear. During dry months the water of Chakmaka is used for the purpose of irrigation. But the sucking of water through pumping set is harmful for Makhana cultivation. Rearing of fishes may be more beneficial as the Machhua society feel. With the rotting of Makhana leaves the water creates skin diseases. Jonk is also a problem in sucking the blood of men and the animals. The 'Argh of Sun' and 'Matkore' at the time of marriage help in religious and cultural ceremonies.

Karmi and lotus flower could also be seen in lake Chakmaka. There is a lot of vegetation in this area. Due to lack of river soil erosion is not found in this lake. During this survey Pancham Singh and Parvin Kumar of Orlaha village helped.

### Chauri Wetland (Nauhatta) Supaul District

Chauri Wetland is located in Nauhatta Anchal of Supaul district. It has been surveyed on 21.2.95 by Navin Kumar and Roshan Kumar. Chauri lake is surrounded by Brahampur in the north, Shahidih in the south, Gola in the east and Hempur in the west. The length of Chauri is 1 km and the breadth is 500 metres. The water temperature was 19°C at about 12.30 p.m. This lake has formed due to the breach of the Kosi embankment. This lake formed on 6th September, 1984 in the flash flood.

In Chauri wetland fishes, Doka, Snail, Frog and Snakes are found. Among the fishes Ichna, Pothi and Kabai are important. Some Harijan childrens are catching crab and snail. Among the plants Lakhwa, Sewar, Makhana and Singhara are produced. The soils of this lake are black, sandy, domat and mixed soil. Due to its location on the side of the Kosi river the nature of soil is always changing. This happens due to the brach of embankment. The birds found and their weight could be seen as follows

| *Birds* | *Weight* |
|---|---|
| Garur | 4000 grams |
| Silli | 500 grams |
| Lalsar | 750 grams |
| Water crow | 1000 grams |
| Duck | 1500 grams |
| Adhanga | 500 grams |
| Bagula | 250 grams |

Near the surrounding area of Chauri lake Garma paddy could be seen besides Makhana and Lakhwa plant. Fishermen are catching the fishes and selling them in the nearby towns and villages. Due to the rotten leaves of Makhana the turbidity is high in the water. With the input of chemical fertilizer the small fishes and frogs die in the lake. In order to check soil erosion specially at the time of flood the afforestation is quite essential. People near the wetlands are of religious mentality. Canal bridge and metalled road are more essential in this water ravaged area. It has been realised that the flesh flood of 1984 has filled some of the bigger wetlands of Nauhatta anchal e.g. Bora Chaur Brahman Toli, English Par and Moradpur. In central part of the lake of Chauri the production of Makhana, Singhara and fishes are done by the people of Machhua society.

The smaller wetlands found in the surrounding of Chauri lake are Bhelahi, Bora Chaur, Sagarmapar and Mohanpur. Irrigation is done with the help of pumping set from the Chauri lake.

## Bengadhasan Wetland (Pipra) Supaul

Lake Bengadhasan originated with the help of Tilaboi and Parbane rivers. Now those two have separated their way due to the erosional process. The length of this lake is 2 km. and the width is 250 metres. The depth of 1.50 to 2.00 metres. Bengadhasan spreads far and wide over the plain land.

Birds and their Weight

| *Birds* | *Weight* |
|---|---|
| Adhanga | 500 grams |
| Silli | 250 grams |
| Lalsar | 500 grams |
| Duck | 1000 grams |
| Pan Silli | 150 grams |

In Bengadhasan the soil is sandy. Except rainy season the water is crystal clear throughout the year. At a distance of 3 meters the depth of water is one metre and at a distance of 12 metres from the shoreline the depth of water is 3 metres.

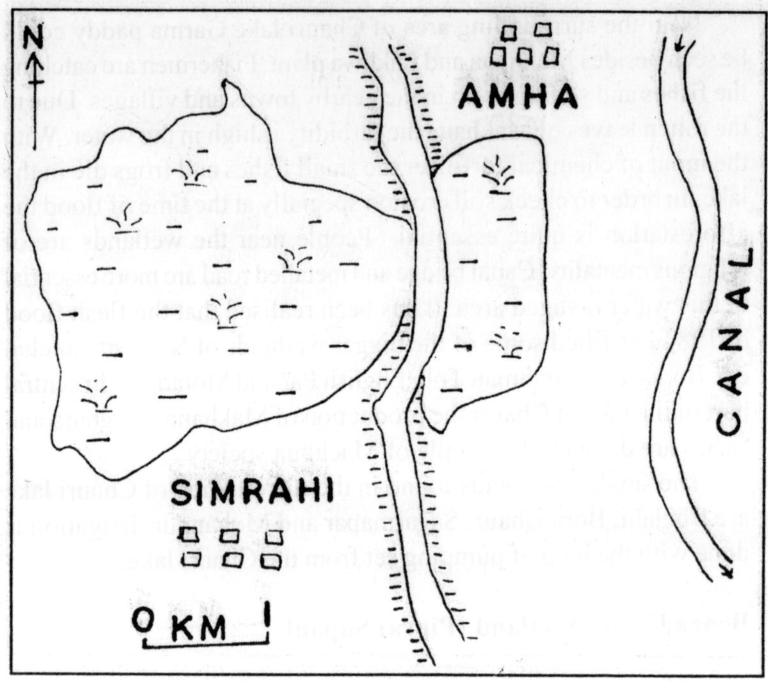


**Fig. 15.33 :** Bengadhasan Wetland (Supaul)

The creatures found in Bengadhasan lake is snail, tortoise, situa, smaller fishes, Phorna snake and Adhpar snake. The plants found on the water of the lake is Karmi, Sewar, Jalkumbhi and others. Although wetland known as Jhanjhatia Mahal but in case of Bengadhasan people quarrel only for the fishes. It is a place for taking bath of animals besides the production of Makhana, fishes and Purain leaves which have been widely used at the time of marriage. Sharadha and other festivals for holding the ceremony of feast to the villagers. But sometimes the villagers are also fighting for the fish catch, collection of Makhana, Purain leaves and lifting of water for irrigation from the pumping set. The input of fertilizers in the field of surrounding area has no impact on water of the lake. The Machhua society is of the opinion that Bengadhasan should be settled with them so that better planning measures could be adopted by the society. This lake has shoothing effect during the summer season on the surrounding area. It keeps the local environment cool. Bengadhasan has formed due to changing courses of the Kosi at the time of flash flood. People wants the construction of bridges and canal on the side of Bengadhasan lake. Flood is the annual problem of this area. The smaller wetlands found around the Bengadhasan lake are : (a) Khariari chaur, (b) Amha chaur and (c) Laipur chaur. (Fig. 15.33). The water temperature was 20°C at 2.30 p.m. on 25.2.1995.

**Sitla Wetland (Kochadhamin) Kishanganj District**

This lake has been surveyed on 30.12.1994 at 11.00 am. The water temperature was 19.50 °C. It is located in Kochadhamin Anchal of Kishanganj district. It may be reached through Kishanganj-Jokihat road at a distance of 40 km.

Lake Sitla is surrounded by Sakitya Bishanpur in the north Andhasur and Surang in the south, Chanpatia in the west and Tangi and Bahakole in the east. Each and every year it produces 250 to 300 quintals of Makhana Guri.

Its length is 750 metres, width 150 metres and depth more than one metre. It expands substantially in all directions especially the during rainy season.

Among the living organisms found in the lake are Prawn, Anahas, Garai, Gothia, Singhi, Gainchi, Bami, Mangur, Burari, Ichna and others. Besides these crabs, snail, frogs and snakes are also found. Among the birds Silli and Bagula are seen. Migratory birds do not visit lake Sitla. Among the vegetation Jalkhumbhi, Sewar, Ghoghua and lotus are important. As the Makhana cultivation is going on in lake Sitla and hence other types of plants are taken out. In the surrounding area mostly agriculturalist reside and the Mallah people are engaged in the cultivation of Makhana. During leisure hour they use to catch fish. Most of the fishermen are poor as this business is not lucrative.

So far as the pollution of lake water is concerned the rotten parts of Jalkumbhi, Makhana and Sewar make the water dirty. During rainy season the water is turbid otherwise it is crystal clear throughout the year. The annual production of Makhana Guri is 250 to 400 quintal. With the input of Jiora the production of fishes is also of the same amount. In the surrounding area of this lake the crops produced are paddy both summer and Bhadai besides wheat, Jute and Tori (Mustard). Sitla lake does not create any problem for the local people.

Lake Sitla provides benefit of Revenue from Makhana Guri and fishes. It gives employment to the local people. Each year it earns a revenue of Rs.52,000. Sitla help in the irrigation of rice fields located in the surrounding area. In order to take more production cowdung and lime are useful for both. Makhana cultivation and fish production as they keep the water clean and productive. The cultivation of Makhana and input of Jiora of fishes is the best utilization of this lake. The protection of the Government in terms of supply of capital as loan for the timely purchase of Jiora and input of Makhana as the local. Mallah are very poor. Due to lack of capital the Machhua Society forced to sell the Makhana Guri in the local market, where the good price cannot be fetched. Second thing is that local influential people irrigate their summer paddy out of the lake water instead of pumping and boring which create problem for the survival of Makhana plant, because without sufficient water the cultivation of Makhana cannot be thought off.

The images of Goddess Kali emersed in the lake. It also help in *Chhat* festival, Sama-chakewa, worship of Kamla Devi, emersion of the idols of Durga and some sort of marriage ceremony took place along the shore of lake Sitla.

The other smaller wetlands connected with the lake Sitla are : (a) Deramari (8 hectare) and (b) Kachan (4 hecrate)

These wetlands are also used for Makhana cultivation only poor menials are living on the side of lake Sitala. The real benefit has been accrued by the middlemen who collects the entire produce of Makhana and fishes out of this lake.

**Dahichal Wetland (Kishanganj District)**

Dahichal Chaur has been surveyed on 22.12.1994 at 11.45 a.m. The water temperature was 19°C. Dahichal is located in Mediadangi Anchal of Kishanganj district. In order to reach this wetland one has to get down at Panjipara railway station of west Bengal from where one has to travel 7 km. west on Kishanganj-Anandnagar road. Dahichal is located 10 km from Tengarmri Chauk, 8 km from Kishanganj, 16 km from Belwa and 4 km from Bihar Security Force camp of Shantinagar.

The surrounding villages of Dahichal Chaur are Piyankuri and Sat in the north, Bhatur in the south. Panjiwara, Dalbasti and Patharbasti in the east and Satkhamhar and Chauandi in the west.

The rural settlements which come under the influence of Dahichal chau, are Bhatur, Satkhamhar, Piyankuri, Singhia, Gwaltoli, Gharghagha, Lohadenga, Chauandi and Bagh Mohar, etc. in Bihar and Panjipara, Haldibita and Banbati in West Bengal.

The length of Dahichal Chaur is 4 km, width 3 km, and depth one metre. It expands its dimensions at the time of flood in rainy season. The living organisms found in Dahichal Chaur are Pothia, Garai, Mangur, Kabai, Jhinga, Singhi, Crab, Snail, Tortoise, Earthworm, Frog, Bagula and Pansilli. Among the migratory birds Rajhans, Garur and varieties of cranes are important. Unfortunately, people kill Rajhans indiscriminately.

The plants of Jalkhumbhi, Sewar, Dhamon to (Marer) and lotus plants are found in the lake. The Harijan and Mallah people of the locality are engaged in fishing and do the work of agricultural labourers. The paddy straw left after harvest, Marer and the rotten parts of Jalkhumbhi are the pollutants of Dahichal chaur. Era and Bankhu varieties of paddy are produced on the side of lake. These varieties have a characteristics that with the rise of water level the stem of paddy grow quickly to cover up the rising trends of water level. This happens especially during the rainy season and at the time of flood. On Jheel land the crops get damaged during the rainy season. But even then farmers have to pay land rent to the government. Only some amount of fishes are available to the Mallah and Harijans and hence they are poor. As the land is slopy and hence irrigation is not possible with Dahichal Chaur. The farmers have to depend on private set. The input of chemical fertilizers on the land of surrounding area has no impact on water of the lake. The people of Machhua Society also want to do agricultural activities as the business of fish catch is not so remunerative. People want reclamation of the whole land for the extension of agriculture. The water of this lake may be taken out to the Mahananda river just located at a distance of 1500 metres west in between Bhatur and Satkhambar chaur. Water area may be left in one corner of the chaur for the purpose of fishing. People of the surrounding area suffer from Malaria, Cholera and Kalazar diseases due to presence of stagnant water around them.

The local people get harassed due to the presence of stagnant water for a longer period. The poverty is looming large. Hence, the agricultural labourers seasonally migrate to Delhi, Punjab, Haryana and the tea gardens of Assam to earn their livelihood. In case the capital is arranged they may be a successful farmer and they may also arrest the tendency of seasonal migration to the distant lands.

## Lake Ghogha (Kishanganj District)

The wetland of Ghogha Beel is located in Singhia Kulmani Panchayat of Kishangarij Anchal and Kishanganj district. It has been surveyed on 25.12.94 at 12.45 a.m. The water temperature was 20.75°C. It is located in village Gwaltoli. Its latitudinal position is 26°N and longitudinal 88°E. Ghogha Beel may be approachable from Panjipara of West Bengal about 6 km west of Kishanganj-Azadnagar road, 8 km from Kishanganj, and 14 km. from Tengarmari Chauk, 12 km from Belwa and 6 km. from Shantinagar BSF camp.

The Lake Ghogha Beel is surrounded by, Gwaltoli in the east; Satghati, Chauandi in the west, Kulamani and Tekna in the north and Piyankuri in the south. Its length is 2.5 km., width 200 metres and depth one metre. It expand in all direction during the rainy season. The living creature found in the lake Ghogha are as follows:

Pothi, Prawn, Garai, Momri, Kabai, Buari and Ichna besides Snails, Tortoise, Earthworn, Frog and Crab. Among the birds Bagula, Duck and Pan-Silli are important. Among the migratory birds Rajhans, Garur, Saras come in the month of October and retires in February and March. The plants of Ghogha Beel are Jalkhumbhi, Lotus, Seinar, Bhent and Motha.

The local people are either agriculturist or fishermen. Rotten parts of Jalkhumbhi make the water filthy but red lotus flower seen here and there amidst lake. The lake has been used for the production of rice, the fishes and yellow maize in the fringe area as summer crop. The huge expense of Jalkhumbhi is only problem of this lake. During rainy season the road link, between Piyankuri and Satghati breaks.

**Finglas Wetland, Raghopur Anchal (Supaul District)**

Lake Finglas in located in Finglas Panchayat of Raghopur Anchal in Supaul District. It has been surveyed by Navin Kumar and Roshan Kumar on 1.11.1994. Finglas lies 3 km. north of Raghopur and east of Bihpur-Birpur road. Its length is 1.5 km from west to east and its breadth is 500 to 1000 metres at places. Finglas is surrounded by Motipur in the north, Parsarma in the south. Imamganj in the east and Bihpur-Birpur road in the west. It expands in areal extent all directions during the rainy season.

The depth of water in Finglas varies from one to two metres. Among the living creatures found in the lake are Pothi, Prawn, Kabai, Katla, Garai, Buari, Rehu and Saura. Besides fishes tortoise, Jonk, Crab, Snail, Dhorna snake and Frogs are important. Among the birds Silli, Lalsar, Karan, Bagula, Garur and Dhanchaha are important.

Makhana the commercial crop available from Finglas. Fishermen are catching the varieties of fishes. People get attracted towards Purain leaves for feast specially on the occasion of Saradh Ceremony, marriage and upnain. The grasses are used as fodder to the animals.

The presence of plants like Chamarhara, Chilmil, Karmi and Jalkhumbhi are harmful for rearing fishes and in the production of Makhana and rice. The smaller lakes found near Finglas are as follows :

(a) Mandal Tank 2 hectare,
(b) Bhular Tank I hectare,
(c) Ganpat Tank 2 hectare, and
(d) Marar Tank 3 hectare

**Table 15.21** : Plants found in Lake Finglas

| Plant | Uses |
|---|---|
| (a) Karmi | Sag |
| (b) Chamarhara | Filthy Plant |
| (c) Sewar | Sort of Green Manure |
| (d) Purain | Leaves for Feast |
| (e) Lotus | Flower |
| (f) Kaka | Flower |
| (g) Makhana | Makhana Guri Source |
| (h) Singhara | Water Fruit |
| (i) Chilmil | Grass |
| (j) Bairi | Grass |
| (k) Doti | Grass |
| (1) Jalkumbhi | Source of Green Manure |

*Source :* Collected from Field Study.

The use of chemical fertilizers in the fields of surrounding area of Finglas lake is harmful for fishes and tortoise. As the tortoise are rarely seen now and the fish production, has declined substantially. The fishes are catched locally by the farmers and hençe middlemen are very active. The Machhua Society wants that the government should settle Finglas to the Machhua society. Flood is an annual feature specially during the rainy season, The annual fish production is 3000 quintal, Makhana 2000 quintal, birds 500 and Singhara 5 quintal only.

## Banbhag Wetland, Krityanandnagar (Purnea)

Banbhag has been surveyed on 3.01.1996 located in Chunapur Panchayat of Krityanandnagar in Purnea district. It is situated along Barhara on Dhamdaha road . It is 8 km. from Purnea in the village of Baribhag. Banbhag is surrounded by Chaur land in the west, railway line in the east, Adampur in the north, and Madhubani Gramghat in the south. The road going from Purnea to Barhara and Banmankhi leads to Banbhag lake. The water of Banbhag is not crystal clear but is turbid in nature. Length of the lake is 5 kilometre, width 500 metres and the depth varies from half metre on the shore to 2 metres in the central part of the lake. During flood season the lake Banbhag expands in all directions.

The creatures found in the lake are fishes, tortoise, Bagula, and Garur. Among fishes some of the important one's are Katla, Pothi, Buari, Rehu and Ichna. Among the plants Jalkhumbhi and Narkat are important. Fishermans of the locality are engaged in fish catch. The rotten parts of Jalkhumbhi is the main pollutant of the lake. The stagnation of water in the lake, the problem of flood and excessive growth of Jalkhumbhi are some of the major problems which the lake is facing. Without cleaning Jalkhumbhi neither fish production nor Makhana cultivation are possible. In this lake the production of rice is considered beneficial in place of fish rearing. With the use of chemical fertilizer the fishes die. Without cleaning the plants of this lake and input of Jiora along with cowdung and lime the better production is not possible.

## Sora Wetland

### *Purnea City (Purnea District)*

It has been surveyed on 4.2.1996. Sora lake is located in Sora village of Purnea city anchal in Purnea district. It is surrounded by Sora village in the east, Rambag chaur in the west, Sora chaur in the north and Manihari river in the south. One has to travel 10 km east of Purnea in order to reach this lake. Water of the lake is crystal clear. Goddess temple and Manokamna Goddess temple are located on the side of lake Sora. Its length is 5 kilometre, width 800 metre and depth 3 metre. During rainy season it expands in all directions.

Among the creatures found in Sora Wetland are Rehu, Katla and Ichna fishes besides Snail, Situa, Crab and Bagula. Chaha bird could be seen in December and January just after the harvest of paddy from the field. Jalkhumbhi and Karmi are found abundantly besides their rotten parts, which have polluted the water severely.

The polluted water is harmful for the animals which drinks it. Stagnation of water for a longer period obstructs timely transplantation of paddy over a vast chunk of land. The tal lands help in Jute cultivation and irrigation of rice field through pumping set. After flood most of the water receeds through the Manihari river. This trend of flow of water should be checked in order to use the available water of the wetland in a much better way. Those who takes regular bath in Sora wetland develop skin diseases like itching and burning which are the cause of polluted water of the lake. The temples of Push Devi and Kali are situated on the embankment of lake Sora.

**Koshwan Jalkar, Manihari Anchal (Katihar District)**

Koshwan Jalkar has been surveyed on 20.2.1995 at 10.30 a.m. The water temperature of the wetland was 18°C. Koshwan Jalkar is located in Maheshpur Panchayat of Manihari Anchal in Katihar district. Koshwan Jalkar is surrounded by the village Mahiyarpur in the east, Banipur Brahmantola in the west, Golaghat in the north and Dilarpur village in the south. One can reach Koshwan Jalkar just 4 km west of Manihari Block Development Office. Just 4 km. west of Koshwan lies the Kosi river and 2 km south flows the Ganga river. The length of Koshwan Jalkar is 2.50 km., width 500 metres and the depth is just 3 metres. It expands in all directions in the rainy season.

Among the fishes Katla, Rehu, Singhi, Pothia, Kabal, Momri, Gainchi, Rewa, Garai, Ichna, Kauwa varieties are most important. So far as the birds are concerned Bagula, Silli, Lalsar and Dighaunch come in the months of September and October and retires to their original place of living in the months of February and March. They consider these wetlands as breeding ground but due to disturbance created by the poachers most of the birds just feel sorry by coming to our wetland. The plants found in the Koshwan Jalkar are Pateba, Pokhra, Rossa, Jalkumbhi and Sewar are important. Karmi is also found on embankment of the lake. These plants are harmful for the growth of fishes and other utilization of the wetland. About 40 per cent part of the lake is full of Jalkumbhi and shore areas with Karmi and hence only 50 per cent parts of the lake is suitable for the rearing of fishes. The fishermen always struggle with the wide spread of Jalkumbhi. The Machhua society purchased Koshwan

Jalkar for Rs. 22,551 in 1995. About 500 fishermen are engaged in catching the fish. As Koshwan Jalkar is always full of water and hence it gives sustenance to the local people without break. Koshwan always help in the irrigation of rice fields through pumping set. The Koshwan wetland has religious significance also as the emersion of the idols of Durga, Kali, Bihula, Sama-Chakewa and the festival of *Chhat* and marriage ceremonies took place along the side of wetlands.

## Wetlands of Vaishali District

There are several wetlands in the district of Vaishali. Baraila is the largest one whose length is 14 kms and breadth is 12 kms. It comprises several anchals in its fold.

## Berain Wetland

Second is the Berain Wetland. It has an area of 300 hectares. It covers the anchals of Mahua, Rajapaker, Hajipur, Goraul and Lalganj. Berain is located in a triangular belt of Hajipur, Muzaffarpur and Mahua road. Due to heavy poaching birds are rarely seen here and the water is found throughout the year. The depth of the water area is not more than 3 metres (Fig. 15.34).

The third wetland in Vaishali is Batra having an area of 200 hectares in the Anchals of Mahua and Goraul. The present excavation site of Vaishali lies in low lying area specially on the southern side near Pushkarni and Baitarni lakes. It has been observed that in the southernside rice fields, tanks and a vast chaur could be seen in between Garh site and Bania Basardh village (Fig. 15.35).

## Baraila Tal

The lake Baraila is the only lake in Vaishali district. It has immense ecological and religious significance. It attracts a large number of devotees and religiously, inclined people. On the other, it holds great attraction for millions of migratory birds who come here from distant regions in the winter season. However, encroachment by the local

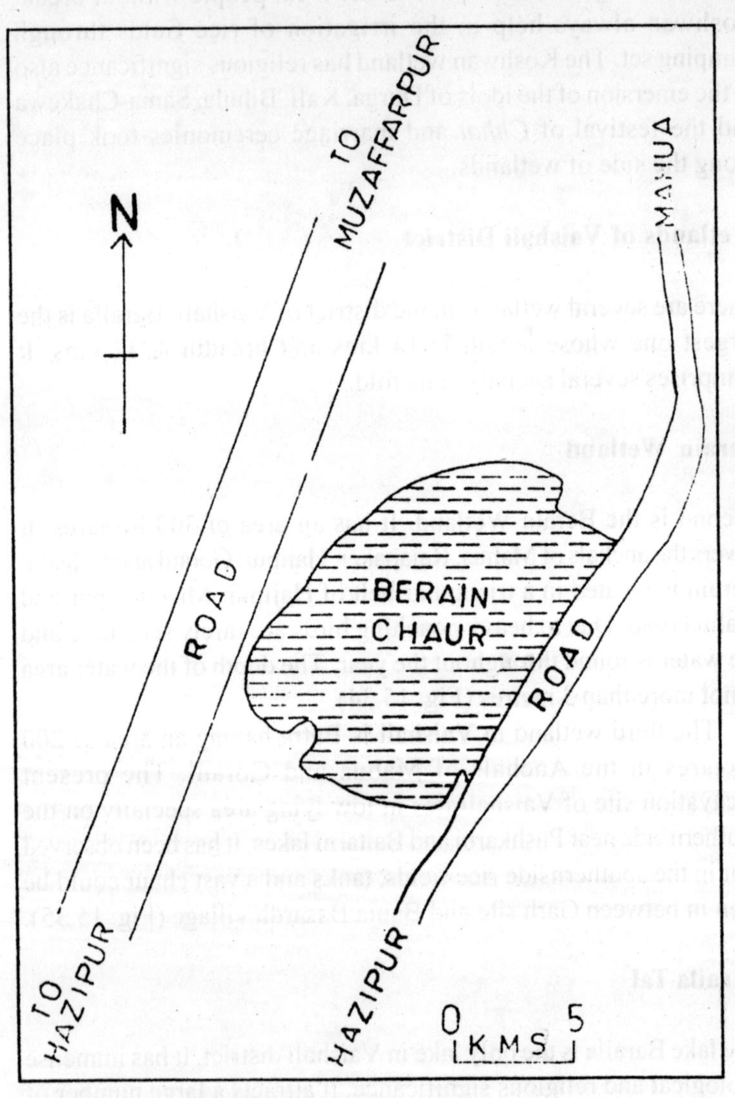


**Fig. 15.34 : Berain Wetland (Vaishali District)**

people in the catchment areas is seriously threatening the very existence of this natural bird sanctuary calling for some serious efforts on the part of the people to save the lake. (Fig.15.35).

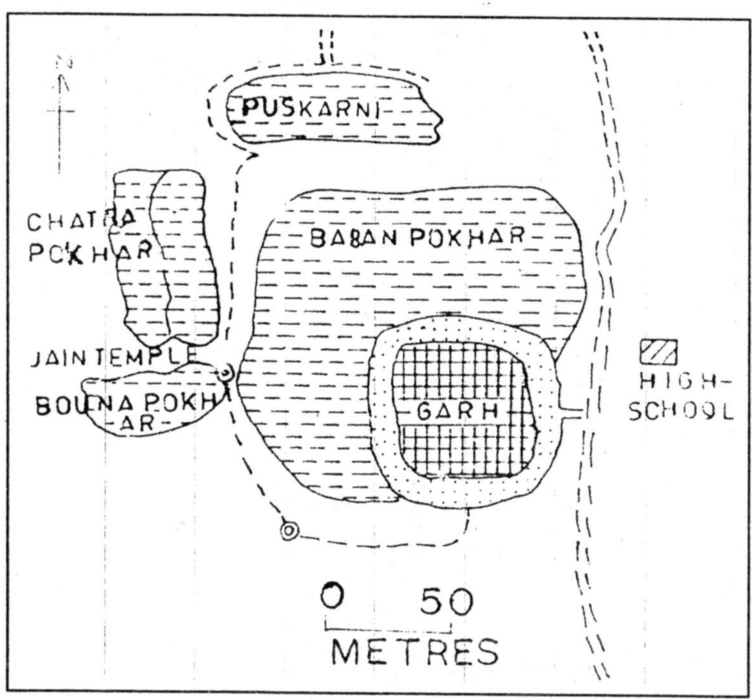


**Fig. 15.35 :** Wetlands near Vaishali Excavation Site

Located in Jandaha Block of Vaishali district about 35 km. north-east of Hajipur town. It starts from Loma-Bijhrauli village. The lake covers and parts of many villages in Vaishali and Samastipur districts. Originally, the Baraila lake was a vast piece of wetland covered with water. The construction of railway tracks from Hajipur to Bachhwara and formation off roadways, in the early 20th century, changed its status says Mr. A.K. Mishra, Head of the Department of Zoology for the betterment of local environment. On the side of Burhi-Gandak river several oxbow lakes are found near meandering channels making the different stages of the formation of wetlands (Fig. 15.36).

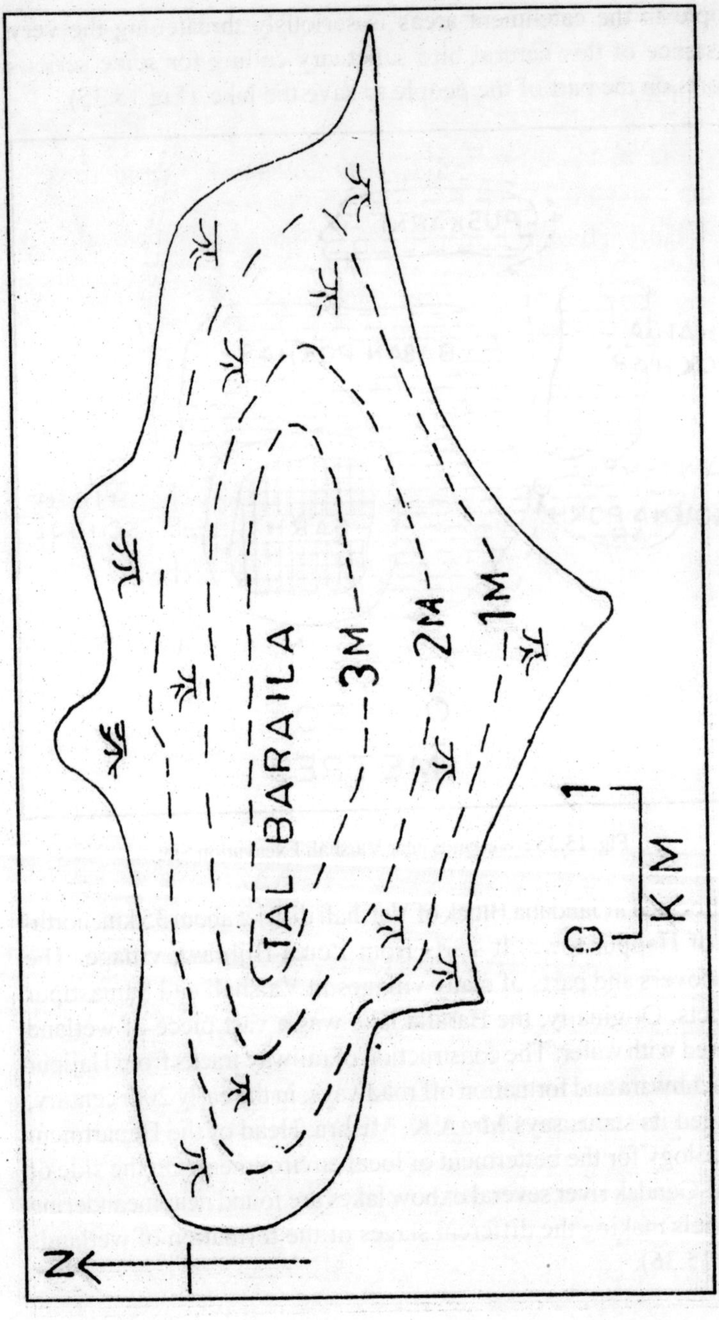

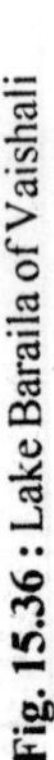


**Fig. 15.36 : Lake Baraila of Vaishali**

**Dhima-Makhnaha (Purnea)**

This lake has been surveyed on 31.1.1996 to 1.2.1996 by D.N. Gupta and Anand Shankar. It covers the villages like Dhima, Makhnaha, Kaji, Hridayanagar and Dharhara. This wetland comes under Banmankhi Anchal of Purnea district. The wetland is surrounded by Dhima Harijan Tola in the east, Dharhara village in the west, Dhima-Makhnaha chaur in the north and Dhima village in the south (Fig.15.37).

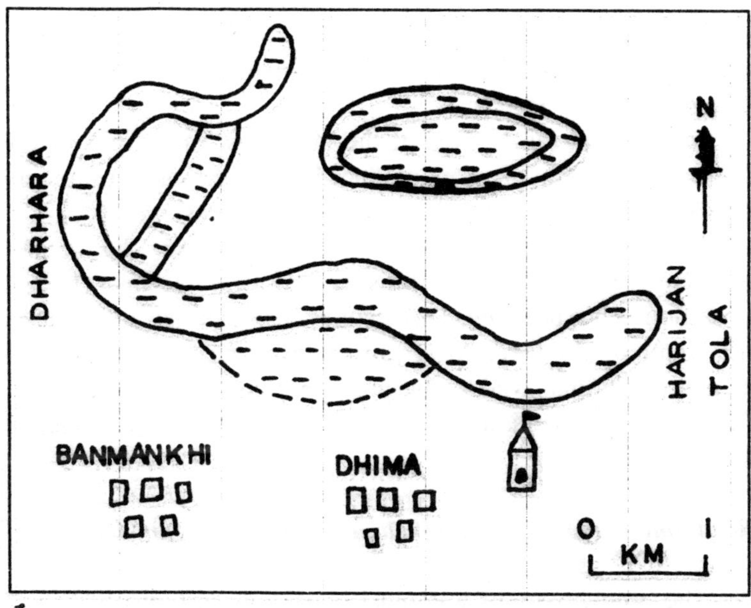


**Fig. 15.37 :** Dhima Makhnaha, Purnea

In order to reach Dhima-Makhnaha one has to get down at Banmankhi station. Dhima-Makhnaha is located 3 kms north-east of Banmankhi. Lake Dhima is located just one km. north of Dhima village. The water of the lake is suitable only for irrigation and washing of animals. It is so dirty and polluted that it is not palatable. Its shape is completely zig-zag. The flood comes each and every year.

During normal period the length of Dhima-Makhnana is 8 kms.; breadth 1.25 km. and depth not more than 3 metres. Among fishes found here are Rehu, Buari Katla, Pothia and Ichna. Buari has a weight of 3 to 4 kg, Rehu 2 to 2.5 kg., and Katla, 5 kg. The price of fish is Rs.25 to Rs. 40 per kg. Among the aquatic plants sewar and water-hyacinth are more common in comparison with others. Due to excessive rotten material of water-hyacinth the water of the lake is dirty. Hence, it is a breeding ground for varieties of worms, snails, crabs, tortoise and snakes as well.

So far as the birds are concerned Bagula and Maina are common ones but among the migratory birds Pan Silli, Crentch, Adhanga and Karan are important. All these come in the month of September and goes back in March.

In the surrounding area of the lake most of the people are cultivators of land. The crops produced in the surrounding. area are paddy, wheat, sugarcane, jute, moong, maize and surajmukhi.

Dhima-Makhnaha produces Bhent, Sadukha and fishes besides Singhara. As the land is relatively low near the lake, hence, irrigation is not possible. The input of fertilizer has no effect on the water of the lake. After proper levelling and reclamation measures Dhima- Makhnaha may be made more productive. People of the surrounding area of this lake suffer from Kalajar and Malaria.

***Recommendations of Rosra Wetland Conference-cum-Exhibition***

(a) The productivity of wetland is very high in terms of fishes, makhana and mothi, therefore it should be conserved and protected at any cost.
(b) Wetland should be saved from devastating flood because it destroys the standing crops and completely uproots the floral and faunal wealth of the wetland.
(c) For cleaning purposes the fish catch may be allowed only once in the month of February and March in the wetland.
(d) The netting of migratory birds should be immediately stopped by the poachers because it will disturb the ecology of the lake.

(e) Wetlands are the pollution filter and saviours of humanity and hence wetland should be cleaned, preserved and protected on regular basis.

(f) Wetlands are considered as marginal land but their environment is highly beneficial for the humanity at large.

(g) It has aroused awareness among people that we should maintain our tanks and ditches for the emanicipation of malaria, influenza, kalajar and asthama diseases.

(h) The exhibition of photographs, maps and wetland products is the centre of attraction of this conference and people have realised that we should not kill the migratory birds, but unfortunately the criminals are still at large in our society, and at times they take the law of the land in their own hands.

(i) The Wetlands should be properly planned in order to systematically develop and beautify our lakes.

(j) The productivity of Wetland should be diversified by the introduction of some more crops, saving of birds from poachers rennovation of our wetlands and make people conscious regarding Wetland environment.

## REFERENCES

Alkuhmi, K.H. (1957): Fish Culture in India, *Farm Bulletin.* I.C.A.R., New Delhi.

Badola, S.P. and Singh, H.R. (1981) : Hydrobiology of the River Alaknanda of the Garhwal Himalaya, *Indian Journal of Ecology*, Vol. 8, No. 2, pp. 269-276.

Banerjee, S. and Ghose, A.N. (1967): Water Quality and Soil condition on the Fish Ponds in some States of India in Relation to Fish Production. *Indian Journal of Fish*, No. 14 (1 & 2); pp. 15 - 144.

Bhagal, M. J. and Dwivedi, S.N. (1979): Ecology of Pawai Lake, Morphology and Topography; *Proceedings of 66th Indian Science Congress*, Part Abstract, pp. 1 - 43.

Bhaskaran, T. R.; Chakarvarty, R.N. and Trivedi, R. C. (1965): Studies on the River Pollution : Pollution and Self-Purification of Gomati River At Lucknow; *Indian Engineers India* 45(6), pp. 39-50.

Birge, E.A. (1913): Inland Lakes of Wisconsin Hydrography; *Wisconsin Geological History and Nature Severy Bulleting*; 27.

Birge, E.A. and Juday, C. (1922) : The Inland Lake of Wisconsin, The Plankton. Its quality and Chemical composition; *Wisconsin Geological History and Nature Survey Bulletin*, No. 64, pp. 1-122.

Chapman, R.N. (1928) : The Quantitative Analysis of Environmental Factor; *Ecology*, No. 9, pp. 111-112.

Das, S.M. (1966): Studies on Fresh Water Plankton from Kashmir; *Proceedings of 42nd Indian Science Congress*, Abstract.

David, A. and P. Ray (1966): Studies on the Population of The River Daha (Siwan) Bihar by Sugar and Distillery Wastes; 1 *Environmental History*; 8; 6-35.

Dutta, Munshi and Rai, D.N. (1981): Ecological Characteristics of Chaurs of North Bihar (India) *Introduction and Ecology of Environmental Science* (70) pp. 89-96.

Ganpati, S.V. (1940): Hydrological Investigation of the Stauley Reservoir and of the River Cauvery at Mettur Dam; *Met. Kem* 6(2), pp. 1-8.

Ganapati, S.V. and A. Sreenivasan (1970): Energy Flow in Natural Aquatic Ecosystem in India, *Arch. Hydrobillogy*, Vol. 66, No. 4, pp. 458-498.

Gupta, B.P. (1966): Soil Characteristics of Bhavanisagar Reservoir; *Journal of Fresh Water Ecology India*, Vol. 14 No. 1.

Khan, M.A. (1986) : Hydrobiology and Organic Production in a Mari Lake of Kashmir, Himalayan Valley, *Hydrobiology*, 135, pp. 233-242.

# 16

# CONSERVATION OF WETLANDS

Wetlands have been identified as one of the most useful and threatened natural resource eco-systems. There are "essential life support systems which plays a vital role in controlling water cycles and cleaning the environment". About the waterlogged wealth Edward Maltby said unfortunately, wetlands are fast disappearing all over the world, including India. Now the time has come to make a coordinated effort to halt this trend and optimise the use of wetlands for the safeguard of natural habitat and human being.

In India, apart from a few surveys and study programmes which are fragmentary and region-specific, little has been done to study about wetlands. At the third meeting of the conference of the contracting parties of the Ramsar Convention in June 1987, it has been said that: "the wise use of wetlands is their sustainable utilisation for the benefit of mankind in a way compatible with the maintenance of the natural properties of the eco-system." The sustainable utilisation means the "human use of a wetland so that it may yield the greatest continuous benefit to present society while maintaining its potential to meet the needs and aspirations of future generations".

The unique characteristic of wetlands is the presence of water and a water saturated soil. This may be either a permanent feature or occurring for a part of the year. Wetland ecosystem is a zone between the dry terrestrial and the wet aquatic systems, having characteristics of both the world besides some unique to itself. Diversity of character, size, type and mode of occurrence of wetlands has given rise to different ways of describing them. Wetlands have been defined from time to time to suit a particular location and the investigator as well.

According to Mitesh and Gosselins, wetlands include three factors: water, unique soil differing from those of uplands and the presence of vegetation adapted to wet conditions.The Ramsar Convention defines wetlands as areas of marsh, peatland or water, natural or artificial, permanent or temporary, with water that is static or flowing, fresh, brackish or saline, including areas of marine water, the depth of which at low tide does not exceed six metres. In India, common people understand easily marshes and swamps, or lakes and mud flats. Lot of people draws sustenance from wetland resources. The wetlands are always evaluated from anthropocentric approach. The wetland's usefulness can be determined from the point of view of the flora and fauna they sustain, their ecosystem values, and the contribution wetlands make in maintaining global air and water cycles. Wetlands utilized in a number of ways: from gathering food to disposal of wastes.

Wetlands are habitat for endangered and are species of birds and animals and are especially important for migratory birds and waders too. They are the habitat for a number of endemic, relict, regional varieties of sub-species of plants, insects and invertebrates, who needs a habitat of aquatic environment. Wetlands as an eco-system are useful for nutrient recovery and cycling, releasing excess nitrogen, deactivating phosphates, removing toxins, chemicals and heavy metals through absorption by plant and also in the treatment of waste water. Retention of sediments by wetlands also reduces siltation of rivers. Wetlands also help in mitigating floods, recharging aquifers and reducing the surface run-off and the consequent erosion. Mangrove wetlands of India and Bangladesh act as beffers against the devastating storms or typhoons of the Bay of Bengal. Wetlands also influence the Micro-climate of a locality besides checking underground salt water intrusion of an adjacent brackish water environment.

On an international scale, wetlands maintain air and water quality including nitrogen, sulpher, methane and carbondioxide cycles. Not all wetland's uses have become definite 'opportunities' in development planning. Wetlands resource opportunities are location-specific and can be defined as socially feasible uses of a resource system. In order to help the task of planning for wetlands resource systems a set of ground rules has been developed. Previous works need to be revised and modified to suit the subjective dimension of the specific area of developing un-utilised and under-utilised wetlands. These postulates are tentative and are based on the author's direct experience in wetland ecosystems. The seven postulates are as follows:

1. Wetlands, in most cases, will have conflicting land use interests and any change contemplated cannot be universally good to all the contending interests.
2. In landuse study no observation is independent of the observer-object relationship and for this fact is become a part of the object. This is why participatory action research is the strongest methodological tool for understanding the use of land and design of better use.
3. The culture of conserving wetland resources and using them in as many ways as possible has been found to thrive among the poor. There is prima-facie an inverse relationship between affluence and the affinity to recycling or reuse.
4. Information about wetland natural resource systems, particularly about those of developing countries, is meagre. Taking decisions on "better use", therefore, will have to use cybernetic models in place of any exercise in pretentious optimisation.
5. All public decisions are political and hence any misuse of natural and biological systems will have its social, economic and environmental backlash.
6. All these reactions are not instant and time-lag provides opportunities to the manipulators and speculators to inflict permanent damage to the ecosystems by forcing wrong land use changes on the society.
7. Wetland damage is identified not by observing the quality of the environment or measuring the external stresses alone but also by evaluating the internal strength and metabolic resistance of the particular group of people inflicted by that of he external stress.

All these postulates are preliminary and their ability to handle the challenge of sustainable development is still amateurish.

There are several areas of land, which need to drain water they collect during monsoons. Some of them are shallow basins with wide shores. These waterlogged areas in the flood plains have almost imperceptible slope of the fringe and the shore lines fluctuate with the seasonal rhythms. Such flooded areas with a few pockets of permanent waterlogging, are some of the least productive lands. In most of such areas, local villagers can at best grow a crop of paddy or jute. An interesting phenomenon of "oscillation" takes place with respect to the cropping pattern with one year interval. Villagers take advantage of the receding shoreline and keep on extending the area under cropping till the whole area is entirely flooded.

The development efforts of these wetland are based on the premise that the land will have to be drained properly. The actions suggested include: modification of the regime is to introduce more efficient resource systems, mainly involving agriculture and fisheries and developing location-specific schemes on the basis of study of existing practices.

There are several wetlands in India, which could be classified into derelict and semi-derelict water bodies prepared by the Directorate of Fisheries.

In 1986, two projects have been initiated to augment fish production. First, a World Bank-aided project for which each district in West Bengal took up some of such water bodies through the Fish Farm Development Agencies (FFDA). The second, a similar project using financial support from the Rural Landless Employment Guarantee Programme (RLEGP). However, the efforts do not as yet match the opportunities and, therefore, these have to be strengthened.

The existing activity links them with the National Mission on Wasteland Development; introducing highly effective system to oversee the technical and financial management of on-going projects and to ensure similar facilities to new projects; by exploring the possibilities of growing blue-green algae in some waterbodies; and ensuring institutional supports in strengthening the project the opportunities should be fully exploited.

In many localities wetlands act as municipal sewage receptacles though without any formal design. The idea is to develop appropriate pond system in such wetlands that will handle a definite range of sewage application rate to obtain the desirable affluent quality and a good harvest of fish to make the system self-sustaining. The wetlands, lying almost derelict, near cities due to lack of sanitation and resource recovery. In fact, they have open up a new vista for low-cost sanitation technology.

Wetlands taken up for the improvement of water quality has been tried in cold climates – in Canada and in the United States of America. Though in its experimental stage, wetland disposal system has been found quite effective in reducing appreciably most of the pollution load. Both natural and artificial marshes have been examined and emergent vegetation has been grown effectively to purify waste water biologically.

In the eastern side of Calcutta, unfortunately the oldest practice but incidentally the largest in the world – uses a back swamp for waste water disposal. It has been possible to draw initial engineering lessons for developing a pond system on the basis of the studies carried out on the Calcutta wetlands. In principle, the pond system is designed on the basis of what is done in designing a stabilisation tank to obtain a desired effluent quality for given waste water loading features. It has also become customary to discuss opportunities of growing fish in the third pond in that series, which is known as maturation pond. In Calcutta wetlands, fish ponds directly ingress raw sewage which has a BOD value between 120-160 ppm. Experiments have shown that fish grown under this condition are less risk prone than those grown in village ponds and not fed with sewage. This is so far as bacterial contamination is concerned the sewage of Calcutta has low metalion concentration which give rise to contamination.

In urban areas untreated municipal sewage contributes a major pollution load to the rivers of India. The relative cost of installation and maintenance of conventional treatment plants are dispro-portionately high in relation to the amount of funds available. This makes the conventional treatment plants non-viable. The disorders in conventional sewage treatment plants are frequent. Wetlands in urban periphery are natural receptacles for waste water and can harness effectively the nutrients available in the waste through fisheries and agriculture.

Therefore, planning for municipal effluent sanitation, through wetland can be more effective if it can follow the above three basic lessons. Sewage treatment plants are essentially non-viable because of the high plant cost, prohibitive operational cost and repeated plant breakdowns. Municipal effluent is a nutrient pool which could be exploited effectively to grow fish and also for irrigational purposes. The cities in India occasionally have contiguous back swamps for waste water disposal.

These ideas expressed in a World Bank/IDRC report on Low-cost sanitation technology options, which has summarised the experiences in developing countries. It has stated *inter alia* : "Universal solution of sewerage and treatment plants does not reach more than 6.5 per cent of the people in developing countries. The reuse of excreta in fish culture, algae production and aquatic plants/ energy production is new and promising technology, that radically changes the context of urban sanitation" I in case properly harnessed.

In fact, the publication of the report in 1978 caused waste water fisheries to gain a quantum jump. The report provides a dedicated pointer towards a 'new approach' which appreciates the role of reuse of human excreta. It is heartening to note that under-utilised marshes around a number of municipalities in West Bengal and Bihar have been identified for being transformed into resource efficient stabilisation tank systems under the Ganga Action Plan.

The National Committee on the Development of Backward Areas has, in a report to the Planning Commission in 1981, identified coastal areas affected by salinity as a backward area. The Committee identified coastal saline areas as places with saline top soil or where the water strata is saline even at great depths. The Committee has appreciated the efforts to develop brackishwater fisheries in mud flats especially in Kerela and Tamil Nadu.

A 'big swing' has taken place in using the land for brackishwater fish culture independently or along with paddy cultivation over a large area in the estuarine region of West Bengal and North Bihar since the flooding of about 40 hectares of Ranigachhi Mauza in South 24-Parganas. A favourable ecological condition and an attractive export market have combined to influence the decision. Although profitable, brackishwater fishery is technically inefficient and comparatively low-yielding.

The plan suggested includes giving effect to the recommendations of the National Committee on the Development of Backward Areas in relation to coastal saline areas. It will remove the policy of uncertainty over land use to introduce brackishwater fishery in such areas, which will be considered as ecologically feasible. The rivers should be channelised to deposit their silt on the plains to the extent that the phenomenon of heaving up takes place on the bed of the river itself and such rivers would loses its conservancy as a wetland.

In India the extent of wetland loss becomes apparent when a comparison is made of the Survey of India topographical maps brought out at intervals of 20 years. This phenomenon is particularly true of urban and semi-urban areas where wetlands have the strongest possibility of conversion. Such fragile areas are in critical need of wetland management, for a few more years of inaction will inflict perpetual damage to the wetland near urban areas.

The wetlands are complex ecosystems and their detailed evaluation is a time-consuming process which require the attention of specialists. The minimum working time is enough for large areas of wetlands to be lost in the meantime. Therefore, a through inventory of the existing wetlands, identification of their potential and existing use is essential. Further, a comparative evaluation using a list of simpler criteria should serve the purpose of deciding landuse options for wetlands.

## Use of Remote Sensing in Wetland Surveys

### *Satellite and Sensors*

The SPOT satellite has been designed by the French Centre of National d'Etudes Spatiales (CNES) and built by French, Belgian and Swedish partners.

The payload of SPOT-1 consists of two identical High Resolution Visible (HRV) imaging instruments and a packege comprising two magnetic tape data recorders and a telemetry transmitter.

The HRV sensors are designed to operate in either of two modes-panchromatic (black and white) or multi-spectral (colour) be visible and near infrared portions of the spectrum. The main characteristics of the sensors are listed ahead.

The capabilities include:

- nadir viewing (vertical) providing a swath width of 117 km.
- off-nadir viewing (oblique) up to 27° from the vertical
- revisit possibilities imaging individual sites
- stereoscopic imaging

SPOT is the first satellite to use pushbroom sensors. These consist essentially of CCD (charged-coupled device) linear arrays. (Fig. 16.1). This approach avoids the problems associated with mechanical means of moving a scanning mirror. With the pushbroom device, the scanning of wetland of a scene is performed electronically by successively measuring the current generated by each detector within the linear array. Each spectral band uses four linear arrays, each array consisting of 1728 elementary detectors (CCD devices). In the panchromatic mode, each detector corresponds to one pixel, while in the multi-spectral mode, each pixel will contain data gathered from a pair of devices (Fig. 16.2)

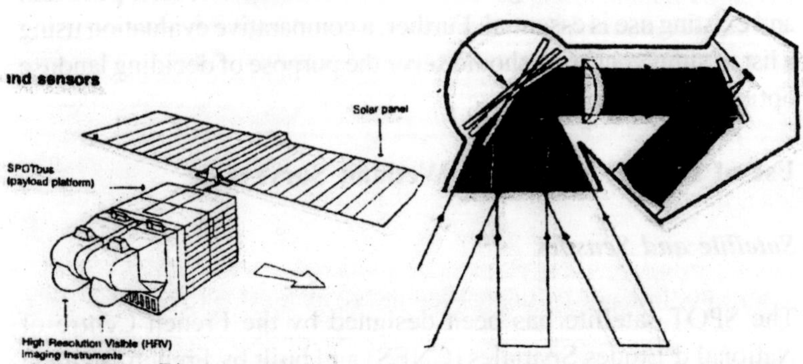


**Fig. 16.1 :** Satellite and Sensors

**Fig. 16.2 :** Stereoscopic Imaging

Launch : 22 February 1986

**Orbital parameters :**

| | |
|---|---|
| *Orbit* | : near polar, sun-synchronous |
| *Altitude* | : 832km |
| *Inclination* | : 98.70 |
| *Timing* | : crossing equator at 10.30 Local sun time (from N to S) |
| *Repeat cycle* | : 26 days |

**Table 16.1 :** Sensors: High Resolution Visible (HRV)

| *Multi-spectral mode:* | *Wavelength (m)* | *Resolution (m)* |
|---|---|---|
| Band 1 | 0.50-0.59 | 20 |
| Band 2 | 0.61-0-68 | 20 |
| Band 3 | 0.79-0.89 | 20 |
| Panchromatic mode : | 0.51-0.73 | 10 |

*Source* : Spot News, NRSC No. 1.

### Sun-synchronous Orbit

The sun-synchronous orbit ensures the satellite always passes overhead at the same (solar) time. In its normal orbit, SPOT crosses the equator, going south, at about 10.30 a.m. and at that time precisely on 15th June of each year. The local solar time of satellite passes over the day side of the Earth is represented in the graph (opposite) as a function of latitude of the point concerned (Fig. 16.3)

Each HRV instrument can be pointed so that two adjacent strips of the Earth's surface are covered (see above), giving a total swath width of 117 km (nadir) and an overlap of 3km. Since, the distance between adjacent ground tracks at the equator is about 108km, complete Earth coverage can be obtained with this fixed setting of instrument fields (Fig. 16.4).

### Off nadir-viewing

It will be possible to steer the mirrors of the HRV instruments to view obliquely (off nadir) up to 27° either side of vertical to cover an area of interest within a 950km wide strip centred on the satellite ground track.

'The width of the observed swath varies between 60 km. for nadir viewing and 80 km. for extreme off nadir-viewing. The programme of planned observations is controlled by the satellite's onboard computer. A sequence of recorded images may include both modes of operation (panchromatic and multispectral) and changes in each instruments viewing directions (Fig. 16.5).

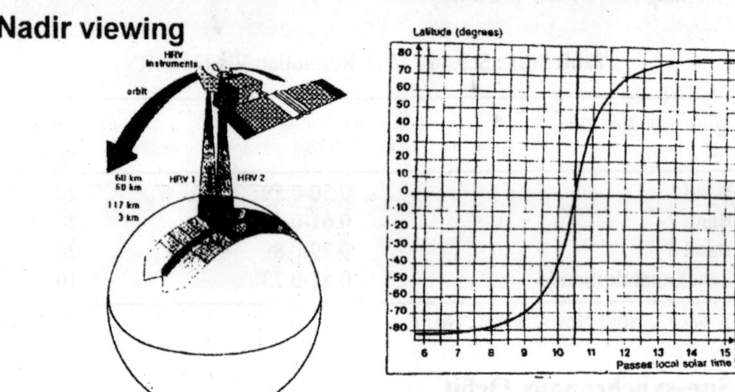


**Fig. 16.3 :** Nadir Viewing **Fig. 16.4 :** Latitude and Local Solar Time

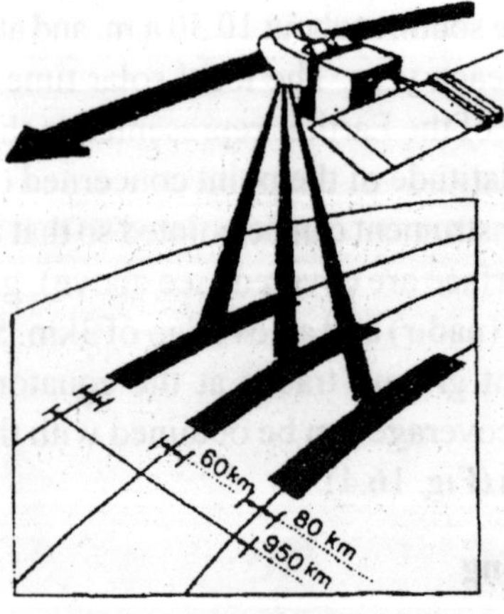


**Fig. 16.5 :** Off-nadir-viewing

## Revisit Capabilities

If the satellite's instruments were only capable of nadir viewing the revisit frequency for any given point would be 26 days. This interval is unacceptable for the observation of phenomena evolving on time-scales ranging from several days to a few weeks, especially where cloud cover hinders the acquisition of usable data.

However, with SPOT, the capability for off-nadir viewing during satellite passes in the vicinity of the area of interest considerably increases the revisit possibilities.

During the 26-day period separating two successive nadir satellite passes over a specific point on the Earth's surface the programmable steering capability of the instruments allows the area to be observed on seven different passes if it were on the equator and on eleven occasions if at a latitude of 45°.

For example, if the day on which the satellite first passes vertically over the point of interest is represented by D, then the other days on which the same point can be observed are as shown in the diagrams. Thus, regions can be imaged on dates separated alternately by one and four (occasionally five) days. The possibility of obtaining image pairs on successive days is of considerable interest for the monitoring of dynamic and rapidly changing environmental phenomena and for stereoscopic analysis (Fig. 16.6 and Fig. 16.7).

**Revisit potential**

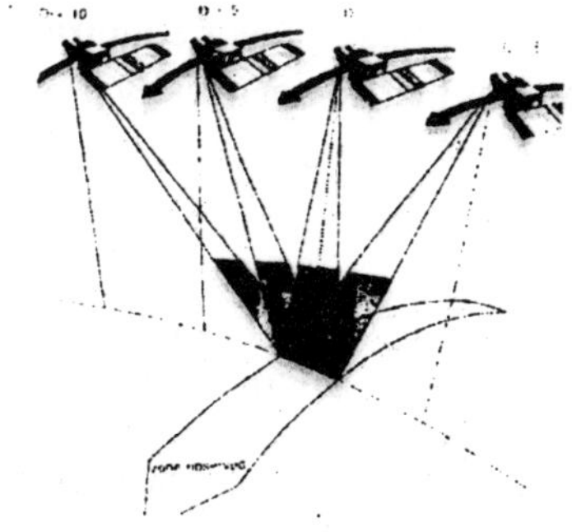

**Fig. 16.6 :** Revisit capabilities

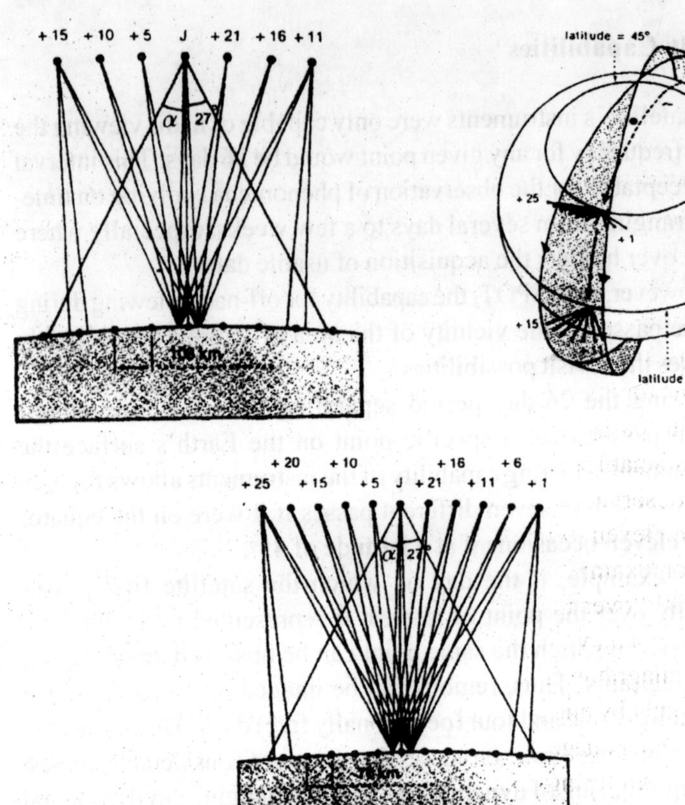


**Fig. 16.7 :** Viewing on successive days

'Viewing on successive days should also improve the chances of obtaining cloud-free imagery over countries, like North Bihar, with weather conditions that do not usually provide long periods for optimum imaging.

## Stereoscopic Viewing

Another important capability offered by off-nadir viewing is that of recording stereoscopic pairs of images of a given scene, i.e. images acquired at different viewing angles during successive satellite passes.

As illustrated under off-nadir viewing, images recorded on successive days are acquired on either side of the vertical. In such cases the ratio between the observation base (or distance between the two positions of the satellite) and the height (or satellite altitude) is approximately 0.75 at the equator and 0.5 at a latitude of 45° permitting stereo viewing (Fig. 16.8).

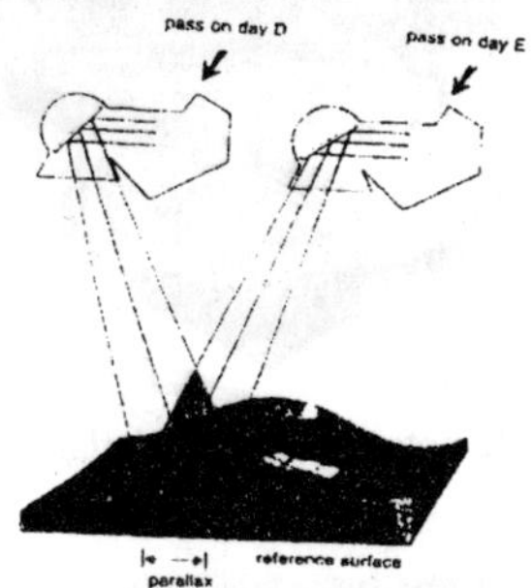


**Fig. 16.8 :** Stereoscopic Viewing

Compared with stereopairs obtained from aerial photographs, the main features of SPOT stereo images are :

***Scene Size*** : large format size - 60 x 60 km compared with 5x5 km or 10 x 10km.

***Scales*** : from 1:400, 000 to 1:25,000.

***Projection*** : SPOT stereo imagery is a cylindrical projection. However, they can be used in virtually the same way as conical projection air photos. Special attention is required to maintain the observation base under the stereoscope perpendicular to the satellite ground track and to ensure that the viewing axis remains as close as possible to the vertical.

***Homogeneity*** : As is the case with all images of the Earth recorded by satellites, SPOT imagery is quite remarkable as regards the uniformity of projection and the conditions of observations.

**Use of Remote Sensing in Wetland Water Management**

In Fig. 16.9 it has been shown that the satellite moving in the sky collects different types of information send it to the ground receiving

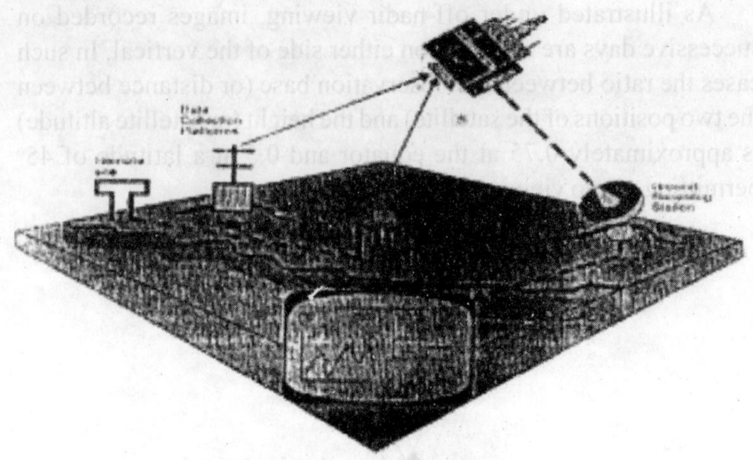

**Fig. 16.9 :** Remote Sensing in Wetland Management

**Fig. 16.10 :** Himalayan foothills at the top, Alluvial Plains of Narayani River

station and data collection platforms besides images to the computers. The image could be seen in Fig. 16.10 in which relief to snow cover the source of wetland has been shown from Ganga plain to Tibet. In lands at Fig. 16.11 the Himalayan foothills at the top, the alluvial plains with series of oxbow lakes as wetlands and the Narayani River (Gandak River) has been shown. In Fig. 16.11 the lands at imagery of the Ghaghra-Gandak rigion has been shown in which the source region of wetland water and stream flow could be seen coming from the Himalaya.

**Fig. 16.11 :** The LANDSAT # MSS (Band 6) imagery of the Ghaghara-Gandak region.

## Conclusion

The task of wetland preservation begin by using a modified technique to achieve workable information in the least possible time and this is where 'rapid appraisal survey' comes in. Such survey involves collection of baseline information. But, in some cases detailed evaluation becomes necessary depending on the resource potential and the ecosystem of wetland. Further, the appraisal will have to be reviewed from time to time to guide the changes necessary in planning for contingencies.

The programme of developing wetlands will have to begin by solving two handicaps. First, weak research support and second, shortage of trained wetland managers and technical assistants.

The research front should be studies on existing resource systems and traditional uses of wetlands; benefit estimates and impact assessment of developmental projects and actions relating to use of wetlands, preparation of classified inventory of unutilised and under-utilised wetlands and training the participants in wetland developmental efforts through minor wetland ecosystems.

## REFERENCES

Choudhary, U. P., "Wetlands in North Bihar", *East-West Geographer*; Vol.1, No.1, 1990, p. 14-15.

Ghosh, D., Wetlands Conserving for the Future, *The Hindu*, 1991, p. 153.

Gopal, B. R. E. *et al., Wetlands Ecology and Management*, National Institute of Ecology and Interrnational Scientific Publication, Jaipur, 1982.

Gopal, B. R. E., *et al.,* 'Wetlands conference in Czechoslovakia' *Nature and Resources*, UNESCO, Vol. XX; No. 2, 1984, p. 22.

# 17

# PROBLEMS AND PLANNING OF WETLANDS

In this chapter the delineation has been made regarding the problems and planning of wetlands in North Bihar. The major problems are land degradation and erosional hazards found in wetlands besides soil pollution, water pollution and the reckless cutting of trees. The management or planning considered the construction of embankment for checking the flood hazard besides the development of afforestation programme and making people conscious about the importance of wetlands. The wetland environment work as pollution filter giving shelter to varieties of birds and fishes. It is productive for medicinal plant besides the production of Mothi, Makhana and provides a ground for boating, picnic and recreation. The planning may have a multifaceted impact on the people of surrounding area especially in terms of rearing fish and producing rice and earning a livelihood by cultivation of land and other means.[1]

The wetlands comprising oxbow lakes, chaurs and other such natural depressions with stagnant water have been for some years, regarded as wastelands and it deserves to be drained. As a result, interesting and biologically rich habitats have become scarce and may practically disappeared. Such drainage results normally in replacement of a hydrophytic community by a mesophytic one, if natural vegetation is allowed to persist. Instance of this type are insignificant in comparison with the areas in which agriculture follows drainage; altogether altering the eco-system in the process.

It is largely the wetlands of North Bihar where the reclamation of land for agriculture through the implementation of Chaui Drainage Schemes is going on for the last 3-4 decades (Fig.17.1).

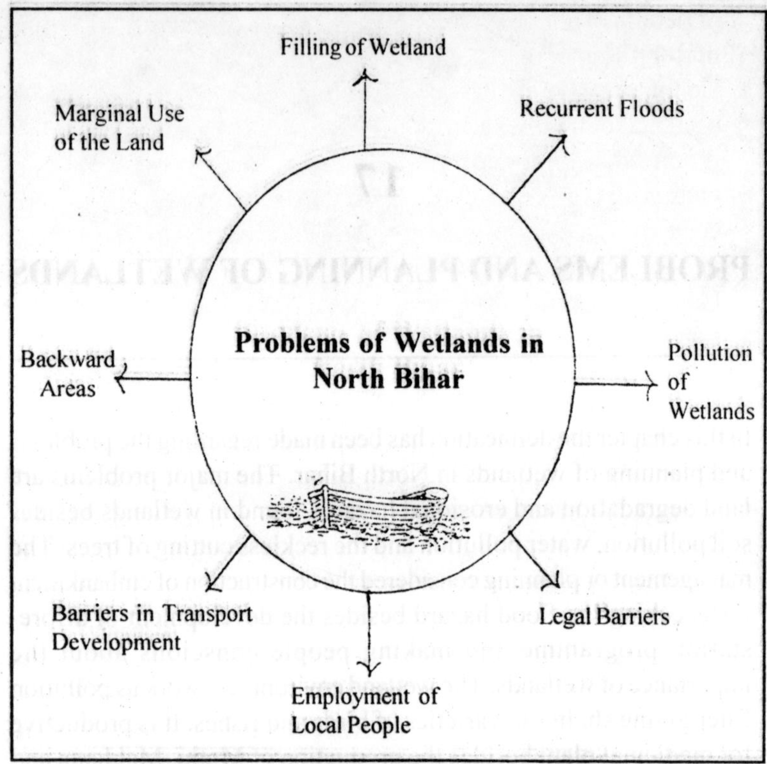


**Fig. 17.1 :** Problems of Wetlands in North Bihar

Conservation, in practice, has gone through five phases, namely the legislative, the biological, the ecological, the sociological and the engineering. With the increasingly obvious need for multiple use of Land and Water Management has taken precedence over preservation and possibly over conservation itself. From 'engineering' point of view taken stock of the fact that virtually all landscape in the country are under some kind of management and this must be done rationally and not left utterly to local unenlightened decisions. But, in practice management is largely the sum of un-planned, un-coordinated, and often cross-purpose pursuits of individuals, groups/communities, and government agencies, all seeking their own objective and seldom with regard to cumulative consequences of their actions. The diversity of interests and values of people in relation to the biophysical environment have also been major factors in the fractionalizing of public responsibility. Comprehensive environmental policy becomes possible only when a sufficient number of these diversities and resulting conflicts are reconciled, adjusted or transcended to permit the degree of consensus needs for public action. This will depend upon the socio-economic conditions and character of society, the political situation and the specific issue on which the level of consensus is sought. Hence, unless the Government acts with vision and discharges its function of leadership backed by adequate comprehension of ecological cause and effect relationships and of a strong and clearly defined concept of environmental values, the general apathy of indifference or inaction on the part of the people involved and affected will continue. However, this apathy is likely to cause incalculable damage to the environment and the creatures living therein.[2] (Fig. 17.2).

The Government policy in respect of drainage and reclamation of wetlands in Bihar is a glaring example of such cross-purpose policies, programmes, apathy and inaction on the part of the people affected. The ownership and management of water resources (including those in Chaurs, mans and oxbow lakes, etc.) is vested in different departments, namely Irrigation, Revenue, Agriculture, Fisheries and Forest. For Agriculture, Irrigation and Revenue Departments, reclamation of the waterlogged areas for agricultural use is important, whereas for fisheries department the protection of the wetlands for pisciculture is valuable. Then, the Environment Department might ask for its conservation together with that of the Wildlife Species living therein or using it. Its another dimension is the interests of the private owners and in turn of the Revenue Department who are responsible for vesting ownership to private persons and local bodies. It is said that during the last 3-4 decades, almost all *gairmazarua* (Public) lands including notified drainage or river courses have been settled with private persons. It is, therefore, necessary that the problems and perspectives of preservation and protection of wetlands is viewed in the back drop of the facts and circumstances briefly mentioned above because in

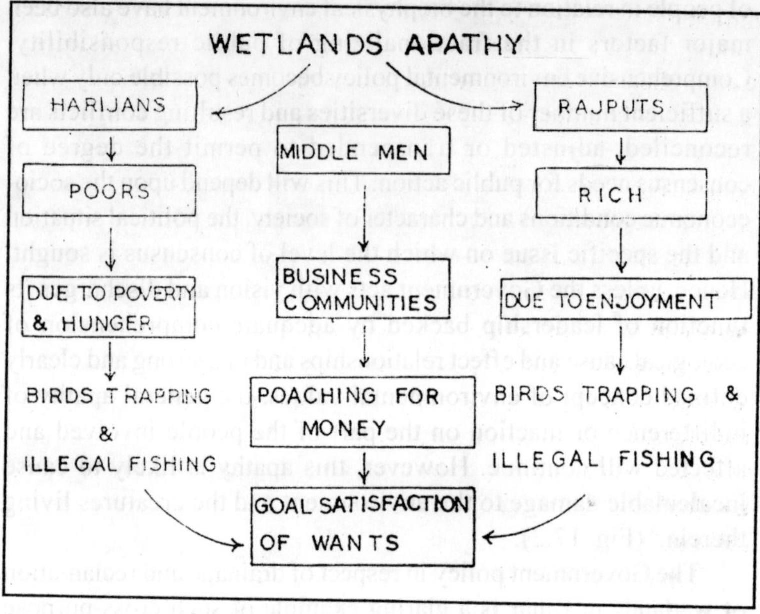


**Fig. 17.2 :** Socio-economic condition and Damage to Wetland Environment

most cases the problem will be first of restoration to status-quo and then action on promotion and improvement, unless of course irreversible drainage have not taken place. It is to be understood in terms of environmental changes or degradation, which are occurring so slowly and perceptibly as to escape attention until some harm is done.[3]

The next important point of relevance is the concept of assigning monetary values to the environmental losses and attempted trade-offs with economic gains. While there is lot of sense and rationality in advocating "wise use" of natural resources, there is equally urgent need for pondering over the dichotomies between economic and ecological view points. The economic concept was concerned with wealth, the ecological with health; the economic with analysis, and the ecological with synthesis. Though there are apparent contracts, even than there is scope for reconciliation through co-ordination of natural resources policies, and by developing institutions that are much more broadly representative of the diversity of people's interests and values than is the present structure of resource administration. It is very necessary that the gap between knowledge of ecology and popular perception or comprehension is bridged because such widening gap is likely to lead to an alineation of public opinion from environmental administration regardless of its ecological soundness or its promises for human welfare. Continuing degradation of wetlands in North Bihar is the result of isolated problem solving policies of government and lack of comprehension on the part of the local people involved and affected. This has been illustrated by the provisions in the Bihar Reclamation, Cultivation and Improvement Act, 1946.[4]

This Act provides opportunities for reclamation and improvement of unproductive lands which are defined as lands lying fallow and recorded in the record of rights as *gairmazarua khas* or *gairmazarua Aam lands* which have been lying fallow for a continuous period of not less than five years preceding the date of possession, or lands which owing to the action of a river or a natural calamity are lying fallow or which have so deteriorated owing to a deposit of sand or accumulation of water or growth of jungle or any other cause as to render its cultivation for the time being unprofitable. It is further provided that the State Government may enter upon such lands and take possession thereof if the Collector is satisfied that it is necessary to bring such lands under cultivation without undue delay. Though this Act was aimed at 'Grow More Food Campaign', there were such seeping provisions in it that even the open spaces and wetlands on which there is so much emphasis today, were not spared. The author have personal knowledge about farmers who prefer broadcasting paddy seeds or transplanting paddy in Chaurs or in that portion of the Chaurs in which never before any attempt to grow crops had been made before enactment of the Land Reclamation Act, for fear of loss of lands under this Act. So was the case with the fallow lands in which trees were cut and camoflage of cultivation started. This trend gathered momentum with Government policies and programmes of draining the Chaurs.

Numerous saucer-shaped depressions occur in the chronically flood prone plains in North Bihar. These are locally known as "Jheels" in U.P., "Chaurs" in Bihar and "Beels" in West Bengal and Assam. Due to meandering nature of the Gangetic river system many oxbow lakes called "Mans" occur in North Bihar. According to the latest figures available, the natural wetlands comprising lakes, Bogs, Marshes and Mangroves, etc. cover about 2248 sq.kms. and Man-made Wetlands cover about 486 sq. kms. In the State of Bihar District-wise area in the division of Darbhanga is given in Table 17.1.

**Table 17.1** : Area Under Wetlands in Darbhanga Division

| *District* | *Area under Chaurs* |
|---|---|
| Darbhanga | 12,1414 ha. |
| Samastipur | 10,000 ha. |
| Madhubani | 13,550 ha. |
| Total | 35,691 ha. |

*Source* : Fishery Department, Government of Bihar, Patna.

Though this list is not complete, it can be seen that the total area very nearly equals, the area under Manmade Wetlands. That is often major reservoirs in South Bihar and Chhotanagpur. According to another survey made by the Fisheries Department, the wetlands comprising tanks and ponds, and Mans measure about 8449 ha. In North Bihar, District-wise break-up is in Table 17.2.

**Table 17.2** : Wetlands of Darbhanga Division, 1997

| *Sl. No.* | *Name of the District* | *Tanks and Ponds* | *Mans in ha.* | *Total area in ha.* |
|---|---|---|---|---|
| 1. | Madhubani | 3,743 ha. | — | 3,743 |
| 2. | Darbhanga | 3,037 ha. | 453 | 3,490 |
| 3. | Samastipur | 1,216 ha. | — | 1,216 |
| | Total | 7,996 ha. | 453 | 8,449 |

*Source* : Revenue Department, Government of Bihar.

This list does not appear to be complete because as per the Report of the National Commission on Floods (1980 March), the area under the oxbow lakes, that the, "Mans" in North Bihar should be 3,845 ha. against 453 ha given in Table 17.2.

It would be clear that the area under wetlands comprising chaurs, oxbow lakes, tanks and ponds, all considered, is cover 8449 ha. The National Commission on Agriculture (1976) had viewed these areas as fishery resource of immense potential, and had recommended that the State Government should consider the fresh water fishery resources, comprising the oxbow lakes, as exclusive fishery resources, while considering the land and water utilization policy, and other interests, if any, should be deemed to be incidental to the fishery development. As per their estimate, the fresh water fishery resources comprising mans, *jheels* and *beels* (in Bihar, U.P. and West Bengal and Assam respectively) which have progressively gone into dereliction, is approximately 4.0 lakh ha. of which about 1.0 lakh hectare could be utilized for the construction of fish-farm ponds. They had stressed the need for augmenting inland fish production on a priority basis appreciating its advantages, such as, its substantial contribution in meeting requirements of low-cost animal protein to the people, low cost on distribution because of the source of production being close to the consuming centers, almost the entire catch being directly utilized as human food, and development of inland fisheries had large potential for employment at the production level besides being an economically viable occupation[5].

According to statistics on fisheries in Bihar, about 21 per cent of the area under Tanks and Ponds, and Mans is under private ownership and about 79 per cent under the Government. As at present, the Fisheries Department earns annual revenue of about Rs.237 lakhs from government controlled/managed tanks covering an area of about 20,235 hectares. The average annual production is about 1,800 kg. per hectares which could be increased to 2,500 kg. per hectare with improved management practices.

Close on the heels of the report of National Commission on Agriculture, came the Report of the National Commission on Floods (March, 1980). This Commission noted the increasing demand for draining of the chaurs permanently for agricultural crops in the Gangetic basin, and recommended that with due consideration to high cost of drainage schemes, alternative use of the derelict water bodies for highly profitable pisciculture and the importance of retaining alley storage for flood moderation, no large scale drainage schemes of reclamation of *jheels*, *chaurs* and *beels* should be taken up without considering their other alternative uses for fishery, irrigation, biological sanctuary and for tourists and a like.

The Technical Committee on Inland Fisheries had earlier suggested a strategy for the Beel fishery development in Brahmaputra valley in Assam. Their suggestions included (i) the promotion of culture fisheries in the marginal areas by construction of ponds, (ii) development of fish catch in the rest of the Beel areas, and (iii) deepening of the connecting channels to the river and providing sluice gates. In Katihar district, Beels occur extensively in the flood plains and occupy about 80,000 hectares. They were mostly under private ownership but due to the implementation of the Estate Acquisition Act, about 50 per cent of the Beel area are now vested with the State Government. Since the Beels had languished over years due to silting up of the connecting links resulting in degradation of the Beels into closed swamps heavily infested with a variety of aquatic weeds, the Government have implemented schemes for development of Beel fisheries. In Bihar, however, the emphasis on drainage and reclamation of the chaurs continues unabated though it is felt that many of such schemes executed have not been successful in draining out the chaurs completely. Perhaps, that is a redeeming feature in as much as the ecological aspects are concerned. As a matter of fact, it is extremely difficult and prohibitively costly proposition to drain out the chaurs in view of flat topography, frequent floods and obstruction to natural drainage ways of the chaur except for the marginal areas. In this context, the Reports of Bihar Irrigation Commission (1971) and the second Irrigation Commission (1972) of the Government of India appears necessary.

The Bihar Irrigation Commission had observed that about lakh hectares waterspread was available in Bihar, which afforded enormous potential for development of inland fisheries. According to the Commission the aforesaid water spread included about 80,000 hectares of tanks and ponds and 40,000 hectares of Mans and chaurs, bulk of which lies in North Bihar. The State Irrigation Commission had recommended that (i) the chaurs whose bed levels permitted outfall into the nearby rivers should be drained out by leading channels; and (ii) the chaurs whose lowest bed levels were so low as not to permit complete draining out but it should be drained out to reclaim the maximum possible areas on the fringe for Rabi cultivation.

Utilization of the portion, which could not be drained out was also suggested by (i) growing water-bearing fruits, (ii) pisciculture, and (iii) irrigation of higher lands through pumping of water in the chaurs.

The report of the second Irrigation Commission (1972) of the Government of India that followed the State Irrigation Commission's Report (1971) made very general, observations on this subject, by stating that large areas of North Bihar suffers from inundation due to floods; and even after the floods recede, water stagnates on large number of depressions known as Chaurs.

Perusal of the observations and recommendations of the four Commission briefly mentioned above will show that:

(i) Comprehensive approach to planned development of the wetlands which had been acknowledged as an important feature of land and water use pattern in North Bihar was not adopted;
(ii) In almost all the reports, the emphasis explicit or implicit was on economics rather than on ecology.
(iii) The wetlands were viewed as valuable resource but differently by different commissions. The National Commission on Agriculture recommended use of wetlands for fishery development whereas the Bihar Irrigation Commission recommended draining out the chaurs and reclaim them for agricultural use. Fishery was suggested as incidental use. The National Commission on floods look

upon these chaurs as a measure for flood moderation through valley storage; and the second Irrigation Commission preferred just to state the problem of water-logging in these depressions and their non-availability for worthwhile agricultural use. This Commission dealt with the problem of drought very extensively but did not consider the problem of wetlands worthy of their attention even though very large areas in the Gangetic plains are covered by wetlands.

(iv) Nothing of the kind of regional planning for development of land and water resources was either advocated or formulated to suggest consideration of the wetlands as an integral part of such development process; and

(v) In none of the four reports, even passing reference was made to the importance of these chaurs and ox-bow lakes as abode of resident and migratory birds, even though it is a matter of both national and international implications and importance.

Thus, it would be apparent that the recommendations of the Agriculture Commission (1976) and Floods Commission (1980) have not affected the recommendations of the Bihar Irrigation Commission (1971); and schemes for drainage of chaurs continue to be sanctioned and implemented. The point of concern is not the implementation of these schemes as such but utter disregard to assessment of their impacts on the Natural Systems and Environmental Quality. The late Prime Minister, Indira Gandhi emphasized the need of natural systems and Environmental quality in project planning by saying that "... survival of mankind depends upon the survival of animal and plant life ..." and since the Stockholm conference, due care is being taken to undertake a biotic inventory of the tract to be flooded in order to identify rare or endangered species, centres of species endemism and to scope out the magnitude of wildlife resources.

The wetlands comprising oxbow lakes and chaurs in North Bihar are natural depressions formed over hundreds of years and contributing to ecological stability of the region. It is not only the large lakes or chaurs alone which deserve attention from ecosystem view-point. It is the whole system comprising natural depressions, big and small, in the region with their in-built inter-relationship and inter-dependence that helps in maintaining the ecosystem. It is to be understood that drainage of such depressions is bound to disturb the ecosystem. Many types of fishes including oysters, crabs and cranes available in these' mans and chaurs are not available in flowing rivers. They will vanish with the drainage of the chaurs. More important than this is the adverse effect it will cause on special types of resident and migratory birds. Considering, the grave risks involved, it becomes a matter of urgent importance that policies and programmes relating to management of the wetlands which are condemned as wastelands in many cases are reviewed and necessary modifications incorporated in order to fore-stall disaster that looms large. With this end in view, a few suggestions are being put forth for consideration by the authorities concerned :

(i) Wetlands should be considered as valuable natural resource, not for agriculture and fishery alone but, more importantly as instrument of ecosystem stability in the region;

(ii) The present standard land-use classification comprise (a) forests; (b) Area put to non-agricultural uses; (c) Barren and un-culturable land; (d) permanent pastures and other grazing lands; (e) Land under miscellaneous tree crops and groves; (f) Culturable wasteland; (g) Fallow lands other than current fallows; (h) current fallows, and (i) Net area sown. It is not definitely known as to which classification is assigned to wetlands of North Bihar in the land-use statistics published by the Directorate of Economics, and Statistics. In order to protect such lands from degradation due to the Bihar State Lands (Reclamation, Cultivation and Improvement) Act, 1946 the wetlands should be classified either as areas put to non-agricultural uses or land under miscellaneous tree crops and groves. It will have to be further protected appropriately by enforcing some provisions of Forest (Conservations) Act, Indian

Fisheries Act, 1897 and Environmental Protection Act.

(iii) Wetlands for the purposes of project planning and enactment of laws for regulation and development need to be defined on following lines:

"All natural depressions known as Mans and Chaurs, etc. and measuring 40 hectares or more at water surface level following the rainy season, say 31st October in 3 out of 4 years; and man-made lakes, tanks, ponds or reservoirs measuring 100 hectares or more at full reservoir levels will be deemed to be treated as wetlands serving as natural flood moderation basins and water recharge areas, aquaculture development including deep water paddy, water-borne flowers and fruits production, fisheries and habitats for flora and fauna including resident and migratory birds."

(iv) Government should regulate development and management of all wetlands through one State Level Agency or Authority.

(v) Wetlands generally covering 200 hectares or more should be declared protected Area or closed Areas, prohibiting bird shooting over the entire area and fishing except in the fringes and through a proper mix of capture and culture fishery. The central portion occupying the deep waters approximately one-third of the total area should not be permitted to be intruded upon for any purpose except for scientific studies and researches.

(vi) In all wetlands excluding protected or closed areas development of deep paddy cultivation, flowers and fruits, fisheries, etc. should be made compulsory. Bird catching and shooting should be regulated and controlled.

(vii) Present policy regarding reclamation of wetlands through Drainage schemes should-be changed keeping with the exhortations by the world Resources Institute (1984) in its report titled "The Global possible" which reads as under in so for as reclamation is concerned:

"Promote intensified production on existing good agricultural lands, rather than expanding agricultural activities into previously un-used usually low potential areas".

(viii) In this context, it is to be noted that eminently sensible actions often are not taken because they appear uneconomical to authority or to independent farmers or the fishermen. Hence, the benefits have got to be demonstrated and trade offs recognised.

(ix) The Committee on Leasing Policies on Inland Fisheries (1970) had pointed out the following shortcomings in the present leasing practices.

(a) Poor linkage with developmental needs; (b) Short range view of the State Government in ensuring maximum fisheries revenue; (c) Leases favouring individual is capable of paying rent; (d) Vested interests of fish merchants in utilizing fisher co-operative societies as a means of obtaining preferential leases; (e) Unauthorised sub-leasing by individuals or Fishery Co-operative Societies in several cases; and (f) Handicaps in the effective utilization of culture fishery resources owing to short span of lease periods and absence of the fish farming community.

The National Commission on Agriculture has recommended that the primary consideration in granting fishery rights in public waters should be the long range interest of strengthening the base for increased production with necessary steps favouring the development activities and improving per capita productivity. It also recommended that for fishing in reservoirs, beels, Jheels and Mans also, the principles governing the grant of fishery rights should be the same as in the case of other capture fisheries and any system viz. licensing, royalty, bifurcated leasing or outright leasing, any be adopted keeping in view the general principles of conservation and exploitation of resources.

(x) The Wildlife (Protection) Act, 1972 passed by the Parliament defines wildlife to include "any animal, bees, butterflies, crustaces, fish and moths and aquatic or land vegetation which forms part of any habitat." It is to be examined how far the provisions of this Act could be enforced in protection of habitats in Jheels, beels and chaurs, that is, the wetlands.

(xi) The words conservation, preservation, protection and promotion will need to be defined in the context of the proposed measures for wetlands management in North Bihar. As it is, not even the correct and up-to-date inventor of wetlands and their salient features such as, its size and present use for various purposes, population of resident and migratory birds, extent of degradation and causes thereof legal status, etc. are available. This is essential for contemplating and initiating action on preventive, protective, remedial and promotional measures.

## Characteristics of Wetlands

Wetlands are characterized by a number of features that pose problems for any attempt to develop highly quantitative nationwide delineation criteria (based upon wetland hydrology such as 15 or 21 consecutive days of saturation or inundation). A major problem is that wetland water levels and vegetation change, from season to season and from year to year in response to precipitation cycles and changes in surface and groundwater elevations. It is understandable that landowners and regulators would prefer a simple approach to wetland delineation, such as a single evaluation of water levels and vegetation at the time of a delineation. But this is not possible if delineation is to reflect basic wetland characteristics, including wetland functions, values, and natural hazards. Unlike lakes, streams, rivers, and oceans, which have relatively fixed shoreline features (at least over a period of decades), the water levels and vegetation found in wetlands shift as a result of short and long-term fluctuations in precipitation, run-off, and groundwater levels. Wetlands may be greatly affected by differences of centimetres in water level. Also, because precipitation varies not only seasonally and annually but also over long term cycles, a prairie pothole or other wetland may be wet year-round for two years, seasonally for the next five years, and then almost entirely dry for five years.

Many wetland functions are dependent upon these fluctuations. The recent drought in western North America demonstrated that wetlands critical feeding and resting functions for ducks, geese, and other waterfowl depend not only upon seasonal wetness but also on wetness in the dry years as well. Thus wetland delineation must incorporate a long-term as well as a short-term perspective on hydrology. Habitats for rat and endangered species often depend on extreme hydroperiod and periodic water level fluctuations. The importance of wetlands to fisheries depends upon periodic flooding of the flood plain systems. Wetland hydrologic functions, such as flood storage and conveyance are also related to periods of fluctuation.

Despite the shifts in water levels and vegetation, wetlands do have permanence in the landscape and relatively certain boundaries over the long-term because fluctuations occur, within relatively fixed ranges, which are partially reflected in vegetable and geomorphological indicators (shape, location, substrata), including soil characteristics. Furthermore, inundation is not an absolute annual, biannual, or triennial even, rather it is periodic, according to the range of hydrologic conditions that occur within a given region or watershed. Hence, the term normal, as used in the proposed manual, is of little use to this concept.

Another problem with developing quantitative hydrologic delineation criteria is that the functions and values of wetlands depend upon a broad range of factors. The primary use of an inflexible number of days of inundation or saturation is, therefore, a poor primary criterion for delineation. Any attempt to delineate wetlands based upon the number of days of saturation alone can only partially reflect wetland values and functions that depend, in many instances, much more upon morphology, location, relative wetness, soils, vegetation, and adjacent land uses. For example, flood storage and conveyance depend upon elevation, configuration, and location; the number of days of inundation or saturation and the kinds of soil and vegetation present are relatively irrelevant.

To understand the importance of location and relative wetness, rather than absolute wetness, to wetlands functions and values, compare, for example, a river in Louisiana and one in Arizona. Many of the driest riverine lands in Louisiana, which annually receive more than 60 inches of rainfall, may be wetter than the wettest riparian sites in Arizona, which receive less than 25 cms. From a national or Louisiana perspective, these Arizona sites would not be considered wetland because they lack 21 consecutive days of saturation. But from an Arizona perspective, the sites are wet in comparison to the rest of the landscape. Because of this relative wetness, these lands are characterized by bands of vegetation, such as cotton, wood and willow trees, that are extremely important habit, but do not meet the proposed manual's wetland vegetation criterion. Moreover, because of their relative wetness and location, these areas serve as flood conveyance and storage, wildlife habitat, food chain support, stream bank stabilization, and in some instances, pollution control functions that are performed by much wetter areas in Louisiana.

Of course, not all of these lands should necessarily be considered wetlands, though this argument has been made. However, regional variations in rainfall and relative wetness and location are extremely important to wetland functions and values, and these factors are not adequately reflected in the proposed manual.

A third problem with the manual's delineation criteria (and, to even a greater extent, those of H.R. 1330) is that the criteria require the simultaneous presence of wetland hydrology, soils and plants.

However, the presence of these three factors is often irrelevant to wetland functions and values. Furthermore, requiring the presence of all criteria will omit substantial natural and altered areas because floods and hurricanes periodically, destroy or damage the vegetation and substantially alter the soils in portions of coastal marshes and mangrove systems, as well as in flood plain marshes and swamps. During long dry periods, fires typically burn the vegetation (and sometimes the layers of peat) in all but the wettest of wetland systems.

Yet such areas include some of the widely recognized "real" wetlands and continue to function like wetlands despite the temporary loss of one or more of the wetland characteristics required by the proposed manual. They also continue to be subject to the same natural hazards — such as flooding, erosion, and subsidence — as other natural wetlands. Similarly, although many altered, artificial, and managed wetlands lack one or more wetland characteristics because of human activities, they continue to serve important wetland functions and continue to be subject to many of the same natural hazards.

Although inundation or saturation for prolonged periods during the growing season is not necessary for an area to serve important wetland functions and values, the proposed manual requires that hydrology be determined during the growing season, which is defined to include 21 days before and 21 days after frost has occurred. As currently proposed, the criteria do not cover the full seasonal range of biotic activity that occurs in wetlands. The use of biological zero (the temperature at which most biological activity ceases in the soil) would more closely define this range because many important wetland functions, as well as many chemical and biological activities (for example, nutrient transformation) within the soil, occur during these times. However, certain wetland functions, such as sediment trapping, flood flow alteration, and wildlife habitat, can occur even when the soils are at or below biological zero. In addition, many wetlands are continuously flooded and provide non-biological functions, such as flood storage and conveyance, during the winter late rainfall in early spring.

Finally, meeting a rigorous, quantitative standard for long-term hydrology in wetland delineation will be exceedingly difficult and expensive, particularly if vegetation and soils cannot be used to infer hydrology. Wetland delineation criteria that incorporate a quantitative approach to wetland hydrology will inevitably result in extremely time-consuming and expensive delineations, particularly if an inflexible, rigid standard is applied and soils and vegetation cannot be used as evidence, albeit inconclusive of long-term hydrology. Except for data on some coastal wetlands with nearby tidal gauges and riverine or lake shore wetlands with long water level records, little quantitative hydrologic data exist for wetlands as a whole. And such data, when available, may not be easy to analyse or correlate with conditions on a particular site.

There are, however, several time-consuming ways of making quantitative projections of hydrology, including measuring the hydrology through repeated field observation or continuous monitoring equipment. Either method is likely to take months or years to complete and cost thousands of dollars. A second approach, though no less costly or time-consuming is to apply a hydrologic model to the system based upon short- and long-term rainfall and topography. The National Flood Insurance Programme has spent more than 5873 million using such an approach to map many of the nation's flood plains. Much more could be spent on wetlands. A third approach is to infer long-term hydrology from onsite indicators. In the past, a number of indicators have been used to infer long term hydrology, but there is little scientific evidence to support their use in determining a particular, quantitative frequency of flooding or saturation as required by the proposed manual. Such long-term indicators include plant, and, soil evidence, and of the two, soil indicators are most useful because they are more likely to reflect what has happened over time. The proposed 1991 manual, however, disallows the use of vegetation and soil indicators to prove hydrology and thus removes the most reliable indicators available.

## Management of Freshwater Bodies

The inland water bodies like rivers, lakes, ponds, pools and puddles are of common occurrences all over North Bihar. They are of great economic value to men and for the water and organisms that abound in them, and with very little ecological view point man has been using these. The demand of growing human population for space and food are ever increasing. Freshwater bodies are being used increasingly for these purposes. Management of freshwater bodies should aim to maintain them in useful form at a high productive level with provision for removal of plants and animals for human use. Thus, a thorough knowledge of drainage, total water runoff, mineral receipts, the biotic communities, the ecological life cycle of economically important species, energy flow pattern, quantitative study of minerals, cycling from abiotic to chains of organisms, turnover, etc. rate of water loss through evapotranspiration should

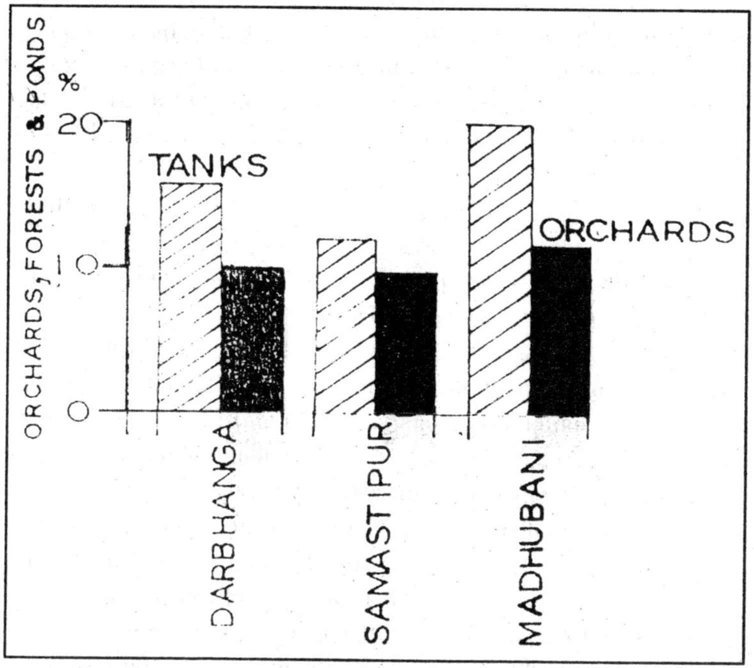


**Fig. 17.3 :** Darbhanga Division Relationship of Ponds and Orchards (1991)

be understood. The Management with regard to its economic use such as quantity and periodicity of water removal for irrigation, maintenance of certain fish and plant crops, the extent of carrying capacity of the water body towards pollutants like town refuge, etc. should be undertaken. A well managed river or lake is one which serves in a multipurpose way the human society without itself degenerating whereas in unmanaged or mismanaged fresh waters the utility is short termed, less efficient and in most cases the system degenerates due to excessive siting, pollution, rapid drying or due to preponderance of poisonous weeds, etc.

Freshwater cover a relatively very small area of earth's surface, but due to their multiple utility, human culture and settlements have developed mostly along rivers. The freshwater bodies like rivers, streams, ponds and puddles are used variously. Rivers are used for (a) irrigation, (b) transport, (c) supply of drinking water, (d) generation of hydroelectric power, (e) aquatic sports and

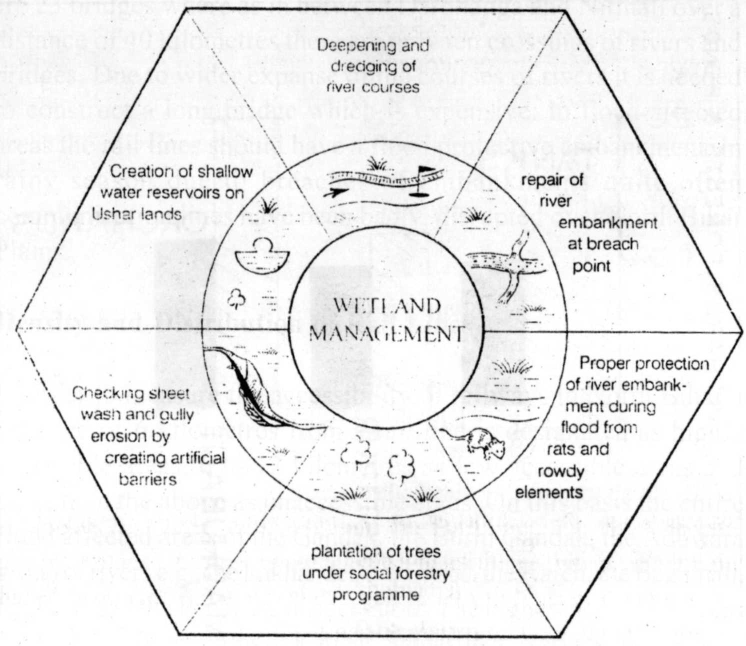


**Fig. 17.4 :** Wetland Management

recreation, (f) bathing, (g) for draining out the municipal and industrial refuge, (h) fishing and so on (Fig.17.3).

There is a range up to which any of these items could be put to use and they are interrelated. For instance excess removal of water for irrigation would effect all other aspects, the pollutants will not be sufficiently diluted due to reduced quantity of water, and may become toxic and injurious for drinking and bathing. It is essential, therefore, that aquatic ecosystems should be properly studied and management should be done considering the interrelations among multiple items of utility (Fig.17.4).

## Soil and Water Pollution

Water bodies such as ponds, lakes and rivers have been used to discharge into them the water of villages, towns and cities. These aquatic bodies have a self-regulatory mechanism of recycling these wastes quickly if the amount of sewage is small. But when the contamination level increases to such an extent that water becomes less useful or harmful, then we regard it as pollution. There are different kinds of pollutants such as sewage, organic chemicals like detergents (washing powders) and pesticides, harmful organisms and sediments. In some places radio active metals are also being dumped.

Normally, if the quantity of sewage received by rivers is in low quantity the organic materials are acted upon by bacteria and turned into minerals in a short time. But if the sewage quantity is higher than the self-purifying capacity of the river, the population of micro-organism acting on it increases considerably and in their respiratory activity consume all the oxygen. In poorly oxygenerated condition, with more of fishes, other animals and plants die and the clean river is turned into a stinking drain.

Pesticides specially the use of D.D.T. in the control of mosquito and pests in agriculture has become the most serious pollutant of soil and water. Many of such pesticides are none biodegradable chemicals which do not decompose or do so very slowly. Therefore, their concentration goes on increasing with successive application.[6]

## Chaur Drainage Schemes

Chaurs are low tracts of land, which remain waterlogged for six to nine months in a year. There are number of such Chaurs in this district. They are useless for growing crops as such and also breed mosquitoes. The Irrigation Department has taken the chaur drainage schemes to make the existing chaurs fit for cultivation. The details of some of the important chaurs are given below:

### *Kanail Chaur*

The Kanail and Arai Chaurs remain waterlogged for nine months in the year for want of effective drainage channel. In 1951 the bed of the channel was desilted and regarded to drain out the waterlogged area to an extent of 1037 hectares at the estimated cost of Rs.57,379.

### *Singia Group Chaurs*

The Singia group of Chaurs falls in Jale Thana and affect a number of villages. To drain these chaurs in the river Kharai drainage channel which falls in Nasu in the village Jahangir tola has been constructed. The estimated cost of the channel is Rs.39,913, which will being under cultivation 562 hectares of land.

### *Madhubani Chaurs*

Chaurs of Mangrauni, Chakdah, Ranti, etc. which are in the vicinity of Madhubani Town remain waterlogged throughout the year and spread malaria. Channels were dug up connecting all these low lands with river Kamla in order to draw silt laden water during high flood. Thus the low areas were almost filled up by heavy silt deposit. The estimated cost of the tapping of channel was Rs. 240,000 and the areas benefited is about 3097 hectares. The scheme was completed in 1959.

### *Kausaur Chaur*

The Kausaur Chaurs in Darbhanga thana remains waterlogged for the most part of the year.

The existing Nasi channel had been re-sectioned and regarded as sluice with marginal embankments along the Nasi had been constructed. The estimated cost of this drainage scheme is Rs. 1,29,696 and the area to be benefited will be about 1036 hectares.

### *Khaira Chaur*

This Chaur remain waterlogged for most parts of the year which falls in Darbhanga thana. The Khaira Chaur drainage scheme was started in 1957 at the estimated cost of Rs. 99,552. A scheme was prepared for the construction of an anti-flood sluice gate to prevent river water entering into the chaur. The chaur is subject to inundation every year by the spill of the river Kamla (Gausaghat branch) which usually destroys the standing crops. Hence, an anti-flood sluice was also made with the estimate amount. The existing channel is being excavated with designed section of 28 feet base width with side slope to cope with the discharge to drain the chaur easily. The work is still in execution.

## Evaluation and Monitoring

This project will evaluate the expenditure made on wetlands even casually and the government is trying to expend crores of rupees for the development of wetlands in North Bihar. The procedure of evaluation will be cost-benefit analysis, etc. The cost-benefit analysis has been done after giving some discount in per cent besides judging the social value and environmental quality of the area.

The monitoring of wetlands development is quite essential in order to :

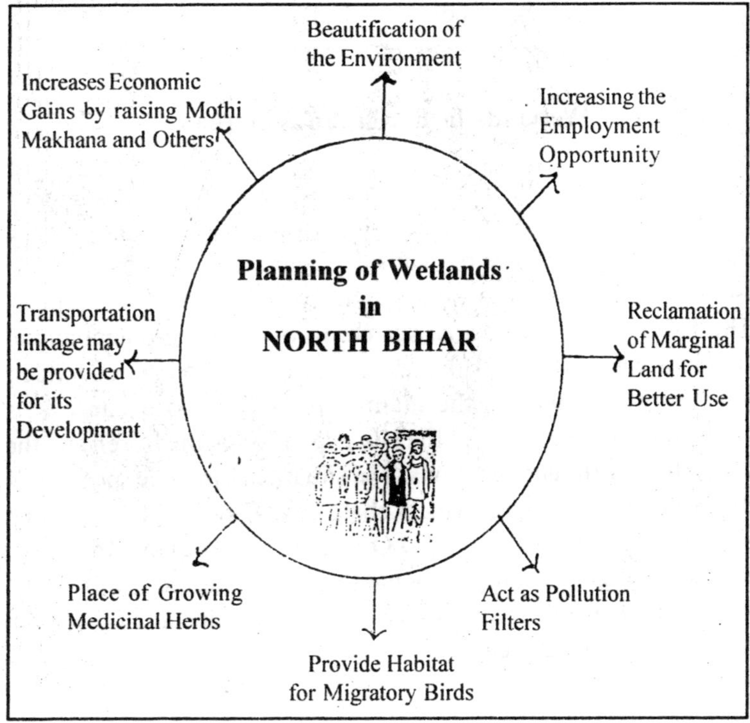


**Fig. 17.5 :** North Bihar : Planning of Wetlands

(a) Sefeguard our wetlands from filling and extinction.

(b) The migratory birds coming to North Bihar seasonally are vanishing slowly due to local prey which needs protection and conservation through proper guidance.

(c) With the rapid increase of population the trees and forest wealth are facing extinction which should be properly monitored for the survival because vegetation has a great power to purify the environment for the survival of living things. The annual flood is a menace in managing the affaire of wetlands because it hampers afforestation work, plugging the breach points, scare away the fishes, birds and disrupts the whole economy of the area.

(d) Monitoring of wetlands are essential because most of the polluted water from towns, villages, industrial establishments and agricultural fields with excess of pesticides and insecticids have a disastrous effect on the living organisms in Lakes, ponds and rivers found in the area.

**Problems of Wetlands in Kusheshwar Asthan**

In Kusheshwar Asthan Anchal a standing crop of 4150 hectare completely damaged by the flood and waterlogging. This area is constantly in the water but subsidy from the Government in the form of flood relief is so meagre that it does not solve the purpose. The fish rearing in this area suffers from greater problem due to stagnant water and so is the cattle rearing due to lack of fodder. Kusheshwar Asthan is the main area of wetland because it is surrounded by the rivers of the Kosi, the Kamla, the Kareh and the Balan from different directions. The situation is pitiable specially in the panchayats of Sughorin, Kebatgama, Dinmo, Chinhaya and Tilkeshwar. The Anchal B.D.O. has reported about the flood menace which has completely paralysed the life and health of the people who visit the area, otherwise there is a change of break out of epedemic in the area.

## NOTES


1. "Wetlands Conference in Czechoslovakia", *Nature and Resources*, UNESCO, Vol. XX, No.2, 1984, p. 22.
2. Mandal, R.B., *Planned Development of Rural Settlements*; Concept Publishing Company, New Delhi, 1982.
3. Dayal, P., "Bihar Plain: A Regional Study", *Transactions of the Council of Indian Geographers*, Vol.V., 1968.
4. Das, K. N., "Population and Land use changes in the Kosi Region, Bihar", Unpublished Ph. D. Thesis, Bhagalpur University, 1969.
5. Ambasht, R.S., *Plant Ecology*, Student's Friends and Co. Varanasi.
6. Choudhary, P.C. Roy, *Bihar District Gazetters*, Darbhanga Secretariat Press, Bihar, Patna, 1964, p. 142-143.

# 18

# THE NATURE OF WETLAND DATA ANALYSIS

## *1. Water Analysis*

- Estimation of hardness
- Qualitative and Quantitative Analysis (Detection of elements and estimation of rare elements.
- Tests of the micro-organisms.
- PH Value of water-Acidic-Alkali
- BOD tests-Bio-chemical oxygen deficiency.

## *2. Monitoring of Wetlands*

- At the interval of 3 months the soanning of depth is essential especially after flood to monitor.
- The free use of chemical fertilisers upto 500 metres around wetland should be banned to check killing of fishes, reptiles and birds.
- The dump of garbage and waste water in the wetland should be channelised to check water pollution from urban areas and industries.
- Filtering of sediment load in the tributaries of wetland at certain interval and distance to be planned.
- To find depth and level of protection needed the use of SONAR technique will be adopted.
- To create awareness among local people.

3. Controlling the flow of nutrients.
4. Removing toxins e.g. heavy metals, pesticids besides under standing biological, chemical and physical process of wetlands.
5. Search of possibilities to prepare plan of Natural Sewage Plant to treat tertiary waste water.
6. Study about pollution filters e.g. water-hyacinth as it absorbs nitrogen, phosphorous, potassium and other substance from water.
7. Storm protection wetlands are natural buffers against storm surges.
8. Reserves of genetic resources such as reserves of plants and animals.
9. Water fowl habitat.
10. Wetlands are not wastelands rather they are among the most fertile and productive ecosystems.
11. The State Irrigation Commission's Report 1971 and 1972 has five recommendations for wetlands.

    (a) Comprehensive approach to planned development of wetland is essential.
    (b) The economic gains emphasised rather than ecological,
    (c) The wetlands were viewed as valuable resources.
    The National Commission on Agriculture recommended the use of wetlands for fishery development whereas the Bihar Irrigation Commission recommended draining out the chaurs and reclaim them for agricultural use.
    (d) Wetlands considered as integral part of regional planning.
    (e) No emphasis is given on chaurs and ox-bow lakes as abode of resident and migratory birds.

12. The government should regulate development and management of all wetlands through one state level agency or authority.
13. The Wildlife (Protection) Act, 1972 passed by the Parliament define wildlife to include "any animal, bees, butterflies, crustaces, fish, moths and aquatic or land vegetation which forms part of any habitat". It is to be examined how far the provisions of this

Act could be enforced in protection of habitats in jheels, beels and chaurs, that is wetlands.

14. The words conservation, preservation, protection and promotion will need to be defined in the context of wetlands management in North Bihar. As yet there is not even a correct and upto date inventory of wetlands, and their salient features, such as its size, present use for various purposes, population of resident and migratory birds, extent of degradation and causes there of besides legal status. This is essential for contemplating and initiating action on preventive, protective, remedial and promotional measures.
15. The factors influencing the development of wetlands are the size, nature, location and sensitivity of the ecosystems to be affected, and the nature and importance of the natural functions and uses of those ecosystems are important.
16. The conservation of wetland may facilitate recreational facility through boating, viewing of birds, fishes, crocodile and wild animals as well.
17. To develop wetland is essential to respect treaty with USSR, and it would attract, scientists and naturalists to study birds behaviour, natural eco-systems, breeding biology besides making a preserve of natural history.
18. The preservation and conservation of flora and fauna of wetland from siltation, soil erosion, deforestation and by landscape modification so that it could attract more birds.
19. The quantitative analysis of topographical sheets, serial photographs and satellite imageries are essential for knowing the changing size and land use pattern around wetlands.
20. The analysis of sample data, the data gathered by filling of questionnaires, the land use data collected on cadastral sheets from field, impact analysis of various economic and socio-cultural processes going on in and around the wetland.
21. The calculation of various correlations, regressions, cost benefit analysis, Cob-Doglas production function, Geographical Information System Analysis, multivariate analysis or factor analysis may not be ruled out besides going on for computer

programming of certain set of data, which are normally unmanageable on small calculators.

22. The analysis of hundreds of maps, charts, graphs, topographical sheets besides aerial or satellite photo interpretation would be implied.

The study of wetland may be contemplated under the following sub-heads through data collection and analysis.

1. Pilot Survey and Inventory Analysis.
2. Statement of Problems and Basic strategies of wetland planning.
3. Historical Evolution of Wetlands.
4. Geological and Geographical setting of the Area.
5. Introducing Individual Wetlands
6. Ecological and Ecosystem Analysis
   (a) Zoo-geographical, and (b) Plant Geography.
7. Economic and social Gains from Wetlands.
8. Chemical Analysis of soil-water-plants.
9. Pollution-Hydrology-Biology.
10. Plan Formulation and Evaluation of Wetlands/Integrated Area Development.
11. Wetlands Management and upkeep.
12. Design and suggestions to Monitor Development Issues of Individual Wetland.
13. Participation of local people, Voluntary Agencies and Government Machinery. Problems of Conservation and Protection by law.
14. Summary and Conclusion.

# 19

# THE DETAILS OF DATA TO BE COLLECTED

1. Yearly measurement of the filling of chaurs, lakes, ponds and rivers under study in the area.

   (a) Nala-Pyne — annual load deposit
   (b) Rate of sedimentation due to flood
   (c) Land reclamation by local farmers withdrawn from wetlands
   (d) Dumping of wastes — rate of deposition.
   (e) Storage place of refuge water from urban areas and amount.
   (f) Depth variations in different parts of wetlands by SONAR. (Measurement by Navigation and Ranging Technique) to find the depth of water and the level of protection required.

2. Measurement and finding of the formation of new wetlands after each year.

3. Rate of deforestation and its impact on filling of wetlands.

4. Feasibility study of waterlogged areas for better utilization:

   - for makhana cultivation.
   - for fish production.
   - for crocodile farming
   - for plantation of medicinal herbs
   - for pollution filter plants
   - for maintaining the ecological balance

- for beautifying the environment
- for reducing the devastation of flood.
- for increasing the population supporting capacity of the region.

5. Tracing the history of the filling of wetlands by back projections of the rate of sedimentation and the time when they completely dwindle in case conservation measurers are not adopted.
6. Measurement of environmental adjustment of wetland with other factors of economic development :

   (a) Land use competition in and around wetland/study of land use pattern and mapping.
   (b) Excess employment generation by construction of ring bundhs, culverts, bridges, development of wetlands to attract tourists.
   (c) Transport development - water - roads - railways around wetlands.
   (d) Relations of human settlements with wetlands distance – direction-slope of the land - levels of wetlands pollution source of pollution local-search of remedies to check pollution,
   (e) Status of tree plantation around wetlands number of trees-area covered.
   (f) Wetlands as sources of irrigation/area covered.
   (g) Wetlands as shelter for local/migratory birds-season — number-species.
7. Measurement of economic gains from wetlands — amount of fish catch, makhana production — collection of medicinal herbs — purain leaves — lotus flower — vent flower.
8. To create awareness among the local people about the conservation and protection of wetlands and its need : Media :

   - Organising seminar and lectures
   - Display of postures
   - Peoples participation.

9. Selection of places to construct embankment - suilicegate - filtering place of sediment load of nalas pouring in wetlands at certain distance and interval of time.
10. Collection of soil samples from wetlands and get them soil tests done for knowing the fertility, chemical status, PH value, sodium presence besides Mhos analysis of soil and crop suitability.
11. Study of micro-climatic conditions of wetlands for knowing the sustenance capacity of plants and living organisms in wetlands. Micro-climatic condition includes the soil-moisture holding capacity and measurment of the rate of evapotranspiration, whether the plants living organisms add something substantial to the wetland ecology or they are extractionist in nature/ measure of absorption rate.
12. What are the plants to be grown successfully in wetlands need to test the rate of germination and selection of better variety to have some economic gain such as Singharas, Mothi, Makhana etc.
13. The functions of plants in wetlands depends upon the contribution of nutrients to the soil, to the living creatures such as plankton for fish, providing employment and sustenance to the local people, amicable to the local birds, animals, micro-biological environment and suitability of the micro-climatic conditions.
14. The wetland inventory includes the role of microphytes and algae in fresh water systems.
15. Measure of eco-system dynamics or changing conditions in continental wetlands shallow waters.
16. The change in wetland ecology is inevitable in response to the managerial system and change in seasons, availability of water stability and instability of water.
17. The seasonal variations of groundwater level, strat chart, acquifer zones thickness and knowing the structural variations of rocks are essential.
18. Plant to construct protective embankment, approach roads, regulation of excess water available during rains and floods.
19. To enact wetland-reform measures for subverting any encroachment on the near by government land and requisition

of coastal lands for the construction of embankment and tourist place.

20. Collection of data of population, occupational structure, dependant population on wetlands required correct estimation.
21. Collection of spot heights, water level, amount of rainfall, temperature, humidity, sun-shine, wind speed, direction of wind blows, types of soil, types of vegetation, types of land use, crops grown, input of fertilizer, sources and amount of land irrigated, mode of transport, types and patterns of drainage and human settlements, etc., will be required.
22. Photography and slide making for the relevant problems.
23. No. of crimes, and the attitude of public/administrators regarding the affairs and management of wetlands (Law and Order Probables), etc.
24. The Geographical Information System should be utilised to know the problems of wetland faced in an area and to adopt proper mode for the solution of problems in relation to the societal needs.

# 20

# ALL INDIA QUESTIONNAIRE FOR THE SURVEY OF WELTNADS

---

**STATE :** ____________________ **DISTRICT :** ______________

## A. GENERAL FEATURES

1. Name of the Wetland ____________________________
2. Ownership : __________Government __________Private
3. Geographic location:
   (a) State ____________________________________
   (b) District __________________________________
   (c) Nearest important town/village ____________
   (d) Geographic coordinates ____________________
   (i) Latitude ______________________________
   (ii) Longitude _____________________________
4. Approximate area of wetland (in hectare) __________

4.A.(a) Shoreline (length in kilometre) ______________
   (b) Kindly attach a map of the wetland

5. Are there any islands in the wetland ? _____Yes _____No.
   If yes, kindly give their number, area, usefulness and ecological importance:

   (a) Number ____________________________________

   (b) Total area (in hectare) ______________________

(c) Usefulness ______________________________

(d) Ecological importance ______________________________

## B. ECOLOGICAL FEATURES

6. Is this wetland natural or man-made? — Natural — Man-made (In contrast to natural wetlands, man-made wetlands are those which are formed by human activities, e.g.irrigation tanks, etc.)

7. (a) Is this wetland temporary or permanent?
   ________________Temporary __________Permanent

   (b) If temporary, in what months does it remain dry? ______

8. Landscape type:

   ______ Forest ______ Scrub______ Grassland _____ Desert
   ____ Delta ______ Estuary ______ Lagoon _____ Mangrove
   _____ Back-Water ______ Coastal Zone ______

9. Water source:

   ______ Spring ______ River ______ Irrigation Channel ___
   Run-off from surrounding areas _____ Estuary ______ Sea
   ____ Any others.

10. Approximate water depth (in metre):
    (a) Minimum
    (b) Maximum
    (c) Average

11. Water quality

    _________ Fresh water ________ Inland brackish/salt water
    _________ Coastal brackish water ________Marine water.

## C. FLORA

12. Please list below the plant species growing in the wetland indicating their common/ scientific names/relative abundance/ economic importance.

| *Sl. No.* | *Common name* | *Scientific Name* | *Abundance** | *Economic Importance* |
|---|---|---|---|---|
| 1. | ________ | ________ | ________ | ________ |
| 2. | ________ | ________ | ________ | ________ |
| 3. | ________ | ________ | ________ | ________ |
| 4. | ________ | ________ | ________ | ________ |
| 5. | ________ | ________ | ________ | ________ |
| 6. | ________ | ________ | ________ | ________ |
| 7. | ________ | ________ | ________ | ________ |
| 8. | ________ | ________ | ________ | ________ |
| 9. | ________ | ________ | ________ | ________ |
| 10. | ________ | ________ | ________ | ________ |
| 11. | ________ | ________ | ________ | ________ |
| 12. | ________ | ________ | ________ | ________ |

* Abundance of the individual spacies may be indicated with the help of appropriate symbols given below:
A = Abundant; F = Frequent; R = Rare; VR = Very Rare.

13. List endengered plant species of Thalophytes, Bryophytes, Pteredephytes, Gymnosperms, Angiosperms, etc. which are endangered:

(a) Locally __________ Yes __________ No

(b) Regionally __________ Yes __________ No

| | *Thalophytes* | | *Bryophytes* | | *Gymnosperms* | | *Angiosperms* | |
|---|---|---|---|---|---|---|---|---|
| | *Local Name* | *Scientific Name* | *Local Name* | *Scientific Name* | *Local Name* | *Scientific Name* | *Local Name* | *Scientific Name* |
| (a) Locally | | | | | | | | |
| | ---- | ------ | ---- | ------ | ---- | ------ | ---- | ------ |
| | ---- | ------ | ---- | ------ | ---- | ------ | ---- | ------ |
| | ---- | ------ | ---- | ------ | ---- | ------ | ---- | ------ |
| | ---- | ------ | ---- | ------ | ---- | ------ | ---- | ------ |
| | ---- | ------ | ---- | ------ | ---- | ------ | ---- | ------ |
| | ---- | ------ | ---- | ------ | ---- | ------ | ---- | ------ |
| | ---- | ------ | ---- | ------ | ---- | ------ | ---- | ------ |
| | ---- | ------ | ---- | ------ | ---- | ------ | ---- | ------ |
| | ---- | ------ | ---- | ------ | ---- | ------ | ---- | ------ |
| | ---- | ------ | ---- | ------ | ---- | ------ | ---- | ------ |
| | ---- | ------ | ---- | ------ | ---- | ------ | ---- | ------ |
| (b) Regionally. | | | | | | | | |
| | ---- | ------ | ---- | ------ | ---- | ------ | ---- | ------ |
| | ---- | ------ | ---- | ------ | ---- | ------ | ---- | ------ |
| | ---- | ------ | ---- | ------ | ---- | ------ | ---- | ------ |
| | ---- | ------ | ---- | ------ | ---- | ------ | ---- | ------ |
| | ---- | ------ | ---- | ------ | ---- | ------ | ---- | ------ |
| | ---- | ------ | ---- | ------ | ---- | ------ | ---- | ------ |
| | ---- | ------ | ---- | ------ | ---- | ------ | ---- | ------ |
| | ---- | ------ | ---- | ------ | ---- | ------ | ---- | ------ |
| | ---- | ------ | ---- | ------ | ---- | ------ | ---- | ------ |
| | ---- | ------ | ---- | ------ | ---- | ------ | ---- | ------ |
| | ---- | ------ | ---- | ------ | ---- | ------ | ---- | ------ |

## D. FAUNA

14. Kindly list below the important migratory and resident birds of this wetland.

| *Sl. No.* | *Common Name* | *Scientific Name* | *(M) Migratory (R) Resident* |
|---|---|---|---|
| 1. | | | |
| 2. | | | |
| 3. | | | |
| 4. | | | |
| 5. | | | |
| 6. | | | |
| 7. | | | |
| 8. | | | |
| 9. | | | |
| 10. | | | |
| 11. | | | |
| 12. | | | |

15. (a) Indicate whether population of migratory water birds has increased/decreased during the last ten years. Increased ______________ Decreased last ten years.

(b) Please list below the migratory birds which have increased/ decreased:

(i) Increased

| *Sl. No.* | *Common Name* | *Scientific Name* |
|---|---|---|
| 1. | | |
| 2. | | |
| 3. | | |
| 4. | | |
| 5. | | |
| 6. | | |

(ii) Decreased

| *Sl.No.* | *Common Name* | *Scientific Name* |
|---|---|---|
| 1. | | |
| 2. | | |

3. ______________ ______________
4. ______________ ______________
5. ______________ ______________
6. ______________ ______________

16. Approximate number of resident birds inhabiting the wetland:

    (a) Number of species ______________
    (b) Total number of birds ______________

17. List of important mammals Rs associated with this wetland.

| *SI.No.* | *Common Name* | *Scientific Name* |
|---|---|---|
| 1. | ______________ | ______________ |
| 2. | ______________ | ______________ |
| 3. | ______________ | ______________ |
| 4. | ______________ | ______________ |
| 5. | ______________ | ______________ |
| 6. | ______________ | ______________ |

18. List of important reptiles associated with this wetland.

| *SI.No.* | *Common Name* | *Scientific Name* |
|---|---|---|
| 1. | ______________ | ______________ |
| 2. | ______________ | ______________ |
| 3. | ______________ | ______________ |
| 4. | ______________ | ______________ |
| 5. | ______________ | ______________ |
| 6. | ______________ | ______________ |

19. List of important amphibian species found in the wetland

| Sl.No. | Common Name | Scientific Name |
|---|---|---|
| 1. | ________ | ________ |
| 2. | ________ | ________ |
| 3. | ________ | ________ |
| 4. | ________ | ________ |
| 5. | ________ | ________ |
| 6. | ________ | ________ |

20. List of important fish species found in the wetland.

| Sl.No. | Common Name | Scientific Name |
|---|---|---|
| 1. | ________ | ________ |
| 2. | ________ | ________ |
| 3. | ________ | ________ |
| 4. | ________ | ________ |
| 5. | ________ | ________ |
| 6. | ________ | ________ |

21. List of important shell-fish found in the wetland.

| Sl.No. | Common Name | Scientific Name |
|---|---|---|
| 1. | ________ | ________ |
| 2. | ________ | ________ |
| 3. | ________ | ________ |
| 4. | ________ | ________ |
| 5. | ________ | ________ |
| 6. | ________ | ________ |

22. Approximate annual fiesh yield (including shell-fish, frogs etc.) in kg/quintal ____________

23. Name of the major fish species contributing to the yield. (including shell fish)

| *SI.No.* | *Common Name* | *Scientific Name* |
|---|---|---|
| 1. | ________ | ________ |
| 2. | ________ | ________ |
| 3. | ________ | ________ |
| 4. | ________ | ________ |
| 5. | ________ | ________ |
| 6. | ________ | ________ |

24. Any other important animal species associated with this wetland.

| *SI.No.* | *Common Name* | *Scientific Name* |
|---|---|---|
| 1. | ________ | ________ |
| 2. | ________ | ________ |
| 3. | ________ | ________ |
| 4. | ________ | ________ |
| 5. | ________ | ________ |
| 6. | ________ | ________ |

25. List of endangered animal species of mammals, birds, reptiles, etc. which are endangered (a) locally or (b) regionally.

| | *Mammal* | *Bird* | *Reptile* |
|---|---|---|---|
| (a) Locally: | ________ | ________ | ________ |
| | ________ | ________ | ________ |
| | ________ | ________ | ________ |
| | ________ | ________ | ________ |

(b) Regionally ________ ________
________ ________ ________
________ ________

## E. Wetland Resources and Socio-Economic Aspects

26. What is the major use of this wetland to the local population?

| | | |
|---|---|---|
| ______ Read gathering | ______ Grazing | ______ Agricultre |
| ______ Cultivation of edible water plants | ______ Fuelwood collection | ______ Forestry operations |
| ______ Fishing | ______ Fish culture | ______ Irrigation |
| ______ Brick making | ______ Pottery | ______ Clay gathering |
| ______ Sewage disposal | ______ Factory effluent disposal | ______ Solid waste disposal |

Any other (Please describe) ________________

27. Indicate (by x mark) the relative importance of this wetland in respect of following resources:

| | *Fish* | *Water bird* | *Fodder plants* | *Edible plants* |
|---|---|---|---|---|
| Very high | ______ | ______ | ______ | ______ |
| High | ______ | ______ | ______ | ______ |
| Medium | ______ | ______ | ______ | ______ |
| Low | ______ | ______ | ______ | ______ |
| Nil | ______ | ______ | ______ | ______ |

28. (a) It this wetland a source of drinking water for:

______ Human beings ______ Cattle ______ Wild animals

(b) Does this wetland provide nesting/roosting/feeding area for water birds.?

______ Nesting ______ Roosting ______ Feeding

29. Is this wetland important as a place of tourist attraction?

__________ Yes __________ No

If yes, please indicate: ________________

(a) Approximate number of tourists visting the area per year —
(b) The main tourist season From ________ to ________
(c) What is the main tourist attraction:
______ Boating ______ Bird watching ______
Fishing ______ Natural Scenery ______ Duck shooting
Any other (Please specify) ________________

30. What is the main occupation of the people living in the vicinity of this wetland?

______________________________

______________________________

31. Is this wetland site being used for any religious purpose / gathering? __________ Yes __________ No

32. Approximate total annual revenue earned from this wetland (in rupees) ________________

## F. Legislation

33. Are there any legislations pertaining to this wetland ? If so, please give details

______________________________

______________________________

34. Indicate whether fising in the area is:

______ Open ______ Regulated ______ Prohibited

35. Indicate whether hunting in the area is:
________ Open _________ Regulated ________Prohibited

## G. Impact of Human Activities

36. Kindly indicate whether any part of this wetland has been drained or reclaimed in the living money ________ Yes ___________ No
    (a) Indicate the approximate area involved
    (b) What is the present land use of the reclaimed area

37. Does the wetlend suffer from any threat due to:

    _____ Domestic sewage ____ Duck shooting ____Drainage
    ___ Deforestation _____Factory effluents ____ Overgrazing
    ____ Overfishing __________ Solid waste __________Silting
    __________________________, Any other human activity.

38. Give your assessment of the impact of human activities on the wetland ____________________________________________

39. Do you know of any other wetland in this area which has been entirely drained, reclaimed or ______________________ Yes ____________________ No lost in the past ?

    If Yes, please give details : _________________________

    ____________________________________________________
    ____________________________________________________
    ____________________________________________________
    ____________________________________________________
    ____________________________________________________
    ____________________________________________________
    ____________________________________________________
    ____________________________________________________

# 21

# CONCLUSIONS

Wetlands are considered as marginal lands but they have the great potentiality of checking the pollution of environment from dust, dirt and abnoxious gases. Hence, the wetlands should be regarded as the saviours of humanity. Wetlands act as pollution filter and they beautify the surrounding environment. In North Bihar right from West Champaran in the west upto Kishanganj district in the east, each district has its own wetland which could be seen in the following (Table 21.1).

**Table 21.1 :** One Important Wetland in each district of North Bihar

| *Sl. No.* | *District* | *Wetland* |
|---|---|---|
| 1. | West Champaran | Lal Saraiya |
| 2. | East Champaran | Kesariya Chaur |
| 3. | Sitamarhi | Ghordaur Tank |
| 4. | Muzaffarpur | Bharthuwa Chaur |
| 5. | Vaishali | Baraila Tal |
| 6. | Saran | Hardia Chaur |
| 7. | Siwan | Ditches |
| 8. | Gopalganj | Ditches |
| 9. | Madhubani | Krishnaraj Sagar |
| 10. | Darbhanga | Narail Chaur |
| 11. | Samastipur | Mehsar chaur |
| 12. | Begusarai | Kabar Tal |
| 13. | Khagaria | Dasin Chaur |
| 14. | Saharsa | Chouri Lake |
| 15. | Supaul | Bengagghasan |
| 16. | Madhepura | Several Chaurs |
| 17. | Katihar | Jangli Tal English |
| 18. | Purnea | Sora Jheel |
| 19. | Araria | Several Chaurs |
| 20. | Kishanganj | Dahichal Chaurs |
| 21. | North Bhagalpur | Marshy Lands. |

Most of the wetlands found in North Bihar are known as Jhanjhatia Mahal as these are the areas of quarrel in between the Government owners of the land and the Machhua society. Recently, the so-called Rangdars are also torturing the Machhua society for forcibly fish catch.

The wetlands as waterbodies help in the irrigation as well as navigation. The agricultural fields in the surrounding area pour the unwanted trace elements in the water which is harmful not only for the migratory birds, fishes and plants found in the water. Although several firms of Calcutta collected medicinal plants from these wetlands. Among the plants litchen, Kai, Sewar and different types of algae and fungi are important.

Different aspects of wetlands considered for improvement are as follows:

1. Keeps Water Level High
2. Haven for Machhua Society
3. Government Receives Revenue
4. Surrounded by vegetation due to high saturation
5. Rich hates it as Marginal land
6. Poors love if for protein supply
7. Repel Drought and Flood
8. Attract Flood as Reservoir
9. Beautifies the Environment
10. Make Ecological Balance
11. Fish Producing Ground
12. Act as Pollution Filter
13. Need Planned Management by Conservation Protection and Promotion
14. Declining due to over siltation
15. Laws of the Land should be adopted for planning and proper management.

The wetlands are areas of Pioneer fringe where the basic human activities have gained purification in terms of fish catch, beautifying the environment, collection of medicinal plants and herbs, development of Birds. Sanctury besides the cultivation of makhana and mothi.

Now-a-days, the studies of wetlands have drown the attention of most educated people and Developed Nations of the world because wetlands act as pollution filter and it is a source of recreations, prolific place for game birds, and wetlands are considered essential for the cultivation of rice and providing employment to a lot of people. Wetlands ecology favours the habitat of plants, birds, fishes, varieties of snakes, insects and lizards as well. Since historic past the people of the world neglected the wetlands and they are still doing so but they are considered essential for fresh water supply, source of irrigation and these are the areas of navigation and a beautiful place for picnic and attraction of tourists. Most of the lakes of world which have formed either due to volcanic eruption, unequal distribution of sands, sheetwash erosion at the time of flood or due to meandering courses of rivers are potential areas for settlements. Silting on natural levee and they are the areas of diverse landscape features to break the monotony of people who are living on the plain lands. In North Bihar most of the cremation ground, temples, bathing place for men and beasts and ferry points are situated along wetlands because people have developed close relations from birth to death with the wetlands. In such a situation, the planned development of wetland is necessary for sustainable growth of economy and the society living near the wetlands.

It could be concluded that wetland are kidney of nature. Therefore, it should be protected, conserved and the regulatory systems identified for the betterment of humanity. The concepts of wetlands study are still in primary stage because these are marginal lands which have not drawn attention of scientists of the world at large. There is still a tug of war between the scientists and the farmers, as the scientist want to protect, conserve and beautify the environment for the emancipation of human society. Whereas farmers think about harnessing and producing more and more from the wetland. Now-a-days, with the excessive increase of population the assessment of the productivity of wetland has increased manifold as the people are in need of judiciously using wetland for providing sustenance to more and more people.

The geographical framework provides us the base for wetland development in terms of suitability of land, soil, climatic conditions, flora and fauna besides mentality of the local people whether attracted towards wetland or not. It has been found that in North Bihar the economy is wholly oriented towards wetland management, as this is represented by the growing of rice, Mothi, Singarhara, Makhana and Bhent besides fish catch and collection of crabs, snails and varieties of medicinal herbs from the wetlands and their surroundings. In areas of wetlands the lines of transport are relatively less developed and one has to walk a long distance in order to reach to these marginal lands. Industrially, these areas are less attractive. The levels of urbanization is very poor only 5 per cent. The density of population is high about 500 to 800 persons per $km^2$ but the quality of population is very poor, as they are illiterate and leading a life of below standard. Only Mallah people does the work of fishermen. The factors of wetlands are surface configuration, high amount of rainfalls, the area prone to floods, the culture which rests on the wetland, along with the problems of sedimentation, erosion of land and the pollution which the wetlands are facing.

It is a sad state of affairs that uptil now the government has no definite policies for the regulation and development of wetlands. Conclusions could also be drawn regarding theoretical background of wetlands found in North Bihar. Although there is a lack of data and proper information on wetlands, but the author is of the opinion that wetlands are remnants of former Indo-Gangetic trough found in pleistocene period in North Bihar. In this period due to deglaciation the wetlands have been filled up and their remnants are still found here and there in the form of lakes, tals, chaurs, moin, man, beels, sand, bars, ditches in North Bihar. This area is quite potential for sheet wash erosion especially during flood and hence wetlands are located in valleys in between interfluves of streams. The Valley location of wetlands have been proposed which have a reality in the flood plains of North Bihar because they lie in lowland areas such as Simri Chaur, Gordah, Jalai-Malai, Dhima-Makhnaha, Simardah, Kusheshwar Asthan and several others.

The North Bihar is a land of rivers and waterways and there

are numerous ferry points like Akharaghat, Baryahighat, Kolhuaghat, Khararighat and Hayaghat, etc. All these are located along the Kareh river and there are several archaeological evidence for their long time continuance. The land around Khagaria is known as ancient Matashyadesh (the land of fish) where *Agni* (Vaishwanara the God of fire) accompanied Videha on their march towards east from the bank of Saraswati river of the Punjab during Aryan period.

In terms of economic value of these wetlands the production of Makhana, herbs besides transportation and tourism are important including the vast amount of fish catch. From cultural side wetland has important role to play in recreation, navigation, religious and ritual performances. Some tanks of this area have archaeological importance as *Jalmandir* (water temple) of Pawapuri where the body of Lord Mahavira emersed in flowry water tank, and from others the statue of Lord Budha, God Barah and others excavated in Rajgir, Kamtaul, Kundagrama, Naulagarh, Tetrawan, Uttra, Bahera and Buxar. So far as the ecological value is concerned wetlands act as pollution filter, maintain ecological balance, offers abode for endangered plants, birds, animals and hence it is obligation on us to conserve, manage and protect wetlands.

From the productivity point of view the value of wetland is immense. For example the Rajorkhar Tank of Narayanpur village in Manigachhi Anchal of Darbhanga district produces fish of Rs. 3.50 lacs and Makhana of Rs. 1.50 over 21 hectares of land annually. The production of no crop on land will be of this value. Hence, the wetlands have physical ecological, economic and social value for the humanity. In this way, for the betterment of humanity the wetland should be conserved, protected and promoted, as they are the saviours of our environment.

# BIBLIOGRAHY

Adam, P., Coastal Wetlands of New South Weles. Report to the coastal council, Sydney, 1985.

Adams, M. Merrony, C. and Sydes, R. E., Excavations at Sutton Common, South Yorkshire, 1988. Unpublished Report, South Yorkshire Archaeology Unit.

Ahmad, S.S., *Ecology of Wetlands of Milkichak*, Darbhanga, Ph.D. Thesis, L.N. Mithila University, Darbhanga, 1993.

Aksorkoae, S., *Ecology and Management of Mangroves*, IUCN, Bangkok, Thailand, 1993.

Aldhouse-Green, S.H.R, Whittle, A. W. R, Allen, J. R. L, Caseldine, A.E., Culver, S. J, Day, M. H, Lundquist, J. and Upton, D., Prehistoric human footprints from the Severn Estuary at Uskmouth and Magor Pill, Gwent, Wales. *Archaeologia Cambrensis*, 141, 1993, pp. 14-55.

Allen, J.R.L. and Rae, J.E., *Late Flandrian shoreline oscillations in the Severn Estuary : A Geomorphological and Stratigraphical Reconnaissance*. Hilosophical Transactions of the Royal Society of London, B 315 ; 1987, pp. 185-230.

Allen, J.R.L., Reclamation and sea defence in Rumney Parish, Monmouthshire. *Archaeologia Cambrensis*, CXXXVII, 1988, pp. 135-40.

Allen, J. R. L. and Fulford, M.G., The Wentlooge Level : A Romano-British saltmarsh reclamation in South Weles, *Britannia*, 17, 1986,pp. 91-117.

Allison, J. Godwin, H. and Waren, S.H., Late glacial deposits at Nazeing in the Lee Valley. *Proceedings of the Royal Society*, series B, 236 : (1952) pp. 169-240.

Andrews, J. and Kinsaman, D., Gravel Pit Restoration for Wildlife : A practical manual. *Royal Society for the Protection of Birds*, Sandy, 1990.

Angel, J. and Heyes, R., *A Guide to lanning for Coastal Wetland Protection in New South Wales*. Total Environment Centre, Sydney, 1993.

Apsimon, A. M, Donovan, D. T. and Taylor, M. B., The stratigraphy and archaeology of the lateglacial and postglacial deposits at Brean Down, Somerset. *Proceedings of the University of Bristol Archaeological Society*. 9, 1961, pp. 67-136.

ARCUS, Sutton Common Environmental Analysis Assessment Report, ARCUS NO. 181. Archaeological Research Consultancy University of Sheffield, 1994.

Armstrong, J., Armstrong, W. and Beckett, P.M., Hragnites Australist : Venturi and humidity induced pressure flows enhance rhizome aeration and rhizone oxidation. *New Phytologist,* 120, 1992, pp. 197 207.

Arthington, A. and Hegerl, E., The conservation and management of Australian Wetlands — A discussion, *In the Conservation of Australian Wetlands* (eds A.J.McComb and P.S. Lake), pp. 62-79. Surry Beatty, Sydney, 1998.

Australian Archaeological Association Minutes of the Australian Archaeological Association AGM 1991. *Australian Archaeology*, 34, 1992, pp. 52-7.

Ayres, M., Classification of Aboriginal heritage sites, as a heritage management tool, in the Lismore-Ballina region, New South Wales. Unpublished Integrated Project thesis, University of New England, Northern Rivers, Lismore, Australia, 1993.

Backeus, I., Ecotone Versus ecocline : Vegetation zonation and dynamics around a small reservoir in Tanzania, *Journal of Biogeography*, 20, 1993, pp. 209-18.

Ball, S.G., The importance of the invertebrate fauna of Thorne and Hatfield Moors an exercise in evaluation. *Thorne and Hafield Papers*, 3 pp. 34-5.

Barhier, E. B., Adams, W. M. and Kimmage, K., *Economic Valuation-Wetland Benefits : The Hadejia Jama are Floodplain*, Nigeria, LEEC Discussion paper pp. 9-30. London Environmental Economics Centre, London, 1991.

Barber, K.E., Peatlands as scientific archieves of past biodiversity. *Biodiversity and Conservation*, 2, 1993, pp. 474-89.

Barnes, I., Second severn crossing : English Approaches : An interim statement on the 1992-93 fieldwork. In Archaeology in the Severn Estuary, 1993, Annual Report of the severn Estuary Levels Research Committee, 1993, pp. 5-20. SELRC, Lampeter.

Batten, L.A., Bibby, C.J. Clement, P. Elliott, G.D. and Porter, R.F., *Red Date Birds in Britain Poyser*, London, 1990.

Bay-Petersen, J. L., Animal Exploitation in Mesolithic Denmark. In the *Early Postglacial Settlement of Northern Europe* (ed. P. Mellars) 1998, pp. 115-45. Duckworth, London.

Bell, M., Brean Down Excavation 1989 and 1991. *In Severn Eatuary Levels Research Committee Annual Report 1991*, 1992, pp. 34-42, SELRC, Lampeter.

Bell, M., Field Survey and Excavation at Goldeliff. *In Severn Estuary Levels Research Committee Annual Report 1992*, pp. 15-29. SELRC, Lampeter.

Bibby, C., Housden, S., Porter, R. and Thomas, G.A., *Conservation Strategy for Birds*. RSPB, The Lodge, Sandy, Bedfordshire, 1989.

Blunden, J. and Curry, N. (eds) *A People's Charter?* Forty Years of the National Parks and Access to the Countryside Act. HMSO, London, 1989.

Bradley, C., The hydrology of a floodplain wetland, Narborough Bog, Leicestershire. Unpublished Ph. D. thesis, University of Leicester, 1994.

Bradley, C. Brown, A. G., Shallow groundwater modelling and the overbank contribution to a small floodplain bog. In *Geomorphology and Groundwater* (ed. A G Brown) , 1995, pp. 37-52. Wiley, Chichester.

Brinkkemper, O., Wetland Farming in the Area to the South of the Meuse Estuary during the Iron Age and the Roman Period. An Environmental and Palaeo-economic Reconstruction. *Analecta Praehistorica Leidensia* 24, 1993, pp. 1-226.

Brookes, A., *Channelized Rivers Perspectives for Environmental Management*. Willey, Chichester, 1988.

Brongers, J.A., Air Photography and Celtic Field Research in the Netherlands. *Nederlandse Oudheden* 6, Amersfoort, 1976.

Brown, A.G. and Bradley, C., Flood plain and palaeochannel wetlands: Geomorphology, hydrology and conservation. *In Conserving our Landscape : Envolving Landforms and Ice-Age Heritage* (eds C. Stevens and C. Bradley) 1992, pp. 101-12. English Nature, Peterborough.

Brown, D.A. and Overend, R.P., Methane metabolism in raised bogs of northern wetlands. *Journal of Geomicrobiology*, 11, 1993, pp. 35-48.

Brown, D.A. Mathur, S. P. and Kushner, D.J., An ombrotrophic bog as a methane reservoir. *Global Biogeochemical Cycling*, 3, 1989, pp. 205-13.

Brundland Report, Our Common Future. *Report of the 1987 World Commission on Environment and Development*. Oxford University Press, 1987.

Buckland, P.C. and Dinnin, M. H., The rise and fall of wetland: recent palaeoecological research on Thorne and Hatfield Moors. Thorne and Hatfield Papers, 4. Doncaster.

Buckland, P.C., Peatland archaeology conservation resource on the edge of extinction. *Biodiversity and Conservation* 2, 1993, pp. 513-27.

Centre for Coastal Management (CCM), National Estuarine Inventory. Report to Australian Recreational Sport fishing Confederation and Australian National Parks and Wildlife Service, Canberra, 1989.

Coles, B. and Coles, J., *People of the Wetlands*. Thames and Hudson, London, 1989.

Coles, B. (ed.)., The Wetland Revolution in Prehistory. The Prehistoric Society and WARP (Wetland Archaeology Research Group), *Occasional Paper 6*. Exter University, 1992.

Coles, B.J., Wetland site protection and preservation. In *A Celebration of Wood* (ed. J. A Springgs) , 1994, p. 3-14. WARP Occasional Paper 8. York Archaeological Wood Centre, York.

Coles, B.J., Wetland Management : A Survey for English Haritage. WARP Occasional Paper 9. WARP, Exeter, 1995.

Coles, B.J., Archaeology and wetland restoration. In the *Restoration of Temperate Wetlands* (eds B. Wheeler, S. Shaw, W. Fojt and A. Robertson). Wiley & Sons, Chichester, 1995.

Coles, B. and Coles, J.M., *Sweet Track to Glastonbury*. Thames and Hudson, London, 1986.

Conservation Foundation; *Protection of America's Wetlands. An Action Agend.* The Conservation Foundation, Washington, DC, 1988.

Cowardin, L. M., V. Carter, F. C. Colet, and E. T. La Roe, *Classificatiion. of Wetlands and deep water habitats of United States*, 1979, U. S. Fish and Wildlife Service Pub. FWS/OBS- 79 / 31, Washington, D. C., P. 103.

Cox, M.J., Archaeology in the mire : Wetland archaeology and nature conservation. In *Rescuing our Historic Environment* (ed. H. Swain) , 1993, pp. 65-70. Reposcue, Rerts.

Cox, M.J., Jones, E. B. G. and Hogan, D. V., Website curation and monitoring in the Somerset Levels and Moors. In *Science and Site* (ed. J. Beavis and K.M. Barker), Archetype, London.

Darvill, T., *Valuing Britain's Archaeological Resource*. Bournemouth University Inaugural Lecture, July 1993. Bournemouth University, 1993.

Darvill, T. Gerrard, C. and Startin, B., Identifying and protecting historic landscapes. *Antiquity*, 67, 1993, pp. 536-574.

Darvill, T., Value systems in archaeology. In *Managing Archaeology* (eds M.A. Cooper, A. Firth, J. Carman and D. Wheatley). Routledge, London, 1995.

Darvill, T. Saunders, A. and Startin, B., A question of national importance: approaches to the evalution of ancient monuments for the Monuments Protection Programme in England. *Antiquity*, 61, 1987, pp. 393-408.

Davies, J. and Claridge, C. F. (eds), Wetland Benefits. *The Potential for Wetlands to Support and Maintain Development*. Publication No. 87. Asian Wetland Bureau, Kuala Lumpur, 1993.

Denny, P., Water management strategies for the conservation of wetlands. *Journal of the Institute of Water and Environmental Managers*, 7, 1993, 387-94.

Denny, P., Wetlands of Africa; Introduction. In *Wetlands of the First World I : Inventory, Ecology and Management* (eds D.F. Whigham, D. Dykyjova, and S. Hejny, 1993, pp. 1-31. Kluwer Academic Publishers, Dordrecht, The Netherlands.

Denny, P., African wetlands. In *Wetlands* (eds M Finlayson and M Moser), pp. 115-48. Facts on File Ltd. Oxford.

Denny, P., (ed). *The Ecology and Management of African Wetland Vegetation.* Dr. W. Junk Publishers, the Hague, the Netherlands 1985.

Den Hartog, C. and Segal, S., A new classification of the water plant communities. *Acta Botanica Neerlandica*, 13, 1964, pp. 367-93.

Denny, P., Biodiversity and wetlands. *Wetlands Ecology and Management*, 3, 1994, pp. 55-61.

Dewilde, M. and Bossu, P., Het Weidegebedies Van Lampernisse. Waar Kulturhistorie en natuur elkar ontmoeten. In *Natuurreservaten jg* 15-2, 1993, pp. 4-7.

Dewilde, M. Ruilverkavelingsb1ok stuivekenskerke. Cultuurhistorische inventarisatie. Unpublished report, 1992.

De Lange, J. Delvosalle, L., Durigneaud, J, Lambinon, J and Vendem Berghen, C., Flora van Belgeie het Grootherttogdom Luxemburg, *Noord-Frankryk en de Aangrenzende Gebieden*, 1988.

De Bruin, D., Ooievaar. De Toekomst van het Rivierengebied. *Stichting Gelderse Milieufederatie*, Arnhem, 1987.

Dinnin, M., Islands within islands: The development of the British Enfomofauna during the Holocene and the implications for conservation, Unpublished Ph. D. dissertation, University of Sheffield, 1992.

Dinel, H., Mathur, S., Brown, A. and Levesque M., A field study of the effect of depth on methane production in Peatland Waters: equipment and preliminary results, *Journal of Ecology*, 76, 1988, pp. 1083-91.

DI (Department of Primary Industries) Edfish; Wetland Education Project, DI, Brisbane, 1989.

Dodson, J., Fullager, R., Furby, J., Jones, R. and Prosser, I., Humans and megafauna in a late pleistocene environment from Cuddie Springs, north western New south wales. *Archaeology in Oceania*, 28, 1993, pp. 93-99.

Doran, G., Problems and potential of wet sites in North America: The example of windover. In *The Wetland Revolution in Prehistory* (ed. B Coles), 1992, pp. 125-34, WARP Occasional Paper 6. The Prehistoric Society and WARP, Exeter.

Dugan, P. J. (ed.) *Wetland Conservation : A Review of Cutrent Issues and Required Action.* IUCN. Gland, Switzerland, 1990.

Dumayne., L. and Barbex, K.E., The Impact of the Romans on the Environment of Northexn England: Pollen data From Three sites close to Hadxian's wall. *The Holocene* 4, 1994, pp. 165-73 .

Dutton, I. N. Jenner, G. G., Specht, A. and Thomson, G., The use of vegetation and water resources monitoring as an input to environmental managements : A case study from North Stradbroke Island. In *Proceedings of the Australian water and Wastewater Association* 15th Federal Convention, 1993, pp. 413-18. Australian Water and Wastewater Association, Brisbane.

Dutton, I. M., Developing a management strategy for coastal wetlands. In *Island Environment and Coast Development* (eds W. Ying and C.T. Schafer) , pp 285-303. Nanjing University Press, People's Republic of China, 1992.

Dutton, I. M. Saenger, P., Perry, T., Luker, G., and Worboys, G., L., An integrated approach to the management of aquatic resources: a case study from Jervis Bay, *Australia. Aquatic Conservation*, 4, 1994, pp. 57-73.

Edwards, K. J. and MacDonald, G.M., Holocene Palaeontology II. Human influence and Vegetation change. *Progress in Physical Geography*, 15 (3), 1991, pp. 261-89.

Eggertsson, T., *Economic Behaviour and Institutions.* Cambridge University Press, 1990.

English Heritage and English Nature : A statement of intent for the conservation of the natural and archaeological environment. *Statement* dated 3.12.1992.

Environment Science and Services; Coastal Zone Inquiry: Queensland Case Study, Resource Assessment Commission, Canberra, 1992.

EPA (Environment Protection Authority); Environmental Protection (Swan Coastal Plain Wetlands) Policy. *EPA*, Perth, 1991.

Eversham, B. C. , Skidmore, P. and Euckland, P.C. Invertebrates as indicators of lowland bogs in eastern England: Some British bogs in a European context. In *Ninth Colloquium of the European Invertebra te Survey: Bioindicators at a pan-European level*, (eds P. T. Harding and I Valovirta). Institute of Terrestrial Ecology, Abbots Ripton.

Evesaham., B.C. and Arnold, H.R.; Introductions: Their place in British wildlife. In *Biological Recording of Changes in British Wildlife* (ed. P.T. Harding), 1992, pp. 44-59. Institute of Terrestrial Ecology Symposium 26. HMSO, London.

Faegri, K., Preface : In *The Cultural Landscape: Past, Present and Future* (eds H. H. Birks, H. J. B. Birke, P. E. Kaland and D. moe), 1988, pp. 1-4. Cambridge University Press.

Finlayson, M. and Moser, M., *Wetlands: Facts on File*, Oxford, 1994.

Flood, J., *Archaeology of the Dreamtime : The Story of Prehistoric Australia.and its People*. (2nd edn). Collins, Sydney, 1989.

Fokkens, H., From Shifting cultivation to short fallow cultivation: Late Neolithic culture change in the Netherlands reconsidered: In *Op Zoek Naar Mens en Materiele Cultuur* (eds H. Follens, P. Benga and M. Bierma), 1986, pp. 5-19. Private edition, Groningen.

Frea, J.I., Methanogenesis: Its role in the Carbon cycle. In *Microbial Chemoautotrophy*, (eds. W R Strohl and O. H. Tuvoinen), 1984, pp. 229-53. Ohio State University Press, Columbus.

Freeman, C., Lock, M. A, and Reynolds, B., Impacts of climate change on peatland hydrochemistry: A laboratory-based experiment. *Chemistry and Ecology* 8, 1993, pp. 49-59.

Fulford, M. Allen, J. and Rippon, S., The settlement and drainage of the Wentloge Level, Gwent Excavation and Survey at Rumney Great Wharf 1992. *Britannia*, XXV, 1994, pp. 175-211.

Gaunt, G. D. and Tooley, M.D., Evidence for Flandrian Sealevel changes in the Humber Estuary and adjacent area. *Bulletin of the Geological Survey of Great Britain*, 48, 1974, pp. 25-41.

Gaunt, G.D., The geology and landscape development of the area around Thorne Moors. *Thorne Moors Papers*, 1, 1987, pp. 6-30.

Gaunt, G.D., Quaternary history of the southern part of the Vale of York. In *The-Quaternary in Britain* (eds J. Neale and J. Flenley), 1981, pp. 82-97. Pexgamon, Oxford.

Gear, A.J., The Holocane Vegetation history and the Palaeoecology of Pinus sylvestris in N. Scotland. Unpublished Ph. D. thesis, University of Durham, 1989.

Geomorphological Services Ltd., *Hydrological Appraisal of Sutton Common*, Askern, South Yorkshire. Unpublished report 1990.

Germany., In *Geomorphology and Groundwater* (ed. A. G. Brown) pp. 21-36, Wiley, Chichester.

Gilliland, M.S., *The Material Culture of Key Marco*. University Presses of Florida, Gainesville, 1975.

Gilvear, D. J. Andrews, R., Tellam, J. H, Loyd, J. W. and Lerner, D N; Quantification of the water balance and hydrological processes in the Vicinity of a small Groundwater-fed wetland, East Anglia, *UK Journal of Hydrology*, 144, 1993, pp. 311-34.

Glasser, N., Earth science conservation and archaeology. *English Heritage Conservation Bulletin*, 22, 1994, pp. 12-13.

Godbold, Sand Turner, R.C., *Second Severn Crossing, Archaeological Response,* Phase 1 — the intert.idal zone in wales, Cadw, Cardiff, 1993.

Godwin, H., *History of the British Flora.* (2nd edn) , Cambridge University Press, 1975.

Godwin, H., *Fenland : Its ancient past and uncertain future*, Cambridge University Press, 1978.

Gopal, B. Turner, R. E., Wetzel, R. G. and Whigham, D. F; Wetlands Ecology and Management. National Institute of Ecology and International Scientific Publications, Jaipur, 1982.

Gorham, E., The development of peatlands. *Quarterly Review of Biology*, 32, 1957, pp. 145-66.

Grieve, I. C. Gilvear, D G and Bryant, R G., Hydrochemical and water source variation across a flood plain mire, Insh marshes, Scotland. *Hydrological Processes*, 9: pp. 99-110.

Grime, J.P., *Plant Strategies and Vegetation Processes.* Wiley, Chichester, 197/9.

Grischek, T. Dehnert, J. Nestler, W. Neitzel, P. and Trettin, R., *Groundwater Flow and quality in an alluvial aquifer recharged from riverbank infiltration*, Torgan Basin, 1995, Germany.

Hall, D. and Coles, J., Fenland Survey: An essay in landscape and persistence. *English Heritage Monograph Series*, 1994.

Hall, J. and Hiscock, P., The Moreton Region Archaeological Project (MRAP) Stage II: an outline of objectives and methods. *Queensland Archaeological Research*, 5, 1988, pp. 4-24.

Halyk, L.C. and Balon, E.K., Structure and ecological Production of fish taxocenose of a small food-plain system Canadian. *Journal of Zoology*, 61(11), 1983, pp. 424-64.

Hammer, D.A. and Bastian, R.K., Wetland ecosystems: Natural water purifiexs? In *Constructed Wetlands for Wasterwater Treatment: Municipal, Industrial and Agricultural* (ed. D. A. Hammer), 1989, pp. 5-19. Levis, Michigan, USA.

Havinga, A. J. and Opt Hof, A., *Physiography and Formation of the Holocene Floodplain along the Lower Course of the River Rhine in the Netherlands.* Mededelingen Landbouwhoge School Wageningen, Nederland 63-8, Wageningen. 1983.

Howard-Daview, C. Stocks, C. and Innes, J., *Peat and the Past.* English Heritage, Lancaster, 1998.

Holcik. J. and Bastl, I., Ecological effects of water level fluctuations upon fish populations in the Danube River flood plain in Czechoslovakia. *Acta. Sc. Nat., Brno,* 10 (9) , 1976, pp. 1-46.

Holmes, N.T.H., River restoration as an integrated part of river management in England and Wales. In *Contributions to the European workshop on Ecological Rehabilitation of River flood plains,* Report Number 11-6 under the auspices of CHR/KHR, 22-24 September 1992, pp. 165-72. Arnhem, The Netherlands.

Hensel, B.R. and Miller, M.V., Effects of wetland creation on groundwater flow. *Journal of Hydrology,* 126, 1991, pp.293-314.

Hollis, G.E. and Jones, T.A., Wetlands of Europe and the Mediterranean Basin. In *Wetlands* (eds M Finlayson, M and M Moser), 1991, pp. 27-56. Facts on File Ltd., Oxford.

HMSO This Common Inheritance, Britain's Environmbntal Strategy, Cm 1200. HMSO, London, 1990.

HMSO; *Biodiversity: The UK Action Plan.* HMSO, 1994, London.

Jacobson, G. L. and Bradshaw, R. H. W. T., The selection of sites for palaeovegetational studies, *Quarternary Research,* 16, 1981, pp. 80-96.

Jose, P. V. The Hydrochemistry of backwaters and dead zones. Unpublished Ph. D. Thesis, Loughboxough University of Technology, 1988.

Jose, P. V. and Self, M., The management of lowland wet grassland for birds. In *The Lowland Grassland Management Handbook* (eds A. Crofts and R. G. Jefferson), 1994, pp. 10:1-10:13. English Nature, The Wildlife Trusts, Peterborough.

Kaoru, Yand Hoagland, P., The value of historic shipwrecks: conflicts and management. *Coastal Management,* 22, 1994, pp. 195-213.

Key, R., Peat Cutting and the invertebrate fauna of lowland Peatlend: Thorne and Hatfield Moors in a national context. *Thorne and Hatfield Moors* Papers, 2, 1991, pp. 19-24.

Khan, I.S.A.N., Socio-economic Values of Aquatic Plants (freshwater macrophytes) of Peninsular Malaysia. *Asian Wetland Bureau,* 1990, Kualalumpur.

Knight, J., The Goldeliff Stone, *Monmouthshire Antiquary* 1 (2), 1992, pp. 34-6.,

Koosi, P. B., Pre-Roman urnfields in the northern Netherlands. Unpublished Ph. D. thesis, Groningen University, 1979.

Kristiansen, K., *Denmark: An Approaches to the Archaeological Heritage* (ed. J. F. Cleere), 1984, pp. 21-36. Cambridge University Press.

Lambrick, G., The importance of the cultural heritage in a green world;, Towards the development of landscape integrity assessment. In *All Natural Things : Archaeology and the Green Debate* (eds L Macinnes and C. R. Wickham-Jones), 1992, pp. 105-26. Oxford.

Larson, J. S., *Wetlands of North America. In Wetlands* (eds M Finlayson and Moser), pp. 57-84. Facts on File Ltd., Oxford, 1991.

Legislative Council (Legislative Council Standing Committee on State Development), *Coastal Planning and Management in NSW : A Framework for the Future,* Maxwell Printing, Sydney, 1991.

Limbert, M., *The Exploitation of Peat at Thorne. old West Riding*, 6, 1986, pp. 9-16.

Limbert, M., Some notes on the landscape history of Thorne Moors. *Thoxne Moors Papers*, 1, 1987, pp. 29-41.

Limbert, M., The Drainage of Thorne waste in The Nineteenth Century. *Thorne and Hetfield Local History Association*, Occasional Publication, 5, 1990.

Lindsay, R. A., Andrews, J, Gordon, J. and Immirzi, C., Lowland Raised Bogs in Great Brita. In, *The National Peatland Resource Inventory*, 3rd Draft. Scottish Natural Heritage, Edinburgh, 1995.

Lindsay, R. A. Charman, D. J. Everingham, F.O., Reilly, R.M., Palmer, M.A., Rowell, T.A. and Stroud, D. A. *The Flow Country: The Peatlands of Caithness and Sutherland*, NCC, Peterborough 1988.

Lindsay, Everingham, F, Fanden-Lilja, Y., Mayer, P., R., Reid, E., Rowell, T. A. and Ross, S., *Raised Bogs Britain.* The National Peatland Rosource Inventory (NPRI) Ist Draft. Scottish Natural Heritage, 1992.

Locke, S., The Postglacial deposits of the Caldicot Level and some associated archaeological discoveries, *Monmouthshire Antiquary.* 3(l), 1971, pp. 2-16.

Louwe Kooijmans, L.P., The Rhine/Meuse Delta. *Analecta Praehistorica Leidensia 7*, 1974, pp. 1-421.

Louwe Kooijmans, L.P., Archaeology and coastal change in the Netherlands, In *Archaeology and Coastal Change* (ed. F. H. Thompson), 1980, pp. 106-33. The Society of Antiquaries, Occasional Paper 1, London.

Louwe Kooijmans, L.P., Sporen in hethand. *De Nederandse' Delta in de Prehistoric.* Meulenhoff, 1985, Amsterdam.

Louwe Kooijmans, L.P., Neolithic Settlement and subsistence in the wetlands of the Rhine/Meuse Delta of the Netherlands. In *European*

*Wetlands in Prehistory* (eds J. M. Coles and A. J. Lawson). Clarendon Press, Oxford, 1987.

Louwe Kooijmans, L.P., Wetland exploitation and upland relations or prehistoric commuities in the Netherlands. In *Flatlands and Wetlands: Current Themes in East Anglian Archaeology* (ed. J. Gardiner) *East Anglian Archaeology* 50, 1993, pp. 71-116, Norwich.

Lowenthal., *The Past is a Foreign Country*, Cambidge University Press, 1985.

Lumb, J., A question of significance: Stone line features in North Creek at Balline, New South Wales. Unpublished Integrated project thesis, University of New England, Northern Rivers, Lismore 1990, Australia.

MAFF. Conservation Guidelines for Drainage Authorities. PB0743, MAFF, London, 1991.

Matsui., Wetland sites in Japan. In the *Wetland Revolution in Prehistory* (ed. B. Coles) , 1992, pp. 5-14. The Prehistoric Society and WARP, Exeter.

Money, R., The restoration of lowland raised bogs damaged by peat extraction with particular reference to sphagnum regeneration. Unpublished Ph. D. thesis, University of Sheffield, 1994.

Mellars, P., Fire ecology, animal population and mans a study of some ecological relationships in pre-history, *Proceedings of the Prehistoric Society*, 42, 1976, pp. 15-45.

Middleton, R., Walls C. E. and Huckerby, E., *The Wetlands of North Lancashire*, North West Wetlands 3, Lancaster Imprints 4, Lencaster University Archaeological Unit, 1995.

Mitch, W. J. and J. G. Gosselink., *Wetlands*, Van Nostrand Reinhold Company, New York, 1986, p. 537.

Mitchell, F. J. G., The vegetational history of the killarney oakwods, S W Ireland: Evidence from fine spatial resolution pollen analysis. *Journal of Ecology*, 76, 1988, pp. 415-36.

Moore, P. D. and D. J. Bellamy., *Peatlands*, Springer Verlag, New York, 1974, P. 221.

Moore, P. D. (ed.); *European Mires*, Acadamic Press, London, 1984, p. 367.

Moore, P. D. and Bellamy, D. J., *Peatlands*, Springer Verlag, New York, 1984.

Moor, P. A., Thousand years of death. *New Scientist*, 113, 1987, pp. 46-48.

Mulvaney, D. J., Past regained future lost: the kow swamp. Pleistocene burials. *Antiquity*, 65, 1991, pp. 12-21.

Nayling, N. Caldicot Castle Lake., In Severn Estuary Levels Research Committee Annual Report, 1992, pp. 11-14. SELRC, Lampeter.

Nayling, N., Tales from the river bank, In *Spirit of Enquiry: Essays forted wright* (eds J Coles, V fenwick and G. Hutchinson), 1993, pp. 72-76, Wetland Archaeology Research Project (WARP), Exeter.

Nayling, N. Maynard, D. and Mcgrail, S., Barlands Farm, Magor, Gwent: A Romano-British Boat Find. *Antiquity*, 68, 1994, pp. 596- 603.

New Habitat Scheme (Briefing Note) , Ministry of Agriculture, Fisheries Food, London, 1993.

Newson, M.G., Conservation management of peatlands and the drainae threat: Hydrology, politics and the ecologist in the UK. In *Peatland Ecosystems and Man: An Impact Assesment* (eds O. M. Bragg, P. D. Hulme. H. A. P. Ingram and R. A. Robertsob) , 1992, pp. 94-103. Department of Biological Sciences, Dundee University.

Noort, R. Van De and Daview. Wetland Heritage. An archaeological assessment of the Humber Wetlands. *English Heritage*, Hull, 1993.

North West Wetlands Survey., Annual Reports. Lancaster University Archaeological Unit, Lancaster, 1990-93.

NRA., *Somerset Levels and Moors Water Level Management and Nature Conservation Strategy,* NRA, 1992, Wessex Region.

NRA., *Conservation Strategy*, NRA, Bristol. 1993.

NRA., Porlock Bay Management Proposals, Nick Stevens (NRA), discussion document, February, 1994.

Nuttall, N. and Jones, T., 800 million airport proposed for Severn Estuary. *The Times* 1 March 1994, p. 7.

Odum, W. E., Environmental degradation and small decisions. *Bioscience*, 32, 1982, P. 728.

O'Sullivan, P., Pollen analysis of mor humus layers from a native Scots pine ecosystem, interpreted with surf ace samples. *Oikos*, 24, 1973, pp. 259-272.

Othman, M. S. H., A Preliminary Economic Valuation of Wetland Plant Species in Peninsular Malaysia, *Asian Wetland Bureau*, Kuala Lumpur, 1990.

Paivanen J., Hydraulic conductivity and water -retention in peat soils. *Acta Forestalia Fennica* 129, 1973, pp. 1-70.

Parkhouse, J. Parry, S., *Runney Alternative Feeding Grounds an Archaeological Assessment.* Glamorgan-Gwent Archaeological Trust, Swansea, 1990.

Parry, S., Caldicot : A late Bronze Age maritime site in Gwent. In *Severn Estuary Levels Research Committee Annual Report* 1990, 1991, pp. 5-11. SELRC, Lampeter.

Pernnington, W., Vegetational history in the North-west of England a regional synthesis. In *Studies in the Vegetational History of the British*

*Isles* (eds D. Walker and R. G. West), 1970, pp. 41-81. Cambridge University Press.

Peterken, G., *Woodland Conservation and Management*. Chapman and Hall, London, 1981.

Plamer, N. E., Treasure trove and the protection of antiquities. *Modern Law Review*, 44, 1981, pp. 178-8.7.

Plantlife Commission of Inquiry into Peat and Peatlands, Commission Report Conclusions and Recommendations, Plantlife, London, 1992.

Posford Duvivier Environment. Porlock Bay Management Study. Economic Benefits Assessment, Fi:ıal Report, March, 1991.

Posford Duvivier. Porlock Bay Coastal Management Study Stage 2, Report, September, 1992.

Prentice, I. C., Pollen representation, source area and basin size. Towards a unified theory of pollen analysis. *Quaternary Research*, 23, 1985, pp. 76-86.

Pryor, F., Glag Fen. *Prehistoric Fenland Centre*. Batsford and English Heritage, London, 1991.

Queensland Government; Integrated Catchment Management : A. strategy for achieving the sustainable and balanced use of land, water and related biological resources. Department of Primary Industries, Brisbane, 1991.

Rackhan, O., *Trees and Woodland in the British Landscape*. Dent, London, 1976.

Ratcliffe, D., *A Nature Conservation Review*. Cambridge University Press, 1977.

Reynolds, W. D. Brown, D. A, Mathur, S. P. and Overend, R. P., Effect of in situ gas accumulation on the hydraulic conductivity of peat. *Soil Sciences*, 153, 1992, pp. 397 -408.

Rippon, S., Landscape evolution and wetland reclamation around the Severn Estuary. Unpublished Ph.D. thesis, Universtiy of Reading 1993.

Rippon, S. and Turner, R., The Gwent Levels Historic Landscape Study. In *Severn Esturay Levels Research Committee Annual Report for 1993*, pp. 113-117. SELRC, Lampeter.

Rippon, S., The Severn Levels in the historic period. In *Severn Estuary Levels Research Committee Annual Report for 1993*, pp. 29-33. SELRC, Lampeter.

Rippon, S., Wetland reclamation and wetland exploitation in the Somerset Levels. In the *Medieval Landscape of Wessex* (eds M. Aston and C. Lewis), 1994, pp. 239-53. Oxford.

Roberts, N., *The Holocene and Environment History.* Blackwell, Oxford, 1989.

Roberts, K.A., Nature conservation in the Lee Valley. In *Conservation in Progress* (eds) F. B. Goldsmith and A. Werren, 1993, pp. 143-59. Wiley, Chichester..

Roberts, K.A., Field monitoring: Confessions of an addict. In *Monitoring for Conservation and Ecology* (ed.) F. B. Goldsmith, 1991, pp. 200-5. Chapman and Hall, London.

Roberts, K. A.. RSB Rye House Marsh: Wetland creation for ecological education, recreation and wildlife conservation. In *Habitat Creation and Wildlife Conservation in Urban and Post-Industrial Environments* (eds J. Rieley and S. Page), pp. 90-7. Michael Packard, Chichester.

Roulet, N. T., Ash, R. and Moore, R. T., Low boreal wetlands as a source of atmospheric methane. *Journal of Geophysics Research*, 97, 1992, pp. 37-49.

Rowell, T. A., *The Peatland Management Handbook.* Nature Conservancy Council Peterborough, 1988.

R. S. B., *Wet Grasslands, What Future?* RSB, The Lodge Sandy, Bedfordshire, 1993.

Rudd, J. W. M. and Taylor, D. C., Methane cycling in aduatic environments. *Advances in Aquatic Microbiology*, 2, 1980, pp. 77-150.

Saenger, P., Managing Coastal Wetlands: Headlong into muddied waters. paper presented to Environment Law Conference, *Coolangatta*, 21 November 1987. Centre for Coastal Management, Lismore.

Samuels, J. and Buckland, P. C., A Romano-British Settlement at Sandtoft, South Humberside. *Yorkshire Archaeological Journal*, 50, 1978, pp. 65-75.

Schinkel, C., Zwervende erven, nederzeting on grafveld uit de brone-en ijzertijd in Oss-Ussen. Unpublished Ph.D. thesis, Leiden University.

Schot, P.P. and Molenaer, A., Regional changes in groundwater flow patterns and effects on gorundwater composition. *Journal of Hydrology,* 130, 1992, pp. 151-70.

Scott, D. A., Wetlands of Asis and the Middle East. In *Wetland* (eds) M Finlayson and Moser), 1991, pp. 149-78. Facts on File Ltd. Oxford.

Scott, D. A., Design of wetland Data Sheet for Database on Ramsar sites. Mimeographed Report to Ramaar Convention Bureau, 1989, Gland Switzerland.

Scotter, C. N. G. Wade, M., Marshall, E. J. P. and Edwards, R. W., The Monmouthshire Level Is drainage system: its ecology and relation to agricultue. *Journal of Environmental Management*, 5, 1977, pp. 75-86.

Severn Estuary Levels Research Committee; Annual Repprts, SELRC, St. David's Unversity College, 1990-93, Lampeter.

Severn Tidal Power Group, Severn Barrage Project Detailed Report, IV Ecological studies, landscape and Nature Conservation. Department of Energy, 1989, pp. Harwell.

Shaw, S.P. and C.G. Fredine., *Wetlands of the United States, Their Extent and other Wildlife,* U.S. Dept. of Interiar, Fish and Wildlife service, Circular 39, Washington, D.C., 1956, p. 67.

Shaw, E., *Hydrology in Practice* (2nd edn) . Van Nostrand Reinhold (UK) Ltd. London, 1988.

Sinden J. A. and Worrell, A.C., *Unpriced Values: Decisions without market prices*. John' Wiley and Sons, New York, 194.

Sir William Halcrow and Partnetrs, Porlock Bay Sen Defences, Preliminary Report, April, 1984.

Sir William Halcrow and Partners, Porlock Bay Sea Defences, Appraisal Study, Final Report, November, 1985.

Sklar, F. H. Costanze, R. and Day J. W., Dynamic, spatial simulation modelling of coastal wetland habital succession. *International Journal on Ecological Modelling and Engineering and System Geology* 29, 1985, pp. 261-81.

Smith, B. M. A., Palaeo ecological study of raised mires in the Humberhead Levels. Unpublished ph. D. thesis, University of Wales, 1985, Cardiff.

Smith R.L., *Ecology and Field Biology*, 3rd.ed. Harper and Row, New York, 1980, pp. 835.

Smith, A. G. and Morgan, L. A., A succession to ombrotrophic bog in the Gwent Levels, and its demise: A welsh parallel to the peats of the somerset Levels, *New Phytologist*, 112, 1989, pp. 145-67.

Smith, A. G., Post-glacial deposits in South Yorkshire and north Linconshire, *New Phytologist*, 57, 1958, pp. 19-49.

Specht, A., *Vegetation Monitoring of Eighteen Mile Swamp*, North Stradbroke Island 1992. Centre for Coastal Management, Lismore, 1992.

Startin, W., The Monuments Protection Porgramme: Protecting what, how, and for whom? In *Managing Archaeology* (eds M. A. Cooper, A. Firth, J. Carman and D Wheatley. Routledge, London, 1995.

Stead, I. M, Bourke, J B and Brothwell, D. Lindow Man, *The Body in the Bog*. The British Museum, 1986, London.

Stephenson, M. A. and Ratnapala, S. Mabo, *A Judicial Revolution : Aboriginal Land Rights. Rights decision and its impact on Australian law*. University of Queensland Press, St Lucia, 1993.

Steward, R. E. and H. A. Kantrud., *Classification of natural ponds and lakes in the glaciated praise region*, U.S. Fish' and wild life service Research Pub. 92, 1971, p. 57.

Stoneman, R. Barber, K. and Maddy, D., Present and past ecology of sphagnum imbricatum and its significance in raised peat-climate modelling, *Quaternary Newsletter*, 70, 1993, pp. 14-22.

Stovin, G., A letter from Mr T G Stovin to his son concerning the body of a woman and an antique shoe, found in a morass in the Isle of axholme in Linconshire. Philosophical Transactions of the Royal Society of London, 44, 1747, pp. 571-6.

Strobbe, M. Runschikkingsvoorstel komgondengebied van Lampernisse. Unpublished Report, 1992.

Surtees, S. F., *Footprints of Roman Occupation in the Southern Parts of North Humber Land.* Baines, Leeds, 1868.

Sydes, R. E., Report on the re-excavation of Teench A/C, Sutton Common, South Yorkshire. Unpublished Report, South Youkshire Archaeology Unit, 1992.

Sydes, R. E. and Symonds, J., Investigations at Sutton Common, South Yorkshire, Unpublished Report, South Yorkshire Archaeology Unit, 1987.

Sylvester, D., *The Rural Landscape of the welsh Borderland*, Macmillan, London, 1969.

Tickner, M. and Evans, C., *The Management of Low land Wed Grassaland on Reserves*. RSB Reserves Ecology/Advisory Publication. R.S.B., the Lodge, 1991, Sandy, Bedfordshire.

Trishal, C.L. and D. P. Zutshi., *Ecology and Management of Wetland Ecosystem in India*, MAE, Department of Environment, Govt. of India, 1985, P. 27.

Turner, J., The Yilia Decline : An Anthropogenic interpretation. *New Phytologist*, 61, 1962, pp. 328-41.

Tyler, S. and Wragg, M., Motorway on the moors, *Natural World*, January, 1994, pp. 20-22.

UNCED; Convention on Biological Diversity. United Nations conference on Environment and Development, Rio de Janeiro, 1992.

UNESCO; Wetlands conference in Czechoslovakia. *Nature and Resources* XX(2) : 22, 1984.

US Federal Intergency Committee for wetland delineation (1989). Federal Manual for Indentifying and Delineating. Jurisdictional Wetlands. co-operative technical publication. U. S. Army Corp of Engineers, US

Environmental Protection Agency. US Fish and Wildlife Service and USDA Soil conservation service, Washington D.C.

Van Heerigen, R. M., The Iron Age in the Western Netherlands. Unpublished Ph. D. thesis, Amsterdum University, 1992.

Van Gijn, A.L. and Waterbolk, T., The colonization of the salt marshes of Friesland and Groningen: The possibility of a transhumant prelude. *Palaeochistoria*, 26, 1984, pp. 101-22.

Van der Woude, J.D., Holocene palaeo- environmental evolution of a perine flurviatile area. *Analecta Preehistorice Leidensia*, 17, 1984.

Van de Noort. R. and Davies, P., Wetland Heritage, An Archaeological Assessment of the Humber Wetlands, *Humber Wetlends Project*, Univeristy of Hull, 1993.

Verhaeghe, F., The late medieval crisis in the low countries: the archaeological viewpoint. In Europa 1400. *Die krise des spatmittelalters* (eds. F. Seibt and W. Eberhard) , 1984, pp. 146-71. Klett-Cotta, Stuttgart.

Wainwright, G. J., Managing change: ancient monuments in the countryside. In *Recuing the Historic Environment* (ed.H Swain), 1993, pp. 17-19. Rescue, Hertford.

Walker, M. and James, J., A rediocarbon-dated pollen record from Vurlong Reen, near caldicot, South Wales. In *Archaeology in the Severn Estuary* 1993, Annual Report of the Severn Estuary Levels Research Committee, 1993, pp. 63-7 SELRC, Lampeter.

Wall, C. and Limbert, M., An annotated checklist of thorne morrs bryophytes. *Thorne Morrs Papers*, 1, 1987, pp. 52-63.

WALSC; Manmouthshire moore Investigation: Draft Report. Welsh Argicultural Land Sub- Commission, Aberystwyth, 1954.

Walker, G. J. and Kirby, K. J., *Inventories of Ancient*, Long- established and Seminatural woodland for Scotland. Research and Survey in Nature Conservation No. 22 NCC, Edinburgh. 1989.

Warren, S. H, Clark, J. G. D., Godwin, H and Macfadyen, W. A., An early Mesolithic site at Broxbourne sealed under boreal peat. *Journal of the Royal Anthropological Institute*, 64, 1934, pp. 101-28.

WCMC, *Global Biodiversity Status of the Earthis Living Resourcs*. World Conservation Monitoring Centre, Chapman and Hall, London 1992.

Welcomme, R. L., A Brief Review of the Floodplain Fisheries of Africa. FAO Committee for Inland Fisheries of Africa. Report CIFA / 12 / S. 17. FAO, ROME, 1972.

Wells, C. and Huckerby E., Macrofossil and pollen investigations at Fenton Cottage, out Rawcliffe, over wyre, Lancashire. *In North-west Wetlands*

*Survey Annual Report 1991.* (ed. R Middleton), pp. 21-5. Lancaster University. Archaeological Unit.

Wetlands Action and Wetlands Meeting the President's challenge. US Department of the Interior and US Fish and Wildlife Service. Washington, DC, 1990.

Wetlands, The Newsletter of Wetlands International, Institute of Advanced Studies, University of Malaya, 50603, Kuala Lampur, Malasiya, 1, 1995.

Whetley, D., The impact of information technology on the practice of archaeological management. In *Managing Archaeology* (eds M A Cooper, A Firth, J Carman and D Wheatley). Routledge, London, 1995.

Wheeler, B. D., Botanical diversity in British mires. *Biodiversity and Conservation*, 2, 1993, pp. 49-512.

Whittle, A. W. R., Two later Bronze Age occupations and an Iron Age channel on the Gwent foreshore. *Bulletin of the Board of Celtic Studies,* 36, 1989, pp. 200-233.

Whiting, C. E., Excavations on sutton common, 1933, 1934, and 1935. *Yorkshire Archaeological Journal* 33, 1936, pp. 57 80.

Wilcox, H. A., *The Woodlands and Marshes of England.* Hodder and Stoughton, London, 1933.

Williams, D H., Goldcliff priory. *Monmouthshire Antitiquary*, 3 (1), 1971, pp. 37-54.

Williams, M., Protection and Retrospection, In *Wetlands : A Threatened Landscape*, 1993, pp. 323-43. Institute of British Geographers, Special Publication, Blackwell, Oxford.

Willis, H. C. Garrod, C. D. and Saunders, C. M., Valuation of the south Downs and Somerset Levels and Moors ESA Landscapes by the General Public, Report under MAFF contract, Newcastle University Centre for Rural Economy, Newcastle-upon-Tyne 1993.

# INDEX


Accessibility of Road, 75-76
Action Plans, 225-26, 229
Adhiwar system, 48
Afforestation, 128
    programme, development of, 451
Afghanistan, 233
*Aghani* crops, 56
Agricultural management, 303
Agricultural productivity, 325-26
    concept of, 326-27
    determination of, 332
    measurement of, 325-30
    problems of, 327-28
Agriculture, 56-57, 300-308, 318-20
Agriculture Commission, recommendations of, 460
Agro-based indiustries, 63-64
Ahmad, Shamin, 11
Air and water quality, 119
Alaknanda river, 230
Alcohol preparation, 66
Alkalimity, 257-58, 260-62
All India Questionnaire, 484-494
Alluvial cones, 39, 134-35
Alluvial landscape, 31-32
Alluviation, process of, 99
Ammonical nitrogen, 263
*Anchals,* 90-93, 200-02
Ancillary industries, 68
Andaman and Nicobar Islands, 131
Anguttarap, 88
Aquatic plants, 167-68
    management of, 180-89
    utilization and management of, 176-79
Aquatic weeds, removal of, 183
Arizona, 466
Artificial embankment, 39-40
Artificial fertilizer, 305
Artificial wetlands, 212
Assam oil fields, 66
*Asthama* disease, 111

Baghmati river, 41
Banbhog wetland, Vritzananda-nagar, 424-25
Bangaon copper plate, 89
Bangaon Mahisi Wetland, 369-72
    problems of, 370-71
Bangladesh, 119, 183, 187, 436
Baraila Tal, 41, 427-28
Barauni fertilizer project, 66
Barauni lake, 378-80, 389-90
Bayons, 208-09
Bayours, 38-39
Bay of Bengal, 436
Beel areas, 458
Begharbeel stream, 216
Begusarai, Kabar Tal in, 310
Belhi Wetlands, crop production of, 351
Beneficiaries, 121
Bengadhasan Wetland, Supaul district, 417-18

Berain Wetland, 427
*Bhadai* crops, 56
Bhagalpur illegal fishing, 407-08
Bharatpur Bird Sanctuary, 233
Bharathua Chaur, Muzaffarpur, 392-93
Bhatsa river episode, 232
Bhimtal, lake, 9, 287-88
    biological organism, 290
*Bhuktis*, 89
*Bhutia Balan*, 137, 222
Bigger Wetlands, 195
Bihar, Wetlands in, 197-98
Bihar Irrigation Commission, 458-59
    recommendations of, 460
Bihar State Lands (Reclamation, Cultivation and Improvement) Act, 461
Biochemical Oxygen Demand (BOD), 123, 224, 228
Biofertilizer/Biogas, 175-76
Biogas production, 181-82
Bombay Port Trust, 229
Brackiswater fish culture, 124
Bridge construction in rivers, 74-75
Brillinger, 114
Burhi Gandak River, 1, 35-36, 84-85, 135, 140, 143, 191-92, 311, 374-75

Calcium hardness, 258
Cash crops, 56
Casf Bow, 181
Cattle feeds, 179
Cauvery, 231-32
Central Ganga Authority, 229
Chakmaka Wetland, Purnea. 415-16
    turbidity, 415
    vegetation, 415
Chambal river valley, 242
Champaran, 6, 406-07
    wetlands in, 200-201, 406-07
Chamra Chaur, 380
Chaudhary, U.P., 10
*Chaurs* lands, 20-22, 28, 132, 152-53, 155-58, 200, 457-59
Chaur drainage schemes, 471-72
    implementation of, 451-52
Chauri Wetland, Supaul district, 416-17
Chilka Project, 237-38
*Chhath* festival, 353
Chhotanagpur, 6
Choudhary, K.D., 9
Clarke, Cohn, 330
Cold storage, 66
Common fresh water bodies, 145
Conservation problems, 126-27
Conserving wetlands, 118-19
Convention treatment plants, 123, 439-40
Cox, Margaret, 10
Crops varieties, 4, 50, 347
Crop contribution, 57
Cropping pattern, 122, 438
Czechoslovak National Academy of Science, 10
Dahichal Wetlands, Kishanganj district, 420-22
Dal Lake, Kashmir, 248, 285-86
    biological organisms, 285
    ecological degradation of, 282
    reduction in area, 284
Dams, 243
Dan Willard, 97
Dandekar, 326
Darbhanga district, Chaur as Wetland of, 155-56
Darbanga Roller Flour Mill, 67
Data, Sources of, 12-13, 22

Deepak Kumar, District Magistrate, 372
Deforestation, 480
Dhima-Makhnaha, Wetland, 431-32
*Diara* lands, 194
Dighi Wetland, 412-14
Drainage areas, 7
 dendritic pattern of, 40-41
 reclamation of, 189-90
 schemes of, 304
Drinking water, 75, 142, 226-28
Drought, 97-98
Drug industry, removal of, 87
Dry-bulb temperature, 43, 47
Dutta, Munshi, J.S., 10
Dying Lake Renuka, Himachal Pradesh, 236
Earthquake, 23
East Champaran, Wetlands of, 374-76
Ecological degradation, 278-80
Ecological factors, 209-10
Economic gains, 167-186
Economic potentialities, 30
Edward Suess, 23
Eighth Five Year Plan, 233
Employment programmes, 67
Endangered Wetlands ecology, 224-250
Environmental functions, 280
Environmental impact, 226
Environmental Protection Act, 462
Epilimnion, 146
Estate Acquisition Act, 458
Eutrophicated lakes, 177
Eutrophication, 278-79, 289-90
Everglades, 110
Factors Controlling Wetlands, 95-104
Farm lands, West Zones on, 303-04
Farming practices, 307-08
Fateh Sagar Lake, 244
 fish production in, 244-45
Fertilizers, 182-83, 303-05
Finglas Wetlands, Raghopur Anchal, 423-24
Fish Development Agencies (FDA), 122
Fish farming, 128, 246
Fish Farm Development Agencies (FFDA), 438
Fish Fauna, 246-47
 stream of, 240
Fish feed, 179-80
Fish production, 168-70, 240-42
Fisheries Development Programmes, 242-43
Fishing, management and methods of, 241-42
Fish production, 168-70, 240-42
Fisheries Development Programmes, 242-43
Fishing, management and methods of, 241-42
Floating gardens, 283
Flood affected areas, 8, 71, 76, 114
Flood Commision, recommendations of, 460
Flood plain areas, 33-34
 system, 465
Florida, 109
Fodder, 174-75
Food chains, mechanisms of, 334
Food for fishes, 174
Food for human use, 173-74
Food production, 300
Foodgrains, types of, 112
Foodgrain storing, 75
Foothills zone, 26
Forest, exploitation of, 222

Forest Conservation Act, 461
Forster, E.M., 47
Free Carbon Dioxide, 257
Free Surface floating hydrophets, 148-49
Fresh water bodies, management of, 469-70
Fresh water wetlands, 40
  pattern formation of, 152
Fringing vegetation, 302
*Gair Mazarna* (Public lands), 453, 455
Gandak river, 41, 209-10
Gandak Project, 61, 63, 376
Gandhi Sagar Reservoir, M.P., 241
Ganga river, 6, 20, 28, 134-35, 210, 226
  pollution of, 229-30
Ganga Action Plan, 229-30, 440
Ganges diaras, 56
Geddes, 31
Ghaghra river, 1, 191, 224
Ghana Birds Sanctuary, Bharatpur, 224
Ghogha Beel Lake, Kishanganj district, 422-23
Giri dam, 79
Godaun and Khadi Gram Udyog Commission, 408
Goga Chaur, 216
*Goonda* elements, 408
Gothra Kannakpur Wetlands, 392-93
Gramadhipatti, 90
Grain Collecting Centres, 71
Grass, types of, 52
Groundwater, nitrozen levels in, 305-06
Grow More Food Campaign, 455
Hajarpanch Wetland, Katihar District, 364-66
  crops grown, 366
  irrigation, 366
  planning, 366
Hardia chaur, 388
Harha valley, 28
Haswell, Margaret, 330
High Resolution Visible (HRV), 442, 443
High Sal Forest, 51
Himachal Pradesh, 79
Himalayan foothills, 26
Holosiene, older alluvium of, 25
Horticulture crops, 182
Hot Westerly winds, 43
Huentsang, 88
Human occupation, socio-economic model of, 320
Human settlement, 316
Hussain Sagar Lake, 227, 248, 291-92
Hydrophytes, classification of, 147-48
Hypolimnion, 146
Hypothesis formulation, 13-15

Illegal ocupation, 408
Indian Fisheries Act, 462
Indian Wetlands, entrophication of, 281-82
Indira Gandhi, 460
Indo-Gangatic plain, 20, 142
Industries, 63-64, 318-20
Industrial activities, 202
  exploitation of, 167
Industrial crops, 182
  pollution of, 231
  potentiality, 66-67
Industrial waste, 227
Industrialisation, 127, 228

Inland waterways, 75
Interface between agricultural development policy and Wetland Conservation, 205
International Association of Ecology, 10
International Biosphere programme, 279-80
International Decade of Drinking Water and Sanitation, 226
Investigating Wetlands, 96, 195-96
Irrigation, 108
  cheap sources of, 61
  facilities, 59-60
Irrigation channels, 194
Irrigational Water Supply, 151

Jaimangla Garh, 215
Jalai-Malai Lake, 95
*Jal Kumbhi,* 168, 368, 419-21, 425
Jalodbhava (land reclamation from swamps), 42
Jambubani Visaya, 89
Jammu & Kashmir, 228
*Janapadas,* 88
*Jatakas,* 87
Jawahar Sagar, 243
Jet stream, 45
*Jhanjhatia Mahal,* 71
*Jheels,* 457-58
Jibachh river, 2, 191-92

Kabar Tal, 41, 95, 152, 154, 214-15
  ecological diversities of, 310-20
  flora and fauna, 318-19
  plan of, 237
  vegetation of, 315
Kamla-Balan river, 1, 41
Kanail Chaur, 471-72
*Kankar,* 23
Kanti Thermal Power, 236
Kanti Wetlands, 384
Kararia lakes, 104
  turbidity of, 378
  weed of, 377-78
Kareh river, meaning of, 35
*Kar Seva,* 236
Katchudhua Wetland, 408-09
Kathra Wetland, productivity of, 340-42
Kausaur Chaur, 472
Kawar Lake Goga Beel, 209
Katihar, 404-05
Keeham Reservoir, Agra, 246
Keolades Ghana National Park, 235-36
Kesharia Wetland, Champaran, 406-07
Khagma Wetland, Saharsa, 38[illegible]
Khaira Chaur, 472
Kharudah lake, Kishanganj, 402-04
Kishanganj, 402-404, 419-20, 422-23
Kosi alluvial cone, 31-33
Kosi Belt, 28, 36-37
Kosi division, wetland, plant resources of, 170-72
Kosi Project, 41, 61
Kosi river, 1, 4, 209-10
Kosi-Mahananda system, 48, 252
Koshwan Jalkar, Manihari Anchal, Katihar, 426-27
Kotla Barrage, 243
Kuleshra Chaur, Muzaffarpur, 400-02
  migratory birds, 402
Kusheshwar Asthan, 95, 129-30, 154
  birds found in, 342-43
  geographical features of, 344-45
  social elites of, 344
  wetlands of, 218-19
    problems of, 4, 75-76
    chaurs and lakes of, 342-43

Laktak lake, Manipur, 233-34
Lakes and rivers, 226-30
Lalsaraiyaman wetlands, West Champaran, 356-58
Land drainage, 304-05
Land and Water Management, 452
Land Reclamation Act, 455
Landforms, pattern of, 98
Landscape features, 133
Land use pattern, 315
Land utilization, pattern of, 54-55
Littoral zone, 147
Louisiana, 466
Low-cost sanitation technology, 124
Lower Pleistocene age, 23
Madhubani chaur, 472
*Mahabharata*, 44, 87, 89
Mahabal Man, Muzaffarpur, 398-401
Mahananda river, 136, 210
Mahananda tista, 31
Makhana, 7, 9, 168-69
    production, 209, 214
Malkayan Wetland Manihari, Katihar, 362-64
    vegetation of, 362-63
Maltby, Edward, 435
Management Action Plan, 132, 225
Mandal, R.B., 11, 101, 199
Mango orchard, 213, 220
Mangroves, 131-32, 225-26
    areas, 101
Mangrove Wetlands, 119, 436
Manikaman Wetland, Muzaffarpur, 394-96
Manjhaul trough scheme, development and beautification, 408
Man-made ditches, 101, 145
Man-made Wetlands, 456
Mansabdari system, 90
Marginal Emergent Hydrophytes, 147-48
Marine environment, 144
Marshes, 37-38, 137, 209-10
Marhy depression, 41
Marshy lands, 29-30, 137-38, 209-10
Masbasi Wetlands, 35-36
    planning measures, 352-53
Massachausetts, 8
Meanders, 33-35
Meandering courses, 207
Medicinal plants, 2, 9, 99, 152
    collection of, 168-69
    varieties of, 189-90
Microscopic plants, 167
Migratory birds, 4, 49-50, 119-20, 233-34, 343, 347-49, 367
Mishra, A.K., 429
Mishra, Lalit Narayan, 165
Mithila, 87
Mithila Woollen Mills, 67
Mithilanchal Chaurs, 153-54
Modern agricultural practices, 306
Moths' production, 7, 168-69
Motihari Lake, 372-74
Moti-jheel Lake, 104, 372, 374
    chemical factors of, 376-77
Muskegs, 107
Mushroom culture, 183
    bedding material for, 180
Muzaffarpur, 85-86, 397-98
    administrative areas, 86
    educational institutions, 85
    industrial areas, 85
    residential areas, 85
    wetlands, characteristics of, 386-87
Nainital, dissolved oxygens, 288-89
    ecological degradation, 287

sewage disposal of, 287-88
Naktidam Project, 113
Nardang Wetlands, 410
Narha Wetland, Supaul district, 360-61
National Commission on Agriculture, 457, 463
National Commission on Floods, 457
National Committee on Development of Backward Areas, 124, 443-44
recommendations of, 124-25
National Flood Insurance Programme, 469
National Hydro Electric Power Corporation, 234
National Institute of Oceanography, 229
National Mangrove Committee, 225
National Mission on Wetland Development, 122, 126, 438
National Policies, 101
National Wetland Committee, 130, 144, 226
Natural Calamities, 28, 133
Natural Environment, 170
Natural habitats, varieties of, 145-46
Natural levees, 39-40
Natural resource systems, 120
Natural System and Environment Quality, 460
Natural Wetlands, 154
Nefarious Act, 408
Neo-tectonic Earth Movement, 1, 191
Nepal, 26, 66, 68, 338
Newer alluvium (*Khadar*), 23
Nile valley, 1
Nitrate Nitrogen, 259
North Bihar, surveyed wetlands of, 252-55
territorial history of, 90
North Ganga Plain, 26

Objectives, 7-8
Off-Nadir Viewing, 443-44
Older alluvium (*Bhanger*), 23
Open air pollution, 248
Open water, sheets of, 301
Optimization, 112
Orbital parameters, 443
Orchards, 52-54, 140-42
Oscillation, 122, 438
Oxbow lakes, 33, 38-40, 103, 135-37, 151-52, 158, 208-10, 338, 457-60

Pachkurba Sahara Lake, 348-49
Palakshappa, 86
Palanithurai, G., 71
Panchob Copper Plate, 89
Paper pulp, sources of, 180-81
Parameters, 6, 144
Peat Bogs, 107
People's Action for People in Need (PAPN), 236
Petro-chemical and fertilizer industries, 63
Philippines, 187
Phoolbhasa Wetland, 384
Phosphorus, 306
Phytoplanktons, 286
Planning Commission, 124, 229
Pokharbhinda village, 137
Polluted Water, 227
Pollution, 9, 95, 111, 123, 189, 439, 451-52
abatement, 182
causes of, 231
Pollution of Lakes, 248
Ponds, 140-42
Population density, 75-76, 83-84
pressure, 144

Postulates, 120, 437-38
Pre-industrial settlements, 63
Profoundal zone, 147
Protein and carotene, sources of, 181
 (*Puranas,* 3)
Purnea, Wetlands in, 2000-01, 425-26

Raghopur Anchals, 423-24
Rail lines, density and distribution, 70-71
Railways, 69-70
Rainfall, 100
 distribution of, 45-46
Rajasthan, Wetlands of, 238-40, 292
Rajiv Gandhi, 321
Rajiv Gandhi Kabar Tal, 311
Rajokhar, Wetlands in, 220-21, 354-55
 economic viability, 356
Ramnagar Dun, 26
*Ramayana,* 87
Ramsar Convention, 118, 346, 435-36
Rana Pratap Sagar, 243
Reed Swamp, 302
Regional economics development, 79
Research coverage, themes of, 5-6
Revisit capabilities, 445
Rhode Island, 8
Rice and fish culture areas, 159
Richhole lake, 227
Rihand Reservoir, 245
Riparian Anchals, 200
River terraces, 32, 39
Rodways, characteristics of, 72-73, 75-76
Rooted hydrophytes, 148
Rosra Wetland Conference-cum-exhibition, recommendation of, 432-35
Ruighasa Wetland, 414-15
Rural Engineering Organization (REO), 72
Rural Landless Employment Guarantee Programme (RLEGP), 122, 438
Rural settlements, 75-79
 area and population of, 316-17
Russel, A., 35, 136

Saharsa, Wetland in, 200
Salt lakes, 109
Salt-tolerant forest eco-system, 131
Samastipur, alluvial geomorphic features of, 30
Sample water test, 272-74
Sandy diaras, 40
Saran district, crop combination of, 57-59
Sat Tal areas, 9
Satellite and sensors, 441-42
Sedimentation, 170
Shallow water surface system, 7
Sharma, U.P., 10
Shikrahara river, 378
*Shramdan,* 236
Siltation, 283
Simardah, Wetlands of, 220, 354
Simri Bakhtly Jhed, 219-20
Simri-Bakhtiarpur Wetland, 367-69
 problems of, 369
Singia group chaurs, 472
Singh, H.R., 9
Singhara, 7
Sisulia chaur, 346-47
Sitla Wetland, Kishanganj district, 419-20
Siwalik Clay, 23, 36
Small Scalle Cottage Industries, 154
Soils, 48-50
 amendment, 180-81

organic matter, 261
physico-chemical analysis of, 260
Soil pollution, 451
Soil and Water, 251-52, 470-72
pollution of, 470-72
Sora Wetland, Purnea district, 425-26
Sowa Lake, Katihar, 404-405
Standard Nutrition Unit (SNU), 327
State Tourism Development Corporation, 237
Stereoscopic Viewing, 446-47
Steward, K.K., 178
Streams, 135-36
Strip-cropping, 128
Sub-Tarai Belt, 31, 205
Submerged Rooted Hydrophytes, 148
Sugar factories, 63
Suhagman Lake, 391
Sumeshwar ranges, 24
Sun-synchronous orbit, 443
Sunderbans, West Bengal, 237
Sustainable development, challenges of, 438
Sustainable utilization, 118-19, 435
Swamps, origin of, 109-10
topography of, 109-10
vegetation of, 105
Swampy areas, 151, 302
Synclinorium, 23

Tal Baraila Wetlands, 218
Tanks, 137-38
digging of, 113
distribution of, 159-60, 184, 210
Tanzania, Wetlands of, 2
Taylor, G., 45
Technical Committee on Inland Fisheries, 458
Telia Chaur, Muzaffarpur, 397-98
Temperature, 100
Tengarmari Wetland, 409-10
Terai region, 23, 45, 127-28
Territorial functional systems, 86
Tethyan basin, 23, 196
Thailands, 187
Thermocline, 146
Thornthwant, 47
Tibet Vaishali, 88
Tidal Marshes, 107-09
Tilabai Moin Wetlands, 358-60
Tilka Manjhi Bhagalpur University, 10
*Tirabhukti,* 89
Tobacco factories, 63, 68
Topographic features, 135
Toponyms, 411
Transportation, 68-69, 79-80
Tribeni Canal, 149-51
Turbidity Water, 373-74
24-Parganas, 124

Udaipur Lake, 239, 292
Unutilised and underutilized wetlands, 126
Uplands, 133
Upper Pleistocene age, 23
Urban areas, 231-32
Urban centres, 75-76
distribution of, 79, 83
growth of, 83
population density, 83-84
Urbanization, 79-80
*Utricularia,* 149
Uttar Pradesh, 43

Vaishali, 41, 87-89
wetlands of, 427-28
Valley Sal forest, 51
Vegetation, 50-52, 80-81, 99-100, 315-16

types of, 192-93
Videha, 87
Vietnam irrigation channels, 187
Village organisation, territorial basis of, 86-87
Virginia, 109
*Vishnu Puran,* 41
Vrijian Confederacy, 87

Wastelands, 222-24
Waste water disposal, 439
treatment of, 436-38
Water, chemical analysis of, 162-63
inflow and outflow of, 318
physico-chemical analysis of, 255-56
Water cycles, 436
Water Boards / Drainage Authority and Farmers, 308
Water-hyacinth, 179-80
Water management insecticide effects, 306-07
Water Moulds, 290-91
Waterlogging areas, 7, 38-39, 71-72, 95, 101, 121, 133, 137, 193-94, 196, 200, 347, 350, 407, 438, 453, 480
development of, 29
problems of, 149-50
Water pollution, 229-30, 451-52
problems of, 227-28
Water and Power Consultancy Services (WAPCOS), 237
Water quality improvement, 123, 439-40
Water sample, chemical analysis of, 264-65
Weeding protection, 168
Westlake, D.F., 178
Wet-bulb temperature, 43, 47
Wetlands, basic information of, 294-95
characteristics of, 464-65
classification of, 281-82
concept of, 96-97, 192-93
conservation of, 307-08, 435-40
cultivation of, 2, 210
determinants of, 101, 194-95
digging of, 100
dimensions of, 3-4
distribution of, 130-143, 232-33, 280-82
patterns of, 139-40
ecology value of, 184, 205
economic value of, 201-02
effect of climation, 48-50
entrophication of, 278-298
fauna of, 302
location and stages of, 112-13
management of, 292-93
meaning of, 4-5
monitoring of, 476-79
origin and evolution of, 190-91
planned development of, 95
problems of, 12
problems and planning of, 451-75
productivity of, 323-38
renovation of, 161-62
sitting of, 28-29
soil and water of, 251-76
sources of, 184-88
types and patterns of, 144-65
value of, 189-220
Wetland areas, biological productivity of, 300
Wetlands data analysis, nature of, 476-79
Wetlands degradation, 455
Wetland development, dimensions of, 190

evaluation and monitoring of, 221-22
socio-economic model of, 114-18, 214
Wetland economy, integrated development of, 12
Wetland eco-system, 120-21
Wetland environment, management of, 1-2, 5
Wetland formation, principles of, 110-12
Wetland management, 221, 292-93
Wetland resources, 202
cultural and indegenous practices of, 320-21
population dependent on, 319-20
Wetland soils, physico-chemical parameters of, 266-71
Wetland surveys, use of remote sensing in, 441-42
Wetland water management, use of remote sensing in, 447-48
Wet zones, 303
Wild plants with ornamental value, 176
Wildlife Protection Act, 311, 463, 477
Wildlife values, 301-03
Willard, Don, 8, 193
Winter seasons, 43
Wood-based industries, 67
Wood lands, 302
Worcester, 35, 135
World Bank, 122, 372, 440
aided projects, 438

Yadav, D.P. (Food and Supply Minister), 165
Yamuna river, 226
Young alluvium non-saline, 252
Young flood plain, 48

Zooplanktons, 286, 291
Zuari river, Goa, 228